Strengthening Family & Self

Sixth Edition

LEONA JOHNSON, EdS
Beldenville, Wisconsin

Publisher
The Goodheart-Willcox Company, Inc.
Tinley Park, Illinois
www.g-w.com

Library of Congress Catalog Card Number 2008051973
ISBN 978-1-60525-108-0

2 3 4 5 6 7 8 9 – 10 – 15 14 13 12 11 10

Goodheart-Willcox Publisher Brand Disclaimer: Brand names, company names, and illustrations for products and services included in this text are provided for educational purposes only and do not represent or imply endorsement or recommendation by the authors or the publisher.

Library of Congress Cataloging-in-Publication Data

Johnson, Leona.
  Strengthening family & self / Leona Johnson.
    p. cm.
  Includes index.
  ISBN 978-1-60525-108-0
1. Family life education—United States—Juvenile literature. I.
Title. II. Title: Strengthening family and self.
  HQ10.5.U6J656 2010
  306.8—dc22
        2008051973

Cover image: Brian Doben/Botanica/Jupiterimages

Introduction

Strengthening Family & Self is designed to help you grow and develop to your full potential. Equally important, this text is designed to assist you in developing skills that contribute to a strong and healthy family unit and success in your future career.

The focus of this text is people—especially you, but also your family, friends, acquaintances, and others with whom you have contact. Each of these individuals is an important part of your life. The text covers skills for relating to others, preparing for and adjusting to marriage, nurturing a family unit, and managing personal resources and multiple roles.

Strengthening Family & Self can also help you develop lifelong skills for managing all areas of your life. With help from the text, you can acquire the skills needed for adjusting to change, choosing and building a successful career, and caring for personal and family needs. You will also learn how to meet the housing, food, health, clothing, and transportation challenges of daily living.

About the Author

Leona Johnson, EdS, is presently the PK-12 Director of Curriculum and Instruction in her district. She is leading the district in new initiatives, including reading across the curriculum K-12, STEM (Science, Technology, Engineering, and Math) initiatives, Formative and Summative Assessments, Six Trait Writing, and differentiated instruction. Johnson has been active in school improvement programs, performing school evaluations in area districts, and presenting workshops on various topics. She is a participating member of several professional organizations and has received recognition for her various academic and professional endeavors, including a Kohl Fellow Scholarship and Award of Excellence for her contributions to education. Johnson previously taught secondary family and consumer sciences in her district, and individual and family relations at the University of Wisconsin-Stout. In addition, she has served as a research specialist for the University.

Welcome to *Strengthening Family & Self*

Each chapter is divided into easy-to-read sections

Life Sketch introduces chapter concepts through an interesting, real-life story.

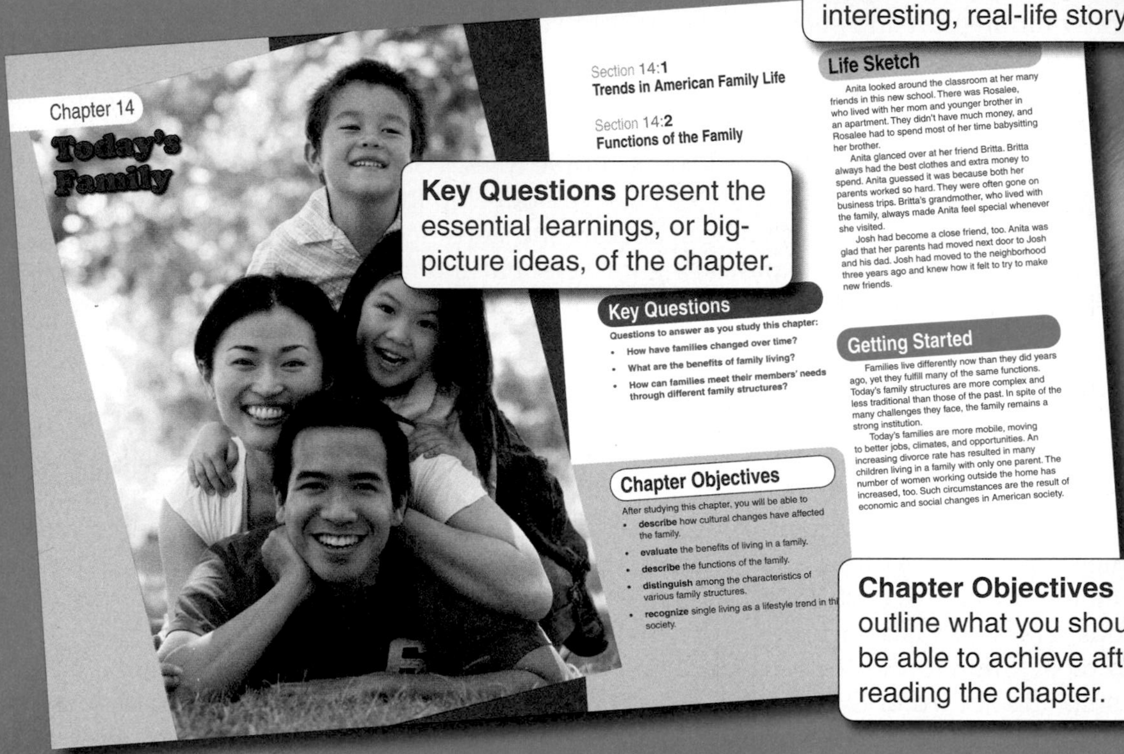

Key Questions present the essential learnings, or big-picture ideas, of the chapter.

Chapter Objectives outline what you should be able to achieve after reading the chapter.

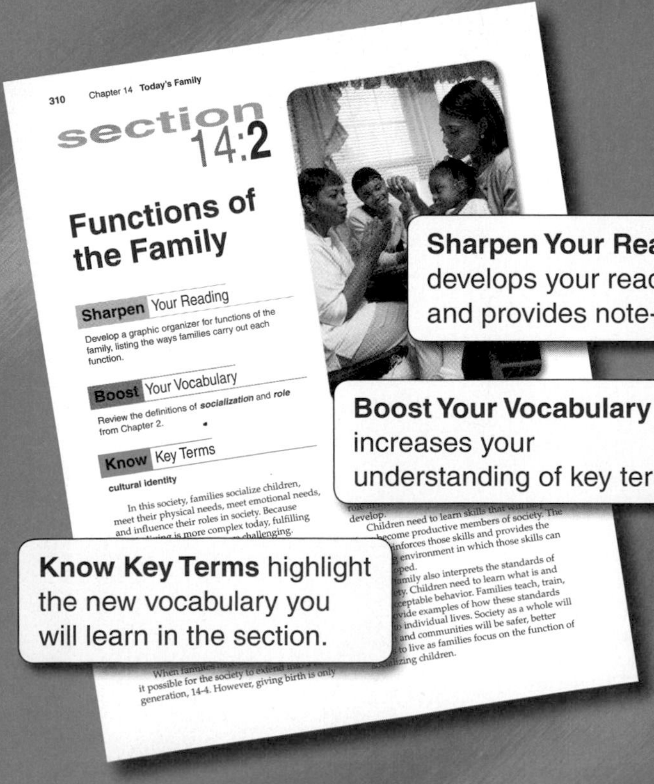

Sharpen Your Reading develops your reading skills and provides note-taking ideas.

Boost Your Vocabulary increases your understanding of key terms.

Know Key Terms highlight the new vocabulary you will learn in the section.

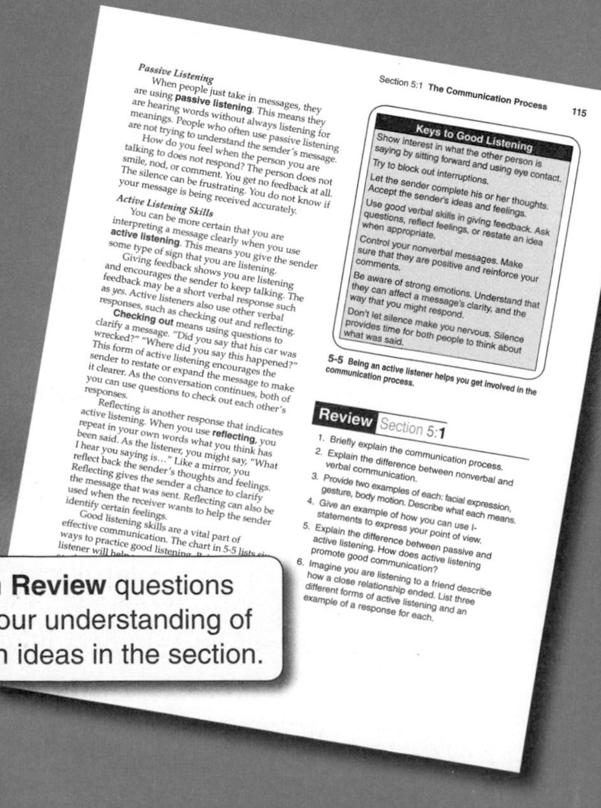

Section Review questions check your understanding of the main ideas in the section.

(Chapter opener page shown)

Chapter 14
Today's Family

Section 14:1
Trends in American Family Life

Section 14:2
Functions of the Family

Key Questions

Questions to answer as you study this chapter:
- How have families changed over time?
- What are the benefits of family living?
- How can families meet their members' needs through different family structures?

Chapter Objectives

After studying this chapter, you will be able to
- **describe** how cultural changes have affected the family.
- **evaluate** the benefits of living in a family.
- **describe** the functions of the family.
- **distinguish** among the characteristics of various family structures.
- **recognize** single living as a lifestyle trend in this society.

Life Sketch

Anita looked around the classroom at her many friends in this new school. There was Rosalee, who lived with her mom and younger brother in an apartment. They didn't have much money, and Rosalee had to spend most of her time babysitting her brother.

Anita glanced over at her friend Britta. Britta always had the best clothes and extra money to spend. Anita guessed it was because both her parents worked so hard. They were often gone on business trips. Britta's grandmother, who lived with the family, always made Anita feel special whenever she visited.

Josh had become a close friend, too. Anita was glad that her parents had moved next door to Josh and his dad. Josh had moved to the neighborhood three years ago and knew how it felt to try to make new friends.

Getting Started

Families live differently now than they did years ago, yet they fulfill many of the same functions. Today's family structures are more complex and less traditional than those of the past. In spite of the many challenges they face, the family remains a strong institution.

Today's families are more mobile, moving to better jobs, climates, and opportunities. An increasing divorce rate has resulted in many children living in a family with only one parent. The number of women working outside the home has increased, too. Such circumstances are the result of economic and social changes in American society.

(Section page shown)

310 Chapter 14 Today's Family

section 14:2

Functions of the Family

Sharpen Your Reading

Develop a graphic organizer for functions of the family, listing the ways families carry out each function.

Boost Your Vocabulary

Review the definitions of *socialization* and *role* from Chapter 2.

Know Key Terms

cultural identity

In this society, families socialize children, meet their physical needs, meet emotional needs, and influence their roles in society. Because ... is more complex today, fulfilling ... is more challenging.

... develop.

Children need to learn skills that will ... become productive members of society. The ... reinforces those skills and provides the ... environment in which those skills can ... ...ed.

... also interprets the standards of ... Children need to learn what is and ... ...ceptable behavior. Families teach, train, ... ide examples of how these standards ... individual lives. Society as a whole will ... and communities will be safer, better ... ...n live as families focus on the function of ...zing children.

When famil... it possible for the society to ex... generation, 14-4. However, giving birth is only ...

(Section page shown)

Section 5:1 The Communication Process 115

Passive Listening

When people just take in messages, they are using **passive listening**. This means they are hearing words without always listening for meanings. People who often use passive listening are not trying to understand the sender's message.

How do you feel when the person you are talking to does not respond? The person does not smile, nod, or comment. You get no feedback at all. The silence can be frustrating. You do not know if your message is being received accurately.

Active Listening Skills

You can be more certain that you are interpreting a message clearly when you use **active listening**. This means that you give the sender some type of sign that you are listening. Giving feedback shows you are listening and encourages the sender to keep talking. The feedback may be a short verbal response such as yes. Active listeners also use other verbal responses, such as checking out and reflecting.

Checking out means using questions to clarify a message. "Did you say that his car was wrecked?" "Were did you say that happened?" This form of active listening encourages the sender to restate or expand the message to make it clearer. As the conversation continues, both of you can use questions to check out each other's responses.

Reflecting is another response that indicates active listening. When you use **reflecting**, you repeat in your own words what you think has been said. As the listener, you might say, "What I hear you saying is..." Like a mirror, you reflect back the sender a chance to clarify the message that was sent. Reflecting can also be used when the receiver wants to help the sender identify certain feelings.

Good listening skills are a vital part of effective communication. The chart in 5-5 lists six ways to practice good listening. Becoming a good listener will help...

Keys to Good Listening

Show interest in what the other person is saying by sitting forward and using eye contact.

Try to block out interruptions.

Let the sender complete his or her thoughts.

Accept the sender's ideas and feelings.

Use good verbal skills in giving feedback. Ask questions, reflect feelings, or restate an idea when appropriate.

Control your nonverbal messages. Make sure that they are positive and reinforce your comments.

Be aware of strong emotions. Understand that they can affect a message's clarity, and the way that you might respond.

Don't let silence make you nervous. Silence provides time for both people to think about what was said.

5-5 Being an active listener helps you get involved in the communication process.

Review Section 5:1

1. Briefly explain the communication process.
2. Explain the difference between nonverbal and verbal communication.
3. Provide two examples of each: facial expression, gesture, body motion. Describe what each means.
4. Give an example of how you can use i-statements to express your point of view.
5. Explain the difference between passive and active listening. How does active listening promote good communication?
6. Imagine you are listening to a friend describe how a close relationship ended. List three different forms of active listening and an example of a response for each.

Boxed features promote reading comprehension and check your understanding

What do you have available to help you carry out your decisions? time? energy? money? a pleasing personality? special skills? Basically, there are two kinds of resources: human and nonhuman. A **human resource** comes from within a person. This includes your personal qualities and characteristics as well as the support you receive from others. A **nonhuman resource** is any item you have available to help you, such as money, a car, tools, time, and information. Some decisions may require several resources.

Human Resources

What personal qualities and characteristics help you carry out your decisions? You may have certain physical resources, such as good health, strength, and energy. Knowledge, talents, and skills are also human resources, 4-5. Your personality and character traits are other examples. These personal traits become resources for making decisions and carrying out a task.

Your character qualities can also be considered resources. Strength in character means that you have personal qualities that will help you carry out your decisions. For instance, if you are self-controlled, you will be more likely to carry out your decisions.

What skills have you developed as resources? Skills for reading, writing, and math are basic resources you can acquire in school. You can also develop skills for communicating with others.

Problem-solving skills and decision-making skills can be learned. In addition, you probably have developed other special skills, such as preparing food or caring for children. Maintaining your car, programming a computer, or playing an instrument are examples of other skills you may have. Each personal skill can be a resource for you in some situation.

Besides your skills and abilities, you may need to use the second category of human resources—other people in your life. Your family members, a friend, teacher, or religious leader can help or support you. For instance, suppose you need help to complete your homework. Would you contact a teacher? Would you ask a classmate to help you?

The people who can help you carry out a decision are part of your human resources. Their support may depend on their own resources. They may offer support by helping you, encouraging you, or giving you other resources. They can combine their resources with yours to help you carry out your goals.

Investigate Further

What human resources could help a person reach a goal of physical fitness? of having good friendships? of personal maturity?

Nonhuman...

4-5 The knowledge gained through education is a human resource.

Investigate Further—
Analyze what you learn and expand your knowledge.

Think More About It—
Extend your learning through critical thinking.

Think More About It
What are some ways that a single-parent family can restore balance to the family system so the needs of family members are met?

Coping with Loneliness

Loneliness is often a problem for single parents. Because they are alone, they tend to focus more on their children than themselves. They feel it is important to succeed at parenting. They devote most of their time to providing for the family and caring for their children. As a result, little time is left to spend building other relationships.

Supportive Friendships

Friendships are especially important for single parents. They need friends who accept them and help them believe in their own abilities. Friends can encourage them to take steps that will help them grow as people. This support increases the single parent's self-esteem and confidence. An attitude of personal growth can lead to the development of new skills. Personal accomplishments will bring feelings of success, 17-11.

17-11 Friendships are important for the single parent. They provide emotional support and help the person gain confidence in his or her ability to succeed.

Link to Your Life

Identify some examples of how the relationships within a family become more complex as more people become involved.

Remarriage and the Stepfamily

Many divorced people remarry within a few years after their divorce. The reasons for this decision vary. They may desire the closeness of a marriage relationship. They may want more financial security. The desire to share parenting tasks with a spouse may be another reason.

When either spouse has children from a previous marriage, they then form a stepfamily. The newly married parent becomes a **stepparent** to the children of his or her new spouse. The stepfamily brings more resources together to meet the needs of family members. However, it also brings more challenges.

Adjusting to th...

Link to Your Life—
Reflect on how the text relates your experiences.

...each other's ...own ...arrangement. ...other's self-esteem. They need to ...children's needs for love, affection, and security.

As a couple adjusts to each other, they are also adjusting to a new parenting arrangement. This means less time for each other. They have less time to communicate with each other, resolve conflicts privately, and develop mutual interests. Setting aside time to develop their personal relationship is an important need for them to fulfill.

Use What You Learn—
Apply what you have read to given situations.

Use What You Learn
What can young adults do to show empathy to parents at this stage? What can parents do to show empathy to young adults at this stage?

The Empty Nest Stage

When the last child is independent and living on his or her own, the family enters the empty nest stage. Parental roles change greatly. No longer are children dependent on their parents for meeting their own needs. The children are responsible for meeting their own needs. Some marry and begin their own families. As a child marries, parents need to accept the child's mate into the extended family.

Role Adjustments

Parents may still be involved in their adult son or daughter's life, but to a much lesser extent. They may still provide some financial help or support in other ways. They may be involved in grandparenting, 15-5. These roles take less time than their full-time parenting responsibilities of the past. This stage may seem lonely for some parents. Developing new interests and setting new goals may fill some needs.

15-5 In many families, grandparenting is a new role of the empty nest stage.

The relationship of empty nesters with their own parents may change. The older generation may need financial support or help with physical care. This new role of supporting older parents requires adjustment from both spouses.

Although this stage can be challenging, it can also be rewarding. Couples have the chance to renew their own close relationship. They return to living as a couple. Strengthening their own relationship is important as they look ahead to the next stage of retirement.

What are some of the challenges of being in this "sandwich generation" between young adults and older adults?

Retirem...

Couples ent...
one or both spo...
Retirement age...
long as they ar...
choose an early...

Many coup...
working to pro...
They have set goa...
some couples, retirement is a time to focus on themselves, hobbies, volunteer work, travel, or leisure activities. More time can be devoted to friendships and grandchildren, too.

Not all people cope well with retirement. Some are unable to adjust to their changed roles. The sense of purpose they felt while working is gone. As a result, their self-esteem may drop. Along with this, health and financial problems can prevent them from looking at the future with hope.

Death of a Spouse

The death of one partner ends the family life cycle. The remaining partner returns to single living. The widow or widower faces two major challenges: dealing emotionally with the loss of a partner and adjusting to a lifestyle change. Personal freedoms may be affected. The loss of income, health, and the ability to live

Weigh the Facts—
Compare and contrast important concepts.

Chapter review pages reinforce concepts and assess your learning

Think It Through

A Breakdown in Communication

It was late Saturday afternoon and Shayla was sitting at the kitchen table, working on her laptop computer. A big research paper was due on Monday for her history class. She was hurrying to get it done so she could go out with friends tonight.

She was annoyed because her brother had friends over and they had just started playing a loud video game in the next room. It was distracting her from focusing on her paper, but she was almost finished so she didn't bother to move to another room. Shayla's dad came into the kitchen and started taking vegetables out of the refrigerator.

"Shayla, would you please set the kitchen table when you finish your homework?" he asked.

"Sure, dad," Shayla replied, half-listening as she continued typing. "I'll be done in a few minutes."

"Thanks," her dad replied. "All the dishes in the dishwasher are clean. I'm going to run up to the store to get some green peppers for the dish I'm making. If your mother gets home, let her know where I am and tell her I'm making dinner."

Shayla was absorbed in typing and didn't respond. She didn't even hear the door shut as her dad left. She had just finished her paper when the phone rang. It was Shayla's mom.

"I'm on my way home from the mall and thought I would pick up a pizza for dinner," she said. "What kind of pizza should I get?"

Shayla told her mom what she wanted, and then hung up the phone. She cleared away her schoolwork and started setting the table. However, there wasn't enough clean silverware or plates to finish. Just as she was wondering what to do, her mom arrived with the pizza. A few minutes later, her dad arrived with groceries. He noticed only half of the table was set and then he saw the pizza box on the counter.

"Shayla, I told you there were clean dishes in the dishwasher," he said. "I also told you that I was making dinner. You should have told your mom she didn't need to pick up a pizza. You need to pay attention and listen better."

Shayla became upset and stalked out of the kitchen.

"All I heard you say was that I should set the table," she muttered as she left the room. "Couldn't you see that I was busy?"

Questions to Guide Your Thinking

1. At what point in the conversation did the breakdown in communication occur?
2. What factors contributed to the communication breakdown?
3. What caused the miscommunication to escalate into a conflict?
4. What could Shayla and her dad have done to make sure they communicated accurately?

Chapter Summary reviews the major concepts covered in the entire chapter.

Chapter Summary

The communication process involves sending and receiving messages. Understanding this process and how it is used is important. It can help you develop effective communication skills and get along with others. As a sender, you need skills in sending clear, accurate messages. As a receiver, you need to listen well and interpret the message correctly.

You use nonverbal and verbal skills every day whenever you communicate. In nonverbal communication, you send messages without using words. Through body language, you express your thoughts, feelings, and emotions to others. Facial expressions, gestures, and body motions are all forms of body language that you use.

You communicate verbally by using words. You can improve your ability to express yourself clearly by using I-messages. This skill gives you more control over what you say to others. Besides sending clear messages, you need skills in receiving messages. Active listening is a skill that helps you to interpret and understand messages clearly.

Your self-esteem, emotional state, and environment can affect the way messages are communicated. In addition, certain factors can get in the way of good communication, such as a closed mind, mixed messages, and prejudice. Once you know how these barriers affect communication, you can work to improve your speaking and listening skills.

Good communication skills are needed to resolve conflicts in a positive way. Conflict resolution is a step-by-step skill you can develop to resolve conflicts successfully and build relationships. First, identify the problem. Next, identify and accept ownership. Finally, reach an agreeable solution to the problem through negotiation and compromise.

Assess...

Your Knowledge

1. What types of nonverbal and verbal messages help communicate a shared message?
2. What are four factors that could interfere with or prevent good communication from taking place?
3. What are the steps for resolving conflict?

Your Understanding

4. How does the communication p___ shared meanings?
5. How could you-statements affe__ communication that takes plac__ people?
6. How could low self-esteem af__ success at communication?
7. How do negative communica__ relationships?

Your Skills

8. Express your own thoughts, feelings, and intentions by using five different types of I-statements.
9. Give an example of how you would use active listening skills to help a friend make a decision.
10. What steps would you take to solve a problem of failing grades in a class?

Think Critically

11. *Writing.* Identify a situation that upset you. Write a paragraph describing this situati___ the self-awareness circle, write I-s__ express your personal observatio__ feelings, intentions, and actions r__ situation. Summarize whether yo__ message you intended to send.
12. As a class, identify several conf__ (consider personal experiences__ or historical references). Choos__ conflicts and describe how it w__ Evaluate the techniques used __ conflict. Explain how the steps __ resolution did or could have enhanced the __ process. *Group option.* In small groups, create a role-play to illustrate how the steps of conflict resolution could be applied to resolving this conflict. Perform the role-play for the class.
13. *Research.* Assess your ability to be an active listener. Try an experiment in which you use the active listening skills of checking out and reflecting when someone is trying to share a confidential message with you. Comp__ conversation to one in which you d__ avoid looking at the speaker and re__

Assess... Your Skills activities evaluate your ability to use and apply the essential learnings of the chapter.

Think It Through case study helps you practice reasoning and problem-solving skills by analyzing a practical problem.

Think Critically activities develop your higher-level thinking skills.

Assess... Your Knowledge and **Assess... Your Understanding** questions evaluate how well you know and understand the essential learnings of the chapter.

Academic skills used in the activities are shown in bold type.

Use Technology activities focus on technology, such as using the Internet and software programs.

Connect With Your Community activities encourage you to seek answers from area resources and apply chapter concepts to your own community.

Choice accommodates different learning styles by giving you the option to complete the activity at a lower or higher level.

Group option explains how to adapt the activity to work with a partner or team.

---

as he or she talks. Describe the __ how these two conversations ar__ arrive at shared meanings. *Cho__* a partner who will record observ__ carry out your research. Post you__ results on your class bulletin board

14. *Research.* Attend a school event or__ and make a list of the different form__ language you observe. Beside each __ identify the nonverbal messages you __ Put each message and your interpretation on a small card. Hand it to the person who sent the nonverbal message. Explain that you are doing a research project, and ask the person to respond to the accuracy of the message. Identify the gaps between the message you received and the message that was sent. Write a paragraph explaining your experiment and the results of your research. *Group Option.* In small groups, share your research and identify similarities and differences in results.

Connect with Your Community

15. Develop a list of words or expressions that are unique to your particular culture, community, or geographic area. Identify other possible meanings for these expressions. *Choice:* Present your information to the class in an electronic presentation.
16. *Writing.* Pretend your report card lists your grade as one level lower than what you understood it to be. Using the self-awareness circle, write five different I-statements that you could use to express yourself positively to your teacher. *Choice:* Using the same process, give an oral demonstration of five I-statements you could use to approach your boss about a possible raise.
17. *Writing.* Choose an on-the-job situation in which communication barriers result in problems between employees or problems between an employee and a customer. Write a short skit to illustrate the problem, ways to overcome communication on the job. *Choice:* With a partner, role-play the problem and solution.

18. __ ps between members __ rrent cultural backgrounds. *Choice:* Prepare a presentation for your local chamber of commerce or school board sharing the potential difficulties and possible steps to help promote clear communication.

Use Technology

19. Use the computer to design and print a poster illustrating the importance of good communication techniques. *Choice:* Choose a target audience: students (preschool, elementary, middle school, or senior high school), families in counseling, workers on the job, or another. Design a poster for your target audience.
20. *Research.* Search the Internet to research the communication skills that are used by a counselor. Identify the skills that you feel are most important for a counselor to be effective on the job.
21. Use a computer program to design and print a brochure that illustrates "Keys for Successful Conflict Resolution." *Choice:* Design a Web page that covers the same information.
22. *Math, research.* Record the various nonverbal techniques that your teachers use during a typical day. Using a spreadsheet, list the names of nonverbal techniques across the top and the different types of teachers down the side. Tally by each teacher (not the total number of times each technique was used). Summarize your findings in a short paragraph, comparing the techniques used with your opinions of each teacher's effectiveness in communicating. Is one or more nonverbal techniques used by all effective teachers? *Group option:* Work with a partner who has the same teachers. Share your findings with another group and compare results.

Career clusters help you plan for the future

Connect with Career Clusters
- Acquaints you with a specific career.
- Relates the career to the career clusters.
- Explains key work factors and the qualifications needed for career entry.

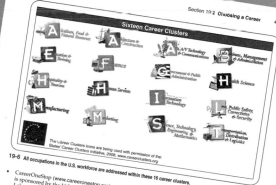

Explore these careers:

Chapter 19
- Overviews the career clusters.
- Explains how the clusters can help you choose the right career.

Apply what you learn through FCCLA

Family, Career, and Community Leaders of America, Inc. (FCCLA) is a student organization that promotes personal growth and leadership development through family and consumer sciences education. As the only in-school student organization with the family as its focus, FCCLA is an ideal companion to *Strengthening Family & Self* and other courses in your school's family and consumer sciences program.

Involvement in FCCLA offers the opportunity to:

- participate in activities and events at local, state, and national levels
- develop leadership and teamwork skills
- learn about careers in family and consumer sciences
- help others through community service projects
- prepare for future roles in your family, career, and community

More information on FCCLA can be found in this textbook in Chapters 19 and 21. For additional information, visit the organization's Web site at **www.fcclainc.org.**

Goodheart-Willcox Supports FCCLA

To champion Family and Consumer Sciences and FCCLA, Goodheart-Willcox sponsors the State Adviser of the Year award. State FCCLA Advisers are dedicated educators that provide organization and leadership to FCCLA chapters and STAR Events Competitions.

At a recent National Leadership Meeting, Julie Bell of South Dakota State University (right) was presented the State Adviser of the Year award by Todd Scheffers, Vice President Sales, Goodheart-Willcox Publisher. Assisting is FCCLA Student Representative, Rachel Remund, National Vice President of Peer Education.

Contents in Brief

Contents

Unit Four
Understanding Families

Unit Six
Managing Your World

Unit 1
Reaching Your Potential

Chapter 1

A Close-Up View of You

Section 1:**1**
Your Life Path

Section 1:**2**
Heredity

Section 1:**3**
Environment

Key Questions

Questions to answer as you study this chapter:

- **What is self-identity?**
- **Why is it important to know who I am?**
- **How did I get to be the way I am?**

Chapter Objectives

After studying this chapter, you will be able to

- **recognize** the unique qualities of your life path.
- **identify** factors that impact your identity.
- **relate** major developmental tasks of the teen years to future changes.
- **evaluate** the influence of heredity on personal characteristics.
- **explain** how factors in the environment can influence growth and development.
- **plan** ways to respond to heredity and environment with resiliency.

Life Sketch

"What are you going to do after graduation?" Ava asked her friend Molly.

Molly's response was eager and excited. "I plan to go to the state college next fall and get a degree in interior design. I'd like to spend a semester in Italy. You know, the state college has a great student exchange program. I'm sure that experience will help me get a good job. I'd like to stay in the Miami area after I graduate from college," Molly said.

"Molly sure has her life together," Ava thought as she listened to all of Molly's plans. Molly was known for setting goals and accomplishing them. There was no doubt she would achieve her dreams for the future.

"I'm still trying to figure out who I am," Ava said to herself. "Where am I going? Will I be a success at what I do someday?"

Getting Started

Have you ever questioned yourself about your future? Almost all young people ask such questions as they try to learn more about themselves. They want to plan for the future and set directions for their lives.

Thinking about the future can be both exciting and scary. Getting a job and living on your own may sound exciting to you. You may be looking forward to getting married and having your own family.

Some events that lie ahead may seem frightening because of the unknown. Will you get the education you need? Will you find a job you like? Will you succeed at that job?

You may feel uncertain about future relationships. Will you know when you are really in love? Whom will you marry? Will your marriage be happy? Will you be a good parent?

Life does not come with a set of directions to answer your questions. However, in this book you will find information related to these important life events.

Looking at the experiences of people who have succeeded in different aspects of life can be helpful. They have learned how to find the information they need and use it wisely. They have developed certain skills that help them in their personal relationships. This book uses the experiences of such people to identify information and skills that can be useful to you.

section 1:1

Your Life Path

Sharpen Your Reading

Outline concepts as you read, listing key points under the following headings: *Definition, Qualities of Your Life Path, Changes Along Your Life Path*, and *Preparing for Change*.

Boost Your Vocabulary

Pick an object that you think describes you and explain how it relates to your identity. Include your strengths and areas you need to improve.

Know Key Terms

life span
gene
developmental task
self-identity

Life can be thought of as a path. Your birth marks the beginning of your path in this world. Death marks the end of this path. Your path from birth to death is called your **life span**, 1-1.

No one knows just how long their life span will be. The average life span today for men is 72 years; for women, it is 79 years. These are averages expected for people who are teens today.

You are unique. No one else is exactly like you. You started your life path with your own set of genes, received from your parents. A **gene** is the basic unit of heredity. Your unique pattern of genes is defined as your *DNA*, which has about three billion base pairs of genetic material. Your DNA is so distinctive that it can be used as a method of identification.

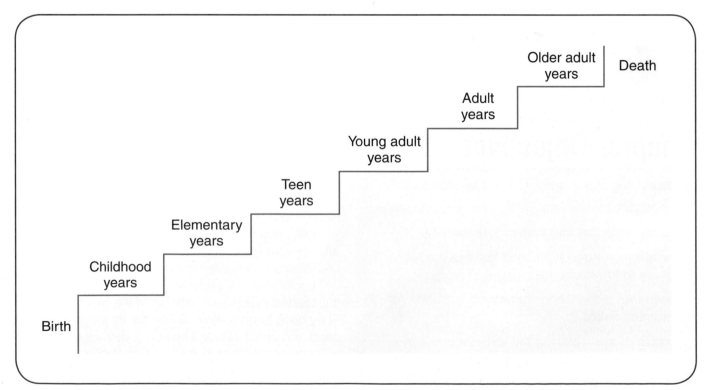

1-1   Although your life path is unique, you will pass through the same growth stages as all people do.

As a unique person, you have your own daily life experiences. You also share many experiences with others. Your life path crosses their life paths every day. You depend on other people and are influenced by them. In turn, they are influenced by you.

Some people have a direct influence on your life path. They may give you food, clothes, and shelter so you feel warm and secure. They may give you a hug or praise so you feel loved. Such actions and words affect you in a direct way.

People's actions can also influence you indirectly. For instance, you may not be invited to a friend's party. As a result, you feel hurt although no one speaks directly to you about it. You can also directly or indirectly impact others. Who you are, what you say, and what you do or do not do are all important.

Use What You Learn

Think of the last item you purchased. Who was indirectly affected by your purchase? Who was directly affected?

Changes over Your Life Span

As a teen, you have major developmental tasks to achieve. A **developmental task** is a skill that society expects of individuals at various stages of life. Accomplishing these tasks successfully helps you become an adult, 1-2.

Understanding and Accepting Yourself

One developmental task of the teen years is to figure out who you are. Asking the question "Who am I?" helps you clarify your **self-identity**. This is a sense of individuality. Exploring the answers to this question will help you feel that you have worth and value.

Identifying who you are can help you accept yourself. When you accept yourself, it is easier to believe that others will accept you as you are.

Developmental Tasks

- Understand and accept who you are.
- Make healthful choices that help you grow to maturity.
- Develop mature relationships with others.
- Prepare for an occupation.
- Prepare for marriage and family living.

1-2 Teens have major developmental tasks to accomplish as they enter adulthood.

There is no need to pretend—you can let others know the real you. Accepting yourself can help you develop relationships with others.

Growing to Maturity

Knowing your self-identity will also allow you to make choices that will help you grow to maturity. When you know and accept yourself as you are, you recognize your good and bad points. You can use your strengths to make choices that help you reach personal goals. You can also make choices to improve the areas in which you are weak.

Developing Mature Relationships

Adolescence is a time for growth toward maturity in many relationships. During the teen years, your position in the family changes. Your relationship with your parents becomes one of decreasing dependence and increasing independence. You gain a new respect for your parents as you mature.

Friendships also change and mature. True friendships, which involve care and concern for a friend's well-being, become important. This is true of friendships with both sexes.

In addition, relationships develop with people at work. As you get your first job and gain work experience, you learn to become a member of a work team. Learning to work well in a group makes it possible to succeed at work.

Preparing for an Occupation

Adolescence is a time to prepare for the future and look ahead to living on your own. One task of the teen years is to choose and prepare for an occupation. When choosing a career, you will need to consider your interests, abilities, personality, and goals. Career education will help you prepare for a job you will enjoy.

Preparing for Marriage and Family Living

Adolescence is a time to learn how to build close relationships with others. What qualities can help you develop a relationship with another person who may become your spouse? What skills are needed to get along with others? How can you work together on a project or solve a problem together? This is a time to develop skills that help you get along with others. These skills will help you experience long-lasting relationships.

You can also learn about growth and development. What is needed to help someone grow to maturity? How can you help others reach their potential? Developing these skills will help you prepare for marriage and family living.

1-3 You may be excited about going to college, yet fear that you will not be able to pass college-level courses.

Investigate Further

How could having a job help you achieve developmental tasks of the teen years? How could being in a school sport or club help you grow in these areas?

Preparing for Change

Change is a normal part of life. Many fear change, though, because it brings unknowns. People prefer individuals and experiences they know are pleasant. When change comes, it brings new experiences. This can make anyone feel uncomfortable or afraid, 1-3. You can avoid these feelings by learning about change and using the right skills to manage it.

Gathering Information

Learning as much as possible about upcoming changes can help you prepare for them. For instance, it is helpful to know what body changes to expect as you grow. Then you will understand that the changes occurring are normal. You will also know that others are experiencing the same things.

You can expect many changes when you get your first job or apartment. Couples experience change when they start going out, get engaged, or get married. Still more changes are involved with parenting.

What information will help you adjust to life's changes? What can be expected? What feelings have others had as they went through these changes? Knowing what to expect is the first step in preparing for change.

Developing Skills to Adjust

Developing skills that help you adjust is the second step in preparing for change. A new job may require skills for managing time. You may need new skills for communicating your thoughts or ideas to others. In a relationship, you may need to develop skills for sharing your inner feelings. With patience and practice, these and many other skills can be learned.

Managing the Change

The third step is to develop a plan to manage change. This step can help make the experience a positive one. For example, what changes might occur when you get your first full-time job? Will your family expect you to buy all your own clothes? If so, you will need to budget so you have money to purchase them.

How would your personal schedule change with a full-time job? You could plan a schedule that includes time to work, relax, and see friends and family. Planning can help you manage the increased demands on your time.

The completion of high school will be a time of change for you. How will you prepare for these changes? What information will you gather to help you grow in a positive way? Will it be information related to college or technical training, getting a job, or living on your own? What skills will you need to be successful in achieving your goals? What plan will you have for managing all these choices?

The more you know about the changes you will experience, the more confident you will be to face them. Planning for change will make you less likely to fear it.

Use What You Learn

Identify a change you will be facing in the near future. What questions would you like answered before this change takes place?

Review Section 1:1

1. List three benefits of knowing your identity.
2. List the five developmental tasks of the teen years.
3. List three ways a person can prepare for an expected change.

section 1:2

Heredity

1-4 These children have physical characteristics similar to their parents' because of heredity.

Sharpen Your Reading

Diagram the concepts of heredity using a graphic organizer. As you read, fill in key points along the branches. Use the following headings: *Who Am I?—Your Identity* and *Hereditary Factors*.

Boost Your Vocabulary

Draw a diagram that shows how information flows in the brain from one nerve cell to another.

Know Key Terms

heredity
genetics
chromosomes
traits
Punnett square
intelligence
neurons
dendrites
synapse
neurotransmitters
carrier
family tree

When planning for the future, it can help to look at the influences that shaped your life in the past. These factors often continue to influence you. One main factor that affects personal development is heredity. Your **heredity** is the sum of the qualities that were passed from your ancestors through your parents to you, 1-4. The qualities you inherit make you a unique human being. Your hair color, facial features, and height are examples.

Besides influencing all your physical qualities, heredity is a major factor in your personality development. Your heredity influences the way you look, feel, and behave. Knowing about the qualities you inherit will give you some insight to your own potential development. You will also pass on to your children part of what you inherit from your parents. The science that studies heredity is called **genetics**.

Genes

Each human being begins life with his or her own set of genetic material. A person normally inherits 23 rod-shaped particles called **chromosomes** from each biological parent. Chromosomes carry hereditary information from each parent. The father and mother each contribute 23 chromosomes. The child inherits a total of 46 chromosomes. This genetic "blueprint" exists in the nucleus of every cell in the body.

Chromosomes contain long, ladder-type strands of DNA that carry genetic information. The parts of the ladder that carry information occur in pairs. These are the genes. There are about 30,000 genes. Genes determine all inherited characteristics, or **traits**.

Physical Characteristics

The genes you inherit affect your body. Your physical appearance may be similar to a brother, sister, or another family member because of inherited genes. However, the genes that come from both parents combine in different patterns in their children. As a result, brothers and sisters have different traits.

Are you tall, short, or average height? Are you male or female? What color are your eyes, hair, and skin? These are some of your inherited traits.

Dominant and Recessive Genes

Some genes are dominant while others are recessive.

- When present, *dominant* genes determine the nature of a certain trait in a person. A dominant gene always overrules a recessive gene. Chart 1-5 lists some examples of physical traits that are dominant.

- *Recessive* genes determine the nature of the trait only when two of them are present. The child must receive one recessive gene from each parent.

Scientists use letters such as *DD* and *rr* to identify a person's genotype for various traits. A *genotype* is the genetic makeup of an individual or group. Capital *D* signifies a dominant trait such as brown hair. A lowercase *r* signifies a recessive trait such as blonde hair. A person with two dominant genes, genotype *DD*, will have brown hair. A person with one recessive and one dominant gene, genotype *rD*, will also have brown hair because the dominant *D* gene is present. A person with two recessive genes, genotype *rr*, will have blonde hair. In the case of eye color, a person with two recessive genes will have blue eyes.

Scientists use a **Punnett square**, invented by R.C. Punnett, to determine what possible gene pairs may result from combining two genes, 1-6. The genes of the parents are identified along two adjacent sides of the square—one parent per side. Each possible combination is recorded in an inner box. A total of four combinations are possible. Consequently, each offspring will have a 25 percent chance of inheriting the characteristic indicated in each box.

Many traits are influenced by more than one pair of genes. For example, height seems to be determined by at least four pairs of genes. When several genes influence a trait, more variations may result in offspring.

Inherited Traits			
Dominant Traits		**Recessive Traits**	
Black or brown hair	Long full lashes	Blond hair	Short thin lashes
Full lips	Curly hair	Thin lips	Straight hair
Free earlobes	Freckles	Attached earlobes	Lack of freckles
Dimples in cheeks	Feet with normal arches	No dimples in cheeks	Flat feet
High and narrow nose	Farsightedness and astigmatism	Broad nose	Normal vision
Brown eyes		Blue eyes	

1-5 This chart shows some of the inherited traits that dominate over recessive traits.

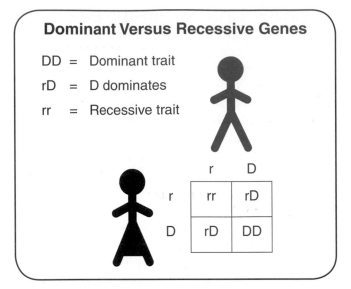

Dominant Versus Recessive Genes

DD = Dominant trait

rD = D dominates

rr = Recessive trait

	r	D
r	rr	rD
D	rD	DD

1-6 A Punnett square illustrates the possible combinations of a pair of inherited genes. The parents in this example each have one dominant and one recessive gene.

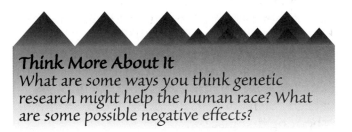

Think More About It

What are some ways you think genetic research might help the human race? What are some possible negative effects?

Brain Development and Intelligence

The way your brain grows, develops, and functions is affected by genes and factors in your environment. Your brain development will affect your intelligence. **Intelligence** is your capacity for mental activity. It affects your ability to learn, understand, reason, and think.

How Your Brain Functions

People are born with over 100 billion nerve cells in the brain called **neurons**. See 1-7. The neurons have many extensions that look like fingers. These fingers are called **dendrites**. Nerve cells send information back and forth through the dendrites.

The space between the dendrites of two neurons is called a **synapse**. The body makes chemicals in the synapses that allow messages to be carried from one neuron to another. These chemicals are called **neurotransmitters**.

Different neurotransmitters result in different types of messages. For example, some messages speed up a body response; others slow it down. Some chemicals produce a positive feeling, while others help information flow to different parts of the brain. The way your body responds is controlled by the neurotransmitters.

The chemicals that are produced in your synapses can be affected by both your heredity and your environment. For example, certain chemicals are produced when you sleep, and different chemicals are produced when you are awake. Other chemicals are produced when you are in danger or in a stressful situation. These responses are genetic. Environmental factors can also affect which chemicals are produced in the synapses. These factors include the food you eat and how physically active you are.

How Your Brain Grows and Develops

Each brain cell connects to thousands of other brain cells. As you grow and develop, your brain increases the dendrite connections in the areas or pathways that are used. Certain stimuli are needed within the environment for this development to proceed.

Parts of the brain that are not used are trimmed back, and those nerve cells die off. This is where the term *use it or lose it* applies to brain development. The critical time for learning to take place is called a *window of opportunity*. If the window is missed, the cells die off and the related development does not take place.

For example, you are born with the capacity to learn any language. The pathways of your brain that are used to learn the language you speak continue to develop, and many dendrite connections form. The parts you could use to learn other languages die off because you do not use them. After age 10, you are still able to learn another language. However, you may not speak it as fluently as you would if you had learned it earlier.

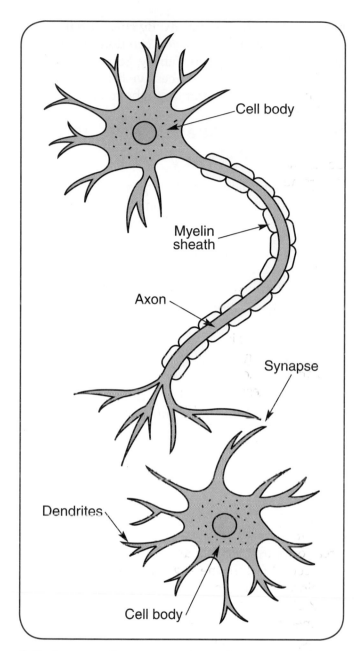

1-7 A nerve cell, or *neuron*, can send 250 to 2500 nerve impulses each second.

Although your heredity determines the number of brain cells you start with, your environment affects the number of connections made. Good nutrition is important for brain development. A stimulating environment is just as important. To reach your full potential, all these factors need to come together. (You will learn more about the parts of the brain and how to stimulate development in Chapter 2.)

Use What You Learn

Give examples of the use-it-or-lose-it rule. Include activities that improve with practice.

Hereditary Diseases

Certain diseases and disabilities are inherited. With advances in medicine, there are new ways to identify these disease traits. Scientists can take a sample of your DNA and identify your particular gene traits. The genotypes of healthy people are compared to those with various diseases. For instance, scientists know that some diseases result from a change in the sequence of genes on a chromosome. This information should help identify causes of and cures for many diseases.

Some people are a **carrier** of a disease. This means they can pass the disease to their children but never have it themselves. This situation occurs because they have one recessive gene carrying the disease trait and a dominant gene carrying a healthy trait. When both parents are carriers, their children have one chance in four of inheriting that disease.

Heredity is also a major factor in mental retardation in children, 1-8. Down syndrome is a chromosome disorder that occurs mostly in children born to women over 40 years old. As women age, their DNA molecules may be altered in some way. Altered DNA passed on to a child may result in hereditary diseases.

Each person is likely to carry some defective genes, but no problems result because the dominant genes are healthy. Defective genes affect a person when they are inherited in pairs. This is why marriage between blood relatives is discouraged. Children of these marriages have a higher chance of inheriting pairs of defective genes, which may result in birth defects and even death.

Investigate Further

How might researchers and doctors use DNA information to help identify causes of and cures for hereditary diseases?

1-8 Down syndrome results when a child inherits an extra chromosome. One of the effects of this condition is mental retardation.

Genetic Counseling

Genetic counselors help people understand how hereditary diseases and disabilities are passed on. Some people may already know that a hereditary condition exists in their family. Couples who have a child with an inherited disease may want to seek genetic counseling before having more children. Also, couples related by blood may want to seek genetic counseling before having a family.

Your **family tree** is a list of your blood relatives for several generations. By tracing your family tree, you can identify conditions that could be hereditary in your family. By checking the life span of past generations, you can determine the average life span in your family. You can also trace other dominant or recessive traits that are passed from one generation to the next.

Medical Research Versus the Right to Privacy

New technologies make it possible to gather information about each person. This ability raises some concerns about the welfare of private citizens. For instance, if you have a genotype similar to a person with Alzheimer's disease, would you want to know this? Would you want your insurance company, your employer, or others to know? Could such information lead to discrimination?

Concerns for the personal well-being of individuals must be considered. The ability to use a technology to gather such information must be weighed against a person's right to keep the information private and confidential. Such issues will continue to be raised as technology becomes more advanced.

Review Section 1:2

1. Name five characteristics that a person inherits.
2. Explain the difference in the effects of a dominant gene and a recessive gene on the way a trait is expressed.
3. Describe how the use-it-or-lose-it rule applies to brain development.
4. Explain why a marriage between close relatives is a health risk.
5. Under what circumstances might a couple seek genetic counseling?

section 1:3

Environment

Sharpen Your Reading

Add to the graphic organizer you prepared for Section 1:2. Include branches listing the environmental factors that affect growth and development. Add the heading *Environmental Factors*.

Boost Your Vocabulary

Find or draw pictures illustrating each of the key terms.

Know Key Terms

environment
sibling
cultural heritage
peers
technology
media
resiliency

Your **environment** includes everything in your surroundings, 1-9. Family, friends, home, and school are part of your environment. Your senses of seeing, feeling, hearing, smelling, and tasting bring you information from your environment. All these factors influence your experiences.

Both heredity and environment influence personal development. You inherit certain traits that affect the way you look and behave, but then your environment takes over. Your heredity determines your potential for development. Your environment determines if or how that potential is reached.

The Influence of the Family Environment

The family is usually the major human influence in a person's life. This is especially true during the preschool years, when children spend most of their time with parents, grandparents, or other family members.

Most families want to provide a *nurturing* environment in which children feel secure and protected. Physical needs for food, clothing, and shelter are met. A child's needs to be with people and to give and receive love are met. Children also have opportunities to learn, explore, and create. In such an environment, family members can grow and develop to maturity.

The Prenatal Environment

The *prenatal environment* is the child's surroundings before birth. The way a woman cares for herself during pregnancy will affect her baby. Eating properly and avoiding harmful drugs and medications are healthful practices. Good health increases a woman's chance of having a healthy baby.

Environmental Factors

- Family
- Cultural heritage and society
- School
- Peers
- Community
- Religion
- Technology
- Media and electronic entertainment
- Stress and violence

1-9 Many factors in the environment influence your growth and development.

Poor health care, on the other hand, can have a negative, long-term impact. Substance abuse by a pregnant woman, poor nutrition, or exposure to harmful radiation can permanently affect a baby's brain development.

The Family in the Early Years

Families need to create a safe environment for a baby to grow and develop. That means they need to take care of the baby, keep the baby warm and fed, and protect the baby from things that are harmful.

However, babies need more from their environment than just physical care. They also need an environment that helps them feel secure and loved. This helps them grow emotionally and socially. Families need to hold, cuddle, talk to, and play with the baby. They need to respond to the baby's cries.

When children receive warm, loving, and consistent care, they tend to feel safe and secure, 1-10. They will want to explore their environment. The sights, sounds, smells, and textures they experience help them grow and develop. With such stimulation, their intellectual development increases.

As they explore, children discover they are independent and can do things on their own. The child's environment should promote the growth of independence. Families can provide tasks for children to do by themselves, such as picking up toys or getting dressed. When children are not allowed to try some tasks on their own, they may

1-10 Reading stories to children makes them feel safe and loved.

doubt their abilities. They may feel ashamed of their lack of skills. Instead of growing toward independence, they become more dependent on others.

Families can also help children learn how to fit into their surroundings. An environment with well-defined limits helps young children learn to control their own behavior. For instance, they discover that when they kick something, it moves. They learn that it is okay to kick balls, but not to kick brothers and sisters! In this way, they learn that some activities are safe and acceptable while others are not.

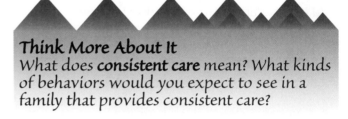

Think More About It
What does **consistent care** mean? What kinds of behaviors would you expect to see in a family that provides consistent care?

The Family in the Teen Years

The family can help teens through the changes of the teen years by providing a loving and caring environment that encourages growth. Such an environment will help both you and your family cope with changes as you become more independent. A caring environment will also help you accept your identity and develop healthy relationships with others.

One way your family can encourage your growth is to allow you more opportunities to make personal decisions. Suppose, for instance, you want to go on a school-sponsored ski trip. You could take the responsibility for making your reservation. Earning the money for the trip could be your responsibility, too. Taking more responsibility also helps you develop your own capabilities for decision making.

Remind yourself that your parents need time to adjust as you change and develop. You may be changing faster than your parents are adjusting. You can help your family maintain a loving family environment through your actions. Show respect for their ideas, requests, and feelings. This will help them listen and show respect for your thoughts and feelings.

Family Structure

The structure of a family can influence many areas of a child's life. A family may include any combination of a father, mother, children, grandparents, or other relatives. Sometimes the family includes stepparents or stepchildren. Not all children grow up with both parents in the family.

Changes in family structure often affect the family's ability to provide a stimulating environment. For instance, there may not be enough money for all the children's needs. There may not be enough time to listen, share, encourage, or guide each child.

Whatever the family structure may be, it is important that the family fulfills its functions and meets the needs of each family member. Sometimes others, such as grandparents, older siblings, babysitters, stepparents, or community youth leaders, help make this happen.

Use What You Learn

What kinds of activities in a family environment could help a teen grow to maturity?

The Influence of Siblings

A **sibling** is a brother or sister. They can be the source of fun and good times together. Siblings can also be the source of conflict and competition.

A family environment that includes siblings can be beneficial. Siblings can learn much from each other. An older sibling may teach a younger sibling. They often play together and can be good companions. They can learn to share as they play. They can learn to work together to do a task. Experiences with siblings can help children learn to get along with others.

Sibling Position

Being the first, the last, or a middle child in the family can make a difference in a child's development. Being an only child may also affect development.

Parents are usually idealistic with their first child. They have high expectations for him or her. Older siblings may be given more responsibility in the family. They may be expected to do things for themselves. They may be required to set an example and care for younger siblings. As a result, oldest children often develop skills for making decisions, organizing tasks, and supervising others, 1-11.

The youngest child often receives a lot of attention. Older siblings may do tasks that the youngest child could and should learn to do alone. As a result, younger children may be slow to develop self-help skills such as dressing themselves. Sometimes younger children may struggle to get a chance to express themselves. When they do get a chance to talk, others may not take them seriously. In some families, the expectations for the youngest child are lower than for the oldest child. Families may provide fewer limits and fewer responsibilities. In these situations, the youngest child may appear lazy or undisciplined. In other families, the youngest child develops skills rapidly to keep up with older siblings.

1-11 Older siblings may be asked to help care for younger children in the family.

The middle child is not always given the same responsibility as the oldest child or the same attention as the youngest child. Children respond to this middle position in different ways. Some middle children become peacemakers. They find themselves trying to settle differences between other brothers and sisters. Some put extra effort into their work, trying to outdo an older sibling. Then, there are others who respond by choosing unacceptable activities that will get attention.

An only child does not experience the daily give-and-take of close sibling relationships. He or she does not experience the conflicts that siblings often have. As a result, this child may take longer to learn to resolve conflicts with playmates. Most families with an only child try to provide opportunities for interaction with other children so these skills are learned.

An only child generally spends more time with adults in one-on-one situations. This can stimulate adultlike behavior at an earlier age. However, an only child is usually the center of attention in those situations. When the attention stops, the adultlike behavior is often replaced with immature actions and attitudes. Interaction with other children of the same age encourages the child to behave more maturely.

Link to Your Life

Do you agree that siblings can be a source of fun and good times? Do you agree that oldest children are given more responsibility in families?

Your Cultural Heritage and Society

Each family environment is strongly influenced by its cultural heritage. Your **cultural heritage** is learned behavior that is passed from generation to generation. Your family's guidelines and beliefs are part of your heritage. The holidays you celebrate, the foods you eat, and the religious traditions or ceremonies you observe are part of your culture.

Every culture in the world has its unique way of life. The families within these cultures pass on their customs and traditions to their children. Within a large society, children are exposed to different cultural experiences. A child in a small farm town has different experiences from those of a child in a large city. From these experiences, children learn the appropriate behaviors of their culture.

Multicultural influences in a society can also affect life experiences within the family, 1-12. Not everyone in a community will have similar views or ways of living. A diverse community can enrich the lives of all. Sharing values and traditions within a community can help members understand one another. This can help them develop mutual respect even though they are different in some ways.

Use What You Learn

What multicultural influences can you identify in your community? In what ways have these influences affected you personally?

The School Environment

School-age children are busy experiencing new situations and becoming more self-reliant. They learn new skills, make new friends, and join group activities. Their interests outside the family grow.

Families can help children adjust to their new environment by providing encouragement, love, and acceptance. They can help children practice skills learned at school. They can attend school events and show an interest in their children's schoolmates. This can help children develop a positive attitude about their schoolwork.

A quality school environment provides a setting that encourages students to learn and grow. School facilities and after-school activities can provide chances for students to interact with schoolmates in clubs or sports. A curriculum should offer a wide range of courses that stimulate students' intellectual growth. Counselors can help students choose courses that meet career needs.

Multicultural Influence on American Families	
African-American	• Husband and wife have more equal roles. • Bonds between relatives are strong. • Emphasis on intergenerational ties is strong. • Children are highly educated. • Extended family households are common.
Hispanic-American	• The extended family is highly valued. • Cooperation and assistance is common among relatives. • Many are bilingual. • Catholicism is an important factor.
Asian-American	• Recent immigrants tend to retain values and traditions of homeland. • Family ties are strong. • Males and females are expected to contribute to family income. • Achievement, education, hard work, and loyalty are valued.
Native-American	• Kin include the clan—a group of related families. • Ceremonies and rituals mark transitions into adulthood and contribute to ethnic identity. • Tribal identities and practices are strong.
European-American	• Values and traditions vary widely. • Kinship groups are important. • Families prefer living close in ethnic neighborhoods.

1-12 Your cultural heritage can give you a sense of identity and strengthen family bonds.

Teachers in a quality school environment encourage students by helping them find areas in which they can succeed. Some students need praise and encouragement. Some need opportunities to lead. Some need slower-paced materials. Others need more challenging work.

Remember the *use-it-or-lose-it* rule as it applies to the developing brain? The school years are a time to stimulate brain development by exploring many different experiences and repeating them. By repeating them, a permanent impression is made so the skills learned in school are not lost in the future.

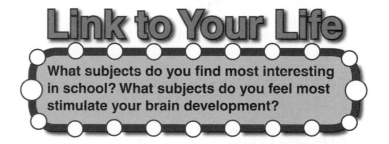

What subjects do you find most interesting in school? What subjects do you feel most stimulate your brain development?

The Influence of Peers

Your **peers** are the people who are your age. The influence of your peers is greatest during the teen years. Your relationships with them are important. You will share many experiences that will influence the way you see yourself. From interacting with your peers, you make judgments about how you look, how important you are, and how successful you are. Your peers can make you feel like you fit in and belong. At other times, they can make you feel left out.

Your peers can also influence the plans you make for your future. You may make decisions about your education based on your peers' choices. You might seek your best friend's opinion of your career or marriage partner. Peers also influence many of your immediate actions since you often face the same decisions that affect them.

Sometimes your peers may make choices that you feel are not right for you. When this happens, you need to make your own choice rather than follow the group. Choices related to sex, alcohol, drugs, and tobacco can affect you for the rest of your life.

Teens can offer understanding to one another as they face similar situations. They can share common experiences and feelings. Peer relationships help you learn what qualities you like or dislike in a friend. You also learn to identify such qualities within yourself. These interactions help teens understand their own identity.

As teens spend time with their friends, they learn to develop close relationships, 1-13. Close friends feel accepted for who they are. They are able to share and communicate deep inner feelings without fear of being embarrassed or laughed at. When young adults have trouble developing such relationships, they feel alone and isolated. Close relationships are important because they help prepare the young adult for marriage.

Your Community's Influence

The community in which you live is part of your environment. Many different types of communities exist, ranging from small towns to big cities. Each community has a particular influence on its residents. A community may influence the jobs that people have, the friends

1-13 Spending time together on common interests can help develop close friendships.

they make, and the activities they join. Most communities offer housing, schools, parks, recreation facilities, police and fire protection, and places to shop and work.

The community environment is influenced by the resources available. A variety of industries or businesses provide job opportunities. A selection of affordable housing allows people to meet their housing needs. Schools with good teaching staffs, facilities, and programs offer quality education. Parks and recreation programs attract families with children.

Other community resources also influence the lives of its residents. Clean air and clean streets provide a healthful environment. A low crime rate makes residents feel more secure and protected. A variety of shopping facilities offer convenience. Opportunities to increase knowledge are provided by libraries as well as technical colleges and universities. Religious institutions draw people of similar beliefs. A community with many resources encourages young people to stay and build a life for themselves and their families.

Link to Your Life

What are the benefits of staying in your home community to raise a family? Are there any drawbacks?

The Influence of Religion

Within a culture, religious beliefs influence your outlook on life and provide guidelines for living. What is the purpose of life? What should you try to accomplish in life? How should you live your life? What happens when you die?

Religious beliefs can provide meaning and direction to a person's life. Associating with others of the same belief and being an active member of the group is usually an important part of a person's environment, 1-14.

Technology and the Environment

Technology is a powerful element in today's environment. It influences every aspect of life. **Technology** is the practical application of knowledge. Technology is also the process of using knowledge to solve problems.

Look around you—technology is part of your everyday world. New technologies influence the food you eat, the clothes you wear, the car you drive, and the work you do. New technologies may even affect your personal growth and relationships.

You may wonder how one aspect of society can have such a far-reaching impact. Changes in technology have resulted in higher standards of living. More goods are available at lower

prices. More information is available faster. Fewer people work at labor-intense jobs. Medical advances result in people living longer. These effects are generally considered very positive.

On the negative side, an emphasis on technology may cause people to judge their quality of life by money or material objects. They may spend all their free time using technology, such as playing video games. This may lead to neglecting personal growth and relationships.

Today, new technologies constantly provide the means for new discoveries. Serious thought should be given to the social and human impacts new technologies may have. An understanding of both positive and negative impacts can help you make choices that will lead to personal growth.

The Influence of Media and Electronic Entertainment

Technology has increased the types of media and entertainment sources available. **Media** include television, radio, newspapers, magazines, and the Internet. These are used to communicate with large groups of people and in many cases provide entertainment as well.

Movies, videos, TV shows, video games, MP3 players, and video phones are forms of electronic entertainment that have changed with new technology. As people have more technology in their homes, the creators of media and entertainment can influence the public—sometimes without people realizing it is happening.

Watching television and movies is one of the most popular leisure pursuits. For many individuals, the people seen daily on television become models to imitate. Television provides models for making friends, developing relationships, and achieving romantic success. Are the models you watch on TV healthy models? Are they realistic? Do you agree with the values they portray?

Some research shows a link between violent, aggressive behavior and watching violent videos or playing violent video games. When you choose movies to watch and video games to play, choose carefully. They may affect the way you control your emotions and actions.

1-14 Religious beliefs impact a family's values.

The Effects of Advertising

Advertising strongly influences how you spend your money. It is designed to stimulate sales of goods and services by giving you information about the items. Ads can provide useful information about food, clothing, entertainment, and other items. You can find out about new or improved products in the market.

Being aware of how ads influence you can help you make wiser choices. Advertisers conduct research to find out why people prefer certain items over others. That information helps them develop ads that display their products in appealing ways. Advertisers constantly try to persuade you to choose their products over others.

You might want to consider how media influences your daily life, 1-15. What information can be useful to you in your personal growth?

Stress, Violence, and the Global Environment

Today's fast-paced society pressures people to succeed at school, work, and home. It is also a society with increased stress from terrorism, war, and violence. This pressure can put stress on the family and on individual lives.

Some stress is positive because it prompts a person to act. For example, feeling stress over a future test will probably cause you to study

1-15 Advertising affects buying decisions, often unconsciously.

hard for it. The more stress you experience personally, the more it can affect your growth and development.

Extreme or long-term stress can have a negative effect on your growth. It can result in special developmental needs. Constant exposure to stress and violence can put the body in a state known as *fight or flight*. This is the body's immediate tendency to defend itself or flee to safety. The biological impact of living in this state during development is negative. A child may react by being impulsive, aggressive, and hyperactive. The ability to think logically and develop language skills may also decrease.

A child who has developed in a stressful environment may have special learning needs. This is not necessarily the fault of anyone in particular. Sometimes unknown factors affect the brain's development. It is important that parents, teachers, and others who work with these children understand their special needs and the best ways to help them learn. This help is necessary for the child to reach his or her maximum potential for growth and development. (Additional information about managing stress and its effects is found in Chapter 3.)

Use What You Learn

What are some ways that violence in your environment could affect growth and development? Do you think movies or video games could stimulate a fight-or-flight response?

The Environment in the Adult Years

A person's job is a very important environmental influence during the adult years. It influences many aspects of the person's life and identity. Just like young children, adults identify themselves by what they are able to do. A person's job has a title that identifies the worker. If a person works at something that he or she feels is important and worthwhile, it increases personal feelings of worth. Doing a job well gives workers a sense of satisfaction.

Many young adults take a spouse and follow the path of marriage and parenting as they create a new generation. They pass their *heritage*—their family guidelines and beliefs—on to their children. Children become a new influence in the adult's environment. Experiences in parenting and later in grandparenting can also influence an adult's identity. All these family experiences can lead to a full and satisfying life, 1-16.

Responding with Resiliency

Many factors impact how you developed into who you are today. As you study the effects of heredity and environment, you may ask,

1-16 For these grandparents, sharing activities with their grandchild provides feelings of fulfillment.

"What can I do about them now?" Scientists are constantly learning new things about the brain and the human body's amazing ability to respond with **resiliency**. That means the body adjusts to setbacks and makes changes to survive and reach its maximum growth and development. For instance, individuals who suffer an injury to a part of the brain respond by using other parts of the brain not specialized for that role. The brain compensates for its loss as much as possible.

Certain aspects of development may have been hindered by your heredity or your environment. The key question is this: In what ways can you respond with resiliency? What can you do to stimulate your own growth to maximum development?

Remember the brain's potential to keep developing as it gets used? You can learn a new skill, read more, or develop new interests. As you learn something new and expand your interests, your brain development increases. Do not worry about the "brain power" you do not have. Make the most of what you have and you will gain more.

Seek positive experiences that enhance your personal growth and development. These experiences will help you progress to maturity. They encourage you to act independently, tackle challenges, develop your identity, and extend yourself into a new generation.

Review Section 1:3

1. List six factors in the environment that might affect a person's growth and development.
2. Give two examples of how a family's cultural heritage influences a person's identity.
3. Name one advantage of being (A) an older child, (B) a middle child, and (C) the youngest child.
4. How can teens help one another mature?
5. Explain the biological effect of a stressful environment on the development of the brain.
6. What are three aspects of the environment that may become part of an adult's identity?
7. Explain what it means to respond to your hereditary and environmental background with resiliency.

Think It Through

A Hereditary Disease

Linda is a sophomore in high school. She has already lived longer than is common for a person in her condition. She has cystic fibrosis. Her parents don't have the disease; neither does her brother or sister. However, the disease is hereditary.

Linda appears healthy to those who meet her, but she doesn't have much longer to live. Every day she undergoes therapy to thin the mucous that affects her breathing and digestion.

Her family members help her with the daily treatments. They have grown very close to one another, realizing that Linda's life will be short. They have also tried to help her live a normal life. She does very well in school. Her grades are high and she has won honors for her achievements.

The stress constantly affects her family. Frequent visits to the hospital strain the family finances. The daily therapy routines take enormous time and energy. Family members also feel the emotional strain of not knowing just how long Linda will live.

Questions to Guide Your Thinking

1. Who in Linda's family are carriers of cystic fibrosis? Using "D" for a dominant healthy gene and "d" for a gene for cystic fibrosis, identify a gene-type for both her mother and her father.

2. What are the chances that each child in this family would have cystic fibrosis? What are the chances that Linda's brother, Dan, and her sister, Tricia, are carriers of cystic fibrosis? (Use a Punnett square to diagram the answer.)

3. Why might Linda's siblings seek genetic counseling before getting married and starting their own families? What information should the counselor be able to provide? How could this information affect a marriage?

4. Linda's family environment has been affected by her disease. How has her family responded to stimulate Linda's growth and development? Because of Linda's disease, in what areas might the growth of other family members be slowed? In what areas might their personal growth be enhanced?

Chapter Summary

As a teen, several major changes in your life path await you. These include living on your own, working at a job, choosing a marriage partner, and raising a family. An important step in preparing for such changes is knowing and accepting your personal identity.

You are a unique person. You inherited unique characteristics from your biological parents. Your heredity influences every aspect about you. Your inherited traits can also be passed on to future generations.

The development of your inherited characteristics is influenced by your environment. Everything and everybody in your environment affect your growth and development. Your heredity and environment work together to make you a unique person. Understanding how these factors impact you can help you make choices. These choices can help you reach your full potential for development.

Assess...

Your Knowledge

1. Define *self-identity*, *heredity*, and *environment*.

2. List the major developmental tasks of the teen years.

3. Identify the hereditary factors that affect development.

4. Identify the environmental factors that impact development.

Your Understanding

5. What can you do to prepare for future life changes?

6. How is your life path unique? How is your life path interdependent with others?

7. How does each developmental task of the teen years relate to future changes in life?

8. How does heredity affect the way a person grows and develops?

9. How does a person's environment affect his or her growth and development?

Your Skills

10. Evaluate your personal characteristics and explain which ones are influenced by your heredity.

11. Analyze how the global environment has affected you personally and explain ways that it has affected your growth and development.

12. Predict ways you could respond with resiliency to various factors in your life.

13. Identify a change that you will face when you graduate from high school. Describe the steps you can take to prepare for that change.

Think Critically

14. **Writing.** Choose one of the following activities and write a paragraph predicting the consequences of the activity. Explain how the action could affect other people, such as family members, friends, classmates, or teachers. Include both direct and indirect effects of the action.

    - Going camping with friends for the weekend.
    - Going out for a school sport.
    - Picking up a part-time job after school.

15. Develop a collage of pictures illustrating the factors that make your life path different from others'. What factors contribute to the differences? Include a description of these factors. *Choice:* Write a paragraph in which you analyze your life and describe how it is similar to and different from others'.

16. Imagine your future and diagram what you hope will occur in your life path. Include the major events you want in your life. Describe three major decisions you must make in order to achieve your goals. *Choice:* Write a song or poem that depicts the three major decisions.

17. Evaluate your present learning environment for factors that stimulate your growth. Consider all areas of growth, including physical, social, emotional, and intellectual. Identify the sights, sounds, smells, tastes, textures, and objects that stimulate your senses. Organize your findings in a graph or chart. *Choice:* Write a two-page paper explaining your findings.

Connect with Your Community

18. *Science.* Investigate a career related to medical genetic research and describe the types of jobs available. What are the educational requirements and job potential for a job in this field? *Choice:* Talk with your family physician to find out which specialist you would see if you had health questions related to your genetic heritage.

19. *Research.* Interview someone who has experienced a hereditary disease. Include questions related to attitudes about the disease, how the disease affects the other family members, and fears about the disease affecting future generations. Consider how the disease impacts a person's ability to live alone or hold a job. *Choice:* Identify community resources available to help people with hereditary diseases. *Group option:* Work with a partner.

20. *Reading, Writing.* Read two news articles from your local newspaper and identify how that information affects you directly or indirectly. Then respond to one article by writing a "Letter to the Editor," expressing your views on that topic. Be prepared to share with the class how your views could impact others in your community.

21. *Writing.* Write a biography, poem, or song describing the life of a typical young person growing up in your community. Include a description of environmental factors that will influence the person's growth and development.

Use Technology

22. Use a computer drawing program to create a family tree that includes you, your parents, grandparents, and great-grandparents. Identify the physical traits you possess that can be traced to members included in your family tree. *Choice:* Determine the average number of years for a life span in your family.

23. Identify a change that a typical teen might expect to experience in the next year. Determine what he or she would need to know about this change. Identify two or more sources of this information, including at least one Internet site; gather information; and identify what skills could help a teen adjust to this change. Use the information to prepare a multimedia presentation and present your findings to the class. *Group option:* Work in a small group to prepare the presentation.

24. *Science.* Search the Internet to explore how technology has expanded the research on human genes and disease traits. Key search terms include *human genome* and *biotechnology companies*. Prepare a one-page report on one aspect of such technology. Present to the class an issue that the use of such technology could raise in the future.

25. *Research.* Develop a questionnaire you can use to survey others' feelings related to future life changes. Survey three classmates, three adults your parents' age, and three older adults. Categorize their responses into *Changes That Are Feared* and *Changes That Are Anticipated*. Using a computer and a graphing program, design a chart or graph showing each age group and the number of changes feared or anticipated. Compare your findings with others in the class. *Group option:* Work in a small group using the total responses of the group.

Chapter 2

Your Growth and Development

Section 2:**1**
Growth Patterns

Section 2:**2**
Your Personality

Life Sketch

Janine stares into space, wishing she could skip gym class. Today the class will be swimming, and she can't bear the thought of wearing a swimsuit in front of her classmates. "They'll see how awful I look and laugh at me!" she says to herself.

She notices Rhonda is already in her swimsuit. Kim, also in her swimsuit, catches up with Rhonda. "Wow, they both look great," Janine thinks.

Janine slowly changes into her swimsuit. A feeling of discomfort grips Janine as the bell rings. She takes one last look at herself in the mirror and realizes it's time to face her peers.

Key Questions

Questions to answer as you study this chapter:

- What choices can help teens reach physical, intellectual, social, and emotional maturity?

- How can people develop strength in character?

- How can teens develop a healthy personality?

Getting Started

Most young people have fears about being different from others. They are afraid they will be rejected or laughed at by their peers.

When you look at your peers, you rate yourself by what you see in them. Compared to others, you may say "I'm too fat (or thin)." "I'm too tall (or short)." "Parts of me are too big (or too small)." These differences in development compared to your peers can be a concern to you.

This concern can make the process of growing seem complex. However, learning more about your own unique growth and development patterns can help you understand yourself. As you grow to maturity, there are certain patterns of development you will follow.

Chapter Objectives

After studying this chapter, you will be able to

- **describe** physical, intellectual, social, and emotional growth patterns of teens.

- **determine** factors that influence character development.

- **identify** factors that influence personality formation.

- **explain** how personality is related to self-concept, temperament, and human needs.

section 2:1

Growth Patterns

Sharpen Your Reading

Organize your notes with a graphic organizer. Create a chart with the headings *Growth Pattern*, *Characteristics During Teen Years*, and *Actions to Promote Maturity.* Chart subheads should include *Definition*, *Physical*, *Intellectual*, *Social*, and *Emotional.*

Boost Your Vocabulary

For each term related to brain structure, draw a picture, diagram, or symbol of the type of brain activity each area controls.

Know Key Terms

physical development
puberty
intellectual development
brainstem
cerebellum
limbic system
cortex
emotional development
social development
socialization
role
character
ethics

Typical growth patterns have been identified in the following four areas:

- physical
- intellectual
- social
- emotional

The chart in 2-1 describes some growth patterns linked to these four areas. Growth patterns follow an orderly sequence—the steps occur in a specific order. For instance, babies move their arms and legs randomly at first. As their muscles develop, they learn to use their arms and legs to pull themselves around. Next, they learn to crawl on hands and knees. Finally, the young child reaches the stage of walking. This is an example of a physical growth pattern. Patterns can be identified in all areas of development.

Although normal growth follows a pattern, each person proceeds along the pattern at his or her own pace or rate of development. For instance, some teens develop physically at an earlier age than others. Some are tall; others are short. Some are well-developed; others are barely beginning to develop.

Your rate of development does not affect the limits of your overall development. If you develop early, it does not mean you will grow taller or bigger or be more intelligent. For instance, one boy in eighth grade may be five feet tall while another is six feet tall. When both finish growing, they may be the same height.

Reaching your full growth potential depends on other factors, too. Heredity and environment both influence your overall growth and personality development. For instance, the way you look and behave are traits inherited from your parents. The way you take care of yourself is an environmental influence.

Think More About It
How do you think different growth rates affect the feelings that young teens have about themselves?

Adolescent Growth Patterns	
Physical	• Hormone production increases.
	• Primary sex characteristics develop.
	• Reproductive organs mature.
	• Secondary sex characteristics develop.
	• Hair grows under the arms and in the pubic area.
	• Male voice lowers in pitch.
	• Males develop facial hair and hair on chest.
	• Breast formation increases in females.
	• Females experience widening of hips.
Intellectual	• Formal thinking skills increase.
	• Abstract ideas are used.
	• Logical reasoning improves.
	• Ability to visualize the future increases.
Social	• Social skills improve.
	• More ideas are shared.
	• Others' viewpoints are considered.
	• Cooperation to complete a task increases.
	• Close relationships with peers develop.
	• Personal identity is formed.
	• Personal standards develop.
Emotional	• Intense emotions are felt and expressed.
	• Emotions fluctuate.
	• Ability to verbally identify emotions increases.
	• Ability to control emotional behavior increases.

2-1 Growth patterns explain the unique way teens grow. In each of these areas, teens grow and develop at their own rate.

Physical Development

Physical growth patterns are the easiest to observe during your teen years. **Physical development** refers to the growth of your body. Growth affects your internal body systems as well as your height and weight. Physical growth and development continues from birth to adulthood.

Adolescent Growth Spurt

Growth patterns during the teen years include dramatic physical changes. Sudden growth as early as age 11 for girls and age 13 for boys marks the beginning of these changes. This is called the *adolescent growth spurt*. Noticeable body changes occur during this growth period.

Boys become stronger as their muscles develop rapidly. Their shoulders widen and their waists narrow. They reach adult height at about age 21. Adolescent girls usually start their growth spurt before adolescent boys. They grow rapidly in height and weight. The average age for girls to reach adult height is 17.

The adolescent growth spurt occurs at puberty. **Puberty** is the time when reproductive organs mature. Hormones bring about sexual maturity and other physical changes within the body. Chart 2-1 lists primary and secondary sex characteristics

Reaching Physical Maturity

Factors such as accidents, disease, and illness can prevent complete growth and development from occurring. To avoid health risks, take good care of yourself and get periodic physical checkups. Get the rest you need. Get regular physical activity. Avoid harmful substances and activities. Take safety precautions. Make wise decisions about what you do and where you go. Eat healthful, nutritious meals. By doing so, you should be able to reach physical maturity and live a long healthy life, 2-2. These topics are so important to your growth that whole chapters in this book focus on these factors.

2-2 Being active and adventurous is natural during the teen years. Following safety precautions will help you reach your physical potential.

Intellectual Development

A second area of growth is intellectual development. **Intellectual development** refers to the growth of the brain and the use of mental skills. These include your use of words, numbers, and ideas. You take information into your brain through your five senses. What you see, hear, taste, touch, and smell all provide information. You then use this information to respond emotionally and socially, as well as reason, solve problems, make decisions, and think creatively.

The Parts of the Brain and Their Functions

The diagram in 2-3 shows the different parts of the brain and the main functions of each. There appear to be three main areas. The brainstem and cerebellum control action activities. The limbic system controls emotion-related responses. The cortex controls thinking responses. As you mature, you develop the thinking part of your brain so it controls your responses to your environment.

- The **brainstem** controls life functions such as the beating of the heart and breathing. The brainstem is made up of different parts that are involved in getting information out to different body parts and producing a physical response. When there is a threat to the body, the brainstem controls the body's responses and ensures survival.

- The **cerebellum** controls automatic movements. For instance, once you learn to ride a bike, you do it automatically. You have stored this information in the cerebellum and use it automatically.

- The **limbic system** consists of four main structures in the brain that control emotions and hormone production as well as eating,

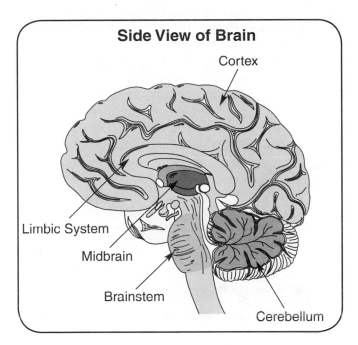

Side View of Brain

2-3 The side view of the brain shows the three major areas: the brain stem and cerebellum, which control movement and motor responses; the limbic system, which controls emotions and their interactions with other parts of the brain; and the cortex, which controls thinking, decision making, and judgment.

drinking, and sleeping. This system is also involved in long-term memory storage.

• The **cortex** is the part of the brain that controls thinking, decision making, and judgment. This is the part of the brain that is most often referred to when people talk about intellectual development. It is divided into different regions. See the diagram of the cortex in 2-4 to learn what brain functions each region controls.

The cortex is also divided in half vertically, so each of the five regions has a left brain half and a right brain half. Each half processes information from a different perspective. The two halves of the cortex "talk" back and forth to each other continuously as you take in information and process it. Together, the two halves help you get a clear picture of the stimuli you are receiving. The *corpus callosum* is the cable of neurons that connects the two halves of the brain. This cord appears to change and grow during the teen years.

The Development of the Adolescent Brain

The *parietal lobe* (touch), *occipital lobe* (vision), and *temporal lobe* (language) are quite developed by the teen years. Your abilities to sense and process touch, vision, and language stimuli are mature.

A major growth spurt takes place in the *frontal lobes* of the cortex around age 11. This is the part of the brain responsible for thinking, problem solving, planning, and making judgments. Growth spurts also occur between ages 14 and 16 and again between 18 and 20. The frontal lobes do not fully mature until young adulthood. Therefore, the teen years are important years in developing this part of the brain.

After a growth spurt, your brain again starts to prune the neural connections. The pathways you use create more dendrite connections with other parts of your brain. The pathways you do not use get pruned, and the connections die off.

The physical growth of brain cells and the connections between them is directly related to mature intellectual skills. When people develop intellectually, they can think in abstract ways. They can use logic and judgment, and are able to visualize the future.

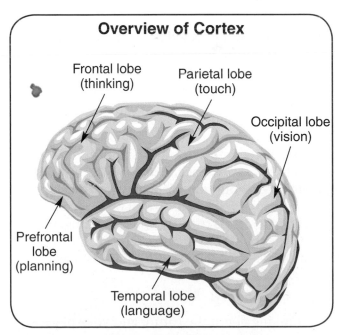

Overview of Cortex

2-4 The overview of the cortex shows five major regions. Each controls different brain functions.

Thinking Abstractly

The development of thinking skills proceeds through stages. Early thinking follows concrete patterns. *Concrete thinking* is related to specific objects that can be seen and touched. The school-age child can think about a cup of water. If the water is heated, rising steam can be seen by the child. Thinking about water turning into steam is an example of concrete thinking.

During the teen years, thinking patterns involve more abstract ideas. *Abstract ideas* refer to thoughts of something you cannot see, touch, taste, smell, or hear. Love is an example of an abstract idea. You cannot touch or taste it. You cannot take it apart and examine it, but you can think about it and experience it. Topics such as love, happiness, friendship, loyalty, and bravery are all abstract ideas.

Developing Logic

As young people mature, they begin to use abstract ideas in a logical manner. This process includes connecting several abstract ideas to support a decision or build a viewpoint. For instance, Doug wonders if he is in love. He likes Erika and enjoys talking to her. He thinks she is friendly and cute. He feels happy when she is around and likes being with her. He concludes that these feelings could be the beginning signs of love. Doug has connected several thoughts about love into a logical conclusion.

Developing Judgment

Maturity also brings an increase in the young person's ability to judge if a viewpoint is strong or weak. New information may cause a change in position. For instance, Doug gains some new information about himself when Melissa stops by his locker to talk. He learns that he likes talking with her, too. She is friendly and interesting, like Erika. After talking to Melissa, he begins to question his first conclusion about his feelings for Erika.

Visualizing the Future

Thinking about the future and your place in it is also part of formal thinking. Doug can think about his future relationship with Erika. He can consider his feelings for her now and how these feelings may change over time. He can even visualize Erika as his wife.

As you mature and develop, you learn to organize and think about your ideas logically. Your skill in visualizing your future will increase. Your ability to predict the consequences of a decision will improve. You will be able to make judgments based on your past experiences by using your maturing thought processes. This is all part of growing.

Link to Your Life

What factors in your environment make it hard to use mature thinking skills?

Reaching Intellectual Maturity

Remember the use-it-or-lose-it principle of brain development? The teen years are the time to expand your knowledge base. You can do this by reading more. Think about new ideas and connect them to what you have already learned. Expose yourself to developing as many new skills as possible.

By learning and developing new skills, you make use of your intelligence. This can help you grow to intellectual maturity. There are eight different types of intelligences, 2-5. Most people possess all eight intelligences in varying degrees. However, some will perform better than others in certain areas. For instance, people with more musical intelligence may excel in playing instruments or writing music. Those with more interpersonal intelligence may interact well with all types of people. By seeking ways to use all eight intelligences, you can reach your maximum intellectual potential.

Link to Your Life

Examine the eight multiple intelligences and then analyze your own preferences for learning. What type of intelligence do you think influences you the most?

The Eight Human Intelligences		
Type of Intelligence	**Description**	**Examples**
Linguistic (verbal)	Using words; communicating through language	Edit, interpret, speak, read
Logical (mathematical)	Using math concepts, logic skills, or abstract reasoning	Analyze, calculate, propose theories
Musical	Using sounds to create meanings; hearing patterns in sounds	Compose, harmonize, sing, play an instrument
Spatial (visual)	Perceiving images and transforming them; recreating images from memory	Draw, design, map, sketch, sculpt, create fine art
Kinesthetic (bodily)	Moving the body in highly skilled ways	Dance, mime, use complex tools skillfully, show athletic talent
Intrapersonal	Understanding oneself	Reflect, set goals, improve behavior
Interpersonal	Relating to other people	Persuade, motivate, teach, inspire
Naturalist	Classifying and using features of the environment	Observe, discover, cultivate, harvest, hunt

Dr. Howard Gardner, Harvard University

2-5 To reach intellectual maturity, seek ways to use all eight of your intelligences.

Emotional Development

Emotional development refers to the ability to experience and express emotions. It also involves the ability to control emotional behaviors.

You have many emotions. During the teen years, they are continually changing. Sometimes you feel loved and accepted. You may feel happy, excited, and successful when others give you positive comments and encouragement. They may laugh at your jokes and invite you to become part of their group. This makes you feel successful.

Then there are times when you feel insecure, left out, and alone. You may think no one really cares about you. At times like these, you may feel depressed, discouraged, and unhappy.

Emotions usually arise from your interactions with others. Understanding how your brain responds to emotional stimuli in your environment can help you understand your own emotions. It can also help you understand how to control your emotional responses.

Your Brain and Your Emotional Responses

When you see an event, you process your emotional reaction to it through the limbic system first. The connections between the limbic system and your actions or responses are fast. It is designed to provide protection to your body. However, in times when you are not in danger, you still may react before your brain has even had a chance to send a response to the cortex. Some people call this brain pathway the *low road*. The brain pathways in the low road travel from the senses to the limbic system to the brainstem and result in quick actions that people may regret later.

Learning to control your emotions and the responses that go with them takes practice. This means getting the high road to function. Some people refer to the connections between the limbic system and the thinking cortex as the *high road*. This brain pathway is a little slower than the low road, so it means you have to force yourself to stop and think—just for a few seconds—so the information has time to get to your thinking brain. As you learn to think about what you are feeling before you respond, you will have a more controlled reaction.

Identifying Your Emotions

Emotional responses will be more controlled as the thinking part of your brain takes over. A first step is to recognize your emotions. Practice sharing your emotions when you are not upset. Then it will be easier to say "I feel angry" or "I feel upset" when you are under stress. Sometimes others can help you recognize your emotions by identifying them for you.

Controlling Your Emotional Responses

Controlling emotional behavior means that you communicate your feelings in acceptable ways. For instance, if you are angry because someone used your MP3 player, you can say "I am really angry because you used my MP3 player without asking." This is an acceptable, healthy response—a high road response. Uncontrolled responses—low road responses—include hitting people or taking something of theirs to get even.

Another controlled response is to remove yourself from the situation. You may decide to take a walk or go to your room until you can handle the conflict. This can give you time to cool down and think through your feelings. Consider what you are feeling and why you are feeling this emotion. In this way, you can activate the high road and think through your feelings. You can think about your response and the effects it will have on others.

Link to Your Life

Think of an example when you responded quickly with an emotional response. What could you have done to slow down the emotional response?

Reaching Emotional Maturity

Emotionally mature persons experience mature emotions such as love, self-esteem, concern, and empathy. They are also able to activate their thinking brain enough to be able to control their emotional responses. What factors help a person grow to emotional maturity?

A strong supportive family network is important in the development of mature emotions, 2-6. Being in such an environment helps you develop positive emotions, like feelings of being loved, cared for, and valuable to others. Positive feedback and warm, affirming touches from others actually affect the chemicals that are produced in your brain. Growing up in such an environment will help you experience positive emotions. However, not every person has a warm, loving, and relaxed environment at home.

A close relationship with at least one significant adult has been found to stimulate the development of mature emotions. Is there at least one adult with whom you can develop a warm and caring relationship—someone who cares about you, and encourages you to grow to be the best you can be? This might be a parent, grandparent, youth leader, religious leader, or teacher. It only takes one close relationship to stimulate the growth of mature positive emotions.

2-6 A warm, loving, and caring relationship promotes the development of the emotional center of the brain.

Another strategy for promoting emotional maturity is to reduce stress in your life. Eliminate whatever stress you can. Consider your choices of music, video games, movies, places to frequent, and friends. Reduce the stressful stimuli that you can control.

Avoid the use of alcohol or other controlled substances. Such substances slow down and dull the functioning of the thinking parts of your brain. When your thinking processes are slowed or dulled, you may express yourself in ways you do not like or want.

Focus on learning new facts and skills that make you feel more positive about yourself. You may like to read, draw, paint, work with tools, or follow some other interest. Find areas in which you can succeed. As you succeed, these positive emotions will be stored in your long-term memory along with the new skills learned. This focus on growth will help you develop more mature emotions and sharpen your ability to control your responses.

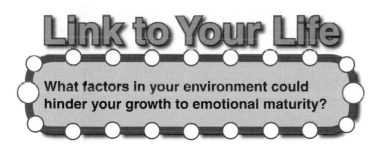

What factors in your environment could hinder your growth to emotional maturity?

Social Development

Social development is concerned with the way you relate to others. Every time your life path crosses another person's life path, you relate in some way. The way you relate to others changes as you grow and develop.

When you were very young, you related to others from your own point of view. Your ideas centered on yourself. You were concerned about your toys, mom, dad, or home. When you began to play with other children, you had to consider their viewpoints. You had to share the ball during recess. You had to take turns jumping rope. You were learning to consider the thoughts and feelings of others. You were beginning to develop social skills.

As you grew and developed, you learned how to share in your relationships with others. Sometimes you were asked to lead a group in a class project. At other times, you were asked to assist and cooperate with others to get a job done. To do this, you had to consider others' thoughts and ideas as well as your own.

During the teen years, you continue to mature socially. You learn give-and-take as you consider others' viewpoints. You use social skills as you try to understand and accept others even though they are different from you. This helps you develop close friendships with them, 2-7.

Social development occurs throughout your lifetime. You will continue to meet new people and face new personalities. You will have to work at understanding them and trying to help them understand you as well.

Investigate Further

Which of the skills involved with social development use the thinking part of the brain—the frontal and prefrontal lobes of the cortex? Which social skills involve the maturation of the limbic system?

2-7 Friendships can help you develop skills for building close relationships.

Socialization and Roles

Socialization is the way you learn the behavior that society accepts. This learning process, which includes the beliefs and standards of your society, begins with your family.

In your family, you learn what will be expected of you in the many roles you will have in life. A **role** is a way of acting to fulfill certain responsibilities. One role you have now is that of son or daughter. In this role, you may be expected to talk to your parents, show them love and respect, and help do household tasks. At school, your role of student means that you must act in a certain way. You are expected to participate in class, read assignments, write papers, and take exams. Your future roles might include husband or wife, parent, employee or employer, and community leader. Each of these roles will have certain responsibilities.

Use What You Learn

What roles do you have in your family?

By observing family members and interacting with them, you learn how to respond to various life situations. You learn what is important, what guidelines to use, and what actions are acceptable.

Young people develop socially as they adopt these beliefs and standards as their own. Part of this process includes thinking about and questioning parents' standards. By providing answers and reasons for their standards and beliefs, parents can help children understand their future roles.

Character and Ethics

Character is developed as part of the socialization process. Your **character** serves as your personal judge for every situation you face. Certain desirable traits are found in persons who have strength of character. These traits help them make choices that benefit not only themselves, but also others around them and society as a whole.

Ethics are the moral principles or standards that you use to judge what is right and wrong. Society sets some of these standards in the form of laws to protect everyone's welfare.

Some of these moral principles are taught to you by parents and family members. They teach you acceptable behavior, which is often based on the family's religious beliefs. These standards serve to guide and protect you, your family, and others.

When people make choices that benefit only themselves, usually someone is hurt. It may even be the person making the choice. For instance, they may be taking work that someone else did and claim it as their own. They may take money that belongs to someone else. In both examples, people are hurt, and problems with the law could result. Ethical behavior protects everyone's welfare.

Character Traits

What are some of the inner traits or moral qualities that define a person's character and contribute to ethical behavior?

- *Self-discipline* is one. This is the ability to control your behavior. For instance, can you control your desire to watch television until your homework is done? This takes self-discipline. Self-discipline is also referred to as *self-control.*

- *Dependability* means that you are reliable and true to your word. If you tell a friend to meet you at a certain time and place, are you always there on time? If you do what you promise, you are dependable.

- Being *responsible* means answering for your behavior and obligations. For instance, how well do you do your part when working on a group assignment? Do you get your part done? Do you complete it on time? Are you careful and thorough so your share of the task is done well? This shows you are responsible, 2-8.

- *Integrity* means honesty. Honest people can be trusted because they are truthful. If you are honest, other people know they can believe what you say. For instance, when honest students say they have done their own homework, their teachers believe them. When an honest person takes a test, he or she can be trusted not to cheat. These are examples of integrity.

- *Motivation* is a drive that moves a person to do a task, sometimes beyond what is expected. Manuel offers to carry Lori's books.

2-8 Doing your part in team class projects shows you are able to be responsible.

He walks her to the door and holds it open for her. The reason is motivation. Manuel is motivated by his desire to know Lori better and maybe date her.

- A sense of *mercy and justice* moves a person to uphold the laws of society and show regard for others' rights and feelings. Your thoughts, feelings, and actions reflect your concern about the rights of others. A sense of mercy and justice is displayed when you treat others in a caring way, with fairness and respect for their rights and views.

These are some of the character traits that may be present or absent in a person's life. People who often show these traits are considered strong in character. They respond with ethical behavior. A person who rarely shows these traits is considered weak in character.

Think More About It
What are some ways that unethical behavior is promoted in society?

The Development of Character

Character development starts when a child is young and continues throughout life. The teaching, training, and examples provided by families are the first influences on a child's

character development. Many character traits are learned through *direct teaching* by parents. Children may be taught to be kind to others or to tell the truth. They may be told to never take what belongs to someone else.

The family also teaches character by setting behavior guidelines. For instance, a teen might be expected to complete his or her homework before going out with friends. When parents require that children follow these guidelines, they are helping the child learn responsibility.

Families reinforce their teachings through *training*. This is a second way that families teach character. Children are provided opportunities to practice how to act responsibly. They may be given responsibilities around the house. They may help with household chores or care for siblings. Caring for a family pet can teach children to carry out daily responsibilities. All these experiences help children develop strength in character.

Families also teach their children by *example*. Certain adult character traits may be modeled, or copied, by young family members. For instance, a sense of justice can be taught by example. When children are treated fairly, they usually learn to treat others the same way. When children see adults act with integrity, they tend to likewise be honest.

Religion can be a strong influence in character development. Various religious faiths teach standards of right and wrong. Many people feel these standards give meaning and direction to their lives. Their religious beliefs serve as a foundation for their character formation.

Schools also influence character development. Students learn dependability and responsibility through homework assignments and group projects. Schools set standards for acceptable behavior, too. Such standards encourage integrity and self-discipline by requiring students to do their own work. Standards of performance help students learn to do a job well. Standards for treating other students with respect and fairness teach a sense of mercy and justice. Teachers influence character development by modeling strong character traits that support these standards.

Encouraging character development is easiest when a child is young. However, character traits evolve over time, and character development continues throughout life.

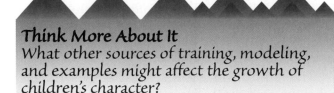

Think More About It
What other sources of training, modeling, and examples might affect the growth of children's character?

Developing Strength in Character

A person's character is not shaped in a day, a week, or even a year. You may have certain traits that you do not like and want to change. Developing new character traits takes effort and time, but it can be done.

1. The first step in improving your character is to identify the trait(s) you want to change or develop. Questions similar to those listed in 2-9 can help you identify some of these areas. Any question to which you answer "mostly never" may pinpoint an area needing improvement.

2. After you identify a weak area, focus on specifics about it. For instance, if dependability is sometimes a problem, identify the circumstances when you are not dependable. Is it when doing homework? Is it when doing a task at home? Is it when trying to be on time for appointments?

3. The next step in improving your character is to develop a plan that addresses a specific trait. List some specific actions to take to improve the trait. Then work on one area at a time.

4. As part of your plan, choose someone to make regular checkups. A person who is close to you could check your progress without offending you. Regular checkups by a friend will help you implement your plan.

Examining Character Traits	
Trait	**Questions**
Self-discipline	Do I accomplish what I plan to do?
	Can I say no to myself?
	Do I keep myself neat, clean, and appropriately dressed?
Dependability	Do I arrive on time for a date or appointment?
	Can I be counted on to get a job done?
Responsibility	Do I do my share of the work when assigned to a group project?
	Do I feel that I have a part in helping others grow to their potential?
	Do I carry out my jobs without being reminded?
Moral principles	Do I respect others' rights and privileges?
	Do I obey the law?
Integrity	Do I try to be honest?
	Do I present a truthful picture?
Motivation	Do I believe that hard work is useful and worthwhile?
	Am I enthusiastic about my work?
	Do I find satisfaction in a job well-done?
Sense of mercy and justice	Do I feel compassion when others are ill-treated?
	Do I help others when I see others in need?
	Am I able to look beyond my own desires to consider the welfare of others?

2-9 These questions help you examine your character traits. Your answers can identify areas that you may want to develop.

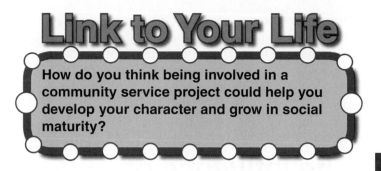

How do you think being involved in a community service project could help you develop your character and grow in social maturity?

Reaching Social Maturity

Developing a strong character will help you achieve *social maturity*. This is a set of qualities that makes you an enjoyable person. When you have social maturity, the important people in your life will be able to count on you, depend on you, and trust you. They know you will also consider their well-being when making decisions. They know you will respond with ethical behavior.

Being involved in community service projects can help you grow socially. Such projects are usually group efforts that focus on helping others and supplying their needs. Community service projects can help you see situations from other points of view. In what group projects have you participated? Is there some type of need in a person's life that you could help fill? Perhaps you could be the one to step in and make a difference. As you help others, you grow socially and become more mature.

Review Section 2:**1**

1. Name the four typical growth patterns and summarize the characteristics of each.
2. When are differences in growth rates most obvious?
3. List three steps that an adolescent can take to promote physical growth to maturity.
4. List three characteristics of intellectual development.
5. List three strategies that could help a person reach intellectual maturity.
6. Describe an emotionally mature person.
7. Describe three characteristics of a socially mature person.

section 2:2

Your Personality

Sharpen Your Reading

Use the equation "All you are + All you do = Personality." Under each part of the equation, summarize the key points from the text that illustrate that part of personality.

Boost Your Vocabulary

For each key term, write an example of words that people use to describe that trait in a person.

Know Key Terms

personality
self-concept
self-esteem
temperament
extrovert
introvert

If your best friend were asked to describe you, what would your friend say? "She's a lot of fun, rather quiet, but a true friend." "He is tall, very outgoing, and a starter on the basketball team."

When your friend describes you, he or she is listing different parts of your personality. Your **personality** is the sum of all your personal and behavioral traits. These traits combine to make you a unique person with your own personality.

Many researchers have studied the factors that affect personality. Some look at the growth of the self-concept and how a person's view of "self" affects behavior. Others study the natural response patterns that people use to express themselves. Still others study personality by looking at how people respond to their human needs. Your personality development will be influenced in some way by each of these factors.

The Influence of Self-Concept

Your **self-concept** is the mental picture you have of yourself, 2-10. If you like the way you see yourself, you will have a positive self-concept. If you do not like what you see, you will have a negative self-concept.

2-10 Your personality is influenced by how you see yourself and feel about that mental image.

If you have a positive self-concept, you feel good about yourself. You accept yourself as you really are—a worthwhile person. When you know and accept yourself, you can be realistic about judging your personal traits. You know your good points and feel positive about them. You also know that you have areas to improve. You feel good about who you are, even though you know you have room to grow.

With a negative self-concept, you do not feel good about yourself. This may cause you to feel insecure or less important as a person. A lack of confidence makes it hard to try to improve. You may not want to try new experiences because you fear failure.

Your self-concept affects your self-esteem. **Self-esteem** is how you feel about yourself. A positive self-concept indicates high self-esteem. A negative self-concept shows low self-esteem. High self-esteem means you respect yourself, have self-confidence, and feel secure in your world. You value yourself as a person.

Three factors influence the development of your self-concept: (1) how you see your physical traits or appearance, (2) what you are able to do, and (3) how people respond to you. Knowing how these factors influence your self-concept will help you understand how your own personality is formed.

Physical Traits

Your height, weight, appearance, and sexuality are traits that influence your self-concept. How do you see yourself? Are you tall, short, or average? Are you thin, heavy, or just right? Are you cute or plain? Your responses to these questions form a part of your self-concept. If you feel good about your appearance, you are more likely to have a positive self-concept.

Skills and Talents

What you are able to do is also a part of your self-concept. Can you play football, tennis, soccer, baseball, or basketball? Can you draw, sing, write, or play the piano? Are you good at math, computer programming, or woodworking? You might include your abilities when you describe yourself. These various skills and talents form a part of your personality.

How do you feel about your skills? Again, these feelings affect your self-esteem. If you feel capable of doing a good job in some area, your feelings of worth increase. Your confidence in your ability to succeed grows. This expression of confidence is part of your personality.

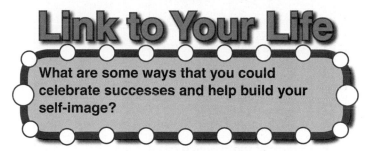

Link to Your Life

What are some ways that you could celebrate successes and help build your self-image?

Responses from Others

Your overall view of yourself is affected by the way others respond to you. Are they friendly to you? Do they compliment you? Do they show you respect? Do they recognize your achievements? Their responses or feedback help you form your self-concept.

If the feedback is positive, you likely see yourself as worthwhile. These feelings add to your positive self-concept and increase your self-esteem.

If their responses are negative, you may judge yourself in a negative way. For instance, your height may be average according to your doctor's chart. If a peer calls you short, though, you may think of yourself as too short.

You can see how your self-concept forms part of your personality. It affects the way you feel about yourself and the way you express your thoughts and feelings to others. Your self-concept also affects your relationships with others and the plans you make for yourself. See 2-11.

Your Temperament's Influence

Individuals tend to relate to others in a consistent manner. In other words, their individual behavior is predictable. Your family and friends generally know how you will respond in given situations. This consistency of behavior is based on your **temperament**, which is an inborn pattern of responses.

A Positive Self-Concept

- I enjoy getting up in the morning.
- I am usually in a good mood.
- I like the way I look.
- Most people like me.
- Others think I am attractive.
- I am happy with my friends.
- I can laugh at my mistakes.
- I am continuing to grow and change.
- I look at the positive side of things.
- I enjoy what I do.
- My life is interesting.
- I plan to do something important in life.
- Others like to have me with them.
- Others care about my opinions.
- I can tell others how I feel.
- I can talk to others with ease.

2-11 This list describes some of the thoughts and feelings expressed by a person with a positive self-image.

Although you inherit your temperament, the environment has a strong effect on how your behavior patterns develop. For instance, behavior patterns that are encouraged and accepted by parents, siblings, or peers are likely to become stronger. Patterns that are ignored or not accepted by others tend to become weaker.

Your environment shapes the way these behavior patterns develop during your life. Temperament patterns are related to basic behavior in the following four areas:
- how you express yourself intellectually
- how physically active you are
- how you feel and express your emotions
- how social you are

Your intellectual behavior pattern relates to how you use words and numbers. It also relates to how you plan and organize your ideas. For instance, you may be able to describe and explain your ideas very clearly when speaking. Another person may be better at organizing thoughts on paper. Yet another person may have difficulty with words and ideas, but ease with math concepts. These differences reflect individual patterns of intellectual expression.

Use What You Learn

What is your strongest response pattern for expressing yourself intellectually? Is it similar to one of the multiple intelligences?

Physical behavior patterns range from being very active to very inactive. You may be a person who is always moving, working on one task or another. You may enjoy active sports such as running, basketball, or tennis. On the other hand, you may be a person who prefers quieter activities such as reading, playing the piano, or building models. Working on projects that require great thought and precision might appeal to you.

Emotional behavior patterns vary widely. Some people are more sensitive to their emotional feelings. They may also be more aware of the feelings of others. On the other hand, some people are considered insensitive. They seem less aware of their own emotions or the feelings of others. Without realizing it, they may hurt other people's feelings or offend them.

Strong emotional feelings can cause some people to anger quickly or lose control and cry. Others tend to hide their emotions, keep everything inside, and cry rarely.

Think More About It
How could a person's emotional behavior patterns affect his or her social relationships?

Social patterns relate to how outgoing a person is. An **extrovert** is a person who is very outgoing and enjoys being with people, 2-12. This person is usually friendly and seems to have a lot of friends. An **introvert** is a person who is more withdrawn. This person may be shy and anxious about meeting new people. An introvert usually likes to be alone or with a very small group of familiar people.

All areas of your temperament—intellectual, physical, emotional, and social—affect your personality. Your intellectual and physical patterns affect the way you approach a task and complete your work. Your emotional patterns affect the way you feel about others' responses to you. This affects your responses to those people. Your social patterns affect the way you relate to others.

Understanding Your Response Patterns

Have you been able to see yourself in any of these temperament patterns? The list in 2-13 identifies some characteristics of two types of common temperament patterns. The first pattern describes an aggressive, hard-working, impatient, and competitive person. A person who tends to respond in a calmer, quieter, and more relaxed manner is described in the second pattern.

One temperament pattern is not better or more desirable than the other. Each pattern of responding has both strengths and weaknesses. For instance, a person may be talkative and enthusiastic. Sometimes that person may be considered loud and obnoxious. A sensitive person may sometimes be considered touchy. The situation may determine whether the quality is a strength or a weakness.

2-12 An extrovert enjoys meeting new people and going to new places.

Behavior Patterns
Type 1: Aggressive, hardworking, impatient, and competitive
I often do several things at the same time.
I ordinarily work quickly and energetically.
I persist at working on a problem even though it seems overwhelming.
I often hurry.
I become impatient when someone slows me down.
In conversation, I often gesture with my hands.
I really like challenges.
I walk quickly.
Sometimes I speak too quickly and put words in another person's mouth.
I often try to persuade others to my point of view.
Type 2: Calm, quiet, relaxed, and easygoing
In comparison to others, I am fairly easygoing.
I usually do not plan more work than I can finish.
I am a good listener and hear people well.
I am relaxed when I work.
I am bothered when people rush me.
Most people consider me quiet.
I like to eat slowly and enjoy my meals.
I can usually wait patiently.
I usually speak more softly than most people.
I rarely worry about being late.

2-13 The natural way people respond to their environment is influenced by their temperament. Some common behavior patterns are described here.

How could you use your knowledge of your temperament to help you choose a project you could complete successfully?

Knowing your typical response patterns can be helpful. You can make choices that will focus on your strengths. This will help you experience success. For instance, you may be required to be a leader in class. If you are a quiet and reserved person, volunteer to lead a small group rather than the whole class. When you know your natural response patterns, you can make choices that will help you achieve success.

The Influence of Human Needs

How you respond to your environment may be based on human needs. All people have certain needs that they strive to fulfill. The manner in which human needs are met influences your personality as well as your physical, intellectual, social, and emotional development. Each person attempts to meet the following needs in different ways:

- *The need for food, clothing, and shelter surpass all other needs.* When people are starving, their only thought is finding food. When they are freezing, they search for warmth and protection. Life's basic physical needs are strong motivators for action. These physical needs must be met before the emotional needs are even recognized.

- *The need to feel safe and secure causes people to act in certain ways.* For instance, if a tornado is near, people seek immediate shelter and stay there until danger has passed. People need to feel secure in their relationships, too. A warm family environment is an example of how this need can be satisfied. Feelings of security develop as you learn you can trust others to care for you and guard your well-being. As you mature, feeling secure helps you reach out to others by showing care and concern for them.

- *The need to be loved and accepted by others is a powerful motivator.* Some teens will join a school club because of their desire to belong to a particular group. The need to feel loved and accepted by family and friends is very important. These feelings help you accept yourself, and in turn, love and accept others.

- *The need for recognition and respect also influences personality.* Why does a person try so hard to be the winner of a game or have the best costume at a party? This inner drive may be a need for personal achievement or recognition. Meeting this need can bring satisfaction and a feeling of success, 2-14. These feelings of success increase as your skills increase. When others recognize your skills and success, you see yourself as a capable and worthwhile person.

When people meet all or most of their needs, they continue to strive to reach their full potential. They try to be the best they can be. They work hard at their jobs. They continue to perfect their talents and skills. They become more concerned for others. Although their personalities are well developed, they continue to learn and grow from their experiences.

Muscular Dystrophy Association

2-14 Sharing experiences with friends satisfies the need to be accepted.

Think More About It
How could a person's needs change over time and, therefore, change the way his or her personality appears to others?

A Healthy Personality

Many parts contribute to a healthy personality. A positive self-concept and a sense of worth and value are important. Accepting yourself, with all your strengths and weaknesses, is also part of a healthy personality. These lead to feelings of "I am lovable" and "I am capable."

A healthy personality means you know you are not perfect but you keep trying to improve. You are aware that learning and growing from your experiences can help you become a better person.

Some people put too much emphasis on a single aspect of their personality. They may be overly concerned about how they look. They may have feelings of importance based on just one area of their lives. Maybe they are too concerned about what others say and do. By focusing on just one part of their personality, they may miss the chance to see other areas that could benefit from change.

How can you develop or change parts of your personality? You can start by looking at yourself. Are there things you can change about the way you look or act? Are there skills that you would like to develop? Would these changes help you think more of yourself? Would they increase your self-concept and self-esteem?

Think about your temperament—how you express your personality to other people. Would you prefer not to be shy in a group of your peers? Does feeling angry when you are criticized by someone bother you? Would you like to be a better listener? If you answer *yes*, you are ready to begin the change. Make a plan for improving that behavior and find a supportive family member or friend to check your progress.

Personality development continues throughout your life. Your self-concept, patterns of interacting, responses to your needs—all these can change. Knowing how personality is formed and how to change it will help you develop a healthier personality.

Review Section 2:2

1. How can personality be defined?
2. Explain how self-concept is affected by physical traits and personal skills.
3. Give an example of a temperament trait in each of the four areas of development: physical, intellectual, social, and emotional.
4. List four human needs that could make a difference in the way a person responds to the environment.

Think It Through

Response Patterns

Gwen was neat and well organized. She was an excellent student at school, particularly in math. At home, her room was the neatest place in the house. She loved to organize items. She had files of all her favorite cards, pictures, and CDs.

Although they shared some interests, Dana was different from Gwen. Dana enjoyed school, but had trouble with math. Her favorite subject was history. She especially liked talking about current affairs. At home, Dana had items all over her room. Her clothes were in one pile. Her homework and favorite magazines were in another.

Gwen and Dana had other friends, but spent most of their time together. Neither had much interest in activities that involved exercise, so they both were a bit overweight. They would go to movies and concerts as well as discuss books they had read. Sometimes they would invite another girl, Roxanne, to join them. Roxanne spent much of her time alone, so they hoped their invitation would help her feel happier.

Questions to Guide Your Thinking

1. What natural patterns of physical activity can you identify in Gwen and in Dana? How were their physical patterns evident in the activities they enjoyed?

2. What intellectual patterns can you identify? How did their intellectual patterns affect their favorite subjects in school and the way they organized their rooms?

3. What social patterns can you identify in Gwen and Dana? what emotional patterns? How did these patterns affect their choice of friends?

4. How might their behavior patterns have been affected by their parents? What behaviors do you think their parents may have encouraged?

Chapter Summary

The growth of the human body follows certain patterns. Each person develops at his or her own rate. Rapid physical growth and development of primary and secondary sex characteristics mark the teen years. Taking care of your health can help you reach physical maturity.

A teen's intellectual growth is related to brain development and greater use of abstract ideas and logical reasoning. These formal thinking skills enable you to make more accurate judgments and predict the future consequences of a decision. Try to learn something new every day to help yourself reach your intellectual potential.

Emotional development in the teen years is characterized by an increased ability to identify feelings and control the responses that go with them. Emotional maturity will help you establish close, long-lasting relationships.

Social development is seen as teens learn give-and-take in relationships and develop close friendships with their peers. They also learn to fulfill the expectations that go with various roles in the society.

As teens grow in all these areas, they develop unique personalities. Your personality is strongly influenced by your view of yourself and your temperament. How you respond to meeting human needs also affects personality. As you learn and grow from your experiences, you may realize a need to change poor behaviors. Feeling good about yourself and continually trying to improve are signs of a healthy personality.

Assess...

Your Knowledge

1. What major physical growth changes take place during the teen years?

2. What is the difference between a person who is emotionally immature and one who is emotionally mature?

3. What can a teen do to help his or her brain reach its full intellectual potential?

4. What three factors affect a person's self-concept?

5. What is temperament? How does temperament affect a person's basic behavior?

Your Understanding

6. How is the development of character stimulated?

7. How does the maturing brain help the development of emotional maturity?

8. How does the development of character traits contribute to long-term relationships?

9. How does a society promote ethical behavior?

10. How does a person's self-concept affect his or her personality?

Your Skills

11. Analyze how a marriage relationship would be affected if both partners were intellectually immature.

12. Evaluate how emotional immaturity could affect a friendship.

13. Describe a socially immature person and analyze how those characteristics could impact the person's performance on a job.

14. Analyze your own personal response patterns in the four areas—physical, intellectual, emotional, and social. Explain how your temperament influences your personality.

Think Critically

15. Bring a variety of shoes to school. Include a tennis shoe, work boot, dress shoe, sandal, loafer, or any other type of shoe. Identify all the different characteristics of each shoe. Vote for your favorite shoe. Decide which shoe has characteristics that match your personality (practical, hard worker, carefree, etc.) Make a list of these qualities. Write a paragraph explaining how the shoe you chose matches your personality. *Choice:* Prepare a musical, spatial, or kinesthetic presentation that describes your personality.

16. Choose an area of character development that you would like to improve. Develop a plan of action that you think would strengthen this area. Identify a person who could check your progress.

17. *Writing.* Write a paper analyzing your personal response patterns in the four areas of development. Include how active you are physically, how you express yourself

intellectually, how you express your emotions, and how you relate socially. *Choice:* Present your information in a format using the multiple intelligence you believe you work with best.

18. *Writing.* Write a paper on "Personal Maturity and Success in Relationships at Home and Work." Explain how personal maturity in social, emotional, and intellectual areas can help you succeed in family relationships at home. Also explain how maturity in these areas could benefit your professional relationships on the job. *Group option:* Complete this paper with two partners, with each of you focusing on one area of development.

Connect with Your Community

19. *Reading.* Evaluate several newspaper articles involving human behavior. For each story, explain how the person's behavior helped him or her meet a need. Try to find articles describing examples of behaviors that responded to each of the following needs:

- basic physical needs (food, clothing, and shelter)
- safety and security

Choice. Find articles describing behaviors that responded to the need for love and acceptance and the need for respect and recognition.

20. As a class, brainstorm a list of community leaders who might be available to come to class for a panel discussion. Your teacher can invite them to discuss the importance of social, emotional, and intellectual maturity for success on the job. Prepare a list of questions to ask that would help you understand the specific qualities these leaders seek in employees. Summarize their responses by writing a one-page paper on "The Ideal Employee." *Group option:* Work in groups to create an oral report using presentation software.

21. *Research.* Interview a community leader on the topic of how to build a strong character. Summarize the interview in a report. Include in your report a list of resources and opportunities in your community for building character. *Choice:* Present your information in a flyer or poster.

22. Choose a community service project and volunteer at least three hours. Describe the project in a one-page report. Include a description of your feelings before, during, and after the project. Also explain how participating in such a project can help a person mature. *Choice:* Present your project in an oral or visual report.

Use Technology

23. Search the Internet for a personality inventory. Take the personality test and print the results. Then, summarize your thoughts about the inventory in a paragraph. Was it thorough enough? Did it provide an accurate picture of your personality? Explain why you agree or disagree with the inventory results. *Group option:* Discuss the results with a partner.

24. Design a flyer to advertise yourself to a future employer. Include your strengths, abilities, skills, interests, and any other information you think would help you get a job. Use a desktop publishing format with at least two folds in your flyer. *Choice:* Insert pictures by using a scanner or a digital camera.

25. *Social studies.* Search for information about a psychology career, such as school psychologist, clinical psychologist, social worker, or a career that focuses on developing young adults. Identify the type of work done, personal qualities and educational requirements needed for job success, and the job outlook for the career. Use word processing software to create your report.

26. *Research.* Survey the senior high school class for height and weight data. Collect current data from every student as well as eighth-grade data. Enter the data in a computer to create a line graph for average heights and weights in grades eight and twelve. Prepare averages for the whole class as well as separate averages for males and females. Were males or females taller or heavier in eighth grade? in twelfth grade? Write a paragraph drawing some conclusions about rate of development and overall growth. *Group option:* Complete the activity as a class project.

Chapter 3

Strengthening Positive Attitudes

Section 3:**1**
Developing Attitudes That Lead to Mental Health

Section 3:**2**
Coping with Difficult Events and Emotions

Key Questions

Questions to answer as you study this chapter:

- How can a person develop attitudes that lead to mental health?

- How can difficult events and emotions be handled in a healthful way?

- How can stereotypes affect mental health?

Chapter Objectives

After studying this chapter, you will be able to

- **explain** how positive and negative attitudes influence behavior and contribute to mental health.

- **describe** positive and negative attitudes.

- **identify** techniques used for building a positive attitude.

- **recognize** sources of stress.

- **identify** ways to manage stress.

- **develop** skills for handling anger, anxiety, and depression.

- **analyze** attitudes toward sex roles and stereotypes.

Life Sketch

The bell rang and the class ended. "You will have an exam tomorrow," the teacher announced.

"Not another test," several students moaned.

"I give up," Lindsay shouted. "The last one nearly killed me. It better not include the hard stuff we covered this week."

"Are you kidding? The last test was a snap," Craig replied. Nan and Vicky nodded their heads in agreement.

"I wonder what the test will be this time," Ryan said. "Will there be a lot of short questions or a few really hard ones? I hope I get a good grade."

"The tests in this class are not all that hard," Kevin replied. "All you have to do is just keep up with your homework."

Getting Started

How many different attitudes would there be in your classroom if an exam were announced? Would some be worried, depressed, or afraid of the results? Would some be confident they would do well? What would be your attitude?

section 3:1

Developing Attitudes That Lead to Mental Health

Sharpen Your Reading

Review the headings in this section. Write some questions that you think will be answered when you read each part of this section. After you read each part, write the answers to your questions. If you have some questions that are not answered, share them with a partner to see if he or she found the answers.

Boost Your Vocabulary

For each defense mechanism, identify the feelings, thoughts, and actions involved.

Know Key Terms

attitude
self-perpetuating cycle
defense mechanisms
projection
rationalization
displacement
conversion

regression
idealization
fantasy
direct attack
compensation
self-talk

Attitudes are learned behaviors that people develop as they interact with their environment. The study of how feelings, thoughts, and actions work together can help you understand your attitudes. Since attitudes affect behavior, they will affect every area of life.

Link to Your Life

What examples can you identify where your feelings about an event gave you a bad attitude?

Positive and Negative Attitudes

Your life experiences and your thoughts about them influence your overall mental attitude, 3-1. If you think positive thoughts about your experiences, your attitude will be positive. If you think negative thoughts, your attitude will be negative. Your mental attitude will be influenced by your thoughts about life, yourself, and your worth to others.

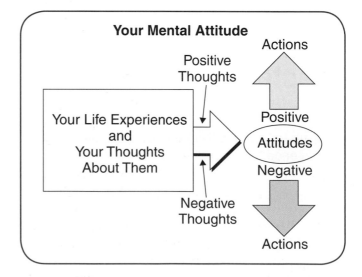

Your Mental Attitude

Actions

Positive Thoughts

Your Life Experiences and Your Thoughts About Them

Positive

Attitudes

Negative

Negative Thoughts

Actions

3-1 Your attitudes are influenced by what you think about your life experiences.

People with positive attitudes think about themselves and their lives in favorable ways. They feel their actions are important. They believe they can have an influence, even if it is minor. These positive thoughts tend to result in positive actions.

Some people have a negative mental attitude. They usually have a low opinion of themselves. They believe that it really does not matter what they do or think. They feel they have no control over the events in their lives. They have no sense of direction and feel powerless. These feelings and thoughts produce a negative attitude.

You may feel positive about some parts of yourself and negative about others. For instance, you may feel confident about your ability to get good grades. However, you may have a negative attitude about your appearance.

Attitudes Affect Behavior

Your attitudes affect how you behave. How you take care of yourself, relate to others, or do your work are all influenced by your attitude.

For instance, when you are feeling down and depressed, you may have negative attitudes. You may not care about what you wear. Acting unfriendly or getting a poor grade on a test may not bother you. Negative attitudes tend to have a negative effect on your actions.

Positive attitudes can influence your actions in a positive way. When you feel good about yourself, you take time to groom in the morning. You greet your friends with confidence. You tackle your work with energy. Your positive attitudes will likely help you experience success in your day.

Attitudes can produce actions that may cause those same attitudes to increase. This is called a **self-perpetuating cycle**. For example, if you start your day with a negative attitude, you may put on sloppy clothes. You feel bad, so you dress the way you feel. When you look in the mirror, you see that your feelings are correct. Not only do you feel bad, you look bad, too!

At school, you may grumble and complain to your friends. They decide to avoid you because of your bad attitude. In turn, their behavior causes you to feel worse about yourself. Later, you get a poor grade on a test. You expected to do poorly, and you did. As a result, your low grade confirms your negative attitudes about yourself. The self-perpetuating cycle continues.

Positive attitudes can produce a cycle of positive actions. For instance, if you start the day by taking time to groom carefully, you would be able to look in the mirror and say, "I look good." Your positive feelings about yourself would increase. Your friendly attitude would help you develop strong friendships.

If you believe you can succeed, you will likely put more effort into your work. Greater effort usually brings more success. Positive attitudes influence you to act in ways that increase your positive feelings.

Use What You Learn

Draw a diagram of a self-perpetuating cycle of positive attitudes and actions. Then draw a diagram of a similar cycle using negative attitudes and actions.

How Mental Attitudes Develop

Past experiences will affect the development of your mental attitudes. Parents influence their children in many ways. As family members spend time together, they share their thoughts, beliefs, and desires. They also model a *mental attitude*, a way of thinking and responding to life situations.

Other people can also influence the development of your mental attitude. Can you think of one person who has made a big impact on your life? Most likely you can identify several people. A teacher, club leader, religious leader, author, or entertainer might have affected you. What particular advice or attitudes did these people express that influenced you? Did they offer special acts of kindness, encouragement, or understanding to show their support?

How would you identify your mental attitude? Do you feel powerless and swept along your life path, or do you see yourself in control of your life path? Teens who adopt a positive mental attitude view themselves as valuable people. They have a purpose and direction for living.

Mental Health

Positive and negative attitudes contribute to your mental health. *Mental health* describes the overall condition of your attitudes. The state of your mental health depends on how well you deal with feelings about yourself, others, and the world around you, 3-2.

Mentally healthy people have a positive mental state. They possess certain qualities that help them deal with life. They can accept themselves as they are, with both strengths and weaknesses. They feel equal to and liked by others. They believe they can handle most situations.

Mentally healthy people can experience hard times that cause negative feelings, too. At times they feel sadness, hurt, or disappointment. The key is how they handle their feelings. A positive attitude even in difficult times is a sign of a healthy mental state.

Think More About It

Think of people who have had a major influence on your life. What kind of attitudes do they portray? How do their attitudes affect their actions?

3-2 Mentally healthy people accept themselves as they are, with both strengths and weaknesses.

The Use of Defense Mechanisms

A positive mental attitude can help people deal with most problems in a positive way. However, dealing with daily problems and situations can be difficult at times, even with a positive attitude. When people have problems they cannot solve, they may react by using defense mechanisms to protect themselves.

Defense mechanisms are methods people unconsciously use to deal with life situations. Sometimes they are used to hide or balance people's feelings and actions. These mechanisms do not resolve conflicts. They provide temporary relief from pain, frustration, or daily pressures. People use them to protect their self-esteem and reduce tension, 3-3.

Everyone has used defense mechanisms at one time or another. Sometimes, however, people use them too often. Instead of resolving conflicts or eliminating problems, defense mechanisms can create more negative feelings and limit personal growth.

Although people use different defense mechanisms in different situations, seven are commonly used. These include projection,

Defense Mechanisms

- **Projection**—placing blame on others
- **Rationalization**—giving excuses to defend a behavior
- **Displacement**—taking out one's feelings on someone else
- **Conversion**—transferring an emotion into a physical symptom
- **Regression**—returning to immature behavior
- **Idealization**—assigning excess value to someone or something
- **Fantasy**—meeting needs through the imagination

3-3 Sometimes people use defense mechanisms as a way to escape the pain of a negative situation. Using defense mechanisms often can limit personal growth.

rationalization, displacement, conversion, regression, idealization, and fantasy.

Projection

Sometimes people place the blame for their failures on others. This is called **projection**. People may project the blame for their problems or shortcomings to someone or something else. They do this to avoid admitting their faults. For example, Steve blames his coach after he loses an important track event. Although Steve did not practice, he feels he would have done better with a different coach. By blaming his coach, Steve is avoiding the real problem—his performance.

Rationalization

Explaining weaknesses or failures by giving socially acceptable excuses is called **rationalization**. People may use excuses to defend their behavior, but they are not being honest with themselves. For instance, Jenny tries out for a singing part in the school play and is not accepted. She responds by saying, "If they had picked a different song for me to sing, I would have been accepted." She is using this common defense to cover her disappointment.

Displacement

When people take out their feelings on someone or something else rather than face the real problem, they are using **displacement**. For instance, your parents may ask you how much gas is in the car. You may respond, "You're always checking up on me." The real problem may be that you do not know and do not want to bother checking. You may be upset about something else. By taking out your frustrations on your parents, you may be creating more negative feelings.

Conversion

Transferring an emotion into a physical symptom is called **conversion**. If you feel anxious about your first day at a new job, you might develop a headache. It is a real physical symptom caused by being anxious, 3-4.

Regression

Returning to childish or immature behavior when difficulties or frustrations occur is known as **regression**. Cindy wants to meet her friends at the basketball game. Her parents want her to stay home to babysit her younger sister. She

3-4 Feeling sick just before exam time often results when a student is not prepared. This is a common example of conversion.

reacts by crying and calling her sister names. This kind of behavior can create more problems for Cindy. She may lose the respect of others as well as her own self-respect.

Idealization

Valuing someone or something far more than it is worth is called **idealization**. If people idealize themselves, they may act conceited. In other cases, they might idealize another person or group. They see the person or group as having more positive qualities than really exist. Material things, such as expensive cars, are sometimes idealized. Spending too much time idealizing someone or some thing can limit personal growth.

Fantasy

Fantasy becomes a defense mechanism when people use their imaginary thoughts as an escape to fill their personal needs. For instance, a young girl who is unhappy with her social life may use TV shows to fulfill her need for love. In her mind, she may pretend to live a romantic life.

Sometimes people use this defense mechanism so often they begin to believe their fantasies. These people may need help in identifying the real needs they are trying to cover up and work on meeting them.

Investigate Further

What are some examples of times when you have used defense mechanisms? Did using the defense mechanism make you feel better? Did it help you solve a problem?

Building a Positive Attitude

Defense mechanisms can help people feel better about a situation, but only for a short time. Negative feelings are temporarily covered up, avoided, or acted out. Using defense mechanisms too often can become a habit that slows personal growth, 3-5. A more positive approach is to recognize and solve the problems that cause negative feelings. This can help in building a positive attitude.

You can use several techniques to help build positive feelings or attitudes. These techniques all involve thinking about yourself in a positive way and taking action to help yourself grow.

3-5 When people use defense mechanisms, they try to cover up a problem rather than solve it.

Direct Attack

Direct attack is a method used to face a problem, recognize it, and try to solve it. For instance, Bailey tries out for first chair in the trumpet section of the band but does not earn the place. She feels bad, but believes that she can improve. She adds 15 minutes to her daily practice. Bailey has used direct attack to address her problem. Her actions will help her reach her goal in a positive way.

Compensation

What is another way you can handle a negative view of yourself? **Compensation** is a technique in which you focus on a strength to make up for a weakness in another area.

For instance, Rico is on the high school football team. He has a small build and is not very muscular. As a result, he feels inferior when he compares himself to other team members. Rico could build his self-esteem by trying another sport for which he is better suited, such as tennis or swimming. He could also develop his skills in some other areas that he enjoys.

Sometimes negative feelings are related to personal qualities that you cannot change. These are times to focus on strengths and abilities you do have.

Set Reasonable Expectations

When people expect too much from themselves or others, their expectations may be difficult to reach. Their chances for experiencing success will decrease. For instance, some students may expect to get *A*s in every subject. If they cannot meet their expectations, they may become discouraged and feel they cannot succeed.

On the other hand, some people choose experiences in which they are certain to succeed. They do not want to take chances. They want guaranteed success. By limiting their opportunities, they may limit their personal growth.

A little challenge is helpful for building self-esteem. When you try something new and do a good job, your confidence grows. You believe that you will probably do well the next time you try something new. Reasonable expectations can help you build positive attitudes.

Use Positive Self-Talk

Little messages that you send to yourself are called **self-talk**. These messages usually are not spoken aloud. When you say to yourself "Good job!" you are sending yourself positive messages. As a result, you will feel more positive about yourself. In the same way, negative messages such as "How stupid!" will increase your negative feelings about yourself. Use positive self-talk whenever you can.

Use What You Learn

What are some of the most common messages that you send yourself? What impact do those messages have on your attitudes?

Interpret the Facts

The way you interpret information can affect your self-esteem and your attitudes. When you try to interpret the facts in a positive way, your self-esteem can increase. For instance, your friend may say "You should have worn a different shirt today." You could interpret that negatively and think "She doesn't like my shirt." You could also interpret that statement positively: "She thinks I should save this shirt for special occasions."

Another way to think positively is to use positive sounding terms that have the same meaning. For instance, *determined* sounds more positive than *stubborn*. Focusing on positive thoughts or speech can increase your positive attitudes.

Select Your Friends

You can stimulate your own personal growth and enhance your self-esteem by your choice of friends, 3-6. Your friends share many feelings, experiences, and interests with you. Friends who accept you help you accept yourself. Their positive attitudes can encourage you to feel positive about yourself. By listening and sharing their thoughts with you, they can make you feel important. Friends can encourage you to reach your potential.

3-6 Choosing friends who share your interests can help you develop positive attitudes.

Friends can also affect your attitudes in a negative way. Their actions can sometimes create bad feelings. In some situations, you may feel left out or inferior to them. Learning to handle your negative feelings in a positive way can help you cope when these situations occur.

Review Section 3:1

1. List two characteristics of people with negative attitudes.
2. Using an example, explain how negative attitudes can produce a self-perpetuating cycle of negative actions.
3. Describe the reaction of mentally healthy people to sadness, hurt, or disappointment.
4. Explain how the continued use of defense mechanisms may slow a person's personal growth.
5. Name and describe five types of defense mechanisms.
6. List and describe five techniques for building positive attitudes.

section 3:2

Coping with Difficult Events and Emotions

Sharpen Your Reading

For each difficult situation discussed, record your feelings and the actions you could take to help you keep a positive attitude during the situation.

Boost Your Vocabulary

Define each key term and give an example of a related life experience that could result in negative attitudes.

Know Key Terms

stress
normative stressors
crises events
anxiety
depression
sex roles
stereotype
sex stereotypes

Many people find that keeping a positive attitude is easy when things are going well. The challenge is keeping that attitude during difficult times. When someone is criticized, made fun of, or yelled at in front of others, how do they handle their feelings then? When they think they cannot succeed, how do they keep a positive attitude?

Many situations can make a person feel hurt, angry, worried, or depressed. It is important to be able to identify these emotions and know how to deal with them.

Stress

Stress is your body's response to the events of your life. Stressful situations cause physical, mental, and emotional tension. Simple everyday events such as oversleeping can be stressful. Major events such as a wedding, divorce, death of a family member, or serious illness especially cause stress. You can feel stress in both good and bad situations.

The physical changes that take place as you react to stress can vary. Your heart rate may speed up and your blood pressure may rise. Your palms may get cold and clammy. Your stomach may ache or feel upset. If stress builds up over time, these physical responses can have harmful effects on your health. High blood pressure, heart attacks, stomach ulcers, and drug and alcohol abuse are often traced to stress.

Stressful events can cause a variety of psychological responses. These are your emotions, such as tension, anxiety, and frustration. Taking a final exam may cause you to feel tense or frustrated, especially if you did not study. In addition to the feelings, you might start to perspire or feel shaky as your body reacts physically. Emotional events can cause both psychological and physical responses, too.

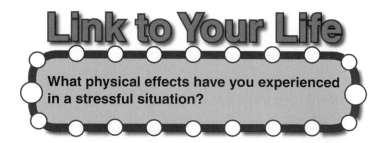

Link to Your Life

What physical effects have you experienced in a stressful situation?

Causes of Stress

You experience some kind of stress every day. Everyday events that cause stress are called **normative stressors**. This is a normal event that occurs and requires some response from you. Stressors can be positive events as well as negative events. The excitement of winning a race is a positive event, but missing a bus can be a negative event. The chart in 3-7 lists other normative stressors.

Other types of experience that cause stress are called **crises events**. These events are changes in your life that require major changes in your behavior. Some common crises events are listed in the chart in 3-8.

The more sources of stress you experience at one time, the greater is their combined effect. Moving to a new neighborhood is an example of a stressful change. Going to a new school after the move causes yet more stress. Having your parents divorce, too, would increase your stress level further.

Stress is a normal part of your life, but too much stress can be unhealthy. Developing skills for handling stress can help you manage and maintain your health and well-being.

Crises Events
• Death in the family
• Divorce
• Marital separation
• Jail term
• Unemployment
• Fired from job
• Loss of home
• Major injury or illness
• Major surgery
• Remarriage in the family

3-8 Stressful events that could lead to crises are often caused by major changes in a person's environment.

Handling Stress

Your ability to handle stress is affected by your attitudes toward yourself and others. A positive mental attitude will help you handle stress in a healthful way. You will more likely learn from the experience. If you accept yourself, you will not be as threatened by these events. You will feel confident that you can work through them.

People with negative attitudes will find it more difficult to handle stress in a healthful way. They may already feel helpless, unaccepted, and worthless. In times of stress, their negative attitudes may lead to increased anger and anxiety. These may lead to more serious mental illnesses such as depression or thoughts of suicide.

Learning how to handle stress is a skill that can help you throughout life. Developing this skill takes time and effort. You can start by learning how to identify stress. Then take the following steps to manage it:

1. Admit any feelings that you have. They are your first clue that some event is causing you stress. You feel this way for a reason. Admitting your feelings will help you accept them.

Sources of Normal Stress
• Change in health of family member
• Change in finances
• Change in friendships
• Change in daily schedule
• Starting school
• Ending school
• Change in social activities
• Personal illness
• Change in eating habits
• Change in work hours
• Change in responsibilities at home
• Change in living conditions

3-7 Normal stress is caused by day-to-day changes in your living environment.

2. Try to identify the event that is the source of your stressful feelings. When you can identify the source of your stress, you begin to feel more in control of the situation.

3. Identify what you can do to manage the stressful situation by considering the following options:

   - Remove the source of the stress.
   - Remove yourself from the stressful situation.
   - Change your response to the stress.
   - Manage the stress by focusing on a part at a time. 3-9.

3-9 Are you tense before an exam? Allowing yourself plenty of time to study can help you control stress.

Reducing the Negative Effects of Stress

No matter what you do to try to reduce the amount of stress in your life, it will still occur. To reduce some of the negative effects of stress, use the following guidelines:

- *Practice relaxation techniques.* Breathing exercises and muscle relaxation can reduce the tension in your body. Take a deep breath and then slowly let it out. Tighten and then relax various muscles in your body whenever you feel tense. Think about a peaceful scene to relax your mind.

- *Do something you enjoy.* Finding an activity that is enjoyable may help reduce your tension.

- *Keep a schedule that includes physical activity.* Exercise can help you release the tension that builds up from stress.

- *Eat nutritious foods.* Stressful situations sometimes affect the way you eat. A healthful diet can improve your ability to cope with stress.

- *Get plenty of rest.* Along with exercise and a good diet, you need rest to help you feel your best during times of stress. When you are tired, you may have more negative feelings than when you are rested.

Anger

Anger is an emotion that occurs when you feel wronged in some way. People of all ages feel anger. A little child may become angry when the tower the child is building falls over. A teen may become angry when parents restrict driving privileges because of high insurance rates. An adult may become angry when his or her car stalls on the highway.

Link to Your Life

Think of a time when you became angry. Identify what made you angry. Was it a situation in which you felt wronged in some way?

Anger is not always a negative emotion. When a situation needs to be changed, anger can motivate people to work on the change. Handling anger in a useful way can bring positive results. For instance, people who are angry about the effects of pollution may fight it by joining environmental groups.

Sometimes anger is expressed in a way that is harmful. Anger can destroy relationships, tear down self-esteem, or even cause physical harm. Some people find it difficult to handle anger in their relationships. They may blame others for their problems and try to get even. They try to increase their own self-esteem by verbally attacking others. Unresolved anger can also lead to violence if an angry person lashes out at others.

Keeping anger inside can have a negative effect, too. Some people try to hide their anger by avoiding the problems. Their bodies may react to the stress by becoming physically ill because anger was not resolved. Headaches, ulcers, high blood pressure, or even heart attacks can occur. Their mental health can be affected, too. Anxiety, fear, and depression may increase under the influence of stress.

Handling Anger

You can respond to anger in a way that builds positive attitudes. The chart in 3-10 lists steps for handling anger in a positive way.

Admitting you are angry is an important first step. You cannot get rid of anger if you try to avoid it. Next, try to identify what is making you angry. Determine what you could do to manage the situation. What action could be taken to reduce your anger? Could you look at the circumstances in a different way?

Refer again to Chart 3-1. If you can think about a negative experience in a positive way, you can build positive attitudes. You might ask "How can I learn from this? How can I grow?"

However, thinking clearly can be difficult when you are angry. Discussing the problem with a friend can be a helpful step. He or she can help you think through your problem with logic and reason.

Even after taking these steps, you may still feel some anger. Dwelling on the problem will only increase your negative attitudes. If another person caused your anger, your willingness to forgive can help you get on with your life.

Steps for Handling Anger
1. Admit your anger.
2. Identify the source of your anger.
3. Identify your choices for managing the situation.
4. Discuss the situation with a close friend.
5. Focus on the positive.
6. Forgive and go on.

3-10 Handling anger in a positive way can help you through stressful situations.

Anxiety

Worries, concerns, or fears of failure produce an attitude of anxiety. **Anxiety** is the uneasy feeling people experience when they believe something terrible will happen. Sometimes the cause of anxiety is real; sometimes it is imagined.

Normal anxiety occurs when you recognize a threat and do something about it. You respond to the threat by either removing it or moving yourself to a safer position. Such anxiety is helpful when it gets people to respond to a real concern.

On the other hand, *high anxiety* keeps people from acting in a way that corrects the problem. Freezing with fear is an example. High anxiety also affects the body physically. It can result in ulcers, headaches, skin rashes, and other problems. Some people have shortness of breath or cannot sleep. Some always feel tired and lose their appetite. Continuous stress and anxiety can cause physical illness.

High anxiety can also influence people in other ways. It can prevent them from getting things done. It may interfere with their ability to think. It may hinder their ability to share thoughts or feelings with others. Anxious people also use defense mechanisms more often.

Think More About It
In what ways do stress and anxiety have similar effects on the body?

Handling Anxiety

The key to handling anxiety is to reduce it so you can respond to the problem. First you need to recognize and accept your feelings. Next, you can look at the cause of your anxiety. Sometimes, it is hard to know just what is making you feel anxious. Some of the most common sources of anxiety are listed in 3-11.

Stressful events that cause anxiety often produce anger as well. People may become angry at the person or event that brought the stress. As they identify causes of anxiety, they may also discover sources of anger in their lives.

How can your anxiety be reduced once the cause has been identified? Sometimes you cannot remove the cause. However, you can work to control the level of your anxiety in several ways.

- Build your self-esteem.
- Increase your communication skills.
- Build relationships with people who support and encourage you.
- Learn techniques for relaxation.

Use What You Learn

What are some actions you could take to build your self-esteem and reduce future cases of anxiety?

Depression

Did you ever have a day when you could not get excited about anything? You just felt down but did not know why. At other times, you were able to identify why you felt blue.

Having occasional negative feelings is normal. Everyone feels this way once in a while. However, if you find yourself feeling this way most of the time, you may be experiencing depression. **Depression** is an overwhelming attitude of sadness, discouragement, and hopelessness. It can cause a person difficulty in making decisions and in trying to lead a normal life.

Causes of Depression

Some cases of depression are mild. The situations described earlier may lead to mild

Causes of Anxiety
• A threat to your well-being
• Fear of failure
• Conflicts
• Fear of the unknown
• Unsatisfied needs

3-11 One way to deal with anxiety is to recognize some of the causes.

feelings of depression. More severe cases of depression often occur when a person suffers a major loss. This loss may be due to the breakup of a relationship, death, or divorce. Other causes of serious depression may relate to money or self-esteem.

Sometimes depression has a physical cause. A chemical imbalance, lack of sleep, or poor diet are possible causes. Low blood sugar or certain drugs can also bring on depression.

Usually there is more than one specific cause for depression. Several factors may combine to bring on the depression. Past negative experiences can build on each other, leading to a feeling of hopelessness. It may seem impossible to change a situation for the better.

Another cause of depression is a pattern of negative thinking. This may lead to feelings of anger and *self-pity*, or feeling sorry for yourself. Self-pity does not lead to positive action. Instead, it leads to more negative thoughts and often no action. This leads to a deeper state of depression.

Use What You Learn

What are some positive things you could do when you are feeling down? How do these activities help you grow?

Coping with Depression

With mild cases of depression, family and friends may encourage the person to relax, get some sleep, or take a break from the daily routine. With such support, the depressed person may be able to return to normal.

When you or someone you know has several of the symptoms listed in 3-12, and these symptoms last for more than a few weeks, professional help should be sought. Persons suffering from severe depression are often too discouraged to solve their problems alone. If the cause of the depression is physical, doctors can prescribe medications to balance the chemicals in the body. Such action should only be handled by a psychiatrist or medical doctor.

Talking about past experiences with a counselor can help a depressed person identify the source of his or her negative feelings. Steps can then be taken to overcome those feelings, strengthen self-acceptance, and build self-esteem.

Warning Signs of Depression

- You feel sad or cry a lot, and these feelings do not go away.
- You feel guilty for no reason or have lost your confidence.
- Life seems meaningless, like nothing good is ever going to happen again.
- You have a negative attitude a lot of the time, or it seems like you have no feelings.
- You do not feel like doing a lot of the things you used to enjoy, and you want to be left alone most of the time.
- You have difficulty making up your mind. You forget things and find it hard to concentrate.
- You get irritated often and overreact.
- Your sleep pattern changes; you may have trouble sleeping or want to sleep all the time.
- Your eating pattern changes; you've lost your appetite or you eat a lot more.
- You feel restless and tired most of the time.
- You think about death or have thoughts about committing suicide.

Source: National Institute of Mental Health

3-12 Professional evaluation and help is needed for major depression.

Suicide

Suicide, the act of taking one's own life, is sometimes considered by a severely depressed person. A person who is considering suicide as an escape often talks about it ahead of time. This can be the person's way of asking for help.

If you hear someone talking about "ending it all" or "giving up," seek help for that person immediately. Your school counselor or religious leader can help. Calling a suicide hotline can help you reach a counselor for such emergencies.

Talking about the problem can help the person think about the finality of such a choice. The goal is to cause the person to stop and think. What other choices are there? What kind of help is available?

Think More About It
Why might people fail to seek help when they hear a friend make comments related to suicide?

Sex Roles and Stereotypes

As children grow up, they learn there are two sex roles in our culture: masculine and feminine. **Sex roles** are the culture's definition of how males and females should behave. The behaviors linked to each sex are learned. You watch your family, other adults, and your peers. From them, you learn how to carry out your sex role.

When society has rigid expectations about how males and females should act, stereotypes form. A **stereotype** is an oversimplified opinion or prejudiced attitude. **Sex stereotypes** are widely held beliefs about the characteristics shared by all members of one sex. The chart in 3-13 lists some common male and female sex stereotype characteristics.

Sex Stereotype Characteristics	
Men	**Women**
• Unemotional	• Emotional
• Decisive	• Indecisive
• Strong	• Weak
• Independent	• Dependent
• Brave	• Meek
• Handsome	• Beautiful
• Muscular	• Slender

3-13 Stereotype patterns for men and women often include these characteristics.

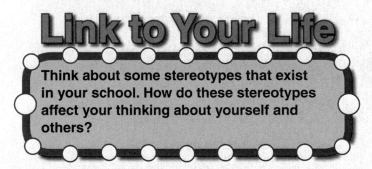

Think about some stereotypes that exist in your school. How do these stereotypes affect your thinking about yourself and others?

Stereotypes and Mental Health

Stereotypes can result in negative attitudes when people do not measure up. They may feel weak, afraid, and unsure. They may think of themselves as failures who do not fulfill expectations. In this way, stereotypes harm mental health.

When you expect people to show stereotyped behavior, you are not accepting them as unique persons with their own personal qualities. Harmful behaviors result when people reject one another. If you are trying to match yourself to your sex role stereotypes, you are not allowing yourself to grow as an individual person.

Most people do not fit into rigid sex-role patterns. All people have unique human qualities and behaviors. People prefer to be themselves and express their own personalities. When they are free to do this, their attitudes toward themselves and their sex roles are positive.

Establishing an acceptable sex role within the society can help you build positive attitudes. It will help you like and accept yourself. You will fit into society and meet your sex-role expectations. Your relationships with others who have similar expectations for you will be positive.

Review Section 3:2

1. Explain the difference between normative and crises-producing stressors.
2. Describe four choices available for managing stress.
3. List five steps for handling anger in a positive way.
4. Explain the difference between normal anxiety and high anxiety.
5. List four ways to reduce anxiety.
6. Identify three possible causes of depression.
7. How are sex stereotypes taught to children?

Think It Through

Coping with Stress

"Would you please go and pick up some milk at the store?" Jon's mother called as he walked in the house.

"Not now!" Jon exclaimed. He threw his keys on the table. "You go get it!"

Jon was tired. His feet hurt from standing and unpacking boxes at the store. He had a lot of homework and studying to do as it was near the end of the semester.

Jon's mother looked up, surprised. She did not expect such an angry reply. She knew Jon was under a lot of stress. They all were.

Jon's father was in the hospital for surgery. He would not be able to work at his construction job for a few weeks. The family finances were strained, and everyone was edgy.

Jon knew he had hurt his mother when he responded. She was under a lot of pressure, too. "I'm sorry," he said. "I was thinking about a final paper that's due tomorrow. I'll pick up the milk before I start on it."

"Maybe I can help by typing it for you," his mother replied. "I know you've been under a lot of pressure lately."

Questions to Guide Your Thinking

1. What were some normative stressors that Jon was experiencing?

2. What was the crisis event in Jon's family?

3. How did the stress in Jon's life affect his mental attitude and behavior?

4. How did Jon's mother handle his anger and negative attitude?

5. How could Jon's family manage the stress they were experiencing?

6. What events in your life cause you stress? How do you respond to the stress you experience? What techniques could you use to manage stress?

Chapter Summary

Attitudes are learned responses that cause people to choose one behavior over another. Positive or negative attitudes can produce actions that cause those same attitudes to increase. Mental health describes the overall condition of people's attitudes. Mentally healthy people who can deal with most life situations show a positive mental state.

Mental attitudes are influenced by people's thoughts about life, themselves, and their worth to others. Learning to build positive attitudes will result in actions that cause positive attitudes to increase.

Keeping positive mental attitudes when you encounter stress may be difficult. Recognizing your feelings and identifying their cause is important. Managing the stressful situation is the next step. As you reduce the effects of stress, positive feelings will replace the negative ones.

People with negative mental attitudes will find it difficult to cope with their emotions in a healthy way. Their feelings of anger, anxiety, and depression may increase and may lead to serious mental illness. Taking steps to replace negative feelings with positive attitudes can improve their mental health.

Stereotyped attitudes toward sex roles can influence your expectations for yourself and others. Overcoming these stereotypes can help you accept yourself and others as unique individuals.

Assess...

Your Knowledge

1. What attitudes lead to mental health?

2. What are seven different defense mechanisms that people sometimes use to deal with problems?

3. What are some causes of stress in people's lives?

4. What are some signs of major depression?

Your Understanding

5. How do feelings, thoughts, and actions work together to portray an attitude?

6. How can stress be handled to reduce its effects on the body?

7. How can stereotypes lead to negative attitudes and poor mental health?

Your Skills

8. Analyze each defense mechanism and explain how it could hinder growth.

9. Give five examples of how you could build positive attitudes in your life.

10. Give four examples of ways you could manage a stressful situation.

11. Write a scenario in which you think through ways to help a friend who shows signs of major depression.

Think Critically

12. *Writing.* List characteristics of events that make you feel positive and identify their common qualities. Do the same for events that make you feel negative. *Choice:* Write a summary of the common qualities in events that make you feel positive.

13. *Writing.* Write a paper comparing various expectations for your life. Include your own expectations, your family's expectations, and your peers' expectations. Identify the main differences. *Choice:* Present the different expectations in a song, poem, or drawing.

14. *Social studies.* List the qualities that you would identify as characteristic of the ideal man and the ideal woman. *Group option:* Work in a small group and compare your lists as a team. In what ways are your lists similar? How are they different? *Choice:* Try to come to a consensus on qualities and write a description of the ideal man and the ideal woman.

15. *Reading.* Evaluate male and female stereotypes in several nursery rhymes, stories, literature, or poems. Describe the stereotypes you find in each. *Choice:* Compare them to stereotypes found in today's media. *Group option:* Work in groups to analyze children's stories for stereotypes and report findings to the class.

Connect with Your Community

16. **Research.** Research resources available in your community for people struggling with suicidal thoughts. List these resources and comment on how accessible each resource is. *Choice:* Identify how often people use each resource, and make a judgment as to whether you think each resource appears effective.

17. **Writing.** Interview a person who has overcome great odds to achieve success in any aspect of life. (The success may involve the person's health, education, job, military service, family life, or community involvement.) Write a report describing the techniques this person uses to adjust to and cope with negative experiences. *Choice:* Present your information in an oral report.

18. **Writing.** Write a "Dear Abby" letter to seek advice for a situation involving anger, anxiety, depression, or defense mechanisms. You can write about a real-life situation or an imaginary one. Have a school psychologist or other resource person respond to the letters by offering advice. *Choice:* Analyze the advice for techniques that build positive life attitudes. *Group option:* Work in a small group to respond to different scenarios; then share your group's advice with the class.

19. **Social studies.** Interview four adults, including both men and women. Ask questions about how they interpret their roles as males or females in your community. Questions could include their thoughts on appropriate behaviors, clothing, childrearing responsibilities, job responsibilities, and housekeeping responsibilities. Write a paragraph summarizing your thoughts on male and female roles in your community. Do the interviewees' roles have anything in common with male and female stereotypes? *Group option:* Share your results with a classmate and discuss similarities and differences in the responses.

Use Technology

20. Prepare a flyer advertising a technology that could be a stress reducer. Use a desktop publishing program in a bifold or trifold format to create the flyer. Present the positive impacts of the technology to the reader. *Choice:* Post your flyer on your class's Web page or network.

21. **Research, writing.** Search the Internet for the physical effects of anger and anxiety and their link to the use of antidepressants. Prepare a report of your findings. Describe the relationship of the physical effects of anger and anxiety to overall health and well-being. *Choice:* Present your information in a poster that you develop using a computer program.

22. **Research, writing.** Research technologies that people could use to help reduce stress and its effects. Then identify technologies that may increase the stress in a person's life. Write a paragraph comparing these two lists. Determine whether technology makes a greater impact on increasing stress or decreasing it. *Choice:* Present your information in a flyer promoting your information with specific examples.

23. **Social studies.** Using a computer, design and print a poster aimed at combating sex stereotyping in your school. Use a scanner or digital camera to add pictures to help emphasize your message. *Choice:* Get permission to post your poster on your school's Web site.

Chapter 4

Developing Decision-Making Skills

Section 4:**1**
Factors Affecting Decision Making

Section 4:**2**
The Decision-Making Process

Key Questions

Questions to answer as you study this chapter:

- **What can help a person make good decisions?**

- **What are the steps in making a good decision?**

Chapter Objectives

After studying this chapter, you will be able to

- **list** factors that influence decision making.

- **explain** how values develop and influence decisions.

- **distinguish** between short-term and long-term goals.

- **develop** plans for reaching your goals.

- **explain** the relationship between standards and goals.

- **identify** human and nonhuman resources.

- **describe** skills for managing your resources.

- **use** the decision-making process to make and evaluate decisions.

Life Sketch

Hector lay on the couch, staring at the wall. His eyes were fixed on a picture, but he wasn't really looking at it. He was thinking about the comment Anna made to him at school that day. "Should be a great game tonight!" she said and smiled. He wondered why she said that to him. Did she like him? Did she want to go to the game with him?

Hector's thoughts were quickly interrupted. "What are you doing, Hector?" his mother called.

"Just thinking," he replied. His thoughts drifted back to Anna.

"Thinking about what?" his mother asked.

"Oh, nothing." Hector grumbled, wondering if his thoughts were important.

Getting Started

All your thoughts are important. When you think about a certain subject, you put together all the information you have about it. You think about the information in different ways. This helps you form opinions and identify your feelings. You review your choices and the possible outcomes. Whenever you make a decision, you use this process.

section 4:1

Factors Affecting Decision Making

Sharpen Your Reading

Create two columns in your notebook. As you read, list each factor affecting decision making in the first column. In the second column summarize how that factor affects decision making.

Boost Your Vocabulary

For each term, identify and describe an example from your own life.

Know Key Terms

routine decision
planned decision
project
values
group values
goal
short-term goal
long-term goal
subgoal
obstacle
standards
resource
human resource
nonhuman resource

You will make many decisions throughout your life. Some will be **routine decisions,** which are made every day without much thought. For instance, every morning you make a decision to get up. Most of the time you will not think about this decision for too long or you will be late. If you feel sick or have a headache, you may think longer about how this decision may affect you.

For a **planned decision**, you use more time and energy to make the best choice. Deciding on a career field or making an expensive purchase are examples of more difficult decisions. They may have long-term effects.

The decisions an individual makes are influenced by the following factors:

- mental maturity
- values
- goals
- standards
- resources

Your Mental Maturity

When you were young, other people did most of your thinking for you. As you grew, your thinking skills developed. At first you needed to see, touch, or experience things to be able to think about them. As you grow and mature, your thinking skills become more advanced, 4-1. You can think about abstract ideas as well as concrete objects. You can *reason*, or examine, and then draw conclusions. You can **project** thoughts about your life. That means you can think ahead and plan ideas for the future.

Evidence of Mature Thinking Skills

- Thinks about abstract ideas
- Uses logical reasoning to draw conclusions
- Projects thoughts about the future
- Predicts possible outcomes
- Compares ideas and thinks about which outcome might be best

4-1 Your ability to make decisions improves as you develop these mental skills.

Growing also brings experiences. You can use past information to think through your decisions and identify possible outcomes. Finally, you can compare your ideas and the likely outcomes of each. As a result, your predictions for the future will be more accurate. Using mature thinking skills leads to more satisfying decisions.

Your Values

Your **values** include all the ideals and beliefs that are important to you. The values you consider important will influence the decisions you make and the actions you take.

How Values Develop

Your values are influenced largely by those around you. The society you live in, the culture around you, and your family all impact your values. Democracy, freedom of religion, freedom of speech, and freedom from fear and want are examples of societal values. Respect for such values are taught openly in the society of the United States.

Various cultures within a society may hold additional values. For example, African American culture places a strong emphasis on intergenerational ties. When people of several cultures live in a society, the values of one culture may influence the members of other cultures.

People within a society have **group values** that are considered important by everyone in the group. Each group that influences you may have different expectations for you. For example, your teachers may have certain ideals that are important to them. They may want you to spend time studying and doing your best in school. Your peer group holds certain values as well. They may encourage you to be more independent or to go to social activities.

The ideals or beliefs that your family emphasizes are your family's values. These will form the base from which you develop your own values. Many of your values will be similar to your family's values while some will differ.

Your personality can influence what is important to you. For instance, if you have an outgoing temperament, then being with people might be important to you. This value leads you to spend more time with your friends. Another family member may like to spend more time alone. Quiet time for thinking and reading may be a value to that person. Such differences reflect each person's unique personality.

Use What You Learn

Identify some societal, cultural, and family values that are evident in your school.

Identifying Your Values

If you were to list your values, they would fall into different categories. You might list good health as one value. Having close friends and a good job may be others. Your values can be divided into three categories—personal, relationship, and work values. Identifying your values in each area is helpful for decision making.

Personal Values

What is highly important to you as an individual? a positive attitude? religious beliefs? physical attractiveness? personal interests and hobbies? fitness? personal growth? Your list may include all these values and more.

Though many people cite these values, they may interpret them differently. For instance, your idea of physical attractiveness may not be the same as your friend's idea. Your idea of personal growth may not be someone else's.

Relationship Values

What values are important to you in your relationships? Values such as respect, acceptance, and kindness might be values you have for all your relationships. In your family relationships, you may have expectations for closeness. Values such as giving and receiving love; showing warmth, caring, and trust; and sharing may be important in those relationships. In certain friendships, you may value honesty and openness. You may also want friends to accept you for who you are. You can see how the values that you identify may vary with different relationships, 4-2.

Work Values

What are your expectations for work? Generally, *work* can be defined as any mental or physical activity to produce or accomplish

4-2 During the teen years, dating relationships can be a high priority.

something. Work affects an individual's identity and self-esteem. As a teen, your main work may be related to school. Some teens may hold part-time jobs as well. For others, a sport or hobby may also be work related.

People have their own values related to work. To some, working within a team of coworkers is important. Others prefer to work alone. Some desire routines while others want every day to be different. Some want work that is exciting and full of adventure, while others seek work that is creative. Identifying what is important to you can help you make decisions related to your future work.

Think More About It
What values might be important for success on the job?

Values Influence Decisions

Knowing your values can help you make decisions. You will feel more confident if you make choices that agree with your most important values. Values may differ in level of importance.

Ranking your values when you make decisions can be helpful to you. List the most important value first. Put the least important value last on the list. Then arrange the others in between. Equally important values could be listed side-by-side. You could use this list to help you think about your most important values when you are making a decision.

Some decisions are more difficult to make when you experience a conflict in values. These conflicts occur every day. In some situations the decisions are simple to make. For instance, should you ride your bike to school or have someone drive you? If you value physical fitness, you might decide to ride your bike for the exercise. Some situations involve conflicting values and are not so simple to decide. This can create stress in your life.

Link to Your Life

How could values sometimes make it difficult to make a choice?

Your Goals

Your values can help you set goals. A **goal** is something you want to have or achieve. Goals identify something you want to do. If it is planned for the near future, it is a **short-term goal**. For instance, Adrianne wants to finish her term paper this week.

If a plan will take longer to complete, it is a **long-term goal**. For instance, one long-term goal is to finish high school. Another may be to finish college or earn a promotion at work.

A long-term goal may be broken down into several smaller subgoals, 4-3. Each **subgoal** is a step leading toward the long-term goal. Libby has a long-term goal to save $1,000 for a car down payment. She has smaller short-term goals of saving $100 each month. Her monthly goals are subgoals that will help her reach her long-term goal.

Subgoals can help you keep a positive attitude as you work toward a long-term goal. As you reach each step, you will feel more confident about your ability to reach your long-term goal. As a result, your success rate for accomplishing your goals will increase.

4-3 You may have to win several qualifying races (subgoals) before winning the state finals (long-term goal).

Developing a Plan to Reach Your Goal

Use your values to set your goals. This will help you make plans that are important to you in each area of your life. See Step 1 of 4-4 to see how Sean set a goal to be physically fit. This is an important value for him. He set subgoals and then broke those down into short-term goals.

Sean then developed a plan of action (Step 2 of 4-4.) His plan of action includes the steps he will take to reach his goal and a time frame for each step. Steps in a plan of action need to be realistic. They need to be something you are willing and able to do.

Even with a plan of action obstacles may interfere. An **obstacle** is something that stands in the way as you try to reach a goal. Watching too much television could be an obstacle if your goal

is to improve your grades. One way to deal with obstacles is identify them as you make your plan of action. Step 3 of 4-4 shows how Sean identified some possible obstacles to his plan of action. He also listed steps he could take to avoid those obstacles.

Your most important values can help you identify the goals that you should work on first. Working on all your goals at one time is difficult. It is easier to choose two or three very important goals. Then take steps to reach them. As you progress toward these goals, you can add others.

Investigate Further

Why are subgoals and short-term goals an important part of a plan to reach a goal?

Your Standards

Standards can help measure your progress toward your goals. They help you identify what *is* and what *is not* acceptable to you. If you value getting good grades, you may set a goal to make the honor roll this semester. To help you reach that goal, you could set certain standards for yourself. These may include getting an *A* on most of your assignments. These standards should help you reach your goal.

Some standards are easily measured while others are based on personal experiences. In school, you are usually required to follow the standards set for all students. For instance, you must earn credits for graduation. To do so, you should do well on tests. These school standards are measurable.

The standards you develop from your personal experiences are not so easily measured. Your standards are unique to you and may be different from the standards of others. For instance, your standard for a good movie will be different from your brother's standards.

Sometimes differences in personal standards cause conflict. Your mom's standard for having a clean room may be different from your standards for a clean room. When setting a goal, it helps to know what the standard will be for measuring success. Then you can include steps in your plan of action to meet the standard and reach your goal.

Using Values to Set and Accomplish Goals

Step 1. Identify a value and use it to set a goal.

Value
_____
Physical fitness

↓

Long-Term Goal
_____
To be physically fit

↓

Subgoals	Short-Term Goals
Lose 10 pounds.	Lose one pound per week.
Develop good muscle tone.	Work out three times per week.
Strengthen heart.	Run three times per week.

Step 2. Develop a plan of action to carry out goal.

Plan of Action

Goal	Steps	Time
To lose 10 pounds	1. Start watching calorie intake.	Monday morning
	2. Identify types and quantity of foods for each meal.	Monday evening
	3. Identify low-calorie snacks.	Monday evening
	4. Purchase low-calorie foods.	Tuesday
To work out three times a week	1. Get workout DVD.	Tuesday
	2. Put time to work out on daily schedule.	M-W-F at 7:00 A.M.
To run three times a week	1. Purchase running shoes.	Tuesday
	2. Put time to run on agenda.	T-Th-Sat. at 7:00 A.M.

Step 3. Identify possible obstacles. List steps to avoid obstacles.

Possible Obstacles	Steps to Avoid Obstacles
• Eating out	1. Choose low-calorie food at restaurant.
• Getting too hungry	2. Keep low-calorie snacks available.
• Sleeping late in the morning	3. Have someone check up on me at 6:55 A.M.
• Not enough money for all purchases	4. Borrow a friend's DVD and use my old shoes to start the program. Make purchases one at a time.

4-4 Sean's personal values can help him set and carry out his goals.

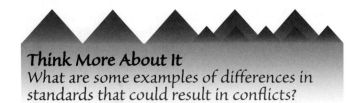

Think More About It
What are some examples of differences in standards that could result in conflicts?

Your Resources

A **resource** is anything available to help you carry out your decisions. When people are aware of all their resources, they are better able to make good decisions and reach their goals.

What do you have available to help you carry out your decisions? time? energy? money? a pleasing personality? special skills? Basically, there are two kinds of resources: human and nonhuman. A **human resource** comes from within a person. This includes your personal qualities and characteristics as well as the support you receive from others. A **nonhuman resource** is any item you have available to help you, such as money, a car, tools, time, and information. Some decisions may require several resources.

Human Resources

What personal qualities and characteristics help you carry out your decisions? You may have certain physical resources, such as good health, strength, and energy. Knowledge, talents, and skills are also human resources, 4-5. Your personality and character traits are other examples. These personal traits become resources for making decisions and carrying out a task.

Your character qualities can also be considered resources. Strength in character means that you have personal qualities that will help you carry out your decisions. For instance, if you are self-controlled, you will be more likely to carry out your decisions.

What skills have you developed as resources? Skills for reading, writing, and math are basic resources you can acquire in school. You can also develop skills for communicating with others.

Problem-solving skills and decision-making skills can be learned. In addition, you probably have developed other special skills, such as preparing food or caring for children. Maintaining your car, programming a computer, or playing an instrument are examples of other skills you may have. Each personal skill can be a resource for you in some situation.

Besides your skills and abilities, you may need to use the second category of human resources—other people in your life. Your family members, a friend, teacher, or religious leader can help or support you. For instance, suppose you need help to complete your homework. Would you contact a teacher? Would you ask a classmate to help you?

The people who can help you carry out a decision are part of your human resources. Their support may depend on their own resources. They may offer support by helping you, encouraging you, or giving you other resources. They can combine their resources with yours to help you carry out your goals.

Investigate Further

What human resources could help a person reach a goal of physical fitness? of having good friendships? of personal maturity?

Nonhuman Resources

What nonhuman resources do you have to help you carry out decisions? Money, possessions, the community, and information are examples of nonhuman resources. Every person has these resources in different amounts.

The one exception is time, the nonhuman resource everyone has on an equal basis—24 hours per day. How do you use your time? Do you use it to accomplish your goals or do you waste it? Do you try to use time productively? Your time is a nonhuman resource that you can learn to manage.

Money is a resource used to buy goods and services. The presence or lack of it will affect the decisions you can make. For instance, if one option costs more money than you have, you know your decision must match what you can afford.

4-5 The knowledge gained through education is a human resource.

Personal possessions can be resources for you in some situations. A personal computer can be a resource if you want to write and edit a paper. The family car can be a resource to travel to and from a job.

Community resources, including parks, zoos, schools, museums, and stores, are shared with others. A park provides recreational services. Your school is a resource for education.

Information is another important resource. Your ability to carry out a decision may depend on information from a reliable source. Books, magazines, newspapers, and databases are reliable sources of information. The Internet provides large amounts of reliable and unreliable information. It is important to check the credibility of your sources.

Investigate Further

What nonhuman resources in a community can help people reach personal goals of maturity?

Managing Resources

Managing your resources means using them wisely. This is a skill that can be learned. First, you must be aware of the resources you have and how they might be developed. Think about your human qualities as resources. Good health, a positive personality, and your talents are examples of resources that are helpful.

Your possessions are easier resources to identify, 4-6. A car can be a useful resource for getting to school or work. Your money can be a resource when you open a savings account and earn interest. The library, park, or other community resources can be useful depending on your goal.

Another skill in managing your resources involves planning. Since many resources such as energy and money are limited, this is an important skill. Planning will help you use each resource in a way that will benefit you. When you do not have the skill to do what you want to do, you may need to substitute another human or nonhuman resource.

4-6 Nonhuman resources such as a computer and money can help you reach your goals.

Use What You Learn

What are some examples of using a human resource to reach a goal when a nonhuman resource such as money is in short supply?

Review Section 4:1

1. Explain the difference between routine and planned decisions.
2. List four factors that influence a person's values.
3. Identify three categories of values and give an example of each.
4. Explain the difference between a short-term and a long-term goal. Give an example of each.
5. What should a person use to measure whether his or her goal has been reached? Give an example.
6. List three examples of nonhuman resources.
7. Identify two skills for managing resources wisely.

section 4:2

The Decision-Making Process

Sharpen Your Reading

As you read the text, refer to the chart that shows each step in the decision making process.

Boost Your Vocabulary

Choose a simple decision and brainstorm all possible alternatives and all possible consequences for that decision. List your ideas under the headings *alternative* or *consequence*.

Know Key Terms

decision-making process
alternative
consequence

Why is it important to develop your decision-making skills? Your decisions should reflect your values. You may be happier with your decisions if they are consistent with your personal beliefs. Your decisions should also help you reach your goals. You will feel better about yourself if you can succeed in carrying out your plans. Finally, you will have greater success in carrying out your decisions if you fully explore all your resources.

The **decision-making process** is a step-by-step method to guide your thinking when you need to make a planned decision. The six steps of this process are outlined with an example in 4-7. Using this process can help you make decisions and solve problems. Each step can help you organize your thoughts so you can make a choice or pick the best solution.

Identify the Issue

What is it about a situation that requires a person to make a decision? Many situations are quite complicated and include several issues. The first step is to clarify what the issue is, as Chandra did.

Chandra's mother works full-time and makes enough money to meet the family's basic living expenses. Chandra, however, would like to have some extra spending money. For her, the issue is to find a way to earn some money of her own. See Step 1 of 4-7.

Identify the Alternatives

The next step is to identify what choices you have in addressing the issue. A choice is called an **alternative**. At least two choices must exist before a person is faced with making a decision. At this step you need to identify as many alternatives as you can.

Chandra thinks about her alternatives for earning money. She identifies four possible job options. See Step 2 of 4-7.

Consider Each Alternative

Think through each alternative. Consider all the factors related to each choice. How does each alternative fit your values, goals, standards, and resources?

To answer these questions, gather information. Seek out facts from reliable sources, such as a family member or someone who faced a similar decision in the past. Your own past experiences can also provide information. Reliable information will help you predict the results of your decision with greater success.

Using the Decision-Making Process

Step 1. Identify the decision to be made.

Chandra wants more spending money. She sets a goal to find a job.

Step 2. Identify all possible alternatives.

Chandra knows that finding a job will be a major task. She has no previous work experience and must work limited hours. She lists four possible job alternatives.

1. Work part-time after school.
2. Work weekends only.
3. Apply for a work-study job at school.
4. Join a vocational co-op program at the high school.

Step 3. Consider each alternative.

1. Work part-time after school.

Pros	Cons
• This option offers a steady work schedule and provides the most work hours. • These jobs are easily available.	• Chandra would not be able to take part in volleyball, softball, and flag squad—all of which she enjoys.

2. Work weekends only.

Pros	Cons
• Work would not interfere with her school schedule during the week. • She would be able to take part in some after-school activities.	• Weekend jobs are harder to find. • Students with after-school jobs are often scheduled to work weekends as well. This would not leave much time for studying. Chandra knew studying was important to her to reach her long-term goal of going to college.

3. Apply for a work-study job at school.

Pros	Cons
• The work location is convenient.	• A limited number of jobs are available. Only a few students with an interest in office occupations are chosen.

4. Join a vocational co-op program at the high school.

Pros	Cons
• Of the several co-op programs offered at school, one includes the health field. This area is her career interest. The teacher would help her find a job related to her career goal. • She could work an average of 15 hours per week. She would be excused from school early to go to work. She would earn credit for the work experience, plus earn an hourly wage. • Job-related classroom instruction would be provided. • She could take part in after-school sports.	• Participating in the program would mean fewer chances to take elective courses during the school year.

(Continued)

4-7 Developing your skill in using this process can help you make decisions or solve problems in your daily living.

Using the Decision-Making Process
Step 4. Make the decision.
• Chandra decided to enroll in an FCCLA co-op class. She would receive job-related classroom instruction and on-the-job training in the health services field. • She would work 15 hours per week. • She would be able to participate in volleyball, softball, and flag squad after school.
Step 5. Carry out the decision.
Chandra identified the following four steps to carry out her decision: 1. Sign up for the FCCLA class. 2. Take the job-related classroom instruction. 3. Work with the teacher-coordinator in finding a job. 4. Work with the coordinator and employer to identify goals for her work experience.
Step 6. Evaluate the decision.
• With assistance from the teacher-coordinator and the employer, she would evaluate her work experience. • She would determine her success in reaching her job-related goals. • She would determine her success in earning more spending money. • Overall, she would think about how well she used the decision-making process in making her choice.

4-7 *Continued.*

How will this choice affect you and others, both now and in the future? This question can help you think about the consequences of each choice. A **consequence** is the end result of a choice. As you think about possible outcomes, you can consider how well each choice would help you reach your goals.

Finally, what resources are needed to carry out each alternative? If you have access to the resources you need, you will have greater success at carrying out your decisions.

Chandra decided to ask some other students at school about their part-time jobs. She felt this added information would help her make a better decision. See Step 3 of 4-7.

Think More About It
How could a person's maturity affect his or her success in considering alternatives?

Choose the Best Alternative

Making a decision takes time as you reflect on each alternative. You may find there is no perfect solution in your choices. One choice may meet your values and help you reach your goals, but you may lack the resources you need. Another choice may involve resources you have, but it does not completely meet your goals. You can weigh all the facts, past experiences, and valued opinions of others. Then you will be able to make the best choice.

Chandra weighed her four alternatives. Her after-school sports activities were important to her. She also wanted to be sure her studies were not neglected. She thought that 15 hours per week would provide the spending money she wanted. Her course schedule would be tight, but she could enroll in a co-op program in place of other electives. She especially liked the idea of gaining work experience that would relate to her career interest. Chandra decided the best alternative would be to enroll in an FCCLA co-op program. This would enable her to work part-time in a health services occupation. See Step 4 of 4-7.

Carry Out the Decision

This stage of the decision-making process requires a plan of action. Identify some of the obstacles you may meet. Then think about ways to overcome them. Assign a time to carry out each step. The more specific your plan of action is, the easier it will be for you to carry out the plan.

Chandra's plan for carrying out her decision involved her teacher-coordinator. Chandra's first step was to contact the teacher of the FCCLA class. Then she had to work with the guidance counselor to set up her classes so she could carry out her plan. There were several human resources involved in helping Chandra carry out her decision. See Step 5 of 4-7.

Evaluate the Decision

Judging how well each decision went is a habit everyone should develop. Your decision-making skills will increase if you evaluate past decisions. You can look back to see if your decision solved the problem. In Step 6 of 4-7, Chandra would evaluate her decision and judge how well it met her goal of earning money.

To evaluate a decision, consider these questions. How well did you predict the outcome of your choice? Were you able to follow your plan of action? Did you think of every possible alternative? Did you have enough information about each alternative? Was the information accurate? Did you recognize other alternatives after you started your plan? Did anything unexpected happen? Did your plan need some changes? Were there some obstacles for which you did not plan or prepare?

In addition to evaluating your decision-making process, you need to evaluate the consequences of your decision as well, 4-8. Sometimes a decision has far-reaching effects when you consider all the people affected by it. A

4-8 A careful evaluation of your past decisions helps you make better decisions in the future.

mature, responsible decision will benefit you as well as those around you. It will have a positive impact on society as a whole.

Evaluating your decisions can help you grow. You can learn from each experience and perhaps prevent future mistakes. Your skills for using each step in the process will increase with practice.

Throughout your life, you will encounter many choices. The decisions you make should help you reach your life goals. Some decisions may not turn out as well as others. Just remember that decision making is part of the growth process. As you mature, your skills for making effective decisions should improve.

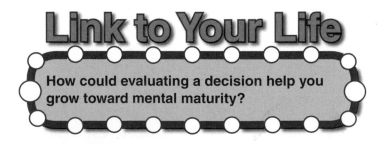

Link to Your Life

How could evaluating a decision help you grow toward mental maturity?

Review Section 4:2

1. List the steps of the decision-making process. In your own words, describe each step.
2. Explain why the decision-making process is an important skill.

Think It Through

Using the Decision-Making Process

Stephanie, a high school student, enjoys her job as a cashier. She works from 3:30 to 7:00 P.M. each day at a local gas station. The gas station is within walking distance of her home. However, the job only pays $8.00 per hour.

Stephanie has been offered another cashier job at a local restaurant that pays $8.75 per hour. She would have to work from 6:00 to 11:00 P.M. daily. The restaurant is located ten blocks from her home. Even though she could walk to work, she would need a ride home each evening.

To help her think through her decision, Stephanie decided to use the decision-making process.

Questions to Guide Your Thinking

1. Identify the issue that is causing Stephanie to make a decision.

2. What alternatives does she have?

3. What information does she have about each alternative? What are the benefits and the disadvantages of each choice? What could be the future outcomes of each alternative?

4. Which choice would you recommend? Explain your reasoning.

5. What plan of action should Stephanie implement? What might be some obstacles that could prevent her from implementing her plan? How could she possibly handle these?

6. What should Stephanie consider in evaluating her decision? What information could she use in the future to help her judge her choice?

Chapter Summary

You will make many decisions throughout your life. Some will be routine; others will be planned decisions that will have long-term effects on your life. Your thinking skills, values, goals, standards, and resources will all influence the decisions you make.

Your decisions should incorporate your values as you try to reach your goals. Some of your values will help you set and carry out goals in your personal life. Other values will relate to your relationships with others or to your work. Your values are important in determining which choices to select from the many alternatives possible.

As you work toward your goals, you use your standards as a measure of your progress. Resources, both human and nonhuman, help you carry out your decisions. Knowing your resources and using them wisely can help you overcome obstacles you may face in the decision-making process.

Making decisions skillfully involves a six-step method. This process helps you to carefully analyze an issue, identify possible answers, and choose the best one. The process also helps you judge the success of your decisions so you develop skill in making them. Successful decision making helps you achieve your life goals.

Assess...

Your Knowledge

1. List four factors that could affect a person's success in making decisions.

2. List the steps that could be used to set and accomplish goals.

3. Describe six steps in the decision-making process.

Your Understanding

4. How is mental maturity related to a person's ability to make good decisions?

5. Why should values be part of setting goals?

6. How can standards help a person know if a goal has been met?

7. How do human resources affect the decision-making process?

Your Skills

8. List and analyze your personal values. How do they relate to your priorities in your schoolwork? How do they relate to your friendships?

9. Identify three goals that you could set that would be consistent with some of your high-priority values.

10. Choose a possible decision that you might make. Work through the problem using the decision-making process, giving examples for each step. Create a diagram to illustrate the steps taken to reach this decision.

Think Critically

11. *Writing.* Write a paragraph describing a situation in which you overcame an obstacle to reach a goal. Evaluate your action for its effectiveness in helping you reach your goal. *Choice:* Create a visual presentation or a rap that expresses your paragraph.

12. List at least three groups to which you belong. Identify each group's values and expectations for its members. Then make a list of your own priorities and expectations for your life. Compare the lists. *Choice:* Choose one group to which you belong and write a paragraph explaining how that group helps or does not help you fulfill your personal expectations.

13. Create three separate lists of your values in the following areas: personal life, relationships, and school. Identify the most important value and a long-term goal related to it from each list. Divide the long-term goals into subgoals. Identify a plan of action that will help you reach your long-term goals. *Choice:* For each long-term goal, identify one possible obstacle and alternatives for how you could overcome it. *Group option:* Discuss your plan of action with a partner for other suggestions.

14. *Writing.* Identify a decision you made regarding a personal, relationship, or work-related issue. List the steps you used to make the decision. Compare your steps to those in the decision-making process. If you had followed the decision-making process, would you have made a better or more-informed decision? Explain your answer.

Connect with Your Community

15. **Social studies.** Create a list of human and nonhuman resources in your community that you could use to help you reach a goal of graduating from high school. **Choice:** Create a collage of pictures or drawings to present your list.

16. **Writing.** Write a one-page paper comparing your personal values with your cultural values. Identify at least three cultural values. **Choice:** Give specific examples of the way your family interprets those three values. Describe how you interpret those values in your own life.

17. **Social studies, writing.** Interview a manager at a local company. Ask the manager to describe the steps he or she uses to make an important business decision. In a one-page report, compare these steps with those in the decision-making process. Identify who is involved in each step of the manager's decision-making process.

18. **Reading.** Evaluate a magazine or newspaper article for different values that motivate people to act. Look for examples of societal, group, and personal values. Write a paragraph summarizing these values and their impact on the person's actions.

Use Technology

19. Use a drawing program to illustrate the steps in the decision-making process in a flowchart format.

20. **Research.** Research three postsecondary institutions. Identify information you could use in making a decision about whether you would want to attend any of these schools. Prepare a multimedia presentation for your class, illustrating the various resources you used and the information you found. *Group option:* Form small groups to prepare the presentation.

21. **Financial literacy.** Interview a cell phone representative and identify the different factors to consider when making a decision to buy a cell phone. In a verbal report, make a recommendation for purchasing a cell phone based on your analysis of the options. **Choice:** Prepare a poster that illustrates the pros and cons of two different cell phone plans.

22. **Writing.** Write a one-page paper explaining how nonhuman technological resources, such as cell phones, laptops, and the Internet, can make human resources more available.

Connecting with Career Clusters

Education & Training

Pathways

- Administration and Administrative Support
- Professional Support Services
- Teaching/Training

Secondary Teacher

Secondary teachers help high school students reach their potential. They often work with students from varied backgrounds and promote learning through a variety of techniques.

Secondary teachers focus on a specific subject area, such as family and consumer sciences, mathematics, English, Spanish, or biology. Most teachers work in a classroom five days per week during the school year. Classrooms for some subjects have labs in which teachers facilitate practical learning. This requires constant interaction with each student as well as continual supervision of the entire class.

A bachelor's degree and completion of an approved teacher education program are needed for a teaching license in the public schools. Most states require teachers to pass competency tests in basic skills.

Career Outlook

This career requires an ability to guide, encourage, and promote learning in others; skill in assessing student needs and designing classroom activities; a capacity for presenting information creatively; and enthusiasm for helping others develop.

Job opportunities in teaching are expected to grow, especially in high-demand subject areas such as science and math. Median annual earnings for all teachers in 2006 were from $43,500 to $48,600. Depending on the degree level and experience, salaries can be as high as $76,000.

Explore

Internet Research

Search the Internet for information on a secondary teaching career in your state. Research entry and top salaries of teachers in your area. Identify two postsecondary schools that offer a program for aspiring teachers. Compare their requirements for entry, the courses of study offered, and the costs of obtaining a degree from each. Prepare a report of your findings.

Job Shadowing

Choose a subject area that interests you and follow a teacher in your school and one in another school. Write a report on the various activities of each teacher, including before-, during-, and after-school responsibilities. Compare the jobs of the two teachers and the programs offered by each school.

Community Service/Volunteer

Spend time tutoring a subject area that you know well. Write a paragraph describing the teaching techniques you will use to help students understand the subject.

Project

Help teach in a boy's or girl's club. Plan several lessons, and for each, write lesson plans identifying the activities to use. Afterward, describe how the activities helped the children grow and develop.

Part-Time Job

Explore a teaching career by working as an aide in summer school, summer camp, a youth program, or a child care center. Develop a journal with daily entries describing the work you do, your interactions with students, the positive aspects of the job, and the frustrations you experience.

Unit 2
Strengthening Relationships

Chapter 5

Developing Communication Skills

Section 5:1
The Communication Process

Section 5:2
Factors Affecting Communication

Section 5:3
Skills for Conflict Resolution

Key Questions

Questions to answer as you study this chapter:

- How can a person develop good communication skills?

- What factors can prevent good communication from taking place?

- How can good communication skills help resolve conflicts and solve problems?

Chapter Objectives

After studying this chapter, you will be able to

- **describe** the communication process.

- **identify** different forms of nonverbal and verbal communication.

- **demonstrate** effective speaking and listening skills.

- **describe** factors affecting communication.

- **apply** the steps of conflict resolution to a problem.

Life Sketch

"Do you know what Sam told me today?" exclaims Ariana. "He was upset because Gabe said that Mary told him we had a fight! Can you imagine that? Why would Mary tell Gabe a thing like that? I think she is trying to break us up! She's always wanted to go out with Sam. I can tell. Now she's trying to stir up problems between us. Sam wanted to know why I told Mary about our disagreement over the movie. Actually, I didn't tell Mary. I told Traci, and she must have told Mary. Besides, I didn't say it was a fight—just a disagreement. Now the whole school is talking about the big fight we supposedly had! Wait till I find Mary; I'm going to make her eat her words. Then I'm going to deal with Traci. I wish those two troublemakers would quit doing so much talking."

Getting Started

Communicating a clear message is not always easy. Poor communication can cause a serious misunderstanding. Sometimes it gives the wrong impression. Somehow the message that was sent was not the same as the one that was received.

Learning to communicate well is an important skill. Effective communication is vital for developing rewarding relationships with family, friends, coworkers, and other people. Besides getting along with others, good communication skills can help you express yourself. Stating your thoughts and ideas clearly will help others understand you. These skills can also help you work through problems and resolve differences with other people. The end result will be improved relationships with others.

You communicate with others every day. Speaking, listening, reading, and writing are all forms of communication. Understanding the communication process will help you improve your skills in all these areas.

section 5:1

The Communication Process

Sharpen Your Reading

As you read, develop a profile of a good communicator. Create a graphic organizer with the heading *A Good Communicator* and two columns underneath. As you read, write qualities of a good communicator in the first column. In the second column, write what skills are needed for good communication to take place.

Boost Your Vocabulary

Share an example with a partner (through words or actions) of how each term can promote good communication.

Know Key Terms

communication
sender
receiver
nonverbal communication
verbal communication
body language
I-statements
passive listening
active listening
checking out
reflecting

Although it may seem simple, communication is a complex process. **Communication** is an exchange of information between two or more people. It is a two-way process that involves both sending and receiving messages.

The **sender** transmits or sends the message. The **receiver** hears and interprets the message. *Feedback* is a sign back to the sender that the message is understood. See 5-1.

Both people need to use certain skills to communicate effectively. The sender needs skills in sending clear and accurate messages. The receiver needs skills in listening to the message and then interpreting it correctly.

Good communication occurs when the sender of the message and the receiver end up with a *shared meaning* about the message. In other words, they both understand the meaning of the message. The receiver signals this understanding back to the sender through feedback. A nod, smile, comment, and direct eye contact are examples of feedback.

Use What You Learn

Why is feedback an important part of making sure that someone understands your full message?

Types of Communication

Two types of communication are used in sending and receiving messages. The first is nonverbal communication. **Nonverbal communication** is a way of sending and receiving messages without using words. This includes body language such as facial expressions, eye contact, and gestures.

The second type is **verbal communication**, which is the use of words to send and receive messages. Speaking and writing are forms of verbal communication.

The way you use both nonverbal and verbal communication affects the messages that you send and receive. As you become aware of how you send messages to others, you can begin to develop better communication skills.

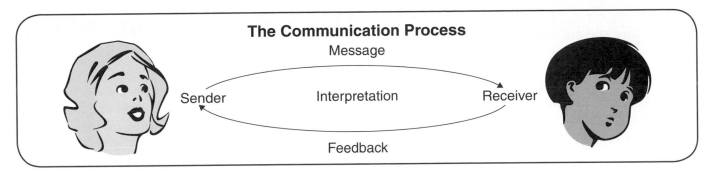

The Communication Process

Message

Sender — Interpretation → Receiver

Feedback

5-1 Communicating effectively means sending and receiving messages clearly.

Nonverbal Communication Skills

People often communicate without speaking. You often know when family members or close friends are feeling happy or sad without a word being spoken. You know by their facial expressions or the way they walk. Nonverbal communication helps you understand their emotions.

Developing your nonverbal skills is important in two ways. First, you become aware of the nonverbal messages you send and receive. Second, you can learn to send clearer nonverbal messages. This means your actions will support the words you say. Overall, your ability to send clear and accurate messages will improve.

Think More About It
When talking on the phone or communicating over the Internet, how does the absence of nonverbal communication affect a person's understanding of the message?

Body Language

One common form of nonverbal communication is body language. **Body language** involves sending messages through body movements. Through body language, people can express their thoughts, feelings, and emotions, 5-2.

Your culture, background, and past experiences can influence how you interpret body language. Considering how others may interpret your facial expressions, gestures, and body motions can help you communicate more effectively.

Facial Expressions
Your facial expressions can communicate a wide range of emotions to others. A smile can encourage others to share their thoughts and feelings. A dull, bored expression tells others you are not interested. A frown or furrowed brow can show that you disagree with what is said.

5-2 A simple hand gesture is a form of body language that sends a message to others.

Direct eye contact helps convey a message that you care and are interested in what a person has to say. Looking away when someone talks can communicate a different message. It can show that you do not care about what the person is saying, or you want to stop talking. For good communication, maintaining eye contact throughout the conversation is important.

Gestures

Along with facial expressions, people use gestures to help communicate their messages more clearly. Perhaps you have seen people who wave their arms or shake their fists when they speak. The use of gestures helps them emphasize their spoken words so others understand the meaning.

Body Motions

The way you sit, stand, or walk while communicating also sends different messages to others. Sitting forward in a chair shows you are alert and listening. Crossing your arms, turning away, or stepping back during a conversation sets up barriers to communication. Good posture or a relaxed stride shows self-confidence.

A person's touch conveys different meanings. A firm handshake sends a message of friendliness. A light touch on the forearm can add emphasis to a message or encourage the receiver to pay close attention. Some people use hugging as a casual way of showing affection. In a serious relationship, embracing sends a message of affection.

Learning how nonverbal messages are sent can help you communicate more effectively. Practicing this skill will help you clearly communicate your message as well as interpret others' messages. However, body language is only one part of the communication process. To convey precise meanings, you also need to understand and develop your verbal communication skill.

Investigate Further

What are some examples of body language that could be interpreted in different ways, depending on your cultural background?

Verbal Communication Skills

Your environment influences the words you use and the way you use them to express yourself. Your family, friends, schoolmates, and other people you come in contact with are all part of that environment. From your family, you learned a certain language. When you are with your friends, you are more likely to use informal language. The school you attend influences the way you speak, read, and write. Listening to others adds to your vocabulary. Even the region of the country where you live influences the way you speak. All these factors produce differences in verbal communication.

Word meanings may vary from one part of the country to another, or from one culture to another. You can send clearer messages by using the language, pronunciation, and words other people will understand.

Even your tone of voice can change the meaning of what you say. The emphasis you place on certain words can also affect the meaning, such as the following: "I said I want to go now" versus "I *said* I want to go *now*." To communicate clearly, make sure your voice conveys the message you want to send.

Communicating well with others begins with you. By developing your skills in expressing yourself, you will send clearer messages. Others will understand you better. Developing your listening skills is an equally important part of effective communication. To be a good listener, you need to develop your skills in active listening.

Expressing Yourself

Do you ever have a hard time telling someone how you really feel? Maybe a friend asked to borrow your car. You were not sure how to say no without hurting his or her feelings. You let your friend use your car, but you worried the whole time it was gone.

How can you express yourself so others understand what you are thinking and feeling? You can start by using I-statements to send clear messages. Learning this skill can give you more control over what you communicate to others.

Use I-Statements

Only you can clearly speak for yourself. Using **I-statements** to express your thoughts, feelings, and ideas can help you speak for yourself—from your point of view. Using these statements gives you responsibility and control over what you communicate to others. Five types of I-statements are outlined in 5-3 to help you express yourself clearly in different situations.

Suppose you do not want to lend your car, but you do not know how to say so. The *self-awareness circle* can help you deal with this situation. It helps you use I-statements to express your point of view in a logical way, 5-4. The circle is a tool to help you think through the action you want to take. Use it whenever you want to express yourself more clearly.

Types of I-Statements	
Descriptive	• Used to report what you have seen or heard. • Describe information taken in through your senses. "I see the scale reads 135 pounds." "I smell smoke." "I heard you say that you are going to the concert." "I can taste a lot of sugar in these cookies."
Thought	• Start with words such as "I think," "I wonder," or "I believe." • Tell others how you interpret what you have seen or heard. "I think Mr. Obley should use a different grading system." "I wonder if it will rain today." "I believe I am gaining weight."
Feeling	• Let others know how you feel. "I feel discouraged because I failed the test." "I feel upset with Mr. Obley's grading system." "I feel worried that it will rain during the ball game."
Intention	• Let others know what you want to do. • Start with words such as "I want" or "I wish." "I want to pass this course." "I want to play ball in the sunshine." "I wish I could lose some weight."
Action	• Let others know what you are doing now, have done in the past, or will do in the future. • Use action verbs. "I studied two hours last night." "I am going to study two hours tonight and again tomorrow." "I plan to memorize that information before the test."

5-3 Using these five types of I-statements can help you speak for yourself.

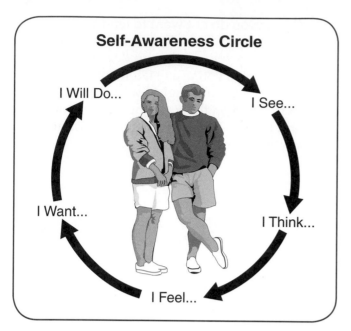

Self-Awareness Circle

I Will Do...

I See...

I Want...

I Think...

I Feel...

5-4 Your personal observations, thoughts, awareness, feelings, desires, and actions make up the self-awareness circle. You can use it to express your point of view.

You can start with the observation, "I see that you want to borrow my car." Then add the thought, "I've worked hard to make the car look nice." State how you feel about someone borrowing your car. "I feel worried when someone wants to use my car. I'm afraid that person may have an accident with it."

Next, you can state what you want to do about the situation. "I really don't want to lend my car." Then end with an action statement. "I plan to stick to my policy of not lending it to anyone."

These statements can help you speak honestly and openly. Your friend now has a clear picture of your thoughts, feelings, and desired actions.

Use What You Learn

Choose a sensitive situation in which you could apply the self-awareness circle. Practice the I-statements that you could use, starting with "I see…" and working around to "I will…"

Avoid You-Statements

Verbal communication is most effective when you speak from a personal point of view. Starting a sentence with *I see*, *I think*, *I feel*, or *I want* lets the receiver know how you really feel.

Although I-statements send clearer messages, many people use you-statements instead. "You are so dumb!" "You should apologize to me." "You should really tell her how you feel!" You-statements attack the person, not the problem. They send messages that judge, command, or blame the other person. Some people use them to vent their personal feelings or give solutions.

You-statements attack the receiver's self-esteem. As a result, the receiver responds in a defensive manner. The person may feel that his or her thoughts, opinions, or plans are unimportant.

Link to Your Life

In what situations would a you-statement be okay? Think of situations in which you expect others to give you advice, and you would not be offended if they used a you-message.

Receiving Messages

Communication is a two-way process. For good communication to occur, you need to speak and listen well. Your skill in listening is an important part of communicating effectively. You receive messages in two parts. First you take in the message; then you interpret it.

If you are a good listener, you do more than just hear the words. You pay close attention to what the person is saying. You try to maintain eye contact in order to share the feelings he or she is sending nonverbally. You make an effort to clearly understand the message. This lets the speaker know you care about what he or she is saying.

Passive Listening

When people just take in messages, they are using **passive listening**. This means they are hearing words without always listening for meanings. People who often use passive listening are not trying to understand the sender's message.

How do you feel when the person you are talking to does not respond? The person does not smile, nod, or comment. You get no feedback at all. The silence can be frustrating. You do not know if your message is being received accurately.

Active Listening Skills

You can be more certain that you are interpreting a message clearly when you use **active listening**. This means you give the sender some type of sign that you are listening.

Giving feedback shows you are listening and encourages the sender to keep talking. The feedback may be a short verbal response such as *yes*. Active listeners also use other verbal responses, such as checking out and reflecting.

Checking out means using questions to clarify a message. "Did you say that his car was wrecked?" "Where did you say this happened?" This form of active listening encourages the sender to restate or expand the message to make it clearer. As the conversation continues, both of you can use questions to check out each other's responses.

Reflecting is another response that indicates active listening. When you use **reflecting**, you repeat in your own words what you think has been said. As the listener, you might say, "What I hear you saying is…" Like a mirror, you reflect back the sender's thoughts and feelings. Reflecting gives the sender a chance to clarify the message that was sent. Reflecting can also be used when the receiver wants to help the sender identify certain feelings.

Good listening skills are a vital part of effective communication. The chart in 5-5 lists six ways to practice good listening. Being an active listener will help you receive and understand the sender's messages.

Keys to Good Listening

Show interest in what the other person is saying by sitting forward and using eye contact.

Try to block out interruptions.

Let the sender complete his or her thoughts. Accept the sender's ideas and feelings.

Use good verbal skills in giving feedback. Ask questions, reflect feelings, or restate an idea when appropriate.

Control your nonverbal messages. Make sure that they are positive and reinforce your comments.

Be aware of strong emotions. Understand that they can affect a message's clarity, and the way that you might respond.

Don't let silence make you nervous. Silence provides time for both people to think about what was said.

5-5 Being an active listener helps you get involved in the communication process.

Review Section 5:1

1. Briefly explain the communication process.
2. Explain the difference between nonverbal and verbal communication.
3. Provide two examples of each: facial expression, gesture, body motion. Describe what each means.
4. Give an example of how you can use I-statements to express your point of view.
5. Explain the difference between passive and active listening. How does active listening promote good communication?
6. Imagine you are listening to a friend describe how a close relationship ended. List three different forms of active listening and an example of a response for each.

section 5:2

Factors Affecting Communication

Sharpen Your Reading

Draw a chart with two columns. Label one column *Factors That Affect Communication Positively* and the other *Factors That Affect Communication Negatively.* As you read, write key concepts in the appropriate column.

Boost Your Vocabulary

Pick one of the communication patterns and write a short skit in which the characters use that pattern. Share your skit with a classmate.

Know Key Terms

blaming
placating
distracting

Certain factors aid good communication while others hinder it. Your self-esteem, emotional state, and environment can influence the message communicated to others. In addition, communication barriers such as closed minds and prejudice can prevent good communication. Understanding these factors can help you improve your communication skills.

Your Self-Esteem

Self-esteem is an important factor in the way messages are sent or received, 5-6. People with low self-esteem send and interpret messages differently from those with high self-esteem.

Low Self-Esteem

People with low self-esteem have more problems communicating effectively. They may not be sure of their own feelings. They often avoid direct eye contact, which prevents them from accurately sending and receiving messages.

People with low self-esteem may fear that others will reject them and their ideas. Therefore, they are afraid to let others know what they really think and feel. To avoid rejection, they withdraw and say little or nothing.

Sharing thoughts and feelings with another person is a good way to build self-esteem. Talking with a caring person who is a good listener can build confidence and improve communication skills.

Think More About It
How could a conversation with a caring person help someone feel lovable and capable?

5-6 Positive self-esteem can help you communicate clearly without the use of hidden messages.

Negative Communication Patterns

When their self-esteem is low, people tend to communicate in negative patterns. They may use lying, blaming, placating, and distracting to avoid saying how they really think or feel. Negative communication patterns result in even lower self-esteem and cause feelings of worthlessness to increase.

Lying is a negative communication pattern in which people are not honest. They do not share observations, thoughts, and feelings in an accurate way. Lying prevents people from building healthy relationships.

Blaming is a pattern in which people accuse others for everything that goes wrong. They find fault with others in order to cover up their low self-esteem.

Placating is a pattern of communication in which people will say or do something just to please others or keep them from getting upset. Going along with the crowd is easier for people with low esteem. They are afraid to do or say anything that might threaten their already low self-esteem.

Distracting is another poor communication pattern in which people just ignore unpleasant situations. They may put the issue aside as not really being important. This is easier than risking an attack on their low self-esteem.

Making encouraging comments and giving positive feedback can improve your communication with someone who has low self-esteem, 5-7. As self-esteem increases, so does the ability to communicate clearly. People with strong feelings of value and self-worth usually feel good about themselves. They are not afraid to share their personal thoughts and feelings with others. They express themselves in a more open manner than those who do not accept or like themselves.

5-7 Giving positive feedback that shows you are listening will encourage a person with low self-esteem.

Your Emotional State

Your emotional state is another factor that can affect communication. Before trying to communicate, you need to recognize your emotional state. Intense emotions get in the way of sharing complex thoughts and ideas. If your emotions are intense, let the other person know you need time to sort out your feelings before discussing the issue. Go for a walk or wait a while before trying to communicate. By doing this, you can think about your feelings, what caused them, and how to control them. You can also avoid upsetting the other person. After you feel calmer, you will have greater success at communicating a message others understand.

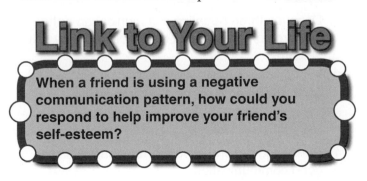

Link to Your Life

When a friend is using a negative communication pattern, how could you respond to help improve your friend's self-esteem?

Your Environment

Along with your emotional state, the environment in which you communicate can affect the communication process. The time of day or the amount of time you have can make a difference.

A relaxed environment helps good communication take place. A quiet place, where it is easy to talk without interruptions, will promote the intimate sharing of thoughts and feelings.

A busy or noisy environment makes it harder. Fatigue or illness can keep a person from showing interest. Distance between the two who are communicating makes it harder to interpret body language and nonverbal signals. Communicating via the Internet or even over a phone makes it hard to get a complete picture of the sender's total message.

Whether you are sending or receiving a message, choose the best environment possible. The choice of time and place is important, especially when communicating sensitive or personal information. An environment that allows direct eye contact and a chance to read nonverbal signals will promote the most accurate interpretation of the sender's message.

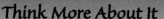

Think More About It
What are some common items used to communicate in today's society? How do you think current technology affects a person's ability to fully understand and interpret another's message?

Communication Barriers

In addition to low self-esteem, intense emotions, and noisy environments, there are other barriers that get in the way of good communication.

People with *closed minds* shut out or ignore opinions and beliefs that are different from their own. As receivers, they may filter out information they do not want to hear. They tune out the message the sender is trying to share, 5-8.

Prejudice is another communication barrier. Prejudice occurs when a person forms opinions about others without complete knowledge or facts.

5-8 People with closed minds prevent good communication by ignoring messages they do not want to hear.

How can you overcome these barriers to communication? First, understand that they do exist and can interfere with communication. Only then can you try to avoid using them. Practicing the following methods will help you develop skills to become a better speaker and listener:

- Keep an open mind. When communicating, listen to others' opinions and beliefs.

- Avoid mixed messages by thinking before you speak and saying what you mean. Use body language that supports your words.

- Overcome prejudice of others by asking questions and getting all the facts before forming an opinion. Try to understand and accept others' differences.

- Practice active listening when others speak. Do not let your mind wander. Pay attention to the speaker and do not interrupt. Respond only when the speaker is finished and it is your turn.

Review Section 5:2

1. Describe three negative communication patterns that are commonly used by people with low self-esteem.

2. Explain how intense emotions affect the communication process.

3. How can your environment affect your ability to communicate verbally?

4. Name and describe two barriers that hinder good communication.

section 5:3

Skills for Conflict Resolution

Sharpen Your Reading

As you read, list the steps for resolving conflicts and summarize the key concepts under each step.

Boost Your Vocabulary

Brainstorm a list of words that are related to each key term. Choose one term and write a paragraph using the key term and related words.

Know Key Terms

conflict
conflict resolution
problem ownership
negotiation
compromise

Many problems occur in relationships because of poor communication. A message may not have been sent clearly. Sometimes the message is misinterpreted or not received accurately. As a result, people disagree or argue. Feelings get hurt.

When conflict occurs, it is important to restore good communication and positive feelings, 5-9. If left unresolved, conflicts can threaten relationships.

5-9 Learning conflict resolution skills will help maintain positive relationships.

Conflict occurs when any two people disagree on some issue. Some conflict is a normal part of most relationships. Even when people attempt to communicate clearly, conflict can occur.

Although conflict occurs for many reasons, it is often due to different personal values. Friends may argue over where to eat. An employer may feel that an employee is spending too much time talking to friends. Family members may disagree over where to vacation. Because people have different personalities, wants, and needs, conflict is common.

People often respond to a disagreement by arguing. This negative form of communication is used to protect their self-esteem. It attacks the person, not the problem. Name-calling or blaming are two types of you-statements commonly used in arguments. "You are so stupid!" or "You never help out!" are examples. Both are destructive to a relationship as they create more hostility. The real conflict is left unresolved.

Use What You Learn

In what ways would conflict be harmful to a relationship?

Steps to Resolving Conflicts

Conflicts cannot always be eliminated from close relationships, but they can be controlled. How can you successfully solve problems and disagreements in your relationships?

Conflict resolution is one skill that can help you resolve conflicts in a positive way. Using this skill builds relationships. It encourages a better understanding of the other person's point of view. Overall, it helps you and the other person deal with the issue and reach a fair solution.

The chart in 5-10 lists some important guidelines to follow when resolving conflicts. These guidelines can set the stage for conflict resolution to occur. Once the stage is set, the following steps must be taken to resolve a conflict successfully:

- Identify the problem.
- Identify who owns the problem.
- Accept ownership of the problem.
- Solve the problem.

Identify the Problem

The first step in resolving a conflict is to identify the real issue. Using good communication skills such as I-statements and active listening can help identify the problem. It is important to take time to analyze and identify the real problem before taking any action.

Guidelines for Resolving Conflicts

Bring the conflict into the open as soon as possible.

Find the right time and place to discuss the issues.

Stay calm. Speak with a moderate tone and at a moderate pace.

Use I-messages to state your thoughts, feelings, and ideas.

Stick to the subject. Don't bring up other issues.

Be specific in stating the facts that relate to the problem.

Avoid you-messages. Name-calling, blaming, or accusing messages won't solve the problem.

Don't walk away from the discussion.

Recognize and accept the other's feelings, ideas, and opinions.

Keep your emotions under control.

Be an active listener when the other person speaks.

Try to compromise in reaching a solution.

5-10 Practicing these guidelines for resolving conflicts promotes positive feelings.

Identify Who Owns the Problem

The next step is to identify **problem ownership**. The person bothered by the situation owns the problem. If the problem affects or disturbs more than one person, both people share it jointly.

Accept Ownership of the Problem

Accepting ownership of the problem is the next step in resolving the situation. If two people own the problem, they must work together to find a solution. Sometimes only one person accepts the responsibility for a joint problem. In this case, reaching a solution that is fair to both people is often difficult.

Think More About It
Why might it be hard for a person to accept ownership of a problem?

Solve the Problem

Once you take ownership of a specific problem, you can take steps to solve the problem. The decision-making process can be applied to solve the problem, 5-11.

When a problem is jointly owned, negotiation is needed to resolve the situation. **Negotiation** is a communication process in which people alternate between sending and receiving messages. The purpose is to reach an agreeable solution. To do this, both people need to send clear and accurate messages. As receivers, both need to understand and consider the message before responding.

When both people own the problem, they may need to negotiate in each stage of the problem-solving process. Maintaining open communication in each stage is critical for success.

Use What You Learn

What attitudes would make it difficult for two people to negotiate effectively?

Reaching an agreeable solution is not always easy. One-sided thinking can hinder negotiation. Sometimes one person takes a stand and refuses to recognize the other's point of view. Then a solution that is satisfactory to both cannot be reached.

Solving a Problem
1. Identify the problem.
2. Identify the alternative solutions.
3. Evaluate the alternatives.
4. Choose the best solution.
5. Implement the solution.
6. Evaluate the solution. Was it effective in solving the problem?

5-11 The steps of the decision-making process can be used to work out a solution to a conflict.

People can overcome obstacles during the negotiation process through compromise. **Compromise** is a give-and-take method that allows both people to express themselves. It is an effective way to resolve conflicts. No one person wins or loses. Both give in a little to reach a solution that is workable to each.

Compromise protects and helps maintain each person's self-esteem. Each person recognizes the worth of the other's opinions, feelings, and desires. People who feel accepted are more likely to work toward an agreeable solution.

Review Section 5:3

1. Explain why conflict resolution can help people handle conflict in a positive way.
2. In a conflict situation, what three steps must occur before the problem can be solved?
3. In conflict resolution, who must own the problem for negotiation to take place?
4. What takes place during the negotiation process?
5. Explain how compromise can help resolve conflicts.

Developing communication skills will help strengthen your relationships.

Think It Through

A Breakdown in Communication

It was late Saturday afternoon and Shayla was sitting at the kitchen table, working on her laptop computer. A big research paper was due on Monday for her history class. She was hurrying to get it done so she could go out with friends tonight.

She was annoyed because her brother had friends over and they had just started playing a loud video game in the next room. It was distracting her from focusing on her paper, but she was almost finished so she didn't bother to move to another room. Shayla's dad came into the kitchen and started taking vegetables out of the refrigerator.

"Shayla, would you please set the kitchen table when you finish your homework?" he asked.

"Sure, dad," Shayla replied, half-listening as she continued typing. "I'll be done in a few minutes."

"Thanks," her dad replied. "All the dishes in the dishwasher are clean. I'm going to run up to the store to get some green peppers for the dish I'm making. If your mother gets home, let her know where I am and tell her I'm making dinner."

Shayla was absorbed in typing and didn't respond. She didn't even hear the door shut as her dad left. She had just finished her paper when the phone rang. It was Shayla's mom.

"I'm on my way home from the mall and thought I would pick up a pizza for dinner," she said. "What kind of pizza should I get?"

Shayla told her mom what she wanted, and then hung up the phone. She cleared away her schoolwork and started setting the table. However, there wasn't enough clean silverware or plates to finish. Just as she was wondering what to do, her mom arrived with the pizza. A few minutes later, her dad arrived with groceries. He noticed only half of the table was set and then he saw the pizza box on the counter.

"Shayla, I told you there were clean dishes in the dishwasher," he said. "I also told you that I was making dinner. You should have told your mom she didn't need to pick up a pizza. You need to pay attention and listen better."

Shayla became upset and stalked out of the kitchen.

"All I heard you say was that I should set the table," she muttered as she left the room. "Couldn't you see that I was busy?"

Questions to Guide Your Thinking

1. At what point in the conversation did the breakdown in communication occur?
2. What factors contributed to the communication breakdown?
3. What caused the miscommunication to escalate into a conflict?
4. What could Shayla and her dad have done to make sure they communicated accurately?

Chapter Summary

The communication process involves sending and receiving messages. Understanding this process and how it is used is important. It can help you develop effective communication skills and get along with others. As a sender, you need skills in sending clear, accurate messages. As a receiver, you need to listen well and interpret the message correctly.

You use nonverbal and verbal skills every day whenever you communicate. In nonverbal communication, you send messages without using words. Through body language, you express your thoughts, feelings, and emotions to others. Facial expressions, gestures, and body motions are all forms of body language that you use.

You communicate verbally by using words. You can improve your ability to express yourself clearly by using I-messages. This skill gives you more control over what you say to others. Besides sending clear messages, you need skills in receiving messages. Active listening is a skill that helps you to interpret and understand messages clearly.

Your self-esteem, emotional state, and environment can affect the way messages are communicated. In addition, certain factors can get in the way of good communication, such as a closed mind, mixed messages, and prejudice. Once you know how these barriers affect communication, you can work to improve your speaking and listening skills.

Good communication skills are needed to resolve conflicts in a positive way. Conflict resolution is a step-by-step skill you can develop to resolve conflicts successfully and build relationships. First, identify the problem. Next, identify and accept problem ownership. Finally, reach an agreeable solution to the problem through negotiation and compromise.

Assess...

Your Knowledge

1. What types of nonverbal and verbal messages help communicate a shared message?

2. What are four factors that could interfere with or prevent good communication from taking place?

3. What are the steps for resolving conflict?

Your Understanding

4. How does the communication process produce shared meanings?

5. How could you-statements affect the communication that takes place between two people?

6. How could low self-esteem affect a person's success at communication?

7. How do negative communication patterns affect relationships?

Your Skills

8. Express your own thoughts, feelings, and intentions by using five different types of I-statements.

9. Give an example of how you would use active listening skills to help a friend make a decision.

10. What steps would you take to solve a problem of failing grades in a class?

Think Critically

11. *Writing.* Identify a situation that upset you. Write a paragraph describing this situation. Using the self-awareness circle, write I-statements to express your personal observations, thoughts, feelings, intentions, and actions related to this situation. Summarize whether you sent the message you intended to send.

12. As a class, identify several conflict situations (consider personal experiences, current events, or historical references). Choose one of the conflicts and describe how it was resolved. Evaluate the techniques used to handle the conflict. Explain how the steps in conflict resolution did or could have enhanced the process. *Group option.* In small groups, create a role-play to illustrate how the steps of conflict resolution could be applied to resolving this conflict. Perform the role-play for the class.

13. *Research.* Assess your ability to be an active listener. Try an experiment in which you use the active listening skills of checking out and reflecting when someone is trying to share a confidential message with you. Compare this conversation to one in which you deliberately avoid looking at the speaker and remain passive

as he or she talks. Describe the differences in how these two conversations arrived or did not arrive at shared meanings. *Choice:* Work with a partner who will record observations as you carry out your research. Post your research results on your class bulletin board.

14. **Research.** Attend a school event or activity and make a list of the different forms of body language you observe. Beside each form, identify the nonverbal messages you received. Put each message and your interpretation on a small card. Hand it to the person who sent the nonverbal message. Explain that you are doing a research project, and ask the person to respond to the accuracy of the message. Identify the gaps between the message you received and the message that was sent. Write a paragraph explaining your experiment and the results of your research. *Group Option:* In small groups, share your research and identify similarities and differences in results.

Connect with Your Community

15. Develop a list of words or expressions that are unique to your particular culture, community, or geographic area. Identify other possible meanings for these expressions. *Choice:* Present your information to the class in an electronic presentation.

16. **Writing.** Pretend your report card lists your grade as one level lower than what you understood it to be. Using the self-awareness circle, write five different I-statements that you could use to express yourself positively to your teacher. *Choice:* Using the same process, give an oral demonstration of five I-statements you could use to approach your boss about a possible raise.

17. **Writing.** Choose an on-the-job situation in which communication barriers result in problems between employees or problems between an employee and a customer. Write a short skit to illustrate the problem, ways to overcome such barriers, and strategies for improving communication on the job. *Choice:* With a partner, role-play the problem and solution.

18. *Social studies, writing.* Write a paragraph explaining how different cultural backgrounds in your community could result in difficulty in communicating a shared meaning. Discuss how these difficulties could affect stereotypes and prejudice in your community. Suggest ways community leaders could help build healthy relationships between members of different cultural backgrounds. *Choice:* Prepare a presentation for your local chamber of commerce or school board sharing these potential difficulties and possible steps to help promote clear communication.

Use Technology

19. Use the computer to design and print a poster illustrating the importance of good communication techniques. *Choice:* Choose a target audience: students (preschool, elementary, middle school, or senior high school), families in counseling, workers on the job, or another. Design a poster for your target audience.

20. **Research.** Search the Internet to research the communication skills that are used by a counselor. Identify the skills that you feel are most important for a counselor to be effective on the job.

21. Use a computer program to design and print a brochure that illustrates "Keys for Successful Conflict Resolution." *Choice:* Design a Web page that covers the same information.

22. *Math, research.* Record the various nonverbal techniques that your teachers use during a typical day. Using a spreadsheet, list the teachers across the top and the different types of nonverbal techniques down the side. Tally the total number of types of techniques used by each teacher (not the total number of times each technique was used). Summarize your findings in a short paragraph, comparing the techniques used with your opinions of each teacher's effectiveness in communicating. Is one or more nonverbal techniques used by all effective teachers? *Group option:* Work with a partner who has the same teachers. Share your findings with another group and compare results.

Chapter 6

Family and Peer Relationships

Section 6:1
Friendships

Section 6:2
Relationships in the Family

Section 6:3
Relationships in the World Around You

Key Questions

Questions to answer as you study this chapter:

* How can people develop close friendships?
* How can strong, meaningful relationships be developed in the family?
* How can positive, healthy relationships be developed with others at school and work?

Chapter Objectives

After studying this chapter, you will be able to

* **identify** the different types of friendships.
* **describe** the qualities of a friend.
* **recognize** ways that friendships can help a person grow.
* **explain** how to develop a close friendship.
* **distinguish** between positive and negative effects of peer pressure.
* **identify** factors that affect family relationships.
* **analyze** ways to improve parent-teen relationships.
* **demonstrate** important relationship skills that can help you succeed at school and at work.

Life Sketch

Everyone was having a great time at the party except Dee. She recently moved to the area and didn't know anyone well. Her only friend at school, Cary, invited her to the party, then got sick at the last minute. Dee sat alone, embarrassed and wondering, "How will I ever get through this? No one wants to talk to me."

As she gazed across the room, Dee recognized Tosha from her biology class. She was standing alone, too. Dee smiled and Tosha waved back. "She probably doesn't like being alone either," Dee thought. She took a deep breath and decided to start a conversation. "What can I lose by trying?" she thought.

As it turned out, Dee and Tosha had much in common and became close friends. Dee was glad she had taken the first step in starting a new friendship.

Getting Started

Everyone needs a friend—including you. A friendship is one type of personal relationship that can help you grow as a person. Friends help you learn and understand more about yourself and others. Friendships usually grow between people who have much in common, but other qualities also matter.

Your peers will most likely be the source of your closest friendships. Choosing friends who can help you grow is important. Relationship skills can help you make such choices.

Families are an important source of close, lifetime relationships. The shared backgrounds, common views, and similar interests help family members form special bonds.

The relationships you develop with your friends, peers, and family are an important part of your life. The way you relate to other people will affect your quality of life, too.

Skills for developing personal relationships can be learned with practice. Developing these skills will benefit you in many ways. You will feel more in control of yourself and the direction your life path is going. Your ability to develop long-lasting relationships will increase. Your future relationships in your family, with your friends, and in the workplace will be affected in a positive way.

section 6:1

Friendships

Sharpen Your Reading

Create a chart with three columns. In the first column, write down what you already know about the topic. In the second column, write down what you want to know about the topic. As you read, write ideas that you learn about the topic in the third column.

Boost Your Vocabulary

Write a paragraph that describes a situation in which you demonstrated empathy.

Know Key Terms

acquaintances
empathy
rapport
passive
aggressive
assertive
bullying
cyberbullying

Friendships usually grow between people who share common interests, goals, and outlooks on life, 6-1. However, developing close friendships takes more than just sharing similarities and interests. Friends have certain qualities in common that build their relationships. These qualities contribute to the growth of the friendship.

Throughout your life, you will probably experience many different types of relationships. These will include your family, teachers, friends, coworkers, and acquaintances. The friendships will range from casual to close. All relationships can affect your personal growth and development.

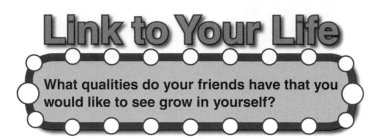

What qualities do your friends have that you would like to see grow in yourself?

Types of Friendships

Think of all the people you know. Some you may have just met, while others are your closest friends. **Acquaintances** are people you know but who are not your close friends. Some acquaintances are casual, such as students you say hi to when passing in the hall. You may see other acquaintances more frequently. Questions such as "What are you doing now?" or "What classes are you taking?" inspire a more involved conversation. However, communication remains brief.

Good friends are people you see often. You spend enough time with them to know each other quite well. Good friends share common interests and experiences. They also share personal thoughts and feelings. Their mutual sharing shows that some measure of trust exists between them.

Usually, only a few people in your life are considered *close friends*. A close friend may also be considered your *best friend*. You know this person will not make fun of you or laugh at your ideas. You can trust this friend to care about what is best for you. You probably have many acquaintances, but only a few close friends.

Investigate Further

Think about your relationships and classify people as acquaintances, good friends, or close friends. Which group is the largest? Why do you think that is?

6-1 Discussing homework assignments and school sports are examples of information you share with a friend.

What Is a Friend?

What qualities do you look for in a friend? Do you look for someone who understands and accepts you? Do you look for someone who is open and honest with you, someone who makes you feel good, or someone you can trust? Each of your friends is likely to have some of these qualities.

For a friendship to develop, you need to have these qualities as well. If you are looking for these traits in a friend, the other person is, too. Both people need to develop similar traits for a friendship to grow. The important characteristics of a friend are described in 6-2.

Why Do You Need Friends?

Friendships take time and commitment to develop. Friends care for, encourage, and support each other. Friends need to contribute to the relationship in order for it to grow.

Friendships offer lifetime benefits to you. They can help you mature intellectually, emotionally, and socially. They can help you get to know yourself better. They can be a source of companionship and closeness. Friendships can contribute to your personal development throughout your life.

- *Friendships can help you know and understand your own thoughts and feelings.* With friends, you share ideas, dreams, and plans for the future. They try to respond honestly and openly to what you say. They help you think through and solve your personal problems. In this way, they help you grow intellectually.

  Sometimes a friend can help you interpret your feelings. "You seem hurt. She really offended you, didn't she?" Such feedback can help you grow emotionally as you identify and then deal with your real feelings.

A Friend Is...
Someone with whom you can talk. You can share your thoughts and feelings and know you are understood. Because you have much in common, you both communicate clearly and with ease. You understand each other's nonverbal messages. You interpret each other's meanings in a similar way.
Someone who accepts you. You are accepted just as you are, for the real you. You don't have to act like someone you're not. You feel comfortable when you are together. A friend does not put you down, laugh at you, or make fun of you when you make a mistake. Instead, a friend makes you feel good about being you.
Someone who supports you. When you need support, a friend gives you the help you need. A friend may encourage you to grow and to do your best by helping yourself.
Someone you can trust. When you share your inner thoughts and feelings, you know a friend will be reliable and honest. A friend won't use what you said in a negative way. A friend will keep your thoughts in confidence. You can count on that person to look out for your well-being.
Someone who is open. For a friendship to grow, both people must take the risk to share their thoughts and feelings. A friend is someone you can count on to be sincere. If you have a personal problem, you can count on a close friend to help you through it.

6-2 Friendships develop and grow between people who share many of the same personal qualities.

- *Friendships can help you accept yourself as a person and increase your self-esteem.* Everyone needs to feel important and worthwhile. A close friend will listen to you, accept your ideas, and include you in activities. They like you for who you are. You, in turn, feel comfortable and relaxed with them. They help you grow emotionally.

- *Friendships can help you develop empathy.* **Empathy** is an emotion in which you feel what another is feeling. Through empathy, you become more sensitive to the thoughts and feelings of that person. You feel as though you are sensing the same experience. You can develop empathy as you listen and learn how others think and feel. Empathy is a mature emotion. Thus, having friends and feeling empathy can help you grow emotionally.

- *Friendships can help you increase your communication skills.* Friends usually spend a great deal of time talking to each other. They share and listen to each other's personal thoughts. They try to understand each other and resolve personal differences. Communicating clearly is an important skill that is part of social maturity. It can help you get along with your friends and others.

- *Friendships can help you learn to work cooperatively.* When friends cooperate, they share their ideas. They consider each other's opinions and viewpoints. Then they choose a solution or plan of action that is agreeable to all concerned. This helps you grow socially.

  In a friendship, reaching such an agreement is easier because both people have similar views. They have mutual acceptance and mutual respect for each other. These qualities make it easier to cooperate. Concern for each other's welfare also makes cooperation easier. A friendship makes a good environment for learning to work with others.

- *Friendships can satisfy the need for companionship.* Most people have a need for someone special with whom they can spend time. They need to feel close to someone, to care and feel cared for, and to love and be loved. These needs continue throughout the life cycle. Close friends can provide companionship and meet many of these needs.

- *Friendships can help you prepare for future long-term relationships.* Your close friendships will serve as a guide in future relationships. As you mature, you develop more caring and less selfish personal relationships. You appreciate your friends for their unique qualities. These deeper feelings carry into adult relationships.

You may also be more selective about your relationships with the opposite sex. If marriage is a consideration, you may carefully evaluate the personal qualities you want in a partner. Who helps you grow as a person? Who encourages you to be the best you can be? Who makes you feel confident, secure, and supported? Many of the same qualities found in a close friendship will help create a lasting marriage.

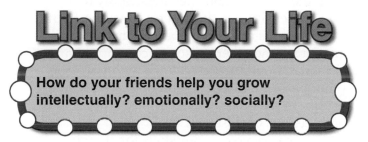

How do your friends help you grow intellectually? emotionally? socially?

Developing a Close Friendship

How can you develop a friendship? What qualities do you have for building such a friendship? Knowing how to develop a friendship is a skill you will always use. You can help a friendship grow in several ways, 6-3.

Be Friendly

"He who has friends must show himself friendly." This old proverb still applies to the development of relationships. Casual acquaintances are based on first impressions and short interactions. To make friends, you must interact with the other person.

Develop Rapport

After a friendly greeting, you then try to develop **rapport**. That is, you create an atmosphere in which the other person feels comfortable and wants to talk. For rapport to exist, both people need to sense each other's friendliness, warmth, and genuine interest in each other.

Saying something interesting can start the conversation and engage the other person. A basic knowledge of several topics can help you start a conversation.

Qualities for Developing Close Friendships
I am friendly.
I can accept others.
I can accept others' viewpoints even if they are different from mine.
I can reveal myself to others.
I have rapport with others.
I like most people.
I feel that most people like me.
I am honest with others.
I have trust in others.
I can keep information a secret.
I can relate person to person.
I like to benefit others.
I like to make other people feel good about themselves.
I enjoy rewarding others.
I am dependable.
I like to learn from others.
I am willing to share power with others.

6-3 Each of these personal qualities can help people develop close friendships with others.

Good friendships take time to develop. For a relationship to grow, you will have to make an effort to get to know the person. When you meet someone you do not know well, start the conversation with some easy-to-answer questions: "Where do you go to school?" "What classes are you taking this semester?" "Where do you live?" "Do you like it here?" Questions that require more than a yes or no can encourage the other person to talk.

Another way to develop rapport is to use direct eye contact. A warm smile shows the person that you are interested in becoming friends. Appropriate gestures can be helpful, too. Do not overdo it. If your body language does not look natural, you may make the other person uncomfortable.

Use What You Learn

How does paying close attention to a person when he or she is talking help build rapport?

Think More About It
Why is it so hard to rebuild trust after it has been broken?

Share Yourself

For relationships to grow, you need to share your personal opinions, thoughts, and feelings. To be open with someone, you risk being accepted or rejected. A fear of rejection may cause uncertainty. You may feel safer by hiding your inner thoughts. However, to develop a close relationship, you must take the risk of sharing your inner self. The benefit comes when others choose to share personal information with you in return. From that point, your relationship can grow.

Build Trust

Honesty and reliability are important parts of trust. Without trust, most relationships do not continue to grow. Most people are not willing to trust a person who says one thing and does another. Trust is developed in stages over a period of time. You can start building trust by sharing information that is not threatening or too personal. In the next stage, you can check for the other person's response. Does your friend show a caring attitude? Is there concern for how you are feeling? Does your friend share similar thoughts with you? In being trustworthy, your friend is helping to build the relationship.

Finally, you can evaluate what your friend does with the shared information. Trust takes time to develop, but it can easily be destroyed. If the information is used in a negative way, trust is broken. If the friend makes fun of your secret or embarrasses you, the trust is broken. If you violate your word to keep a friend's secret, you will destroy that friend's trust in you.

For trust to develop and grow, both people must believe the other person is honest. An attitude of care and concern for each other must be there. Also, both must believe that the information will not be used against them in any way.

Respond with Empathy

Learning to respond with empathy can help you develop closer relationships. Try to identify with the other person's feelings. Show that you are sensitive to the other's concerns. Show interest in his or her well-being. Empathy will encourage the other person to continue sharing personal thoughts and feelings with you. The other person will feel accepted. You will build esteem in the other person. You will develop trust and feelings of closeness.

You can develop your skills for showing empathy with practice. Use good listening skills. Using eye contact, focus on the speaker. Show a genuine interest in what the speaker is saying through your body language. A smile, a nod of the head, or a raised eyebrow—all can show that you are interested and concerned. A touch on the hand, an arm around the shoulder, or a hug can also send messages of caring and concern, 6-4.

Verbal feedback can also show empathy. "Tell me about it." "Go ahead, I'm listening." "Let me hear the whole story." These comments let others know you are really interested in what they have to say. Phrases such as "I see," "I understand," and "good idea" assure the sender that you are listening with concern.

Be Open to Growth

In a close relationship, you can learn more about yourself as well as the other person. As you share personal information with each other, you may become aware of *blind spots*. Your blind spots are factors that you did not know about yourself. As a relationship grows closer, each person can point out the other's blind spots without fear of rejection. Both grow from the experience.

6-4 Being a good listener can encourage the speaker to keep sharing.

Link to Your Life

Why might a person become defensive when you point out a blind spot to them?

The Goal of a Close Relationship

Not all relationships become close. Close relationships most often develop between persons who have common interests, priorities, and goals. The goal of a close relationship is to experience fulfillment through sharing. Sometimes the sharing is intellectual, emotional, spiritual, or physical. A marital relationship can provide closeness in all these areas. Other types of relationships may provide closeness in one or two areas.

Developing a close relationship requires a commitment from both people. That means taking time to get to know each other. Both need to share openly and to respond with empathy. Both need to be committed to helping each other grow.

Some relationships may grow in closeness, but then eventually end. Sometimes trust is broken and, as a result, one person feels hurt. Then that person no longer confides in the other. If the conflict is not resolved in an acceptable way, the relationship may end.

Some close relationships may change over time as people grow and mature. People who were very close may grow apart later as their lives change. They may have less time to spend together. Their emotional needs may be met through other relationships. Relationships sometimes end, or change to a different level.

In what ways would it be more difficult to develop rapport with someone through a long-distance relationship? In what ways would it be easier to build rapport through a long-distance relationship?

Peer Relationships

You will most likely develop your closest friendships with others in your peer group. Your peers are at the same stage of their life path as you. They often have similar needs, fears, interests, and goals. Peers can both positively and negatively affect each other.

Peer Pressure

Peers have a strong influence on one another throughout life. They can affect the way others in the same age group think or act. Teens make choices to be like their peers because they want to be part of the group. To most teens, belonging to a group is important. In order to belong, the peer group member must conform to certain standards of appearance, dress, and behavior.

Sometimes you will agree with these standards and what the group wants to do. When the group's standards and conduct are positive, peer pressure can have beneficial effects on your behavior.

Use What You Learn

What examples can you think of where peer pressure is positive?

Negative Peer Pressure

At other times, peer pressure may be negative. Peers may pressure you to do something you do not believe in or do not want to do. They may want you to join in activities that could be harmful to your health and well-being or to others. Sometimes young people want friendships so badly that they give in to negative peer pressure. Close friendships are hindered by negative peer pressure. Such pressure does not encourage open, honest sharing or acceptance of individual differences. In addition, it threatens the personal growth of all concerned.

Handling Negative Peer Pressure

How can negative peer pressure be handled? Teens may respond to peer pressure in three different ways. They may be passive, aggressive, or assertive.

Some teens respond to peer pressure in a **passive** way. That is, they just go along with whatever is said or done in the group. They will not risk being different. Such passive responses will not help them handle negative peer pressure in a positive way. It will not lead to growth and deeper friendships.

Sometimes people respond with **aggressive** behavior that can harm or hurt others. Aggressive behavior includes yelling, calling names, criticizing, pushing, shoving, and more violent behavior. Aggressive behavior increases problems in relationships. It breaks down good communication. It often leads to fighting and more intense violence, not good friendships.

The best way to respond to peer pressure is to be **assertive**. That is, you let peers know what you think and feel by using good communication skills. You use I-statements to describe how you feel, what you desire, or what you intend to do. You use eye contact and look directly at the person to whom you are talking. You speak clearly, with even tones.

People who are assertive do not let others take advantage of them. They are not afraid to disagree, say no, or express what they believe. They are not afraid to ask questions to make sure they understand a message. They communicate clearly, yet show respect for others' thoughts and feelings.

If peers pressure you to do something you really do not want to do, try an assertive response. Tell them, "No, I'm not interested." Stand firm for what you think is right for you. The more you assert your own thoughts and say what you believe, the easier it will become.

Handling Bullying

Using aggressive behavior to intentionally harm another person is called **bullying**. People may bully in several ways, 6-5. Any form of bullying harms the growth of a relationship. It destroys feelings of caring, nurturing, and safety in the relationship. Bullying is a sign of social immaturity because bullies are not concerned about the well-being of others.

An assertive response can help you stand up for yourself when around a bully. However, being assertive is not always easy, especially if you are unsure of yourself. The first time you stand up for yourself may be difficult, but with practice it will become easier.

Think More About It
Why might a person tolerate bullying in a relationship? What effect could constant bullying have on a person's growth and development?

Types of Bullying	Examples of Behavior
Physical Bullying	Punching, poking, hair-pulling, beating
Emotional Bullying	Rejecting, defaming, humiliating, blackmailing, manipulating friends, isolating, pressuring peers
Sexual Bullying	Exhibitionism, requests for sexual activities, sexual harassment, abuse involving physical contact and assault
Verbal Bullying	Name-calling, teasing, gossip

6-5 Bullying appears in many different forms.

Cyberbullying

Cyberbullying is using technology, such as the Internet or cell phones, to send hurtful or threatening messages to another person. Cyberbullying can include the following actions:

- spreading lies or rumors through e-mail or instant messaging
- pretending to be someone else online
- registering another person for something online without their permission
- posting pictures without the subject's permission

Aggressive behavior at any time or place destroys relationships. Demonstrating behavior that respects yourself and others will help you develop healthy and long-lasting friendships.

Review Section 6:1

1. Friendships often develop when people have common _____, _____, and outlooks on life.

2. What are the different types of friendships? In your own words, briefly describe each and give an example.

3. When friends help a person think through and solve a problem, that person can grow _____.

4. When friends help a person interpret his or her real feelings, that person can grow _____.

5. Friendships can help a person grow _____ by providing opportunities to increase communication skills, to see others' viewpoints, and to work cooperatively.

6. Explain how peers may influence a person's choices. Include a positive example and a negative example.

7. What actions are considered cyberbullying?

section 6:2

Relationships in the Family

Sharpen Your Reading

As you read, list each key factor affecting family relationships. For each factor, identify what you can do in your family to contribute to growth in the relationships between your family members.

Boost Your Vocabulary

Define your support network by listing the people you can rely on to help you with a problem.

Know Key Terms

support network

The family can be a source of strong, meaningful relationships. Relationships with parents, siblings, and extended family members help people learn about themselves and others. Lifelong relationships often provide love, affection, sharing, acceptance, support, and trust. Such family relationships can provide a model for you to develop your own long-lasting adult relationships.

Several factors influence the development of close family relationships. However, even the closest families experience some conflicts as each person grows and develops within the family. Learning to handle these conflicts in a positive way can strengthen family relationships. It can also help you learn how to resolve conflicts in your future adult relationships.

Factors Influencing Family Relationships

Family members get to know one another as a result of living together. How well they know each other depends on how involved they are in one another's lives. Also, their cultural background may influence their common interests and patterns of relating. Changing past patterns, if desired, can be hard. Communication and empathy skills influence a family's ability to resolve conflicts and grow closer.

- *How well do family members know each other?* Each family member is a unique individual. Each has personal likes, dislikes, needs, and goals. Each person also changes over time as he or she grows and matures. For close relationships to develop in the family, members need to know and understand each other.

- *How much time do family members spend together?* The type of sharing that helps family members really get to know each other takes time and effort. Quality time is needed for closeness to develop. Different cultural backgrounds may affect the amount of time adults spend with the children, 6-6. Family members must make an effort to contribute to the relationship or it will not grow.

Use What You Learn

What can interfere with a family spending quality time together?

- *What common interests do family members share?* If family members develop shared interests, finding time for building closer relationships is easier. Whatever the activity, doing things together can provide time for sharing. This will help you build your communication skills and prepare you to develop long-lasting future relationships.

- *What kind of communication occurs in the family?* Skills for communicating clear and accurate messages are very important between family members. Using I-statements can let family members know how you

6-6 The roles that family members take may vary from one culture to another. Being aware of cultural differences can help you understand how families interact.

feel without destroying self-esteem. Avoid you-statements that hurt others, and lead to conflict and fighting. Identifying problem ownership can help family members resolve many conflicts. Practicing active listening skills will help you clarify family members' messages.

Think More About It
Why might family members use negative communication patterns with each other, yet use good communication skills at work or with friends?

- *Does acceptance and support exist in the family?* Close relationships are developed in an atmosphere of acceptance and support. Strong family support can help members

succeed. Listening and caring about what each member says and does builds feelings of worth and acceptance in the family.

- *Does love and concern exist in the family?* Saying "I love you," being helpful, or doing small favors for each other shows love and concern. A warm hug or a pat on the arm can also make each member feel secure in the family.

Use What You Learn
Why would words of love need to go hand-in-hand with loving actions in order for family members to feel secure?

Relating to Your Parents

The above factors help build strong, meaningful relationships between family members. Even so, relationships between parents and teens often become strained. Understanding the parent-teen relationship can help you manage the changes that occur during the teen years.

Understanding Your Parent's Point of View

Mutual understanding between you and your parents could lead to a better relationship. To have that mutual understanding, you need to try and look at things from your parent's point of view. Consider how the issues they face impact their thinking, their feelings, and their responses to you.

In raising their children, parents are influenced by cultural role expectations. In this society, parents may feel pressured to raise perfect children. Fulfilling these expectations is unrealistic for most parents. Few parents have been trained to help children grow to physical, intellectual, social, and emotional maturity. Most parents rely on their past family experiences to help them raise their children. Knowing what their parents experienced as they grew up can help teens understand how their parents relate to them.

Most parents put considerable time and effort into providing for their families. Living expenses are high. Many people are competing for the same jobs. They are expected to perform at their best during the workday. Parents may be required to work overtime, take work home at night, or travel, 6-7. These activities leave less time to spend with the family. Moving may be required to get promotions. That also means a move for the family. Too much pressure from work can place a strain on relationships between family members.

In today's mobile society, many families have moved away from the **support network** provided by close relatives. In past generations, this network consisted of grandparents, aunts, uncles, and other relatives. When relatives lived nearby, they tended to help each other with daily problems. They assisted with child care and discussed common questions about parenting. Many families today do not have that support group nearby.

6-7 Work demands can reduce the amount of time parents have to spend with their family.

When families move far apart, maintaining this support is difficult. Family members do not have the benefit of sharing common concerns about parenting, their jobs, or household chores. They have fewer resources in emergencies. Children have fewer family role models. Such situations add more pressure on parents.

Parents must make decisions that protect the well-being of all family members. As you recognize the scope of their responsibilities, you will begin to see why they make certain decisions. You will recognize their concerns for you, your health, and development. Your efforts to understand this will help you resolve conflicts that may arise.

Parent-Teen Conflicts

Both teens and their parents are adjusting to changes. As teens grow to maturity, they become more independent. Teens' abilities to think for themselves increase. They have strong opinions and ideas they want to express. Teens develop their own personal friendships and want to choose their own social activities. As teens become young adults, they emotionally separate from the close dependent bond with the family. This separation process enables them to develop other personal relationships in the future.

Most parents desire growth and independence for their children. The actual process, however, forces parents to change as well. They must learn to gradually let go and allow teens to become independent. The result is often conflicting feelings between parents and teens.

Parents and teens often have different views on how much independence is appropriate for a maturing teen. Maturity occurs gradually, but some teens want total independence, whether ready for it or not. Sometimes parents do not want to recognize their teen is maturing. They may keep a tight control even when the teen is able to handle the responsibility of independence. These differences can lead to conflict.

Negotiating Solutions

When parents and teens desire to keep close family relationships, they can negotiate solutions to their conflicts. A willingness to negotiate shows a positive attitude. There is respect and concern for the thoughts and desires of both parties.

Good communication skills can help parents and teens understand one another's viewpoints. To negotiate a solution, both parties need to give-and-take. Everyone needs to benefit from the solution.

How can you plan ahead for negotiating with your parents? Set a time to talk about an issue. Think about exactly what you want to say and how you can express yourself most clearly. Consider the following questions:

- What end result do you desire from the discussion?
- What aspects of the solution can you negotiate?
- Are some aspects more important to you than others?

Family meetings can provide a time and place to talk, share feelings, set goals, or make plans related to family living.

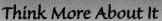

Think More About It
Why would families who hold weekly family meetings demonstrate stronger communication skills in stressful situations?

One-on-one interaction between parent and teen can also keep the door open for good communication. Personal time allows them to know each other better and develop a close friendship, 6-8.

In some families, parents and their adult children become close friends. Siblings, grandparents, aunts, and uncles can also be a source of close friendships.

Relationships with Siblings

At times, siblings may have a close relationship. They learn from and encourage one another. At other stages of life, they may spend less time with each other and more time with peers.

6-8 Doing tasks together is an opportunity for teens to develop a close relationship with their parents.

Just as siblings can be close friends, they can also be rivals. Sibling rivalry is common between brothers and sisters because they are growing through different stages. Some struggle with self-esteem, peer pressure, new roles, or new responsibilities. Siblings may be trying to compete with one another or for their parents' attention. Parents have the responsibility to help siblings work out their relationships in a positive way.

Sometimes, close relationships are not maintained between siblings. The breakdown may occur just as it would in other relationships. It may be due to a violation of trust, unwillingness to work together, or an attack on personal value and worth.

Most siblings have the chance to spend time together and share many experiences. Sibling relationships can become strong and close, lasting a lifetime. They can become the core of a strong support group.

Review Section 6:2

1. Identify five factors that can help build close relationships within the family.

2. Name three things family members could do to communicate more clearly with each other.

3. When planning to resolve a conflict with parents and negotiate a solution, list four things a teen can do.

section 6:3

Relationships in the World Around You

Sharpen Your Reading

Summarize how positive, healthy friendships in each relationship area could help with personal growth.

Boost Your Vocabulary

Identify specific groups who add diversity to your community, and describe the ways in which they contribute to the multiculturalism in your area.

Know Key Terms

significant adults
multiculturalism
diversity

Good relationship skills will help you interact with people in your community and in the workplace. Knowing how to relate to people who are older than you is a valuable skill and can lead to rewarding friendships. At work, developing good relationships with supervisors, coworkers, and customers will help you succeed. In today's global society, it is important to know how to build relationships with people of other cultures. Building positive relationships with people in all areas of your life will help you experience personal growth and success.

Relationships with Significant Adults

Adults other than parents who play an important part in your life can be called **significant adults**. They may be grandparents, aunts, uncles, teachers, youth leaders, religious leaders, coaches, or neighbors. They are people who take the time to get to know you. They care about you and what happens to you in life, 6-9.

Relationships between significant adults and teens usually are less stressful than parent-teen relationships. Parents feel responsible for what their teens do, but significant adults do not have that pressure. Thus, they often relate to teens with more empathy.

Sometimes you may find that important relationships in your family are damaged. Talking to a significant adult in your life may be helpful. You may find it easier to share your point of view as well as listen to what they have to say. A good friendship can develop with a significant adult, even if that person is much older than you.

Link to Your Life

What are some examples of relationships with significant adults that have helped you grow as a person?

6-9 Significant adults can offer valuable friendships to a teen.

Work Relationships

Good relationship skills will help you succeed on the job. No matter what job you hold, nearly all aspects of your work will be affected by the way you relate to others. Whether your job brings you in contact with customers, or just coworkers and your supervisor, it is important to use good relationship skills.

Customer Relations

Friendly service is the key to good customer relations. Chatting with customers while serving them can make them feel comfortable and welcome. Employers also expect their employees to be courteous to customers.

Relating to Fellow Employees

Your boss will expect you to be able to work cooperatively with others to get the job done. Employees are also expected to be able to discuss problems and negotiate solutions. Using good relationship skills will help you contribute to a positive work environment. Because friendships develop between people who have much in common, you may develop some close friendships with your coworkers. If you do, remember that your personal life should not interfere with your job performance. The work you are doing on the job must come first.

Use What You Learn

How could personal relationships at work interfere with good job performance?

Relationships with Supervisors

Becoming extremely close friends with your supervisor is not likely. However, the work atmosphere will be more positive if you are friendly, show interest in your work, and do your very best. Always listen to directions carefully and follow them. Ask questions about anything you do not understand. Your supervisor's main focus is getting the job done well. Consequently, you will be valued to the degree that you contribute to this goal. Above all, show respect for employees who hold positions of authority.

Relationships with People of Other Cultures

The United States includes people from many different cultures—all of whom influence each other and society in general. This influence is known as **multiculturalism**. The impact of multiculturalism is expected to increase as minorities become a larger share of the U.S. population.

Some of the individuals you meet at school, at work, or in your community probably have a cultural background different from yours. This difference may be apparent in their customs, language, traditions, or racial background. They may have different beliefs, personal and family values, or religious practices. All these factors can reflect a person's unique cultural heritage.

When focusing on the differences that exist between people of different cultures, sometimes the term **diversity** is used. It simply is another term to describe multiculturalism.

Investigate Further

In what ways could a friendship with a person from another culture help you grow?

Accepting Differences

Getting to know people who are different from you can have a positive effect on your personal growth, 6-10. Your knowledge of human nature will increase. Your understanding of others and the qualities that all people share can deepen. You will gain a new perspective on life.

Meeting people of other cultures may seem challenging at first. In fact, you may feel uncomfortable associating with someone

6-10 Spending time with people from other cultural backgrounds can help you learn more about other views of life.

who seems to share nothing in common with you. This is quite natural. Everyone prefers being with friends or acquaintances instead of strangers. Remember the other person feels just as uncomfortable as you. Try to consider how that person feels and respond with empathy.

Take the initiative to introduce yourself and be friendly. Reach out and try to develop rapport. Listen to his or her ideas. Show respect for the person's cultural background. If the individual is new to the school, the job, or the neighborhood, offer to help them become acquainted. Building positive relationships with people of other cultures will strengthen you, your school, and your community.

Review Section 6:3

1. Give two examples of significant adults in your life outside your family.
2. What relationship skills should employees in the workplace use with customers? with supervisors?
3. List three steps teens can take to develop relationships with people of different cultural backgrounds.

Think It Through

Peer Pressure

The telephone rang and Marc's dad picked it up. "Would you please come down to the police station?" an officer asked. "Your son has been picked up for stealing a car." Marc's dad turned pale and swallowed hard as he responded, "Yes, we'll be there." His mind raced as he wondered how this all came about.

Marc was outgoing and friendly. He liked to be with people. He wanted his peers to like him and to include him in their groups. He especially wanted to belong to a certain popular group.

To try to get the popular group to notice him, Marc would pick on others in his classes. He would break a pencil or rip a notebook. He would poke others in the back or push them in the hall. He would laugh at them, tease and make fun of them, and call them names. Instead of making friends, however, Marc was becoming a bully. Nobody liked him.

Rebelling against authority was Marc's next attempt at getting the attention and friendship he wanted. He ignored his parents' requests and did not carry out his chores at home. He didn't bother with homework. Marc's parents were frustrated with his lack of responsibility. They pleaded with him to do better. They ordered him to do what they asked. They yelled at him for getting poor grades, telling him all the consequences of failing in school.

Marc tuned them out. He also ignored his teachers and talked constantly in class. He proudly served his detentions, which brought him more attention. The attention he was getting, though, was from other students who were also serving detention. They started to hang out together, looking for new excitement and new things to try. This time, however, Marc and his friends had gone too far— and had ended up at the police station.

Questions to Guide Your Thinking

1. Why did Marc's attempt to build friendships fail? What factors did he not consider?

2. How did Marc respond to not being part of the popular peer group? What other responses might a young person make when important relationships fall apart?

3. What communication techniques did Marc's family use to try and solve Marc's problem? Identify some examples of ways they could have responded with empathy.

4. What qualities of real friendship were missing in Marc's new group of "friends"?

Chapter Summary

Friendships often develop between people who have common interests and share their personal thoughts and feelings. Sharing with openness, trust, acceptance, understanding, support, and encouragement creates this special bond. Close friendships help people grow intellectually, emotionally, and socially. The experience helps them prepare for future long-term relationships.

Friendships often develop between peers as they tend to have much in common. Peers also may pressure each other to make certain choices in order to identify with a peer group. When teens feel pressured by their peer group, thinking about and asserting their own priorities and goals is important.

The family is an important source of close relationships. Several factors affect these relationships. Family members who develop common interests are likely to spend more time together sharing, having fun, and building friendships that can last a lifetime. Even healthy family relationships experience parent-teen conflicts. Empathy and understanding are the keys to resolving these conflicts in a positive way.

Good relationship skills have a positive impact on workplace performance. Also, skills for developing good relationships are very important in building strong ties with people from other cultures.

Assess...

Your Knowledge

1. What are the qualities of a good friend?

2. What are three steps families can take to build strong relationships within the family?

3. What relationship skills are needed to succeed in the workplace?

Your Understanding

4. How can friendships help a person grow to maturity?

5. How are close friendships developed?

6. How does negative peer pressure hinder the growth of close friendships?

Your Skills

7. Analyze a friendship for the qualities needed for this relationship to develop into a close friendship.

8. Write an assertive response to a peer pressure situation where a peer asks you to steal money from another student's locker.

9. Write a scenario in which you negotiate a solution to the following problem: your family cannot agree on a location for a family vacation.

Think Critically

10. **Writing.** Keep a daily journal for one week to note the times you could have been assertive but were not. For each, write down some I-messages you could have said. What differences in the outcome of each situation might have occurred with an assertive response?

11. **Writing.** Evaluate your own opinion of what constitutes an ideal friend. List the personal qualities, desirable interests and goals, and the priorities you would like to see in an ideal friend. Compare your list to the qualities described in Figure 6-2 of the text. Write a paragraph describing how the lists are similar or different. *Choice:* Present your comparisons in a chart.

12. Create a real or fictional scenario of a teen-parent conflict. Evaluate the conflict for types of communication used. What listening skills were used? What items were negotiated? Explain how this conflict is related to parents "letting go" and teens "becoming independent." *Group option:* Work with a partner.

13. **Research, writing.** Observe and then write a list of all the ways your peers meet each other in the school halls. Include their verbal greetings, gestures, facial expressions, and other body language. Can you identify differences based on cultural backgrounds? Can you identify differences in how your peers communicate versus adults in your community? Write a paragraph describing the similarities and differences you discover through your observations, and any conclusions you can make about peer and adult communication. *Group option:* Work in a small group and create a digital presentation of your combined results.

Connect with Your Community

14. *Writing.* Identify a significant adult who has played an important part in your life. In a paragraph, describe the relationship you have with this person. What type of activities do you do together? How well do you communicate with this person? *Choice:* Use a collage of drawings or pictures to depict the characteristics of this relationship.

15. Invite a social worker or juvenile police officer to discuss the relationship between young people's feelings and social problems such as bullying, alcohol and drug abuse, and crime.

16. *Writing.* Observe various peer pressure situations (in the cafeteria, the hallways, before class, after school, etc.) in your school for one day. In a paragraph, describe one example of each of the following responses: passive, aggressive, and assertive. Did each response cause you to feel more or less respect toward that person? Summarize by explaining how attitudes are shaped by the responses people make. *Group option:* Share your observations with a partner, analyze them together, and report your summary to the class in an oral report.

17. *Social studies.* Briefly describe in one paragraph a method you use to develop rapport when meeting someone you don't know very well. Compare it to the method presented in the text. Then interview a person in the community who is outgoing and well known. Ask this person what methods he or she uses to get to know a new person. Summarize this person's responses and compare his or her methods with the method you use. What changes could you make to improve your rapport-building skills?

Use Technology

18. Use a computer program to create a poster that depicts the qualities of a good friend and display it in the classroom

19. Observe three television programs that emphasize friendships. Rate them according to how well they illustrate the qualities of a friend, as described in Figure 6-2 of the text. Prepare a checklist of the qualities to use in rating the programs. Summarize your findings in a paragraph.

20. *Research.* Using the Internet, research the characteristics of three successful people whom you admire. Using your rating sheet developed in the previous activity, check their qualities. Note any comparisons between the qualities that attract you to a person and the successes these people achieved. *Group option:* Work with a partner.

21. *Math.* Using a computer spreadsheet, make a list of first impressions that attract you to a person and inspire you to know that person better. Use your spreadsheet checklist to rate several strangers you observe at school, in a shopping mall, a grocery store, or anyplace else. Create a graph that shows how many people had each characteristic. *Choice:* In a paragraph, write some generalizations about the qualities you identified and the number of people who actually had such characteristics. *Group option:* Share your findings with a small group and identify common generalizations.

Chapter 7
Dating

Section 7:**1**
The Dating Process

Section 7:**2**
Love

Key Questions

Questions to answer as you study this chapter:

- How does dating help people learn more about themselves?

- Why is it important to evaluate a dating relationship?

- Why wait to be sexually Involved in a relationship?

Chapter Objectives

After studying this chapter, you will be able to

- **explain** the functions of dating in our society.

- **recognize** the stages in thc dating process.

- **describe** beginning and ending dating relationships.

- **distinguish** between mature love and romantic feelings.

- **analyze** dating behaviors for long-term effects.

Life Sketch

The students silently waited for their next assignment. As the teacher began to explain it, Sandy glanced at Nathan. Their eyes met, and he raised an eyebrow and smiled. "He is so cute!" Sandy said to herself as she smiled back.

The teacher suggested that students work in pairs on the new material. Nathan moved closer to Sandy. "Want to work together?" he asked.

"Sure," she calmly replied, but her heart was pounding fast.

At the same time, Dan slid over by Kyla. "Hi, Kyla! Need a partner?"

"No thanks. I think I'll work with Jed," she replied as she moved closer to Jed's desk.

Dan's smile faded. His stomach felt like lead. He wished that the ground would open up and swallow him.

Getting Started

You have probably experienced feelings similar to those felt by Sandy and Dan. These feelings may be both exciting and discouraging. Most teens spend a lot of time thinking, talking, and dreaming about dating. They feel elated when their attempts to develop relationships are successful. However, they often feel hurt when their attempts are rejected.

In our society, young people generally make their own dating choices. They often decide who they will date, where they will go, and what they will do on a date.

Parents and peers do have some influence on these dating decisions. During the early dating years, parents often set guidelines and limits. Both parents and peers may influence a young person's decisions by their approval or disapproval. In many cases, the final decision is left to the young person. As you face these types of decisions, it is helpful to understand the purpose and process of dating in our society.

section 7:1

The Dating Process

Sharpen Your Reading

Develop a graphic organizer with *Dating* at the center. Use the headings *Functions of Dating*, *Stages of the Dating Process*, and *Evaluating a Dating Relationship* as main lines off the center topic. As you read, add key ideas under each main line.

Boost Your Vocabulary

With a partner, brainstorm examples of dates for each dating stage. As you read about each dating stage, evaluate if your examples are appropriate.

Know Key Terms

group dating
pair dating
steady dating
personal boundaries

Understanding dating's purpose and process helps you in the following ways:

- *You keep a positive attitude about yourself.* Dating relationships include both positive and negative experiences. Your overall attitude toward yourself can remain positive because you realize these experiences are part of growing.

- *You avoid a long-term commitment too early in life.* Since feelings come and go, they are not a good basis for making lifetime choices.

Growing takes time—to learn about yourself and what you like and dislike in dating partners.

- *You make decisions that are consistent with your long-term goals.* You may have goals to finish a college education, develop a career, or save some money before marriage. Your efforts to reach these goals can be hindered by the long-term consequences of some dating decisions.

Use What You Learn

What examples can you identify in which a poor dating choice affected a person's life goals?

Functions of Dating

In our society, dating is the pathway that leads to engagement and marriage. Most adults will eventually marry. Through the process of dating, young people can choose a suitable marriage partner. In addition, a healthy dating relationship should provide experiences through which you learn about yourself and others.

Understanding Others

Dating is a socially accepted way for young people to develop close romantic friendships. In the process of dating, you can learn how others think and feel, what they like to do, and what their goals are.

Understanding Yourself

As you date and get to know others, you get to know yourself better. Developing a relationship requires that you also share your ideas and feelings. As you share, and they reflect back what you say, you will learn more about yourself, 7-1.

Link to Your Life

What are some things you might learn about yourself through dating?

7-1 Feedback from others can help you learn more about yourself.

Providing Companionship

Dating gives you the opportunity to spend time with someone who shares your interests. You may need a tennis partner, so you call someone who plays tennis and make a date for a tennis game. You may want to see a movie, so you call a friend to go with you to the theater. Feelings of friendship may develop into a deeper relationship as you spend more time with the other person.

Improving Communication Skills

Dating provides opportunities to talk and listen to your dating partner. You may feel comfortable around most of your peers. It is easy to talk about common interests and goals. On the other hand, how do you communicate with someone you want to date? Open communication is an important part of building any relationship. As you share your ideas, others will get to know you.

When you communicate, your messages should be clear. Your verbal and nonverbal messages need to match. You also need to practice active listening skills to be sure you understand the other person's meaning.

Think More About It
What are some reasons that a message might be interpreted differently than intended in a dating situation?

Learning to Negotiate

Dating requires that young people consider others' opinions when decisions need to be made. This give-and-take process requires that each person be sensitive to the other's ideas and feelings. Such practice helps you develop empathy for what another person thinks and feels. Thus, your dating experiences can help you grow socially and emotionally.

Investigate Further

If one person always gives in when making decisions about where to go on a date, what effect will this have on each person's growth in the relationship?

Learning to Be Responsible

Dating provides opportunities to take responsibility for your decisions. At first, the commitments are small. "I'll be there at four o'clock," you may say. That is a commitment to be reliable and to meet your date on time.

In dating, you will also need to take actions that show responsibility for other commitments you have made. Some of these commitments will be to yourself, based on your values. For instance, taking the responsibility to say no to drugs, alcohol, and sex can help you fulfill a commitment to health. Other commitments will be to your parents.

Dating also provides experience in showing another person that you care about them. You are willing to help them grow, solve a problem, or meet a need. Selfish interests can be put aside. Personal plans can be changed. For instance, a friend calls with a problem. You suggest getting together to talk about it. You are taking the responsibility to help your friend. Kindness and caring are two qualities that help keep a relationship growing.

Use What You Learn

How would irresponsibility on one person's part affect the overall growth of the relationship? Why would a person stay in a relationship with a person who is irresponsible?

Evaluating Personality Traits

One of the main benefits of dating is the chance to find out what personality traits you most like in a partner. If you have dated only a few people, you do not have much information to use in making comparisons. However, if you have dated several people, you have more experience to make judgments. You learn to evaluate qualities and find those that do or do not appeal to you. You become more aware of what it takes to get along with your dating partner. The qualities you would like to find in your ideal mate for marriage become easier to identify.

Stages of the Dating Process

Most dating relationships pass through several stages. They often begin informally in group situations. In **group dating**, a group of people spend time together and develop friendships. As teens get older, a couple will usually separate from the group and spend time as a pair. In **pair dating**, a couple will develop a relationship with each other. Pair dating may lead to **steady dating**, which is a commitment to date only one person. Eventually, the couple may make a serious commitment—to become engaged for marriage.

Group Dating

Most teens develop their first dating relationship during informal group dating. This is a chance to interact with potential dating partners without making a commitment to one person. Activities are planned by the entire group, so everyone can socialize and have fun. This gives everyone the chance to enjoy the friendship of others, 7-2. Group dating can provide positive growing experiences. You can get to know several of your peers. You can gain experience communicating with many different people, sharing your ideas, and listening to theirs. You can improve your social skills and have fun with others without making a commitment to one person.

7-2 This group is getting to know each other in a relaxed atmosphere.

In what ways can dating as a group provide more opportunities for growth than pair dating?

Pair Dating

Young people usually pair off when they are attracted to one particular person. In pair dating, two people spend time as a couple building their friendship. They may go on a formal date in which they attend a planned event together. At other times, they may just meet and spend time together on an informal basis. Sometimes they may *double date*, when another couple joins them on the date.

Double dating can be a good transition from group dating to pair dating. It can help reduce the nervous feelings of first getting to know someone. Since the date is usually planned around some type of activity, the atmosphere is more relaxed. In fact, many activities are more fun when several people are involved.

When two people make a commitment to date only each other, they are steady dating. Steady dating, sometimes called *going out*, is a statement to others that the couple has spent a great deal of time together. They have discovered each other's interests, attitudes, ideas, values, and goals in life. They both feel committed to build a relationship with each other.

Use What You Learn

What are some common events that people attend on a date?

The Advantages and Disadvantages of Steady Dating

Young people often feel that steady dating has advantages in a relationship. Besides knowing they care for each other, the couple feels secure with each other. They feel comfortable in knowing what to expect from each other. In building the relationship, they can develop trust, openness, and respect for each other. They can relax and be themselves when they are together. As a couple, they may feel more committed to resolving and handling conflicts in a positive way.

Steady dating can have some disadvantages as well. In some cases, young people go steady for reasons other than building a long-term relationship. Some go steady to increase their sense of self-esteem. It makes them feel important. They may go steady to keep up with their peers. However, the desire to have a steady companion can hinder growth. It can limit your experiences with other friends and, thereby, hurt those friendships. It can limit your opportunities to meet new people who can help you learn more about yourself.

Link to Your Life

What are the reasons that young people you know choose to go steady?

Breaking a steady dating relationship can be difficult. If you decide that you really are not ready for the commitment, you may feel trapped. You might even feel used or controlled by your partner. Your relationship may not be growing, yet you may be afraid to break it off. You may want to avoid hurting your partner. These are the risks that go with making a commitment to one person too early in life.

Beginning a Dating Relationship

The desire to build relationships and have friends is part of the human need to feel accepted by others. Perhaps you have taken part in group dates, but there is someone you would like to get to know better. How can you get him or her to notice you?

- *Make your appearance count.* Good grooming helps a person make a positive first impression, 7-3.

- *Be friendly, confident, and courteous.* By being courteous, you can show others that you respect, care about, and value them as people. They will more likely respond to you with respect.

- *Start a conversation.* Asking open-ended questions encourages other people to talk about their interests. As you find common interests, you can then guide the conversation into more personal topics.

- *Listen intently to what the person shares.* Use eye contact and show that you care enough to pay attention to what the other person is saying. As personal information is shared, you can discover whether you want to get to know this person better.

- *Plan some time together.* As you share and take part in activities, your relationship may become closer. Trust and understanding may develop as your friendship grows.

7-3 Looking your best will help you feel confident and will make a positive impression on others.

If you discover that you really do not have much in common, the relationship may not grow. Personal sharing by one person or the other may stop. At that point, you may decide to end the relationship.

Use What You Learn

How can good conversation skills help you begin a dating relationship?

Evaluating a Dating Relationship

Evaluating your relationship can help you decide whether or not to continue dating. When you are in the midst of a relationship, it can be difficult to view the situation objectively. Asking the following questions can help you determine if your relationship is healthy.

- Does spending time together help both of us be the best we can be?
- Do we think things through together, both sharing our thoughts equally?
- Does spending time together help us both grow socially (learning to give and take, compromise, solve problems, and communicate openly)?
- Do we express empathy for each other?
- Do we both enjoy being together?

Personal Boundaries

Personal boundaries are limits for behavior that you will accept in your relationships. These limits apply to what you are willing to say, think, or do in your relationships with other people. They also apply to what you are willing to allow others to say or do to you. Personal boundaries can help you know when a relationship has crossed the line.

When one person in the relationship forces the other to do something outside of his or her personal boundaries, it is a sign of abuse. People who focus only on their own wants, desires, and wishes make demands on their partners. These demands often are abusive and do not allow the other person to grow and develop. Such behaviors are listed in figure 7-4.

Signs of an Unhealthy Relationship

- Any kind of physical abuse.
- Verbal abuse (name calling, yelling, demeaning criticism).
- Demands on your time so you cannot maintain relationships with other friends and family.
- Demands for sexual favors.
- Disrespect for your ideas, feelings, and person.

7-4 Unhealthy behaviors signal that it is time to end a relationship.

Think More About It
What are some personal boundaries that a person could list to help them recognize an unhealthy relationship?

Ending a Dating Relationship

Dating relationships end in many ways. Sometimes a couple will date a few times, and then one person just never hears from the other again. That person may have decided they did not have enough in common.

In other cases, the couple simply drifts apart. The two date less and less. One or both may become interested in someone else. If a relationship ends in either of these ways, you may feel hurt and disappointed. However, you probably will not be devastated by the experience.

If you have been going steady, ending the relationship can be painful. Close relationships rarely end by mutual consent. Usually one person wants the relationship to break up but the other does not. The least interested partner may have found someone else or thinks the relationship is not growing closer.

Breaking up is most difficult for the person who wants to keep the relationship going. However, breaking up is not easy for either partner. When dating relationships do end, the adjustment can be made easier by focusing on growth. Making the best of the situation is a positive approach. The following suggestions may help.

- *Realize your partner will feel hurt.* If you are breaking off the relationship, be sensitive to the other's feelings. Show empathy. Explain why you feel the relationship needs to end. If you continue the relationship to avoid hurting your partner, you are not being honest. The relationship will suffer and your partner will be hurt anyway.
- *Change your dating patterns.* Once a relationship is over, it is difficult to keep on seeing each other. After the pain of the

breakup has lessened, you may be able to be friends with your former partner. Being friends will be easier if you both have developed new relationships.

- *Recognize your feelings as normal.* Feelings of pain and loneliness do not mean that you made a wrong decision. They are part of the grief feelings that go with ending a close relationship. These feelings are a sign that the relationship was valuable to you. They are not a sign that you made a mistake.
- *Emphasize other aspects of your life.* If you are the person who wanted the relationship to continue, you may feel lonely or depressed for a while. Doing something that you enjoy can help, 7-5. The pain will pass, and you will be able to put your energy into building a relationship again.

7-5 Talking to a friend can help ease the pain of ending a close relationship.

Think More About It
What are some reasons why it is difficult to maintain a friendship with a former dating partner?

Commitment to Marry

Although relationships vary among couples, most people follow the dating process through engagement to marriage. This formal commitment is the final stage before marriage. At this point in your life, do not be surprised if you feel you are not ready to consider marriage. That feeling is very common. Marriage takes much preparation and a total commitment to the relationship.

In many relationships, a type of magnetism exists that draws the two people together. It may be physical attraction or common interests. Steady dating leading to engagement and marriage should be approached slowly. It takes time for a couple to develop a relationship and identify whether the attraction will last.

Review Section 7:**1**

1. Briefly list four functions of dating.
2. List three reasons why group dating can provide positive growing experiences for young teens.
3. List two advantages and two disadvantages of steady dating.
4. Describe three ways a teen can get noticed by someone he or she wants to get to know.
5. How can personal boundaries help a person recognize an abusive relationship?

section 7:2

Love

Sharpen Your Reading

Compare the similarities and differences between infatuation and mature love.

Boost Your Vocabulary

Research one sexually transmitted infection and summarize your findings in a paragraph.

Know Key Terms

romantic love
mature love
infatuation
abstinence
sexually transmitted infections (STIs)
human papillomavirus (HPV)
genital warts
gonorrhea
chlamydia
genital herpes
syphilis
hepatitis B
acquired immune deficiency syndrome (AIDS)
human immunodeficiency virus (HIV)
rape
date rape

How would you define *love*? A simple definition separates love into two main categories. One is the exhilarating feeling that can be called **romantic love**. The other is the long lasting, caring, and giving type of love that can be called **mature love**. Sometimes romantic love sparks a relationship that grows into mature love. Sometimes a caring and giving friendship grows into a romantic relationship as well.

Romantic Love

The outward signs of romantic love are easy to recognize. You may have seen couples walking hand in hand, staring into each other's eyes, 7-6. They are so focused on each other, they tune out the rest of the world. They want to spend all their time together and even dream about each other. These blissful feelings may lead them to think about marriage because they want the feeling to last forever.

Sometimes this strong feeling of attraction between two people is called **infatuation**. Infatuation tends to be self-centered or one-sided.

7-6 Initial feelings of romantic love may draw two people together. As couples get to know each other better, mature love may develop.

A person may think, "This is the greatest thing that ever happened to me." Such feelings focus on the self rather than on the well-being of the other person. The other person may not share the same feelings, either.

Feelings of infatuation begin and often end quickly. "I loved her as soon as I saw her." "It was love at first sight." These statements refer to the strong attraction that one person feels for another. Such feelings may be based on a few attractive traits. When someone more attractive comes along, the feelings leave as quickly as they came.

Sometimes a couple will base their entire relationship on infatuation and move ahead quickly to marriage. Then they are hurt and disappointed when their feelings fade. Their first disagreement may produce some unkind thoughts, words, or actions. They start to see character flaws in the other person. The feelings of infatuation start to fade. One may say, "I thought you loved me" or "I thought I knew you."

Romantic love alone is not enough to build a long-lasting relationship. At times these feelings increase, then decrease. Mature love, even without romantic feelings, can keep a relationship together. Consequently, it is important to determine whether or not mature love exists in a relationship.

Think More About It

Why might it be hard to tell if a relationship is based only on romantic attraction and infatuation?

Mature Love

Mature love is different from infatuation, 7-7. Mature love is characterized by a giving, unselfish attitude. Each person cares about the well-being of the other. People who have mature love for each other like to do things that please each other. They are committed to finding and doing what is best for each other. They may give up personal desires to bring benefits to the partner or to both of them as a couple.

You cannot "fall" into mature love. Mature love grows as a relationship grows. It takes time and effort to develop mature love in a relationship.

The Growth of Mature Love

The growth of mature love can be described in four stages. Each stage stimulates the growth of the next stage, 7-8.

Infatuation	Mature Love
• Based on an instant desire for each other.	• Based on sharing interests and ideas.
• Decreases over time.	• Deepens and grows as a friendship grows.
• Self-centered with attitudes like, "I don't want to lose you. You're the best thing that ever happened to me. Let's hurry up and get married."	• Other-centered, giving of the self to benefit the other person.
• Possessive and one-sided.	• Encourages growth in the other person.
• Leaves nagging doubts, unanswered questions, or areas that you don't want to question.	• Accepting of each other, even with imperfections.
• Lacks confidence and trust in each other's commitment.	• Trusting and secure.
• Often involves pressure to be sexually involved.	• Patient, kind, and willing to take time to make wise decisions.

7-7 This chart shows how you can tell the difference between mature love and infatuation.

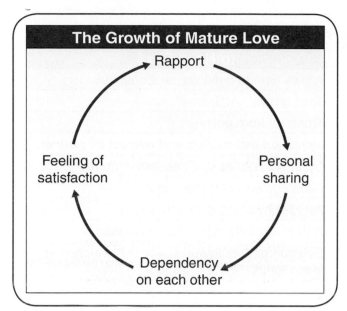

The Growth of Mature Love

Rapport

Feeling of satisfaction

Personal sharing

Dependency on each other

7-8 The growth of mature love can be described as a cycle, with each stage stimulating the growth of the next stage.

First, the two individuals develop rapport. They care about each other and enjoy being together. They want to spend more time getting to know each other.

As rapport grows, the couple shares more personal thoughts, ideas, and feelings. Through this personal sharing, each person exposes the inner self and finds acceptance by the other. Trust develops. If one or the other does not feel accepted, mutual sharing and the growth of love stop.

In the third stage, the couple are becoming attached to each other, and depend on each other for support and encouragement. They miss each other when they are apart. They look forward to being together. They both contribute to the relationship to meet each other's needs.

In the fourth stage, both feel their personal needs are being met in the relationship. The two are important and valuable to each other. As their needs are fulfilled in the relationship, their love grows deeper.

How does the cycle continue? As needs are met, the couple is motivated to spend more time together. Times of deep personal sharing increase. They share empathy, feeling what the other is feeling. They become more attached to each other. They depend on each other to meet more and more of their emotional needs.

As these needs are met, more interaction is encouraged. In this way, the cycle continues. Mature love grows deeper.

As couples grow in mature love, they become committed to each other's happiness and well-being. This commitment remains strong even if romantic feelings decrease. To keep love growing, though, couples must continue giving to the relationship throughout life. They must continue to spend time together, share, depend on each other, and meet each other's needs.

Use What You Learn

How might premature sexual involvement in a relationship affect the growth of mature love?

Expressing Affection

As feelings between two people grow, a couple may find themselves drawn into a desire to give physical expression to their love. Physical expressions such as close hugs and affectionate kisses are normal. However, as a relationship grows, sexual feelings may grow more intense. Teens may feel confused and even pressured to yield to their desires.

Making a Decision to Wait

Though the physical desire to be sexually involved may increase, this does not mean you have to give in to your desires. Thinking about your choices, considering the consequences, and making a logical decision based on your standards is important. Think through this decision ahead of time, before you find yourself under emotional pressure, 7-9. Your response to this decision can have lifelong effects.

Decide now what is acceptable to you. Set your personal boundaries. If you become involved in a serious relationship, be honest with your partner. Talk about what your limits are concerning sex. It is important, too, that you respect each other's feelings. If your partner truly cares for you, he or she will respect your decisions concerning your body.

Teens sometimes feel pressured by their dating partners. They are made to feel that they must prove their love by having sex. However, such demands are not a part of a true loving relationship.

Consequences of Not Waiting to Have Sex	Consequences of Waiting Until Marriage to Have Sex
• Increased fear that the relationship may end.	• Allows time to build the relationship.
• Increased doubts about the relationship.	• Trust grows.
• Increased feelings of guilt.	• Freedom from guilt.
• Decrease in self-esteem and self-respect.	• Increased self-respect and respect for partner.
• Decrease in verbal communication.	• Contributes to sexual freedom in marriage.
• Slows growth of mature love.	• Allows growth of mature love.
• Possible pregnancy and early parenting.	• Avoids unwanted pregnancy.
• May contract a sexually transmitted disease.	• Avoids sexually transmitted diseases.
• May affect physical ability to have children in the future.	• Safeguards health and ability to have children in the future.

7-9 Consider the consequences of having a sexual relationship before marriage.

Teens sometimes feel pressure from peers to have sex. They may feel that "everyone is doing it." Some teens may worry about what their friends will think of them if they are not having sex. However, statistics show that some who say they are having sex are not.

Teens also are pressured by the constant reference to sex in the media. Advertisements, TV, movies, videos, and music all suggest the casualness of sex. Songs may refer to "one-night stands." Many TV shows, movies, and videos present sex as a casual activity between any two people who have the desire. This constant reference to sexuality makes it difficult for teens to play down the role of sex in their lives. Unfortunately, the media seldom show the true consequences of such activity—the negative emotional consequences as well as pregnancy and disease.

Some Reasons to Wait

There are several good reasons for choosing not to have sex. The consequences of premarital sexual activity are both psychological and physical. They affect the persons involved, as well as other family members, future spouses, and the community as a whole.

Psychological Consequences

Many people are brought up to believe that sexual intimacy belongs in marriage. Values

learned from family, friends, and religious beliefs concerning this issue may be very strong. Going against these values can cause intense feelings of guilt, regret, and anxiety. A person may sacrifice feelings of self-esteem if strongly-held family and personal values are disregarded.

Having a sexual relationship does not signify commitment. Only marriage signifies commitment. Without the marriage commitment, a partner could be gone tomorrow. The fear of that happening and doubts about the other's love can eventually destroy a relationship. Either partner could be left feeling used, unwanted, or worthless. Trust is vital to a fulfilling relationship. Complete trust is only possible within the commitment of marriage.

The negative consequences of self-doubt, guilt, feeling used or abused, fear, and lack of trust are psychological. These can hurt the growth of mature love in a relationship. There are also physical consequences of sexual activity in a relationship.

Think More About It
What are the fears that keep people in unhealthy relationships? How can they overcome those fears?

An Unwanted Pregnancy

One of the physical consequences of sexual activity is pregnancy. There is no contraceptive that is 100 percent effective in preventing pregnancy. Some are more effective than others. Some have various side effects. **Abstinence**, not having sexual relations, is the only 100 percent effective method to avoid pregnancy.

If pregnancy occurs, the couple may face the decision whether or not to marry. Marriage is a long-term commitment and needs the full participation of two mature people. Most teens are not socially and emotionally ready to commit themselves to a marriage, 7-10. With a baby involved, the adjustment is extremely difficult. One or both parents may be required to leave school. Also, most teens are not able to make it financially.

What if the partners do not marry and the young mother decides to keep the baby? If she does not finish her education, her income will be limited. Her social growth will also be affected since much of her time will be spent caring for the baby.

Teenage pregnancy poses health risks for the mother as well as her baby. Because a young woman's body is not yet fully developed, the strain of pregnancy creates more health risks for her. Many pregnant teens ignore or deny their condition. As a result, they do not always receive proper prenatal (before birth) care. Pregnant teens are more likely to experience complications such as *anemia*, which is iron deficiency. Babies born to teen mothers are often premature or have low birthweight. These factors can lead to increased health risks at birth and throughout childhood.

7-10 Caring for a new baby is a 24-hour responsibility that requires social, emotional, and intellectual maturity.

Investigate Further

Statistics indicate that many teen parents are single and struggle with poverty. Why is it so hard to break the cycle and change this statistic?

Sexually Transmitted Infections

Sexually transmitted infections (STIs) are passed from one person to another by sexual contact. They are also referred to as *sexually transmitted diseases (STDs)*. In many cases, there are no obvious outward signs of the infections, yet they can be spread from one partner to another. Many STIs have a harmful effect on a person's reproductive organs and some can result in early death. The most common STIs are human papillomavirus (HPV), gonorrhea, chlamydia, genital herpes, syphilis, hepatitis B, and acquired immune deficiency syndrome (AIDS).

The **human papillomavirus (HPV)** infects the skin and mucous membranes. Most people who become infected with HPV do not even know they have it. Certain types of HPV cause **genital warts**, or small bumps or clusters of bumps in the genital area. Some HPV types can cause cervical cancer as well as other types of cancer of the sexual organs. A vaccine is available for females that protects against some types of HPV. However, the only sure way to prevent all types of HPV is to avoid sexual activity.

Gonorrhea is a bacterial infection that can damage the male and female organs, resulting in sterility. It grows in the warm, moist areas of the reproductive tract, and also in the eyes, mouth, or throat. The infection can be treated with antibiotics. However, some strains of the bacteria are becoming resistant, making them more difficult to treat.

Chlamydia is a bacterial infection that can damage a woman's reproductive organs. It is one of the most common bacterial STIs in this country. Detection of the infection may be difficult because many men and women have no obvious symptoms. Chlamydia can be treated and cured with antibiotics. However, if it is left untreated,

it can cause sterility. An infected mother can pass the disease to her unborn child. After birth, the child may develop serious infections.

Genital herpes is a widespread, incurable virus. It stays in the body and reappears periodically, producing painful sores or blisters. A person with the disease may experience repeated outbreaks of blisters. Genital herpes can be spread even when sores are not present. It can also be passed from an infected woman to her newborn infant at birth.

Syphilis, caused by bacteria, can be treated with an antibiotic such as penicillin. The early stages of the disease are not easily recognized. A sore, called a *chancre*, appears in ten days to three months after infection has occurred. Because it heals, the disease is not suspected. After the chancre heals, the disease spreads to other parts of the body. Rash, fever, sore throat, and headache are common symptoms. The later stages of the disease damage other parts of the body including the liver, skin, heart, or nervous system. If left untreated, it may result in death.

Hepatitis B is caused by a virus that attacks the liver. It is spread by sexual contact with an infected person or by exposure to infected blood.

Acquired immune deficiency syndrome (AIDS) is caused by the **human immunodeficiency virus (HIV)**. This virus attacks the cells that normally help a person fight infection and disease. The virus is passed from one person to another through body fluids such as blood, vaginal secretions, and semen. The virus can be spread from an infected person in two main ways: through sexual activity or sharing intravenous needles. During pregnancy, at childbirth, and while breastfeeding, an infected woman could pass the virus to her child.

The AIDS virus can live in the body for many years before symptoms appear. However, an infected person can spread the virus to another person before or after symptoms appear. Symptoms in the early stages include fatigue, swollen lymph glands, dry cough, shortness of breath, fever, diarrhea, and rapid weight loss. Once a person contracts the virus, he or she remains infected for life and symptoms may recur. That person's immune system continues to weaken until it can no longer fight disease. At present, most AIDS patients die from serious infections or cancer.

When young people are sexually active prior to marriage, the chance of becoming exposed to an STI is great. Even one relationship may be the source of an STI. Sexual activity with more than one partner is especially risky. Blood tests, however, can identify the presence of STIs.

Use What You Learn

Do you think many teens fully understand the health risks associated with having more than one sex partner?

Responding to Pressures

If you have made a decision to avoid sexual relations before marriage, how can you stick to your decision? Waiting until marriage is sometimes difficult, especially when others around you are not. How can you respond to such pressure? There are several ways, 7-11.

The most important step is to set your personal boundaries ahead of time. What is acceptable behavior? What is not? Think through the consequences of various behaviors. Make choices that will help you stick to your decision and reach your life goals.

Talk to your partner before you become sexually involved. Plan what you will say. Do not give mixed messages by dressing or acting in a seductive manner.

Ways to Say No to Sexual Pressures

"No, I don't want to."

"If you really loved me, you wouldn't ask."

"I respect myself too much."

"I believe in waiting for marriage."

"AIDS is forever."

"I make lifelong decisions."

7-11 Practicing these responses can help teens stick to their decision to say no to sexual pressures.

Avoid situations that may cause you to be tempted, such as parking a car in a quiet area or going home when no one is there. Try not to spend as much time alone. Instead, find alternative activities that involve other people. Go out with friends or participate in sports activities. Also avoid alcohol and drugs, which decrease your ability to think and to say no.

It is never too late to make a decision to wait. Even if you cannot change past actions, a decision to wait can help you avoid continued psychological and physical risks. Saying no now can help you develop a future relationship based on sharing, caring, mutual respect, and trust, 7-12.

7-12 Choices you make during the dating years can affect the rest of your life. Making responsible decisions now can help you develop healthy relationships and achieve future goals.

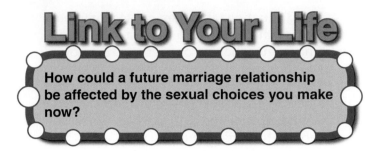

How could a future marriage relationship be affected by the sexual choices you make now?

Date or Acquaintance Rape

Sometimes people find themselves in situations in which a *no* reply is disregarded. Forced sexual intercourse is called **rape**. Sexual intercourse with a dating partner against one person's will is called **date rape**. The use of force or the threat of force is often involved. *Acquaintance rape* can occur between friends, classmates, or coworkers. It is the most common form of rape.

Studies show that alcohol and drugs are often involved when date or acquaintance rape takes place. A rape might occur during or after a party that includes drugs or alcohol. When alcohol or drug use is involved, some people become more aggressive and their judgment is impaired. Those who become victims may not be able to fight off an aggressor or flee a potential rape situation. The best way to avoid becoming a victim of rape is to avoid alcohol and drugs while dating or attending parties. If others around are using these substances, ask to be taken home or leave the party. Call a parent or friend if you need a ride home.

"Date rape drugs" cause victims to become physically helpless and unable to remember forced sexual intercourse. These drugs often have no color, smell, or taste, and are usually slipped into a beverage. To protect yourself when you are on a date or in a group, never trust anyone with your drink. Open your own beverages and do not drink out of a large punch bowl or other open container if you are at an unsupervised party. If something seems suspicious, throw it out.

Teenagers sometimes have a hard time interpreting the nonverbal messages that are given by a dating partner or acquaintance. Be careful that your nonverbal messages and your spoken messages match. Be verbal about what activities you want to avoid. Clarify that your *no* means *no*, and watch out for your own safety and well-being.

Review Section 7:2

1. Describe how mature love grows through a four-stage cycle.
2. List two psychological consequences of premarital sexual activity.
3. Describe how an unwanted pregnancy could affect a teen couple's life.
4. Describe two long-term consequences of STIs.
5. Name three STIs that can be treated with antibiotics.
6. List two main ways that the AIDS virus is spread.
7. List three comments teens can use to respond to sexual pressures.

Think It Through

A Dating Relationship

Al and Marietta have been dating for six months. They believe they are in love with each other. When they first started dating, they planned ahead and went to many different places. They had fun being together as they went to the museum, on biking trips, and on picnics. However, now they find themselves spending a lot of unplanned time together. They meet after school and spend evenings in one or the other's home. They don't spend much time with their friends either.

When they are alone it's hard to control the passionate kissing and hugging. The pressure to become more and more sexually involved gets greater. Marietta finds herself feeling angry and confused. She does not want to give in to the sexual pressures. She misses the times they spent just having fun, laughing, and doing things together. In fact, she almost dreads the evening dates because the same problem occurs over and over. Marietta is not sure how to deal with it.

Questions to Guide Your Thinking

1. In what situations do the sexual pressures become the greatest for Al and Marietta? What could they do to decrease these pressures on themselves? How could discussing the problem help them find solutions?

2. When one dating partner pressures the other to become sexually involved, does it mean that he or she really cares for the other person? Why or why not? How can you tell if a dating partner is considering the happiness of both people rather than personal or selfish interests?

3. Are Al and Marietta feeling romantic love for each other or mature love? What actions and feelings suggest that their love is romantic love? What evidence is there that this could be mature love?

4. Using I-statements, write a script in which Marietta confronts Al about her desire for less pressure to be sexually involved.

Chapter Summary

In this society, formal and informal dating serves many important functions. Dating is a way for young people to learn more about other people, themselves, and the qualities they desire in a marriage partner. It can increase their social skills for communicating and negotiating with other people. Also, dating provides companionship and opportunities to take responsibility in relationships.

Dating usually proceeds through several stages. Group dating gives teens the chance to develop their first relationships. Pair dating lets teens get to know another person better. Some dating relationships develop into friendships; others may end after one date. Ending a relationship can be painful, but it can also be a growing experience.

As a couple becomes more attracted to each other, they focus on building their relationship. Their attraction may be short-lived if it is based only on romantic feelings. Mature love grows as the couple spends time together, share, depend on each other, and meet each other's needs.

As dating relationships become more serious, young couples may feel pressured to deal with sexual feelings. Learning to control these feelings can help them avoid serious psychological and physical risks. Saying no is a healthy, responsible, and mature response.

Assess

Your Knowledge

1. Identify the purpose and functions of the dating process.

2. Explain the difference between infatuation and mature love.

3. Name five different sexually transmitted infections.

Your Understanding

4. Explain how mature love grows and develops.

5. How can a person identify if a dating relationship is healthy?

6. How can waiting until marriage to become sexually involved contribute to your overall well-being?

Your Skills

7. Evaluate a dating relationship (yours, a friend's, or someone you know) for the growth that should be taking place in a healthy dating relationship. Write a paragraph about why you think this relationship is healthy or unhealthy.

8. Who do you know who thinks they are in love? Analyze their relationship for evidence of mature love.

9. Create a list of three assertive responses that you could use to say no to unwanted sexual pressures.

Think Critically

10. Plan a group dating activity. Analyze the activity and identify the various ways this activity would fulfill the functions of dating. *Group option:* Work in a small group.

11. Watch a TV sitcom in which marital or dating relationships are portrayed and identify the relationship qualities you observe. Evaluate the qualities for characteristics of mature love or infatuation. Discuss your observations with an adult or a classmate. In a paragraph, summarize your evaluation of the type of love depicted in this TV sitcom.

12. *Math.* Consider your own views on the qualities of a good dating partner. Include your ideas on appearance, responsibilities, desirable attitudes, and expected behavior. Report your views to a group of three or four classmates. In your group, tally the number of group members who mentioned each quality. Create a bar graph that depicts the number of times each quality was identified. Share your group's graph with the class. As a class, create a list of qualities that the entire class agrees on. Then write a paragraph comparing your original list with the final class list, commenting on similarities and differences.

13. *Social studies.* Write scenarios of various dating concerns in your community. Analyze the scenarios for the root problem behind each concern. Working with three or four classmates, consider some healthy ways to handle each of the concerns. Identify healthy responses that partners in each scenario could make to help them grow as people.

Connect to Your Community

14. Clip articles related to dating and love from an advice column in a newspaper or teen magazine. Analyze each article. Are they talking about mature love or feelings of infatuation? What evidence is there to support your analysis? *Group option:* Work in a small group.

15. Invite a guest speaker to discuss issues related to teen sexuality and sexually transmitted infections. *Choice:* In advance, prepare a list of questions to ask the guest speaker.

16. Survey your community for opportunities for healthy dating activities. Refer to the Yellow Pages of the phone book and community bulletin boards or event calendars for ideas. Create a report listing the options that promote healthy dating activities in your community. *Group option:* Divide the community into sections and have one group member prepare a list for each section. Combine your findings into one report.

17. **Social studies.** Contact someone in your community who counsels couples planning marriage. Ask the counselor for a definition of love and some clues to identify when couples are really in love. Share this information with the class. After several students report their information, list the common aspects of the definitions reported. Compare this list to your own definition of love. *Choice:* Interview a target population (teens, young adults, married couples, older adults) and ask the same questions. How does that group's definition of love compare to the counselor's and to your own definition?

Use Technology

18. Use a computer program to design a flyer or poster illustrating creative ways to say no to unwanted dating pressures. Post the flyers and posters on a bulletin board by the school office.

19. Assemble a collage showing healthy dating activities that include places to go and things to do in your community. Use a scanner to incorporate the pictures into an electronic presentation. Summarize how these activities can help persons grow and mature. Share your presentation with the class. *Group option:* Work in a small group.

20. **Research.** Search the Internet to learn more about one of the sexually transmitted infections. Prepare a report using word processor software, and create a graph showing the incidence rate of this disease over the last five years.

21. **Math.** Survey parents to learn what they expect from responsible daters. Include questions related to dating activities, places to go, ideal hours for dates, age for dating, and opinions related to group or pair dating. Compile the information on a computer spreadsheet, analyze the data, and prepare a report on parents' attitudes toward dating. Use charts or graphs to illustrate your findings.

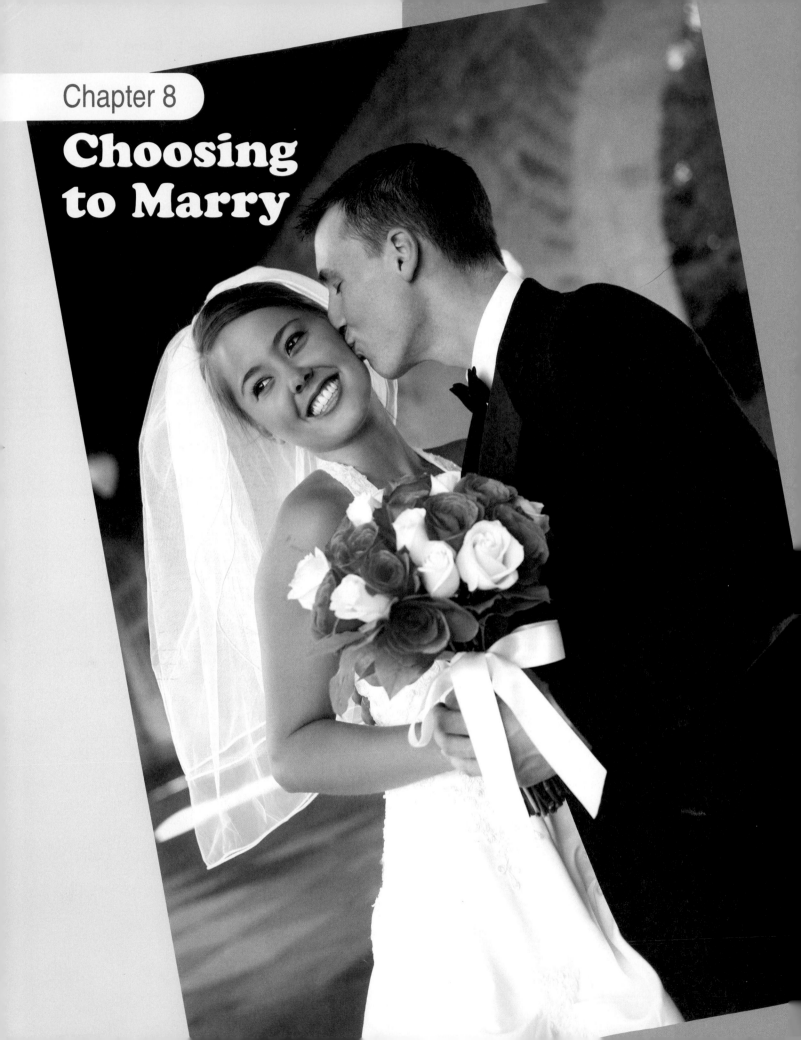

Chapter 8

Choosing to Marry

Section 8:**1**
What Qualities Can You Bring to a Marriage?

Section 8:**2**
Evaluating a Relationship

Section 8:**3**
Preparing for a Long-Lasting Marriage Relationship

Key Questions

Questions to answer as you study this chapter:

- What qualities help to make a marriage happy and long lasting?

- What skills can help build a satisfying marriage relationship?

Chapter Objectives

After studying this chapter, you will be able to

- **identify** personal qualities that can help you build a happy and stable marriage.

- **explain** how similarities and differences between spouses can affect a marital relationship.

- **analyze** how skills for communicating, making decisions, and solving problems can help a relationship grow.

- **identify** important decisions to be discussed during the engagement period.

- **recognize** the legal aspects of beginning a marriage.

Life Sketch

"Did you hear about Jason getting married?" Ethan asked.

"Are you kidding?" Matthew replied. "He always seemed so focused on helping his dad run the family business. I didn't think he had time to date."

"I ran into him yesterday," Ethan said. "That's when he invited me to his wedding. His future wife has worked for their business for two years, and last spring they got engaged. You'll probably get an invitation, too."

"What's the bride's name?" Matthew asked.

"Laurie," Ethan replied. "Jason said he didn't think he would ever find the girl of his dreams until he met Laurie."

Getting Started

Many young people are concerned about how to prepare for a happy marriage. They may know some broken marriages or may have lived in unhappy family situations. They have seen conflict in marital relationships, and they want to know how to avoid similar problems.

In a happy marriage, both people feel satisfied. Many factors can influence happiness in a marriage. Some are personal qualities that relate to a couple's maturity. Some factors relate to similarities and differences between a couple. Other factors relate to how close the relationship has developed.

In this chapter, you will learn more about the positive qualities needed to build a strong marriage. You will also learn about ways a couple can honestly evaluate their relationship before becoming engaged. Once a couple becomes engaged, they continue to evaluate their relationship. You will learn more about the important issues they need to identify and discuss. Finally, you will learn how a wedding satisfies legal requirements and symbolizes the beginning of the couple's new life together.

section 8:1

What Qualities Can You Bring to a Marriage?

Sharpen Your Reading

As you read this section, write a description of a person who demonstrates the qualities needed for a strong and stable marriage.

Boost Your Vocabulary

Give an example of how a couple could demonstrate each personal quality listed in Figure 8-1.

Know Key Terms

flexibility

Think of a marriage like a house built of bricks. Each factor in a marriage relationship is like a brick in the wall, 8-1. Combined together, these factors strengthen the relationship and make it stable. If a marriage is missing too many of these factors, the relationship may become weak and break apart.

You have certain qualities that can help you build a happy and stable marriage. Your personal qualities, skills, and resources all accompany you into a marriage relationship. Some qualities can make married living quite difficult. Others can add to and strengthen the relationship.

Marriage		
Personal Qualities	**Homogamous Factors**	**Relationship Skills/Abilities**
Sensitive	Similar attitudes and life views	To disclose inner thoughts and feelings
Empathic		
Loving	Similar priorities	To communicate clearly
Emotionally stable		To actively listen
Positive	Similar goals	To accept each other
Trustworthy		To give for each other's best interest
Caring	Similar interests	To build mutual respect
Giving		
Flexible	Similar backgrounds	To build trust
Logical		To give and receive mature love
Reasonable		To negotiate
Thoughtful		To make joint decisions
Dependable		
Responsible		

8-1 The combined effect of these factors helps make the structure of a marriage strong and stable.

Certain personal qualities make it hard to build a satisfying relationship. These include being self-centered, insensitive, rigid, unwilling to change, and unreasonable. Such qualities hinder a couple's ability to communicate clearly or solve problems fairly. They are signs that more time is needed for personal growth to maturity.

Link to Your Life

Think about a couple you know who struggle to get along in their relationship. What qualities do they have that make it hard to develop a strong marriage?

Some personal qualities make it easier for a couple to build a satisfying relationship. Many of these qualities tend to increase with maturity. The questions in 8-2 can help you evaluate the growth of these qualities in your own life. As two people mature and develop these qualities in their relationship, they will experience greater happiness and satisfaction.

The Ability to Give and Receive Love

The ability to give and receive love is vital to a happy marriage. Expressing your love and showing that you care will strengthen your relationship. You need to be willing to commit yourself to help meet your partner's needs. You also need to be willing to do what is best for the other person. That means taking time to share, listen, and build trust and mutual respect.

Accepting love includes being willing to let your partner meet your needs. It means allowing yourself to depend on another person. It also means accepting your partner as he or she is. The ability to give and receive mature love in these ways will add to marital happiness.

Use What You Learn

How can self-acceptance help you develop mature love for another person?

Are You Ready for Marriage?

Am I able to unselfishly give love?

Am I able to receive love?

Am I sensitive to the hurts and needs of others?

Am I willing to try to see and experience the world from the other person's point of view?

Can I recognize my own emotions?

Can I accept my emotions and control them?

Can I express my emotions without hurting another?

Am I able and willing to adjust to change?

Can I accept differences in a partner?

Can I give and take in resolving differences?

Do I usually respond logically?

Am I able to define issues?

Do I think through the alternatives when making a decision?

Am I reasonable when evaluating alternatives?

8-2 A person's honest responses to these questions can help determine his or her readiness for marriage. A mature person would answer "yes" most of the time.

The Ability to Express Empathy

Empathy is an important quality for the growth of a satisfying relationship. For two people to share in each other's lives, they must be sensitive to each other's thoughts and feelings. They must share their inner thoughts and feelings openly. They must also be willing to see a situation from the other's point of view.

Empathy keeps a relationship close. The couple identify with each other's inner thoughts and feelings. They know how to respond and meet each other's needs. As their needs are met, they become more attached to each other. In this way, empathy helps mature love grow in a relationship.

Use What You Learn

What are some examples of situations where a couple would express empathy for each other?

Emotional Stability

Emotional stability is an important personal quality in marriage. Without it, good communication is difficult. Unclear verbal and nonverbal messages may be sent and received. Intense emotions may cause couples to respond defensively. They may resort to name-calling, using defense mechanisms, or making irrational statements. They may attack each other's esteem and break down trust in the relationship. The ability to control emotions can help couples avoid such negative communication patterns.

Emotional stability comes with maturity. In any relationship, you are likely to feel a variety of emotions. With maturity, you will be able to control your responses to those emotions. The ability to handle your emotions helps you keep a positive attitude in a relationship.

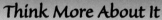

Think More About It
How could developing empathy help you control other emotional responses?

Flexibility

Many problems in marriage result because a couple has difficulty adjusting to each other's needs and wants. They may be unwilling to change. They may both insist on having their own way. Such rigid attitudes make it almost impossible to keep a relationship healthy and growing.

Flexibility means being willing to change. You do not always need to have your way. You are willing to negotiate differences with your partner. You can agree to a decision that benefits both rather than just you. If both you and your partner are flexible, you can resolve your differences. Each of you can reach a compromise that is satisfying to both, 8-3.

8-3 Being flexible often involves compromise. Both partners show they are willing to adjust to satisfy each other.

Flexibility also means accepting and learning to tolerate certain personality traits you do not like in the other person. When you marry, you cannot expect your partner to change to suit you. You must be willing to accept that person as he or she is.

Decision-Making Skills

Many of your decisions will have long-term effects on a relationship. Some decisions will relate to you personally. Some will involve your relationship with your partner. Other decisions will relate to your family, children, career, or community.

Being able to think through a decision is an important skill to bring into a marriage. In marriage, many decisions are made together. Shared decision-making skills will help a couple make decisions that match their priorities and help them reach their goals. This adds to a satisfying relationship.

Review Section 8:**1**

1. List four personal qualities that make it easier for couples to build satisfying relationships.
2. Explain how empathy strengthens a relationship.
3. Give one example of how emotional stability is an important quality in a relationship.
4. Describe three qualities of a flexible person.

section 8:2

Evaluating a Relationship

Sharpen Your Reading

For each heading in this section, predict how that factor could impact a marriage relationship. As you read evaluate the accuracy of your predictions.

Boost Your Vocabulary

Build a concept diagram for the term homogamy as it applies to developing close relationships.

Know Key Terms

homogamy
complementary qualities

Two young adults may bring many mature qualities into a relationship. However, it still takes time to build a successful marriage.

Many factors can affect a couple's marital relationship. Some factors relate to the couple's age, financial status, and common interests. Others relate to how well they communicate, make joint decisions, and resolve their differences. The thoughts and feelings of family and other friends can also affect a relationship. Evaluating a relationship for these qualities before marriage is an important first step.

Age at Marriage

The link between age and marital success is related to emotional, mental, and social maturity. A young couple's ability to meet their financial needs is also a factor. Generally, a person is better prepared to make a lifetime commitment after the teen years.

During the late teen years, much personal growth still occurs. You continue to learn more about yourself and to accept yourself for who you are. You learn more about what you like and dislike in others. You decide what qualities you desire in a long-term relationship. You begin to see your life goals more clearly and make plans to reach them. You choose a job or career and make plans to become financially independent. This period of growth is important in the young adult's life.

Marrying during the teen years adds more stress to a relationship. Many teens are not mature enough to handle the responsibilities and make the adjustments required in the early years of marriage. Developing into a mature person takes time. It also takes time to develop your skills and resources for living on your own. As you plan for a successful future, give yourself the time you need for personal growth.

Think More About It
What do you think the ideal age range would be for marriage? Why?

What Do You Have in Common?

Researchers who have studied marriage relationships have formed a principle called **homogamy**. That principle suggests that people who have many similarities, or much in common, are more likely to have a satisfying marriage, 8-4.

You will most likely be attracted to someone who has much in common with you. People often spend time with others who have similar backgrounds. They generally are attracted to those who have similar interests. When they find they share similar life goals, they are more closely drawn together.

8-4 Couples with similar interests and backgrounds enjoy their time together.

Similar Interests

Common interests can help a relationship grow. They can be a source of topics for discussion. They often are the center of joint activities. Couples who are about the same age are more likely to have similar interests. They will find it easier to develop leisure activities they both enjoy. Their friends will likely be similar to them in age and interests. Similar interests help enrich relationships through the years as well.

Link to Your Life

What are some interests you have that you hope to share with a life mate?

Similar Goals and Values

People are often attracted to those who have similar life goals. Your values affect what you do and the way you do it. They affect the goals you set, the choices you consider, and the decisions you make. Choosing a partner with similar goals and values can reduce future conflict areas in the relationship.

However, that does not mean you and your partner need to think alike on every issue. In many areas of your lives, you both will have your own values and goals. Some issues may be more important to you; some will be more important to your partner. Some will be equally important to you as a couple.

Top priority areas for many couples include children and parenting, family roles, education, work expectations, and religious beliefs. Expectations and goals in these areas need to be shared. Determining which goals and values the individuals have in common will help reduce future conflicts. Knowing their common goals and values will help them make satisfying decisions.

Think More About It
What goals and values do you hold that are essential for you to have in common with your partner?

Similar Backgrounds

People are often attracted to others with a similar background. They usually feel comfortable around each other. Acceptance comes more quickly. Their backgrounds may be a source of similar interests, values, and goals.

Similar backgrounds can also make it easier to establish good relationships with each other's families. Acceptance of in-laws may come more quickly. Family customs may be similar. Social and economic expectations may be alike.

When couples from different backgrounds choose to marry, they will have more adjustments to make. Adjusting to differences in family attitudes, customs, and expectations takes time. Common interests, values, and goals help a couple to endure family differences.

Complementary Qualities

Sometimes a person is attracted to another who is quite different. When these differences benefit the relationship, they are called **complementary qualities**. That means the strengths of one person make up for the weaknesses of the other. The couple's qualities balance each other, and the relationship benefits, 8-5.

Couples who do not share complementary qualities may find it difficult to work together as a team. Conflicts may not be easily resolved. If couples cannot balance their differences, they will not find agreeable solutions to conflicts.

Use What You Learn

What are some examples of complementary qualities?

Racial Differences

Couples in an interracial marriage may face additional challenges. Differences between the spouses may cause conflict. Family members and friends may support an interracial relationship, or they may object to it. They may be open to different views on family customs and children, or they may not. They may extend their friendship and include the spouse, or they may leave that person out. Interracial couples need to consider these factors in depth before marriage.

In addition to the effect on their own lives, those considering an interracial marriage need to consider the effect on their future children. In some communities, children of mixed race may feel less accepted by either race or by either family.

These challenges can cause a couple to think through their decisions more thoroughly. Their differences can cause them to evaluate areas of interests, priorities, and goals even more closely. Similarities in these areas can help them work through the challenges they face.

Differences in Religious Views

When young people date, their different religious views may not seem important. However, it is an important factor to consider before marriage. A person's faith can strongly influence his or her beliefs and practices. Marrying someone of a different faith can cause problems unless the couple discusses the issue first.

Differences in views usually become more important when children are born. Dealing with the question of raising a child in a certain religious faith is the biggest problem interfaith couples may face. Each partner may wish to raise the children to follow his or her beliefs. That can result in increased conflict between spouses and within the family unit. Discussing this issue before marriage can help a couple make decisions that will avoid future problems.

8-5 Complementary qualities can benefit a relationship if both people are open to growth and willing to make adjustments.

Investigate Further

Consider all the areas of homogamy and describe which are most important to you in a relationship.

How Well Do You Communicate?

Your satisfaction with a relationship will be related to the quality of communication that takes place in it, 8-6. Good communication means that messages are sent, received, and understood. Verbal messages are clear. Nonverbal messages such as facial expressions and body language support what is said. Both use active listening skills to be sure a shared meaning is reached. If misunderstandings occur often in a relationship, these skills need to be developed.

Think More About It
Is it possible for a relationship to be satisfying if misunderstandings occur often?

How Do We Communicate?

1. I feel free to share my personal thoughts and feelings.

2. My partner freely shares deep and personal thoughts with me.

3. I feel that my ideas are accepted.

4. I accept my partner's point of view.

5. I listen actively, making sure I understand what is shared.

6. My partner listens actively to me.

7. I trust my partner.

8. I don't spread what my partner has shared confidentially with me.

9. Our communication helps us know each other intimately.

10. We communicate clearly, with few misunderstandings.

8-6 Couples can use this checklist for evaluating how well they communicate with each other. If they answer "no" to most questions, they need to spend more time developing their relationship before considering marriage.

For communication to be satisfying, it also needs to be personal. A couple needs communication skills for sharing their personal thoughts, feelings, and inner desires. Both need to feel their views are accepted and valued by the other. If either feels ignored or unaccepted, the relationship will not grow.

Quality communication in a marriage relationship is based on trust. The couple can trust each other with their most intimate thoughts and feelings. They know the other will respond with their best interests in mind. There is no fear of being hurt or rejected. Trust leads to freedom and acceptance in a relationship. In this way, high-quality communication helps mature love grow.

Skills that foster such growth can help a relationship continue to be satisfying. That does not mean there will not be any more misunderstandings. However, those occasions should become rare. Good communication skills can help a couple clear up misunderstandings, make joint decisions, and solve problems in a marriage.

How Well Do You Make Decisions Together?

As a relationship grows, you and your partner should improve your skills for making important decisions together. Within a marriage, many decisions must be made, both small and large. Using decision-making skills as a couple improves with practice. Then you are able to identify an issue and talk about various alternatives. You choose one alternative that satisfies both and develop a plan to carry it out. Later, you evaluate your decision together.

This process can help both partners feel they have contributed to making the decision. They will more likely support each other in carrying it out. They will also have greater success in reaching the goals they have set for their marriage.

Use What You Learn

How will a relationship be affected if one person makes all the decisions or makes decisions without consulting the other person?

How Do You Solve Problems Together?

Evaluating your skills for solving problems and settling differences before you consider marriage is important, 8-7. These skills will affect your satisfaction with the relationship.

Problem-solving steps are much like those used for decision making. However, greater self-control is needed in communication. Problems need to be identified in a mature way. As a couple, that means waiting until your emotions cool down to resolve your differences. Using I-statements to express observations, thoughts, and feelings will help reach a solution without damaging the relationship.

Disagreements are normal in a relationship. In a growing relationship, your skills for solving problems together should improve. There should be fewer times of arguing or fighting. Attitudes of respect and sensitivity to each other should increase. Your skills for negotiating acceptable solutions should increase.

Evaluate Your Decision-Making and Problem-Solving Skills

1. We disagree about little things.

2. We both like to make our own decisions.

3. We make decisions on impulse.

4. We go by our gut-level feelings when we make decisions.

5. We both want to prove our point when we disagree.

6. We expect each other to keep quiet when we disagree about personal matters.

7. We use comments such as, "You should..." when we disagree.

8. We get angry when we don't get our own way.

9. We yell and call each other names when we get upset.

10. We try to figure out who's at fault to take the blame for a problem.

8-7 A couple who responds "yes" to these questions will have difficulty resolving problems in a marriage.

What Do Your Families and Friends Think?

Your chances for a successful marriage are increased when family and friends approve of your marriage partner. You and your partner may have evaluated your relationship in all the above areas and agree that you are ready for marriage. When family and friends also agree, you are more likely to feel confident about your decision.

Link to Your Life

What are some activities that you enjoy doing with your family that you would like your spouse to enjoy as well?

Receiving love and acceptance from both families is another benefit. Your family loves and cares for you. When they extend love and acceptance to your partner, his or her feelings of self-esteem and confidence will increase. Yours will, too. When both families express love, the couple's relationship will be strengthened.

Family support can help a couple through the adjustments of the early years of marriage, 8-8. They can be a source of friendship, counseling, or financial help. A good relationship with both families can help a couple make satisfying choices about family matters.

The approval of friends can also increase satisfaction in a relationship. They may extend their friendship to include your partner. Also, there will likely be fewer conflicts over time spent with friends.

Couples who choose to marry without the approval of family and friends face more challenges. In this situation, their relationship must be strong. Developing new mutual friendships will help. The couple will need well-developed skills for resolving conflicts with each other, old friends, and family members.

In addition, the couple will need greater flexibility to find solutions that are satisfying to both. They will need to encourage each other often so their esteem and confidence remain high. With good communication skills,

8-8 Friendships with family members strengthen relationships.

positive attitudes, and a willingness to work out problems, relationships with family and friends may improve.

What Is Your Reason for Wanting to Marry?

People decide to marry for many different reasons. Infatuation and other one-sided emotional needs are negative reasons. To be successful, a marriage must be based on positive reasons.

Negative Reasons

Some people want to marry because they like being together. They want those feelings to last for a lifetime so they choose marriage. This infatuation can cloud a couple's judgment of their relationship. They may overlook personal differences. One may give in to make the other happy, or keep quiet rather than express personal opinions. When infatuation fades, they begin to feel dissatisfied with the relationship. Even minor differences soon become major issues. If they cannot resolve them, the relationship may fall apart.

Some marry to avoid loneliness. Some may marry for the financial security that a partner may bring. To some, marriage may seem to be a way to achieve adult status. Some use marriage as an escape from problems at home. Sometimes, young people marry because of a pregnancy. All of these are poor reasons for marriage.

Positive Reasons

Mature love, intimacy, companionship, and a desire to grow together throughout life are healthy reasons for marriage. They contribute to a satisfying relationship. As satisfaction increases, the couple's desire to stay together does, too.

A mature relationship based on love is a good foundation for a successful marriage. In addition, a commitment to one relationship is an expectation in this society. Both partners need to be willing to turn aside from all other possible romantic relationships. They need to be committed to keeping this relationship growing and satisfying for both. This commitment begins with the engagement.

Review Section 8:2

1. Explain why marrying as a teen may add more stress to a relationship.
2. Couples who have many similarities are more likely to have a strong marriage. List and briefly describe three possible areas of similarities.
3. Give two examples of complementary qualities in a couple's relationship.
4. List three ways in which good communication skills help a couple's relationship.
5. Briefly describe two ways in which a family's support can help a couple's relationship.
6. List two negative reasons and two positive reasons why people choose to marry.

section 8:3

Preparing for a Long-Lasting Marriage Relationship

Sharpen Your Reading

Create a checklist of questions that a couple could use to evaluate if they are ready for marriage.

Boost Your Vocabulary

Define role sharing, give examples and identify the benefits of sharing roles.

Know Key Terms

engagement
complementary role
role sharing
ceremonial wedding
civil ceremony
vows

As a couple prepare for marriage, they will need to continue evaluating and growing in their relationship. They will need to communicate clearly, set goals, make decisions, discuss expectations, resolve problems, and continue to build a loving relationship. These experiences will help prepare them for the adjustments in the early years of marriage.

Engagement

The **engagement** is the final stage in the dating process leading to marriage. The engagement period signifies the start of a couple's plans for married life. It usually begins with a formal announcement to family and friends that the couple intend to marry. A person may either give or receive a ring to identify this commitment to marry.

The engagement period provides time for a couple to discuss important issues and expectations. Both will have expectations for each other, for children, for relating to their families, and in other areas of their shared life.

Role Expectations

Roles describe particular patterns for daily living. Some common roles of a marriage partner include being a friend, lover, companion, wage earner, cook, housekeeper, bill payer, or nurse. The expectations you have for your spouse are strongly influenced by the roles your parents took in your family, 8-9. Your spouse's expectations will likely be based on his or her family experiences. Thus, if a couple has similar backgrounds, many role expectations will be similar.

Link to Your Life

What are your expectations for your spouse? What roles do you think he or she will fill?

It is necessary for the couple to discuss each other's role expectations. Together, they need to determine what roles make sense for each of them as a couple. Living up to personal roles is easier if a couple knows what is expected. Thus, communication about roles is important.

Dividing Roles

Sometimes, a couple may choose **complementary roles**. That is, each person takes on a role that supplies what the other person lacks. Some couples choose **role sharing** as a

8-9 Roles are certain patterns that each family member identifies and shares.

way of handling some responsibilities. Through role sharing, they work together to carry out the task. Role sharing allows couples to keep in touch with one another's thoughts and feelings while sharing responsibilities.

Use What You Learn

How are roles divided in your family? Give some examples of how family members carry out different roles and identify whether these are complementary roles or shared roles.

Planning Finances

Finances are often a major area of conflict in a marriage. Future income, expenses, paying bills, saving for desired purchases—all these areas of money management should be discussed before marriage. A couple may find it helpful to develop

a spending and saving plan. They also need to decide who will actually pay the bills and who will make certain purchases.

Think More About It
How important is it to have a steady income before getting married?

Planning for Housing Needs

A couple's choice of housing will depend on the money they have to spend. Most young couples rent housing since a large sum of money is needed to buy a home. Apartments, which are available in a range of prices, are the most popular choice. A couple should consider the cost of utilities, furnishings, and rental insurance in addition to the cost of the rent.

Other housing factors they consider include a convenient location close to work or public transportation. The neighborhood, closeness to child care facilities, or closeness to family and friends may also be considered.

Link to Your Life

What are your expectations for your first home? What kind of income will it take to maintain such a home?

Planning for Career Goals

As they plan for the future, couples need to discuss their career goals. Each person's career will affect family living. The demands of work will influence the amount of time a couple have together. Their schedules may affect the way they divide or share roles in the home. Their incomes will influence the amount of money they have to spend. Other career issues that will affect the family include promotions, pay raises, job relocations, or future educational expenses.

A couple should discuss their expectations for each other and their top-priority issues. If their commitment to their relationship is a top priority, their marriage can be healthy. They both can grow individually, and they will work to balance the pressures of their lifestyle. If either partner puts personal goals ahead of the relationship or family goals, the marriage will likely suffer.

Weigh the Facts

How important is it to you to complete your education before getting married? What would be the advantages? Why might it be more advantageous for some to finish school after they get married?

Planning for Sexual Fulfillment

The security of marriage allows a couple to express their love in physical intimacy. They are confident their relationship will last. They have established trust and are totally committed to each other. Sexual satisfaction in a relationship goes hand-in-hand with love, caring, mutual respect, trust, and commitment to each other.

An engaged couple should be informed about sexual roles and expectations in marriage. However, that does not mean either partner must have previous sexual experience before marriage. Experiences during the engagement period are often not satisfying because the security and commitment of marriage are missing. Premarital relations may be accompanied by fear, doubts, or guilt. The couple may feel disappointed because they do not experience the satisfaction they expected.

To make sexual adjustment easier in marriage, any concerns and anxieties about the sexual aspects of marriage should be discussed by the couple. Talking about sexual expectations before the wedding can make physical sharing after the wedding more meaningful. Sensitivity to each other's physical and emotional needs can help a couple make the sexual adjustments to marriage.

Planning for Children

Another area that needs to be discussed before marriage is whether to have children, 8-18. Does each partner want to be a parent? How many children do they want? When do they want to

have children? How will children affect their income, expenses, roles, and careers? What if they learn they cannot have children?

In addition to planning for children, a couple should discuss their viewpoints on raising children. Who will have major responsibility for child care? What expectations does each spouse have for the other's involvement in child care? What are their attitudes toward child guidance and discipline? These need to be discussed before marriage so the couple is united in their approach to child rearing.

Link to Your Life

Do you want to become a parent some day? How many children would you like to have? How important is it that your spouse has similar feelings about parenthood?

Planning Your Relationships with Families and Friends

Families and friends are both important areas to be discussed during engagement. What family obligations does each spouse have? Will they celebrate birthdays, anniversaries, and holidays with family members? Which holidays will be spent with which family? Good relationships with families can strengthen a couple's relationship.

Couples also need to discuss their personal friendships and joint friendships. Engaged couples may find that as they spend more time together, their friendships with others may change. In some cases, they may spend less time with their present friends. Some friendships will remain strong while others just drift apart. Mutual friends of the couple may take the place of individual friends. Discussing expectations about friendships before marriage can decrease future conflict in this area.

Use What You Learn

What could a person do to find out whether current friendships could cause conflict in a future marriage relationship?

Premarital Counseling

Sometimes couples will consult a counselor before marriage. This person may be a licensed marriage and family counselor. Often couples consult a religious leader or the person who will be performing the marriage ceremony, 8-10. The counselor may discuss topics as personal readiness for marriage, expectations for each other, skills for communicating, skills for making decisions and problem solving, and even money management.

Most marriage counselors recommend an engagement period of six months to two years. The time depends on several factors. These include how well the couple know each other, if they can handle the responsibilities of marriage, and if they can support themselves financially.

An attitude that may become evident in the counseling process is a "me-oriented" attitude rather than "we-oriented." Such focus on personal wants and desires may be evidence of immaturity. In this case, it may be a sign the couple should wait before considering marriage.

8-10 Many couples seek premarital counseling to help them evaluate their relationship and their plans for the future.

Think More About It
What are some reasons that a couple may hesitate to pursue premarital counseling?

Breaking an Engagement

The engagement period is a time of preparation for marriage. For most couples, this is a happy time as partners prepare for a new life together. As some couples plan for the future, however, they may discover they are not ready for marriage.

A couple may decide to break the engagement for various reasons. One person may sense a need to grow personally. The couple may recognize poor communication patterns or an inability to make decisions together. They may discover they are not suited for each other. If either partner doubts the relationship will be successful, the couple would be wise to break the engagement. Ending a relationship is difficult at any time. However, a broken engagement is better than an unhappy marriage.

Planning the Wedding

The engagement period allows time for a couple to complete their wedding plans. The customs and traditions of the couple's families often influence the wedding celebration. The couple's personal desires and social and economic status may also influence the wedding plans. In the midst of all the planning, the partners need to continue developing their relationship as a couple.

Marriage

In this country, marriage is a legal contract involving the couple and the state. The state sets minimum standards for the contract. These standards are designed to establish some order and stability to the institution of marriage. Once these standards are met, the couple can proceed with the wedding ceremony.

Marriage Laws

All states have certain requirements concerning the marriage contract. They require that both parties must be competent and eligible to enter the contract. Also, both parties must enter the marriage contract willingly, or by *mutual consent*. The contract cannot be legally dissolved without state action.

Although all states have marriage laws, particular details may differ. A person planning to get married should check the laws in that particular state. Many couples seek this information from the licensed official who will perform their marriage ceremony. Most marriage laws specify certain physical requirements, minimum ages, licensing necessities, and legal officiates.

Investigate Further

What are the legal requirements for getting married in your state?

The Wedding Ceremony

The wedding ceremony serves two purposes. First, it meets a requirement that a couple be legally joined together by a licensed official. Secondly, the ceremony symbolizes the couple's commitment to their relationship.

Some couples choose a **ceremonial wedding** performed by a religious official. Family members and friends usually share in the ceremony. They also witness the couple's vows of commitment to each other. They celebrate this commitment by sharing gifts to help them establish a new home.

Some couples may choose a **civil ceremony**. For this type of ceremony, family members and a few friends witness the couple's vows taken before a judicial or public official.

Sometimes exceptions exist in the laws associated with certain weddings, as in the Quaker community. Instead of having a legal official, the couple marry themselves. The members of the congregation sign the marriage license as witnesses.

The vows are a traditional part of the marriage ceremony, 8-11. The **vows** are statements that specifically express the couple's

8-11 During a wedding ceremony, couples exchange vows by stating their commitment to each other.

commitment to each other. The marriage official will have a copy of the marriage ceremony, including the vows, and will discuss this with the couple. Sometimes couples like to write their own vows as a way of making the ceremony unique for them. This needs to be discussed with the marriage official.

The Honeymoon

A honeymoon allows time for the couple to relax after the wedding and adjust to their new life. Some couples may use this time to travel. Others may just spend some time alone, away from the pressures of work and other responsibilities. The length of the honeymoon may vary, depending on the couple's finances and time schedules.

Review Section 8:**3**

1. What is the purpose of the engagement period?
2. Identify three important issues a couple needs to discuss during their engagement.
3. Describe two ways of dividing roles in a marriage relationship.
4. List three reasons why a premarital counselor may suggest that a couple make their engagement longer.

Think It Through

A Growing Relationship

Jennifer and Samuel felt they were ready for marriage. They were deeply in love. Their relationship had grown close. They shared many common interests and were truly committed to each other. They knew they had some differences, but they believed they could work them out.

Both of them had promising careers. Jennifer worked as a manager for a local restaurant chain. She was organized and efficient as well as friendly and outgoing. She enjoyed her work, but she knew she would have to relocate for a promotion. Samuel was also an organized person and very attentive to detail. He was less social than Jennifer, preferring to spend time alone with her. He worked as a computer technician for a large company. This company located employees throughout the U.S. and in other countries as well. Jennifer and Samuel realized their jobs could pull them in different directions.

Jennifer and Samuel both wanted to have children, but they weren't sure when. They weren't sure how children would affect their career choices either. That seemed like a decision they would make later.

Questions to Guide Your Thinking

1. What personal qualities can you identify for Jennifer and for Samuel that could add to a marriage relationship?

2. What similarities could have attracted them to each other? In what ways might their personality differences cause conflicts?

3. In what ways could Jennifer and Samuel's careers pull them in different directions? How could this affect their marriage? How important would it be to agree on a potential solution before they marry?

4. What are some questions that Jennifer and Samuel should discuss about parenting? If they do not agree in these areas, how could having children increase conflict in their relationship?

Chapter Summary

Certain personal qualities can help couples build a stable marriage. Many are qualities that tend to increase with maturity. Couples who develop these qualities in their relationship will experience greater satisfaction in married life.

Couples should honestly evaluate their relationship before becoming engaged. Since certain factors affect marital happiness, this evaluation can help a couple determine their readiness for marriage. Some factors are related to similarities and differences between the couple. Other factors include a couple's ability to communicate, make decisions, and solve problems together. Each of these factors will affect the way the relationship grows.

An engagement period provides time for continued evaluation and growth in the relationship. It also allows time for planning future needs such as finances and housing. Couples need to discuss role expectations, career goals, and sexual expectations. Deciding whether to have children and assessing family relationships are other issues in this planning process.

A premarital counselor can assist couples in evaluating their relationship and identifying marriage practices required by law. After evaluating their relationship, some couples may discover they have doubts about the upcoming marriage. They are wise to break the engagement at this point. The final part of the engagement period involves planning the wedding. Wedding plans are often based on family traditions and customs, personal desires, and finances.

Marriage is bound by a legal contract and is a commitment to give fully to one relationship. A couple must accept the responsibility of following certain laws to fulfill the marriage contract. The wedding ceremony legally joins a couple. Ceremonial weddings are chosen by many couples, although some couples prefer civil ceremonies. After the wedding, a couple may go on a honeymoon.

Assess...

Your Knowledge

1. What are the personal qualities that contribute to a happy and healthy marriage?

2. What factors should be evaluated when considering a marriage relationship?

3. What are the areas in which couples should plan before getting married?

Your Understanding

4. How can personal qualities and skills affect the quality of a marriage relationship?

5. How can similarities and differences between a couple affect their marital relationship?

6. How can planning for married living affect a couple's relationship?

Your Skills

7. Write a paragraph in which you evaluate your development of the personal qualities needed for a long-lasting marriage.

8. Identify a problem in your school that you can address. Work with a partner to solve this problem and present your solution to the class. Develop a checklist to evaluate your personal skills for communicating, decision making, and solving problems with your partner. Evaluate each other's skills using your checklist.

Think Critically

9. *Writing.* Write a paragraph describing a person who could be a homogamous partner for you. What qualities would this person have in common with you?

10. *Writing.* Write a scenario describing your idea of the ideal wedding for you. Include the following points:
    - cultural preferences or traditions
    - roles you and your spouse will take
    - roles your families will take in your wedding

    Choice: Present your information in an electronic presentation or narrated video.

11. Make a list of the qualities you desire in your ideal mate. Include both general and specific qualities. Compare your list with other classmates' lists. Are there any differences between the qualities desired in males or females? Are there any qualities desirable for all spouses? Summarize in a paragraph which qualities you think are most important, and assess the differences between your list and those of your classmates. *Group option:*

Identify three other classmates to be your partners, and together, write a one-page paper in which you identify qualities that all of your group members think are important in a life mate.

12. *Writing.* Analyze the following statement: If your family and friends do not approve of your potential marriage partner, you should not get married. Write a paper stating your position of either agreeing or disagreeing with the statement. Use specific arguments to support the position you take. *Choice:* Debate your position with a classmate who chose the opposite position.

Connect to Your Community

13. *Research.* Interview a marriage official. Ask the official to explain the marriage laws in your state. What type of ceremony does the official use? What vows does the official recommend? Have the official describe any symbolism related to the traditional wedding ceremony. Prepare a one-page report summarizing your findings from the interview. *Choice:* Work with a partner, each interviewing a different marriage official. Then prepare a report together, summarizing both interviews.

14. *Social studies.* Compare the marriage roles of two different families in your community. What differences are there in the two families? What similarities are there in the ways the couples fulfill roles in their families? Discuss your findings with two other classmates. Look for differences and similarities with the families they compared. Then work with the class to prepare a class list of roles most commonly taken by spouses in your community. Are there any generalizations you can make about such a list?

15. Invite someone from the community to join a panel to discuss recommendations for preparing for marriage. (Your classmates will invite other guests from the community who together will form the panel.) Guests may include a religious leader, marriage counselor, wedding planner, or parent who recently had a child marry. Prepare questions to ask the panel.

16. *Research.* Form teams of four to five students and research a career area that focuses on helping couples build strong marriage relationships. Have each team prepare a summary of the services provided by professionals in that career area. Appoint one person on each team to present their findings in a symposium on "Local Services for Building Strong Marriages in our Community."

Use Technology

17. *Writing.* Using a word processing program, write a marriage contract listing the expectations you have for yourself and for your spouse. Include your ideas about the roles you both should take in marriage. Try to be specific. Submit a printed copy of the contract to your teacher.

18. *Research.* Use the Internet to research the wedding customs of two different cultures. Write a report comparing each culture's wedding customs to those you have observed. *Choice:* Present your information in an electronic presentation or video.

19. Use a computer spreadsheet to prepare a checklist to use to evaluate a relationship. Include the factors affecting the quality of a marital relationship. Identify factors you feel are very important, somewhat important, and not very important. Survey three married couples, asking questions about the importance of each item on your list. Gather their responses as to whether they agree with your rating of very, somewhat, and not very important. Summarize your findings, comparing their responses with your first list. *Group option:* Work in a group of 4 to prepare the lists, gather data from married couples, and then prepare a graph showing the number of persons rating each factor as very important, somewhat important, and not very important.

20. Identify a TV sitcom or a movie that has married couples as main characters. Evaluate the qualities that are modeled in the relationships between the characters. In a one-page paper, summarize your evaluation. Include a description of the qualities you see modeled. *Choice:* Use your checklist from the previous activity to evaluate the relationships you observe.

Chapter 9

Adjusting to Marriage

Section 9:**1**
Patterns of Adjustment

Section 9:**2**
Interpersonal Adjustments

Section 9:**3**
Adapting to Financial and Social Changes

Key Questions

Questions to answer as you study this chapter:

* What patterns of adjustment contribute to a high-quality marriage relationship?

* What personal adjustments are needed for a strong marriage?

* What other adjustments are common in the early years of marriage?

Chapter Objectives

After studying this chapter, you will be able to
* **identify** patterns a couple may use to handle their differences.

* **relate** patterns of adjustment to the quality of a marriage relationship.

* **determine** interpersonal, financial, and social adjustments that add quality to a relationship.

* **identify** outside sources of help for strengthening a marriage.

Life Sketch

Carey and her cousin Sasha were watching Sasha's brother and his new wife cut the cake at their wedding reception.

"I can't wait to get married," sighed Carey. "Your brother and his wife seem so in love and she looks like a fairy tale princess in that beautiful dress."

"Well, this is just the beginning of their life together as a married couple," Sasha replied. "They are really happy, but marriage certainly isn't a fairy tale."

Sasha's older sister had been married for several years, and Sasha knew that marriage wasn't always easy. Her sister and her husband worked hard to maintain their healthy, happy marriage. In addition, Sasha's parents were divorced and she had observed many arguments between her mother and father. Sasha knew there was a lot to consider before getting married.

Getting Started

You have probably observed a variety of marriage relationships in your family and community. Some marriages may seem more successful than others, with qualities you admire. These couples seem to thrive. They are able to work together and be happy. You have probably seen other marriages in which couples do not get along well. Their relationships seem to be divided, unstable, and unhappy. You may wonder why some marriages succeed and others fail.

No one formula will guarantee a perfect marriage. However, couples can develop a quality relationship in the following ways:
* dealing effectively with conflicts in their day-to-day living
* learning to balance interpersonal relations
* adapting to changes in financial and social areas

As you will see in this chapter, all couples must make some adjustments in their marriage relationship. As they grow and change over time, they will need to continue to make adjustments to keep the quality of their relationship high.

section 9:1

Patterns of Adjustment

Sharpen Your Reading

As you read this section, summarize how a person would deal with conflict using each pattern of adjustment.

Boost Your Vocabulary

Write a scenario in which a person uses one of the patterns of adjustment. Role-play the scenario with a partner.

Know Key Terms

marital adjustment
continuum
hostility
concession
accommodation

All married couples experience conflict in their relationships. Whenever two people live together on a day-to-day basis, some disagreements will occur. Couples deal with these conflicts by making adjustments. **Marital adjustment** is the process couples use to modify their relationship as needed throughout their married life. The goal of making these adjustments is to develop and maintain a high level of quality in the relationship. As quality goes up, the relationship is more likely to last.

The quality of most marriage relationships is somewhere on a continuum. The **continuum** represents changes in the feelings and attitudes that a couple might have about their relationship. At one end of the continuum, the relationship is happy, satisfying, and fulfilling. At the other end, the relationship is unhappy, dissatisfying, unfulfilling, and empty. Most marriage relationships move back and forth somewhere in the middle of the continuum.

When conflicts occur, couples make adjustments in their marriage by using certain methods. These basic patterns of adjustment include hostility, concession, accommodation, and compromise, 9-1. The method they choose may depend on the situation. A couple's success in making fair adjustments will determine the degree of happiness in their marriage.

Hostility

Sometimes couples handle their differences with **hostility**. They never really settle conflicts and do not agree on solutions. They continually quarrel about these areas. Sometimes they may hit or be physically abusive in their anger and frustration. Unresolved hostility has negative effects on a relationship. If it begins in one area of the relationship, it will gradually spread to other parts of it.

This method of handling differences produces the lowest quality in a relationship. Because the couple does not find any satisfactory solutions, the marriage relationship often weakens.

Use What You Learn

Where do you think a relationship would fall on the continuum if all conflicts are handled with hostility?

Concession

There will be times in a marriage relationship that you or your spouse just give in to the other. Rather than work to reach a joint agreement, you give in to agree with your partner. This method is known as **concession**. If both spouses give in some of the time, the quality of the relationship can be quite high. However, if you or your

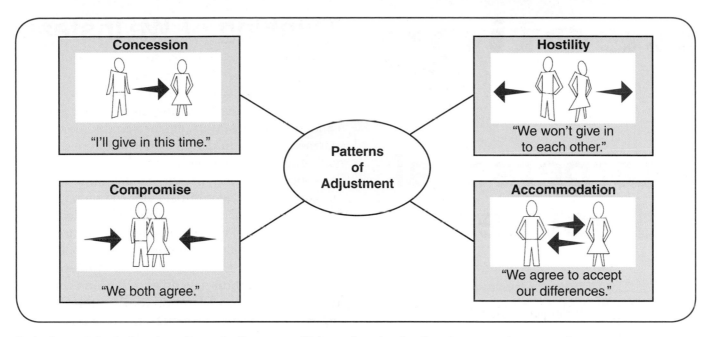

9-1 A couple's choice of a pattern of adjustment will depend on the situation they are trying to resolve.

spouse feel that you are giving in all the time, dissatisfaction will grow. The quality of the relationship will then decrease.

Accommodation

Sometimes you and your spouse may not be able to find an agreeable solution. Instead you may use **accommodation**. You accept each other's differences and agree to live with them. You put up with each other's behavior or opinion. No mutual agreement on the issue is reached. The differences still exist, but they do not obstruct the relationship. This method does not increase the quality of the relationship, but it helps couples work around their differences.

Compromise

Compromise tends to be the most satisfying way to resolve differences in a marriage. When couples compromise, they find a solution to which they both agree. Both must be willing to give-and-take to reach an agreeable solution.

Of all the methods described, resolving differences through compromise will bring the greatest satisfaction to a relationship. A couple will feel their ideas have been expressed and accepted. No one wins or loses. Both will feel they have taken part in finding a positive solution.

Couples most likely will use all the above methods at some time in their marriage. However, no one method can be used all the time since conflicts vary. Looking at the pros and cons of each possible solution will enable you to choose the best method for handling the problem. The better you become at choosing the best method for your situation, the more satisfying your relationship will become.

Review Section 9:1

1. In your own words, briefly explain how the quality of marriage relates to a continuum.
2. Explain the difference between *accommodation* and *compromise*.
3. Give an example of how a couple can compromise to resolve their differences.

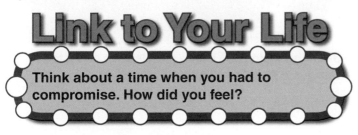

Think about a time when you had to compromise. How did you feel?

section 9:2

Interpersonal Adjustments

Sharpen Your Reading

Imagine you are a marriage counselor. As you read, develop questions that you could ask a couple related to each area of interpersonal adjustment.

Boost Your Vocabulary

Give four examples of what a person might say if using the sandwich approach to express an opinion in a sensitive situation.

Know Key Terms

interpersonal adjustments
pair adjustment
sandwich approach
active interaction
passive interaction
marital roles

Marriage is the joining of two unique individuals. Each person has his or her own personal preferences and opinions. These differences do not change after marriage. The couple must learn to adjust to each other. The changes they make as they learn to live with each other are called **interpersonal adjustments**.

Thinking of *We* Instead of *Me*

When couples adjust their individual lifestyles to have a satisfying life together, it is called **pair adjustment**. It starts in dating as partners seek to find similarities in interests, values, goals, and expectations.

Once you marry, the day-to-day adjustments of being a couple continue. Prior to marriage, you have a great deal of independence. You decide when you will eat, shop, or sleep. After marriage, these matters make a difference to someone else as well, 9-2. Even trivial habits can become subjects for joint discussion and decision making.

Sometimes consideration for the other's desires and feelings is enough to settle a difference. If either spouse sticks with self-centered *me* attitudes, hostility can increase. If hostility expands and spreads to other areas of the relationship, then it becomes more difficult to resolve any issues.

9-2 After marriage, a couple must learn to adjust to changes in their daily routine.

Think More About It
Why do you think pair adjustment is an ongoing task for a couple?

Accepting Habits

No one is perfect. You are not, and your spouse will not be. You may overlook each other's irritating habits while dating. You may even think your partner will change these habits after you are married. However, after marriage, habits do not always change or go away. Instead, habits often become more irritating.

When you first marry, you are learning new behaviors and establishing new routines. Many everyday behaviors can cause friction as you adjust to living with someone else. It is normal that a few of your habits will irritate your spouse as well. In a marriage, accepting minor irritations is easier when both people focus on the positive aspects of their relationship.

Use What You Learn

Why is it often difficult to change a habit? What are some habits that could cause conflict in a marriage?

Showing Appreciation

Praise, sincere compliments, and thoughtfulness are ways of showing appreciation. Both verbal and nonverbal expressions of appreciation can keep a positive atmosphere in the relationship and also keep the romantic spark alive. When couples show appreciation for each other, the quality of their relationship will increase.

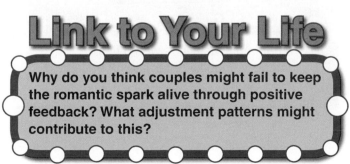

Why do you think couples might fail to keep the romantic spark alive through positive feedback? What adjustment patterns might contribute to this?

Keeping Communication Lines Open

Open and honest communication needs to take place often in a marriage. Daily sharing of events, situations, frustrations, or successes can help you keep these communication lines open. Planning a set time each day just to talk can help make communication a priority. Deep, interpersonal sharing takes time to develop, so couples also need to plan for longer periods to talk. A relaxed environment free of distractions and away from interruptions is best.

Sometimes you may need to express an opinion to your spouse about a sensitive topic. Planning what to say before discussing sensitive issues can help avoid an argument. If you have a criticism to make, use the **sandwich approach** by putting a negative comment between two positive comments. Taking time to develop patterns of honest, open communication will help keep the quality of a marriage relationship high.

What elements of communication are missing when a couple try to carry on a conversation while one person is focused on another task?

Resolving Conflicts

If a couple is in the habit of taking time daily to share their thoughts and feelings, it will be easier to resolve differences when they come up. If handled right away, the source of the problem is easier to identify. Then, as a couple you can use problem-solving skills. You can identify possible solutions, discuss them, and choose one solution with which you both agree. Then you can develop a plan to carry it out.

Use Problem-Solving Skills

In each stage of the problem-solving process, you may need to negotiate. That includes listening to each other's opinions and considering the views of both. Give-and-take is needed to compromise and come to a solution agreeable to both.

Some differences can become major disagreements. They will weaken the relationship if they are not resolved. If disagreements build on each other, hostile feelings are more likely to grow. Hostility may result in anger and placing blame on each other. Using the problem-solving process is difficult when the couple is tense.

When upset, allow time for your emotions to calm down. You will have greater success in reaching a compromise if you both keep your emotions calm. Use empathy and try to see the issue from your partner's point of view. Keep your voices even and use good listening skills. Respect and acceptance of each other's opinions help both persons maintain a positive self-esteem throughout the discussion.

Use your skills for identifying the source of the problem. Think about the real cause of your disagreement. You may discover the issue that brings on the conflict may not be the real cause.

Once an issue is identified, you need to stick to that issue and resolve it. Do not bring up past arguments. When resolving your differences, no one person wins or loses. You both win if you can resolve the difference in a way that benefits your relationship.

Staying Actively Involved with Each Other

You and your spouse will continue to grow and change throughout life. Time spent together will help you keep in touch with each other's thoughts and feelings. This will help your relationship continue to be strong.

Active Versus Passive Interaction

Active interaction involves physical and verbal exchanges between two people who are doing something together. When you actively do things together, you learn more about what your spouse is thinking and feeling. Your marriage relationship will be strengthened if you and your spouse spend time in active interaction, 9-3.

9-3 A couple can actively interact by enjoying a bike ride. Taking part in joint activities can help them keep their relationship growing.

In **passive interaction**, you are involved only as an observer or listener, such as watching television or reading books. Passive activities can become active if you discuss the programs you watch or the books that you read. Active interaction produces more growth in a relationship than passive interaction.

Use What You Learn

What family activities would fit the category of active interaction? passive interaction?

Meeting Emotional Needs

People experience satisfaction when their emotional needs are fulfilled. Your satisfaction in marriage will increase as your emotional needs are met through the relationship. The need for love, respect, and self-actualization are some of these emotional needs.

The Need to Be Loved

The primary emotional need met in marriage is the need to love and to be loved. In a strong relationship, mature love continues to grow as you spend time together and share personal thoughts, ideas, and feelings. Such sharing cultivates feelings of acceptance, belonging, and importance. Through deep, intimate sharing, you become more attached to each other. You depend on each other and you meet each other's needs.

Think More About It
How could failure to share thoughts, feelings, and ideas result in the loss of love in a relationship?

The Need for Respect and Self Actualization

As mature love grows, other emotional needs are being met. The need for respect and acceptance is met when your spouse makes you feel that you are an important part of his or her life. Once this need is met, you can strive to grow and reach your full potential in other areas of your life.

Each spouse needs to find some emotional satisfaction in personal accomplishments. The person who continues to develop in other areas of life adds vitality to the relationship. In this way, the quality of a relationship is strengthened.

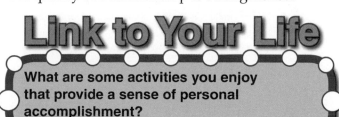

Link to Your Life

What are some activities you enjoy that provide a sense of personal accomplishment?

Experiencing Sexual Satisfaction

An important aspect of sharing love in a marriage is the sexual experience. Sexual satisfaction increases as the partners become emotionally bonded to each other. Trust and commitment to each other can help the couple experience a more meaningful sexual relationship. Mutual respect and appreciation can build positive esteem through the sexual experience. Showing sensitivity to each other's thoughts and desires can also help a couple experience sexual fulfillment.

For most couples, sexual satisfaction increases as the relationship develops. Love grows and trust builds. Respect and empathy are shared. The couple continues their commitment to each other.

Keeping Balance in the Relationship

Balance is maintained when both spouses work to contribute fully to the relationship. In a balanced relationship, both feel important to the relationship and to each other. There is no need to compete since both partners know that each has strengths and weaknesses. They are committed to cooperate for the benefit of their relationship.

A relationship could become unbalanced if one spouse has expectations that the other cannot meet. Some people count on having all their emotional needs met by their spouse. Such an unrealistic hope can put too much stress on a relationship.

Think More About It
What type of interactions might take place in an unbalanced relationship?

Adjusting to Marital Roles

Many of the roles you have before marriage will continue after you marry. After marriage, these roles change somewhat. You become a married son or daughter, living independent of your family perhaps for the first time. You will also be a son-in-law or daughter-in-law, roles for which different expectations apply.

The **marital roles** you may be expected to fulfill after marriage include spouse, friend, wage earner, cook, caregiver, or housekeeper. If you decide to have children, you also acquire the role of mother or father. Each role carries certain responsibilities and expectations.

9-4 Cooperating to carry out a task shows teamwork in the relationship.

> ## Investigate Further
>
> **How might the work of the family (cooking meals, doing laundry, cleaning house) result in conflict in early married life?**

Keeping a Cooperative Attitude

Adjusting to new roles is easier when a couple cooperates and works together, 9-4. Before a couple marries, they usually discuss their expectations for each other. When partners are able to live up to each other's expectations, their relationship is enhanced. They are happier with themselves and each other. Living out these expectations will be easier if the couple has a cooperative attitude, is sensitive to each other's needs, and is willing to adjust.

Periodic Evaluation

Couples need to talk about their roles often. Roles do not stay the same. Sometimes new roles

are added, such as the role of parent. With new roles come new responsibilities. Taking time to communicate openly and reevaluate expectations can help couples adjust to changing roles.

Review Section 9:2

1. List eight ways a couple can improve the quality of their relationship in interpersonal areas.
2. Explain how pair adjustment affects a couple's relationship.
3. Describe what is meant by the sandwich approach.
4. Explain how active interaction improves the quality of a relationship more than passive activities do.
5. Give three examples of common marital roles.

section 9:3

Adapting to Financial and Social Changes

Sharpen Your Reading

List the financial and social changes you would experience if you got married. As you read, identify strategies that would help you adjust to these changes.

Boost Your Vocabulary

List people that a couple might consider substitute family after moving into a new community.

Know Key Terms

substitute family
marriage enrichment programs
marriage counseling

As a couple adjust to married life, different views about money management and social commitments may surface. A couple will need to agree on how much money each person will spend, who will pay the bills, and how much income should be saved. As a couple establishes their identity as an independent unit, relationships with family members and friends may change. Discussing financial and social

issues before marriage can help a couple adjust more easily. Participating in marriage enrichment programs or counseling can also help a couple maintain their marriage relationship and resolve conflict.

Financial Adjustments

Different views about money management can be a major source of conflict in a marriage. Before you marry, you will likely experience the freedom of handling your own money. After marriage, both partners are responsible for the family finances. That is, both have the right to know what the family income totals are and where, how much, and why money is spent. After marriage, lifestyle adjustments may be needed in order to live on the income available.

A couple should jointly manage their money. This approach provides accountability and can help each partner keep track of the family funds. Chapter 23, "Managing Your Money," will discuss money management in detail.

Investigate Further

Why do you think that money issues are the number one source of arguments in marriages?

Social Adjustments

Throughout dating and engagement, a couple becomes identified as a pair. After marriage, the couple needs to establish their pair identity and grow as an independent unit. They need to make their own family decisions and be responsible for their own lives.

A couple establishes their own identity as an independent unit by living on their own, 9-5. They make their own decisions based on discussion between the two of them. They take responsibility for the consequences of their decisions. If they make a mistake, they learn from it together and go on. At this time, family and friends can be supportive and offer encouragement. Newlywed couples need this independence for their relationship to grow.

9-5 Choosing an apartment and living on their own can help newlyweds develop their own identity as a couple.

Use What You Learn

How could a couple's growth in pair identity be affected if parents interfere too often?

Relating to Family

A couple's marriage joins two families. A person's family is a very integral part of oneself, as are family ties. These strong attachments, which are formed during infancy, continue to some degree throughout life.

In the marriage relationship, the partners seek to develop a similar type of attachment with each other. At the same time, some feelings of attachment to family members naturally continue. The marital relationship improves when good relationships are maintained with family members.

Keeping a Balance

Good relationships with family members are balanced. Spending too much time with family members takes away from the pair relationship. On the other hand, too little contact with family members causes hurt feelings. Parents can feel ignored. As a result, conflicts may develop. A couple can discuss in advance how they will handle family occasions, such as vacations and holidays. After they have come to a joint decision, they can share their decision with both spouses' families.

Keeping Family Counsel in Perspective

Good family relationships occur if the couple can show respect for both sets of parents. This does not mean the couple does whatever the parents ask. Instead, they can listen to family members' suggestions and advice. They can be courteous and thank parents for their concern. However, the couple needs to be firm in making their own decisions.

Link to Your Life

What communication skills will help you speak for yourselves as a couple when handling pressures from parents and family members?

Supporting Parents in Their Adjustment

Parents also have adjustments to make when their children marry. The new role of family members is one of encouragement and emotional support. When asked, the family can share their opinions as suggestions, not commands.

Sometimes this new role is hard for parents. They may be accustomed to giving guidance and being heavily involved in their children's decisions. It takes time for them to adjust to their new role.

Adjusting Friendships

A strong network of *mutual friends* can add to the quality of a marriage. As a couple builds their identity as a pair, they may find their friends will change. They will more likely spend time together with joint friends. Sincere friends can listen with empathy and provide constructive advice. They can share with a couple in both easy and tough times. In addition, both spouses will have personal friendships they will want to maintain. Good friends can strengthen a marital relationship.

Use What You Learn

What could a couple do to develop mutual friends?

Adjusting to a New Community

Young married couples sometimes move from their home community into a new community. Substitute family relationships often develop when relatives live far away. A **substitute family** is a group of nonrelatives who encourage or help you in a way that family members would if they were present. Most communities have several organizations where people can meet others with similar interests. Clubs or recreational programs provide opportunities to share common goals and work together for the community's benefit. Through these activities, a couple can find new friends and adjust to their new community, 9-6.

Sources for Help

A stable and happy marriage does not automatically happen. Some couples have more success than others in adjusting to their relationships. Others do not adjust well or resolve conflicts easily. Their marriage may be troubled. Couples may seek to strengthen or improve their marriage by attending marital enrichment programs or marriage counseling.

Marriage Enrichment Programs

Organized programs designed to help couples maintain or improve their marriage relationships are called **marriage enrichment programs**. Their main purpose is to keep marriages strong and help them grow. These programs are usually sponsored by community service agencies, religious groups, or educational groups. They usually seek to help couples in the areas of personal growth, growth as a couple, and financial planning.

9-6 Getting involved in community events is one way for a couple to adjust to a new community.

Choosing a Marriage Enrichment Program

Couples should seek a marital enrichment program designed for their particular need. Couples should also check to be sure the program leader is a qualified professional in the family counseling field. Recommendations from past participants may also be helpful in making a choice.

Marriage Counseling

Marriage counseling is somewhat different from marriage enrichment. **Marriage counseling** also seeks to improve marriages, but usually focuses on helping couples identify and resolve existing problems. As part of the counseling, marital enrichment programs may be used to strengthen various areas of the relationship.

When looking for a marriage counselor, couples should seek a qualified, licensed marriage counselor. Since many states do not require marriage counselors to be licensed, some counselors may be practicing without professional training. Couples interested in finding a qualified counselor in their area can contact the American Association for Marriage and Family Therapy for a list of accredited marriage counselors.

Many religious institutions also provide family and marriage counseling and enrichment programs. Couples can also check the Internet or Yellow Pages for listings of government or private social service agencies that offer marriage counseling. In every case, it is important to check the program's purpose and cost as well as the counselor's qualifications.

Review Section 9:3

1. How should a couple adjust to financial changes after marriage?
2. Explain why a couple needs to establish pair identity when relating to others.
3. Name two issues a couple should discuss to help keep family relationships balanced.
4. Describe how parents can help a young couple establish their pair identity.
5. List three ways in which marriage enrichment programs may increase the quality of a marriage relationship.
6. Explain how marriage counseling is different from marriage enrichment.

Think It Through

Adjusting to Marriage

Salvador and Isela have been married for a year. Their first few months of married life seemed so exciting. They spent most of their time together. They would shop together, meet each other for lunch, watch a movie, or have friends in for dinner.

As the weeks passed, however, they found themselves spending less time together. Isela had to work late at the office a few evenings. She also accepted a position on the board of a volunteer organization, which involved evening and weekend events. Salvador joined a bowling league and was gone a few evenings with his friends. He also enrolled in a weekend class at the local community college. Isela and Salvador found they were together less and less. Both were feeling hurt that the romantic spark was disappearing from their relationship.

Arguments became frequent and usually they ended with each blaming the other for the situation. Salvador thought Isela should work fewer hours so she could be home earlier. Isela thought Salvador should quit bowling so they could at least have evenings together. They did not invite their mutual friends over anymore. They did not feel very romantic toward each other as their relationship gradually got worse. Sometimes they wondered why they ever got married.

Questions to Guide Your Thinking

1. What are some of the areas in which Salvador and Isela are having difficulty adjusting?

2. What adjustment patterns are they using to resolve their differences?

3. How are their patterns of adjustment affecting the following areas?

   • trust

   • communication

   • cooperation

   • the growth of mature love

   • the quality of their relationship

4. How could they use compromise to improve the quality of their relationship?

5. In what areas could Salvador and Isela's relationship benefit from marriage counseling?

Chapter Summary

A marriage that is high in quality is happy, satisfying, and fulfilling. The quality of most marriage relationships varies from time to time. The goal of making adjustments in married life is to try and maintain a high level of quality.

Marriage partners will differ in many aspects of their lives because they are two unique people. The way they handle their differences will affect their relationship. When they can settle their differences and find agreeable solutions, the quality of their relationship will be higher.

As a couple adjust to living together, they will need to resolve differences in many interpersonal, financial, and social areas. Sometimes they may seek marriage counseling or marriage enrichment programs to help them make adjustments and improve their relationship.

Assess...

Your Knowledge

1. What are four different ways that people could handle conflict?

2. What are common areas of adjustment in the early years of marriage?

3. What are some sources of help for couples who have difficulty adjusting to a marriage relationship?

Your Understanding

4. How can a couple handle conflict in a way that will build their relationship?

5. How can a couple make day-to-day choices that will increase the quality of their marriage?

6. How can marriage counseling help a couple improve their relationship?

Your Skills

7. Identify a scenario in which you used concession to resolve a conflict. Then give an example of how you could have used accommodation or compromise to resolve the same conflict.

8. Explain how you would resolve the following dilemma in a way that builds relationships: You have been looking forward to attending a playoff game with your close friend. A week before the game, your spouse asks you to attend an important event at the same time as the game.

Think Critically

9. **Writing.** Reflect on your personal feelings and desires about spending quality time with your family after you are married. Identify specific occasions for which it is important for you to be with them. Summarize your thoughts in a paragraph expressing how you expect to carry out your personal desires for family involvement after you are married.

10. Observe a family TV sitcom that depicts interactions between a married couple. In a paragraph, describe the interactions that you observe. Analyze those interactions for patterns for communicating, making decisions, and solving problems. Then evaluate the interactions for their potential impact on the quality of the marriage relationship. *Group option:* Work with a group and observe the same TV program. Analyze the interactions together and prepare a group report to share with the class.

11. **Writing.** Write a paper titled "Planning for Quality in My Marriage." Explain how premarital choices could help decrease potential conflicts in each of the three areas of adjustment: interpersonal, financial, and social.

12. Write a scenario depicting a problem in the early years of marriage. (This may be a true-to-life situation you observe or one you predict will result in a problem.) Share your scenario with a classmate. Read and analyze the other's scenario and write a paragraph identifying some steps the couple could take to improve the quality of their relationship. *Choice:* Read your scenario aloud and have your partner share the improvement steps with the class.

Connect to Your Community

13. **Research.** Interview a marriage counselor or religious leader. Ask questions about the major conflicts and difficulties couples experience in the early years of marriage. Summarize the counselor's responses.

14. Invite a marriage counselor to be a guest speaker and respond to some scenarios that you have written that depict common problems in a marriage relationship. *Choice:* Have the speaker respond to scenarios created by the class for Activity 12 of the *Think Critically* section.

15. **Reading, writing.** Clip an advice column from a newspaper that deals with marital problems. In a paragraph, evaluate the situation and identify what type of adjustment pattern is being used by the couple. Identify what type of adjustment pattern the columnist is suggesting. Do you agree with the column writer's advice?

16. **Research.** Over a one-week period, analyze how students in your school use the four patterns of adjustment in their day-to-day relationships. First, create a chart with the four patterns of adjustment listed down the left side. In the second column, draw a picture that depicts how each pattern might play out in real life. Then add columns for five days. Record a short description each time you observe students using a pattern of adjustment. At the end of your observation period, write a paragraph describing which pattern you observed being used most often.

Use Technology

17. **Research.** Using the Internet, research the various marriage counseling services available. Include both marital enrichment programs and marriage counseling services. Locate a minimum of three different programs, and identify the purposes of each program and the credentials required for the leaders. Identify specific services that are available in your community.

18. **Math.** Survey three married couples: (A) a young couple, (B) a couple with young children, and (C) an older, retired couple. Ask each couple to list the top five issues likely to cause conflict or irritation with their spouse. Use a computer program to create a bar graph showing the results for each age group. Compare your findings with a partner in your class.

19. **Social studies.** Search the Internet to identify different role expectations for married couples in other cultures. Choose one culture and identify how their marital role expectations differ from yours. Imagine what your life would be as a spouse of a person from that culture. In a paragraph, describe the role expectations that would exist for you if you lived in that culture.

20. Using a word processing program, create a questionnaire to use in an interview to identify how couples make decisions related to money management. Interview each partner separately. Create a table showing their responses. Compare their responses to your questions. Write a paragraph summarizing your findings. Then describe how you would like to handle money management in your marriage relationship. *Group option:* Work in a small group, compare your findings, and combine your data into one table.

Connecting with Career Clusters

Human Services ♥

Pathways

- Early Childhood Development & Services
- Counseling & Mental Health Services
- Family & Community Services
- Personal Care Services
- Consumer Services

Marriage and Family Therapist

Marriage and family therapists (also called counselors) work with individuals, couples, and families to resolve emotional conflicts. The goal is to improve communication among members of the family, change individual perceptions of one another, modify behavior, and thereby help families and individuals avoid crises in their lives.

These specialists work with clients to set goals and carry out therapy plans, often collaborating with other professionals. Many are self-employed, working out of their homes or private offices.

Marriage and family therapists and counselors often work flexible hours so those in crisis can obtain help when needed. Evening or weekend counseling sessions are common.

A master's degree is usually required to enter the field. Supervised field experience plus a license or certificate may also be required.

Career Outlook

A job in this field requires high levels of physical and emotional energy; an ability to work under stress and maintain the confidentiality of clients; and a desire to help people improve their lives.

Faster-than-average job growth is expected because more people are seeking help for their marital and family problems. Social service agencies employ the largest number of marriage and family therapists. Salary can range from around $25,200 to above $69,000. Median annual earnings in 2006 were $43,210.

Explore

Internet Research

Research your state's requirements for credentialing marriage and family therapists or counselors. Locate an accredited university that offers marriage and family therapist or counselor training and identify the courses required. Prepare a report summarizing this career information.

Job Shadowing

Ask your school counselor to recommend a counseling open house or workshop that would present a clear picture of a typical day for a marriage and family therapist. Write a report describing what you learned about the profession and whether such a career might suit you.

Community Service/Volunteer

Connect with the local office of United Way and volunteer your services to work with children whose families are in crisis. Keep a journal of your activities and analyze your conversations with the children. Again, remember confidentiality.

Project

Do a case study for experience in gathering information as you maintain utmost confidentiality throughout the project. Research what data should go into a case study. Choose a friend (someone willing to talk to you openly) who has a family-related conflict. List the questions you could ask to help identify the root of the problem. Write up your case study.

Interview

Interview a local religious leader who provides marriage and family counseling for congregation members. Inquire about the frustrations, challenges, and rewards of the job.

Part-Time Job

Apply for a part-time job as a receptionist for a social services agency or clinic that provides family counseling. Keep a journal of your work experiences and record any relevant career information you learn from the job.

Unit 3
Establishing a Family

Chapter 10

Choosing to Parent

Section 10:**1**
Understanding Parenting

Section 10:**2**
Qualities Needed by Parents

Section 10:**3**
Parenting Issues

Key Questions

Questions to answer as you study this chapter:

- How does becoming a parent impact a person's life?
- What does It take to be a good parent?
- What are your choices if you cannot become pregnant?

Chapter Objectives

After studying this chapter, you will be able to

- **recognize** the importance of the parenting role.
- **evaluate** factors affecting the decision to become parents.
- **identify** personal qualities needed by parents.
- **explain** the positive effects children have on parents.
- **describe** parenting options for infertile couples.

Life Sketch

"Jessica is so cute and fun!" everyone said about Catina's new baby. Catina smiled but said nothing. She couldn't let her friends know that sometimes she resented the baby. How could one tiny person require so much work? Jessica had to be fed every three hours around the clock, rocked and held often, and changed and bathed several times a day.

Her husband Roland spent little time at home. He worked during the day and took college classes in the evening. He often studied late at the college library because the baby was too noisy.

Roland and Catina had married young. Catina planned to work while Roland finished college, but an unexpected pregnancy sure changed their plans! Catina became ill, missed too much work, and lost her job. The medical bills wiped out their savings. Now Catina and Roland argued often. Their relationship was becoming more tense by the week.

Getting Started

How would parenthood affect your life? Would your daily schedule and free time change? How would your finances be affected? Would you still have time for your friends? How would your plans for an education or a career be affected? As you will see in this chapter, parenting is an important decision that deserves careful thought.

section 10:1

Understanding Parenting

Sharpen Your Reading

Review the headings in this section and write some questions you have for each topic. Then, as you read, write the answers to your questions.

Boost Your Vocabulary

Describe what *parenting* means to you.

Know Key Terms

parenting
anemia
preeclampsia

Becoming a parent causes major changes in a person's life. Many of these changes relate to the responsibilities that go with caring for a child. New demands would be made on your time, energy, money, and emotions.

A *parent* is anyone who is biologically or legally a father or a mother. Once you become a parent, you are always a parent. You cannot reverse that status even if you do not fulfill the parenting role.

The Parenting Role

Parenting means using skills to care for and raise a child to adulthood. The biological parents usually fulfill the parenting role in their children's lives. Sometimes, one biological parent carries the responsibility alone. In other cases, grandparents, other relatives, foster parents, or adoptive parents take on the parenting role.

Becoming a parent is one of life's roles that a person can acquire with no preparation. Experience is not required to become a parent, yet parenting is perhaps the most important role you might fulfill. Parents shape the lives of the next generation. Parenting practices have a long-term effect on the future. You and your spouse can be effective parents if you are prepared to have children and be responsible parents.

Parents are not the only influence on their children. Other factors also play an important part in a child's life. Family members, teachers, a child's friends, society, and media all have some effect on a child. However, a child's family and home have the greatest effect on his or her development.

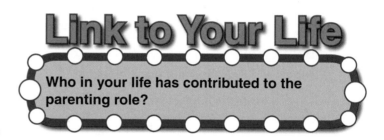

Link to Your Life

Who in your life has contributed to the parenting role?

Deciding Whether to Become a Parent

Are you ready to have children? Do you both want to become parents? These questions should be considered by couples as they think about parenthood.

As a couple decides whether they are ready for parenthood, they will consider many personal questions, 10-1.

- *Their goals and what they want to accomplish.* How would children fit into those plans?

- *Their relationship as a couple.* Is the relationship strong and growing? Would a child enrich that relationship?

- *How they relate to children.* Do they enjoy children and communicate well with them? Do they both want children?

Parenthood Decisions

What are our life goals?

Do we have a secure and stable relationship?

Do we both want children?

Can we accept changes in our lifestyle?

Do we have any hereditary health problems that our child might inherit?

Are we in good physical health so we can handle the physical and emotional stress of raising children?

At what age should we start having children?

Do we understand how a child grows and develops?

How do we view child care and guidance?

Are we prepared for child-related expenses and lifetime changes in our budget?

How will children affect our career plans?

10-1 To make wise decisions about parenthood, couples should carefully consider these questions.

At some point in your life, you may face decisions about parenthood. Using decision-making skills is one approach you and your spouse can use to make a responsible decision. This process can help you review the alternatives and consequences of each choice. An understanding of the factors that may affect each choice will help you reach a satisfying joint decision.

Think More About It

Why is it important that a couple make a parenting decision jointly?

Reasons for Not Parenting

Although many couples choose to have children, others choose not to become parents. After evaluating their individual and joint feelings, they may decide not to have children or to delay having children.

Some couples choose not to become parents for personal reasons. They may enjoy the freedom of a childless lifestyle. They do not want to commit themselves to raising a child. They may want to invest more time in their careers than in parenting. They may have diseases that could be inherited. They may have had an unhappy childhood and fear that they will repeat the cycle in their family.

Other couples may choose not to have children for less personal reasons. They may feel that the world is overpopulated. They may look at the economic problems in the world and feel they could not care for a child. High divorce rates, high crime rates, or an increase in child abuse may be other reasons for their choice.

Sometimes a couple choose not to have children, but their decision is temporary. They decide to delay parenting for a short time. They may feel they are not ready to become parents now. Perhaps they have goals they want to reach first. Goals such as a better job, more income or savings, further education, or better housing are common.

A couple's decision to delay parenting should be discussed periodically. They need to evaluate their progress toward goals or discuss their reasons for waiting. Then they should identify when they do want to have a child. Sometimes a couple wait too long. If the wife is older than the safest childbearing years, risks to her health and the baby's health increase.

The Age of the Mother

Age is quite important for the prospective mother. The health and well-being of mother and child may be at risk if a mother is too young or too old. The safest childbearing years for women are between the ages of 20 and 35.

Although women can bear children before and after this range, the health risks for both mother and child increase. Babies born to women over 35 have an increased risk of complications such as Down syndrome. This condition is caused by abnormal chromosome formation.

Teenage girls can have problems with pregnancy because they have not fully developed physically. A pregnancy places an added strain on the young mother's body. Also, a teen mother does not always receive proper medical care or nutrition. She is twice as likely to miscarry the baby during the first few months of pregnancy. Some of the greater risks faced by young mothers include the following:

- **Anemia** is a condition of weakness and fatigue caused by an iron-deficient diet. An anemic mother has too few red blood cells to carry oxygen to all parts of her body and to the growing baby.

- **Preeclampsia**, also called *toxemia* or *pregnancy-induced hypertension (PIH),* includes swelling and high blood pressure. This can cause damage to the mother's organs as well as risk of premature delivery or stillbirth.

- *Placenta abruptio* is the separation of the growing baby from the wall of the mother's uterus. Once this separation takes place, the baby cannot survive. Excess bleeding may result, endangering the mother's life as well.

Teen mothers often have low-birthweight or premature babies. These problems often pose increased health risks for babies at birth. Chances of birth injuries and mental retardation increase. The risk of illness and death within the first year of the baby's life is also higher for babies of teen mothers, 10-2.

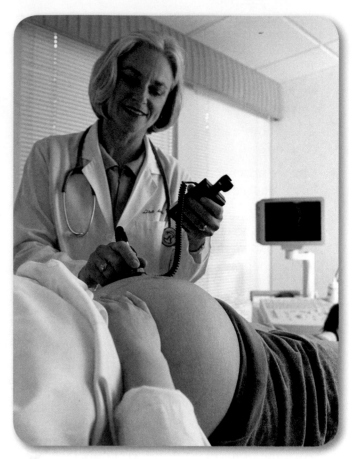

10-2 Pregnancy poses fewer health risks when a mother is between the ages of 20 and 35.

Think More About It
What are some common risks to pregnant teens?

Parenting in the Teen Years

Age is an important factor for potential mother and father when considering parenthood. A couple should be mature enough to handle the related roles and responsibilities. Most teens are not ready to face the emotional, social, and financial problems involved.

Normally, the teen years are a time of gaining independence and developing close relationships. An unplanned pregnancy can cause emotional stress as the couple try to cope with new roles. For teen parents, the arrival of a baby greatly limits their social life. They soon find out that a baby is a full-time responsibility. They see that their friends have more freedom and are not tied to any major responsibility. As a result, the teen parents may find it difficult to fit in with their teen friends.

Teen parents also face financial difficulties fitting into the adult world. The demands of child care can keep them from completing an education or making future career plans. Teen parents are more likely to be unemployed or have low-paying jobs. Sometimes the teen father offers no financial support, so the mother must be dependent on others. Stable financial resources could help teens in their adjustment. However, it is difficult for teen parents to acquire them.

Link to Your Life

How would becoming a parent today affect your life?

Reasons for Parenting

One of the most important decisions a couple must make together concerns parenthood. After considering the effect this decision will have on their lives, most couples decide they want to have children.

Healthy Reasons

For many couples, parenting is a means of personal extension. It is a way to pass on a part of themselves into the future. They are able to share their lives with a new and younger life, 10-3. They can extend the family into a new generation.

Some couples want the personal experience of having children. They want to know how it feels to bring a child into the world. Sharing their love and nurturing and guiding a child to adulthood is important to them. They believe parenting will be a rewarding experience.

These are positive reasons for wanting to parent. Attitudes of sharing and giving to benefit another will increase a couple's effectiveness as parents. Healthy reasons are evidence of the emotional maturity needed to be responsible parents.

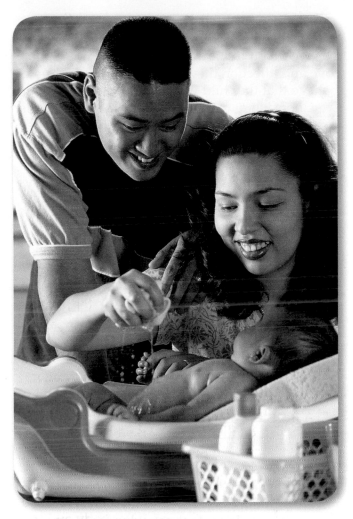

10-3 The desire to share their life and love with children motivates many couples to become parents.

Unhealthy Reasons

Other reasons for parenting are not so positive. Some people may want to parent because having children brings prestige. Others react to outside pressures from family or friends. For example, the couple's parents may want to be grandparents.

Sometimes couples choose to become parents to show their physical competence. They want to prove to others that they are adults and can produce children.

For some, parenting is a means of gaining personal power. Having a child depend on them gives them a sense of power. In some cases, they may desire to have power over the child. Sometimes having children gives one parent power over the other.

To gain love is another reason that some couples choose to become parents. They may believe that the child will provide them with the love and affection they need. Some couples may believe that the child will improve their marriage.

Choosing parenthood because of what a child can do for the couple is a sign of immaturity. The need for esteem, power, or love are best met through the couple's adult relationships and other areas of accomplishment.

Weigh the Facts

What are the key differences between the healthy and unhealthy reasons for parenting?

Having Realistic Expectations

A decision to parent needs to be based on realistic expectations. These expectations should be based on facts. If parents have unrealistic expectations, they can hinder the child's development. They may be too protective and not allow the child a chance to learn to do things alone. On the other hand, they may not be protective enough, which could result in the child getting hurt.

Suppose a couple decides to have a child because they want power, greater self-esteem, or a fix for a troubled marriage. What happens when a child cannot fill those needs? Unrealistic expectations can result in abuse, disappointment, rejection, and unhappiness for all involved.

Preparing for parenthood can help married couples develop realistic expectations for parent-child relationships. It can help them understand how to nurture a child's growth and development. This can lead to healthy relationships within the family.

Review Section 10:1

1. Explain the difference between the terms *parent* and *parenting*.

2. List three reasons couples give for not wanting to parent.

3. A teen mother and her baby face many health risks. Name two for each.

4. List the safest childbearing years for women.

5. Briefly describe how the responsibilities of parenting may hinder the growth and development of a teen.

6. List three healthy reasons and three unhealthy reasons couples give for wanting to parent.

7. Explain why parents' unrealistic expectations for children can be unhealthy for a child.

section 10:2

Qualities Needed by Parents

Sharpen Your Reading

As you read this section, create a checklist that couples could use to assess whether they are ready to be parents. In the first column, list the qualities that parents should have. In the second column, list a brief description of each quality.

Boost Your Vocabulary

Choose one of the key terms and write a parent-child scenario that demonstrates the qualities of that term.

Know Key Terms

unconditional love
responsible parenting

Besides considering their reasons for wanting to parent, couples should consider the personal qualities needed to be effective parents. Emotional maturity, unconditional love, flexibility, and responsibility are some of these qualities, as well as the readiness to allow children to change your life forever.

Being Emotionally Mature

As people mature, their emotions become more stable, 10-4. They can think before they act, so they control their responses better. This is important in parenting for several reasons.

First, children respond to the parent's emotions. If the mother feels tense, the baby will feel tense. If the father feels upset, the baby will feel upset. Emotions are communicated to children even without words.

10-4 Emotional maturity can help prospective parents prepare for their first child. As a couple, they realize their lifestyle will change.

Second, emotional maturity helps parents identify their own emotions. Parents should label their emotions so children in turn can learn to identify their own feelings. A parent should be able to say "I really feel sad when you and your sister fight," or "I'm getting upset with the noise you two are making." Being able to identify and label their emotions also helps parents take steps to deal with their emotions before the emotions get out of control.

Third, emotional maturity helps parents control strong emotions. Emotional immaturity may be the cause of some abuse to children. Although parents may love their children, some immature adults may respond with violence when emotions are high. Anger over a childish response—which is normal for children—may cause a parent to explode. Parents need to be able to control their emotions and their reactions. Also, emotional maturity will help parents guide and control their children's emotional responses.

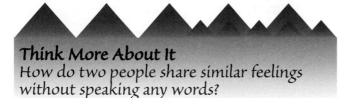

Think More About It
How do two people share similar feelings without speaking any words?

Giving Unconditional Love

Unconditional love is the ability to love another under any circumstance. This is the kind of love parents must have for their children. Children need to know they are loved for who they are. They should not feel a need to perform or pretend they are someone or something else to get love. When children experience unconditional love, they are able to accept themselves as being lovable. Their ability to give love in return is influenced by the love they have experienced.

Being Flexible

Parent-child relationships will change throughout the life cycle. During the early years, children are dependent on their parents to provide for all their needs. As children grow,

they learn to meet some of their own needs. As teens, they need to take more responsibility for themselves and for their actions. Through all these changes, parents need to be flexible. They must be willing and able to change as the child grows.

Being Responsible

Most parents want to help their children grow to become mature adults. **Responsible parenting** means making choices that will help a child develop fully in all areas of life, 10-5. It includes providing an environment in which the child's needs are met and growth is stimulated.

A couple's effectiveness at responsible parenting will be influenced by several factors. These include personal maturity, a mature relationship, financial resources, and preparation for parenting. Their own personal growth will affect the qualities that their children see and imitate. Their own relationship should be strong so they can love and support a child. Their financial resources should be adequate to meet a child's needs for food, shelter, clothing, medical care, and a safe environment. Their preparation for parenting should help them understand how to encourage a child's growth and development.

Being Ready for Children to Change Your Life

Parenting requires giving—giving of time, energy, money, and skills to meet a child's needs and encourage development. As parents give, a child receives and responds as well. These responses can give parents much satisfaction and hope. Children can also help parents grow in various ways.

- *Children can give parents satisfaction.* For most couples, parenting is a satisfying experience. It is enjoyable to have a child return love and affection. Parents enjoy seeing a child learn new skills, accomplish new feats, and grow as a person. The bond that develops between parent and child can last a lifetime.

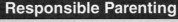

Responsible Parenting

Responsible parents need to provide

- **mature role models** of how people live and act

- **a nurturing environment** in which a child feels loved and supported

- **a secure environment** in which a child's physical needs for food, clothing, shelter, medical care, and safety are met

- **a stimulating environment** in which a child learns new skills and concepts by interacting with people and objects

10-5 Responsible parents provide for their children's growth and development in all these areas.

- *Children help parents mature.* Parenting is a growth experience. Parents learn to be responsible for the needs of another. The give-and-take of parenting causes love to grow between parent and child. In this way, parents stimulate growth in their child. The child's growth encourages the parents to keep on adjusting. Both parent and child experience growth in their relationship.

- *Children help parents recognize their human weaknesses.* Many times parents are disappointed with what they learn about themselves. They may not control their emotions as well as they thought. These are times for parents to learn and mature. The parent-child relationship will grow stronger if parents admit their mistakes and learn to adjust.

- *Children can help parents enjoy family leisure time.* Playtime activities involving children help parents have fun. These shared activities can help the parents' relationship as well as the parent-child relationship.

- *Children can give parents hope for the future.* Parents feel satisfaction in seeing their children develop and mature. Sometimes children make mature choices and succeed in reaching a goal. At other times they respond with more insight than the parents have.

Review Section 10:2

1. Name three reasons why emotional maturity is an important quality in parenting.

2. Identify four things that responsible parents provide to a child.

3. List five ways that children can affect parents.

section 10:3

Parenting Issues

Sharpen Your Reading

Summarize the key points under each heading. Then choose one of the topics and prepare an oral presentation to give as a community service project.

Boost Your Vocabulary

Compare and contrast the terms related to adoption in a three-column table. List the terms in the first column. In the second column, list ways the terms are alike. In the third column, list ways they are different.

Know Key Terms

infertility
endometriosis
ovulation
artificial insemination
in vitro fertilization (IVF)
surrogate mother
agency adoption
independent adoption
open adoption
closed adoption
home study
international adoption

The decision to become parents and have a family is of major importance. Couples who have thought through this decision will take steps to plan and prepare for children.

Some couples are not able to conceive a child. There are several options that couples may pursue to become parents.

Preparing for Children

Once a couple decide to have children, they need to plan for changes in their lifestyle. They should check their health insurance plan to see what coverage is provided for prenatal and newborn care. The financial costs of having and raising the child should be included in their budget. They should also discuss how parenting could affect their careers, leisure activities, and their own relationship.

Considering Child Care

Child care takes much time and energy. The couple needs to discuss how they will handle child care responsibilities, 10-6. How will they adjust their schedules? What does each expect from the other in terms of sharing responsibilities?

Some couples choose to have one parent stay home with the young child. They want to be the young child's main caregiver and role model during these early years. Stable finances can help the young family in this situation.

10-6 Children benefit when both parents are involved in providing their care.

Often the young family needs the income of both parents. Sometimes the parents are able to adjust their schedules to provide child care themselves. In some cases, other family members help out with child care. Some families choose to hire in-home child care for their young children. This may take place in the caregiver's home or in the couple's home. Some choose to use licensed child care centers. The couple needs to discuss their options for child care and agree on a solution.

> ## Use What You Learn
>
> What resources are needed to provide care for a growing child?

Planning for Financial Changes

Pregnancy and the birth of a child may require adjustments to the family income. One of these changes may involve adjusting to one income. Most women can work up to a few weeks before their due date, depending on the type of work that they do. Sometimes complications occur in pregnancy. In those cases, women may be required to reduce their activity and stay home.

Couples will find it easier to adjust to parenting if they feel their income is adequate. Once they feel financially secure, they are more likely to feel ready to be parents.

The arrival of a child puts increased strain on the family budget. Medical care for pregnancy and childbirth plus doctor's services for the infant are major costs. These may be covered by a health insurance plan. Next, consider the costs of providing care for the child for at least the next 18 years. Some experts estimate that families will spend two-and-a-half times their income to support a child to age 18. Additional expenses for raising a child need to be included in the family budget.

Preparing for Lifestyle Changes

Before children are born, couples devote their time and energy to careers, friendships, or leisure activities. Children place new demands on a parent's time and energy. Parents will have less time to spend with each other and other adults. They will have less money to spend freely. These losses can be very frustrating.

Couples adjust to parenting more readily if they feel they have satisfied their goals for the childless stage of their lives. Perhaps they wanted to complete their education, establish a home, and advance in their careers. If they have accomplished these goals, they will look forward to parenting.

Also, couples who have developed a mature relationship find it easier to adjust to parenting, 10-7. Making adjustments for a child is easier when the couple has learned to adjust to each other and resolve conflicts.

> ## Investigate Further
>
> **How does becoming a parent impact a person's life?**

10-7 Couples who have developed a solid relationship will find it easier to provide a loving and secure environment for their child.

Infertility

Most couples look forward to having children when they marry. They hardly consider the possibility that they might not be able to have children. Many couples who want to have children find they are not able to conceive, while others have fewer children than they want. For some, the problem is infertility.

Infertility is defined as a couple's inability to conceive a child or carry a child to full term. A couple is usually not considered infertile until they have tried to have children for a year or more. The heartache of not being able to have a child affects 10 to 15 percent of all couples.

Causes of Infertility

Infertility problems are common to both males and females. For men, the main causes of infertility are low sperm count or a blockage in one of the tubes that carries sperm. The leading causes in women are hormonal factors or blocked fallopian tubes resulting from disease or infection.

Endometriosis is the second major cause of infertility in women. **Endometriosis** is a disease in which uterine tissue grows outside the uterus. The tissue may appear on the ovaries or block the fallopian tubes. The disease is most commonly diagnosed in women between the ages of 25 and 35.

Other harmful factors contribute to infertility in both sexes. These include exposure to radiation or toxic chemicals, smoking tobacco or marijuana, and sexually transmitted infections.

Link to Your Life

How would discovering you are infertile affect your long-term goals?

Treatment for Infertility

Most causes of infertility are physiological. Males and females are affected equally, so both should be examined by their physician if problems of infertility exist. A doctor may refer the couple to a fertility specialist for further tests to diagnose the problem. Once the problem

is known, many couples are successfully treated and able to bear children. Following is a description of the most common infertility treatments:

- *Medications and hormones can stimulate or improve ovulation.* To conceive, a woman's ovaries must release a mature egg. This process is called **ovulation**. The egg enters the fallopian tube where it is most successfully fertilized. The fertilized egg then travels to the uterus. Hormones are involved in maturing and releasing the egg and in preparing the uterus for a fertilized egg.

- *Surgical therapies can open blockages.* With new medical technology, blocked fallopian tubes can be identified and opened with minimal trauma to the patient. A *laparoscopy* is a procedure that allows the doctor to look inside the patient and take pictures internally. With lasers and special equipment, surgery can be performed if needed during the procedure, 10-8.

- *Artificial insemination of the husband's sperm can promote conception.* To help a couple achieve pregnancy, a doctor can use a syringe to deposit the husband's sperm directly into the uterus. This procedure, known as **artificial insemination**, can make conception more likely. It is a painless and relatively inexpensive procedure. It is most commonly used if low sperm count is causing infertility.

10-8 When infertility results from a blockage, surgery can correct the problem in most cases.

Section 10:3 Parenting Issues   **219**

- *Assisted reproductive technology (ART) can increase the rate of conception.* New technologies make it possible for most infertile couples to experience an excellent chance of conception. These technologies may be costly, and success is not always certain.

The most commonly performed ART procedure is **in vitro fertilization (IVF)**. This treatment can be used to overcome blocked fallopian tubes. It involves stimulating multiple eggs to mature. The mature eggs are removed from the ovaries and fertilized in the laboratory with the husband's sperm. After cell division has begun, the fertilized eggs are placed directly into the uterus. More than one fertilized egg is placed to ensure success. All may not implant into the uterine wall, but if they do, multiple births result. Extra fertilized eggs are usually *cyropreserved* (frozen) for later use by the couple, should they try again to achieve a pregnancy.

In this society, reproductive technology raises many legal and ethical questions. When the partners involved are married, however, such technology is generally accepted since it allows infertile couples to have children. Sperm or mature eggs from donor parents can be used, or a fertilized egg can be transplanted into a surrogate mother. A **surrogate mother** is a woman who is hired by the couple to carry the couple's child to birth. In all these situations, legal and ethical questions about tampering with a biological process may be raised.

Think More About It
What ethical questions can you identify related to using technology to produce a child?

Emotional Effects of Infertility

Infertility is crushing for many couples. It is common for them to ask why this is happening to them. They may look for a cause to blame. Feelings of anger, bitterness, and sadness may be overwhelming. They mourn the loss of the children they will not be able to bear.

Some adjust to infertility and accept childlessness. For others, the desire to have a child may become even more intense. Some couples may consider expensive reproductive technologies. Others consider adoption.

Investigate Further

How might infertility affect a couple's mental attitudes?

Adoption

Many people seek to fulfill their dreams for children through adoption. Their reasons for adopting vary. Some adopt because of infertility problems. Some couples already have children but would like more. Some may have inherited problems in their backgrounds. Others are single but still want to share their love with a child who needs a family. An emotionally stable adult who can love and provide for a child has a good chance of adopting one.

Because most couples prefer an infant, fewer infants are available for adoption, 10-9. The wait for adopting an infant can last up to five years. Check with each agency to determine the waiting time.

Rights of Birthparents in an Adoption

Birthparents must consent to the adoption. If the birthparent refuses to consent, the adoption cannot take place. If parental rights are ended due to abandonment or unfitness, then adoption can occur. Abandonment in most states means the birthparent has not contacted, communicated with, or supported the child for a certain period of time (usually a year).

Sometimes a couple cannot pay for the medical care during pregnancy. In this case, potential birthparents can contact human services in their local community. Medical care can be obtained through the agency. If the potential birthparents are interested in having their child adopted, counselors will help them through the steps. The cost of prenatal care and the delivery are usually passed on to the adopting parents.

10-9 Many couples seek to adopt infants, but few are available. Most of these couples never fulfill their dreams of becoming parents.

Investigate Further

What would be the benefits of receiving counseling if you or your girlfriend were pregnant and considering finding adoptive parents for your child?

Agency Adoptions

Most adoptions are arranged through adoption agencies and are called **agency adoptions**. Public adoption agencies usually do not charge for their services since they are tax supported. Private adoption agencies usually have a fee. In some cases, the adoption fee is based on income. Legal fees are usually extra.

Adoption agencies are licensed by the state. That means they meet certain minimum standards set by the state. They should also provide psychological counseling and guidance.

Not all adoptions take place through an agency. **Independent adoptions** are arranged privately. The adopting parents may agree to pay medical expenses for the pregnant mother's care and the birth of the baby. The arrangements are made through a lawyer or doctor. Such adoptions are legal in most states as long as the lawyer's fees are reasonable and no payment is made for the baby. Baby selling is illegal.

Think More About It
What are the benefits of using an adoption agency if you are trying to adopt a child?

Types of Adoption

Adoptions may be open or closed. In an **open adoption**, birthparents may select and meet the adoptive parents. The child will have information about his or her birthparents. The child may have some ongoing contact with the birthparents.

In a **closed adoption**, the child does not know the identity of the birthparents. Birthparents can specify some requirements for the family selected for their child. However, the adoption agency will make the final decision.

All adoptions fall under state regulation. In some states, the birthparents may change their minds within 30 to 60 days after the adoption consent forms are signed. In other states, after forms are signed, the birthparents do not have this opportunity. After the court issues a final adoption decree, the adoption is final. Before making a decision, birthparents should receive counseling from social workers who are familiar with the legal aspects of adoption.

Weigh the Facts

What are some benefits of open adoption for a pregnant teen considering finding a family to parent her child? What could be some disadvantages?

Steps in Adoption

The adoption process involves several steps, 10-10. These steps help the adoption agency make

10-10 Before proceeding with adoption, both spouses should be certain they want to adopt a child.

sure the family is able to provide a warm, secure, and loving home for the child. The agency's goal is to be certain the family will be able to provide the nurturing environment the child needs.

- *A couple contacts an adoption agency.* For example, Lin and Sam had many questions about adopting a child when they contacted the agency. The agency worker explained the policies and described the adoption process. Lin and Sam also had an opportunity to share what they expected from the agency.

- *The agency conducts a thorough screening.* All states require that an agency or licensed person conduct a thorough screening before a couple is allowed to adopt. Healthy reasons for wanting to have a child are important to determine. In addition to wanting a child, being able to provide for the emotional, physical, intellectual, and social development of the child is an important factor. Do the couple understand how a child grows and develops? How would they provide child care? What are their views on guidance and discipline? Are they prepared for child-related expenses and lifetime changes in their budget?

- *The agency conducts a home study.* Many states require a **home study**. The social worker visits the home to be sure the parents can provide a safe, roomy environment for a growing child.

- *The agency worker meets with potential parents to discuss possible children.* Lin and Sam were excited when they received notice that they had been accepted to be adoptive parents. They had expressed an interest in an infant with a physical disability. The worker showed them pictures and talked about the history of several different children.

- *Potential parents get acquainted with the child.* Lin and Sam decided they would like to meet one-year-old Jon. The first meeting was arranged in Jon's foster home. More meetings took place afterward—some in the foster home and others in their home. Usually a child lives with the adoptive family for a while before the adoption is finalized legally. This lasts six months to a year, depending on the state.

During this period, the agency worker visited often and helped them work through their many questions about Jon. Because Jon had a disability, they were also able to get aid to help with his medical bills. Through the time of adjustment, Jon and his new family became strongly attached to each other. The agency worker was prepared to submit a written recommendation of approval to the court.

- *The adoption becomes legal in court.* The final stage came when Lin, Sam, Jon, the agency worker, and their lawyer went to court to make the adoption legal. The lawyer had made certain that all legal requirements were met. They decided to make this special day—the day that Jon became a member of their family—an annual celebration. They knew that Jon would have questions in the future about why his birthparents had found other parents for him. Lin and Sam wanted him to know that he was specially chosen to belong to their family.

Investigate Further

How do the steps in the adoption process help secure a good home environment for a child?

Costs of Adoption

Adoptions can cost a lot of time and money, 10-11. Agencies are allowed to charge adopting parents certain expenses. These are specified by state laws. The adopting parents may be asked to pay for the medical expenses incurred by the birthmother. Living expenses during pregnancy and costs of counseling may also be charged to the adopting parents. The adoption agency may

10-11 Couples who want to adopt a child through a private agency must have sound finances to afford the high costs.

pay these costs for the pregnant girl, then recover them through the adopting parents.

An agency may charge a set fee for an adoption. Some may add the birthmother's expenses to the flat rate. Others may charge the adopting parents according to their income. Adoptions may cost the adopting family anywhere between $10,000 and $30,000.

Single-Parent Adoption

When a single parent wishes to adopt a child, the agency worker will ask the single person the same questions as couples. The interview process may be more intense as the single parent would have to meet all the roles of both parents rather than sharing the roles with another parent. The single person would need to prove his or her ability to provide for the child financially, just as couples do. Questions related to health, personal and family relationships, and the quality of home life would also be asked.

When considering who should be allowed to adopt, all states look to the best interests of the child. Often the social worker or the judge makes that judgment.

International Adoption

An alternative to domestic adoption is **international adoption**. Some countries have many children living in orphanages. Agencies that specialize in international adoptions may also provide counseling and support groups.

This helps families adjust to raising a child from another culture, 10-12.

Whether a child is born into a family or adopted, the responsibilities, challenges, and joys of parenting are similar. Parents need to provide a loving and secure environment in which a child's needs are met and growth is stimulated. In turn, parents can gain satisfaction relating to their children and seeing them grow and mature.

10-12 When adopting a child from another country, parents take on the added challenge of helping the child adjust to a new culture.

Review Section 10:3

1. Name three areas a couple can plan to help them adjust to becoming parents.
2. Identify the main causes of infertility in men and women.
3. Give three reasons why people adopt children.
4. Briefly describe the steps in the adoption process.
5. Name three ways that an adoption agency might help a pregnant girl during her pregnancy.

Think It Through

Parenting Decisions

Eun and Tia had decided they wanted to become parents. Month after month they continued to hope for signs of a pregnancy. They wanted to have a child so much. Even their parents openly talked about the day Eun and Tia would give them grandchildren.

The fear that they would not be able to have children haunted them. They really had not believed that it would be a problem for them. However, the doctor told them they were one couple in many who had infertility problems. They had high hopes that treatment would be effective. The doctor told them the success rate for treating fertility was 70 percent. As time continued to go by with no results, their hopes dimmed.

Questions to Guide Your Thinking

1. How might this couple feel pressured into having children?

2. What are some of the feelings a couple may have if they are not able to have children?

3. What are some options that Eun and Tia could consider?

4. There are few babies available for adoption. How might that fact influence Eun and Tia's parenting decisions?

Chapter Summary

Parenting is an important role in the lives of many couples. The couple's mutual decision to have children requires careful thought. This decision is based on several factors. A couple may or may not choose to have children for various reasons. Some choose to delay parenting while they develop a career or seek to reach certain goals. As part of their decision, couples should evaluate the personal qualities needed to be effective parents. They must also consider the positive effects children have on parents. Overall, most couples look forward to having children in their family.

Preparing for parenting can help a couple fulfill the roles of responsible parents. Their ability to carry out such roles is increased by planning who will care for the child. The future financial and lifestyle changes should also be planned.

Some couples who desire to share their love and life with a child are hindered by infertility problems. Infertile couples can seek medical help and possibly find a treatment that helps them have a child. For many couples, infertility has strong emotional effects, which include feelings of loss and grief. Many adjust to childlessness, while others apply for adoption to fulfill their desire to have a child.

Assess...

Your Knowledge

1. List three risks associated with a teen pregnancy.

2. What do responsible parents provide for their children?

3. List two types of treatments for infertility.

4. Explain the difference between an open adoption and a closed adoption.

Your Understanding

5. How would becoming a parent affect your life?

6. What are some reasons people should wait to become parents?

7. How can infertility affect a couple's parenting decisions?

Your Skills

8. Develop a decision-making tree that could be used for making the decision to start a family. Include alternatives, the pro and con of each alternative, and a possible plan of action.

9. Write a scenario in which you describe a person who has qualities needed to be a responsible parent.

Think Critically

10. Develop a checklist entitled *Readiness for Parenting*. Include criteria that you think are important for parents to have. *Group option:* Work as a group to complete the checklist.

11. *Research.* Assess your peers' attitudes about placing a child in adoption. Develop questions you could ask to help gather this information. Then interview 10 of your peers about their attitudes toward adoption. Tally the results in a spreadsheet and create a bar graph showing how many of your peers have the same attitudes. Write a summary of the responses. *Choice:* Include a paragraph about why so few infants are placed in adoption by teen mothers and what influences them to try to raise their children themselves.

12. *Writing.* Create a scenario describing the changes in a couple's life during their first week of parenting. *Choice:* Write the scenario from the viewpoint of new parents in one of the following groups:
    - an adoptive couple
    - teen parents
    - first time parents in their mid-20s
    - first time parents in their mid-30s
    - first time parents in their mid-40s

13. Analyze current media depictions of attitudes toward children. Choose a TV show or movie to critique. List the attitudes that the adults show toward children in the show. Explain what actions, words, or nonverbal messages depicted these attitudes. Then compare your list of attitudes to the list of qualities that are needed by parents. Summarize your analysis in a report.

Connect with Your Community

14. Interview a grandparent about the ways technology has made a difference in parenting decisions. Request one example of *then versus now*. Summarize your findings in a paragraph.

15. **Math.** Interview several parents about their parenting experiences. Include questions about what they enjoy most about parenting, what they find most challenging, how prepared they were for parenting, and what preparation they would have found helpful. Tally the number of similar responses and present this information in a bar graph. Discuss your findings in a paper, including the graphs as illustrations. *Choice:* Present your information to the class using presentation software.

16. **Reading.** Find an article from your local newspaper illustrating the legal and ethical issues related to the use of reproductive technology. Be prepared to cite your article and discuss its key issues in class.

17. **Social studies, research.** Research the procedures for adoption in your state. Present your information in a poster. *Choice:* Post your information on your class Web site.

Use Technology

18. **Writing.** Use a word-processing or drawing program to create a tri-fold flyer providing information on one cause of infertility in either males or females.

19. **Research.** Conduct a survey, asking students in your school how many children they think they would like to parent. Tally your results by grade in a spreadsheet. Convert the spreadsheet to a bar graph showing how many children the students in each grade want to parent. Discuss your findings in a paragraph. *Group option:* Complete the assignment in groups, with each group interviewing a different grade.

20. **Science, writing.** Research the Internet for information on reproductive technologies. Choose one technology and write a paper on the social and legal issues that might be related to its use.

21. **Research.** Search the Internet for a list of agencies in the region that serve as a resource for parents seeking to adopt a child. Include addresses and phone numbers for each.

Chapter 11

Pregnancy and Childbirth

Section 11:1
Pregnancy and Prenatal Development

Section 11:2
Prenatal Care

Section 11:3
Preparing for the Baby

Section 11:4
The Baby Arrives

Key Questions

Questions to answer as you study this chapter:

- What takes place during pregnancy?
- How can a mother help her unborn child grow and develop?
- What happens during childbirth?

Chapter Objectives

After studying this chapter, you will be able to

- **identify** the signs of pregnancy.
- **describe** the stages of prenatal development.
- **determine** the importance of healthy prenatal care practices.
- **explain** preparations parents can make for childbirth.
- **identify** the stages of labor in childbirth.
- **describe** the parents' postpartum adjustments.

Life Sketch

"I'm just too tired to get up!" Phaedra thought as the alarm clock buzzed for the third time. "How could it be morning already?"

Adam walked in, grinning. "Breakfast, anyone?" he asked.

As the aroma of breakfast entered the room, Phaedra felt her stomach churn. "Oh no! None for me again, thanks," she replied.

The smell of food didn't agree with Phaedra now that she was two months pregnant. Of the many changes taking place in her body, only the tiredness and nausea showed. Inside, she knew that her baby was growing and changing rapidly. She knew how important her health, diet, and lifestyle were during this period of her pregnancy. She and Adam had many dreams they hoped would be fulfilled with the birth of a healthy baby.

Getting Started

For most couples, pregnancy is a shared experience filled with many different emotions. It is a time of happiness and fear for both. They may feel excited about becoming parents, yet wonder whether they will be *good* parents. They may be overwhelmed by concerns for a healthy baby and worries about being unprepared for future changes. These feelings are common as pregnancy triggers dramatic changes in their lives.

Learning about prenatal care and development can help soon-to-be parents prepare for the challenges ahead. A mother-to-be who takes care of herself is more likely to have a healthy baby. The more she knows about the emotional and physical changes she will experience, the better she will be able to cope. A father-to-be can support his wife by sharing in the emotions and experiences of this special time.

section 11:1

Pregnancy and Prenatal Development

Sharpen Your Reading

Outline the stages of prenatal development, starting with conception and going through the birth of the child.

Boost Your Vocabulary

Draw and label the embryo stage of development, including the support system between the child and the mother.

Know Key Terms

conception
zygote
cervix
embryo
fetus
amniotic fluid
placenta
umbilical cord

Pregnancy is the condition of carrying a developing child within the uterus. It begins with conception and implantation.

Pregnancy

Conception occurs when one sperm and one egg unite, 11-1. Their chromosomes combine, producing a cell with 46 chromosomes. This cell is called a **zygote**. The zygote increases in size by cell division and travels to the uterus. The five-day zygote is called a *blastocyte* and attaches itself into the lining of the uterine wall. Two groups of cells develop from the blastocyte; one group forms the placenta and the other forms the baby.

Multiple conceptions occur in two ways. For one, the mother produces more than one egg. The two different fertilized eggs result in *fraternal twins*. Releasing more than two eggs is uncommon unless the mother has been undergoing fertility treatment. *Identical twins* result when a single fertilized egg divides into two identical zygotes. If there is a three-way split, the result is identical triplets.

Signs of Pregnancy

How can a woman tell if she is pregnant? Although answering that question during the early stages is not always easy, a woman will notice several signs. The most common sign of pregnancy is a missed menstrual cycle. However, pregnancy is not the only reason a woman may miss a period. Stress, illness, or an emotional upset can also have such an effect.

Two to three weeks after the missed period, other symptoms of pregnancy usually occur. Hormonal changes may cause a woman to feel very tired. Some women require more rest during this time. Nausea, sometimes called *morning sickness*, is common during the early months of pregnancy. For some women, the nausea may cause vomiting. Usually by the twelfth week of pregnancy this feeling disappears.

Think More About It
Why should a woman who suspects she is pregnant make an appointment to see her doctor as soon as she can?

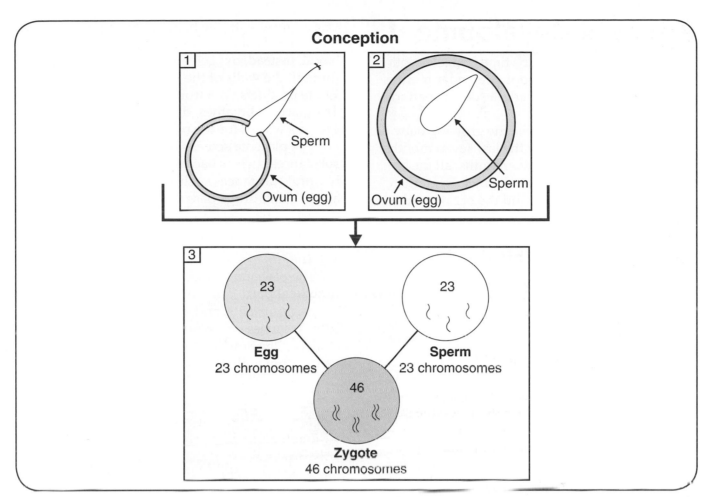

Conception

11-1 In conception, one sperm penetrates the egg's protective membrane. (See diagram 1.) It then sheds its tail (see diagram 2) and begins cell division. A normal sperm and egg cell each have 23 chromosomes, which combine to produce a zygote with 46 chromosomes. These chromosomes contain the genetic information that directs the child's growth and development. (See diagram 3.)

Pregnancy Tests

The most accurate test for pregnancy is a chemical test. It is most accurate if used at least 7 to 10 days after the missed menstrual period. The test is done in a doctor's office, medical lab, or health clinic using a sample of the woman's urine. If certain hormones are present in the urine, the pregnancy is confirmed.

Pregnancy test kits can be purchased and used at home. These tests are not always accurate. Movement, dust, or checking the results too early or too late could give an incorrect result. Inaccurate results are usually negative, indicating no pregnancy. Tests rarely show positive results for a woman who is not pregnant. However, early stages of uterine cancer can produce positive results. Scheduling a physical checkup with a doctor as soon as possible is important.

Six to eight weeks into pregnancy, a pelvic examination by a doctor can also help confirm the pregnancy. During the exam, the doctor will check for changes in the woman's reproductive organs. The increased size of the uterus and a softening of the cervix are two positive signs. The **cervix** is the opening to the uterus.

Proper prenatal care should begin early in the pregnancy. The first three months are the most critical for proper development of the growing baby. Therefore, a woman should be in good health to provide the best environment possible.

Investigate Further

What problems could develop if a woman relies on the results of a home pregnancy test to determine if she is pregnant?

Prenatal Development

The prenatal period is the time from conception until birth. It is usually about 9 calendar months or 280 days. Each month marks a specific pattern of development.

For the first two months, the growing baby is called an **embryo**. During the last seven months, it is called a **fetus**. After two months, all the baby's body organs become distinct. From then on, the fetus grows larger and the organs and muscles begin to function.

The Support Systems

Once the zygote implants itself into the uterine wall, the support systems begin to function, 11-2. The embryo's support system consists of four parts: the amniotic sac, amniotic fluid, placenta, and umbilical cord.

The Amniotic Sac and Fluid

The *amniotic sac* is a membrane that surrounds and protects the baby until birth. Inside the sac is the **amniotic fluid**. This fluid serves some important functions. It acts as a cushion for the fetus to protect against injury. It provides an even temperature for the fetus. The fluid enables the fetus to move easily. Finally, the fluid aids in the birth of the baby.

The Placenta

The placenta also begins to function. The **placenta** is an organ in which the mother's blood

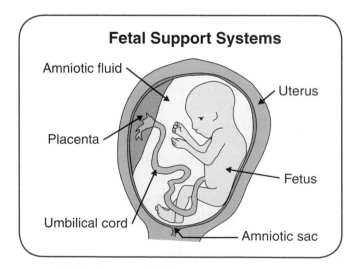

Fetal Support Systems

Amniotic fluid

Uterus

Placenta

Fetus

Umbilical cord

Amniotic sac

11-2 **The fetal support system provides protection and nourishment for the developing fetus.**

vessels meet with the baby's. During pregnancy, the mother's blood does not mix with the baby's blood. Instead, oxygen and nutrients pass through the walls of the blood vessels to the baby. Waste products pass from the baby to the mother. The placenta breathes, digests nutrients, and excretes wastes for the baby.

The placenta screens out some harmful substances such as bacteria. However, other harmful substances such as gases, viruses, alcohol, and drugs pass through the placenta into the baby's bloodstream. These substances can affect embryo development.

The Umbilical Cord

The placenta connects to the embryo by the **umbilical cord**. This cord of blood vessels carries oxygen, nutrients, and antibodies to the growing baby. It carries waste products away from the embryo. The flow of blood through the cord keeps it untangled.

Think More About It
How do the support systems meet the growing baby's needs?

The Embryo Stage

The first two months of development is the embryo stage, 11-3. Specific development takes place during this time. The heart, eyes, and ears appear during this stage. Hands and feet take form. Proper development at this stage is vital—growth that does not take place cannot be made up later.

The embryo's development is rapid and occurs even before the mother knows she is pregnant. By the twentieth day, the foundations for the brain, spinal cord, nervous system, and eyes are formed. By the end of the first month, the heart is pumping blood. At eight weeks, all the internal organs are developing. The brain coordinates their functions.

During this stage, the embryo's development is affected by factors in the mother's environment. Poor nutrition and harmful substances can adversely affect the developing embryo. The mother must provide certain nutrients. If she is undernourished, her baby's growth will not occur as it should. If the mother is exposed to radiation or toxic substances, permanent damage to the embryo may occur. This stage is an extremely critical period in the formation of the growing embryo.

Prenatal Development

Embryo Stage

One month

- Fertilized egg divides rapidly, creating a ball of cells.
- Cells become attached to the wall of the uterus.
- Foundations for brain, spinal cord, nervous system, and eyes are formed.
- Heart is pumping blood.
- Buds develop that are the beginning of arms and legs.
- Embryo length is ¼ inch.

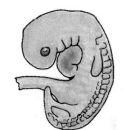

Two months

- Face forms.
- Embryo shaped with a *C*.
- Back grows faster than front.
- Ridges of fingers and toes begin to appear.
- Eyes are forming.
- Indentations where nose and ears will be appear.
- Embryo length at the end of 2 months is about ½ inch.

Fetal Stage

Three months

- Part of intestines has formed.
- Kidneys function and produce urine.
- Bones and muscles start to grow.
- Ribs and backbone are soft.
- Swelling shows where ears will develop.
- Beginning of eyelids.
- Male (testes) or female (ovaries) reproductive organs begin to form.
- Arms and legs long enough to bend.
- Fingers and toes are more distinct.
- Fetus may reach 4 inches in length.

(Continued)

11-3 Embryo and fetal development follow a precise pattern, starting with conception and ending at birth.

Prenatal Development

Fetal Stage

Four months

- Fetus flexes arms and legs.
- External sex organs become distinctly male or female.
- Facial features are distinct.
- Ears appear in proper place on side of head.
- Soft downy hair (lanugo) covers fetus's body and face.
- Eyelashes and eyebrows are growing.
- Weighs about 4 to 7 ounces.
- Fetus is about 6 to 8 inches long.

Five months

- Hair begins to grow on fetus's head.
- Number of nerve cells in brain increase rapidly.
- Fetus can hear sounds.
- Sucking reflex develops.
- A pasty substance (vernix) covers fetus's skin.
- Nails form.
- Fetus turns, stretches, and kicks.
- Length varies from 8 to 12 inches long.

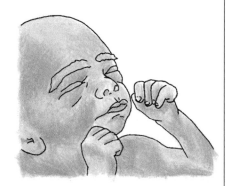

Six months

- Looks like a newborn.
- Fetus is thin.
- Skin is wrinkled and translucent.
- Bones are hardening.
- Movements are definite.
- Heartbeat is stronger.
- Fetus's lungs begin to prepare for breathing at birth.
- Eyelids open and shut.
- Weighs about 1½ pounds.
- Length varies from 9 to 14 inches.

(Continued)

11-3 Continued.

Prenatal Development

Fetal Stage

Seven months

- Takes a fetal position with legs curled up on chest.
- Fetus can see changes in light and dark.
- Fetus's hearing develops.
- Skin is less wrinkled as fat forms.
- Hands can make grasping motions.
- Hair on scalp grows longer.
- Taste buds are developed.
- Weighs about 2 to 3 pounds.
- Length varies from 11 to 15 inches.

Eight months

- Brain and nerves mature.
- Limbs become smooth and plump.
- Skin is a healthy color.
- Fingernails have grown longer.
- Fetus can hiccup—makes rapid, jerky movements.
- Eyes are open.
- Lungs are maturing.
- Weighs about 4½ to 5½ pounds.
- Length varies from 16 to 18 inches.

Nine months

- Lanugo is almost gone.
- Much of vernix has fallen off.
- Organs can function on their own.
- Assumes position for delivery.
- Weighs about 6 to 9 pounds.
- Length varies from 17 to 22 inches.

11-3 Continued.

Investigate Further

Why is the health and nutrition of women of childbearing age so important?

The Fetal Stage

The fetal stage lasts from the third month to birth. During this stage, organs grow and function. Systems develop and work together.

By the end of the third month, the fetus is quite active. It can kick its legs and turn its head. The male or female genital organs have appeared. By this time, the greatest dangers to the fetus's development from the outside environment are past. The baby begins to move in the third month, but it is usually the fourth month when the mother begins to notice movement. In the fifth month, the heartbeat is loud enough to be heard with a stethoscope.

If the baby is *premature* (born before development is complete), it has a chance of survival after six months of development. Late in the seventh month, the organs have developed so the baby has a 90 percent chance of surviving if born at this time. The specialized areas of the brain that control hearing, sight, smell, and movements are working.

By the ninth month, the fetus has reached full term and is ready to be born. The first step in birth occurs as the fetus shifts so the head is down toward the pelvic cavity. As a result, the uterus shifts downward and forward. This shifting process is called *lightening* because the mother's breathing becomes easier and abdominal pressure is eased. The birth process is started when the placenta releases a hormone called *oxytocin*. Doctors can also *induce* labor (cause labor to start) by giving the mother oxytocin. The actual birth process is covered later in this chapter.

Investigate Further

Based on the development that takes place in the 8th and 9th months, what health problems do you think are most common for children born 4-6 weeks early?

Review Section 11:**1**

1. List three common symptoms of pregnancy.
2. Identify and describe the functions of the embryo's support systems.
3. Explain the difference between the embryo and fetal stages of pregnancy.

section 11:2

Prenatal Care

Sharpen Your Reading

For each topic under *Prenatal Care*, list two suggestions for a pregnant woman to follow to protect her unborn child.

Boost Your Vocabulary

Compare the pros and cons of using each type of health care provider for a pregnant woman.

Know Key Terms

obstetrician-gynecologist
certified nurse-midwife (CNM)
birth defect
ultrasound
amniocentesis
fetal alcohol syndrome (FAS)

To provide a healthful environment for her developing baby, the mother needs to keep herself in good health. This is because the fetus's environment is controlled by the mother's body. Substances that reach the fetus enter through her body. Therefore, she should avoid substances that could harm her or her unborn baby.

Professional Health Care During Pregnancy

As soon as a woman thinks she is pregnant, she should call for an appointment with her doctor. This first prenatal visit is important. If the father-to-be can go with her, they can both benefit. The doctor will discuss questions they may have.

At the first visit, the doctor usually gives the mother a complete physical exam, 11-4. This includes a check of the mother's weight, height, and blood pressure. A urinalysis and blood test are sent to a lab. In the pelvic examination, the doctor will check for the size of the uterus and a softening of the cervix.

Once pregnancy is confirmed, the doctor will estimate a due date for the baby's birth. The due date is about 266 days after conception. This is figured by the date of the woman's last menstrual cycle. Most women deliver within two weeks of their due date, but some vary even more. As the predicted due date draws near, the doctor can be more exact about the actual delivery date.

11-4 A woman should visit her doctor as soon as she thinks she may be pregnant.

Regular medical checkups throughout pregnancy are important for the mother and her developing baby. The doctor will check the fetus's growth and watch for any abnormalities. A monthly checkup is recommended for the first six months. During the seventh and eighth months, the mother should be checked twice a month. Weekly visits are scheduled in the final month.

Think More About It

Why does the doctor check a woman's weight and blood pressure during pregnancy?

Sources of Health Care

A woman can obtain health care during her pregnancy from the following sources:

- An **obstetrician-gynecologist** is a specialist who provides medical and surgical care to women. The obstetrician provides mainly pregnancy care.

- A *family practitioner* is a medical doctor who provides health care for all family members. A family doctor will provide care during a normal pregnancy and refer a patient to a specialist if problems arise.

- A **certified nurse-midwife (CNM)** is a registered nurse who is trained to provide health care for normal pregnancies and births. The services provided by the CNM may vary from one state to another.

Some health care services for pregnant women may be available through a maternity clinic at a hospital, a public health clinic, or a prenatal clinic. The services available through these clinics may vary as well as the fees for service.

What are some benefits of receiving health care during pregnancy from an obstetrician? from a CNM?

Testing for Birth Defects

At some point during her pregnancy, the woman's doctor may need to obtain data about the condition of the fetus. Conditions such as high blood pressure or fluid retention alert the doctor to possible complications.

The doctor may have a concern about a possible **birth defect**. This is a condition that exists from birth and limits the ability of a person's body or mind. Birth defects are usually caused by outside factors, such as drug use or radiation exposure. Research suggests that more folate in the mother's diet can prevent some brain and spinal defects. Genetic disorders, on the other hand, are inherited through the genes. Abnormal development of the fetus may be a concern if the mother is over the age of 40 or one parent is a carrier of a genetic disease.

AFP Screening

A pregnant woman can choose to have an AFP blood test done between the fifteenth and eighteenth weeks of pregnancy, 11-5. This test measures the amount of *alphafetoprotein (AFP)* produced by the baby and passed to the mother's blood.

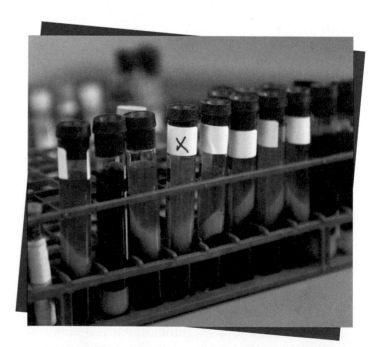

11-5 An AFP blood test can give doctors much information about the developing fetus.

The AFP test provides important information about the fetus's condition. The doctor can tell if the mother is carrying twins and, if so, in what stage of pregnancy she is. The test can also give indication of possible neural defects in the fetus. *Spina bifida* is a birth defect in which the nerves are open along the spine. *Anencephaly* is the absence of all or a major part of the fetus's brain. The causes of these birth defects are not known.

If the AFP test indicates that a birth defect may exist, further tests can be done. Ultrasound and amniocentesis can provide more information about the fetus.

Ultrasound

The use of ultrasound in pregnancy is considered a safe practice. **Ultrasound** involves the use of sound waves that bounce off the fetus. An image of the fetus is then projected onto a monitor. Doctors can use this test to learn about the position, size, and development of the fetus. They can see the movement of organs such as the heart. In this way, they can detect potential problems.

Amniocentesis

To detect birth defects, doctors use a test called **amniocentesis**. A sample of the amniotic fluid is removed from the woman's uterus. This fluid contains cells that have been cast off by the fetus. By studying these cells, the doctor can detect abnormal development in the child.

Investigate Further

What environmental conditions might increase a couple's chance of having a child with birth defects?

Diet and Nutrition

Good eating habits are important at all times. A woman should not wait until a pregnancy is confirmed before starting to eat healthful foods. Much of an embryo's development takes place early in the pregnancy, before a woman even knows she is pregnant. A growing baby gets its nourishment from the mother's bloodstream. The mother must eat enough of the right foods to meet her nutritional needs and the baby's needs, 11-6.

11-6 Maintaining good eating habits will help a woman meet the extra demands of pregnancy.

Some nutrients have added importance in preventing certain birth defects. The U.S. Food and Drug Administration recommends a diet high in folate or folic acid (the manufactured version) for women of childbearing age. A diet low in this B vitamin complex can affect the baby's brain and spinal cord development and cause mental retardation, paralysis, and premature death. Sources of the vitamin include dark leafy greens, broccoli, oranges, cantaloupes, legumes, and enriched grain and flour products. Overall poor nutrition increases the chances of miscarriage, stillbirth, premature birth, and birth defects.

Eat a Well-Balanced Diet

During the months of pregnancy, a mother's diet should follow a food plan for a balanced diet. She should eat a variety of foods from all the food groups to help get the nutrients she needs. After the baby is born, a mother will need even greater quantities of certain nutrients if she breast-feeds the baby.

A woman who has followed a healthful diet throughout her life will not need to make many changes during pregnancy. Her calorie needs increase by about 300 calories per day during the last six months. See the chart on page 550 to identify how many cups or ounces are needed for each food group. Pregnant women can also view recommended quantities at www.MyPyramid.gov in the section for pregnant and breast-feeding women.

For teenagers, whose own bodies are still growing, greater quantities of calories are needed. Demand for all vitamins and minerals is high, but especially so for several of these. Her doctor may recommend taking vitamin and mineral supplements or increasing the intake of specific foods. (Food groups and nutrients are discussed in Chapter 27, "Managing Food Needs.")

If the mother is poorly nourished, both the mother and her unborn baby can have health problems. Unless the mother improves her diet and eating habits, she may not be prepared for the physical stress of pregnancy. Her baby may be born prematurely, have birth defects, or be undernourished.

Think More About It

Why is eating a healthful diet one of the easiest steps an expectant mother can take to prevent birth defects? Why might a pregnant teen have trouble eating a healthful diet?

Weight Gain

During her regular prenatal checks, the mother is monitored for her weight gain. The doctor's guidelines for healthy eating and weight control should be observed by the pregnant woman. An average gain of 25 to 35 pounds is recommended, 11-7.

Pregnancy is not a time for a woman to try to lose weight. If she does, her body may use some of the nutrients needed for the baby. Underweight mothers may also deprive the baby of nutrients needed for proper development. An undernourished baby may have low birthweight, fewer brain cells, or slowed development.

Physical Activity

Regular physical activity is important for the general health and well-being of a pregnant woman. Physical activity helps her develop good muscle tone needed for delivery. Another benefit is an increased energy level from improved blood circulation. Exercise can also help her relieve tension and relax.

Weight Gain During Pregnancy	
	Weight in pounds
Weight of baby	7½
Placenta	1½
Amniotic fluid	2
Increased size of uterus	2
Increased breast size	2
Extra blood	4
Extra fluid in body tissues	4
Extra fat stored in body	7
Total Average Weight Gain	30 pounds

11-7 Normal weight gain during pregnancy has a positive effect on the health of the fetus.

A pregnant woman should discuss any exercise program with her doctor. A moderate exercise routine is beneficial. Walking and swimming are among the best and the safest physical activities for a pregnant woman.

During pregnancy, intensive exercise causes heart rate and body temperature to rise rapidly. Early in pregnancy, this could cause problems for the fetus. High hormone levels also make the pregnant woman's joints more susceptible to injury. Overall, doctors advise against strenuous exercise during pregnancy.

Special exercises are often taught in childbirth classes. These may be designed to strengthen muscles in preparation for delivery. Some exercises are designed for after the delivery. They help the uterus contract and strengthen muscles in the abdomen.

Investigate Further

Why is moderate physical activity a better plan for weight control during pregnancy than dieting?

Rest and Sleep

A pregnant woman may become tired more easily and need extra rest. Eight hours of sleep each night with a short rest during the day can help a mother-to-be handle fatigue. The first three months and the last few weeks of pregnancy are usually the most tiring.

Handling Stress

A pregnant mother should try to avoid long periods of continued stress. High degrees of stress produce physical changes in her body. Her heart rate and breathing speed up. Her brain may signal the production of certain hormones.

Short-term reactions are not likely to affect the fetus. However, if the stress continues, the chemicals produced in her body can affect the development of the fetus. Also, under stress, the pregnant woman will become tired and fatigued. She may become more susceptible to illness as her body is less able to fight disease.

Illness

Although most pregnancies are normal, complications caused by illness sometimes occur. The causes vary, but include infectious diseases or poor prenatal care and nutrition. These illnesses or conditions can harm the fetus if the mother contracts them during pregnancy. Proper care during pregnancy can reduce the risk of serious complications, 11-8.

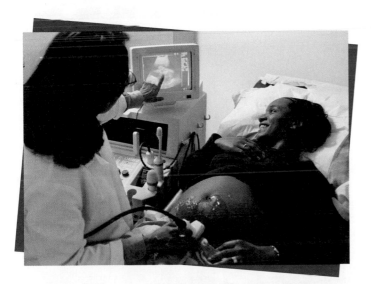

11-8 Regular checkups can help the doctor identify early signs of complications and take steps to protect both mother and baby.

Common Infectious Diseases

Infectious diseases that a mother may contract can damage the fetus. Measles, polio, mumps, chicken pox, or influenza can affect the unborn child. They may stunt the fetus's growth, cause deafness, or cause other serious birth defects.

If a mother gets *rubella* (German measles) during the first three months of pregnancy, the baby can be affected. This virus can cause miscarriage, stillbirth, or birth disorders. *Stillbirth* is the birth of a dead fetus. If a pregnant woman thinks she has been exposed to the virus, she should see her doctor. A blood test can determine if she is infected.

STIs

Sexually transmitted infections (STIs) must be treated to protect both the mother and the baby. However, it is important that the doctor know the woman is pregnant before treatment is given. Some antibiotics used to treat STIs must not be taken during pregnancy. (The most common STIs are discussed in Chapter 7, "Dating.")

Preeclampsia

Another serious complication of pregnancy is *preeclampsia*, also known as *toxemia* or *pregnancy-induced hypertension (PIH)*. This condition causes high blood pressure, swelling, and protein in the urine. Poor prenatal care and poor nutrition are linked to preeclampsia. If left untreated, the condition is dangerous to the health of the pregnant woman and the baby.

Preeclampsia occurs most often in the last half of a pregnancy. If diagnosed early, it can usually be controlled. Signs include a sudden weight gain, swelling of feet and hands, dizziness, severe headaches, or blurred vision.

Investigate Further

What are some key signs that a pregnant female should consult a doctor about her health or the health of her unborn baby?

Use of Drugs

If a mother uses drugs during her pregnancy, her baby will be affected. Drugs cross from the mother's bloodstream into the baby's blood. The baby's liver is not able to break down drugs until some time after birth. The developing baby has no way to get rid of the drug or its effects.

Any drug that harms the mother will also affect the unborn baby. Drugs such as tranquilizers, heroin, and LSD may cause severe birth defects. A baby can be born deaf, with heart and joint defects, a cleft palate, or malformed limbs.

If a mother is addicted to a drug, her baby will be, too. The baby may die of severe withdrawal symptoms if drug treatment is not given. Babies of addicts are likely to be born premature and underweight. They may cry often and not respond when held.

Other drugs such as hormones, sedatives, and some common antibiotics have also proven to be harmful. Sometimes these effects are seen at birth. On the other hand, some drug effects may not appear until many years later. Effects such as sterility and some forms of cancer may not be apparent until the children are older.

A pregnant woman should consult her doctor before taking any over-the-counter medications. Most prenatal specialists agree that the best policy for pregnant women is to take no drugs at all. That way possible side effects, now or in the future, can be avoided.

Use What You Learn

Identify possible long-term effects of a mother's use of drugs on the baby's development.

Other Harmful Effects

Tobacco, alcohol, and exposure to radiation pose serious health risks for a pregnant woman. All have harmful long-term effects on the developing baby.

The Effects of Smoking

Tobacco smoke contains poisonous gases that enter the mother's bloodstream, pass through the placenta, and enter the fetal bloodstream. Two of these harmful gases are nicotine and carbon monoxide. Nicotine constricts the blood vessels in both the mother and the fetus. Carbon monoxide cuts down the amount of oxygen carried by the blood. As a result, the fetus receives fewer nutrients and less oxygen.

Studies show that maternal smoking during pregnancy increases the risk of having a child with mental retardation. Also, the reduced supply of oxygen and nutrients tends to affect the baby's birthweight, 11-9. Low-birthweight babies have a high mortality (death) rate. Mothers who smoke have a greater risk of having a miscarriage, a stillbirth, or an infant who dies soon after birth.

Studies also show a high rate of infant deaths in nonsmoking mothers whose spouses smoked. Smoke from the lit end of a burning cigarette or exhaled by smokers is called *secondhand smoke*. This smoke actually contains more toxic chemicals than smoke inhaled through the cigarette. The smoke can enter a pregnant woman's lungs and have harmful effects on the developing fetus.

Link to Your Life

Why is it important that a person of childbearing age not use tobacco products?

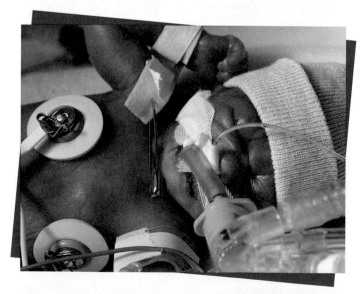

11-9 Heavy smoking triples the risk of delivering a premature baby. If born too early, the newborn will struggle to survive on its own.

The Effects of Alcohol

What happens when a pregnant woman drinks one 12-ounce can of beer or 1.5 ounces of liquor? She is giving her baby the equivalent of a full, intoxicating adult dose. Alcohol passes through the placenta and enters the fetal bloodstream quickly. The fetus feels the effects of alcohol as quickly as the mother. Because the fetal liver has not developed enough to break down the alcohol, the effects remain for a long time.

Alcohol is the third leading cause of birth defects in this country. If a pregnant woman drinks alcohol regularly, her baby can develop eye, heart, limb, and joint problems. Alcohol can influence the development of the fetus's brain and result in mental retardation or poor bone and muscle development.

Some children of alcoholic mothers develop patterns of disabilities known as **fetal alcohol syndrome (FAS)**. Children with FAS are affected both physically and mentally. They are short in stature. Their heads may be small. They have certain facial features such as small eye openings. Their physical development is slow, and they are mentally retarded. Many have behavioral problems.

The birth defects described thus far result from excessive alcohol use. However, even moderate use during pregnancy can affect unborn babies. Moderate amounts of alcohol can lead to short attention spans and slower reaction times in children. Since there is no safe level, pregnant women should avoid alcohol completely.

Think More About It
How can a couple make sure that alcohol will not have an effect on the development of their unborn child, even during the first two months?

The Effects of Radiation

The effects of radiation are known to be harmful at several stages of prenatal development. Even before conception, radiation can cause mutations in the father's and mother's cells. These changes in the gene structure can result in birth defects.

If a pregnant woman is exposed to radiation, her child's growth may be slowed. The central nervous system may not develop as it should. The risk for cancer tumors or leukemia increases. Large doses of radiation cause severe birth defects and death.

Women who suspect they are pregnant should not have X-rays. Women of childbearing age and younger should avoid X-rays of the lower abdomen and pelvic area. Lead shields are used to protect the reproductive organs whenever X-rays must be taken of another part of the body, 11-10.

Miscarriage

Sometimes a baby is born before the sixth month, too early to have developed enough for survival in the outside world. This is known as *miscarriage*. Miscarriages are not uncommon;

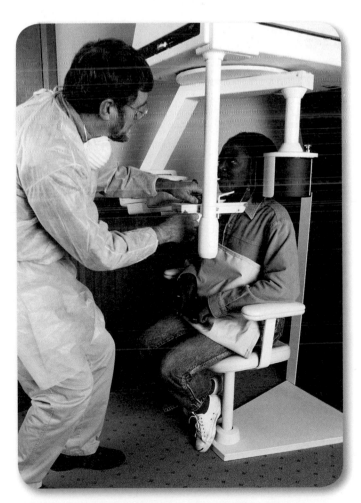

11-10 Pregnant women should avoid all forms of radiation. If dental or other X-rays are needed, a lead shield should be used to protect the fetus.

many occur during the first three months of pregnancy. About 15 to 20 percent of all pregnancies end in miscarriage. Many women who miscarry early in pregnancy are not even aware they are pregnant.

Miscarriages can have different causes. Most take place because of an imperfect embryo. This is the body's natural way of removing an embryo that is not developing properly. Other miscarriages may be caused by disease, infection, hormonal problems, vitamin deficiencies, or accidents.

One miscarriage should not discourage a woman from conceiving again. She should not feel guilty, thinking it happened because of something she did or did not do. In most cases following miscarriage, a woman can have a full-term pregnancy.

The Couple's Relationship During Pregnancy

A couple may work at providing a healthful environment for their unborn baby. They may be conscious of the pregnant mother's needs for a good diet, physical activity, and rest. They may be careful to avoid sources of harmful substances. Equally important is the relationship between the two of them.

The sharing and intimacy of a couple's relationship should continue throughout the pregnancy. A couple can discuss their sexual relationship with their doctor if they have fears or questions. A warm, close, and supportive relationship can help both adjust to the pregnancy, 11-11.

Helpful Tips for a Father-to-Be

- Communicate openly with your partner. Share feelings and support each other.
- Eat healthful foods. In that way you can encourage your partner to eat nutritious foods as well.
- Do not create secondhand smoke for your partner, and try to keep her out of a smoke-filled environment.
- Help your partner avoid the use of alcohol.
- Handle daily chores, child care, and other tasks to help your partner get the rest she needs.
- Go to childbirth classes with your partner. Be informed so you can support her through the delivery.

11-11 A supportive father-to-be can help ensure the arrival of a healthy baby.

Review Section 11:2

1. List three types of specialists who provide professional health care for pregnant women.
2. Identify three tests that can be used to detect possible abnormalities in the fetus.
3. Explain the importance of eating a well-balanced diet during pregnancy.
4. Explain why a woman should not try to lose weight during pregnancy.
5. List five common infectious diseases that can harm the fetus if the mother contracts them during pregnancy.
6. List four possible effects on the unborn child of alcohol use during pregnancy.

section 11:3

Preparing for the Baby

Sharpen Your Reading

Develop a chart with three columns: *Decisions to Be Made*, *Options to Choose*, and *Pros and Cons of Each Choice*. Complete the chart with decisions that parents need to make as they plan for their baby's arrival.

Boost Your Vocabulary

Explain the differences between the three most common methods of delivery.

Know Key Terms

sudden infant death syndrome (SIDS)
Lamaze method
Leboyer method
cesarean delivery
breech birth
lactation

Most couples approach pregnancy as a joint experience. They share the emotions and experiences of pregnancy together. Planning and preparing for the baby's arrival should be a joint experience, too.

As the woman's pregnancy progresses, other family members may find it easier to become involved in her pregnancy. They may see and feel the active movements of the fetus, especially kicking. This involvement tends to increase the bond between the growing child and the parents. Such bonding is also important for the couple's other children. As they are involved in preparing for the new baby, they are less likely to feel jealous, 11-12.

Planning for the Baby's Physical Needs

During the middle months of pregnancy, most families begin to prepare for the items the baby will need. Newborns do not have many clothing needs as they grow quickly. However, what they do wear should be comfortable. Clothes should be loose so the baby can move around easily. They should be easy to put on and take off. Also, they should have no buttons or snaps that could cause choking.

11-12 When children are spaced three or four years apart, less sibling rivalry occurs. Older children will enjoy helping care for the new baby.

The new baby will also need a place to sleep. Bassinets, cradles, or baby beds can all be used. The pad or mattress in the baby's bed should be firm to reduce the risk of **sudden infant death syndrome (SIDS)**. SIDS is the unexplained death of a healthy baby. The infant stops breathing and dies in its sleep. Experts recommend that placing an infant to sleep on his or her back reduces chances of a SIDS-related death. In addition, do not place pillows, blankets, or toys in the bed with the infant. This can increase risk of suffocation.

Any slats in a cradle or bed should be close enough so a soft drink can will not fit through. Wider gaps may allow a baby's body or head to become wedged. For the same reason, the edges of the bed pad should be close to the walls. No space should be wider than two fingers.

Planning for Delivery

As a couple prepare for the arrival of the baby, they have options about how the baby will be born. They should discuss the method of delivery they desire with their doctor. The three most common methods of delivery are natural childbirth, the Lamaze method, and the Leboyer method. Two other important issues should also be discussed with the doctor: the situations that require a surgical birth and the preferred location of the birth.

Most hospitals, clinics, and some private organizations offer classes to help couples prepare for childbirth. They help the parents understand the birth process so they can feel more in control of the situation. The classes are designed so both parents are involved, 11-13.

Natural Childbirth

Some childbirth classes teach parents the techniques of natural childbirth. In natural childbirth, little or no anesthesia is used to block the mother's labor pain. The mother learns how to breathe and relax to help with the labor and delivery. The father is taught how to support and coach her through the birth process. It is helpful for single mothers to ask a friend or family member to attend childbirth classes with them. The support and encouragement of this coach can help her with the birth experience.

11-13 Natural childbirth can be considered an educated childbirth since both parents understand the birth process. The father can assist and support his wife during labor and delivery.

The Lamaze Method

The **Lamaze method** of childbirth is named after Fernand Lamaze. In the 1950s, he developed this method to help mothers control the pain of childbirth. In a Lamaze class, the mother is taught to focus on breathing techniques to relax her muscles. She also learns how to shift her position to help ease the labor pains. The father or support person is taught how to coach her to relax using these techniques.

The Leboyer Method

Frederick Leboyer developed another approach to childbirth. In this method, the focus is on making the baby's transition into the world more gradual and less shocking.

With the **Leboyer method**, a comforting outside environment similar to the fetus's environment is provided at birth. The delivery room lights are dimmed. Soft music is played. The baby is placed on the mother's body right after birth. The umbilical cord continues to supply oxygen until the baby breathes alone. The cord is not cut until several minutes after birth. Then the newborn is gently placed in a warm water bath. There the baby can kick and move about as it did in the uterus. Afterward, the baby is dried and wrapped in a warm blanket.

Cesarean Delivery

A **cesarean delivery** (or *C-section*) is a surgical method of delivering a baby. The mother's abdomen is opened and the baby is removed. Because this is major surgery, a C-section is not performed unless the mother or baby's health is in danger. A C-section may need to be performed in the following cases:

- Labor is abnormal and the infant is in danger.
- The baby's head is very large and the mother's pelvis is small.
- The mother had a previous C-section. (This does not mean that future babies cannot be born naturally.)
- The baby is in the wrong position. In a **breech birth**, the baby is positioned for birth buttocks first. Doctors usually try to turn the baby to make the delivery easier.

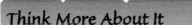

Think More About It
Which of the three methods of delivery do you think would be the least stressful on the baby?

Place of Delivery

Most babies are born in hospitals. The hospital chosen often depends on the doctor. The services offered at hospitals may vary. A couple may want to discuss this with their doctor early in the pregnancy.

Most hospitals have a labor room and a separate delivery room. In the past, fathers waited in a separate room while the mother went through the labor and delivery. Now, most hospitals encourage the father or support person to be with the mother during the entire process.

Today, more hospitals arrange for *family-centered childbirth*. This allows fathers, children, and other family members to be in the labor room. Some hospitals may allow them in the delivery room as well.

Some hospitals have *birthing rooms*. The labor and delivery all take place in a room with a homelike setting. This arrangement allows more freedom in determining who can attend the birth. The sounds and lighting in the room can be controlled. The mother's delivery position may be varied as well. Some centers have a birthing chair so the mother can sit upright during delivery.

If complications develop, most hospitals reserve the right to move the mother and limit those attending the birth. The mother and baby's health are always their first concern.

Many hospitals have a *rooming-in* service where the mother can have the baby stay in her room. This allows the mother to spend more time holding and feeding her newborn. Most hospitals will take the baby back to the nursery if the mother wants time to rest and sleep.

Breast-Feeding or Bottle-Feeding

Most couples discuss the method they will use to feed the baby before the baby arrives. The baby can be breast-fed or bottle-fed. In making their decision, the couple can look at the benefits of both methods, 11-14. Their choice usually depends on their desires and schedules.

Breast-Feeding

A mother's hormones will change and cause lactation about three days after the baby is born. **Lactation** is the production of milk in the breasts. If the mother is breast-feeding, the baby's sucking stimulates the nerve endings. This causes another hormone to start the milk flow. If she does not choose to breast-feed, her body will soon stop producing milk.

Low-birthweight babies especially benefit from mother's milk. Breast-fed babies are less likely to have stomach upsets since the milk is easy to digest. They have fewer problems with constipation, too. Other benefits include fewer skin disorders and less respiratory infection.

Breast-Feeding Versus Bottle-Feeding	
Breast-Feeding	**Bottle-Feeding**
• Breast milk has the right amount of nutrients to meet the baby's needs. • Breast milk is easy for the baby to digest. • Breast milk contains substances that protect the baby against certain illnesses. • Breast milk is always clean and at the right temperature. • Breast-feeding costs less than formula. • Breast-feeding helps the mother's uterus return to normal more quickly. • Breast-feeding uses the extra nutrients the body stored during pregnancy and helps the mother lose weight. • Breast milk contains the mother's natural antibodies to help the newborn fight off illness and disease.	• Bottle-feeding allows the father to share in the feeding of the baby. • Formula can be purchased that provides nutrients similar to those found in mother's breast milk. • Bottle-feeding provides a consistent amount and quality of milk at all times. • Bottle-feeding puts less demand on the mother and is less tiring for her.

11-14 Both of these feeding methods offer advantages. Whatever their choice, parents should create a relaxed atmosphere to strengthen the bond with their baby.

Most of the responsibility for feeding the baby is put on the mother when she chooses to breast-feed. Some families also use a bottle to supplement breast-feeding. Then the father can also share feeding time with the new infant.

Bottle-Feeding

Some mothers choose not to breast-feed or cannot use this method. Instead they choose to bottle-feed their newborn. Formulas are similar to breast milk. They meet the baby's nutritional needs for growth and development. Bottle-feeding also puts less strain on the parents' schedules because others can easily feed the baby.

Think More About It
What factors do you think affect a couple's choice about breast-feeding or bottle-feeding their newborn?

Review Section 11:**3**

1. Compare natural childbirth and cesarean delivery.
2. Briefly describe the types of delivery services a hospital may offer.
3. List three ways in which breast-feeding benefits the newborn.

section
11:4

The Baby Arrives

Sharpen Your Reading

As you read this section, list the steps that take place as labor occurs and the baby is born.

Boost Your Vocabulary

Compare what you would see if you observed a newborn who scored low on the Apgar scale and one who scored high on the Apgar scale.

Know Key Terms

labor
Apgar scale
bonding

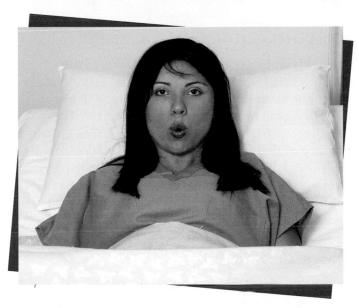

11-15 A woman's breathing can help her relax during labor pains.

Television and movies often give the impression that labor is short and fast. In reality, the process of giving birth is long, hard work. When a woman's labor begins, most couples know what to expect and what to do. After long months of planning and anticipation, they are ready for the delivery!

The Stages of Labor

The birth of a baby is divided into three distinct stages. These stages of labor differ in length and intensity of pain. **Labor** is the term used to describe the contractions of the uterus, 11-15. During labor, the lengthwise muscles of the uterus contract or shorten. This pulls open the circular muscles around the cervix and expels the baby.

First Stage of Labor

The first stage lasts the longest, averaging 4 to 16 hours. The mother's body first expels a pinkish plug of mucous. This is an early sign that labor is beginning. The amniotic sac may break early in labor. When this happens, about one cup of amniotic fluid is discharged. The mother should notify her doctor immediately when the amniotic sac breaks. Once this happens, the baby has lost its protection against infection. The doctor will want to be sure that delivery occurs soon.

When the uterine contractions are regular, true labor has begun. They should continue at regular intervals. As labor progresses, the contractions will become more intense and last longer.

Most doctors will discuss with the couple when they would like the mother to be at the hospital. Most suggest timing the contractions first. The couple should keep track of the time from the beginning of one contraction to the beginning of the next contraction.

The first stage of labor continues until the contractions have fully *dilated* (opened up) the cervix. For most women, the dilated cervix opening is about ten centimeters. During the last part of this stage, the baby's head enters the birth canal.

Second Stage of Labor

When the cervix is fully dilated and the baby's head is in the birth canal, the second stage of labor begins. It ends when the baby is born. This stage is much shorter than the first stage, lasting from 5 to 45 minutes. Labor pains are most severe at this point. With each contraction, more of the baby appears. After the baby has been delivered and helped to breathe, the umbilical cord is cut. Then the baby is examined and weighed.

Third Stage of Labor

In the third stage of labor, the uterus continues to contract. This causes the *afterbirth* (the placenta) to be expelled. The doctor or midwife will examine the placenta to be sure it is whole. If parts of the placenta are left in the mother, it could cause her to *hemorrhage* (uncontrolled bleeding). The uterus will continue to contract as it begins to shrink in size. It takes about six weeks for the uterus to return to its normal size and shape.

The Newborn

As soon as the baby is born, doctors assess the condition of the newborn to see if emergency care is needed. The **Apgar scale** is often used as a measure of the overall physical condition of the newborn, 11-16. At one minute and then five minutes after delivery, five vital signs are checked: the newborn's color, heart rate, reflexes, muscle tone, and breathing. The newborn receives a rating of *0, 1,* or *2* for each. Most newborns receive a total score of *7* or higher, which indicates average adjustment. Newborns who receive a score of *4* or less need emergency treatment to survive.

Newborn Screenings

Research has shown that some newborn deficiencies can be corrected if detected early. Once detected, the appropriate adjustment can be made at the ideal future time. The period when an adjustment can be made is called a *window of opportunity* because it must occur at a specific stage during growth. Because human development occurs in patterns, scientists now know the different periods when various adjustments should be undertaken for best results.

The importance of early detection has led to several newborn screening tests. These tests may be automatically given as part of your state's newborn screening program. Other tests may be recommended by your doctor. Discuss these tests in advance to learn the reasons for them. The information gained by using newborn screenings can help new parents remain calm and make logical decisions related to the growth and development of their newborn.

The Apgar Scale			
Vital Signs	**Score**		
	0	**1**	**2**
Heart rate	Absent	Slow (below 100)	Rapid (over 100)
Respiratory effort	Absent	Slow, irregular	Good, crying
Muscle tone	Limp	Weak, inactive	Strong, active
Color	Blue, pale	Body pink, arms and legs blue	Entirely pink
Reflexes	No response	Grimace or cry	Coughing, sneezing, crying vigorously

11-16 Each of the newborn's vital signs is rated and scored one minute after birth and then five minutes after birth. The highest score is 10. Most newborns score 7 or higher.

Investigate Further

What are some newborn screening tests required in your state?

Adjusting to the Newborn

Bringing a baby into the world is exciting for new parents. However, bringing the baby home into their family can require some immediate adjustments. The few weeks after childbirth are called the postpartum period. This period is marked by several changes.

The mother and father begin to adjust emotionally to the newborn. As they care for their baby, the interaction helps them become attached to the child. It also helps the baby attach to the parents. This feeling is called **bonding**. As the newborn focuses on his or her parents, these close feelings of attachment increase.

Most parents bond readily with their new baby, 11-17. However, mood swings are common for the mother during this period. Her hormones change after the birth of the baby. The loss of blood and lack of sleep may leave her feeling tired. At times she may feel depressed or have the "postpartum blues." This feeling is common and usually does not last beyond the first few weeks.

Fathers may also feel the postpartum blues. They may not sleep well. They may be concerned about being a good parent and husband. Fathers may need to adjust to helping care for and feed the baby. Financial pressures related to paying hospital bills may worry them.

After the excitement of delivery, parents may finally realize the responsibility of parenthood is a reality. They must learn to cope with and care for their newborn. More than ever, they need each other's understanding and support as they adjust to their new parenting roles.

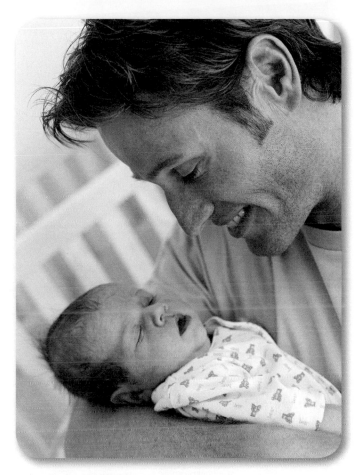

11-17 This father is developing a close bond with his newborn as he shares caregiving responsibilities with the mother.

Review Section 11:4

1. Briefly explain the three stages of labor.
2. Why do some states require several tests automatically be given to newborns?
3. Name two emotional adjustments a mother makes during the postpartum period.

Taking precautions during pregnancy can help prevent complications during the birth and result in a healthy child.

Think It Through

Three Parents-to-Be

Dr. Ranney stopped at the coffee shop for a quick break. She had three patients at different points in their labor.

Tony and Rosanne were expecting their third child. They were both confident having been through this twice before. They brought some CDs with their favorite music. They even brought some pictures for Rosanne to concentrate on when the labor became hard. Tony was giving Rosanne a back massage when Dr. Ranney last checked them. Rosanne's labor was progressing quickly, and she would soon be ready to deliver.

Jermaine and Latrice were first-time parents. Latrice had been in labor for nine hours. She still had not dilated much, yet seemed very tired. Jermaine was very anxious, pacing up and down the hall outside the labor room. Sometimes he sat for a few minutes with Latrice, then resumed pacing. Dr. Ranney wondered how many childbirth classes Jermaine had attended with Latrice and how he would react if complications occurred.

Angie, a young teen, was soon to become a single mother. Dr. Ranney was most concerned about the small size of her baby. Angie seemed to be handling her labor well. A good friend was acting as her coach, timing the contractions, and massaging her back to relax her. They seemed to make a good team. Dr. Ranney called to alert the "preemie" unit to prepare for a low-birthweight newborn. Then she returned to check her patients.

Questions to Guide Your Thinking

1. What observations did the doctor make in each case regarding how prepared the parents were for childbirth?

2. What relaxation techniques did Tony and Rosanne and Angie and her coach use to make labor easier?

3. How would prepared parents be helpful to Dr. Ranney?

4. What could result from couples not being prepared for childbirth?

5. If Jermaine and Latrice had not planned for their child, how might their relationship be affected by a difficult labor and delivery? How might their feelings toward the newborn be affected?

6. Why is a support person so important for Angie at this time?

Chapter Summary

A woman may suspect she is pregnant based on certain physical changes. A pregnancy test and physical exam by a doctor is the best way to confirm this.

The prenatal period is the time from conception until the birth of a baby. Throughout this period, a specific pattern of development takes place. After nine months, the baby is ready to be born.

The health of the developing baby is greatly affected by the health of the mother. Professional health care is important through the prenatal period and childbirth to help the mother deliver a healthy baby. Eating properly and avoiding harmful substances are key factors in her baby's growth and development.

As the due date nears, both parents can be involved in preparing for childbirth by planning ahead. This involves making decisions about the baby's physical needs. A method of delivery must be chosen. The choice of breast-feeding or bottle-feeding must be discussed. Sharing these decisions helps strengthen the couple's relationship.

The birth process begins with the onset of labor, which progresses through three stages. The arrival of a newborn forces parents to make immediate adjustments. Emotionally, both parents begin developing a bond of attachment to the newborn. This encourages them to work together to care for the infant and meet its needs.

Assess...

Your Knowledge

1. What changes take place in the female body during pregnancy?

2. What changes take place in the female body during childbirth?

3. What key development takes place in each stage of prenatal development?

Your Understanding

4. Briefly explain what happens after an egg and sperm unite.

5. How does prenatal care affect the growth of the unborn child?

6. How can couples prepare for childbirth and delivery?

Your Skills

7. Analyze your community and identify at least three possible scenarios in which an unborn child could be at risk.

8. Create a daily "to do" list that a pregnant woman could follow to help her and her unborn baby stay healthy.

Think Critically

9. *Social studies.* Interview a mother with a newborn. Ask her questions about the adjustments of parenting and the care of the baby. Write a paragraph discussing the impact these parenting adjustments would have on the roles of a teenager in high school. *Choice:* Invite the parent to speak to the class and demonstrate the care of a newborn.

10. **Writing.** Write a report summarizing the effects of smoking, alcohol use, or the use of a particular drug on the development of the unborn child. Identify resources available to help pregnant women struggling with these problems. Include a discussion of why you think women continue to use these substances when they know their harmful effects.

11. *Science, research.* Prepare a report on one birth defect and create a list of steps a parent-to-be should take to help avoid its causes. *Choice:* Present your information in a flyer or a poster.

12. Identify at least 10 healthful foods within each of the food groups that a pregnant woman could select in designing a menu plan. Also list foods that you believe she should avoid and explain why. *Choice:* Present your information in a collage or other visual.

Connect with Your Community

13. Interview a doctor, nurse, or registered dietitian. Prepare questions related to the importance of prenatal care both before and during pregnancy. Include questions on diet; weight gain; exercise; sleep; stress; the effects of drugs, alcohol, or smoking; possible birth disorders; and the doctor's role in childbirth. Summarize the professional's advice in a newspaper column called "Tips for Parents-to-Be." *Group option:* Work in groups to complete the assignment, with each person reporting on one aspect for the newspaper column.

14. **Writing.** Interview a midwife. Ask questions about the training and education required for a career, and the procedures used in both emergency and nonemergency situations. Prepare a one-page written report of your findings. *Choice:* Include reflections on why people might choose to use a midwife for delivering a baby.

15. Visit a local childbirth class. Prepare a brief report based on your observations of the following techniques taught: handling the pain of childbirth, involving both parents in the birth process, and handling the baby immediately after birth. *Choice:* Present your information using a flyer or presentation software.

16. **Science.** Obtain permission from a hospital facility in your area to tour its birthing facilities. Report on the types of facilities and the delivery methods available to prospective parents. *Choice:* Present your information in a video or with presentation software.

Use Technology

17. Use the Internet to find current pregnancy tests available over-the-counter. Print the list, including the cost of each test and the name of the manufacturer. Also include a review of the test's reliability if available. *Choice:* Present your information in a chart or table.

18. **Research.** Search the Internet to locate menus for a pregnant woman for one week. Contact a reliable source, such as the American Dietetic Association. Print the menus. Using word-processing software, write a paper describing what changes you would need to make to your diet in order to follow the menu plan.

19. **Science.** Using the Internet, research current tests available for detecting birth disorders early in a pregnancy. Write a report on one of these tests and include a discussion of legal or ethical issues that may be raised by the use of these tests. *Group option:* Form two teams and hold a debate on the issues.

20. **Math.** Research statistics related to birth disorders and prepare a chart using a spreadsheet program. Illustrate the frequency at which these defects have occurred over the last five years. Print the chart and turn it in with a summary of the trends shown in the chart.

Chapter 12

Helping Children Grow and Develop

Section 12:1
Factors Affecting a Child's Development

Section 12:2
Areas of Growth and Development

Section 12:3
Stages of Growth and Development

Key Questions

Questions to answer as you study this chapter:

- How do children grow and develop?

- What factors stimulate a child's growth to full development?

Chapter Objectives

After studying this chapter, you will be able to

- **recognize** hereditary and environmental factors influencing children's development.

- **identify** patterns of physical, intellectual, social, and emotional growth in a child.

- **describe** characteristics of a child in each stage of development.

- **determine** how parents can stimulate their child's development in each growth stage.

Life Sketch

"What do you think, Mom? What's wrong with Jason? Why won't he sleep? Why does he cry so much? What should I do?"

"Guess what? Jason finally slept through the night! Eight whole hours! I can hardly believe it!"

"Dad, Jason rolled over from his back to his stomach! He really is getting stronger."

"He can sit up now all by himself. He likes to pull himself to his feet. He stands there and bounces up and down like he's trying to dance!"

"He's really getting into things now. He crawls all over the place, under the table, and behind the chairs. His favorite place to play is my drawer of pots and pans. He empties everything onto the floor!"

Getting Started

From day to day, proud parents marvel at the growth and development of their child. Along with this excitement are the challenges of parenting. Many new parents have questions about what to do and how to handle new situations.

Many parents feel some anxiety about their new roles. They want to do a good job of parenting because they know this is a one-time experience. They cannot take a practice run and then try again. Each child will go through the process of growth and development just once.

Learning how children grow and develop from birth to adolescence can ease some parental concerns. Understanding this growth process can help parents do the following:

- ***Understand and accept children at different stages of development.*** Children mature over a period of several years. Their behavior will change as they grow and develop. Behavior that is normal for a two-year-old is not average for a six-year-old.

- ***Know how to stimulate a child's growth to full development.*** The environment holds many influences that can either stimulate or slow a child's growth.

- ***Feel confident about parenting.*** Being prepared for the developmental changes of a growing child will make it easier to adjust to those changes. Parents will know what to expect and how to make it a positive experience.

section 12:1

Factors Affecting a Child's Development

Sharpen Your Reading

Create two columns on a sheet of paper. As you read each topic in the section, identify a key concept that parents should understand and write it in the first column. Then discuss with a partner what parents might do if they did not understand this concept. Write your thoughts in the second column.

Boost Your Vocabulary

Identify an example that illustrates how two children proceed through a growth pattern at different rates of development.

Know Key Terms

maturation
rate of development
obesity

Development occurs little by little over a long period of time. The major impacts on development are the long-term factors. This fact can be encouraging to parents and others who are trying to help children grow, but occasionally make mistakes. Most mistakes of parenting do not cause permanent damage. However, if patterns that prevent or slow growth are continued, the child's development can be affected.

Patterns of Development

In all children, normal development follows certain patterns. These patterns consist of several events that take place in a certain order. Infants first move their arms and legs. Next, they learn to roll over. Then they learn to sit up alone. Later they begin to crawl and walk. Similar patterns can be found in all areas of children's development.

Within a developmental pattern, new learning builds on what was learned in earlier steps. In the earlier example, children learn to control their arm muscles first, then their leg muscles and back muscles. Finally, they learn to use the arm and leg muscles together.

Maturation

Learning cannot occur until the body is physically ready. **Maturation** is the emergence of physical characteristics through the growth process. Physical maturing must occur before certain skills can be learned. For instance, arm muscles and leg muscles must develop before a child can use them to crawl. Brain cells and nerve cells must develop to coordinate the activity, 12-1.

12-1 A toddler will enjoy riding a scooter toy, which requires fewer muscles and less coordination than a tricycle.

For parents, understanding how maturation influences their child's development is helpful. Sometimes parents get anxious because their child has not learned a new skill, such as walking or speaking. They must realize their child will follow the same developmental patterns as others, but at his or her own rate.

Think More About It
What might a parent expect a child to do before the child is physically ready or able to do it?

Rate of Development

A child's **rate of development** is the speed at which that child proceeds through a developmental pattern. The age at which a child begins a growth spurt will depend on that child's own rate of development. Most children have a rate of development similar to others the same age. However, each child is a unique individual—heredity will control his or her rate of development.

A child's rate of development is not constant. It varies throughout the child's eighteen years of growth. This change in the rate of development is seen in the growth curve in 12-2. From the chart, you can see that the rate of development is most rapid during the first year of life. Then again in adolescence, growth is quite rapid.

Sometimes parents compare their child's progress with others and feel discouraged. They may interpret their child's slower rate of development as a lack of intelligence. However, the rate of development is not related to intelligence. Slower development just means the child will progress through the pattern more slowly than a child with a faster rate.

Investigate Further

Why is it hard for parents to avoid comparing their young child with the child's peers?

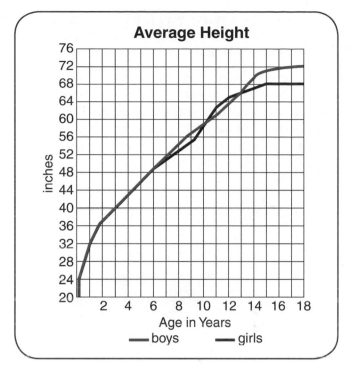

12-2 This growth chart gives the average height of boys and girls for each year from birth to age 18. The steep slope indicates a faster growth period.

A child's heredity lays the basic plan for growth. The limits of many physical traits are set by a child's genes. Whether those traits develop to their fullest is affected by factors in the child's environment.

Stimulating Environment

What happens in the environment surrounding the infant and young child affects the development of the brain. The newborn depends on the environment to provide sounds, smells, touch, tastes, and sights to the senses. This input stimulates the brain's development according to the use-it-or-lose-it principle. The parts that are stimulated develop and mature; those not used gradually die. Therefore, it is important that the growing child has an interesting and interactive environment. It needs to include people who provide loving and consistent care as well as stimuli for all the senses.

Stress in the Child's Environment

Although many parents are concerned about giving their child too little stimulation, either too much or too little stimulation can negatively impact development. An excess amount of loud noises and constant sensory bombardment causes stress for the infant. When the body is under stress, the stress hormone *cortisol* is produced. This washes over the developing brain, producing an acid-wash effect. The child needs adequate calm and rest in the environment to give the brain time to integrate all that it is learning.

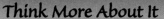

Think More About It
In what situations might parents allow their child too much sensory stimuli and not realize it?

Nutrition

A child has daily needs for nutrients. Parents need to plan healthful meals for their children and make sure they eat a variety of healthful foods. Every day, children need good sources of protein in their diet. They need fruits and vegetables, whole grain breads and cereals, and dairy products. A child will be malnourished if one or more needed nutrients are left out of the diet on a regular basis.

The Effects of Poor Nutrition

Poor nutrition can affect a child's development. Within the first three years of life, 85 percent of the core brain structure develops. The foods children eat affect which brain chemicals are produced. In turn, these brain chemicals affect how the brain develops. They also affect the child's behavior, emotions, and ability to learn.

The food a child eats can influence maturation. This affects the time the child is ready to go on to the next stage of development. Severe malnutrition can result in poor muscle control in children. They may appear clumsy. Their language development may be slow. They may appear quiet and without energy. On the other hand, they may be fussy and cranky. It all depends on the specific nutrients the child is lacking.

A child's physical appearance and long-term health are affected by poor nutrition. Too many fats in the young child's diet can lead to obesity. **Obesity** is a condition marked by excess body fat. Once formed, the number of fat cells cannot be decreased through diet. This can lead to difficulty with weight problems in later years. Also, too many fats in the diet may mean an absence of other nutrients. These may be the nutrients needed for the growth of bone cells, nerve cells, and muscle cells.

Use What You Learn

Have you observed that certain foods make a difference in children's behaviors? If so, which ones?

Disease

Children who do not receive a proper diet are more prone to illness. This means they may get sick more often and have a harder time recovering from illness. With good health care, most childhood diseases do not cause permanent damage to a child. Immunizations are given to children to protect them from common childhood diseases.

People in the Child's Environment

How do the people in a child's life affect growth and development? During the first few years, parents tend to be the main influence in a child's life. Other family members, teachers, caregivers, and peers also play an important part in the child's environment.

Parents

Parents are responsible for providing an environment in which the child's needs are met. Parents need to provide a nurturing environment in which a child feels loved and supported. This is crucial for the development of the limbic part of the brain. A lack of love not only affects the development of emotions, but physical development as well. Studies have shown that babies who do not receive love can be stunted in their growth. A lack of affection causes their pituitary glands to malfunction so they do not produce enough growth hormones. These children do not gain height or weight as they should.

The environment should be safe and secure and meet a child's physical needs, 12-3. Proper nutrition, clothing, shelter, medical care, and a safe environment are important for the child's health and well-being. In the first year of life, illness or accidents could bring harm and even death.

Parents are also responsible for introducing the child to the outside world. A child's view of this world is based on what is learned at home. To stimulate growth, parents must learn to manage the child's environment. This will help make it an interesting and safe place to learn and explore. If parents do not manage the child's environment, the world may be presented as a

12-3 As parents care for their children and meet their needs for love and security, they stimulate growth and development.

fearful place full of danger. Then the child may be afraid to explore the environment. In other cases, the child may be overprotected and not allowed to explore and learn.

Another parental responsibility is to provide a role model of how people live and act. The time they spend interacting with a child helps the child grow socially. The child learns what behaviors are acceptable and unacceptable. When parents do not fulfill this responsibility, a child may find it difficult to fit into society.

Other Adults

Parents are the primary but not *only* adults who affect a child's development. Children will spend many hours with other family members, caregivers, and teachers. These adults can help meet some of a child's needs and be sources of love and affection. They can also provide physical care, enrich the child's environment, and serve as role models. A child's experiences in the extended family, school, and community are important to growth and development.

Peers in the Environment

The young child's friends, or lack of them, also have an impact on the child's development. Friends help children grow. When they play with others, children learn social skills. They learn to communicate their thoughts and feelings and consider the thoughts and feelings of others.

This growth process takes time and can be painful. Children are very competitive with one another. They want to be the best, the fastest, and the smartest. They often pick those who appear the most skilled to be their friends. The children who do not measure up often feel left out or picked on.

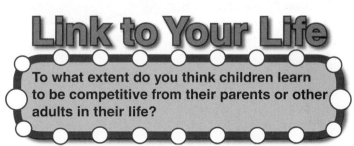

Link to Your Life

To what extent do you think children learn to be competitive from their parents or other adults in their life?

When a child feels rejected by his or her peers, it can have a negative effect on that child's development. Sometimes parents need to intervene. They may need to change the environment so the child has some positive peer experiences. They may be able to help the child increase his or her social skills.

When parents become aware of problems, they need to take action. They should not let harmful conditions for their child continue over time. Children are resilient, and in most cases, can bounce back when negative experiences are replaced with positive ones.

The Child's Responses to the Environment

Parents soon learn that each child responds to the environment in his or her own way. One child may be content to sit and build with a pile of blocks. Another child may run around the room, kicking or throwing the blocks. Each child has patterns for responding physically, socially, emotionally, and intellectually. These patterns form the child's temperament, 12-4.

12-4 Temperament is often the reason for children reacting differently to the same situation.

A Child's Temperament

Being aware of differences in a child's temperament is important for parents. A child's temperament may influence how parents and others respond and care for him or her. All children need to be loved and cared for in a consistent way. For some parents, it may be much easier to provide warmth and love to the quiet, sensitive child. A busy, noisy child may cause the parent or caregiver to respond with more control and less love. However, the active child needs affection just as much as the quiet child. Differences in children's temperaments may cause some differences in their needs. What helps one child learn self-control may not work with another.

A child's temperament will affect how that child approaches learning situations. One child may need only a little encouragement to explore the environment. Another may need to be coaxed and helped to take the first step. Understanding a child's response patterns can help parents and caregivers know how to stimulate growth and development.

Review Section 12:1

1. How does heredity influence a child's growth and development?

2. Explain how physical maturation influences the development of new skills.

3. Name the two stages when a child's rate of development is most rapid.

4. Give three examples of how a child's diet can affect development.

5. List four responsibilities parents have regarding their child's development.

6. Explain how a child's temperament may influence his or her particular needs.

section 12:2

Areas of Growth and Development

12-5 Learning to walk is a milestone in a child's physical development.

Sharpen | Your Reading

As you read, use either words or pictures to develop a sequence for each area of growth and development. Illustrate milestones or major accomplishments in each sequence.

Boost | Your Vocabulary

Give an example of a milestone for each area of development.

Know | Key Terms

milestones
motor development
symbols

Each child grows and develops in four areas: physical, intellectual, social, and emotional. Major accomplishments within each area are called **milestones**. Learning to walk, talk, and care for oneself are all milestones in development, 12-5.

Physical Development

The first and most obvious area of growth is a child's physical development. Observing and measuring physical growth is easy. Height and weight measurements are taken often to check a child's progress.

A child's physical body needs to grow and mature before growth can be seen in other areas. The maturation of brain cells, muscle cells, nerve cells, and bone cells is part of physical development. Although you cannot see these cells growing, you can see the results of their growth. The child moves around, learns to talk, thinks in more complex ways, and grows taller.

Physical Patterns of Development

Physical development follows certain patterns in all children. These three patterns dictate which parts of the body develop first:

- The body develops from top to bottom (or head to tail). For example, the brain develops before the legs and feet.
- The body develops from the central part of the body to the outer parts. For example, the spinal column matures before arms and fingers.
- Development proceeds from the simple to the complex. Children can wave their arms before they can pick up objects.

These patterns are easy to see as children develop motor skills.

Motor Development

The physical movements that a child makes as development proceeds are known as **motor development**. Motor development requires that muscles, nerves, and brain cells mature and work together to enable the child to reach each new milestone. Motor development occurs from head to foot and from the center of the body outward. Children learn to control large muscles before they learn small-muscle control.

Gross-motor behavior describes movements that use the large muscles. For most children these behaviors follow in the same order, but occur at different times. Simple kicking movements proceed to rolling over, sitting, creeping, and crawling. Walking, running, pedaling, and skipping are more advanced skills in the sequence.

Fine-motor behavior describes the movements of the hands and fingers. These proceed from simple grasping of objects to coordinating the movements of the fingers. Picking up small objects proceeds to holding a pencil or crayon and scribbling. Then children progress to drawing, buttoning, cutting, tracing, and other manipulative tasks.

Use What You Learn

Give examples of how motor development occurs from head to foot and from the center of the body outward.

Intellectual Development

The growth of mental skills is referred to as *intellectual development*. The sequence of steps that achieves intellectual development starts with taking in information through the five senses. This information is then imprinted on the brain. The child continually takes in information and later uses it. In this way, the child develops memory.

How Language Develops

With information in memory, the child begins to develop thought-pictures of objects. These are called **symbols**. A toddler may point to a

water faucet and grunt. In the toddler's mind is a symbol of water and an understanding of its source. The next step in the development of language is identifying those symbols, 12-6.

Stages of Language Development
Crying
• The newborn's only means of communicating needs
Different types of crying
• Hunger
• Attention
• Pain
Cooing
• Squeals, gurgles, bleats
• Vowel sounds
Babbling
• Playful repetition of sounds: "Ma-ma-ma-ma" and "Da-da-da-da"
Imperfect imitation
• Takes place from six months to one year
• Listens to sounds, then repeats sounds and syllables
Imitation of others' sounds
• Imitates sounds even though not understood
Expressive jargon
• Uses a string of syllables that make no sense
One-word sentences
• Uses one word to mean a whole sentence: "Wa" means "I want a drink of water"
Two or more words in a sentence
• "Me go" and "All gone"
Correct speech
• Uses all parts of speech in a sentence

12-6 Language development follows a definite sequence. During this period, children learn to speak the language they hear.

The muscles in the mouth and tongue must develop for language development to proceed. Children learn by imitating and repeating the sounds they hear. They need to hear labels for all experiences with people, objects, feelings, sights, and sounds.

Language development proceeds from the simple to the complex. A child can understand words two to four months before actually using those words.

The use of language should be rewarding for a child. Language should help the child express thoughts and desires and should bring responses from parents. When parents and others respond to the child with more speech, that also is a form of reward.

Think More About It
What is the benefit of using correct grammar when talking with a child?

Concrete Thoughts

When children can do in their heads what they used to do in actions, they are using concrete thought. They think about real objects or real people. They think about the qualities they can see and observe. They test concepts to see what will happen. They order and categorize this information in the brain. Their ability to use information in a logical way increases.

Social Development

The developmental process in which children learn to adapt to the world around them is known as *social development*. A child's first relationships are very important during this time. Close and nurturing relationships help a child feel secure and develop trust in other people. The child needs to be held, cuddled, and talked to while care is provided. These interactions help the parent-child bond grow.

Bonding

Bonding is a strong feeling of attachment that develops between the parent and the newborn. Parents interact with their newborns by looking

into their eyes, talking, smiling, and caressing the skin. These interactions stimulate the neurons in the newborn's brain. The newborn responds to the parent, and this communication creates a close bond of attachment. This attachment is critical in the development of the child.

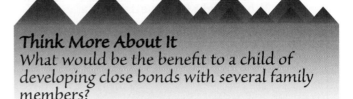

Think More About It
What would be the benefit to a child of developing close bonds with several family members?

Developing Peer Relationships

From the trusting family relationships, the child learns to reach out to others. Young children become interested in their peers. At first, peers are just objects to watch or explore. Soon young children enjoy one another's company and will play beside each other. They are still very self-centered since their actions revolve around their own desires.

Children's social skills continue to develop as they learn to play with one another. As they learn to share and take turns, they also learn that others have a point of view. These social skills develop as parents and other adults guide their behavior.

Through guidance and teaching, parents pass on their standards for living to their children. Children first comply with these standards in order to avoid trouble. Later, their responses are aimed at pleasing or helping others. As they mature, children respond as a result of concern for the rights and welfare of others, 12-7.

Emotional Development

Children pass through many stages of emotional development as they grow. Early emotions are connected to the parent-child bond and feelings of attachment. They are also related to the care the infant receives from caregivers. Children pick up emotions from the adults around them. They also learn to control their emotions as they see parents model the expression of emotions. Thus, a child's relationships have a major impact on emotional development.

Investigate Further

What might be the effect on a child's development of living in an environment where fighting and yelling are common?

12-7 As she shows concern for the younger child's well-being, this girl shows she is maturing socially.

Developing Positive Emotions

Children need to feel secure. These feelings develop as parents provide care for young children's needs. Children learn they can trust those around them to provide that care.

Children need to feel loved. They feel loved when family members meet their physical and emotional needs. As children feel loved, they are able to love others.

Children need to experience feelings of success. These feelings come from success in doing tasks, such as putting on their own clothes, feeding themselves, and learning to talk. Successful experiences help the child think "I am capable."

Children who feel lovable and capable develop a positive self-concept. Children with high self-esteem will likely build friendships and develop close relationships. Such warm, loving relationships provide close bonds of attachment, and the cycle continues. Therefore, emotional growth is tied to the relationships that a child develops.

Review Section 12:2

1. Identify three principles that describe how physical growth proceeds.
2. Give an example of a physical sequence for gross-motor movements and for fine-motor movements.
3. Identify two milestones in intellectual development.
4. Name three results of positive emotional development on a child's growth.

section 12:3

Stages of Growth and Development

Sharpen Your Reading

Develop a chart with the four main areas of development as headings (*Physical*, *Intellectual*, *Social*, and *Emotional*). Going down the side, list each stage of development. As you read, fill in the chart with key characteristics of each stage.

Boost Your Vocabulary

Identify how each reflex helps the newborn survive.

Know Key Terms

fontanels
rooting reflex
grasping reflex
startle reflex
swimming reflex
Babinski reflex
states of the newborn
stranger anxiety
separation anxiety
autonomy

The stages of growth and development include behaviors that are common for children of a certain age. All children progress through patterns of development at their own rate, yet they share many similarities.

Both boys and girls progress through these stages in a similar manner. Children's growth is a gradual yet continuous process. There is no exact time at which they leave one stage and enter another. In the following sections, the examples of Alex and Lauren show an average child's needs at various stages of development.

The Newborn: Birth to Three Months

The newborn baby is a unique individual. For example, one-day-old Alex has five senses to take in information from his new environment, 12-8. He has reflexes for responding to his environment. Also, he responds with different patterns to let others know his needs.

Appearance of the Newborn

As an average-size newborn, Alex weighs about seven pounds and is about 20 inches long. His head is almost one-fourth of his body length. On his skull are six soft spots called **fontanels**. This is where the skull bones have not yet fused together. The fontanels allowed his head to flex as he traveled through the birth canal. These soft spots are covered by a tough membrane. Like many newborns, Alex has a misshapen head and a squashed nose from the trip down the birth canal. His head will return to a normal appearance in a few days.

Reflexes

A newborn arrives with built-in reflex behaviors to adjust to the new environment. What will happen if Alex's mother strokes his cheek? Alex will turn his head toward her. As he begins searching for food, he opens his mouth and starts sucking. This is called a **rooting reflex**. This survival instinct helps Alex find food and prepare for feeding.

Alex can really hang on if he gets hold of his mother's finger—or her necklace or hair! This **grasping reflex** enables Alex to hold on tight enough to even hold his own weight.

The **startle reflex** is seen if Alex is put down suddenly or if someone makes a loud noise. He will throw out his arms, draw back his head, and stretch out his legs. When he is bathed, the **swimming reflex** causes Alex to make swimming movements in water. The **Babinski reflex** causes him to extend his toes when the soles of his feet are stroked.

As a newborn, Alex has some other useful reflexes. Some cause him to blink his eyes or cough. One helps him eliminate waste products when his bladder or bowel is full. Some reflexes that protect his body will continue throughout his life. Others will disappear as his brain and nervous system develop. Then Alex will take control of his own responses.

Investigate Further

What area of development is most influenced by the reflexes? Why would maturation of this area result in the reflexes disappearing?

States of the Newborn

Newborn Lauren demonstrates responses that are common to all newborns. These responses are called **states of the newborn**. Each state

The Newborn's Abilities
Sight
• Sees best at an eight-inch distance
• Likes to look at a human face
• Follows a moving target with eyes
• Responds to light
• Likes to look at patterns with sharp outlines and contrasts of dark and light

Sound	
• Sensitive to voices	
• Prefers high-pitched voices	
• Turns head toward a sound	
• Tries to focus on the source of a sound	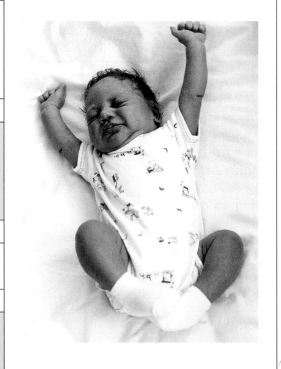
Touch	
• Sensitive to touch	
• Comforted by closeness, warmth, and touching	
• May kick or cry at changes in air temperature	
• Responds to pain, rough textures, and moisture	
Taste and smell	
• Puckers lips after a strong flavor	
• Breathes faster and kicks when smelling strong odors	
Communication	
• Communicates by crying, cooing, and smiling	
• Responds to parents' moods and feelings	
• Develops attachment to caregiver	

12-8 Newborns show remarkable abilities at birth. They respond to their environment through the use of all five senses.

describes patterns in which the newborn responds to the environment. A total of six states exist, 12-9.

- Three states refer to the newborn's activity when awake: quiet-alert, active-alert, and crying.
- Two states refer to sleeping patterns: quiet sleep and active sleep.
- One state refers to the transition between sleep and being awake: drowsiness.

Watching a newborn like Lauren while she is in the *quiet-alert state* is enjoyable. It is fun to talk to her and see how she responds. She may coo and look into your eyes. She may follow your hand as you hold a brightly colored ball and move it about. Most newborns are awake and quiet for one to two hours a day.

If Lauren is uncomfortable or close to feeding time, she will move into the *active-alert state*. Usually, a newborn like Lauren can be quieted by having her needs met right away.

States of the Newborn	
Quiet-Alert	• Newborn is awake and content • Eyes are open wide • Eyes try to focus on objects • Enjoys an interesting environment • May maintain this state if full, warm, and dry
Active-Alert	• Movement increases • May move arms, legs, body, or face • May kick and cry
Crying	• Newborn's way of communicating needs • Cry of pain is sharp and intense and may be followed by holding the breath • Crying an hour or so after feeding may be a sign of a digestive problem • Hunger cries usually start with whimpering, then become more intense
Drowsiness	• The state between being awake and asleep • Movement may occur • Facial expressions may change • Eyes do not focus
Quiet Sleep	• Newborn sleeps soundly • Not disturbed by most noises • Does not move much • Breathes deeply and evenly
Active Sleep	• Eyes will flutter • Movement is common • Newborn will smile, frown, suck, or chew • May make snorting noises

12-9 These various states describe the patterns newborns follow for the first three months of their lives.

Crying is Lauren's way of letting her parents know her needs. If it is close to feeding time and she starts to fuss, she should be fed before she breaks into a hard cry. Responding to her cry right away will not spoil her. Instead, it will help her feel secure.

If she has a wet or dirty diaper, she needs to be changed. If she is bored, she needs someone to talk, sing, walk, or play with her. If she appears to be in pain, she may need to burp or pass some gas.

Sometimes, newborns do not quiet easily. Lauren may be fed and burped, her diaper changed, and still be fussy. Usually movement and stimulation will quiet her. Her parents may rock or hold her or walk with her. They may use a ticking clock or a rhythmic swing to quiet her. Sometimes they may wrap her tightly in a blanket, swaddling her. This can help her feel secure. If Lauren is easy to quiet, her parents will feel that it is easy to care for a newborn. If she is often fussy and difficult to quiet, it may be frustrating for her parents.

Sometimes a fussy newborn causes the parents to become nervous and tense. The newborn senses this and becomes even more fussy. Some new parents may find it hard to relax as they adjust to caring for their newborn. They need to take steps to relax, call someone to talk or seek help, and at all costs, avoid becoming angry with a crying baby.

Newborns spend about half their sleeping time in *quiet sleep*. Lauren may sleep soundly for about 30 minutes. Then she may move into *active sleep* for 30 minutes. When Lauren's parents are aware that she will make movements and sounds when sleeping, they can relax. They know she is not about to wake up. After Lauren stirs for a while, she will return to a quiet sleep unless it is near feeding time.

Think More About It
How would understanding the states of a newborn help new parents adjust to parenting?

The Infant: Three Months to One Year

Infants grow rapidly, 12-10. Even on a daily basis, Lauren's parents notice changes in her. As her body matures, she will explore her environment with all her sensory powers. As she takes in information, patterns are imprinted on her brain.

Physical Development

As Lauren develops her motor skills, she will reach out for items around her. She will explore her mother's mouth, nose, ears, hair, and skin. Toys are objects she can touch, put in her mouth, and squeeze. She also explores her own hands, fingers, feet, toes, and other body parts.

As she gains control over her muscles, she learns to coordinate her movements. She can pick objects up and play with them. She learns to move her body and masters sitting, creeping on all four limbs, and even walking. Most children learn to walk alone at about one year of age. This can vary by several weeks as each child is unique.

Intellectual Development

Over the next several months, Lauren's reasoning and language abilities quickly advance. She delights in playing games such as peek-a-boo with her parents. She becomes skilled at imitating others' behavior. In just a few months, her language skills increase. She progresses from imitating sounds to saying several words and "singing" along with her favorite songs. She responds to words and can follow simple directions. At night, she likes to look at the picture books her parents read to her.

Social Development

Lauren becomes very attached to her mother and father, who provide most of her care. If another main caregiver is used during this first year, it is important that one person consistently fill this role. Lauren needs to feel secure in this close relationship before she will reach out to explore the world around her.

The Infant: Three Months to One Year	
Characteristics of Development	**Suggestions to Stimulate Development**
Holds head erect Reaches for object Recognizes mother Rocks like an airplane on tummy Rolls over	• Provide sensory stimuli such as colorful mobiles; pictures on wall; objects hanging in crib; soft fuzzy toys to touch, squeeze, and explore; and soft, rhythmic music.
Grasps objects	• Provide objects to grasp, bang, drop, or mouth.
Expresses many emotions: jealousy, sympathy, and affection	• Display calm and stable emotions in response to child.
Imitates faces	• Play peek-a-boo games.
Likes to play	• Talk and sing to child.
Fears strangers Attached to mother	• Show confidence and positive attitude around other people.
Sits alone, hitches around, creeps on hands and knees, stands alone, and may walk	• Provide space to move around, objects to crawl on, and objects that allow infant to pull up to a standing position.
Turns and manipulates objects Uncovers toys that have been hidden	• Provide toys that encourage investigation.
Points to body parts	• Play "Where's your nose?" and other games.
Uses a few words	• Name objects in the child's environment.
Holds crayons and makes marks	• Provide large crayons and large pieces of blank paper to accommodate the infant's large motor movements.

12-10 Infants pass through many stages of physical, intellectual, social, and emotional development as they grow.

Other siblings or relatives should be involved with Lauren as well. She will enjoy the attention. Also, she will benefit from the extra stimulation as they talk to her, hold her, and play with her.

Emotional Development

Lauren quickly learns to recognize those who care for her. When someone unfamiliar comes near, she expresses **stranger anxiety**. She reacts by crying in fear. If she is not secure in her parent-child relationships, this fear will be even greater. As she learns that others can be trusted, her fears subside.

Her ability to move about marks a new phase of learning. Lauren starts to explore her environment. At first she fears moving too far from her mother. This is called **separation anxiety**. Instead, she crawls over to a toy and then brings it back to her mother. She plays with the toy by her mother's side. As she becomes more confident, she moves further and further from her mother to explore her new world.

Separation anxiety may also occur when Lauren's parents leave her with a caregiver. Lauren fears that her parents will not return.

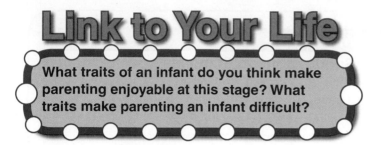

What traits of an infant do you think make parenting enjoyable at this stage? What traits make parenting an infant difficult?

The Toddler: One to Three Years

The toddler's approach to learning is by exploration. A rapid increase in motor skills opens up a whole new world for the toddler to explore. As a toddler, Alex will tackle exploring his new world with vigor.

Physical Development

As a toddler, Alex needs constant watching. He does not know what parts of the environment offer danger. By taking walks or special trips with Alex, his parents can give him a chance to safely explore his larger environment, 12-11.

Alex is developing a sense of **autonomy**. In other words, he is learning he can do some tasks on his own. He knows he is a separate person. He is learning that he has control over his own body. He can make his body climb, walk, and run.

Intellectual Development

Alex is also learning that he can exercise control over his environment. He can move objects or make them come apart. He can stack

The Toddler: One to Three Years	
Characteristics of Development	**Suggestions to Stimulate Development**
Attempts to solve simple problems	• Provide toys that reward exploration using principles of cause and effect (hop when pulled, squeak when pushed, puzzles, nesting buckets, stacking toys).
Learns via exploration	• Take walks or trips to explore surroundings.
Vocabulary increases	• Identify objects you can see, hear, smell, touch, or taste.
Identifies objects by names	• Read to child and name objects in pictures.
Enjoys sound patterns and music	• Teach nursery rhymes and finger plays. • Clap and swing to music.
Learns to walk well, run, kick, jump, and climb	• Provide opportunities for gross-motor development—balls to kick, small riding toys.
Fine-motor control develops in hands and fingers	• Provide blocks for stacking, large crayons for coloring, toys to manipulate, finger paints, and clay.
Becomes interested in self; learns self-identity	• Talk about gender and sex differences; teach about body parts.
Learns to feed and dress self	• Provide opportunities to feed self, choose clothing, and dress self.
Develops control over sphincter muscles for bladder and bowel control	• Encourage toilet training for toddlers aged 24 to 30 months.
Plays alongside friends in parallel play	• Provide opportunities to play with friends.
Develops independence	• Set safe limits to provide a secure place for exploration.

12-11 The toddler needs opportunities to explore the environment.

objects and knock them over, making a loud noise. His success in his environment makes him feel important. He is developing self-esteem. The development of language and new self-care skills increase this sense of control.

Social Development

Alex looks forward to going to preschool. There he plays games with his new friends. One of their favorite activities is playing house. Because his physical and intellectual skills have improved, he now plays alongside the other children. He also enjoys playing on his own, inside and outside. He loves water activities and playing in the sandbox. Sometimes he even helps his teacher pick up the toys.

Emotional Development

Sometimes Alex becomes frustrated. He may not be physically able to carry out the ideas in his head. For example, sometimes his blocks fall over when he tries to build a tower. Other times he cannot have what he wants, such as playing in the street or having a cookie. Alex may respond by lying down on the floor, kicking, and screaming. Then he may stop his tantrum just as quickly as he began.

Alex needs understanding as guidelines are set for his behavior. He needs experiences that are at his level so he can feel success. He also needs limits that protect him yet allow him to explore. Limits help Alex see that his world is a safe and secure place to live. Sometimes he may test these limits. However, he needs to see them enforced in a consistent way. Limits help Alex learn self-control and increase his feelings of security.

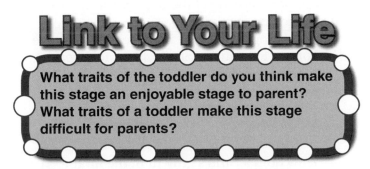

Link to Your Life

What traits of the toddler do you think make this stage an enjoyable stage to parent? What traits of a toddler make this stage difficult for parents?

Early Childhood: Three to Five Years

The period from three to five years of age is also referred to as the *preschool years*. Much learning takes place during these years, 12-12. It is very important for children to fully develop opportunities for play and exploration since learning occurs through these.

Physical Development

During the early childhood years, a child like Lauren will be very active. Her control over her muscles will increase. Her balance and stability will improve. Her small muscle skills will become more refined. She will master skills that enable her to provide some of her own care.

Intellectual Development

Through all her activity, Lauren is learning. She is taking in all sorts of information. She is learning to deal with symbols. She is understanding more about how words can stand for objects. She learns best if she can actually see and touch objects as she hears the labels for them. Through such hands-on activities, Lauren learns concepts. She learns about her world, and she learns words to describe it.

Lauren needs a chance to talk. She also needs to hear someone talking to her. Her language will increase quickly if others talk to her and explain things to her. Others can also help her label items in her environment.

Lauren's basic approach to her environment is through play. She plays with almost everything. This includes crayons, scissors, puzzles, dolls, trucks, blocks, dress-up clothes, mother, father, siblings, or animals. She also plays with words, using silly talk, rhymes, or poems.

Social Development

The early childhood years are a time when children become more social. Lauren's interest in playing with her playmates increases. Lauren also likes to imitate the roles she experiences in her life. She likes to play house, sometimes acting as the mother, the father, a baby, or an older sibling.

Early Childhood: Three to Five Years	
Characteristics of Development	**Suggestions to Stimulate Development**
Develop language, including more vocabulary and longer sentences	• Encourage child to describe activities, pictures, and feelings. • Identify new words; explain reasons. • Explain concepts related to color, numbers, seasons, relationships. • Read stories and talk about concepts.
Fine-motor control becomes more refined: • Draws figures with head, body, arms, and legs • Adds eyes, hair, ears, hands, and feet to drawings • Uses scissors and cuts on a line • Ties shoelaces and fastens buttons	• Provide toys that allow matching for sizes, colors, and shapes. • Provide various art materials to cut, paste, paint, or color. • Provide puzzles, beads to string, and crayons.
Gross-motor control improves: • Walks a straight line • Jumps, climbs upright, turns, somersaults, hops, and skips	• Provide riding toys with pedals. • Provide opportunities for active outdoor play. • Use park facilities; provide opportunities to play in sand and water.
Sensitive to praise and blame	• Emphasize positive accomplishments.
Imaginative and creative Likes to pretend and recreate roles in play	• Provide props for dramatic play with dress-up clothes, homemaking toys, construction toys, and building sets.
Needs to develop initiative	• Have child participate in household duties.
Shares and understands fair play Wants to make friends	• Provide opportunities to play with friends and in small groups.

12-12 Preschoolers are busy discovering the world around them. Parents and children can have fun sharing in these discoveries.

As Lauren plays in her environment, her feelings of independence increase. She learns that she can initiate actions and see results. If she cannot carry out her thoughts in real life, she often does it through her imagination.

Emotional Development

At this age, childhood fears are not uncommon for Lauren. She may not understand why certain things happen. Her imagination makes things more fearful than real. Lauren needs understanding and explanations to help her overcome her fears. If she fears the neighbor's dog, her parents can pet the dog and show Lauren the dog is friendly.

Developing confidence in herself at this stage is important for Lauren. She is about to enter the school years. Her abilities will be challenged by others.

Investigate Further

How does a child's growth in the infant-toddler years affect the way he or she approaches the environment during the preschool years?

Elementary Years: Five to Twelve Years

The elementary-school years mark significant changes in growth and development. In the early years, each area of growth is gradual. Rapid growth, especially physical, is seen in the later years. More information is added to a child's store of knowledge. Children's skills improve in all areas, 12-13.

Physical, Intellectual, Social, and Emotional Changes

A child's rapid physical growth is more obvious in the later elementary years. Both boys and girls grow taller and thinner, taking on more of an adult figure. Children in this age group are developing more interest in learning. They tend to be more curious and have a longer attention span. Many are good at problem solving.

| The Elementary Years: Five to Twelve Years ||
Characteristics of Development	Suggestions to Stimulate Development
Learns by experimenting Figures out problems	• Suggest reasons relating to cause-effect; give explanations.
Needs to see and touch items to understand concepts	• Provide opportunities to test problems and understand them. • Help child focus on qualities of what is seen.
Learns systematically through ordering of facts	• Encourage collections of plants, rocks, stamps, etc.
Develops skills in reading, writing, and physical dexterity	• Encourage reading for enjoyment.
Needs to develop a sense of industry	• Help child develop skills.
Develops sense of self from relationships and abilities	• Relate reasoning to life experiences. • Provide positive feedback. • Encourage friendships.
Grows physically at rates that vary widely	• Emphasize positive body image. • Encourage participation in group games.
Internalizes family rules and values	• Stress real values and point out what is really important.
Attaches strongly to adult who models desired behavior	• Model desired behavior.
Adjusts moral behavior by what happens to others	• Keep guidance constant. • Explain rules and consequences.
Adjusts to school setting	• Listen to teacher's perception of child. Be interested in child's work. Provide praise and acceptance.

12-13 Parental guidance and support is important as elementary school children make adjustments in their school and home lives.

Emotional and social changes are closely linked during this period. School-age children like to participate in group activities. They want to belong to a group. In addition, they want to look and act like their peers. As both boys and girls try to cope with their growth, their emotions shift. Younger elementary children still act childish at times. They experience mood swings. Sometimes they are cooperative; at other times they are stubborn. As they get older, their emotions gradually stabilize.

Think More About It
What are some strategies parents can use in the preschool years to help their child prepare for kindergarten?

Adjusting to a New Environment

Most children begin kindergarten at the age of five. This does not mean they magically become ready to learn by sitting at a desk. Learning by experimenting is still important. Children still need to see and touch things as they grasp new concepts. They still need to practice newly learned skills. However, the freedom of the early years is exchanged for a more structured environment.

The school environment brings many changes into a child's life. For some children, school is a new social experience. They may have more contact with other children and adults than ever

before. They have new rules to follow and a rigid schedule to keep. Activities are stopped and started by bells.

A child like Alex may have a hard time adjusting to this rigid structure. He may stop along the sidewalk to watch a toad hop in the grass, just as he did before going to school. However, he is no longer praised for his creativity and exploration. Instead, he may be punished for being late for school.

Children like Alex need love and understanding as they make the adjustment to the school environment. Alex's parents can help him by showing an interest in every stage of his development. He needs praise for what he does accomplish. He needs encouragement to believe he can adjust.

All school-age children go through the awkward and sometimes painful stages of social and emotional growth. Parents can help stimulate growth by providing a positive, supportive family environment. This can help children develop feelings of confidence and security.

Review Section 12:3

1. Explain the difference between the rooting reflex and the Babinski reflex.
2. Compare stranger anxiety and separation anxiety in an infant.
3. Briefly describe how toddlers develop a sense of autonomy.
4. List two ways an average child develops intellectually in the preschool years.
5. Give one example of how parents can stimulate a child's growth during the elementary years.

Think It Through

Deona and Sherice

When Deona was born, her mother found it easy to care for her. She seemed easy to keep happy and content. She would only fuss a little when she was hungry, and her mother would feed her right away. After her feeding, she would watch the dancing clowns mobile hanging from the ceiling until she got drowsy again and fell asleep. When she woke up, she would coo at the pictures on her crib.

As she grew older, she still was easy to keep busy. She would sit and play with blocks, puzzles, or toys. At nap time, she would sit in her bed and look at books until she fell asleep. She complied with her mother's requests.

When Deona's sister was born, her parents were shocked at the differences in their children. Sherice was just the opposite of Deona. She was full of energy right from the start. She expressed her desires with loud, lusty cries, even when her mother came right away. She liked to be held and carried. As soon as she was put in her crib, she would cry. Not even the dancing clowns mobile would quiet her.

As Sherice got older, her mother found it hard to keep up with her. She was not content to stay in one place. Instead of building with blocks, Sherice would throw them. When Deona built a tower, Sherice would delight in seeing it crash to the floor. With her endless energy, she was always moving! She seemed to get into everything.

Questions to Guide Your Thinking

1. How can two children in the same family be so different?

2. Describe Deona's approach to her environment.

3. How is Sherice's approach to the environment different?

4. How do the needs of these children differ?

5. How are their needs the same?

6. How can parents respond to differences in their children so each child's growth to full development is stimulated?

Chapter Summary

Patterns of development can be identified in all areas: physical, intellectual, social, and emotional. Children progress through the sequences in each area at their own rate of development. Environmental factors such as nutrition, disease, and interactions with others may also affect a child's growth potential.

Stages of development describe behaviors that are common for children of a certain age. The first three months of life are called the newborn stage. Then children progress through the stages of infant, toddler, early childhood, and elementary years. As children develop through these stages, they share many similarities. Understanding the needs of children as they progress through each stage can help parents take steps to stimulate growth and development.

Assess...

Your Knowledge

1. What factors in a child's environment impact growth and development?

2. What are the stages of growth and development that children go through?

3. Name one milestone for each type of a child's development: physical, social, emotional, and intellectual.

Your Understanding

4. How can parents help a newborn feel secure?

5. Why is an environment that invites exploration important for the toddler's development?

6. How can parents promote intellectual growth in their preschool child?

7. How can too much stimulation negatively affect a child's development?

Your Skills

8. Analyze your school environment and identify factors that help you grow and develop.

9. Think back over the past and analyze various factors in your environment that were *not* positive experiences. Evaluate whether these negative experiences helped you grow to maturity or hindered your growth.

Think Critically

10. **Research.** Observe a child and record examples of physical, social, emotional, and intellectual behaviors that display the child's stage of development. Write a one-page paper describing the behaviors observed. *Choice:* Use pictures to create a visual presentation depicting the child's stage of development in each area. *Group option:* Compare your observations with those of a classmate who observed a child of the same age. Discuss the similarities and differences between your observations.

11. **Research.** Prepare a checklist of the sequence of events that one should observe or each of the four areas of development. Then observe a child of any age in a child care center. Compare the child's growth and development with the items on the checklist. Record your observations, the child's age, and the activities observed. *Group option:* Work as a group to prepare the checklist.

12. *Social studies, research.* Interview a parent who has more than one child. Ask questions related to each child's patterns for responding to the environment. Summarize your interview in a one-page report. Include a description of each child's temperament. Discuss any differences in the parent's responses to each child.

13. Create a "quiet-time" booklet with activities that would be age-appropriate to stimulate a preschool child's development. *Choice:* Create a booklet for a toddler or school-age child.

Connect with Your Community

14. *Social studies, writing.* Visit a mother with a newborn or the young infants at a child care center. Observe the following:
    - reflexes of a newborn
    - experiences with the states of a newborn
    - caring for a newborn

    In a paragraph, summarize how the reflexes of a newborn help the child respond to and connect with the parent. *Group option:* Invite the mother to visit the class with her newborn.

15. *Writing.* Take a field trip to a preschool or child care center. In a one-page report, summarize how the physical, social, emotional, and intellectual needs of the preschool child are met in that setting. *Choice:* Report on how the needs of an infant or toddler are met in a child care setting.

16. Visit an elementary school classroom. Identify an example of how that classroom meets a child's needs in each of the four areas of growth and development. Develop a poster to present your information to the class. *Choice:* Use presentation software to illustrate your findings.

17. *Science.* Choose one age group of early childhood and identify a parent who can record for you everything his or her child eats in one day. Analyze the child's diet. Identify changes the parent could make to better meet the nutritional needs of that child's stage of development. *Choice:* Use a nutrient analysis program to help you analyze the child's diet.

Use Technology

18. Choose a stage of development and design a toy or game that is developmentally appropriate (one that would promote the growth of a child). Make a model of the item, if possible, or draw a picture of it. Present your toy or game to the class and explain how it matches the stage of development you chose. *Choice:* Observe how a child interacts with the model of your toy or game. Use descriptions in your presentation.

19. *Math.* Find four classmates who observed the same age child that you did in activity #11 above. As a group, create a spreadsheet listing the physical behaviors from your checklist and the number of children exhibiting each behavior. Convert the spreadsheet into a graph showing the number of children at each step in the sequence. Write a paragraph describing the results of your comparisons. *Group option:* Compile all the results from everyone in the class who observed children of the same age.

20. *Research.* Search the Internet to learn about new technologies that are designed to stimulate a child's growth and development. Choose one of these technologies and explain how it claims to promote growth and development. Then analyze those claims, comparing them to your knowledge about what it takes to stimulate the growth of a child. Write a paragraph in which you critique this technology and its potential.

21. Prepare a checklist that could be used for evaluating children's computer programs, considering factors that would contribute to a child's growth and development. Then use your checklist to evaluate two children's computer programs. Summarize your findings in a short paragraph. *Choice:* Choose software targeted for a specific age group: preschool, grades K-1, grades 2-3, or grades 4-5.

Chapter 13

Caring for and Guiding Children

Section 13:**1**
Providing a Nurturing Environment

Section 13:**2**
Providing Guidance

Section 13:**3**
Providing Opportunities for Play

Section 13:**4**
Providing for the Health and Safety of Children

Key Questions

Questions to answer as you study this chapter:

- **How can a parent create a nurturing environment?**

- **What methods can be used to help children learn self-control?**

- **What play experiences are vital for a child's growth and development?**

- **What steps should parents take to meet their child's needs for health and safety?**

Chapter Objectives

After studying this chapter, you will be able to

- **identify** techniques for helping children feel loved.

- **describe** various methods of guidance.

- **explain** the importance of play in children's development.

- **select** toys that stimulate development.

- **determine** practices that promote the health and safety of children.

- **identify** community support resources available to parents.

Life Sketch

"Of course I love my children. I provide them with good food, nice clothes, a comfortable house, and a good education."

"We work all day and half the night just to take care of them and buy all the things they need."

"I don't have a lot, but I give them as much as I possibly can. I want them to know that I love and care about them."

"Our children know we love them because we tell them so."

Getting Started

If you asked most parents "Do you really love your children?" you might expect these comments. Most parents do love their children. However, do they show their love in a way that makes the child feel loved?

Children need to feel loved and supported. Feeling loved is the key to the child's responses to the parents. Parents provide a great deal for their children—food, clothing, shelter, health care, education, and toys. These items will have a greater effect on the child's development if the child feels loved. Also, the techniques that parents use for guiding a child will be more effective if used in love.

section 13:1

Providing a Nurturing Environment

Sharpen Your Reading

Develop a graphic organizer for this chapter with four main branches extending from your main heading, *Caring for and Guiding Children*. Add the section title, *Providing a Nurturing Environment*, to the first main branch. As you read the section, list the key ideas for each heading in this section.

Boost Your Vocabulary

Draw an analogy between nurturing a growing plant and nurturing a growing child.

Know Key Terms

nurturing environment

All children need a nurturing environment to help them grow and develop. In a **nurturing environment**, children feel secure, protected, satisfied, and loved. How can parents fill children's emotional needs so they feel loved? Children who feel loved can conclude "I am lovable." This evaluation becomes part of the child's self-concept.

Sending Messages with Love

Children want to hear their parents say "I love you," but they also need to hear love expressed in other nonverbal messages. Children respond to the nonverbal messages of their parents—the tone of voice and amount of attention.

Some messages show respect, acceptance, or concern for the child as a person. These messages will help the child feel loved. Some comments make a child feel worthless or unimportant. Then the child will feel unlovable.

Use What You Learn

What are some nonverbal messages that can attack a person's self-esteem?

Making Direct Eye Contact

How often do people look directly at you when they speak to you? That is one of the first rules of good communication. When parents speak to their child, it is easy to look down at the child's head. However, parents can send a message of care and love by looking directly into the child's eyes, 13-1. This may mean lifting the child up to the adult's eye level or squatting down to the child's eye level. To talk with older children, it may mean sitting across from them at a table.

Children want to make eye contact with people they care about. Newborns seek to focus on the eyes of the person providing care. Young children will try to make their mothers look directly at them. Eye contact meets children's emotional needs. It also helps children learn to make direct eye contact with others as they begin to build relationships with peers.

Link to Your Life

How does direct eye contact contribute to communication with your parents?

Spending Time Together

An important way for parents to help their children feel loved is to spend time with them. Doing activities together does build bonds within the family. However, the kind of time that really conveys love to children is undivided and uninterrupted. This is time spent one-on-one between parent and child. No one else is interrupting. The television is off. The child has the full attention of the parent.

During such focused time, listening to a child is important. Parents can learn how their child thinks and feels. They can learn about the child's opinion or what problems the child is having in school or with friends. Sometimes the child just needs someone to listen and show empathy.

To find time, parents may need to consider their values. What is truly most important to them? Even with busy schedules, parents need to set aside time to spend alone with their child. It may be a few minutes at bedtime. As children get older, parents may set aside time on weekends for a special outing together. Even if the undivided, uninterrupted time together is short, it is important for the relationship.

13-1 Direct eye contact is one way for a parent to send a child a message of love and concern.

Providing Close Physical Contact

The messages sent by physical contact usually signal caring, concern, support, and love. When someone talks to you, leans over, and touches your arm, there is an immediate message of closeness. Sometimes it may be an arm around the shoulder. Of course, a hug or kiss on the cheek signals a great deal of closeness. Parents can help their children feel loved by using such types of physical contact regularly.

Review Section 13:**1**

1. Give examples of four ways a parent can help a child feel loved.

2. Why is making direct eye contact with children important?

section 13:2

Providing Guidance

Sharpen Your Reading

Add this section title to the second branch of your graphic organizer. Extend your organizer, listing the key ideas for each heading in this section.

Boost Your Vocabulary

For each method of guidance, give an example of a parent using this strategy with his or her child.

Know Key Terms

guidance
modeling
redirecting
reinforcement
natural consequences
time-out

13-2 Parents provide guidance as they lead their child to use acceptable behavior.

Children do not automatically know what they should or should not do. While busy exploring their world, toddlers will play in the street, reach out to a fire, or hit a sibling. They do not know which choices may be harmful to them or to others. They have not learned that some actions are acceptable while others are not.

Children need guidance from their parents so their choices will lead to growth and development. A *guide* is someone who leads the way. Guidance is not something that is done to a person, but *with* a person, 13-2. **Guidance** is all that parents do and say as they influence their children's behavior in a positive way. The goal of parental guidance is to help children grow to maturity and learn to be productive members of society.

With proper guidance, children will learn self-control. *Self-control*, also called *self-discipline*, is the ability to control your own behavior in a responsible way. Parents train their children to use certain behavior that is acceptable to them and others. No matter which guidance method is used, it should incorporate these three guidelines:

- Love should always be the key ingredient.
- A child's self-esteem or value as a person should always be upheld.
- The method should help the child learn self-control.

There are eight guidance methods described in this chapter. Each follows these three guidelines.

How are guidance and self-control similar? How are they different?

Modeling

If parents knew that every word they said was being recorded or every action photographed, would they act or speak differently? In the mind of a child, the words and actions used on a daily basis are recorded.

Modeling is acting in a way that sets a good example. This encourages children to use good behavior. Children learn best by example—they imitate what they see others doing.

Parents are a child's first role models. Children love to imitate their parents and pretend to be like them. They imitate their parents' roles in play and carry out the actions they see in real life.

Through modeling, parents can help their children develop relationships, make decisions, and control emotions. Parents can also help children develop healthful habits and strong character. The most important and often difficult part of this task is for parents to model the desired behavior. Children will imitate bad behavior as well as good behavior.

Link to Your Life

What examples can you give of habits you have picked up from people with whom you spend time?

Setting Limits

Parents also set limits or rules to guide the child's behavior. Limits should be well defined and clearly explained. Children need to know exactly what is expected of them. They should have no doubts about what *is* acceptable behavior and what *is not*. As a child gets older, some limits will need to be changed to match the child's level of development.

Parents may find it helpful to write down the limits they have set for the children. Then it is easier for them to keep in mind what the limits should accomplish.

- *Be consistent.* Parents need to be consistent in their expectations. If a behavior is allowed one time and not another, a child becomes confused.

- *Keep both the child's and parents' welfare in mind.* What is needed for the child's safety? Will the limits help the child's personal growth? In addition, the needs of other family members should be considered.

- *Use positive reinforcement.* This will reinforce and encourage desired behavior. Positive reinforcement lets children know their behavior pleases their parents.

Establishing Routines

Learning to follow some regular routines is important for children. Routines give a feeling of security to a child's life. They help children know what to expect.

Routines also help parents show parental control. In turn, this helps children develop self-control. Children learn to be independent within accepted limits. Once children know what is expected of them, they can learn to control their behavior.

Developing a routine that works takes time. However, once the routine is established, it can save much time and conflict between parent and child.

Link to Your Life

Think of an example in which one of your routines has helped you develop self-control.

Redirecting

Sometimes parents can guide their child from one activity to a more acceptable one. This method is called **redirecting** the child's behavior. Redirecting is accomplished by focusing the child's interest on something else, 13-3. With a young child, a parent may need to physically move the child to another place to play.

The key to redirecting is to replace the unacceptable activity with one that is acceptable and equally as interesting. Redirecting is a good technique to use with toddlers, whose main desire is to explore. Parents can redirect older children by offering other alternatives. Reasoning and logic may be used to persuade them to follow their parents' advice.

Link to Your Life

What form of guidance do you think you would be most comfortable using with your children?

13-3 Parents can sometimes guide behavior by redirecting the child's attention to a substitute toy or activity.

Making Requests

One of the simplest ways a parent can guide a child's actions is to express personal desires. "Karin, I would like you to put your toys on the shelf," is one example. This gives the child a chance to please the parent by responding with the behavior. Karin's feelings of worth and importance increase because she is able to please her parent.

Negative commands or you-statements tear down a child's self-esteem. "Don't leave your clothes on the floor!" is an example. Hearing such commands continually will cause the child to have negative feelings of worth. Children are less likely to develop self-control if they do not believe they can carry out acceptable behavior.

Reinforcing

When a child performs a desired behavior, **reinforcement** can influence the child to repeat that behavior. For instance, when Karin picks up her clothes or cleans her room, her parents can reinforce that behavior. They may praise her for doing a good job. They may give her some special privilege.

Reinforcing Desired Behavior

Reinforcement needs to occur right after the desired behavior is displayed. The child needs to remember the good feelings that result from that response. Then the desired behavior will be repeated. The method a parent uses to reinforce behavior depends on the child's interests and level of development, 13-4.

Reinforcing Negative Behavior

Sometimes parents reinforce negative behavior without realizing it. Think of some behaviors that a child may use to get his or her own way. In the grocery store, Chor has learned that if she keeps asking for what she wants, her mother will buy it. She has also learned that it only works to beg for one item; the second item will be a definite no. Chor's mother does not

13-4 Giving children total responsibility for caring for the family pet is one way to reinforce responsible behavior.

realize that she reinforces this behavior. Chor, however, has learned that begging usually brings results.

Desirable behavior often goes unnoticed. When siblings are playing together without conflict, a parent will probably not stop to praise them. If these siblings are pushing and tugging on the same toy, they will attract a parent's attention. If the child needs or desires a parent's attention, the negative behavior will bring it.

Most children want their parents' attention but also want to please. The reinforcement that parents give can be a strong motivator. Parents need to watch their responses to be sure they reinforce desirable behavior only.

Think More About It
Why do adults often fail to reinforce positive behavior?

Using Natural Consequences

Sometimes the natural consequences of an action are effective in helping a child control behavior. **Natural consequences** are the normal result of an action. For instance, if Jeremy steps on a balloon, it will burst.

Sometimes natural consequences are dangerous to the child's health or welfare. Parents cannot let a child play in the street to learn this behavior is harmful. They cannot let a child get burned to learn what *hot* means.

A direct relationship must exist between the child's choice of action and the result of that action. For instance, Abe spends all his money on a large box of popcorn at the movies. The natural consequence of his decision is thirst. Now Abe must wait until he is home to get a drink.

Use What You Learn

Think of an example in which guidance with natural consequences is a good choice to develop a child's self-control.

Punishing

Punishment gives the child a reason to regret engaging in behavior he or she knew was wrong. For punishment to be effective, the child needs to be old enough to understand wrong behavior. Punishment is not appropriate for a very young child.

Parents should only use a punishment that *fits* (or directly links) to the wrong behavior. For example, parents might take a bike away for a time if a child repeatedly rides in the street instead of staying on the sidewalk. Other parents require that the child take a short **time-out** away from others to think quietly about the behavior. The time-out should take place in a room where the child has no toys or other distractions.

If some form of punishment is necessary, parents should discuss it with the child first. They need to make sure the child understood that the behavior was not acceptable. As they talk about the behavior, they can help the child realize they love him or her, but not the behavior.

Discussing behavior is difficult for parents if they are angry. The goal of punishment is *not* to give the parents a chance to vent their anger. Punishment dealt under these circumstances will likely tear down the child's self-esteem and may be abusive. Angry parents need to take time to calm down and control their emotions so they can address the child's behaviors in a calm, firm, and loving manner.

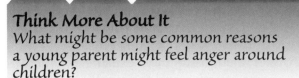

Choosing a Guidance Method

When a child misbehaves, parents need to ask themselves two questions: *Why did the child act this way? What can I do to help the child learn appropriate behavior?* Identifying the problem can help parents choose an effective method of guidance, 13-5.

13-5 When children misbehave, they should be given a chance to explain their behavior.

Identify the problem first. Sometimes what appears to be undesirable behavior is really normal for the child's age. The child may just need to be redirected to play that is more acceptable. The child may be bored from not having enough to do. At other times, there may be too much activity for the child to handle. In such cases, parents may need to change the child's environment.

Sometimes a child misbehaves to receive attention. If so, the child should be given love to fill that emotional need. Parents need to reassure a child that he or she will be loved even during periods of misbehavior.

If the problem resulted from a misunderstanding, the child may need some clear and simple instructions about what is acceptable. Sometimes the problem is a child wanting his or her own way. Then parents needs to ask if they are reinforcing the behavior by using punishment.

Parents should then identify which guidance method will help the child learn self-control. Parents will most likely use all forms of guidance at some time during their parenting years. Limits, routines, positive models, and positive reinforcement help set guidelines for children's behavior. Sometimes children will step outside those guidelines. Parents can guide them by redirecting them. At other times, natural consequences or punishments such as a time-out may be effective in helping children learn not to repeat a behavior.

Investigate Further

Why do you think parents often have a difficult time choosing an appropriate form of guidance?

Review Section 13:2

1. Name and briefly describe four methods of guidance.
2. When choosing a method of guidance for their child, what two questions should parents consider?

section 13:3

Providing Opportunities for Play

Sharpen Your Reading

Add this section title to the third branch of your graphic organizer. Extend the organizer, listing the key ideas for each heading in this section.

Boost Your Vocabulary

Draw diagrams to illustrate each type of play.

Know Key Terms

solitary play
onlooker play
parallel play
associative play
cooperative play

Parents are responsible for providing an environment that stimulates their child's development. For children this means having opportunities to play at their own level. What stimulates a child at one level may bore a child who is at another level. Therefore, knowing what type of experiences a child needs is important.

The Importance of Play

Play is an important activity for all children because children learn as they play. To children, learning and playing are the same activity. Play helps children grow in all areas of their development, including the following:

- *Build self-esteem.* Feelings of control and success develop when children realize they can make things happen. When they push a truck, it rolls. When they pedal a tricycle, they can make it move.

- *Encourage creativity.* In play, children have the freedom to choose the action they desire, 13-6. They can use blocks to make a city. Then they can use the same block and pretend it is a plow.

13-6 Through art or drama, children can express themselves creatively.

- *Learn about different roles.* Play gives children a chance to learn about other people's roles. They may pretend to be a mother, father, baby, police officer, or mail carrier.

- *Build relationships.* As they play with others, children learn how to give and take to get a task done. They learn how to share and cooperate. They also learn to follow rules, take turns, and express their feelings.

- *Practice new skills.* Through play, children practice the many new skills they are developing. Physical skills are easy to notice as children learn to run and jump. They also practice new mental skills as they sort out colors or shapes that match.

- *Focus on tasks.* Children often become very involved in their play activities. As they play, they learn to think and reason. Such concentration on a task is important as children become ready for the school years.

One stage builds onto the next stage as children progress through the five stages of play. These stages are based on how children interact with others in a play situation.

- In **solitary play**, babies tend to play alone and ignore other children.

- In **onlooker play**, toddlers watch other children play but will not join in.

- In **parallel play**, children play side-by-side without interacting with each other.

- From age three into the elementary years, children enjoy playing with each other. In **associative play**, two or more children play at one activity. They may share toys and ideas, but do not really organize their play.

- Around age ten, children can usually work together in **cooperative play** to reach common goals. The roles they take complement each other. Cooperative play also enables them to play as team members in organized sports.

Link to Your Life

Think of a leisure activity you enjoy. Identify any area in which this "play" activity helps you grow.

Think More About It
How could a child's self-concept affect the type of play in which he or she engages?

Types of Play

Children approach their environment through many different types of play. Eight of these are described in the chart in 13-7. Understanding the various types of play will help parents provide appropriate activities for their developing children. Each type involves basic developmental skills. The physical skills gained include gross- and fine-motor skills. Intellectual skills increase through the processing of information that the child takes in through play and the development of language skills. As children learn to play together, they also develop social and emotional skills.

Stages of Play

Children's play reflects the changes taking place in their development. As children grow older, their stages of play change and advance.

Choosing Toys for Children's Play

Children can be strongly influenced by the media. Many TV shows for children are flooded with toy ads. With so much competition from the media, how does a parent choose toys wisely?

One point for parents to remember is that children do not need expensive toys to make playtime a valuable experience. With a little of their own imagination, parents can provide many play experiences for their children at little or no cost. Often the simple toys—blocks, dolls, crayons, paints, chalk—spark a child's imagination. They can be used in many ways. Many common household items can be recycled to provide hours of imaginative play. Games such as hide-and-seek and hopscotch are fun to play, cost nothing, and provide gross-motor exercise.

Types of Play	
Characteristics	**Guidelines for Parents**
Manipulative play Use small muscles. Put beads on a string. Run yarn through a sewing card. Stack, take apart, or put together toys.	• Provide toys that child can manipulate with success. • Provide toys that offer a new challenge. • Allow child to repeat skills over and over to master them.
Large-muscle play Crawl over objects. Climb over jungle gym. Walk, run, jump, kick, hop, skip, or pedal.	• Provide opportunities for play, both indoors and outdoors. • Provide adequate space for large-muscle movements. • Provide toys that promote gross-motor skills, such as riding toys, tricycles, and bikes.
Play with art materials Explore colors, paints, brushes, and other art materials. Use play dough, clay, yarn, and other textures.	• Provide opportunities for child to use as many senses as possible while playing. • Allow child to experiment and be creative with materials.
Water and sand play Learn science concepts. Pour, shake, sift, stir, or measure. Build bridges, plow roads, navigate boats.	• Allow child to be creative and use his or her imagination. • Provide equipment to measure, pour, shake, stir, and sift. • Include toys such as boats, trucks, diggers, or plows to expand the pretend play.
Blockbuilding play Build a tower and knock it down. Build detailed structures. Create cities, adding people, cars, and other objects.	• Provide sturdy and stable blockbuilding materials. • Allow child to control how building will be built. • Provide other toys to stimulate pretend play.

(Continued)

13-7 Different types of play involve using different types of skills.

Types of Play	
Characteristics	**Guidelines for Parents**
Housekeeping play Act out homelife experiences. Imitate different roles. Pretend to cook, care for the baby, clean house, or wash clothes. Pretend to go to work, a movie, bowling, a religious service, etc.	• Provide child-size equipment, such as kitchen sets, dishes, beds, strollers, and dolls. • Model positive behavior as children will pretend to do whatever they see parents do.
Dramatic play Act out real or television events. Act out stories in books. Try solving problems. Express needs or release frustrations.	• Provide props for dramatic play; dress-up clothes, hats, umbrellas, briefcases, and books.
Table games Learn concepts such as colors, numbers, matching, and counting. Learn about themselves as they measure their own skills against others. Learn to play together, take turns, play fairly, work as a team, and follow the rules of the game.	• Play games that use concepts the child can grasp. • Plan child-centered games for the young child. • Allow preschool children to play games in which they can run, chase, and capture one another. • Encourage school-age child to take part in organized games.

13-7 Continued.

Guidelines for Toy Selection

When selecting toys for children, parents should consider several factors. Besides being safe, fun, and easy to clean, they should be right for the child's age and level of development. Good toys generally have the following qualities:

- *Are safe to use.* See 13-8. Read toy labels carefully. Removable parts such as doll's eyes or buttons are especially dangerous to young children.
- *Have interesting color, shape, and texture.* Bright colors, textures, and shapes add interest.
- *Stimulate new kinds of exploration.* Choose toys that have parts to manipulate, sounds to explore, or different options for assembly. Toys that come in a variety of sizes are good choices as well as toys that can be sorted by different parts. Avoid mechanical toys that do all the work for the child.
- *Fit a variety of play settings.* Toys that can be used in many ways will be more interesting to children.
- *Help a child express creativity.* Toys that promote housekeeping play or dramatic play and encourage the child to practice gross- and fine-motor skills are good choices.
- *Are durable.* Toys need to be sturdy and well constructed.
- *Match the age of the child.* As children develop, their skills increase. Toys that are too complex for a certain age will frustrate the child. Toys that no longer offer a challenge will bore a growing child.

Safety Features for Infant-Toddler Toys

- Nontoxic paint or finish
- No sharp edges, jagged edges, or points
- Nonbreakable materials
- Larger size than the child's two fists
- No long cords or strings
- No small removable parts that a child could swallow
- Nonflammable or flame-resistant materials
- Washable materials

13-8 To protect their child's health and safety, parents should select toys carefully.

Investigate Further

What are some toys for a preschool-age child that would meet the above criteria?

Technology and the Development of a Child

How much television should children watch? How many video or computer games should they play? How much time should they spend surfing the Internet? Such questions plague parents in today's society. When trying to answer these questions, some additional questions need to be asked.

- What are the physical, social, intellectual, and emotional needs of a child at this age? If too much time is spent on any one activity, other areas of development do not occur.
- What types of experiences will meet those needs and enhance the child's growth and development?

Parents should limit the time children spend on any one activity. Children can spend hours with electronic entertainment. Playing with a friend can enhance social learning. Working together to solve a problem can enhance thinking skills. A balanced blend of activities is important so children grow in all areas of development.

Control exposure to violent images. The television programs, movies, video games, and Internet sites that children see need to be monitored. Programs that show violent images should be off-limits for young children. Parents should seek programs that promote character development.

Review Section 13:3

1. List six reasons why play is important for a child's growth and development.
2. Give eight examples of different types of play.
3. Describe each of the stages of play.
4. List seven guidelines parents can follow when selecting toys.

section 13:4

Providing for the Health and Safety of Children

Sharpen Your Reading

Add this section title to the fourth branch of your graphic organizer. Extend your organizer, listing the key ideas for each heading in this section.

Boost Your Vocabulary

Explain the differences between a pediatrician and a family doctor.

Know Key Terms

pediatrician
immunizations
germs
contagious disease
quarantine
individual education plan (IEP)

All parents want their children to stay healthy. Good health habits need to be started when children are young. These include eating right and getting enough sleep and physical activity. Medical care should be sought when needed. Childhood illnesses should be recognized and proper care provided. Steps must be taken to ensure a safe environment and avoid accidents.

Health Habits

Eating right, getting enough sleep, and being physically active are important health habits for everyone. Children are no exception. Good health habits developed in childhood will become lifelong habits.

Establish Good Eating Habits

Children's eating habits are important right from the start. Proper nutrition is needed for children's growth and development. Children's eating habits are influenced by different factors, 13-9. These include how active they have been, the food's appearance, and the meal schedule. Nonetheless, parents can establish good eating habits for their children with the following helpful tips:

- Choose the recommended amounts from each of the food groups. (Refer to Figure 25-8 in Chapter 25.) The total daily servings are commonly divided into three meals, a morning snack, and an afternoon snack.

- Serve nutritious snacks.

- Avoid serving foods with too much sugar, salt, and fats. Since children have more taste buds than adults do, foods taste stronger, sweeter, and saltier.

- Make food look appetizing by combining different colors, textures, and shapes. This can encourage children to eat nutritious foods.

- Involve children in food preparation. This experience can promote an interest in eating and trying new foods.

- Encourage children to try new foods. Keeping a positive attitude sets a good example for the child.

Sleeping Habits

How much sleep do children need? This may vary among children. Many important activities take place in the body during sleep. The brain sorts and stores information. The body builds and repairs cells.

Making sure that the young child has time for adequate sleep is important. Observing behavior can provide some clues that help parents determine if their children are getting enough

13-9 Offering finger foods in interesting shapes and sizes encourages a child to try healthful foods.

sleep. Does the child have a hard time waking up in the morning? Is the child sick often? Does the child sit or lie around, not interested in playing? Is the child fussy, cranky, and uncooperative? These may be signs that a child needs more sleep. A healthy, alert, and active child is most likely getting enough sleep.

Physical Activity

Physical activity is important for children's health and well-being. Exercise increases muscle strength, including the heart. It aids in weight control. If a child is overweight, physical activity is a great way for the child to burn calories. If a child is not gaining enough weight, exercise can improve a child's appetite.

Parents need to help their children develop life habits that include physical activity. They should limit the time allowed for sedentary activities. They should emphasize that physical activity includes any movement during the day,

not just structured exercise or sports. However, they can encourage active leisure activities such as participation in sports, 13-10.

Dental Health

The nutrients needed for forming good strong teeth should be supplied through a child's diet. Milk and dairy products are good sources of calcium and phosphorus needed for building teeth and bones. (Fluoridated toothpaste helps provide the mineral fluorine, which is also important.)

Brush Regularly

Teeth will decay when in prolonged contact with sugars and starches. That is why candy or any foods that stick to the teeth should be avoided, if possible. Set up a daily brushing routine. Brushing after meals and snacks is always a good dental practice. Brushing at bedtime is especially important. Food that remains in contact with the teeth for a long period can cause decay.

Schedule Regular Checkups

Dental checkups should begin at three years of age. Visits to the dentist before problems occur will encourage a child's positive attitude. Fears

13-10 Children need active play for developing their gross-motor skills. Outdoor activities encourage children to run, jump, kick, and climb.

will not have a chance to develop. A checkup every six months is a good practice. If a cavity does develop, it can be caught in the early stages.

Medical Care

A child's health can benefit from regular medical care. The family doctor or a pediatrician may provide the child's medical care. A **pediatrician** is a medical doctor who specializes in the care of children. Some community health clinics also provide low-cost health care for children.

After the baby's birth, most doctors recommend regular checkups. These should be continued as a child grows. From age two to six, a child should visit the doctor every six months. From age six to 18, a once-a-year checkup is recommended.

Immunizations

Giving injections or drops to a person to prevent a specific disease is called **immunization**. As a result of the immunization, the person's body produces agents that resist the disease. Some of the deadliest childhood diseases have been controlled in this country through immunization programs. As part of a child's regular checkups, the doctor will suggest an immunization schedule, 13-11. It is important for parents to follow this schedule so their child develops the needed protection. Parents should keep a record of the immunizations that have been given. Proof of immunizations is a requirement for enrolling a child in school.

Childhood Illnesses

Children will come in contact with many germs in the environment. **Germs** are disease-causing organisms. Some germs are spread by insects. Some are spread through the air by sneezing or coughing. Other germs are spread through contact with an ill person or with objects that person has contaminated. Diseases that are easily spread from one person to another are called **contagious diseases**.

A parent or caregiver will most likely notice if a child is not feeling well. When a child has an illness, parents should follow the doctor's advice for the child's care. If the disease is highly

Childhood Immunizations		
DPT	•	Protects against diphtheria, pertussis (whooping cough), and tetanus.
Oral Polio	•	Protects children against polio, a crippling disease.
MMR	•	Protects against measles, mumps, and rubella (German measles).
HIB	•	Protects against Haemophilus b, a bacterium that causes a number of infections in children
Hepatitis B (HBV)	•	Protects against hepatitis B, an inflammation and infection of the liver.

13-11 A regular schedule of immunizations helps protect children against common childhood diseases.

contagious, such as chicken pox, the doctor may **quarantine** the child for a period of time. This means that the child must be confined to the home or kept away from other people until the contagious stage is past.

Avoiding Accidents

Accidents kill more young children than any one disease. Car accidents, fires and burns, and drowning are the three major causes of accidental death for children. Safety precautions for dealing with these and other dangers are described in chart 13-12.

- Use proper car restraint systems. Toddler car seats and infant carriers are common child-restraint systems.
- Learn first aid and emergency treatment.
- Never leave children alone. Young children should especially not be left alone near or in water or near a fire.
- Never play roughly with infants, throw them in the air, or swing them upside down. These activities can cause brain damage.

Child-Safety Precautions	
Car accidents	• Always buckle up for safety. • Use a restraint system that meets federal safety standards. • For children under 40 pounds, use a certified child-safety seat. • For children between 40 to 80 pounds, use a booster seat. • For a larger child, use a regular seat belt.
Fires and burns	• Place guards in front of fireplaces and open heaters and around registers and floor furnaces. • Keep hot liquids and foods out of children's reach. • Keep pot handles turned away from the edge of the stove or counter. • Avoid long tablecloths that a child could pull down to spill hot liquids. • Set hot water heater to no more than 120°F. • Put covers on unused electrical outlets. • Keep matches out of child's reach. • Keep smoke and fire detectors working. • Keep fire extinguishers in the home.
Drowning	• Watch children when they are in or near water. • Never leave a baby or small child alone in sink or tub. • Use life preservers at the beach, in or near a pool, or in a boat.
Falls	• Do not leave baby unattended on a changing table, dresser, bed, etc. • Put safety gates at top and bottom of stairs. • Remove ladders or objects that a young child may be tempted to climb.
Poisons	• Put poisonous substances such as the following out of child's reach or in locked cabinets: 　• Cleaning agents (bleach, all-purpose cleaners, furniture polish, auto polish, or plant sprays). 　• Garage and garden products (antifreeze, fertilizers, gas, oil, paints, and pesticides). 　• Medicines, vitamins, and personal products (perfume, nail polish and remover, and lotions). 　• Poisonous plants or plants with poisonous parts.
Large plastic bags	• May cause a child to suffocate if child puts bag over face.
Unused freezer or refrigerator	• Fasten door when appliance is not in use so children cannot crawl in and shut the door.
Firearms	• Keep firearms and ammunition locked in separate places. Keep key out of child's reach.
Broken glass	• Pick up and dispose.
Tools	• Sharp or heavy tools should be put away where children will not play with them.

13-12 Children face safety risks every day. Many of these risks can be avoided with proper adult supervision.

Community Resources

Most communities offer support services to parents. These services are available to answer questions, teach new skills, or provide help. The services are provided by local support groups, the education system, and government agencies.

Support Groups

Some parents will find themselves in special parenting situations. They may have a child who has a physical disability, who is gifted, or has a certain illness. Their child may have a learning disability and not be doing well in school. A child may have emotional problems because of a death or separation in the family. Parents with similar interests and concerns may form community support groups. Members can help and encourage one another.

How can parents find a support group? The Internet or Yellow Pages are good sources. Local social service organizations such as United Way can be contacted to suggest a suitable group within your area. Religious institutions, social workers, welfare agencies, and medical or community health clinics can also provide information.

The Education System

Parents can contact the local school district for information and answers to their many questions. The school district may offer special classes for parents as well as for children. Parents may also choose to get involved with school events or parent-teacher groups.

Children with Special Needs

When special needs are noticed in a child, the parent or teacher can ask to have the child tested. If a problem is diagnosed, parents and school staff members work together to help the child.

A special plan for this child's education can be developed. This plan is called an **individual education plan (IEP)**. School staff members and parents are involved in designing the IEP. Older children are sometimes involved in designing their own plans. The plan must be reviewed on a regular basis to see if the child is making progress or if changes should be made.

Education specialists use technologies to help students with special needs. These can be included in the IEP. For example, computers with programs that check for spelling and grammar can help students with disabilities affecting their writing skills. Auditory aids can be used for students with reading disabilities. Devices that enhance vision or hearing or address physical disabilities may be available to help a child with special needs.

Government Agencies

Sometimes parents have difficulty providing for the economic needs of their children. In these cases, they may be able to get some help from social service or welfare agencies. Some programs offer nutritious food, either free or at reduced costs. Some provide low-cost medical care for those who cannot afford a doctor's fee. Assistance with dental care and eye care is sometimes available.

Review Section 13:4

1. Name four ways parents can encourage a child to eat healthful foods.
2. List two reasons why physical activity is important to children's health.
3. List the nutrients that are important for the development of strong teeth.
4. List six common childhood diseases prevented by immunizations.
5. Name the three major causes of childhood deaths caused by accidents.

Think It Through

Caring for Victor

Margarita and Ramon sat in the emergency room while the doctors quickly worked to pump Victor's stomach. Victor was their three-year-old son. Just a short time earlier, he had swallowed a whole bottle of vitamin pills.

The hospital was a common site to Victor and his parents. They had nearly lost him as a baby when he developed problems breathing. They could not forget the oxygen tent draped over his hospital crib. After that, they let him sleep in their bed so they could watch for any problems that might arise. That was two years ago, and he still insisted on sleeping in their bed—right between them.

Victor had really become a handful. Margarita wondered if they had spoiled him while he was recovering from his illness. They felt sorry for him and usually let him do what he wanted. He cried when they laid him down for a nap so they let him get back up and stay awake. Sometimes he would get so tired playing that he would fall asleep on the lawn or the floor.

Margarita had to watch Victor all the time. She could not trust him for a minute. When he began climbing and walking, she never knew what he might do. He would tear the paper before they got a chance to read it. Once he crawled on top of the counter and emptied a jar of honey on the floor. He fell and, fortunately, only broke a leg.

Another time, he flushed a toy down the toilet and played in the water as it overflowed. She wondered if he would ever outgrow these pranks. Now she and Ramon had to deal with this crisis. How did Victor manage to eat the whole bottle of vitamins?

Questions to Guide Your Thinking

1. How could a child's serious illness cause parents to treat the child in a different or special way?

2. What techniques did Margarita and Ramon use to show their love for their child?

3. What techniques did they use to provide guidance?

4. Cite some specific examples of actions that Margarita and Ramon could take to help Victor learn self-control.

Chapter Summary

As parents provide care and guidance, they help their children mature physically, intellectually, socially, and emotionally. For children to develop to their full potential, they need to live in a nurturing environment and feel loved.

Children need parental guidance so they can learn self-control. Parental guidance can also help them learn to be productive members in society.

Children need a stimulating learning environment. Much of their learning is through play. A variety of play experiences and toys can stimulate development and learning.

Parents also need to provide for the health and safety of their children. They do this by helping children establish good health habits and providing medical care. They also need to help children avoid accidents.

Parents who need support in their parenting role have access to many community resources. Community support groups, local schools, and government agencies are some of the resources available for their use.

Assess...

Your Knowledge

1. Which guidance strategies are appropriate for very young children?

2. Name three types of play activities parents could provide for their child in order to stimulate growth and development.

3. List four community resources parents can use to find a local support group.

Your Understanding

4. Why should parents be consistent when setting behavior limits?

5. Why is punishment not appropriate for very young children?

6. In what ways can parents promote good health habits in their children?

Your Skills

7. Analyze the following play activities for their impact on a child's growth and development during ages 5-8. Identify some guidelines for their use in a play environment.

   A. toy action figures

   B. video games

   C. computer programs

8. Choose a selection of toys for a preschool-age child that are age-appropriate for stimulating development. Include a variety to promote growth in all areas.

Think Critically

9. *Writing.* Write a paper describing the methods of nurturing and guidance that you have experienced in your family. Summarize your paper by discussing which methods you feel were most effective in helping you learn self-control.

10. Locate a toy catalog (online or paper) and prepare a news report in which you analyze popular toys for preschool children. Consider toy selection and guidelines and what children learn through play as you make recommendations for these popular toys. *Choice:* Analyze toys for children of different ages.

11. *Research.* Research various technologies that are used for children's toys and entertainment. Choose five and make a judgment about the impact that each could have on a child's development. Include the positive and negative effects that you predict the technology could have on a child.

12. *Social studies, writing.* Write a paper addressing the impact of violence in our society on the development of children. Include examples of ways that young children are exposed to violence on a daily basis. Make recommendations for ways parents can limit their children's exposure to violence.

Connect with Your Community

13. Visit a child care center or nursery school. Observe and write down examples of these situations: using guidance techniques, using nurturing behavior, and following a routine.

14. *Writing.* Visit a nursery school. Write a one-page paper describing the equipment that promotes gross-motor play, manipulative play, pretend play, and game play.

15. *Science.* Attend a presentation of a professional in the medical field who speaks on the special health needs and care of children born to a parent having a sexually transmitted disease. Take thorough notes and report the key facts to the class. *Choice:* Research additional information on the Internet and present your report in a flyer, poster, or chart.

16. *Research.* Using the Internet, research and prepare a report on one community organization that offers educational or economic support to parents. Include a description of the following: the type of support or resources provided, eligibility requirements, and application requirements.

Use Technology

17. *Math.* Interview three adults about strategies they have found successful in helping children learn self-control. Form small groups. Combine your strategies in a spreadsheet, identifying the number of adults using each strategy. Convert the spreadsheet into a graph that shows how many adults use each strategy. Prepare a report for the class summarizing your findings. *Group option:* Create a graph that includes all the statistics found by the entire class.

18. Create a catalog in which you show developmentally appropriate toys for different age groups. *Group option:* Exchange catalogs with a partner and evaluate the choices for each age group. *Choice:* Post the electronic files for your catalog to your class Web site.

19. *Research.* Search the Internet for environmental dangers, such as poison ivy rashes or tick bites, that affect a relatively high percentage of children in your area. Using a drawing program, design a poster illustrating these dangers. Include a description of the symptoms, possible complications, and care that an affected child needs.

20. Using a computer, develop a chart to reinforce desirable behavior for a preschooler and for a fourth grade child. Include specific behaviors for each age (such as feeding the dog or picking up toys) that a parent might be trying to reinforce. With the chart, suggest a possible reward system to use. *Choice:* Use clipart or other features to illustrate the chart.

Connecting with Career Clusters

Human Services

Pathways

- Early Childhood Development & Services
- Counseling & Mental Health Services
- Family & Community Services
- Personal Care Services
- Consumer Services

Child Care Provider

Child care providers nurture children in small- or large-group settings. They provide custodial care (food, shelter, and a healthful and safe environment) and play an important role in a child's physical, emotional, intellectual, and social development. They help children develop their interests, independence, and self-esteem.

These professionals need to know the various stages of human development and methods for promoting growth through age-appropriate activities. Most children in child care are under six, but ages range from infancy to teenage. Preschoolers generally spend full days in child care, while school-age children participate in before- and after-school programs.

Work hours are generally long and usually set for the convenient drop-off and pick-up times of working parents. The turnover rate is high as workers change jobs for better pay and work hours. With additional education and training, child care providers may become teacher assistants, teachers, or program directors—jobs with higher pay, better benefits, and shorter workdays.

Licensing requirements for child care providers vary by state. Most states require some formal training and work experience.

Career Outlook

Child care providers must be interested in children; have immense energy; provide fair but firm treatment; communicate effectively with children, parents, and administrators; anticipate and prevent problems; and be patient and alert.

Employment for child care providers is expected to grow because many working parents seek quality child care for their children. The increasing number of early childhood education centers, which only hire preschool teachers, may adversely affect job prospects. In May 2006, the median annual earnings of child care providers were $17,630. Depending on the number of hours worked and the size and location of the facility, income may range up to $27,000 annually.

Explore

Internet Research
Identify the Web site of the licensing agency in your area and review your state's procedures for making sure that caregivers meet those requirements. Research and report the requirements for operating a licensed child care facility from your home.

Job Shadowing
Spend one day in each licensed facility: a preschool and a child care center. Compare the facilities in a report, explaining their differences and giving specific examples. Identify when you would suggest either care setting for a working parent.

Community Service/Volunteer
Assist a local child care center after school. Keep a journal describing your activities, the effectiveness of the activities in which you participate, and suggestions for improvement.

Project
Organize a field trip for children in a child care program, with the consent of the center's director. Plan transportation, food accommodations, and age-appropriate activities. Identify ways (intellectual, social, emotional, and physical) in which the field trip will stimulate the children. Take steps to obtain all required permission slips. Participate in the trip and write a summary, evaluating whether the planned activities met your learning objectives.

Interview
Interview working parents who use child care for preschoolers. Find out the extent of their child care needs, the ease with which they can obtain quality care, their concerns about available care and its costs, and what they expect from the care provider for their money. Summarize their responses in a report.

Part-Time Job
Start your own small business and offer babysitting services with an educational component. Prepare activities—physical, social, emotional, and intellectual—that match each child's level of development and promote growth. Develop lesson plans for these activities, including a description of how each activity will help a child grow and develop.

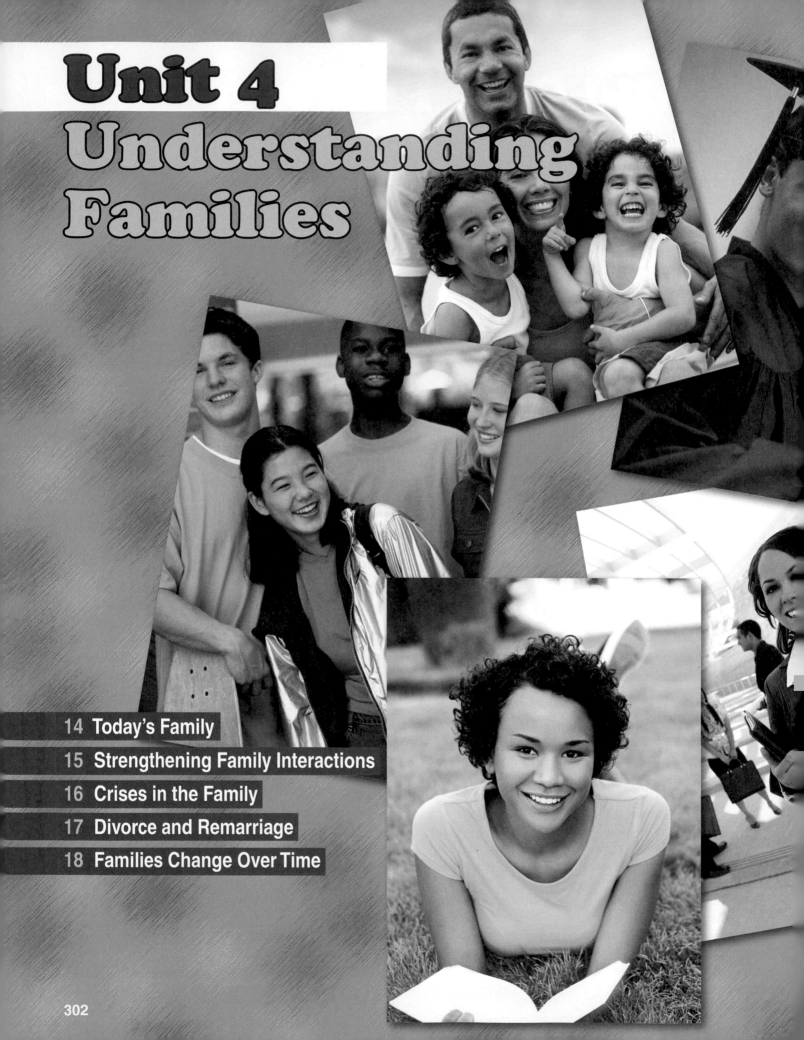

Unit 4
Understanding Families

Chapter 14

Today's Family

Section 14:1
Trends in American Family Life

Section 14:2
Functions of the Family

Section 14:3
Family Structures

Section 14:4
Single Living

Key Questions

Questions to answer as you study this chapter:

- How have families changed over time?
- What are the benefits of family living?
- How can families meet their members' needs through different family structures?

Chapter Objectives

After studying this chapter, you will be able to
- **describe** how cultural changes have affected the family.
- **evaluate** the benefits of living in a family.
- **describe** the functions of the family.
- **distinguish** among the characteristics of various family structures.
- **recognize** single living as a lifestyle trend in this society.

Life Sketch

Anita looked around the classroom at her many friends in this new school. There was Rosalee, who lived with her mom and younger brother in an apartment. They didn't have much money, and Rosalee had to spend most of her time babysitting her brother.

Anita glanced over at her friend Britta. Britta always had the best clothes and extra money to spend. Anita guessed it was because both her parents worked so hard. They were often gone on business trips. Britta's grandmother, who lived with the family, always made Anita feel special whenever she visited.

Josh had become a close friend, too. Anita was glad that her parents had moved next door to Josh and his dad. Josh had moved to the neighborhood three years ago and knew how it felt to try to make new friends.

Getting Started

Families live differently now than they did years ago, yet they fulfill many of the same functions. Today's family structures are more complex and less traditional than those of the past. In spite of the many challenges they face, the family remains a strong institution.

Today's families are more mobile, moving to better jobs, climates, and opportunities. An increasing divorce rate has resulted in many children living in a family with only one parent. The number of women working outside the home has increased, too. Such circumstances are the result of economic and social changes in American society.

section 14:1

Trends in American Family Life

Sharpen Your Reading

As you read each section, compare family life during the era discussed to family life today.

Boost Your Vocabulary

Identify a timeframe for each time period discussed: colonial times, the industrial revolution, and the technological age.

Know Key Terms

family

A **family** consists of two or more people living in the same household. They may be related by blood, marriage, or adoption. A family may include any combination of mother, father, stepparents, children, stepchildren, adopted children, grandparents, or other relatives.

Every period in history has presented challenges to families trying to make a life for themselves. To survive, families have learned to adjust to these challenges. They survived by learning to change as the economic and social needs of their society changed. The needs of the U.S. society in earlier periods were very different from those of today.

The Colonial Family

Ole and Martha were a typical young family, ready to face the hardships of colonial life. They grew up together in the same community. Their families farmed land nearby. Ole visited Martha's home often, helping the men put up a building or harvest crops. Martha went with her mother to help Ole's mother sew quilts and preserve food. When Ole was old enough to get his own farm, he asked permission to marry Martha. After all, he needed a wife and family to help him survive colonial life.

Ole owned a small plot of land when he married Martha, his young bride of sixteen. Martha learned many skills while growing up and was prepared for her new role as wife. She knew how to raise food and preserve it for the long winter months. She could spin yarn, weave cloth, and sew garments for every family member. She could make candles and soap. She helped care for younger brothers and sisters at home so she knew about child care. She was ready when her own baby arrived that first year of married life.

Ole and Martha always worked from sunrise to long past sunset on the farm. Many chores needed to be done so a large family was the norm, 14-1. Ole hunted turkey and venison, which she cleaned and prepared for meals. They and their children dug the fields, planted seeds, and harvested crops. Eventually they acquired a few farm animals to provide labor, food, hides, and wool for clothing.

14-1 Before farming machinery was available, large families were needed to do the work.

The Effects on the Family

The work of most families in colonial times—and for many generations to follow—centered around agriculture. Families worked to obtain and own land. All family members worked together to provide for the family's needs.

The work done by both spouses was important and necessary for the family's survival. Their roles were similar to those they saw their parents fulfill. Children were valuable, for they helped with farm chores at a very young age. Relatives lived nearby. They worked together, helped one another in times of trouble, and celebrated special events together.

Think More About It
What are some examples of characteristics of families today that are similar to those of the colonial family?

The Family During the Industrial Revolution

Fritz knew that his ancestors had farmed his land for years. His parents wanted him to continue farming, but Fritz had heard about good jobs in the big cities. Fritz and his wife, Maria, moved to the city for a job.

Life in the city was very different from what they expected. Fritz found a job in a factory, but it paid less than he hoped. They found an apartment, but the rent took much of his pay. They had to buy food as they no longer had land to raise it. Maria stayed at home and cared for their two small children.

Maria's homemaking skills stretched the money Fritz made. She spent most of her time baking, washing, and ironing. The children's care was almost totally hers. Fritz had little time to spend with the children because he worked such long hours.

Maria missed the times when they worked together on the farm. She missed being able to walk over to her parents' place to talk or work on a project. She missed her sister who was always eager to help her take care of the children. This new city life had brought many changes to her family.

The Effects on the Family

During the industrial revolution, many families moved from rural areas to large cities. They found work in factories, 14-2. Families no longer worked the land for their survival—they worked for someone else. Families became dependent on others as they adopted the role of consumers. Now that their lives were free of farm chores, large families were no longer an advantage.

Parenting roles changed, too. A man worked long hours away from his family and became the main provider. Because he was gone from the home so much, his role in parenting decreased. Raising the children became a major part of the mother's role since she was the one whose full-time job was homemaking. Women worked long hours alone in the family. The stress on the marriage relationship was high. Support from other family members was not available since many families no longer had relatives living nearby.

In what ways was family life in the industrial revolution similar to family life today?

14-2 As in the industrial revolution, some family members are involved in producing manufactured goods.

The Family in the Technological Age

Monique finished college and was teaching when she met Andre. They dated for a year before they decided to marry. They both continued to work, saving enough for a down payment on their own home. Their careers kept them both quite busy. They managed their busy schedules by sharing household tasks while working full-time.

When Jackie was born, Monique and Andre were excited to become parents. Monique wanted to spend more time with her newborn so she requested leave for one semester. Not wanting to give up her teaching position, Monique returned to work when Jackie was only six months old. It took some time to adjust to the new schedule, but Andre and Monique shared both household chores and parenting tasks. Andre's mother was delighted to babysit while Monique taught school.

The Effects of Technology on the Family

As industries grew, so did the production of goods. Jobs were easy to obtain. Families bought appliances and cars to make life more comfortable. Housekeeping became easier with these new conveniences, but the demand on family income increased. As a result, many women joined the workforce.

When mothers went to work outside the home, their child-rearing role changed. They shared the role with babysitters, child care workers, and teachers. Eventually new services became available to handle household tasks formerly done by family members. Although family income increased, there were many more goods and services to buy.

The marriage relationship changed. It became based on mutual love and affection rather than a need for one person to provide and care for another. Couples who were not happy with their marriage separated, and the divorce rate increased. As a result, many families became headed by a single mother or father. New family structures emerged as divorced persons remarried and merged their families.

With the advance of technology, many industrial jobs changed. Workers were replaced with machines. Computers made complex jobs simpler. New jobs emerged in service and information industries. Many jobs required less physical labor but more technical skills, 14-3. Time and energy for leisure activities became more common.

Higher education was no longer a goal just for men. More women obtained college degrees and higher-paying jobs. A shared wage-earner role led to both sexes sharing the work at home. More couples divided parenting, child care, and housekeeping tasks to balance work and home responsibilities.

14-3 In this technological age, many work at providing services for others.

Investigate Further

What resources did the colonial family have that families in the age of technology do not have? What resources do families have today that colonial families did not have?

The Changing Family

Family functions change in response to economic and social pressures. Families that were self-sufficient (meeting their own needs) in an agricultural economy went to work for others in an industrial economy. The value of a large family decreased when work moved away from the farm into the factory. As a result, families had fewer children and established the small-family trend that still exists today. Throughout past economic and social shifts in society, family roles varied and relationships changed.

Today's families face some old challenges, such as balancing work and family responsibilities. They also face some new challenges, such as caring for older parents and retraining themselves to work in the computer era and a global economy. Throughout these challenges, the family adjusts and survives. It continues to be a strong and important unit of society.

Think More About It
What past changes have made family living easier or better today? What changes have made family living today more difficult?

Benefits of Family Living

Family living offers several benefits to its members. These benefits help to keep the family unit strong, even through many years of change. A family can do the following:

- *Satisfy physical needs.* These include food to eat, clothes to wear, medical care when needed, and a place to live.

- *Be a source of protection.* Parents and older siblings can protect you from experiences that could bring harm or danger.

- *Provide long-lasting relationships.* Even though many changes occur in the outside world, the family can provide a sense of belonging.

- *Be a source of love and affection.* Some family members show affection outwardly. Others show they care by being there when you need them. Such bonds of affection can remain strong throughout a lifetime.

- *Provide support and encouragement.* The ties between family members can be strong. They want to see you succeed and will help you if they can. It can be encouraging to know they are there to help you if you need it.

- *Provide companionship.* Family members have similar backgrounds. You may enjoy similar interests, hobbies, or leisure activities. As family members share experiences, they build ties that remain strong even through change.

Review Section 14:1

1. Briefly describe two major cultural changes before the technological age that affected families.

2. Name six benefits of family living.

section 14:2

Functions of the Family

Sharpen Your Reading

Develop a graphic organizer for functions of the family, listing the ways families carry out each function.

Boost Your Vocabulary

Review the definitions of *socialization* and *role* from Chapter 2.

Know Key Terms

cultural identity

In this society, families socialize children, meet their physical needs, meet emotional needs, and influence their roles in society. Because family living is more complex today, fulfilling these functions may be more challenging.

Use What You Learn

In what ways do you think it is more challenging to fulfill these functions today than in times past?

Socializing Children

When families have children, they make it possible for the society to extend into a new generation, 14-4. However, giving birth is only

14-4 Families reproduce and socialize children, extending their family tree into a new generation.

the beginning. Children are born helpless, needing others to provide and care for them as they grow to maturity. The family fulfills a major role in meeting children's needs as they grow and develop.

Children need to learn skills that will help them become productive members of society. The family reinforces those skills and provides the nurturing environment in which those skills can be developed.

The family also interprets the standards of the society. Children need to learn what is and is not acceptable behavior. Families teach, train, and provide examples of how these standards apply to individual lives. Society as a whole will benefit and communities will be safer, better places to live as families focus on the function of socializing children.

Meeting Physical Needs

The family is responsible for providing care and protection for family members. This includes providing food, clothing, shelter, and protection from harm, injury, and disease. Usually one or more family members hold a job to earn the salary to pay for these needs.

Inside the home, physical needs are satisfied by accomplishing certain tasks, such as cooking, cleaning, providing transportation, shopping, and more. Usually these tasks are shared by various family members. Families may divide these tasks in various ways. With the cooperation of all members, families will have greater success in fulfilling this function.

Meeting Emotional Needs

The family can be a source of close relationships in which people live together and love and care for one another. They provide companionship for one another. Through these close, intimate relationships, each member's emotional needs are met.

Developing Close Relationships

Family members can work together to develop strong family ties. They need to spend time together talking, listening, resolving disagreements, and taking part in family activities. Children need to experience the love and acceptance of such nurturing relationships in order to mature.

If technology fills too much of a child's time, quality family relationships will not develop. Families need to monitor children's activities and take time to be involved in what they are doing. They also need to show love and affection for each other while they are working and playing together. Such joint activities in a caring atmosphere will foster the growth of close relationships between family members.

> ### Investigate Further
>
> **How does work in the technological age impact the development of close intimate relationships in the family?**

Influencing Roles in Society

Your family can influence the place you take in society. They may influence the educational path you choose and the career you eventually select. In this way, the family affects your role as a future adult in the workforce.

Your family gives you your **cultural identity**, too. This is the way you see yourself as a member of your specific cultural group. Through your parents, you inherit physical traits unique to their cultural background. Your family also influences the religious beliefs you have. In addition, it can influence the customs you observe and the traditions you will continue in your own family, 14-5.

Your Changing Roles

Your family also influences the *personal roles* you have and the expectations that go with them. Currently, you have the role of a son or daughter. The expectations for that role changed as you grew from infancy through childhood into adolescence. They will continue to change as you become an adult. When you marry, you will acquire a new role as husband or wife. If you become a parent, you will acquire another role. The expectations for each of these roles are influenced by your family and the society in which you live.

14-5 Families pass on their beliefs, traditions, and expectations to the next generation.

Link to Your Life

What expectation do you have for your own personal roles of the future?

Review Section 14:2

1. List four functions of the family. Then briefly explain how the family carries them out.
2. What is cultural identity?

section 14:3

Family Structures

Sharpen Your Reading

Create a chart with three columns labeled *What You Already Know*, *What You Want to Know*, and *What You Learned*. On the left side of the chart, record each type of family structure. Before you read, fill in the first column with what you already know about each family structure. If some questions come to your mind, write them in the second column. As you read, write what you learn in the third column.

Boost Your Vocabulary

For each family structure, draw a diagram showing whom you would find in a household with that family structure.

Know Key Terms

nuclear family
single-parent family
stepfamily
extended family
dual-career family

Even though families have different structures, they try to fulfill the same functions for family members. The six common family structures are nuclear, single-parent, stepfamily, extended, childless, and adopting. Several of these family structures may also be dual-career families. Each structure has unique challenges in fulfilling family functions.

The Nuclear Family

The most traditional family structure in this society is the **nuclear family**. It includes a married couple and their children. The children were either born into the family or adopted. Neither parent has children from a previous marriage.

Benefits of the Nuclear Family

A nuclear family tends to be the most supportive family structure for children. This type of family structure has strong bonds. Most activities center around the family and family goals. Children benefit by growing up in a nuclear family in the following ways:

- They have both parents present while they grow up, 14-6. They have two adults to encourage their growth and development and provide support.

- They have a parental model for both male and female roles. Children will develop expectations for a future spouse based on their parental models.

- They have the opportunity to relate socially to both sexes. Such interaction can help them learn to develop friendships with members of both sexes.

- They tend to have more family resources available, including financial resources.

14-6 In a nuclear family, children have the benefit of frequent interaction with both parents.

Parents also benefit in a nuclear family structure. They have the advantage of an adult partner to help with the many tasks of parenting and providing for a family. They can support and help each other in times of stress. They can meet each other's needs for love and intimacy.

> ### Investigate Further
>
> **If the nuclear family has such benefits for raising children, why is this structure less common today than it was in the past?**

Parental Roles in a Nuclear Family

Parents may take different roles in a nuclear family depending on their skills, time available, and choices made regarding work. There are many ways that family tasks can be shared to provide a quality environment for children to grow and develop.

In some nuclear families, mothers fulfill the traditional role of "mothering." This includes taking the main responsibility for child care, meal preparation, housekeeping, laundry, and maintaining a loving and nurturing environment. Many mothers who work full-time at a job outside the home still assume the mothering role.

The traditional role of "fathering" is to provide for the financial needs of the family. It also includes taking part in the guidance of children. Fathers are seen as authority figures in the family. Most fathers fulfill this role in a loving and nurturing manner.

The Single-Parent Family

A **single-parent family** includes one parent and one or more children. The parent may be a mother or father. A single-parent family may result from divorce, separation, death, or a birth to an unmarried woman. The most common form of this rapidly growing structure is headed by the mother. The number of single-parent families is increasing.

The Parent's Role

The single parent is responsible for all the adult roles in the family. The role of provider is a major role. Along with this role come other financial responsibilities, such as budgeting and paying the bills. The roles of child-caregiver, housekeeper, cook, shopper, nurse, and decision maker all belong to the single parent. A single parent may sometimes feel overwhelmed. Often there is not enough time, energy, or money to handle all these roles.

Children's Roles

Children are often given more responsibility in a single-parent family, 14-7. They may be required at a young age to get themselves up, dressed, and off to school on time. They may cook for the family, care for younger siblings, and help with household tasks. With such responsibilities, children learn to be independent quite early.

14-7 In a single-parent family, children learn to be independent by taking responsibility earlier for helping with family tasks.

Children in a single-parent family have fewer resources to help them handle the stresses of daily living. Only one parent is there to meet their emotional needs for love and affection. Money may be in short supply if only one parent provides an income. Children may have only one role model to help them learn acceptable social roles.

However, a single-parent family can fulfill the same functions as other family structures. It can provide a warm, positive setting so children feel love and security. As physical needs are met and activities shared, children can become responsible individuals, just as they do in other family structures.

Support Resources

Many single-parent families turn to outside sources to seek help in managing all their responsibilities. Assistance and support is often available from community social service organizations, businesses, and religious organizations. Sometimes the absent parent can help with finances or child care.

Other family members or friends can help with child care, too. They can spend time with the children, listening to them, giving love and affection, and encouraging them in their achievements. They can also be role models for the children. Such assistance gives the single parent time to enjoy other interests, improve job skills, and develop new relationships.

Think More About It
What strategies can a single parent use to help carry out the functions of a family?

The Stepfamily

The challenges of living and parenting alone often lead single parents to seek out a new partner. When they join in marriage, a stepfamily is formed. A **stepfamily** consists of a husband and wife, one or both of whom have been married before. It also includes children from one or more previous marriages.

The stepfamily has the advantage of two parents working together to fill the parenting role and maintain the home. There is less strain on each parent's time and energy. The couple has their marriage relationship to meet their own emotional needs for intimacy.

The children in a stepfamily have access to more resources. They have the benefit of two parents in the home. They have both male and female role models. Relationships with stepparents take time to develop, but can be the source of love, affection, encouragement, and understanding.

The stepfamily is a more complex structure. Two different family structures combine to make a new family unit, creating new family roles. These include the roles of a newly married husband and wife as well as stepparent and stepchild. The absent parents, grandparents, and other relatives also have roles in the life of a stepfamily. Working out the role expectations to meet family needs takes time.

Think More About It
In what ways does the combining of two families help the parents fulfill the functions of the family?

The Extended Family

In an **extended family**, several generations of one family live together, sharing the home and family activities. Grandparents, aunts, uncles, or cousins live with the family in the same household, 14-8. This structure is much more common in other countries.

This type of family structure can benefit family members. As children interact with older family members, they learn to trust and appreciate them. Older members gain a respected position in the family. They can offer experience in childrearing and participate in family activities.

Extended families can be formed in different ways. One common form is the *modified-extended family*. Relatives live near one another, but not with one another. They are involved in each other's lives, helping out when needed. They may help with child care and housekeeping tasks. They may work together on large projects. They may celebrate social events together. Such cooperation and support strengthens the relationships within the family.

14-8 In this extended family, three generations live in the same house.

Investigate Further

How could an extended family structure help the family fulfill its functions?

The Childless Family

Some families do not include children in their structure, just husband and wife. Their reasons for remaining childless vary. They may delay having children, be unable to have children, or plan to never have children.

The childless family may have more financial resources. They do not have the expenses that go with child-rearing. Both adults often work. They may pursue challenging career goals because they can give more attention to their jobs. The spouses tend to share their roles in the home, working together to reach their goals.

Some childless families choose to devote some of their time to working with others' children. By doing so, they become involved in socializing children. They may work with children in community clubs or organizations, recreation programs, youth groups, or schools.

The Adopting Family

When children are adopted, they may become part of a nuclear family, a stepfamily, or a single-parent family. An adopted family has unique

challenges to face. The first is adjusting to the parenting role. The second is talking to the child about the adoption.

Usually adoptive parents must adjust to the new role of parenting quite suddenly. In most cases, the adopting family has waited for the child for quite a long time, sometimes years. The date of arrival is often uncertain and may occur suddenly.

Another challenge is deciding how to talk about the adoption. Children should be told early that they were adopted. Parents can emphasize the child was wanted, specially chosen, and brought into their family. Children will have questions about their birthparents, especially as they get older. There may be times when they feel insecure or uncertain about their identity. They may want to find out who their birthparents are and even meet them.

Close relationships within the adopting family can help meet these challenges, 14-9. As a couple model a strong marital relationship, adopted children will feel more secure. Then parents can build the child's esteem and affirm that the child is loved and wanted.

Investigate Further

What challenges might an adopting family have in fulfilling the functions of the family?

The Dual-Career Family

In a **dual-career family**, both husband and wife pursue careers outside the home while maintaining their family roles. This is not a separate family structure but a type of arrangement based on work roles. A dual-career family may be any family structure.

Both spouses can develop individual interests and pursue their professional roles in a dual-career family. The roles of earning a living, keeping a home, and raising children are divided between husband and wife. Children may become more independent as their busy parents assign them greater household responsibilities.

Family teamwork and cooperation makes this type of family arrangement work. Perhaps the key benefit of this type of family is the greater family income provided by two wage earners.

While relationships in a dual-career family tend to benefit from the sharing of roles, sometimes the sharing causes problems. If spouses do not agree on how to share household responsibilities and child care tasks, one spouse may feel overburdened. Physical stress and tension can result from trying to fulfill too many roles.

Review Section 14:3

1. Identify two benefits of living in a nuclear family.
2. List four ways a single-parent family may be formed.
3. Explain the difference between an extended family and a modified-extended family.
4. Name two challenges faced by the adopting family.

14-9 As the adopting family freely shows love, affection, and acceptance, the child's feelings of security increase.

section 14:4

Single Living

Sharpen Your Reading

Outline the reasons and advantages of not marrying. Add common concerns of those who do not marry.

Boost Your Vocabulary

Look up the different definitions of **single** in a dictionary. Do you think the different definitions apply to single people?

Know Key Terms

single living

Single living refers to a lifestyle in which a person lives alone. The household consists only of one person. This trend is becoming more common as the singles population continues to grow. At some time in their lives, most people will experience single living, 14-10. The period of single living may be temporary or permanent. For many young people, single living is a transition period between living with parents and later with a spouse.

Reasons for Single Living

Sometimes living alone is the chosen lifestyle. Often this choice is short-term—to delay marriage. However, living single may be a long-term choice—to never marry. On the other hand,

14-10 More young people remain single for a longer period of time than in the past. For many, single living is a transition period from one stage of life to another.

single living may not result from a decision, but as a result of circumstances in life.

Delaying Marriage

More young people are postponing marriage until they are older. Some choose to finish their education before they get married. Others desire to establish themselves in a good job or become financially stable. Some want to fulfill lifelong dreams, such as extensive traveling, before making a commitment to another person.

When older singles do marry, their maturity helps them to work harder at developing a good marriage relationship. They have determined that friendship and companionship are more important than anything else they might want in life. Since they are older when they marry, they tend to have children at an older age. When the mother is over age 35, the health risks of pregnancy increase. Older couples sometimes remain childless, have only one child, or attempt to adopt a child. These couples tend to be more financially established, which helps them succeed in reaching their goals.

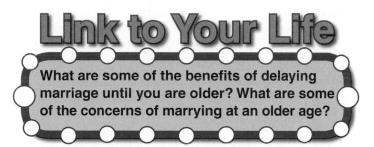

Link to Your Life

What are some of the benefits of delaying marriage until you are older? What are some of the concerns of marrying at an older age?

Choosing Not to Marry

Some people prefer the independence and flexibility of single living. These singles never seek a marriage partner. Since social pressures to marry have lessened, they are less likely to feel they must get married.

Some people are intensively involved in their careers and do not want to commit to a relationship. They may not want the responsibility of marriage or parenting to take time away from their careers.

Some people have been hurt in previous relationships. To avoid being hurt again, they decide to remain single.

Yet other single people have a dependent family member who is ill, is older, or has a disability. Because they devote so much time tending to the needs of that person, they may not want to burden a spouse with the responsibility.

Changes Leading to Single Living

Divorce and a spouse's death are leading reasons for an increase in the number of singles. Many divorced people who do not have children or custody of their children return to single living. The loss of a spouse also forces many people to live their remaining years alone. Although circumstances make them single, they may choose to stay single rather than risk an unwise marriage.

In addition to these life circumstances, there is one more—never finding a suitable marriage partner. Some who want to marry may not find that special person. As a result, they live alone all their lives even though their intention was to marry.

Advantages of Single Living

For many people, single living is an attractive lifestyle for the following reasons:

- Singles may have more freedom, independence, and time to do whatever they want, 14-11.
- Singles usually have fewer living expenses than a person with a family.

14-11 Some adults view the freedom of single living as attractive and desirable. They often have more time to spend on their hobbies and interests.

- Singles often have more mobility than married people. They can easily make career changes or move to another city.
- Many singles gain self-confidence in knowing they can take care of themselves, emotionally and financially.

Many singles work to build a strong support network of family and friends. They meet others through friends, work, or other social activities. Their social life can be structured as they wish—either busy or relaxed.

Think More About It
In what ways are the roles of singles different from the roles of married couples?

Concerns of Single People

For some singles, living alone may have disadvantages. Social relationships or dealing with stereotyped images of their lifestyles are two concerns.

Social Relationships

Some singles may need to make more of an effort to develop social relationships. Demanding careers can make it difficult to meet others. The field of dating partners may shrink. Some may feel uncomfortable trying to fit into society, especially when so many events are geared toward couples. The single person may feel increasing loneliness as others the same age marry and develop lives around their children.

Some singles may feel they are missing out on part of life. They may desire the closeness and sharing of married life. They may want to have a child, but not as a single parent. These factors may draw the single person toward marriage.

Stereotyped Images

Singles must deal with the stereotypes associated with single living. Singles are sometimes viewed as self-centered because

they pursue their own interests. They may be considered irresponsible and unstable.

Some people believe that a person must be married to be happy. As a result, a single person may feel pushed toward marriage. Some parents believe that single living is not an acceptable lifestyle. Friends may want the single person to experience the fulfillment they have found in marriage.

Singles have the same needs as others for friendships and emotional support, 14-12. Once they possess these, they can be happy and experience personal fulfillment. Singles who are self-confident believe they can make a worthwhile contribution to society. If they remain single, such positive attitudes will help them live a complete life. If they eventually marry, they will have a rich background to bring to the relationship.

14-12 Getting involved in social activities is one way for singles to develop friendships.

Review Section 14:**4**

1. List four reasons why some people choose to remain single.
2. List four advantages of choosing single living as a lifestyle.

Think It Through

Different Family Structures

Trista hurried home as soon as school was out. Her mother worked the late afternoon shift at the assisted living facility, and she had to babysit her little sister, Tara. Ever since her parents had separated, Trista had the responsibility of caring for Tara while their mother worked. After Tara went to bed, Trista would do her homework or watch TV. She usually fell asleep on the couch waiting for her mother to come home. She liked to wait up so she and her mother could talk before they went to bed.

Noah rushed to his locker as soon as the bell rang. He had to hurry to his after-school job. He worked at the local supermarket from the time school was out until 9:00 each night. He stocked shelves and sometimes bagged groceries at the checkout.

With his schedule, Noah found it hard to get his homework done. However, he knew that the money he made really helped his family. After Noah's dad was laid off from his job, he found work at a much lower pay. Noah's mom looked for a job, too, but could only find work paying minimum wage. The cost of a babysitter for Noah's little brother was so high that she decided to stay home and care for him herself. Noah's grandmother lived with them, but her health was poor. Sometimes she needed care as well.

Noah's income was a real help to the family, but his parents insisted that he save some each week. They were determined that Noah would go to college.

Dominique and his brother lived with their parents, who worked until 6:00 each night. Both boys were responsible for getting their homework done by the time their parents came home. Then they both had to do household chores. Sometimes Dominique had to help cook supper. At other times, it was his turn to clean the kitchen or do laundry. They all had to work until the chores were done.

Questions to Guide Your Thinking

1. Identify the type of family structure in each situation. List the family members who make up the structure of each.

2. What roles did family members take in each of these families?

3. In each family, were the roles affected by the structure of the family or by other changes in the society? Explain your answer.

4. What are the differences in the ways each family fulfills its functions?

5. What are the similarities between these families?

6. How are these families similar to the early American families of colonial times? How are they different from the colonial families?

Chapter Summary

The family is a flexible institution that constantly adjusts to economic and social changes in society. Throughout this country's history, the types of work and roles of family members have changed. Relationships with relatives, views of children, and expectations for the marriage relationship have also changed. Through all these changes, the family continues to be an important unit in society.

The family fulfills several important functions. It is the main societal unit for the reproduction and socialization of children. In the family, physical needs are met, close relationships are developed, and personal roles are influenced.

Several types of family structures are common in this country. Though today's family structures vary, most families try to fulfill the needs of family members.

Although many people do plan to marry and form their own family, single living is more common today. For many singles, this lifestyle offers more advantages than disadvantages.

Assess...

Your Knowledge

1. What is a family?

2. What are the benefits of family living?

Your Understanding

3. Throughout history, how have families adjusted to meet the needs of family members?

4. Explain how each type of family structure fulfills the functions of the family.

Your Skills

5. Identify some of the successful adjustment strategies that past generations made in the family as technologies and careers changed. Which of these strategies could be helpful for families adjusting to a global economy?

6. What resources are available in your community to help single-parent families fulfill their functions?

Think Critically

7. *Writing.* Write a paper, song, or poem that describes the family of the future. Include ideas about how the family will fulfill its functions.

8. *Writing.* Interview a grandparent or other older adult about the early years of married life. Include questions about the type of work he or she did, the family's structure, and the roles carried out by members of the extended family. Then interview a parent and ask the same questions. Record answers for both interviews. In a paragraph, compare and contrast your grandparent's responses with your parent's responses. How are they similar? How are they different? *Choice:* Present your findings orally to the class.

9. *History, writing.* Pretend you are growing up in a family during the colonial period or the industrial revolution. First, research this period of history at the library. Then write an autobiography describing your role in the family and how your family fulfills its functions.

10. Compare two television shows that emphasize family living. Identify the family structure each family illustrates. List the family members in each show, identify their roles, and describe the relationships between members in each family. *Choice:* Evaluate how well each family fulfills its functions. Write a brief report summarizing your findings. *Group option:* Complete the activity with a partner.

Connect with Your Community

11. Analyze your family and your friends' families to identify examples of the benefits of family living. Include your examples in a one-page paper titled "The Benefits of Living in a Family." *Choice:* Present your analysis in a poster, song, rap, or poem.

12. *Social studies.* Prepare questions to ask a social worker about services available in your community to help families fulfill their basic functions. Interview the social worker and write a report identifying these services. *Choice:* Search the Internet for further information on local family services.

13. *History, research.* Search the Internet to identify the types of jobs common in your community in the past. Write a report that compares past trends in your community to the trends described in the text.

14. *Social studies.* Interview a farm family in or near your community. Write a one-page report comparing the roles of these family members with the roles of family members in the colonial years. Describe ways they are similar and ways they are different.

Use Technology

15. Using the computer, prepare a chart on the functions of the family. Create four columns for the chart. List one main function of the family as the heading for each column. Under each, list five examples of what families do to fulfill that function.

16. *Math.* Take a class survey of family structures. Using the computer, prepare a pie chart showing the percentage of nuclear, dual-parent, single-parent, step-, and adopting families. Also, what percentage of the families are a type of extended family?

17. *Research.* Interview a single person and ask questions about the advantages and disadvantages of single living. Work with a small group of classmates to identify common responses in each area. Create a spreadsheet listing the advantages and disadvantages identified, and the number of singles reporting each. Create a graph showing your findings. *Choice:* Write a paragraph summarizing your findings. *Group option:* Gather data from several groups so your graph reflects a larger population.

18. *Math.* Create a survey to discover who carries out which roles in the families in your class. List various roles in the left column and various possible family member titles across the top. Tally the results and create a graph for each title of family member. *Choice:* Write a paragraph discussing any generalizations you can make about the roles family members take in your community.

Chapter 15

Strengthening Family Interactions

Section 15:1
The Family as a System

Section 15:2
The Family Life Cycle

Section 15:3
Patterns of Interaction in Families

Key Questions

Questions to answer as you study this chapter:

- How do family interactions affect the family system?

- How can families maintain balance amidst the changes of the family life cycle?

- What interaction patterns lead to strong, healthy families?

Chapter Objectives

After studying this chapter, you will be able to

- **identify** various roles in the family.

- **recognize** challenges and rewards of each stage of the family life cycle.

- **describe** patterns of communication and decision making that increase positive family interactions.

- **determine** measures for preventing violence and abuse in the family.

- **relate** how family activities can strengthen the family.

Life Sketch

Rowena's dad opened the door leading to the auditorium as Rowena and her mother hurried inside. He helped them remove their coats and quickly checked them. The three politely smiled and thanked the usher who escorted them to their seats. Side by side they sat through the play, laughing and clapping with the rest of the audience.

Afterward, they pleasantly chatted with friends, neighbors, classmates, and teachers. No one could tell that the three were involved in a big argument before hurriedly leaving home. Only they knew about the heated words that were exchanged over Rowena's late date the night before. This was a matter that the family members intended to keep private. To everyone in the auditorium, this family appeared happy and content.

Getting Started

What goes on inside your family is usually private. Others may not know how your family members treat one another when no one else is around. Your family may have private patterns for communicating, solving problems, or making decisions.

These private interactions affect your self-confidence and self-esteem. They can influence the development of your personal skills for communicating, making decisions, and resolving conflicts. They can affect the way you handle stress. Finally, they can influence the interactions you will experience in your own future family.

section 15:1

The Family as a System

Sharpen Your Reading

Draw a diagram of a balance scale. As you read this section, list the two parts that need to balance in the family system, one on each side of the scale.

Boost Your Vocabulary

Draw a diagram that includes all the members of your family system.

Know Key Terms

family system

The family is a system because all family members interact with one another. In a **family system**, every member has an effect on every other family member.

Family Systems Are Complex

The more people in the family, the more complex the family system. When a family system is composed of two people, interactions occur in two directions. As families add members, the number of relationships multiplies. In a family of four, there are 12 different relationships, 15-1.

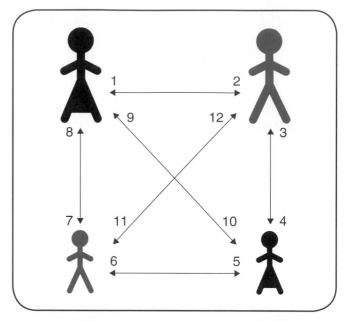

15-1 In larger families, interactions become very complex. Each arrow in the diagram represents two relationships in the family.

Think More About It
How many different relationships are added to a family when a couple has their first child?

Family relationships tend to have their own distinct patterns of interaction. For instance, your mother may relate to your father in one way and to you and siblings in another. When the extended family enters the picture, even more relationships exist. Learning more about these interactions is one way to help you understand and strengthen your family relationships.

Rights and Responsibilities

Being a member of a family usually involves both rights and responsibilities. These are interrelated—one cannot exist without the other. Meeting these expectations takes a combined family effort. Some of these rights and responsibilities are described below.

- *Satisfying physical needs.* Members have the right to eat the family's food, live in the household, and share other family resources. They may be expected to help with household chores and contribute to the family income.

- *Promoting emotional support.* Giving and receiving love tend to go hand-in-hand. For members to receive love and affection, others must provide it.

- *Speaking and being heard.* Family members have the right to voice their feelings and be heard by others. Such a right also requires that each person willingly listen to others in the family.

- *Supporting and encouraging.* Support and encouragement is provided by family members. In return, each family member is responsible for offering encouragement and support to the others.

Families can balance member's rights and responsibilities by making sure all members have chances to grow to their potential. This means managing family resources such as time and money so the needs of all family members can be met. Children need opportunities to learn new skills, take in new information, be creative, and express themselves. Parents also need opportunities to keep on learning and growing. They need time to enhance their relationships with others, improve old skills, and learn new skills.

> ### Investigate Further
>
> **What might happen in a family if everyone claims to have rights, but no one is willing to fulfill any responsibilities?**

Balancing Roles

Families balance their family system by defining each member's roles. Family members have various roles. Your family has expectations for each family member's role. These are based on family needs and should be clear and realistic. For instance, if the family needs more income, all members may be expected to work. Each person in the family system needs to know what actions or behaviors are expected.

Members should have responsibilities that match their skills and abilities. Then they will have greater success fulfilling them. As family members are able to fulfill their roles, they help keep the family balanced.

> **Think More About It**
> How might the family be affected if members do not fulfill their expected roles? Are there any family needs that might be left unmet?

Adjusting to Changes Inside and Outside the Family

The expectations for family roles may change as the needs of family members change. For instance, a parent's role changes as children grow older, 15-2. Adjusting to these changes helps keep the family system balanced.

Sometimes changes inside or outside the family affect a member's ability to carry out expected roles. For example, unemployment, illness, or an accident may prevent a person from accomplishing some aspects of his or her role well.

15-2 When children enter the teen years, the roles of both parent and child change.

Sometimes, family members do not fulfill their roles or carry out their responsibilities. For instance, a parent may abandon the family, or a teenager may rebel against the parent's expectations. By neglecting their responsibilities, one family member affects every other family member in a negative way.

Investigate Further

What resources could help a family adjust to the loss of a job and help meet the needs of family members?

Restoring Balance in the Family System

When roles are not fulfilled in a family, the family becomes unbalanced. As a result, the family is not able to function smoothly. Then the family system must adjust. This is done in one of two ways. Either the members not fulfilling their roles are helped so they can, or the other members work together to handle the neglected role.

For instance, a father may develop an alcohol abuse problem. Because of his problem, he is unable to carry out his role as the family's income provider. Family members may provide support to the father so he can fulfill his roles. By giving such support, they are helping return the family to balance.

In the second way, family members work together to carry out the unfulfilled roles. For instance, if unemployment or illness is the problem, another family member may try to find work. The family tries to return to a balance so the needs of family members are met.

The impacts of family interactions are far-reaching. If families cannot fulfill their functions and meet the needs of their members, society suffers. Broken relationships, emotional problems, child abuse, family violence, and poverty can result when the family cannot fulfill its functions. Therefore, the family's ability to fulfill its functions should be a primary concern to communities and society.

Review Section 15:1

1. Describe how a family functions like a system.
2. Briefly explain why expectations for family members need to include both rights and responsibilities.
3. Describe how a family can restore balance to the family system.

section 15:2

The Family Life Cycle

Sharpen Your Reading

Create a chart and list each stage of the family life cycle in the first column. As you read, identify the changes that occur in each stage in the second column. In the third column, record the adjustments family members must make to maintain balance in the family system.

Boost Your Vocabulary

Draw a picture depicting the family makeup for each stage of the family life cycle.

Know Key Terms

family life cycle

Families continue to change throughout the family life cycle. The **family life cycle** is composed of five stages that extend from marriage to the death of a spouse, 15-3. Right now, you are a part of your parents' family life cycle. When you marry, you will begin your own family life cycle.

Most families go through similar stages in the family life cycle. In each stage, family members have different roles to fill, tasks to carry out, and challenges to meet. Along with the challenges, each stage has its own rewards.

The Newly Married Stage

This stage begins when a couple marry. They will live on their own and provide their own housing, food, and clothing. They need to work together to establish their own family of two.

Developing New Roles

During this stage, a couple take on new roles of husband and wife. Responsibilities include making an income, caring for their own home, and managing their time and money.

The couple need to develop good communication patterns and learn to solve problems together. They need to set goals and plan for their future. Their success in these tasks will affect their family through all other stages.

During the early years of marriage, couples often share many responsibilities. They may both work as wage earners. They may share housekeeping roles and make decisions together. These roles may change when children are added to the family.

Think More About It
How is the family system affected if a newly married couple cannot adjust to their new roles of living on their own?

The Early Parenthood Stage

Pregnancy and the birth of the first child mark the early parenthood stage. This stage continues through the child's toddler, preschool, and elementary years.

Role Adjustments

Adjusting to the new roles of mother and father can be a challenge. The tasks include caring for young children and meeting their needs. That means that parents need to understand child development and learn how to stimulate the young child's growth.

The Family Life Cycle		
Youthful Marriage (ages 20-40)	**Newly married stage**	**Wedding**
		Adjustments to being a pair
	Early parenthood stage	**Birth of first child**
		Infant/toddler stage
		Birth of second child
		Preschool years
		Birth of third child
		First child starts school
		Elementary years
Middle-Age Marriage (about ages 40-60)	**Later parenthood stage**	**Oldest child begins adolescence**
		Puberty
		Junior high years
		Senior high years
		Dating
		First child moves out of house
		Second and third child follow
		First child may marry
Aging Marriage (about age 60+)	**Empty nest stage**	**Last child leaves home**
		Renewal of spousal relationship
		Grandparenting
		Caring for elderly parents
	Retirement Stage	New interests/hobbies
		Extended family relationships
		Death of spouse

15-3 Each stage of the family life cycle is marked by a series of different events. Most families follow similar patterns in their life cycle.

In many families, two or more children are born during this early parenting stage. Relationships become more complex. As children begin school, expectations from teachers, peers, and others in the community also influence family roles.

During the early years of parenting, the family budget often seems stretched to the limit. The need for income increases as children are born, and the family budget is expanded to meet their needs.

In the young family, there is a need for flexible roles. Often the tasks are nonstop. Keeping a positive attitude in the family is easier when spouses work together to meet the family's needs.

The parent and work roles take up much of a couple's time in this stage of the family life cycle. What time is spent together is usually child-centered. Little time alone is available, so having quiet moments together becomes a major need for a couple with young children.

Rewards of Parenting

Although the tasks of parenting are demanding, this stage of the family life cycle is very rewarding. It is exciting and satisfying to see children grow and learn new skills.

The time spent with children can be rewarding for the family as a whole. Good patterns of communication lead to trust between family members. Relationships grow stronger. Such activities have the potential for building a strong bond between family members, 15-4.

During this stage of the life cycle, grandparents and other relatives can help with the heavy load of parenting responsibilities. Such involvement meets needs in both families and builds relationships within the extended family.

Use What You Learn

What resources can help a young couple handle the heavy demands of parenting during these early years?

Later Parenthood Stage

When children reach adolescence, major changes take place in the family. These changes mark the beginning of the next stage of the family life cycle.

15-4 In the early parenting years, most parents find the close relationships with their children rewarding.

Parent-Teen Role Adjustments

The onset of puberty brings about rapid changes in physical growth and sexual development. The adolescent begins to appear more like an adult and less like a child. This time of transition requires that parents let go of some responsibilities, while teens take on more responsibilities. This process continues to the completion of the later parenting stage. At that time, the young adult is independent, living on his or her own.

Conflicts tend to arise when parents and adolescents do not agree on how much responsibility should be given up or taken on. Children often demand more freedom. However, parents are still legally responsible for their children until the children reach age 18. Parents often continue in the provider role while their children attend college. This stage of later parenting can extend for several years before children become completely independent.

Other parent-teen issues may cause conflicts during these years. Teens' dating habits and choices of friends and clothing may become sources of conflict. Performance in school and future goals can be other areas in which teens and parents have disagreements.

Rewards During This Stage

During the later parenting years, communication skills are important in the family. Patterns of clear and open communication, joint decision making, and conflict resolution are vital. These skills can help families manage the changes in a way that brings rewards. The goal of these years is to launch a self-sufficient new generation. Seeing children reach that goal is rewarding.

The key to this stage of the life cycle is empathy in communication and decision making. Communicating with empathy can help keep channels open between family members. Respect for one another's feelings and desires can be maintained as decisions are made. Then relationships can continue to be close, and family members can become adult friends.

The Empty Nest Stage

When the last child is independent and living on his or her own, the family enters the empty nest stage. Parental roles change greatly. No longer are children dependent on their parents for meeting their needs. The children are responsible for meeting their own needs. Some marry and begin their own families. As a child marries, parents need to accept the child's mate into the extended family.

Role Adjustments

Parents may still be involved in their adult son or daughter's life, but to a much lesser extent. They may still provide some financial help or support them in other ways. They may be involved in grandparenting, 15-5. These roles take less time than their full-time parenting responsibilities of the past. This stage may seem lonely for some parents. Developing new interests and setting new goals may fill some needs.

15-5 In many families, grandparenting is a new role of the empty nest stage.

The relationship of empty nesters with their own parents may change. The older generation may need financial support or help with physical care. This new role of supporting older parents requires adjustment from both spouses.

Although this stage can be challenging, it can also be rewarding. Couples have the chance to renew their own close relationship. They return to living as a couple. Strengthening their own relationship is important as they look ahead to the next stage of retirement.

Retirement Stage

Couples enter the retirement stage after one or both spouses retire from their career. Retirement age varies. Some couples work as long as they are physically able, while some choose an early retirement.

Many couples plan ahead while they are still working to prepare financially for these years. They have set goals for this time of their life. For some couples, retirement is a time to focus on themselves, hobbies, volunteer work, travel, or leisure activities. More time can be devoted to friendships and grandchildren, too.

Not all people cope well with retirement. Some are unable to adjust to their changed roles. The sense of purpose they felt while working is gone. As a result, their self-esteem may drop. Along with this, health and financial problems can prevent them from looking at the future with hope.

Death of a Spouse

The death of one partner ends the family life cycle. The remaining partner returns to single living. The widow or widower faces two major challenges: dealing emotionally with the loss of a partner and adjusting to a lifestyle change. Personal freedoms may be affected. The loss of income, health, and the ability to live independently are hard to accept. Self-esteem may decline. Fears of being used or abused increase.

Many older adults choose to remain in their own homes as long as possible. Some live with a child, other family members, or a roommate. Others move to communities developed exclusively for older adults. A small percentage live in a group-care facility.

Family members and friends are very important to the older person, 15-6. They can bring joy, meaning, and hope into the person's life. Keeping them active in community groups, religious groups, or educational settings also helps the older person stay in contact with others.

Investigate Further

How do retirement and the death of a spouse unbalance the family system?

Government Assistance

Some government programs have been set up to help those with limited incomes. Social security provides some income. Medicare helps pay for medical expenses. Meal-assistance programs offer help with nutrition. In some areas, low-income housing is available for older adults. These programs are designed to help older adults live independently.

15-6 Older family members can pass on their knowledge and skills to the younger generations.

Review Section 15:2

1. List the stages of the family life cycle.
2. Identify one particular challenge couples face in each stage.
3. Identify one unique reward for each stage.

section 15:3

Patterns of Interaction in Families

Sharpen Your Reading

Outline the key skills that are needed in each area of interaction in order to build strong families.

Boost Your Vocabulary

Locate one example of each source of emergency help for abused family members in your community.

Know Key Terms

democratic decision making
scapegoating
violence
assault
battery
child abuse
physical abuse
Shaken Baby Syndrome
emotional abuse
sexual abuse
neglect
crisis-care centers
shelters
group homes
foster care
independent living
family routines
family traditions

As the needs of family members change, expectations and roles change. The overall goal of keeping the family unit strong, however, remains the same.

Strong families have good communication skills. They make decisions, deal with conflict, and resolve their problems together. They avoid family violence and focus on family activities that build strong family bonds.

Developing Family Communication Skills

Open, honest communication among family members is key to developing close relationships. Family members take the time to talk to each other. They use active listening skills. They show respect for others' viewpoints. They appreciate one another. Positive communication builds strong feelings of attachment between family members, 15-7.

15-7 When a family member cares enough to listen, positive feelings grow.

The techniques for building good communication skills are discussed in Chapter 5, *Developing Communication Skills*. The techniques discussed there also apply to family communication.

Developing a Sense of Trust

A sense of trust within the family helps keep communication lines open. When members trust each other, they are more likely to share personal thoughts. They may look for advice or counsel from each other. They know that private thoughts will be kept confidential. They know others in the family can be trusted to protect their well-being.

Loyalty grows in the family when members have proven themselves to be trustworthy. They can be counted on to tell the truth and carry out their duties. They can be relied upon to be responsible in their actions. They have shown genuine concern for one another and respect for members' privacy. These experiences build trust in the family.

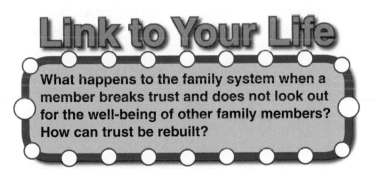

Link to Your Life

What happens to the family system when a member breaks trust and does not look out for the well-being of other family members? How can trust be rebuilt?

Making Family Decisions

There is just not enough time for one person to gather information for every decision, evaluate all alternatives, and carry out all plans of action. In healthy families, everyone makes decisions. When everyone in a family takes part in making decisions, all members feel important. Everyone's esteem increases. The basic steps for making good decisions are also used in family situations. You may want to review this information in Chapter 4, *Developing Decision-Making Skills*.

Democratic Decision Making

Some decisions can be made by all family members together through **democratic decision making**. Members offer suggestions for alternatives and even take part in gathering information. They discuss the advantages and disadvantages of each choice. They jointly select the best choice and help carry out the plan of action.

All members can be involved in the evaluation of the decision, too. Was it a good choice for the family? Why or why not? Such involvement is a learning process for younger family members. Through these experiences, they can learn how to use the decision-making process to make choices that will help them reach their goals.

Selective Decision Making

Sometimes it is best *not* to involve the whole family in making a decision—just certain members. For example, the responsibility for some decisions is given directly to the individual member best able to handle it. Also, parents may divide responsibilities according to each family member's interests or expertise.

Parents can have children make decisions on small matters to help them develop decision-making skills. Young children may be given a choice between two simple items. Deciding between two acceptable choices can help a child develop skills to make difficult choices later, 15-8.

Sharing Decision-Making Responsibilities

A family can be considered an organization. Every organization needs a system for carrying out decisions. In a business, the president is responsible for the whole system. That does not mean the president makes all the decisions or carries out all the tasks. However, the president is the one held responsible.

A family operates in a similar manner. Ultimately, someone must take responsibility for what is done. However, all members provide information, ideas, feelings, and different points of view. Each family should identify its own organizational plan for sharing decision-making

15-8 Young children can build their decision-making skills by handling small questions, such as which game to play.

responsibilities. Once this is decided, members know what is expected of them regarding planning and carrying out family decisions.

Recognizing the Impact of Cultural Differences

Sometimes a family's communication and decision-making patterns are influenced by their cultural background. For instance, it may not be common to listen to the input of children in some cultures. In others, the input of men and women may vary in importance. In yet others, the voice of older adults carries great weight in family decisions.

Investigate Further

What can families do to increase a young teen's success with making decisions?

Knowing the influence of your cultural background can help you understand the communication and decision-making patterns

in your family. By recognizing that past habits impact current family relationships, families can take steps to build open communication patterns.

Dealing with Conflict in the Family

Whenever two or more people live together, there are disagreements. How those disagreements are handled can affect family members' growth. It can make a difference in whether the family atmosphere is positive or negative. It can affect family unity and the degree to which the family sticks together and supports each other.

Who Owns the Problem?

Disagreements often arise when one family member tries to solve a problem that belongs to someone else. Such help is often given with a you-message: "You shouldn't let her go out before her homework is done!"

Such helping comments often do just the opposite. Children may feel that parents do not trust them to solve problems on their own. A parent may resent the hidden message that he or she is not capable of solving the problem without help.

Think More About It
How can I-statements help family members identify who owns a problem?

Using Active Listening

Encouraging each other to work through personal problems is the best way to help family members grow. This takes active listening skills. It also requires giving feedback. By showing empathy, family members can encourage each other to solve their own problems, 15-9.

As family members become better at handling conflict, their skills for solving problems increase. Negative feelings are expressed in words instead of being bottled up for a future explosion. A deeper sense of caring grows between family

When certain family members are made into scapegoats, their self-esteem suffers. They will feel unloved and unaccepted by the family. Failures, real or imagined, cause them to believe they cannot do anything right.

Learning to Compromise

When family members use compromise to resolve arguments, both sides benefit because no one loses. If you fight for your point of view and win the argument, then the other person loses. That person may feel defeated, worthless, and ill-treated. You may win the argument, but you tear down a relationship. When people refuse to compromise, the issue may never be resolved fairly.

To compromise, you may need to admit to a misunderstanding. You may need to accept that you both see the issue from a different point of view. You may even need to admit that you could be partly wrong. If both people give a little to reach a compromise, all will feel better about the solution, 15-10. The fear of failing or being wrong is reduced for all involved.

15-9 Solving other family members' problems for them does not help them to grow. Encouraging or helping them to solve their own problems does.

Investigate Further

How could learning to solve problems together help reduce family violence?

members. They begin to trust the others. Self-esteem increases. It becomes easier to accept and respect each other as individuals who can handle their own problems.

Problems of Scapegoating

Sometimes family members will not take ownership of a problem and blame others instead. This is known as **scapegoating**. The person who gets blamed for the problem is the scapegoat. Blaming may make it seem that one person is responsible for all the family problems. Family members accuse that person and at the same time defend their own actions. Because they do not claim ownership of the problem, they do not take action to change and solve the problem.

15-10 Siblings first learn to compromise when sharing during playtime.

Preventing Family Violence and Abuse

Sometimes a family conflict becomes more than a disagreement. Family members become angry and lash out at each other. They may abuse each other verbally or physically. **Violence** is any physical act intended to harm another person.

Assault and Battery

Assault is the threat to cause physical harm to a person. For instance, threatening someone with a weapon is assault. **Battery** is the use of force resulting in physical contact with a person that the individual did not permit. This includes physical acts of violence such as slapping, choking, hitting, punching, kicking, and stabbing. Reported cases of battery show that millions of women are abused by spouses or boyfriends each year. Cases of battering a husband have also been reported. The terms *assault* and *battery* are often used together.

Use What You Learn

Think of a recent news story involving family violence. How were the family relationships described?

Child Abuse

Child abuse is a serious form of family violence. **Child abuse** is any physical or mental threat or injury to a child under the age of 18. Thousands of children die every year from abuse and the number of reported cases is increasing. Often the abuse is part of a cycle. People who were abused as children often become the abusers themselves. It is important to learn to identify what abuse is, who abuses, why, and what characteristics can break the cycle.

Abuse can take different forms. **Physical abuse** is the intentional hurting of a person's body, causing physical injury. For example, Hosea's father spanks him with a belt because he refuses to do chores. Hitting with a belt can cause injury and is considered physical abuse.

Infants are particularly susceptible to a form of physical abuse called **Shaken Baby Syndrome**. This is brain damage caused by a fast and forceful shaking. Caregivers sometimes shake an infant in anger or because they mistakenly think shaking will stop the infant from crying. However, shaking an infant is child abuse. The shaking whips the infant's brain around within the skull. This causes damage to the nerves because the protective tissue within the brain has not yet developed. This condition can leave an infant deaf, blind, or mentally retarded.

Emotional abuse includes actions by a parent or caregiver that interfere with a child's development and damages self-esteem. Emotional abuse occurs when parents constantly make demands that a child cannot meet. They continue to criticize the child for not meeting their expectations. Children feel inferior and guilty.

Sexual abuse includes any sexual contact or interaction by an adult with a child or teenager. Sexual interaction can be physical or nonphysical. Physical sexual abuse includes rape as well as all forms of sexual touching. Nonphysical sexual abuse refers to actions such as exposing oneself, taking pornographic pictures of children, and using obscene language.

Neglect is failing to give a child proper shelter, clothing, food, medical care, supervision, love, and affection. Neglect can be either physical or emotional. All forms of abuse have long-term effects on children.

All states have passed laws that require suspected child abuse cases be reported by teachers, child care workers, and medical staff. Statistics show that millions of American children suffer from abuse each year. Violence at the hands of parents is a leading cause of death for children under three years of age. However, many cases of neglect or abuse are not easily identified.

Signs of Child Abuse

Signs of possible physical abuse are unexplained bruises, welts, burns, fractures, joint injuries, cuts, or scrapes that repeatedly occur, 15-11. Signs of possible emotional abuse are more varied and difficult to detect than physical abuse. A child may regress in development. A child who is hostile and aggressive, or an extremely compliant child who does everything that is asked without any response, may be showing

15-11 An occasional mishap occurs to all growing children and does not signal physical abuse. An uncommon number or frequency of injuries may signal abuse.

signs of abuse. Also, a child who is dependent, withdrawn, and portrays a poor self-image may also be emotionally abused.

Signs of neglect include such behaviors as begging or stealing food, constant fatigue, or failing to attend school. A child who always arrives early at school or leaves late may have no place to go. Young people who are sexually involved with many partners or in trouble with the law may not be receiving needed supervision.

Signs of sexual abuse include bed-wetting, torn or stained underclothing, or difficulty walking or sitting. Frequent urinary infections or sore throats may be signs of sexual abuse. Along with these physical signs, children who have been sexually abused may suffer from poor self-esteem. They may withdraw socially or show a lack of emotional control. Some show fear of closeness, and others regress to childlike behaviors.

Investigate Further

Children become emotionally attached to their main caregiver, even if it is an abusive parent. How does this make it harder to identify child abuse?

Reporting Child Abuse

People are often afraid to report suspected child abuse. They may be anxious about possibly sending the abuser to jail. Perhaps the child will be taken away from the parents, which sometimes happens, especially in cases of sexual abuse. It is important to remember that not reporting abuse results in problems for the child. If not reported, the abuser will continue to abuse. The abuse will likely get worse. The child may be permanently harmed or even die. Abuse almost never stops on its own.

Sources of Help

Cases of suspected child abuse should be reported to your local police or social service agency. During a crisis, call a hotline number or the police emergency number, 15-12. Help can be obtained for the abuse victims to get away from the immediate danger of a crisis situation. The care options include the following:

- **Crisis-care centers** are safe shelters for abused children and are short-term care resources. Children may be placed in these centers for two to four days. Crisis nurseries are usually open 24 hours a day. Social workers and the courts attempt to protect abused children. State agencies provide medical care, child care services, and foster care.

- **Shelters** provide short-term safety to escape from a family crisis. The most common shelters are for women and children.

- **Group homes**, also called *residential care*, may be available for teens or children who live in abusive families. They live in these homes along with counselors who provide care and counseling.

- **Foster care** is temporary care for children under 18 years of age. A child or teen is placed with foster parents who meet state requirements. It is important that their situations are reviewed often by social services to be sure their needs are being met.

- **Independent living** is sometimes an option for teens whose parents agree to give up legal control. This option is only for mature and emotionally stable teens who can provide for themselves financially.

15-12 Trained hotline personnel offer support 24 hours a day.

Families at Risk

Some families are more likely to suffer violence and abuse than others. Research indicates that an abusive childhood can lead to being abusive as a parent. Adults whose parents abused them as children often treat their children the same way. They also then teach their children to respond to a future generation in an abusive way.

Immaturity contributes to abusive situations. Adults who have not developed mature emotional and social traits may respond by yelling and hitting. Parents who have low self-esteem may feel they—and their children—are not worth much.

Poor parenting skills are another factor. A parent may not know what behavior to expect or how to guide the child into acceptable behavior. The parent may lash out in anger or frustration.

Poverty, job loss, and marriage problems increase levels of stress in a family. Stress can decrease parents' ability to handle situations calmly. Single parenthood can increase stress since the parent must handle the child's guidance alone. Such situations have a higher risk of being abusive.

Substance abuse in families increases the risk. Alcohol is a depressant and adults under the influence of alcohol may respond in ways they would not normally.

The factors just described do not cause child abuse; they are risk factors. The more risk factors present in a family, the greater the risk that a caregiver might lose control and engage in abusive behavior.

Investigate Further

What resources are available to help families who are at risk of family violence?

Breaking the Cycle

A more effective deterrent to violence and abuse in the family is to strengthen the family unit. Good communication, decision-making, and conflict-resolution skills help break the cycle of violence from one generation to the next. Experiences that encourage family members to mature can help develop self-esteem, self-acceptance, and self-control.

Sometimes families need professional help to work out their problems. A professional family counselor can help families identify steps for changing patterns of violence and abuse. They can help families develop skills for resolving their problems in a nonviolent way. Other resources such as therapy programs are also available. These are sponsored by private, community, religious, or government groups. With help, the cycle can be broken.

Family Leisure

Busy schedules tend to make family leisure time scarce in today's families. However, benefits of spending time together are greater than the disadvantages. For most families, the desire to strengthen their family unit through family leisure activities is important, 15-13.

The Importance of Sharing

Families need time to communicate so family relationships will grow. The evening meal is a good time for some families to share the day's events. However, work schedules do not always allow that. Instead, the family must set aside other time when they can share their thoughts, ideas, feelings, and activities.

Family meetings can be one way to plan for family communication. These can be times to gather input from the members on future plans, current decisions, or impending problems. One advantage of having family meetings regularly is that small items will be handled while they are still small. If families wait until the need is obvious, the conflict may be more difficult to resolve.

Time for Playing

Family fun times build family relationships. Memories of good times spent together draw the family closer. Family outings can be educational

15-13 Spending time in family activities helps build long-lasting relationships among siblings.

as well as fun. Family hobbies such as camping or fishing give members something to do together. They learn to cooperate to carry out a joint task. Opportunities to communicate increase. Even work activities can be fun when members find creative ways to get a job done.

Time for Meaningful Family Routines

Family routines are small events that are repeated on a regular basis. Meaningful routines strengthen the family and provide opportunities for sharing and showing affection. Mealtime routines are an example. These may involve preparing the food, eating the meal, and cleaning up afterwards. Bedtime routines are especially common in families with small children.

These regular events in the family add security to the family environment. Children know what to expect and when to expect it. They know they can count on a time to talk and a time when others will listen to them.

Traditions in the Family

Most families enjoy celebrating special events and holidays together. These become family traditions. **Family traditions** are established patterns of behavior or customs handed down through generations. Most families have their own religious and cultural traditions. Other repeated activities can also become family traditions. For instance, the family may plan a special camping, hunting, or fishing trip every year.

Benefits of Family Traditions

Family traditions can help members develop common interests. They may be planned so the family has uninterrupted time for communicating and sharing. The time may be spent in family activities or recreation.

Family traditions can also build a sense of family identity. Often they are celebrated with grandparents and other relatives. Such

celebrations can provide a link with the past. Younger members feel connected to their roots. Older members have hope for the future.

Family traditions are a source of strength and unity for the family at all stages of the family life cycle, 15-14. Meaningful traditions bring family members together, strengthening the bonds that exist. These patterns of interaction are part of a strong and healthy family.

15-14 A family's traditions are often passed from one generation to another. These valued traditions add meaning to family life.

Review Section 15:3

1. Briefly explain what is meant by *democratic decision making*.

2. List two negative effects of scapegoating on family members.

3. Name one benefit of family members using compromise to resolve their arguments.

4. Identify four common forms of child abuse.

5. Explain the difference between family routines and family traditions.

Think It Through

Family Interaction

Cameron was nervous all through supper. He knew his math teacher had called his parents about his failing grade. His parents didn't say a word—not until after supper, that is.

Cameron's brother was already in bed when his parents called Cameron to come in the study. "I hear you are having some trouble with math," Cameron's dad said. "Would you like to talk about it?"

Cameron really didn't know what to say. "I'm trying, Dad. It's just a hard subject for me."

"What do you think would help?" his mom asked.

"Well, I could use some extra help with my homework assignments."

"Do you think your teacher could give you some help?" Cameron's dad asked.

"Maybe, but she's pretty busy."

"When she called, she said that she would be willing to stay tomorrow after school. Would you be willing to talk to her then?" Cameron's dad asked.

"I guess so," said Cameron. "What time?"

"She said 3:30 would be fine. Why don't you give me a call when you're done, and I'll pick you up."

Randy's mother also received a call from the teacher that day. As Randy walked in the house, his mom called to him. "Your teacher called today, and you are in trouble! You're failing math! How can you do that? Don't you know you have to pass math to graduate?"

Randy threw his books on the table. "That dumb teacher! She never explains anything. Besides, I hate math—I don't care if I never graduate!"

"Well, I have to go in to talk to her tomorrow. You'll just have to work harder. I don't have time to keep going in to see the teachers."

Questions to Guide Your Thinking

1. How did Cameron's parents control the environment for their family discussion?

2. What types of messages were used to communicate in Cameron's family? What types were used in Randy's family?

3. In Randy's family, who took ownership of the problem with the math class?

4. How did Cameron's parents help him take ownership of his problem?

5. What solutions did each family find? Who will likely be most successful in solving his problem?

Chapter Summary

Interactions within the family tend to be private, complex, and long-lasting in their effects on individual family members. The family identifies expectations for each member's roles and the rights and responsibilities that go with each role. The family balances various roles in order to carry out its functions.

Throughout the family life cycle, the needs of family members and expectations for their roles will change. Skills for communicating clearly, making decisions together, and resolving their conflicts will help families adjust to these changes. Family leisure activities help bring family members together. The family unit will be strengthened as bonds between members grow and a sense of family identity increases.

Assess...

Your Knowledge

1. List two rights and two corresponding responsibilities of family members.

2. What is the difference between neglect and abuse?

3. Name three skills that can help a family break a cycle of violence.

Your Understanding

4. Give one example of how two stages of the family life cycle might overlap.

5. Explain how the loss of a parent's job would affect the family system.

6. How would scapegoating affect the way a family solves problems?

Your Skills

7. What are some steps you could take to help your family plan a vacation using democratic decision-making skills?

8. Describe a situation in which a family member uses active listening to help diffuse anger and restore balance to a family system.

9. What are some activities that would help a family with teens build strong relationships in the family?

Think Critically

10. *Writing.* Choose one major event, such as a teen's first date, that is commonly experienced by a family in the later parenting stage. Write a scenario describing the interactions in the family. Include examples of communication, decision making, and handling conflict. Use either negative or positive examples of interactions. Write a summary explaining how the interactions affected the outcome of your scenario. *Group option:* Present the scenario as a role-play.

11. *Social studies, writing.* Working with three or four classmates, discuss the number of interaction patterns that exist in each teammate's family. Find out how many siblings were in the families of each teammate's parents and grandparents. Then write a one-page paper comparing family interaction patterns today to past generations. What generalizations can you make?

12. *Writing.* Write a paragraph describing how your family balances the rights, responsibilities, and roles of various family members to maintain balance in the family system. *Choice:* Present your information in an alternative format as a song, rap, poem, drawing, picture, video, or presentation.

13. *Writing.* Think about the routines and traditions that you would like to develop when you begin your own family life cycle. How are these similar to or different from your own family routines and traditions? Summarize your thoughts in a paragraph.

Connect with Your Community

14. **Social studies.** Prepare survey questions to ask teens and adults about the rights of a child, parent, and grandparent in a family. Then develop questions to ask about their views on the responsibilities of various family members. Survey five teens and five adults and record their answers. Write a paragraph describing the similarities and differences between the teens' and adults' views. *Group option:* Complete the activity with a partner or in a small group.

15. **Research.** Using the Internet, research and prepare a report on one area of violence and abuse in the family. Describe the types of communication, decision making, and conflict-handling methods related to this area of violence. Identify resources available in your community for victims of violence and abuse. *Choice:* Present your information in a flyer or poster for your classmates' reference.

16. **Speech.** Organize a panel to present information to the class on "The Challenges and Rewards of the Family Life Cycle." Form groups with each group responsible for one of the family life cycle stages. Invite a guest to discuss one of the stages. Develop questions that you want the presenter to answer. Summarize the presenter's information in a paper. *Choice:* Present your summary in a song, poem, or visual portrayal.

17. Contact a crisis care center in your community. Find out what their policies are, who they serve, what services they provide, and when and how they refer calls to other sources of help. Present this information in a report to the class. *Choice:* Research this information on the Internet.

Use Technology

18. Using chart-making software, draw a diagram with a different block representing each person in your family. Use arrows to indicate all the possible interaction patterns that could exist between family members. Count the arrows to determine the total number of interactions. *Choice:* Describe in a paragraph how this number could affect the relationships among your family members.

19. **Math.** Using a spreadsheet program, prepare a checklist of at least 20 leisure activities in which families might participate. Survey your class to identify how many families participate in each activity. *Choice:* Use software to prepare a bar graph, indicating what percentage of your class participates in each leisure activity.

20. **Research.** Use the Internet to locate a technology-based game that family members can play together to build communication, decision-making, and problem-solving skills. Create a report describing how this game could build these skills and what specific age levels the game targets.

21. **Math.** Gather data from 10 classmates regarding the total number of interaction patterns that exist in their families. Using a computer, develop a scatter plot to present the number of classmates with each number of interaction patterns. Write a summary of your information, including the average number of interaction patterns existing in the families of the students surveyed. *Choice:* Explain how increased interaction patterns affect the family system.

Chapter 16

Crises in the Family

Section 16:1
The Impact of Crises on the Family

Section 16:2
Preventing a Crisis

Section 16:3
Coping with Crises

Key Questions

Questions to answer as you study this chapter:

- How does a crisis affect the family?
- What can a family do to prevent crises?
- How can a family restore balance to the family system in a crisis?

Chapter Objectives

After studying this chapter, you will be able to

- **identify** characteristics of life events that could lead to a family crisis.
- **explain** how a crisis affects the family system.
- **distinguish** between internal and external sources of family stress.
- **recognize** factors that help families prevent crises.
- **evaluate** family coping skills.
- **identify** community resources that aid families in crises.

Life Sketch

Glenda put her hand to her head as she tried to sit up in bed. Where was she? She started to call out, but feelings of nausea overtook her. As Glenda's body started to shake, a nurse hurried over and lowered her back onto the bed. Glenda's parents stood by her bedside, too nervous to talk.

Glenda's family was in a crisis. Glenda had nearly died from a drug overdose. Fortunately, when the police were called to break up a loud party, they found Glenda unconscious and rushed her to the hospital. She was not merely sleeping, as her friends had thought.

When Glenda's parents were called, they were shocked. This really wasn't happening, was it? For a few hours, they feared she might die. When she finally regained consciousness, they had mixed emotions. They were relieved, yet angry and hurt. Why did she do it? Were they somehow to blame? Even worse, would she do this again?

Getting Started

Families experience many changes in life. Most of these changes are minor enough for family members to deal with them. These changes are only stressful enough to motivate family members to take action. However, a crisis can happen when a family experiences so much stress that members are unable to carry out regular functions.

section 16:1

The Impact of Crises on the Family

Sharpen Your Reading

As you read, list the ways that a crisis affects the family.

Boost Your Vocabulary

List events that currently are stressors in your life. Then analyze figure 16-2 to see if any of the items on your list are in the diagram.

Know Key Terms

crises
stressors
pileup effect
alienated

Crises are experiences or events that cause people to make major changes in their lives. Life events that change or have the potential to produce change in the family cause stress, 16-1. Such life events are called **stressors**. Whether stress leads to a crisis depends on the following four factors:

- the event itself
- number of stressful events experienced at the same time

16-1 The pressure of studying for a final exam can be a stressful event. As a result, the stress felt by one family member can affect others in the family.

- how the family identifies and interprets the event
- resources available to manage the stressful event

Crises-Producing Life Events

The following four types of events often cause crises within families:

- *Devastating events that cause a great loss.* Events that cause great losses are more likely to lead to crises than events that cause small losses.
- *Very stressful events that widely impact members.* A stressful event that affects several

or all the members in a family is very likely to produce a crisis.

- *Sudden, important events.* When an event is unexpected, the family has no time to prepare for the change. If they have no previous experience with such a change, they often feel the situation is out of control.
- *Events requiring major adjustments.* Events that require little or no change are less likely to result in crises than events that require major adjustments.

Investigate Further

Why can a hurricane be a crisis-producing event in a community?

The Pileup Effect

Sometimes crises result when several changes occur at the same time, or one after another, 16-2. Each event in itself is too small to produce a significant loss. Each event may not affect all the family members. The changes may be expected and occur slowly.

Small changes do not have the characteristics of crises-producing events. However, the stress from each event continues to build, producing a **pileup effect**. The end result is a crisis. For example, the stress from poor grades on a test, an argument with a friend, conflict with parents, and pressure from peers can all add up.

How Crises Affect the Family

An individual's crisis can also be a crisis for the family. Every member in a family affects every other member. When a member is unable to function, the whole family can be negatively affected.

The Family System Becomes Unbalanced

When the family is functioning smoothly, it is balanced. Each member carries out his or her roles. The family works together to meet the needs of each member. The family is able to fulfill its functions in each member's life.

In a crisis, one or more changes disrupt this balance. Individual family members are unable to fulfill their functions. Suddenly the family is not functioning smoothly as a unit. The family needs time, resources, and support as it works to adjust to the changes and restore balance.

A Loss Affects Family Functions

In most crises situations, some type of loss has taken place. The loss may involve a family member, skills or abilities, a job, income, or a home.

A loss usually hinders the family's ability to fulfill its normal functions, at least for a period of time. The family function of reproducing and socializing children is hindered by illness, divorce, hospitalization, or loss of a family member. A job loss or a natural disaster could hinder the family's ability to meet physical needs. The family function of assigning roles may be slowed by any crisis that prevents members from carrying out their roles. Finally, the family's ability to carry out the function of providing close relationships and intimacy may be hindered by a death, divorce, or move away from relatives.

Think More About It
In a crisis, why is it important that a family have access to resources that can help them return to a balanced family system?

The Grieving Process

When family members experience a loss, even though small, they go through a grieving process. When they are able to identify and accept their feelings, they will be able to handle them and go on with their lives.

When a loss occurs, family members pass through certain emotional stages. First, they may deny it. "This isn't really happening." Then they often experience feelings of anger. "Why is this happening to us?" This may be followed by

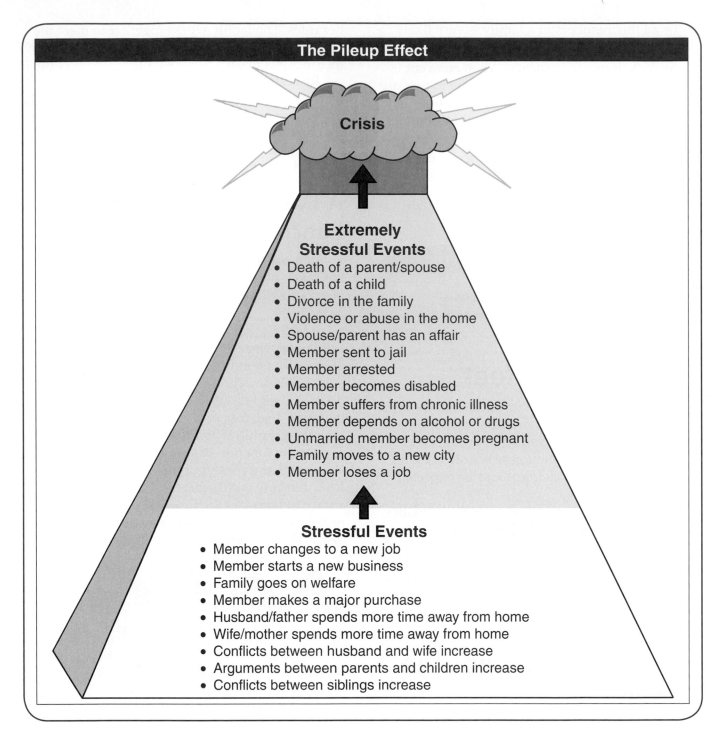

The Pileup Effect

Crisis

**Extremely
Stressful Events**
- Death of a parent/spouse
- Death of a child
- Divorce in the family
- Violence or abuse in the home
- Spouse/parent has an affair
- Member sent to jail
- Member arrested
- Member becomes disabled
- Member suffers from chronic illness
- Member depends on alcohol or drugs
- Unmarried member becomes pregnant
- Family moves to a new city
- Member loses a job

Stressful Events
- Member changes to a new job
- Member starts a new business
- Family goes on welfare
- Member makes a major purchase
- Husband/father spends more time away from home
- Wife/mother spends more time away from home
- Conflicts between husband and wife increase
- Arguments between parents and children increase
- Conflicts between siblings increase

16-2 Many life events bring changes and increase stress in a family. The combined stress of several events at the same time can lead to a family crisis.

feelings of guilt. "What did we do to cause or deserve this?" To try and get rid of these feelings, they may blame others for the problem. At this point, they may feel sorry for themselves. These feelings may lead to depression.

Such feelings are normal responses in the grieving process. However, it is important that family members move on and accept the reality of the loss. "This has happened to our family and we are sad, but we can and will move on."

Investigate Further

What family strengths can help its members move through the grieving process to acceptance?

Accepting a Loss

Acceptance is needed so family members can take action and adjust to the changes brought about by the loss. They need to work together so the functions of the family can be carried out. Roles may need to be adjusted. Financial resources or help from others may be needed.

Unhealthy Adjustment Patterns

If the family does not adjust, unhealthy behavior patterns may develop, 16-3. Feelings of anger, blame, and guilt will continue. Members may feel depressed. They may stop eating, withdraw from others, or fail to show up at work. They may abuse alcohol or other drugs to cover up their feelings. In anger, they may lash out and abuse other family members.

When the family does not function normally, the physical and mental health of members may suffer. Parents may ignore their parental responsibilities. As a result, children may be neglected, malnourished, or abused. Their emotional development will suffer if they do not experience love and acceptance. They may feel **alienated**—alone, without hope, or cut off from others who care. This feeling is listed as a major factor in teen suicide. Responding to crises with unhealthy behavior patterns may hinder the growth and development of family members and cause serious long-term results. Developing skills for preventing a family crisis is important for all family members.

16-3 When a family cannot adjust to a loss, all members are affected. Some may find it difficult to carry out daily tasks.

Review Section 16:1

1. Explain how stressors can bring on a crisis in the family.
2. List four types of crisis-producing events.
3. Briefly describe how the pileup effect may result in a crisis.
4. Briefly explain how a loss could hinder a family's ability to fulfill its normal functions.
5. Identify four emotional stages that are experienced during the grieving process.

section 16:2

Preventing a Crisis

Sharpen Your Reading

Outline ways a family can identify and manage stress and develop family resources.

Boost Your Vocabulary

List examples of internal and external stress in your own life.

Know Key Terms

internal stress
external stress

Family members who are prepared to adjust and handle stress-producing life events are more likely to do so. They use the following methods to help prevent stress from becoming a crisis:

- Identify sources of stress in the family.
- Use outside resources to help handle the stress and its effects.
- Foster good interaction skills with family members so they will cooperate in times of stress.

Identifying the Source of Stress

Identifying the exact source of stress can be hard for a family. Sometimes the stress comes from within the family. At other times the stress is from outside sources. See 16-4.

Internal Stress

Stress that comes from inside the family is called **internal stress**. Normal growth and development or unresolved conflicts are the two main sources of this type of stress.

- Internal stress from normal growth and development takes place slowly over time. For example, adolescents may continually ask for a little more independence. Parents may then feel frustrated, but not really know the exact cause. Each new request puts a little more strain on the family.

- Internal stress resulting from unresolved conflicts continues to build tension in the family. When old conflicts are not resolved, new problems add to the already existing stress.

Internal sources of stress are more likely to pile up into a crisis situation. Arguments and fighting are more frequent. The good communication that could help family members identify and decrease the stress does not take place. Headaches, colds, sleeplessness, and other physical problems tend to increase under stressful situations. Family members may take

16-4 Stress from outside sources may increase tension in the family.

more medication to try to handle their problems. The source of the stress becomes even harder to identify. Sometimes families need to seek help from a professional counselor to identify the real source of internal stress.

External Stress

When stress is caused by factors outside the family, this is known as **external stress**. Pressures from work, a natural disaster, or war are examples of external sources of stress. External stressors that produce crises usually happen quickly without notice. They are likely to affect the whole family and sometimes whole communities.

External stress is usually easier for family members to identify than internal stress. They can see it as a threat to the family unit. Finding a solution to which all family members agree is easier when the source of stress is outside the family.

Link to Your Life

What are some normal sources of internal stress during adolescence?

Managing Stress

Families learn to manage stress in two ways. First, they may reduce the amount of stress they experience at one time. Second, they may reduce the effects that stress has on them. When they cannot manage stress or its effects, they are more likely to experience a family crisis.

Reducing the Amount of Stress

Living in a busy society makes it hard for families to reduce the amount of stress they experience. However, choosing to reduce the stress in your life will contribute to your health and well-being, as well as your family's.

- *Remove the source of stress.* Sometimes it is hard to identify any one cause of the increasing stress in the family. Families may

need to make several small changes to reduce the total stress.

- *Remove family members from the source of the stress.* Sometimes a family chooses to remove all the members from a stressful source affecting one or a few members, 16-5.

- *Break down the stressor into smaller parts.* Sometimes the family is able to break down the source of stress into smaller, easier-to-handle parts. Responsibilities may be divided among members as well.

Think More About It
Is it easier to reduce the amount of stress from some sources more than others?

Reducing the Effects of Stress

At times, families are not able to reduce the stress they experience. Instead, family interactions increase the stress. Communication breaks down. Members do not share their thoughts and feelings as readily. They are more sensitive to what others say and do, yet respond with less sensitivity. They react more quickly with anger. Stressful events lead to more stress in the family unless steps are taken to change such responses.

- *Change responses to stressful events.* A little humor may be appropriate to lighten a tense situation. Laughter can help everyone relax. Exercise together. Make sure that everyone is eating a healthful meal.

- *Set aside time to communicate.* A quiet place, away from the normal setting, can help family members take time to talk. At home, maybe the phone can be disconnected for a short time or the ringer turned off. Interruptions need to be eliminated so members can focus on one another.

- *Take part in a family activity.* Recreation can help reduce stress. Sharing hobbies and playing sports or games can be enjoyed by the whole family. These provide an outlet for reducing the effects of stress.

16-5 Visiting a favorite place in the old neighborhood after a move takes the family away from the source of the stress, if only for a few hours.

Many of these responses are not normal under stress, but they can be specific plans for action. Such responses help families manage the effects of stress and maintain balance in the family.

Use What You Learn

What routines would you recommend for a family with a lot of stress?

Developing Family Resources

What resources can help families handle stress and avoid a potential crisis? A positive family view of life, financial resources, personal characteristics, interpersonal skills, and strong support or community groups can all aid the family in times of stress.

The Family's Viewpoint

A family's viewpoint can make a difference in whether changing life experiences lead to crises or are merely seen as manageable problems. Small changes and small problems cause little stress. Extreme changes and big problems cause enormous stress. Sometimes the difference can be just the way the family looks at the situation.

Financial Resources

Financial resources can help families handle stressful events, 16-6. A savings plan can help during times of disaster or loss of income. Insurance plans can protect against large losses of income or property. Financial resources can help families obtain counseling to help with internal stresses as well.

Flexibility

Family members will handle stress better and avoid a crisis if they are flexible and able to adjust. Flexibility is a personal characteristic. It will help family members cooperate as they adjust to changing roles and balance the needs of the family.

Commitment

Family members need to be committed to meeting one another's needs and showing support and encouragement. They need to show love and affection for each other, thus fulfilling emotional needs in the family. Finally, they need to be willing to make choices that consider the well-being of others in the family. Such commitment will help family members stick together to find solutions to family problems.

Investigate Further

Why is it hard for families with a lot of internal stressors to consider the well-being of others around them?

16-6 Having adequate financial resources can relieve the stress of a poor economy.

Good Communication Skills

Good communication skills need to be practiced all the time. Then when changes occur, the family will be able to share personal thoughts and feelings without offending or hurting each other. They will use good listening skills to make sure that clear and accurate messages have been received.

Positive communication between family members can build esteem in each member and a sense of unity in the family. When changes occur, family members can continue to encourage and support each other. Confidence in the family's ability to adjust will increase.

Joint Decision-Making Skills

As families make decisions together on a regular basis, they set patterns for decision making under stress. As they take time to listen to each other, they encourage input from every family member. They know how to identify and evaluate their alternatives and can use this skill to solve a problem. They know how to develop a plan of action and divide tasks among the members. In turn, each person feels important and is more willing to help the family handle the stressful life event.

Negotiation Skills

As families resolve conflicts through negotiation and compromise, they build mutual respect among members. They learn to take ownership of their problems. They learn to work together to reach solutions that benefit all concerned. They learn to be family-oriented rather than self-oriented. In times of stress, they can use these skills to resolve problems that could build into crises situations.

Family Support

Family members can build a strong social support group within a family. They do this by spending time together, taking part in leisure activities, celebrating special events, and starting their own traditions. Strong bonds between the members can help a family work together to handle stressful life events. The family members are committed to helping each other grow and succeed. They build esteem in one another and help the others feel capable of handling their problems. They stick together, providing love and affection, companionship, social support, and other types of aid, 16-7.

Think More About It
Why is it that strong and healthy families have the best chance of restoring balance to their family system in a crisis?

16-7 Celebrating special events helps family members build strong bonds that serve as a resource in times of stress.

Community Support Groups

Involvement in a community can result in strong support from friends and neighbors. In times of stressful life events, community members can offer encouragement and understanding. Some can provide aid, such as help with child care, cleanup, or food.

Community groups are especially helpful to families because the people in these groups have experienced similar situations. Such support groups can help family members understand their feelings and identify their needs. With their support, family members are encouraged to believe they can handle the problems facing them. Sometimes a community group includes professionals who are qualified to provide information specific to a family's situation. In addition, they can help family members develop skills for handling the changes they are experiencing.

Review Section 16:2

1. Explain the difference between internal and external stress.
2. List three ways families can reduce the amount of stress they experience.
3. List three ways that family members can reduce the effects of stress.

section 16:3

Coping with Crises

Sharpen Your Reading

Prepare a chart with two columns. In the first column, list the four behaviors that families can use to cope with a crisis. In the other column, give an example of that behavior being applied in a family coping with a drug abuse crisis.

Boost Your Vocabulary

List examples of coping behaviors that would strengthen the family unit. Contrast with examples of behaviors that harm the family unit.

Know Key Terms

coping behavior
chronic illness
disability
substance abuse

Even the most well-prepared family will experience some crises-producing events during the life cycle. Chronic illness, the death of a loved one, drug or alcohol abuse, and unemployment are types of crises many families face.

Often these events occur suddenly, without time for preparation. They will be unexpected and inconvenient. Most likely, the family will not have prior experience dealing with them.

Family Coping Behaviors

When a crisis occurs, the family needs to use coping behavior. **Coping behavior** is planned behavior that helps the family adjust as quickly as possible to changes that have taken place. Notice the word *planned*. That requires a logical process, and that is the key to the family's response. Chart 16-8 lists the following four behaviors that a family can use to cope with a crisis:

- Understand the situation.
- Seek solutions to the problem.
- Strengthen the family unit.
- Emphasize personal growth for individual family members.

Coping behavior helps stabilize the family so it can again fulfill its functions within the lives of family members. As family members take steps to identify and implement a solution, they need an attitude of tolerance for each other. It takes open lines of communication and flexibility to do whatever needs to be done to cope with a crisis. It also takes a commitment from members to find a solution that benefits everyone in the family.

In a crisis, the family's own interactions can be the most valuable resource for coping. Actions that encourage the growth of family members and strengthen the family unit are important. Healthy, growing family members are more likely to succeed at working together to solve problems.

Think More About It
Why is it important to practice the behaviors that you will need in a crisis situation before a crisis occurs?

Chronic Illness and Disability

Chronic illness is a problem experienced by many families during the family life cycle. A **chronic illness** is a medical problem that cannot be cured. Some illnesses require changes in eating or activity patterns, while others end in death.

Coping with Crisis

1. Understand the situation.

- Ask what changes have taken or will take place.
- Identify how the family is affected.
- Use good communication skills.
- Seek professionals who can provide information.

2. Seek solutions to the problem.

- Ask what can be done to handle the changes.
- Keep a tolerant attitude.
- Do not blame others for the problem.
- Avoid the use of drugs and alcohol as coping aids.
- Be open and flexible.
- Look for a solution that benefits all family members.
- Identify available resources in the family and community.

3. Strengthen the family unit.

- Set aside quiet uninterrupted times to talk.
- Share thoughts and feelings openly.
- Accept each other's thoughts and feelings.
- Encourage each other.
- Take time for family leisure activities.

4. Emphasize personal growth for individual family members.

- Encourage all members to pursue individual interests.
- Keep involved with friends and community.
- Set goals for the future.
- Make plans to reach personal and family goals.

16-8 Coping behaviors are positive steps that enable family members to deal with a crisis.

A **disability** describes an impairment that interferes with certain abilities. It may refer to a physical or mental condition. A physical disability may result in a problem with a person's vision, hearing, speech, or motor movements. A mental disability may result in a delay in mental skills.

A disability or chronic illness may affect a family member of any age. A chronic illness is a permanent condition, but a disability may be temporary or permanent.

Children with Disabilities

Some children are born with a physical or mental disability. A child with a learning disability has difficulty learning to carry out certain skills even though intelligence is average. Some children struggle with behavior disorders, such as hyperactivity.

Children with disabilities need special help to reach their full potential for development. A pediatrician, family doctor, or school psychologist can recommend special tests to determine the exact nature of the child's disability. Then ways to help the child can be identified.

The Effects of Chronic Illness or Disability on the Family

Learning to live with chronic illness or a disability can be difficult. It is emotionally stressful on the family. One family member may have to stay home to provide care. Tension may increase, and members may withdraw from one another. Conflicts over extra demands on time and money for medical care may occur. Other family members' needs may be put aside.

Coping with Chronic Illness and Disability

In order to cope with these challenges, family members must continue showing love, support, and affection. They need to listen to each other with empathic listening skills. Such communication skills can help members accept the illness or disability and the effect it will have on the family. An attitude of cooperation and flexibility is important. Each family member also needs to keep involved in activities that promote personal growth, 16-9.

16-9 Family members with disabilities should be encouraged to engage in hobbies and explore personal interests.

Community Resources for Coping with Chronic Illness or Disability

Understanding the illness or disability and its long-term effects is an important part of adjusting. Community resource people are available to make this process easier.

Medical professionals are key resources in providing basic information. They can educate family members to understand the situation and related medical procedures. Counselors and religious leaders can help family members adjust emotionally to the stress of chronic illness. Educators and school psychologists also help the chronically ill or disabled person develop to full potential.

Think More About It
How might a severe illness affect the functioning of a family? What coping behaviors could help the family cope with such a crisis?

Drug and Alcohol Abuse

One example of a potential crisis for families occurs when family members use illegal drugs or abuse prescription drugs or alcohol. Drug or alcohol abuse is also called **substance abuse**.

The Effects of Substance Abuse on the Family

Drug and alcohol abuse lead to increased stress in a family. A major area of stress is the constant concern for the health and safety of the abuser. The person's physical health is in danger as brain cells are destroyed and body organs may be damaged. There is danger of accidents resulting from the choices the person makes with impaired judgment. Because of this lack of judgment, the person may also have trouble carrying out family roles.

Another concern for the family is the person's influence on others. The use of drugs or alcohol by parents tends to encourage it in their children. Teens may also influence the choices of younger siblings.

When a family member abuses drugs or alcohol, others in the family may feel they are to blame. Rather than seek information or help, they may try to cover up the user's problems. They may feel embarrassed and ashamed when contacted by law enforcement or hospital officials about the member's abuse.

Drug and alcohol abuse tend to be used as coping mechanisms to hide from problems. The abuse tends to increase in families when both spouses or parents and teens do not resolve conflicts. Other cases of abuse occur when parents are not involved in their children's lives at a young age.

Family interaction patterns—good communication, joint decision making, and problem solving—usually break down before the abuse takes place. In such situations, families have a hard time strengthening the family unit. Encouraging personal growth and taking steps to regain control of the situation is difficult. Therefore, outside programs are important resources for coping with drug and alcohol abuse, 16-10.

16-10 A serious alcohol or drug problem often requires the assistance of a professional to help the abuser and his or her family return to a normal life.

Community Resources for Coping with Substance Abuse

Neighborhood groups, schools, and government agencies want to help families avoid drug and alcohol abuse. Professionals in health, education, social services, and law enforcement work together nationwide to provide solutions for these problems.

Families experiencing substance abuse can seek help from such local agencies. They often provide immediate help with food, clothing, shelter, and medical assistance. These steps are necessary to help the family restore its functions.

Long-term family therapy may be needed to handle the stress and resolve the problems that contributed to the drug or alcohol abuse. Therapy may be obtained through drug counseling centers, religious organizations, health care systems, psychologists, and other community programs. In an effort to help everyone affected by the problem, counselors often work with all family members. This will help family members learn to support each other so individuals can fulfill their roles in the family again.

Prevention is the best resource a family has for coping with alcohol and drug abuse. Educational programs that address three different goals help families deal with these issues.

One goal is to help families handle problems that could lead to future abuse. Some education programs are designed to help families handle problems due to lack of education, health care, housing, and child care. By helping families manage these problems, community agencies can reduce the amount of stress that family members experience.

Another educational goal is to educate people about the serious consequences of drug and alcohol abuse. The effects of substance abuse and the factors that influence people to make such decisions are covered. Various professionals in education, health, and law enforcement are involved.

A third goal is to help people develop skills that serve as personal resources during times of stress. In addition to learning decision-making and communication skills, people learn assertiveness skills to stop others from using or abusing them. Assertiveness skills can help young people withstand the peer pressure to join in drug and alcohol use.

Investigate Further

What services are provided to families with drug or alcohol problems through your local community?

Unemployment and Financial Crises

The loss of a job can occur anytime. No matter what the reason is, it can be stressful for the whole family and result in a family crisis. This is especially true if income is sharply decreased or stopped. Emotional stress may cause the unemployed person to feel a sense of failure, isolation, and despair, 16-11.

Family Resources During Financial Crisis

Family members' skills and abilities are important resources in adjusting to the stress of lost income. The family needs to stick together and believe that they can find ways to cope and handle the problem. Some family members may be able to find work or work extra hours. They may be able to cut expenses by avoiding unnecessary items and activities.

Social support from family members, friends, and relatives is an important family resource during a financial crisis. They can offer encouragement and aid until a new job is found, which helps the family system become balanced.

Outside Resources During Financial Crisis

Help with providing basic food, shelter, clothing, and medical services is available locally through government and social service agencies. Community and religious organizations in the area may also provide similar help.

16-11 Unemployment and searching for a new job can cause stress for all family members.

Through a state's labor/employment department, unemployed workers may be able to get unemployment compensation. This is a portion of their previous earnings received while seeking a job. If a financial crisis affects an entire community, such as a natural disaster or the closing of a leading employer, state and federal aid programs are often available.

Personal Coping Behavior

High self-esteem, positive self-concept, and positive life attitudes can help you believe in your ability to adjust. These qualities will help you look for ways to achieve personal growth with each experience. Flexibility can help you make the adjustments.

Your skills for communicating with others can help you build and maintain friendships. Friends will encourage you through hard times. They can help you relax as you spend leisure time with them. They can also encourage you to stay active in your community.

Your personal management skills are also important resources. You can learn to manage both your time and your money. Your skills for making decisions can help you find solutions when problems arise. Your problem-solving skills will lead you to community and government resources that are available in times of crises. All these resources can strengthen you to cope with changes that will affect you and your family.

Review Section 16:3

1. List four coping behaviors that can help families adjust to a crisis event.
2. Identify three ways in which educational programs are designed to prevent drug and alcohol abuse.
3. List three main resources that can help an individual cope with a crisis.

Think It Through

Facing Unemployment

Carlos's family knew that the construction season was almost over. Soon his dad would be out of work. Thinking about another long winter with no income was causing everyone in the Sandoz family to be edgy. One Saturday evening, Carlos asked for a family meeting.

"Isn't there something we can do to help Dad keep his job?" Carlos asked.

His dad shook his head. "I don't think so, son. I'm a road builder and not too many roads are built in the winter."

"But you have so many other skills, Dad," Carlos said. "You know how to drive those big road building machines. Couldn't you drive trucks in the winter?"

Carlos's dad thought quietly for a minute. "That might be worth a try, Carlos. You may have a good idea. I thought I was too old to try something new, but maybe that wouldn't be too difficult for me to try."

"They offer truck driving courses at the technical college. I saw it on a bulletin posted at school. Do you want me to check?" Carlos asked.

Mr. Sandoz was beginning to catch Carlos's excitement. "Yes, I'd be willing to look into it," he said.

Questions to Guide Your Thinking

1. Explain how the upcoming layoff could be a potential crisis-producing event for the Sandoz family.

2. Was the source of stress for the Sandoz family external or internal?

3. What factors made it seem difficult for the Sandoz family to handle the stress and prevent the potential crisis?

4. What family resources did the Sandoz family use to help them prevent a crisis?

5. List four actions Carlos took to cope with the potential crisis.

6. What could Carlos have done if his father had been less willing to adjust and consider something new? What other alternatives could they have taken to avoid a crisis?

Summary

A crisis is an experience or event that causes a person to make a change in his or her life. A single life event or combination of events can cause a crisis in the family. When a crisis occurs, the entire family is affected. As a result, it may not be able to carry out it functions for some time. This situation can hinder the growth and development of family members. Developing coping skills will enable them to adjust to the crisis and handle family functions again.

Families can take steps to prevent a crisis. First, they can learn to identify sources of stress. Then they can learn to manage stress before a crisis develops. Developing and using family resources can help them return balance to the family system and avoid the negative effects of a crisis.

When a crisis does occur, family members need to use good coping skills. These skills can help families adjust to changes so that the family can return to normal, meeting the needs of its members.

Assess...

Your Knowledge

1. What four factors determine if stressors lead to a crisis?

2. Identify six resources families can use to handle stress and thereby avoid a crisis.

3. List three common events that can produce stress in a family.

Your Understanding

4. How do crises affect the family system?

5. How can families prevent crises?

6. How can families cope with the crisis of unemployment?

Your Skills

7. What steps could you take to reduce stress in your life before a big exam?

8. What resources are available in your community to help families through the crisis of a major illness?

Think Critically

9. Analyze sources of stress in your life and in your own family. Identify resources both inside and outside the family that could be used to help you handle the stress and its effects on your life.

10. *Writing.* Write a one-page scenario of how several normal events could contribute to the pileup effect, resulting in a crisis for a family. Include a description of coping strategies that could help the family handle the crisis.

11. *Social studies.* Write a one-page scenario of a possible neighborhood disaster. Describe how the disaster would affect families in the neighborhood. Include families who had prepared for such a disaster and families who had not. Describe the resources that would help families adjust to the changes brought about by the disaster. *Group option:* Present your scenario as a role-play.

12. Use the cycle of the grieving process to describe the feelings a family may go through when learning of a child's addiction to drugs. *Choice:* Describe what resources are available to help them at each stage of the grieving cycle.

Connect with Your Community

13. Interview a school counselor and ask questions about how to reduce stress in your life. Summarize the interview in a one-page paper.

14. **Reading.** Clip a newspaper article that describes a family in crisis. Identify the source of stress that led to the crisis. What resources did the family have (or not have) to handle the stress? How did the family cope with the crisis?

15. **Writing.** Contact your local emergency center and interview workers about the guidelines for handling a major emergency in your community. List possible external sources of stress that could contribute to such an emergency for families in your neighborhood. What community resources are available to help handle these sources of stress? Write a report on your findings. **Choice:** Deliver your report to the class using presentation software.

16. **Social studies.** Form a small group and research information on drug or alcohol abuse in your community. Have each person in your group present information from the perspective of a different community service worker: a law enforcement officer, a social worker, a school counselor, and a hospital employee. Present your information to the class as a panel.

Use Technology

17. **Social studies.** Choose a potential crisis situation for a family. Use the Internet to research and prepare a report on government and community resources available for families in such a crisis. **Choice:** Post your report to your school Web site as a resource for families.

18. Using a desktop publishing program, prepare a flyer with tips for reducing stress in the family when undergoing a crisis in your community.

19. **Social studies, writing.** Using the Internet, research the effects of drug or alcohol use and abuse on the family. Prepare a paper describing these effects and relate them to possible crises a family may experience as a result.

20. **Science.** Use the Internet to research a chronic illness and identify treatments or technological resources for coping with the illness. Using a word processing program, write a report describing the illness and treatments as well as the impact that such an illness could have on balance in a family system. **Group option:** Form groups based on the illness chosen. Compile your information and present it to the class.

Divorce and Remarriage

Life Sketch

Four-year-old Marcia sat on the steps by the door of the child care center. Her eyes were open wide as she tried to hold back her tears. The lump in her throat just wouldn't go away.

Seeing Marcia sitting alone, her child care teacher walked over and sat beside her. She put her arm around her and gave her a warm hug. Trying to sense Marcia's feelings, she said, "You're feeling pretty sad, aren't you?" Marcia nodded her head and the tears began to flow.

"Daddy packed his suitcase last night and left," she sobbed. "He even took his winter coat! He said he would be gone for a long time."

Key Questions

Questions to answer as you study this chapter:

- **What are some causes of divorce?**

- **How does a breakdown in a marital relationship affect the family?**

- **What can families do to adjust to divorce and strengthen the family system?**

Getting Started

A child's understanding of what happens when parents separate is often dim. What children see is a dearly loved parent leaving. They feel hurt, rejected, insecure, and uncertain of the future. They may wonder if the remaining parent will leave, too. They often feel at fault for the problems in the family.

Separation, divorce, and remarriage bring about major changes in families. Changes occur in the family structure and members' roles. Financial changes take place. Close relationships within the family change.

Studying the effects of separation and divorce may seem a negative way to build strong marriages. However, it points out the importance of making careful, mature choices in dating and choosing a marriage partner. Couples who are aware of the causes and effects of divorce may think more carefully about the commitment of marriage.

Studying this chapter will also help you understand the issues of single parenting, a common result of divorce. Single parents face many problems and challenges as they try to reorganize their lives to meet the needs of family members. Sometimes this includes remarriage, which brings more adjustments as families work to build a strong stepfamily unit.

Chapter Objectives

After studying this chapter, you will be able to

- **recognize** the factors that contribute to divorce.

- **identify** the legal terms associated with divorce.

- **describe** how divorce affects the lives of family members.

- **determine** the challenges facing single-parent families and stepfamilies.

section 17:1

Divorce Trends

Sharpen Your Reading

Divide your paper into three columns, one column for each main heading in this section. Identify what you already know about each topic. After you read, fill in key concepts for each topic.

Boost Your Vocabulary

Draw a picture of something you think could be a barrier to divorce.

Know Key Terms

barrier to divorce

Statistics clearly show that divorce is common. Young people, at some point in their lives, have a 50 percent chance of living in a family that has experienced divorce. It may affect their parents or their own marriage. They may experience a divorce or marry someone who has been divorced.

This does not mean that divorce is inevitable in a marriage relationship. It does mean that there are many factors that can lead to a divorce. Couples need to be alert to these factors and take steps to nurture and strengthen their relationship. A close, intimate marriage is the best protection against the hurt that divorce brings to a family, 17-1.

17-1 If you plan to marry in the future, making mature relationship choices during the dating years is important.

The Effects of Divorce

A divorce in a family affects many people: parents, children, relatives, friends, and even the entire society. Remember how interdependent people are. What happens in your family affects you and other people around you.

Investigate Further

How does divorce affect different people?

Divorce brings about an imbalance in the family system. There are fewer resources to meet the needs of the family. Since the family tends to be split between two households, the needs of the family actually increase.

Most often, divorce results in poor communication between family members. Making any type of adjustment is easier when family members understand the changes taking place. Good communication skills can help family members work out all the details. However, in the case of separation and divorce, understanding and good communication are often missing.

The adjustments resulting from divorce can be very difficult for adults and children. There will be adjustments in physical living arrangements, emotional ties, finances, social ties, and parenting arrangements.

Ending a marriage relationship is a legal matter. Obtaining a divorce can be a long, stressful process. Recognizing that divorce is not a quick and easy way to end a relationship is important.

Divorce does not end a relationship if children are involved. It only changes the relationship. An ex-spouse is still a parent. Parents still need to work together to fulfill the functions of the family and meet the needs of their children.

Barriers to Divorce

Many people feel the pressure to stay married, even when their relationship is not growing or healthy. They may feel they cannot break the commitment to stay together "until death do us part." They may stay married for the sake of children or to avoid the disapproval of family and friends. Some fear the loneliness of being single. Some hope the happiness of the past will return. Others fear they cannot afford to live alone.

These fears or pressures serve as barriers to divorce. A **barrier to divorce** keeps a couple from moving ahead with a divorce. Such barriers can result in a person living in a situation of abuse for a lifetime. In contrast, barriers may influence a couple to try and rebuild their relationship.

Most people who divorce do remarry. Such trends indicate that people are seeking to find an intimate and fulfilling marital relationship, 17-2. The key to the problem of divorce, then, is the breakdown in the marriage relationship.

Think More About It

How might living in an abusive situation be more harmful to the development of a child than divorce?

17-2 The desire for companionship and a close relationship often leads a divorced person to remarry.

Factors Contributing to Divorce

Researchers have identified several factors that often contribute to divorce. Background differences, personal immaturity, and a lack of relationship skills can lead to divorce. Marrying into problem situations or marrying to escape problems at home are other significant factors. Frequent financial conflicts may also increase the chances of divorce.

Differences in Backgrounds

Major differences in backgrounds can result in differing views and expectations for marriage. These differences can increase conflict in the relationship and then be hard to resolve. If a couple disagrees on most aspects of the relationship, divorce is quite likely. However, similar and realistic expectations for marriage can help a marriage stay intact.

Immaturity

Immaturity can also lead to a marital breakdown. The growth that leads to maturity may result in changes in a person's thoughts, feelings, and goals. If this growth takes place after marriage, a couple may find they do not have as much in common with each other as they once did. Their personal readiness for marriage can affect the stability of their relationship.

Investigate Further

How might intellectual immaturity affect a couple's relationship?

Poor Relationship Skills

A lack of relationship skills makes it difficult for a couple to adjust to each other during the early years of marriage. They need to communicate clearly, make decisions together, and solve problems in a way that both are satisfied. These skills are important for living as a pair. If a couple do not develop these skills, the chance of divorce will increase.

Problem Situations

Marrying into problem situations also increases the chance of divorce. For instance, a premarital pregnancy may influence a couple to marry even if they are not ready. Then they must adjust to parenting as well as to each other during the early years of marriage.

Marrying to escape problems at home does not help a marriage, either. Past conflicts with parents may be brought into the marital relationship.

Financial Conflicts

Finances tend to be the major source of conflict in a marriage. Financial problems increase if a couple is unemployed or lack the training or education to get good jobs. Such problems can increase the chance that a marriage will end in divorce.

Even if both spouses have good jobs, strong differences may exist regarding money matters. Personal habits related to spending and saving money may differ sharply. How the household budget is handled may cause additional conflict, 17-3. If one spouse brings money or property to the marriage, arguments may arise over "his car" or "her bank account." Divorce often results from disagreements over how to handle money and other valuables in the marriage.

17-3 Arguments about finances can cause ongoing conflict between spouses.

Think More About It
How would good communication and decision-making skills help couples handle financial conflicts?

Teen Marriages

Many teen marriages end in divorce. This is closely related to the above factors. During the teen years, much personal growth takes place. Personal views and goals are still developing. Relationship skills are developing, too. Career goals and steps to reach them are being identified. Financial independence is not likely. As a result, many teen marriages do not survive.

Review Section 17:1

1. What are two barriers that might keep a couple from getting a divorce?
2. List six factors that may contribute to divorce.

section 17:2

A Breakdown in the Relationship

Sharpen Your Reading

As you read, develop a graphic organizer that follows the path from the breakdown of a relationship to a divorce. Include key concepts for each stage of divorce.

Boost Your Vocabulary

Identify the terms used in court proceedings that you have heard in the news or on TV shows.

Know Key Terms

emotional divorce
legal separation
legal divorce
petitioner
respondent
impotency
no-fault divorce
custody
visitation rights
joint custody
split custody
alimony
child support

How can a loving, caring relationship change so much? A couple may ask themselves that question and wonder how it happened. When did it start to fall apart?

Failure to Nurture a Relationship

A marriage relationship needs regular loving care. It needs a commitment from both partners to provide that care. To keep the relationship alive and growing, couples need to spend time together. They need to share their thoughts and feelings and do things together. In these ways, spouses build and strengthen their marital relationship.

Think More About It
Do you think that nurturing stops suddenly in a relationship or fades slowly? Why would a couple stop nurturing their relationship?

Emotional Divorce

What inside or outside factors could attack a marriage relationship? Spouses who cover up their hurts and do not share their inner feelings build walls between them. Their emotional needs are not met. One or both may withdraw from the relationship. They may seek to fulfill emotional needs outside the marriage. Such responses attack and tear apart the relationship from the inside. This first stage in the breakdown of the marriage relationship is called **emotional divorce**.

Skills for communicating and resolving conflicts can help couples renew and strengthen the relationship. They may seek marriage counseling to help them identify areas of their relationship that need to improve. With effort, many couples do work out their problems. They rebuild their marriage into a healthy and growing relationship.

Separation

Couples may struggle with their relationship for some time before they decide to separate. Separation is the second stage of the breakdown. Exactly what causes couples to stop trying to hold the relationship together varies. One partner usually moves out of the home while the other stays. The partner who leaves may seek separate living quarters or move in with family or friends.

The Effects of Separation

For parents with children, a separation produces a divided family structure. Mother and father live in different places. Children may live with one parent or the other, 17-4. They may be moved back and forth between the parents. In some cases, the children may be split up. Some may live with the mother and some with the father.

One partner may file papers for a legal separation. A **legal separation** is a legal agreement for the couple to live apart, divide their property, and provide for their children. However, the couple are still legally married. A couple may use this approach if they do not believe in divorce.

Sometimes the spouses move back together after a period of separation. The reasons for doing this vary. They may be lonely. They may remember the warm, close times they shared together. Professional counseling may have helped them resolve their differences. They may decide their differences were not as great as they thought. Sometimes couples do work out their differences and reunite the family. However, in many cases, separation ends in divorce.

17-4 When parents decide to separate, they need to discuss this with their children honestly. Children need to be reassured that the parents will still love them and take care of them.

Divorce Counseling

For many couples, the thought of divorce brings fear and uncertainty. Sometimes couples seek a divorce counselor who acts as a third party. Predivorce counseling is aimed at resolving differences with a goal of saving the marriage. Some states require predivorce counseling. The court then requires a letter stating that counseling was obtained. The letter also must state whether the counselor believes the marriage can be restored. The counseling may be obtained through the court system, from social workers, or through private counselors.

When a couple decides to divorce, the divorce counselor assists. This person helps the spouses understand the legal procedures and the alternatives they have. The counselor also helps the couple cope with the feelings that tend to surface in a divorce. After the divorce is final, the counselor can help each person adjust to the changes created by the divorce.

Investigate Further

Why do you think that separation usually ends in divorce?

The Legal Divorce

The final stage of a divorce can be a lengthy legal process. In each state, certain laws and procedures govern a legal divorce. A **legal divorce** is the ending of a marriage through the legal process. This is usually done through lawyers, one representing each spouse, 17-5.

Legal Procedures

All states have legal procedures for divorce. Although the exact laws differ somewhat from state to state, they follow a general pattern. First, a residency requirement must be met. The couple must have lived in the state for a certain length of time before they can apply for a divorce. The length of time varies from state to state. Three months, six months, or a year are the most common residency requirements.

Divorce Proceedings

In the divorce proceedings, there are two parties. The person who files for divorce becomes the **petitioner**. The other spouse is the **respondent**. Most persons filing for divorce seek legal counsel.

Grounds for Divorce

All states have laws concerning divorce. However, the *grounds for divorce* (valid reasons) differ in each state. In many states, the couple is required to just state that their marriage is "irretrievably broken." This means the relationship cannot be restored. Adultery is considered evidence of a broken marriage in all states. Cruelty, desertion, alcohol or drug addiction, impotency, or insanity have also been accepted as grounds for divorce. **Impotency** is the inability to have sexual relations.

If one spouse does not want the divorce, he or she *contests* (fights) it. Then a battle may develop over determining the grounds for divorce. If one partner requests certain child care arrangements or money settlement, the grounds for divorce are very important. It can affect the judgment.

No-Fault Divorce

A **no-fault divorce** is a legal term used to identify a divorce in which neither spouse is being blamed for the divorce. If the couple both agree to the divorce, the court does not inquire into their reasons. Instead, the spouses must make a statement that their marriage has broken down and cannot be saved. Also, if they agree to a fairly even division of their property, most courts do not interfere.

Think More About It
How could no-fault divorce benefit families? Can you think of any negatives of having no-fault divorce laws?

17-5 During a legal divorce, each spouse retains a lawyer. The lawyer represents that spouse's interests and advises him or her about legal issues.

Custody Settlements

The court is responsible for awarding legal custody of children in a divorce settlement. The person given **custody** has the rights and responsibilities of providing for the children's care until the children reach age 18. This person also has the authority to make important decisions in matters affecting the life and development of the child, 17-6.

Three different types of custody settlements can take place during a legal divorce. They include one-parent, joint, or split custody. Depending on the situation, the court will try to set up fair custody arrangements.

17-6 Custody settlements determine with whom the children will live. Depending on the circumstances, children may live with the mother or father.

One-Parent Custody

In most cases, the person who provided the major share of child care will continue to do so. The mother is often granted custody of the children. That means the children live with their mother, and she has the major responsibility for them. The father may be required to help pay for their support. Today, however, more fathers are being granted custody of their children.

The court also establishes **visitation rights**. These are arrangements for the noncustodial parent to visit the children. Changes to this arrangement must be sought through the court. It is a felony for a parent to interfere with the custody and visitation rights that are established by the courts. If a child is in danger of physical harm, those rights can be suspended.

Joint Custody

Sometimes parents request **joint custody**. This may be granted when both parents want to be involved in the children's lives. In addition, they both want to share the rights and responsibilities of legal custody.

Both parents must be judged as fit and proper people to have legal care, custody, and control of the children. They both must agree to have a full and active role in parenting. They are required to consult with each other in major areas, such as religious upbringing, education, and health care. They must agree to work cooperatively for the best interests of the children in all decisions.

Joint custody keeps both parents involved in their children's lives. They both continue their parenting roles. It also forces the parents to continue relating to each other. For couples who have had problems relating in the past, this arrangement may not work very well. They may continue to argue and fight, but through the children.

Split Custody

An arrangement in which the children are divided between the parents is known as **split custody**. In most of these cases, the father takes the boys and the mother takes the girls. This arrangement splits the children as well as the parents.

 Which custody arrangement do you think is the best environment for children in a divorced family? Why?

Financial Settlements

Financial settlements are often part of the divorce proceedings. Two types of financial settlements are alimony and child support.

Alimony

One spouse may request alimony as part of the divorce settlement. **Alimony** is a financial settlement paid to a spouse, 17-7.

17-7 Finances to pay for more education may be part of an alimony settlement.

Judgments for alimony are based on need. Need is determined by factors such as income, assets, debts, previous standard of living, and a person's ability to be self-supporting. Some settlements are lump sum judgments. Some are monthly payments given for a period of time or for specific purposes such as going to college.

Investigate Further

How would alimony payments benefit children living with the custodial parent?

Child Support

The court also sets **child support** payments. These are payments that a noncustodial parent is legally required to pay toward the expense of raising children under 18. The court assumes that the custodial parent shares his or her income directly with the children. Child support payments are required to maintain the child's standard of living. The court considers the parents' incomes and other factors in determining the amount of this payment.

Review Section 17:2

1. Briefly explain how emotional divorce affects a marriage relationship.
2. Explain the difference between a legal separation and a legal divorce.
3. Describe a no-fault divorce.
4. List and describe three types of custody settlements.

section 17:3

Strengthening the Family After Divorce

17-8 Divorce requires adjustments from both parents and children.

Sharpen Your Reading

Draw a graphic organizer with branches going to at least three family members: mother, father, and children. As you read, list the adjustments each family member goes through as a result of a divorce.

Boost Your Vocabulary

Draw a cartoon strip that depicts a single parent experiencing role overload.

Know Key Terms

role overload
stepparent

Adjusting to Divorce

Legal divorce is a traumatic experience for all involved. Many changes result, leaving a lifetime effect on parents and children. Adjusting to these changes takes time. Family members struggle with the emotional trauma, new living arrangements, lower family income, and new parenting arrangements, 17-8.

Adults adjust more easily if they can reasonably work out the details of their new relationship as ex-spouses. Children adjust more easily if their parents can cooperate in carrying out parenting tasks. They also benefit when both parents continue to be involved in their lives.

Emotional Adjustments

When a divorce occurs, parents and children struggle with their mixed feelings. They each may feel the divorce was their fault and blame themselves. They may be angry that the divorce occurred. They may feel hurt and rejected by the absent parent or spouse. Self-esteem and self-confidence may be low. They may wish life would return to the way it was before the problems began.

Think More About It
How is the loss of a relationship from divorce different from the loss of a relationship due to some other outside factor?

The Divorced Adult

Mixed feelings are common after a divorce. Feelings of loneliness may be combined with feelings of rejection and hurt. A divorced person may wonder if anyone will ever want to marry him or her again. The desire for a close friend and close relationship is strong. Such emotions often influence a newly divorced person to jump into a new relationship too soon. Before getting involved in a relationship, this person needs to take time to reevaluate the qualities desired in a partner.

Rebuilding self-esteem and self-confidence is an important part of the adjustment process. This adjustment is helped by looking for ways to grow and learn through the divorce experience. A person may need to learn more about himself or herself and develop personal skills. Thinking about life goals and perhaps training for a new occupation are other needs to consider.

Children of Divorced Parents

Children must deal with mixed emotions. They may feel angry that their parents have divorced. They may feel hurt and rejected by the parent who does not have custody. They may blame a parent or themselves for the divorce. Feelings of insecurity are common since the family unit is broken and their source of love and nurturing is divided.

Think More About It
Why do you think it is important that children have someone they can maintain a strong close attachment to during a breakup in the family?

Emotional adjustment can be helped if both parents continue to be actively involved in their children's lives. They both need to spend time with each child, showing love and affection. They need to let the child know that he or she is still loved, even though the family is not together. They both can show interest in the child's friends, achievements, and activities. Also, grandparents and other extended family members may be able to offer security and affection at this time, 17-9.

New Living Arrangements

Along with handling the emotional stress, family members must adjust to new living arrangements. Their home may need to be sold so the money can be split between the divorced couple. The family may need to move, relocate

17-9 Close relationships with grandparents and other relatives can help children adjust emotionally to the parents' decision to divorce.

in a new neighborhood, and find new friends. Children must adjust to living with one parent and visiting the other. Adults must adjust to managing a household alone, without help from the ex-spouse.

Lower Income

For most families, both spouses have less income after a divorce. This shortage of money can be a major source of stress. Since women tend to earn less than men, female-headed families tend to have less household income. They cannot always count on child support payments, either. In many cases, fathers do not fulfill their responsibilities to pay child support. By federal law, not paying child support is a felony. Even so, many fathers do not pay or have such low incomes that they cannot pay.

17-10 Even when divorced, each parent should continue to be involved in the child's life.

Investigate Further

How could family members work together to help restore balance to the family system after a divorce?

New Parenting Arrangements

Parents and children need to adjust to the new parenting arrangements. The parent with custody of the children takes on the new role of single parent. The noncustodial parent must adjust to the new role of being a visiting or part-time parent.

Children often have less access to both parents after a divorce. The custodial parent may be gone more due to work, school, or dating. The noncustodial parent may visit often at first, but less often as time goes on. Visitations usually must be arranged ahead of time.

Parenting roles must be adjusted, too. Questions of how to relate to the children, what to do with them, and what needs should be met may arise. Questions about differences in guidance between one parent and the other must be settled.

Deciding livable solutions to finances, visitations, and parenting questions is an important task for ex-spouses to complete. Children benefit most when their physical and emotional needs are met. They need to know that both parents will still provide love and affection and spend time with them, 17-10. This can help children rebuild feelings of security within the new family arrangement.

Think More About It
What are some ways family members could reduce the stress that goes with adjusting to a divorce?

Single-Parent Families

Usually the parent who has legal custody also has physical custody of a child. This means the child lives with that parent most of the time. Most single-parent families struggle with financial and parenting responsibilities as well as loneliness.

Role Overload from Added Responsibilities

Most of the time, the single parent carries the responsibility for child care alone. Many parenting decisions need to be made. What should the parent do when the child is sick, grades are poor, or the child misbehaves? Even when the parent is tired or angry, reasonable parenting decisions still need to be made. No one else is there to fill in while the parent calms down or thinks over the situation.

All financial needs of the family must be handled by the single parent as well. Often the single person's income does not cover all the family's needs.

Working, parenting, and managing the household alone often result in role overload for the single parent. **Role overload** means the single parent has too many roles and responsibilities to carry them all out well.

Grandparents, other family members, and friends may help the single parent with child care responsibilities. Such support can help the single-parent family fulfill its functions and meet the needs of each family member.

In some cases, government aid for parents with dependent children may be obtained to help the family provide basic shelter, food, clothing, and health care. Also, in some communities programs are available to help single parents upgrade their skills and education to obtain better-paying jobs.

Think More About It
What are some ways that a single-parent family can restore balance to the family system so the needs of family members are met?

Coping with Loneliness

Loneliness is often a problem for single parents. Because they are alone, they tend to focus more on their children than themselves. They feel it is important to succeed at parenting. They devote most of their time to providing for the family and caring for their children. As a result, little time is left to spend building other relationships.

Supportive Friendships

Friendships are especially important for single parents. They need friends who accept them and help them believe in their own abilities. Friends can encourage them to take steps that will help them grow as people. This support increases the single parent's self-esteem and confidence. An attitude of personal growth can lead to the development of new skills. Personal accomplishments will bring feelings of success, 17-11.

Remarriage and the Stepfamily

Many divorced people remarry within a few years after their divorce. The reasons for this decision vary. They may desire the closeness of a marriage relationship. They may want more financial security. The desire to share parenting tasks with a spouse may be another reason.

When either spouse has children from a previous marriage, they then form a stepfamily. The newly married parent becomes a **stepparent** to the children of his or her new spouse. The stepfamily brings more resources together to meet the needs of family members. However, it also brings more challenges.

17-11 Friendships are important for the single parent. They provide emotional support and help the person gain confidence in his or her ability to succeed.

Link to Your Life
Identify some examples of how the relationships within a family become more complex as more people become involved.

Adjusting to the Marriage

In a second marriage, newly married couples need time to adjust to each other. The early years of a second marriage are full of adjustments, just as they were in the first marriage. However, these adjustments are even more complicated.

Feelings of hurt and rejection that carry over from the divorce may still exist. To deal with this, both spouses need to experience acceptance and unconditional love. They need each other's full support and encouragement. They need to build each other's self-esteem. Fulfilling their own emotional needs will help them meet their children's needs for love, affection, and security.

As a couple adjusts to each other, they are also adjusting to a new parenting arrangement. This means less time for each other. They have less time to communicate with each other, resolve conflicts privately, and develop mutual interests. Setting aside time to develop their personal relationship is an important need for them to fulfill.

Stepparenting

The most challenging role in a stepfamily is that of *stepparent*. The relationship between a stepparent and stepchild can be fulfilling, yet it can also be strained.

Building this relationship takes time. A stepchild may express fears, doubt, mistrust, and insecurity. The child may purposely misbehave as a way of expressing these feelings. Anger and rejection are still felt over the divorce. The child may resent the stepparent trying to take the place of the absent parent.

Although stepparents cannot take the place of absent parents, they can fill the gap the absent parents leave. The stepparent can provide a listening ear. Listening with empathy is important. Messages such as "I understand" can encourage the child to talk about feelings.

Reflecting, or repeating in your own words what you think was said, can help the child identify feelings. "It hurts when things like that happen, doesn't it?" Reflecting can help the child identify the feelings that are deep inside.

As more experiences are shared, feelings of love will grow, especially when acceptance and affection are shown, 17-12. All this does take time, however.

It is important that the parent and stepparent support each other in parenting decisions. They can work out rules ahead of time and support each other in enforcing them.

17-12 Given time, members of the stepfamily can build close bonds of affection.

Think More About It

How can stepparents and children develop rapport and trust so children's needs are met and feelings of attachment can grow?

Needs of the Stepfamily

First and foremost, a stepfamily must adjust to a new marriage, family structure, and parenting situation. These adjustments take time. Besides these adjustments, the stepfamily must also do the following:

- *Allow time for family unity to grow.* Stepfamilies need time to develop bonds that build a sense of togetherness. They also need time for love to grow between family members.

- *Provide personal space for each family member.* Children are especially possessive of their space. Establishing some personal space for each member may help the stepfamily feel "at home."

- *Make workable visitation arrangements for the absent parent and other people important to the children.* Grandparents and others involved in the lives of the children also need to be included in these arrangements.

- *Accept all family members in the stepfamily structure.* The household members need to accept each other and the reality of the situation. Together, they are a family and can fulfill the functions of a family in each other's lives.

Review Section 17:3

1. Name three common emotional responses to a divorce.
2. Explain how parents can help their children adjust to new parenting arrangements after a divorce.
3. Identify four challenges faced by a single-parent family.
4. List two emotional adjustments that are unique to a couple in a stepfamily.
5. Briefly describe how a stepparent can fill the gap an absent parent leaves.
6. Give four suggestions to help a stepfamily meet the unique needs of its members.

Think It Through

Adjusting to Divorce

"Mommy, look what Tara did to the coloring book!" Joel exclaimed as he turned the pages. Tara had marked a big black *X* across the father's face in each picture.

Katie looked across the table at her five-year-old daughter. She knew the divorce had been hard on all of them, but she had thought they were adjusting well.

Tom had paid for her to complete an accounting course at the technical college. Since she had found a job at the bank, she felt life had improved for her and the children. Now this!

Katie wondered what she should do. She also wondered if Tom's decreasing visits had anything to do with Tara's anger. Since meeting his new girlfriend, Tom hadn't visited his children even once.

Katie decided to talk to Tara's kindergarten teacher. Perhaps she had shown some unusual behavior there as well. She hoped the teacher might have some suggestions.

Questions to Guide Your Thinking

1. Identify and describe the custody arrangements in this family.

2. What evidence is there of an alimony settlement?

3. What steps had Katie taken to adjust to the problem of lower income in single-parent families?

4. Considering the stages of grieving over a loss (explained in Chapter 16), what do you think might have been the reason for Tara's action?

5. What other behaviors might a child use that could be evidence of the grieving process?

6. What could Katie do to help her daughter with the emotional adjustment to a divorce?

Chapter Summary

A family faces change when a marriage relationship breaks down. Various factors can contribute to this event. Breakdowns that cannot be resolved often result in divorce. Divorce is a legal procedure in which a marriage is ended. It does not, however, end parenting responsibilities. During the divorce proceedings, certain legal issues must be settled. Custody settlements, visitation rights, and child support payments are handled by the court.

Adjusting to the changes caused by divorce is difficult for both adults and children. Emotional adjustments must be made as well as new living arrangements. Often both spouses have less income to live on as a result of maintaining separate households.

When there are children in the family, divorce produces a single-parent family structure. Often a divorced parent remarries, producing the stepfamily structure. Both these family structures have unique challenges in fulfilling the functions of a family in the lives of the members.

Assess...

Your Knowledge

1. What are the stages that indicate that a relationship is breaking down?

2. What happens to the family system when there is a divorce in the family?

Your Understanding

3. Through all the steps in the breakdown of a marriage and a divorce, how can a family meet the needs of children and adults and restore balance to the family system?

4. How can stepparents develop close relationships with their stepchildren?

Your Skills

5. Reflect on a family you know that has experienced divorce. Which of the factors that can contribute to divorce were evident in that family?

6. What are some skills that could possibly have helped family members from Question #5 improve their relationships and strengthen their marriage and their family?

Think Critically

7. *Writing.* Think about your family and families you know. List five actions that you think would contribute to a breakdown in a marriage relationship. Explain why you see the cause and effect relationship between these five actions and such a breakdown.

8. *Social studies.* Identify a television show that has a stepparent as a main character. Write a paragraph discussing the following questions: Is the stepparent presented from a positive or negative view? How does the stepparent relate to the children in the family? What conclusions could be drawn about stepparent relationships from this TV show? Are those real-life conclusions? *Choice:* Analyze a cartoon, child's story, or novel.

9. *Social studies.* Create a scenario depicting the family interactions that might exist in a family with one of the following types of custody: one-parent, joint, and split.

10. *Writing.* Write a scenario of a dinner scene in the custodial family one week after a legal divorce. In a paragraph, explain how your scenario describes the adjustments the family members are making. *Choice:* Write your scenario into a play. *Group option:* Role-play the scenario.

Connect with Your Community

11. *Social studies.* Prepare questions related to grounds for divorce, divorce procedures, custody arrangements, or other legal aspects of divorce in your state. Invite a lawyer or legal assistant to speak to your class on the legal considerations of divorce and participate by asking your questions. *Choice:* Summarize the presentation in a written report.

12. Prepare questions about the challenges of parenting in today's families. Help arrange a panel of four or five guest speakers to discuss such challenges. Invite parents of single-parent families and stepfamilies to serve as the guest speakers. *Choice:* Summarize the presentation in a written report.

13. *Social studies.* Interview a social worker to identify what resources in the community are available to a single-parent family while the head of the household is going through the process of a divorce. *Choice:* Use the Internet to research available community resources.

14. Identify a list of concerns that teens may have when their families are going through the stages of divorce. Consult with your guidance counselor about these concerns and identify school resources available for teens facing these issues. *Choice:* Start a peer support group for students whose families are going through divorce.

Use Technology

15. Create a tri-fold flyer that illustrates the stages of divorce. Identify possible school and community resources for families going through each stage. *Choice:* Post your flyer to your school's Web site.

16. *Research.* Using the Internet, research the differences in grounds for divorce in various states. Describe these in a paragraph. Include your opinion on why you think there might be variations in grounds for divorce from one state to another.

17. *Research.* Search the Internet for information about the attitudes and divorce patterns in at least two cultures outside the United States. Write a paper comparing the attitudes toward divorce in these cultures with the attitudes of this society.

18. *Math.* Survey students in your school for those who have experienced divorce in their immediate family and in their extended family. Survey your parents asking whether they, as teenagers, experienced divorce in their family or extended family. Then develop a graph indicating divorce statistics and trends in your community.

Families Change Over Time

Key Questions

Questions to answer as you study this chapter:

- How can families adjust to the challenges of aging?

- How does grandparenting benefit both generations?

- How does understanding the grieving process help people accept a loss?

Chapter Objectives

After studying this chapter, you will be able to

- **describe** how aging affects middlescence.

- **recognize** the benefits of grandparenting.

- **identify** the challenges of retirement.

- **determine** the challenges faced by older adults.

- **locate** federal and community resources to assist older adults.

- **explain** the concept of hospice.

Life Sketch

Vi and Walter weren't going to work, since both were retired, yet they still led busy lives. Vi wanted to leave by 7:30 a.m. because she would give her granddaughter a ride to school. Then she had to be at the Bergstroms' home by 8:00. Martha Bergstrom, who was 84, had fallen a few weeks earlier and broken her leg. Vi visited Martha three mornings a week. Sometimes she took Martha to the doctor, did some housework, or went shopping for her. On Tuesdays and Thursdays, Vi baby-sat two little girls. Vi enjoyed keeping busy and making a little money to cover her extra expenses.

Walter's first stop was the churchyard, which he kept mowed. After that, he planned to meet Rollie and Adolph for lunch at the senior center. There he would attend an afternoon meeting to help plan a bus trip to the Ozarks. Walter was a member of the center's planning committee.

Getting Started

Aging does not mean that life becomes meaningless. Friends, family, and neighbors are all sources of meaningful relationships throughout a lifetime.

Aging does affect the family system. Needs change. Resources often decrease. A strong family system can help people adjust to change and make the aging years enjoyable and rewarding.

section 18:1

The Middle Years

Sharpen Your Reading

Develop a chart with three columns. Label column one *Changes that Take Place*. Label column two *How Changes Affect the Family System*. Label column three *How Family Members Can Help Adjust to the Change*. As you read this section, fill in information under each column.

Boost Your Vocabulary

Compare middlescence with adolescence and list ways they are similar.

Know Key Terms

middlescence
midlife crisis

Between the ages of 35 and 40, most adults begin to notice the first physical signs of aging. They may notice a few more wrinkles or gray hairs. Their reflexes may seem a little slower. Perhaps they cannot run quite as fast or as far as they did in the past. In a person's life span, these physical changes tend to mark the beginning of the middle-age years.

The middle-aged years between 40 and 65 are sometimes called **middlescence**. This is because many adults look back at their lives, questioning their purposes and goals for living. Similar to the years of adolescence, many of the same questions are often repeated. "Who am I?" "What have I

done so far in my life?" "Will I reach the goals I have set?" "Will I ever own my own business or travel around the world?" Such questioning usually increases as the signs of aging become more evident.

Weigh the Facts In what ways do you think a person's answers to these questions are different at age 50 versus age 15?

The Effects of Change During Middlescence

Several changes take place in adults' lives during middlescence. The family life cycle advances to a new stage. Parental roles change. Working adults reach the peaks of their careers and look ahead to retirement. Each of these changes can trigger the questioning that takes place during middlescence.

Family Life Cycle Changes

Changes in the family life cycle remind the adult that time is passing. The children leave home. Parents may feel the effects of the empty nest stage. A child gets married. A grandchild arrives. The roles of grandparenting begin. Parents have more time for their own relationship and interests. These events may trigger more questioning for the middle-aged adult.

Parental Relationship Roles

Changes in relationships with their own parents also take place. The parent roles may even switch as the older adult loses some self-care abilities. The middle-aged adult may then have to provide care and support for the aging parent. This reminds the adult just how short life really is. The aging process cannot be avoided; it is inevitable.

Changes Affecting Careers

Changes in an adult's career may also influence questioning during middlescence. Some reach the peak of their career achievement in middle age. On the other hand, the middle-aged adult may feel threatened by a younger employee who is climbing the career ladder. Self-esteem may drop. Such experiences can influence the adult to question his or her own self-worth.

For the middle-aged adult, this period of questioning can be beneficial. It can encourage the adult to evaluate progress in reaching life goals. This can lead to revising goals or forming new goals. It can also lead to planning and preparing for the retirement years. Questioning can encourage a couple to work together to strengthen their own marital relationship. They can establish closer relationships with their children, 18-1. Also, it can help them relate to their parents who are coping with the effects of aging.

 What resources increase for the family during middlescence? Which resources decrease?

Midlife Crisis

Some adults have problems adjusting to the changes of the middle years. Some experience a midlife crisis during this questioning period. A **midlife crisis** is brought on by the stress from changes in the middle years of life. This stress is increased when the adult views youthfulness as more desirable than aging. To these adults, the

18-1 As middle-aged adults reflect on the importance of life, they may focus more attention on personal relationships.

signs of aging are proof that they are losing their youth. Their feelings of esteem are under attack. They may see themselves becoming less attractive and less desirable, with little self-worth.

During this midlife crisis, some middle-aged adults try to regain their youthfulness. They may seek friends among youth, wear teen fashions, and listen to teen music.

Some adults blame their loss of youthfulness on others. They may blame their family. Some desert their families and the responsibilities that go with their middle-aged roles. Some may blame their job situation and change jobs or careers.

Most adults in middlescence are able to work through their questioning and avoid midlife crises. Understanding from family members can help the adult cope with the stress and adjust to the changes of middle age. These adults can revise and set new goals. They may develop new interests and start a hobby they have always wanted to try. They may focus on areas of personal growth, learn a new skill, or take classes for enrichment. They may set aside more time for important relationships. These experiences are enriching. They can help the adult rebuild feelings of esteem and enhance the years of retirement ahead.

Use What You Learn

What could family members do to help a person who was experiencing a midlife crisis?

Grandparenting

When adults are in their middle years, their children will likely be having children. The adults take on the new role of grandparents. For most families, this is an exciting transition filled with many joys.

Most families look forward to welcoming a new baby into the extended family. Grandparents may want to help the new parents with baby care expenses such as clothing and furniture. They may help the new parents during the early weeks of adjusting to a baby's schedule. Help with household chores, such as cooking, cleaning, and laundry, are often welcomed by the new parents. Most grandparents enjoy babysitting so the new mother can get some extra rest.

Grandparent Roles

As children grow, grandparents can play important roles in their lives. As a teen, you may find it easier to talk to a grandparent about some topics. Grandparents usually have more time to sit and listen or play with grandchildren. Close relationships benefit both grandparents and grandchildren. If you do not have a grandparent living nearby, an older neighbor may enjoy being a substitute grandparent.

Provide Love and Acceptance
Grandparents can have a nurturing role. Their attention can make a child feel special. As they offer affection, they can help the child feel loved and wanted. Grandparents may attend special events in which the child takes part. They may celebrate the child's birthday with the family. Those who live far away can call or send letters, cards, or gifts to help make the child feel important. In these ways, they help build the child's esteem and feelings of self-acceptance.

Give Focused Attention to Grandchildren
Grandparents who spend time with children can give them focused attention. They can center their attention on the child, taking time to talk and listen. They may not have all the responsibilities that take most of the parents' time. Through such focused attention, grandparents build close bonds with their grandchildren.

Provide Child Care
Grandparents may also take part in the role of caring for children. They may provide child care while the parents work. At other times, they can give the child's parents some time alone by offering to take care of grandchildren. These experiences help them build relationships with their grandchildren.

Continuing Family Traditions
Grandparents often play a role in keeping family traditions alive. They may take part in special celebrations on holidays. They may organize family reunions.

Grandparents help establish bonds between members of an extended family. Grandparents serve as a link to the family's past history, helping grandchildren feel a sense of belonging to the family.

Provide Some Financial Assistance

Sometimes grandparents help with the provider role as well. They may help purchase clothing and other gifts for their grandchildren. If they are financially secure, they may be able to help out with loans or finances for the children's education.

Benefits of Grandparenting

Grandparenting not only benefits the children and parents; it also benefits the older adult. It is a role most older adults enjoy.

Grandparenting relationships can be rewarding. They provide a source of love and affection for aging adults, 18-2. When grandparents become involved with their grandchildren's lives, they share many experiences together. Strong bonds can develop. In return, most young children will openly express their feelings of love.

The role of grandparenting also provides the older adult an opportunity to feel needed and important. Helping with child care is a way in which they can give support to their own children. Their time and experience become valuable resources to their children.

Grandparenting provides a feeling of satisfaction. Older adults feel satisfaction in helping a child learn and watching the child grow. Contributing to the development of a new generation helps older adults feel their lives are complete.

18-2 Grandchildren can be a source of love and affection for their grandparents.

Review Section 18:1

1. Briefly describe what is meant by the term *middlescence*.

2. List four changes that take place in an adult's life during middlescence.

3. Identify four characteristics of the grandparent role.

4. List three benefits that the older adult can gain from grandparenting.

section 18:2

The Retirement Years

Sharpen Your Reading

Continue the chart from Section 18:1, filling in the same information about the retirement years.

Boost Your Vocabulary

Interview a grandparent and ask questions about retirement income, social security, pensions, and Medicare. Summarize how each of these helps meet a retired person's needs.

Know Key Terms

retirement
social security
Supplemental Security Income (SSI)
Medicare
pensions

When a family member retires, more changes occur. **Retirement** is the ending of paid employment. For most adults in this society, retirement occurs around age 65. The trend to retire earlier has increased as companies replace those nearing retirement with younger workers.

Retirement affects people's lives in different ways. It brings changes in their daily schedules, social activities, and income, 18-3. If they can adjust to these changes easily, then retirement will be an enjoyable stage of their lives.

18-3 People of retirement age look forward to having more control over how they spend their time.

The Challenges of Retirement

"I can't wait to retire!" Many workers make that comment several times in life. However, when the reality of retirement draws near, the feelings may not be the same.

Changes in Work Roles

Many people are not ready to face this stage of their lives. The loss of their job equals a loss of part of their identity. They have found satisfaction in their work. Others have respected them for their experience and expertise. Within one day, that can change. They may find themselves getting up in the morning with no place to go and no schedule to keep. They may feel worthless and suffer from a loss of self-esteem. Often they are faced with having less income. Some miss the daily contact with other people they had when they were working.

Some may have less severe feelings. This may be related to the many roles they fill in the home. Many look forward to having more time to spend on personal interests as well as the role of grandparenting.

Adjusting to changes in work roles is easier if a retired person has other interests or hobbies to pursue. Some develop a hobby into a business. Others go to school and pursue some other type of work. Volunteering in community and religious organizations is another option. These newfound interests provide satisfaction. They may also provide some income, as well as social contact with other people. Such interests can help people adjust to retirement.

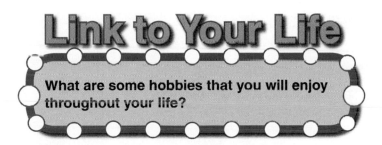

Link to Your Life

What are some hobbies that you will enjoy throughout your life?

Financial Changes

Adjusting to the loss of income is easier if people planned ahead for their retirement years. Now they have time to pursue the activities they always wanted to do. Savings, investments, pension funds, and social security can all provide income during these years. When people have enough money to pay living expenses and pursue leisure activities, their retirement years will be more enjoyable.

Investigate Further

At what age should a person start saving for retirement and invest in a pension plan?

Changes in Social Life

Keeping socially active and continuing relationships with others is important as people age, 18-4. Relationships with children and grandchildren can provide closeness and bring much satisfaction. Relationships with other retirees can provide companionship. Involvement in organizations can help the retiree keep active in a community and develop friendships with many different age groups.

Planning an Active Retirement

Making plans for an active retirement can help older adults enjoy these years. However, the belief that older people are limited in what they can do stops many from exploring new interests and activities. Older adults may need to be encouraged to step out and try new things.

Maintaining a Positive Attitude

One factor other than poor health that might keep older adults from being active during retirement is attitude. Some retirees have a negative attitude. If they believe they are weak, have a poor memory, and cannot learn something new, they will likely act that way. Those who

18-4 Without the demands of work, a retired couple will have the time to renew the closeness in their relationship.

have a positive attitude about themselves, their abilities, and their worth can do almost anything they choose.

Link to Your Life

What could you do to encourage a grandparent or other older adult to be active?

Staying Healthy Through Diet and Physical Activity

Diet and physical activity are important factors in staying active. Older adults need to continue eating a nutritious diet. Older adults who are physically active are more likely to stay healthy and retain ease of movement.

Planning for Financial Needs

A worker's paycheck stops at retirement, but living costs continue. Unfortunately, few adults actually save and invest enough money during their working years to prepare for retirement. As a result, their standard of living may change when they retire.

Wise money management, including savings and investments, is one key to security in the later years, 18-5. In addition, some financial assistance is available through federal and community programs. Learning about these programs before retirement can also help older adults meet some of their financial needs.

18-5 Financial planning can help couples have the money they need for activities during retirement.

Federal Programs

Social security is a federal program that is run by the Social Security Administration. This program is designed to give retired or disabled people some source of income. At age 65, retired workers who paid social security taxes for a certain period are eligible for benefits. These benefits are paid monthly. A spouse, widow, or widower of an eligible worker can also receive social security benefits. Retired workers can file for social security benefits as early as age 62. However, the amount they receive each month will be less than if they wait until age 65 to file for benefits.

People should apply for social security benefits about three months before they turn age 65. They should apply in person at their local social security office, making sure they take certain documents with them. Common documents needed include their social security number and a copy of their latest federal income tax form or wage statement from an employer (a W-2 form).

Supplemental Security Income (SSI) is another federal program administered through local social security offices. Many people are not aware that this income source is available. The purpose of this program is to help people who are age 65 or older, blind, or disabled with extra income. It is not necessary to have worked and paid into social security to receive these funds. To find out if they are eligible, people should contact their local social security office.

Medical expenses can take much of an older person's income and savings. Planning for health insurance can help with these expenses. All retiring employees and spouses can remain on an employer's group health plan for up to three years after retirement.

Three months before they reach age 65, older persons receive **Medicare** information. Medicare is a federal program that helps older people in paying their medical bills. Some people purchase insurance to supplement what Medicare pays.

Pension Income

About one-third of retired Americans receive a pension check from their employers. **Pensions** are funds paid by employers to former employees who contributed to a special retirement fund while they were employed. Persons who do not have a company pension should build their own retirement account by saving and investing throughout their working years.

Through a local social service agency, older adults may also be able to receive help with some of their expenses. Aid such as food stamp programs or fuel assistance may be available if they qualify.

Review Section 18:2

1. Identify the changes retirement brings to a worker's life.
2. Describe the benefits provided to a retired person by social security and Medicare.

section 18:3

The Elderly Years

18-6 Due to medical advancements, people are living longer, healthier lives than ever before.

Sharpen Your Reading

Summarize the changes of the elderly years, the effects on the family, and strategies the family can take to adjust to these changes.

Boost Your Vocabulary

Research one of the four sources of care (adult day, community-based, home health, and hospice) for elderly adults. Prepare a report with visuals to describe the care provided.

Know Key Terms

agencies on aging
elder abuse
material abuse
adult day care
community-based day care
home health care
hospice care

Just how long will each person live? No one knows that answer. If your past relatives lived long lives, your grandparents have a greater chance of living to an old age as well. Generally, each generation averages a slightly longer life span than the previous one, 18-6. This means that you have a greater chance of facing the many challenges of old age.

Physical Health

Adults between the ages of 60 and 75 are healthier today than the same age group was in the past. The average life span of the population overall (including those with poor and good health) is over 76 years. Many outlive this estimate, even to 100 years.

As the result of aging, many physical changes take place during the elderly years. Increased illness, loss of strength, loss of vision and hearing, and loss of mental abilities are common. For most people, the physical changes linked to aging do not increase until after age 75.

Think More About It
What are some examples of increased needs in the family when grandparents lose their physical health?

Dealing with the Effects of Aging

What can older people do to counter their physical decline? Regular physical checkups can help detect some physical problems. With early detection, there is a greater chance of cure for some illnesses.

Proper diets are important for the elderly. They need to eat nutritious meals with foods from all the food groups. This provides proper nutrients so their bodies can continue the repair and rebuilding process.

Regular exercise is also important for staying healthy, but the elderly may avoid activity. Because of physical limitations, some may feel they cannot or should not exercise. Those who are alone may have no motivation to exercise. However, lack of physical activity does affect the aging process. Muscles and bones weaken quickly in the elderly if they are not used.

Plenty of rest in addition to good eating habits and regular physical activity can also help slow some of the effects of aging. A healthful lifestyle not only helps deter physical problems, but also enables the elderly to keep active in society. Regular health care and a healthful lifestyle can help the elderly keep active and remain independent longer.

Community Resources

Various **agencies on aging** bring many services to the elderly to help them overcome problems. The agencies plan, fund, and coordinate senior citizen services. Some of these services include transportation, home-care workers, counseling, recreation, and information. The agencies also support community centers that provide activities and meals for the elderly. Meals are served in community center dining rooms and also in individuals' homes through the Meals on Wheels programs. Information about these agencies can often be found online or in community telephone directories under *Senior Citizens' Services*.

Investigate Further

Why do you think more elderly people do not use community services such as Meals on Wheels?

Changes in Social Life

As physical health declines, so does the elderly person's social life. Their spouse may have died. Their children may be busy with work

or live far away. Older people may not be able to get out as often to visit friends and family. Those in poor health may be confined to their homes or bedridden.

Elderly family members still need the warmth and companionship of family relationships. Family visits and extra attention are important during these years. Parents and children can help elderly members by visiting regularly, running errands, doing housework, or providing transportation to medical appointments.

Most elderly like to continue living in their own homes as long as possible, 18-7. This keeps them in a familiar environment, near neighbors, friends, and family. Familiar surroundings and family support meet their needs for security.

Use What You Learn

What might family members need to do to help grandparents continue to live on their own?

Protecting the Rights of the Elderly

When the elderly feel lonely and isolated, they may open the doors of their home to anyone who knocks. They are so glad to have someone to talk to that they are prime targets for fraud. Many are curious about products and services

18-7 Most elderly adults want to continue living independently in their own homes.

that promise to improve their lives. Even cautious people have been tricked by someone they thought they could trust.

Consumer Fraud

Door-to-door salespersons may exploit the elderly with their bargains, good deals, and cure-all remedies. The elderly may pay in advance for the promised goods, miracle drugs, repairs, or financial services.

Finances are usually limited for the elderly. Salespersons with "deals that can't be beat" or "get rich quick" schemes often sound convincing.

What can you do to help an elderly person avoid becoming a victim? Encourage them to talk with a family member before making a commitment or signing a contract. Identifying community experts they can contact about finances, health, and consumer services would help build the older adult's personal resources.

Cases of fraud or suspected fraud should be reported to the police. Often the elderly are embarrassed when they learn they have been victims of fraud. They do not want to appear foolish or incompetent. Fear of losing their independence keeps them quiet. Reporting the fraud, however, may protect others from being victimized.

Use What You Learn

What are some ways you could help an older relative avoid consumer fraud?

Elder Abuse

There is the chance that some people will take advantage of the elderly because they cannot see, hear, or move well or think clearly. Perhaps the older person is part of a family relationship that was not healthy in earlier years. Maybe the extra care needed by the older person is more than the financial resources available. Such situations increase the risk that abuse might take place.

Elder abuse refers to intentionally or knowingly causing the elder person to suffer physical harm or injury, unreasonable confinement, sexual abuse, or a lack of services or medical treatment to maintain health. **Material abuse** means the misuse of the elder person's property or financial resources. A person cannot misuse the elder's money, take valuables, or obtain property. Material abuse also includes denying the elder's right to personal funds and interfering in financial decisions.

Elder abuse may also take the form of neglect in which the elder's physical or mental health is in danger. It refers to cases in which the caregiver fails to provide adequate food, shelter, clothing, medical, or dental care. Elderly persons may also cause self-neglect by taking actions to jeopardize their health.

Such offenses should be reported to a local agency on aging. The agency can also be contacted for free or low-cost legal service or other consumer problems. The federal government provides funds to every state to operate free or low-cost legal services for people over 65.

Loss of Independence

As people age, they become more dependent on others. Many of those over 85 years old live in special care facilities that are equipped to handle the challenges of old age. For the safety and well-being of an elderly person, families must eventually make decisions about how to provide the best care.

Becoming an Extended Family

Sometimes families choose to move a grandparent into their own home. They want to help with the physical, social, and financial problems that the elderly person faces. This can have a major effect on the family and should only be done after much thought and discussion. The elderly parent, other children, and all the family members should be included in the discussion.

Think More About It

What are some factors that a family should consider before moving an older relative into their home?

Community Resources for Providing Care

Many community programs are designed to help elderly people remain as independent as possible in their own homes. These programs also help families who have taken an elderly relative into their homes to live with them. Three common programs are available:

- **Adult day care** is a program that transports older adults from their homes to centers that provide daytime group activities. These services are for elderly people who are impaired by physical or mental conditions. The centers provide activities, lunch, health screening, and counseling.

- **Community-based day care** is a program of activities for older people who are still somewhat independent. It may be sponsored by the local agency on aging and held at a senior center. Social workers, nurses, and aides are involved in providing a full program of activities.

- **Home health care** may be a solution for the very elderly. Nurses or aides go to the elderly person's home to provide assistance with health care, 18-8. Services can involve helping the elderly take medicine, monitor blood pressure, and change dressings on a healing wound. Help with housekeeping chores and laundry is sometimes available through home care services.

Sometimes the elderly require frequent care. Assisted living can provide the around-the-clock care they need. Nurses, doctors, dietary specialists, rehabilitation staff, and recreation workers offer the many services the elderly need. Every state requires assisted living facilities to be licensed. Even so, the choice of assisted living should be researched and made with care.

Death and Dying

You may have already experienced the death of someone you love. Death can come suddenly and unexpectedly. On the other hand, a death may be expected as a result of a long illness.

When someone dies, the people affected by the loss must adjust. However, when someone

18-8 Home health care nurses or aides provide assistance to elderly adults in their homes.

becomes ill with an incurable condition, the adjustment is harder. Both the dying person and the loved ones must eventually accept the fact that the person's life will end.

Hospice

Hospice care is designed to help a dying person live the final days of life in comfort. Such physical, emotional, and spiritual care can help the person face death with dignity. Hospice programs also offer support to families as they face the death of a loved one.

When a person feels that life has been full, death is easier to face. A hospice program helps a dying person focus on fulfilling experiences. These may be memories of special events or hobbies that can still be enjoyed in some way.

Hospice programs also focus on showing love and affection. Taking time to talk, listen, and touch the person can help meet social and emotional needs. Physical contact such as holding a hand can give the person enormous comfort.

A doctor supervises the hospice care program. A team of nurses, volunteers, a home health aide, a social worker, and a clergyperson provides the care. Support and involvement of both the patient and the family are needed. The dying patient remains an important member of the family. Family members receive counseling to help them accept the approaching death.

Investigate Further

How are family members an important part of hospice care?

Coping with Death

When death occurs at a very old age or after a long illness, family members find it easier to accept. They can view the person's life as full and complete. Even then, they experience a grieving process.

The Grieving Process

The first stage of grieving brings feelings of emptiness and numbness even though death has been expected, 18-9. Feelings of sorrow and loss may cause family members to weep without control. Because this stage has such a numbing effect on family members, it is helpful if funeral and burial plans have been prearranged.

In the weeks following the death of a loved one, family members pass through another stage. They may feel anxious, fearful, and abandoned by the loved one. They may feel angry that the loved one left them alone. Sometimes a grieving person wants to talk and share memories of the lost loved one. Sometimes he or she wants to sit alone. Family members can help one another through this stage by listening and offering quiet support and understanding when someone needs to talk.

Brief periods of depression are normal after a loss. Talking with other people who have gone through similar experiences can help. Grief support groups may be located by contacting a local mental health agency or religious organization.

People who have mourned the loss of a loved one will gradually accept the loss and adjust to living without that person. However, they

18-9 People experiencing the first stage of grief may have feelings of numbness or disbelief.

will continue to feel times of loss and sadness. Birthdays, anniversaries, or certain events will bring back the pain of the loss.

Friends and family members are important to each other throughout the life cycle. In difficult times, they can provide support and encouragement. They can help each other focus on positive thoughts and memories. They can offer each other love and affection. They can help each other find satisfaction and fulfillment in living.

Review   Section 18:3

1. List four examples of physical decline that can cause problems for the elderly.
2. Give three reasons why the elderly are susceptible to fraudulent sales practices.
3. Describe three community programs that provide care services to the elderly.
4. Describe two techniques used in hospice programs to help people cope with dying.
5. Identify the feelings that are common during the grieving process.

Think It Through

Carmen's Grandparents

Carmen felt concerned as he left his grandparent's home Sunday afternoon. He knew that Grandpa's leg was really bothering him. Convincing his grandfather to go to the doctor hadn't been an easy task. Grandpa was afraid the doctor would put him in a hospital, and he was worried about leaving Grandma home alone. Who would take care of her? What if she forgot something important like turning off the oven?

Carmen's dad feared that the time had come when his parents no longer could live alone. How could the family handle this? His own home was already too small for his family of six. There just was no room for two more people. Also, who would care for Grandma and Grandpa during the day while everyone else was at work or school?

Carmen's dad thought about his brother in California. They had a large house, but that was thousands of miles away. His parents would be far from the friends and community they had known all their lives. He was sure that his parents did not have

enough money to live in an assisted living facility very long. What else could they do? He also thought about his plan to give Carmen some financial help as he started college next semester. He knew he couldn't afford both assisted living for his parents and college for his son.

Questions to Guide Your Thinking

1. What factors did Carmen's dad consider as he thought about his parents' inability to take care of themselves?

2. What alternatives would there be in your community for a family in this situation?

3. How do you think each alternative might affect Carmen, his immediate family, and his grandparents? Consider both the positive and negative aspects of each alternative.

4. What alternative do you think would be best for this family? Explain your answer.

Chapter Summary

Aging is inevitable; so are the effects that go with the aging process. In midlife, when these effects begin to appear, adults often find themselves questioning their purposes and goals for living. Such evaluations can help adults set new goals for the years ahead.

The family continues to change as adults grow older. Two major events may take place during this part of the life cycle: grandparenting and retirement. Many parents with married children become grandparents. At the same time, they may also provide care for aging parents who struggle with failing health and loss of independence.

Retirement brings changes in practically every aspect of life. The extended family continues to be an important resource for adjusting to these changes in the life cycle. Close relationships with children and grandchildren can help adults adjust to the changes that go with aging and retirement. Close relationships in the family can also help members adjust to the grief and loss experienced over a death.

Assess...

Your Knowledge

1. How do the changes of middlescence affect the family system?

2. How do the changes of retirement affect the family system?

3. How is the family system affected by the changes of the elderly years?

Your Understanding

4. How can the family help members cope with the changes of middlescence and keep the family system balanced?

5. How can the family help members cope with the changes of retirement?

6. How can the family adjust to the changes of the elderly years and meet the needs of all family members?

Your Skills

7. What questions would you use to open conversation with an adult going through a midlife crisis?

8. What resources would you use to help make sure an elderly grandparent gets nutritious meals? to help with health care costs?

Think Critically

9. Make a list of activities that you could do with a grandparent or another person of retirement age. For each activity, explain how it could provide mental, social, or physical stimulation for the older adult. *Choice:* Explain how you or other teens could benefit from each activity. *Group option:* Form small groups and present your activities in a song, poem, rap, or visual presentation.

10. **Writing.** Interview a grandparent or another older adult. Ask questions about how their family members help them (or could help them) with different aspects of aging. Summarize the responses and write a paragraph on how aging affects the family system. *Choice:* Present your information in a video or using presentation software.

11. **Writing.** Interview a middle-aged person. Ask questions related to the person's goals for the next 20 years and retirement plans. Discuss the person's goals and plans in a written report. Judge whether you feel this person will be prepared for retirement. Identify any areas in which you think the person might struggle.

12. **Social studies, writing.** Write a paper describing your community thirty years from now, considering the future increases in the older population. Describe how this increase will impact the local economy, health care services, home care services, housing needs, and the job market. *Group option:* Work in small groups, with each group member researching one of the topics. Present your information to the class.

Connect with Your Community

13. Visit a local assisted living facility. Write a paragraph describing your visit. Include a description of the physical conditions of the residents, the activities available to them, and the care they received. Summarize your overall impression of life in an assisted living facility.

14. **Social studies.** Choose an older adult and carry out an activity with him or her. (You may choose an activity you previously listed in #9.) Summarize in a paragraph your feelings about the experience. *Choice:* Share your reflection in a speech to the class.

15. Contact a local agency on aging and identify services that are available in your community to help older adults. Develop a poster describing these services and give it to your local agency on aging for the public to see. *Choice:* Research the Internet to identify the services that are available in your community.

16. **Writing.** Interview a retired person in your community and ask questions about what he or she does to keep active. What resources does your community offer for retired people? Summarize your interview in a written report. Evaluate the person's behavior and hobbies for effectiveness in keeping mentally and physically active. *Group option:* Work with a small group to tally all the resources identified in your community that might attract retired people. Prepare a handout summarizing these resources. *Choice:* Present your summary to your local chamber of commerce to post on their Web site.

Use Technology

17. Identify a new technology that is designed to help older adults keep active. Prepare a report that describes how this technology works and analyze the product for its potential to be effective. *Choice:* Obtain access to the technology and try it out with an older adult.

18. **Research.** Using the Internet, gather information on a hospice program. Prepare a report describing the services offered, their costs, and the qualifications of the people providing the services.

19. **Math.** Inquire at your local social security office for statistics on the average monthly payment for people retiring from various careers. Using a software program, prepare a chart with the statistics for the ten careers that interest you most. *Choice:* In a written paragraph, evaluate what kind of lifestyle these monthly payments will support.

20. **Research.** Using the Internet, research careers that will grow due to expanded services to the older population. Choose five different services. For each, explain the nature of the work, potential employment sites, working conditions, average earnings, training and education needed, and potential job outlook for your community. Present your information in a table. *Group option:* Complete the activity as a group with each team member researching one service.

Connecting with Career Clusters

Human Services

Pathways

- Early Childhood Development & Services
- Counseling & Mental Health Services
- Family & Community Services
- Personal Care Services
- Consumer Services

School Counselor

School counselors help students identify school and career goals that match their interests, abilities, and personality traits. They also help students learn to resolve conflicts, make good decisions, and develop healthful life habits. They work with individual students, small groups, and entire classes.

At the elementary level, counselors help students identify strengths, weaknesses, or special needs. Working with parents, school personnel, and social workers, they help students handle various social, behavioral, and personal problems. They also try to identify cases involving abuse and assist student clubs that oppose drinking and driving, drug use, and tobacco use.

In high school, counselors advise students on career planning, educational and training options, and job-search skills such as résumé writing and interviewing techniques. At the college level, counselors focus on job placement and career development.

School counselors are usually required to have a master's degree and the appropriate certification. Some states also require a teaching certificate.

Career Outlook

A job in this field requires high physical and emotional energy; a strong interest in helping students; the ability to inspire respect, trust, and confidence; and good communication, listening, problem-solving, and conflict-resolution skills.

Employment for school counselors is expected to grow, but job opportunities may be affected by school budget constraints. Median earnings of school counselors averaged $47,530 in 2006. Overall, salaries for school counselors range from $27,200 to $75,900.

Explore

Internet Research

Research the requirements in your state for a school counselor. Identify the coursework needed, schools that offer the training, requirements for practical experience, and the total length of the educational and training period. Contact one of the schools and learn what job opportunities exist in your area.

Job Shadowing

Spend a day with your guidance counselor. Identify various resources counselors use to guide students in their career choices. List these resources and teach how to research a career.

Community Service/Volunteer

See your guidance counselor about becoming involved in peer counseling. Take peer conflict-resolution training and join a peer conflict-resolution team. Help resolve peer conflicts, keeping a journal of your experiences and techniques.

Project

Assist your school counselor with a student club that opposes drinking and driving, drug use, or tobacco use. Become a member of the club and help carry out a project. Complete a report describing the club, its mission, the involvement of the student body, and the goals and effectiveness of the project.

Interview

Interview a counselor in your school or another for advice to students wishing to enter the career field. Find out his or her recommendations for good schools to attend, valuable internship opportunities, and the jobs offering the most prospects for someone eager to work hard and get ahead. Summarize your interview in a report.

Part-Time Job

Seek a part-time job assisting the camp counselor in a youth summer camp or recreation program. Identify the responsibilities of the counselor and the effectiveness of the role you played.

Unit 5
Fulfilling Career and Community Roles

Choosing Your Career Path

Section 19:1
Learning About the World of Work

Section 19:2
Choosing a Career

Section 19:3
The World of Work

Life Sketch

Ilsa watched her teacher count the money from the school carnival. To her nine-year-old eyes, it looked like a huge sum. "I think I'll be a teacher," she whispered to her sister. "I would like to have lots of money."

"Don't be silly," replied twelve-year-old Tanya. "That's not her money. She's only counting it for the school. Why don't you become a rock singer like me? They really make lots of money."

Key Questions

Questions to answer as you study this chapter:

- How does work help people meet life goals?
- What factors should be considered when choosing a career?
- What does it take to be successful in a job search?

Getting Started

Your thoughts about work change as you grow and develop. You may ask yourself, "What type of work do I really want?" In this chapter, you will learn more about work, the career world, and the personal factors that affect career choices. You will learn about the resources available for exploring careers. Knowing how to conduct a job search is a valuable skill that will help you get the job you want. All this information will point you toward a career decision that is right for you.

Chapter Objectives

After studying this chapter, you will be able to

- **list** reasons people give for working.
- **recognize** factors that may influence your career choice.
- **identify** sources of career information.
- **prepare** a career plan.
- **explain** the steps of a job search.

section 19:1

Learning About the World of Work

Sharpen Your Reading

Create a graphic organizer with the heading *Why People Work*. Make branches for each heading in this section. As you read, write key points under the appropriate branches.

Boost Your Vocabulary

Create a chart with each key term listed on the left. In the first column, write your own definition for each term. Then ask a parent, grandparent, or other adult how they would define the term and write the response in the second column. As you read, write the text definition in the third column.

Know Key Terms

work
job
occupation
career
career ladder
lifestyle

Choices must be made about where you will fit into the workplace. You may have a part-time job now. You may be given jobs to do at home, to help out with the work of the family. You may do volunteer work in your community. There are many different types of work. By considering as many different types of work as possible, you will recognize several jobs that interest you.

What Is Work?

Work can be defined as any activity that results in a useful product or service. In many cases, people are paid for their work. However, sometimes work is done for personal reasons rather than money, 19-1. This chapter focuses on work that is part of a job.

A **job** is a position held by a person working to earn a living. You may have several jobs over your lifetime. For instance, you may mow lawns, take fast-food orders, or give piano lessons. For each job you hold, you will have a job title. A job title refers to an **occupation** or type of work. You may be a housekeeper, nursing assistant, nurse, or business manager.

A **career** refers to the work done over several years while holding different jobs within a particular field or area. A career requires careful thought and planning. Usually, each new job builds on the experiences and skills of a previous job. In this way, a person moves up a **career ladder**. Each step on the career ladder builds on the experiences of the previous step.

19-1 Much of the work that people do is for personal needs, satisfaction, or comfort. Often such work is not compensated with money.

Are there some jobs you have held that others might have as a career?

Why Do People Work?

People work for many different reasons. One reason is to earn an income. An income is needed to pay for food, clothing, and shelter—all necessities of life. People also work to satisfy personal needs such as satisfaction and recognition.

Another reason that people work is to support their **lifestyle**. This is the way a person chooses to live. Lifestyle is affected by a person's work and includes the following aspects:

- family relationships
- friendships and social contacts
- the area and neighborhood chosen
- the type of housing and furnishings chosen
- schools attended
- leisure activities enjoyed
- the type of food eaten
- the car(s) driven

A job affects a person's status in the community and, as a result, the friends and social life one has. Work also affects family life. Some jobs require working in the evening or at night. Some require weekend work. Some may require traveling away from home frequently. People who work at night or away from home have less time to spend with family members.

How is your lifestyle affected by the work your family does?

Earning Income

A person's job determines his or her income. Many of your lifestyle choices—clothing, housing, transportation, food, and leisure activities—will be influenced by your income. The following factors can affect a job's pay:

- *Education and training.* Usually work that provides higher pay requires greater training or education, 19-2.

- *Experience.* People with more experience generally have more skills. For their advanced skills and knowledge, they usually receive higher pay.

- *High-demand and high-risk jobs.* Often advances in technology create new jobs faster than workers can be trained to handle them. Until enough workers fill all available jobs, those who are qualified are eagerly sought and well paid. High-risk jobs that involve danger often command higher pay as well.

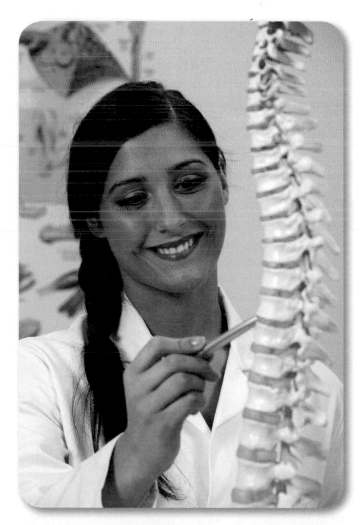

19-2 Doctors are required to have six or more years of education following high school; however, their incomes are above average.

Investigate Further

Identify and describe some high-paying jobs in your community.

Personal Reasons

If you asked several people why they work, you would likely hear different responses. Besides earning an income, they would probably mention some personal reasons for enjoying their work. The following reasons are the most common:

- *Work provides personal satisfaction.* A worker feels a sense of pride when goals are achieved at work. If a worker really enjoys the job, there is great satisfaction in seeing it done well.

- *Work brings recognition.* Other people notice good work and may praise you for your accomplishments. Their respect for you and what you can do increases.

- *Work increases feelings of worth.* By working on something you believe is worthwhile, you feel important, too. Your self-esteem will increase as you succeed at such work.

- *Work provides opportunities for personal growth.* You may be creative in your work. You may sharpen your abilities and learn new skills. Work can help you become a more capable person.

- *Work provides social contacts.* Work often brings you into contact with people who have similar interests. This is why close friendships often develop on the job.

It is not likely that every job you have will fulfill all these reasons for working. As you make career choices, you will need to decide which of these factors are most important to you.

Review Section 19:1

1. Explain what is meant by the term *work*.
2. Explain the relationship between jobs and a career.
3. List three personal reasons people give for enjoying their work.

section 19:2

Choosing a Career

Sharpen Your Reading

Outline this section using the headings as a guide. As you read the section, write an example of how each topic relates to your life.

Boost Your Vocabulary

Ask a guidance counselor if you could take an activities preference inventory to help you choose a career pathway.

Know Key Terms

interests
activities preference inventory
aptitudes
abilities
transferable skills
career clusters
entrepreneurs
career plan
apprenticeship
portfolio

How can you know what type of career to choose? This is an important question as there are so many choices available. Choosing a career requires personal evaluation to see what type of work best suits you. Once you know what type of work you prefer, you can begin gathering information and developing a plan.

Learning About Yourself

How well do you know yourself? Recognizing your unique talents and traits, examining your likes and dislikes, and deciding what you want to achieve can help you find the right career. The following personal factors should be considered when choosing a career:

- personality traits
- values
- goals
- interests
- aptitudes
- abilities

Taking time to assess yourself in each of these areas will help you achieve satisfaction and success in a job.

Personality

If the nature of your work matches your personality traits, you will find it easier to succeed, 19-3. You will also find the work more satisfying. Try to identify your personality traits and choose an occupation that suits them.

Your personality is influenced by several factors, one of which is your temperament. As you read in Chapter 2, your temperament includes your basic patterns for interacting with your environment.

19-3 An outgoing person who likes working with people might enjoy a creative, team-oriented job.

Everyone's personality has both strengths and weaknesses. To experience success, try to match your strong qualities with the demands of your work. You will experience even greater success when you choose work that is not demanding in your weaker areas.

Values

The beliefs or ideals that you feel are important are your personal values. They affect your decisions, actions, and choice of a career.

You may believe it is important to have a job helping others. You may also believe that it is important to work at a job that is challenging or fulfilling. How do you determine which qualities are most important to you? You can try prioritizing them. List the qualities in order of importance, putting those most important first. Ordering your values can help you identify jobs that will match the qualities most meaningful to you. When the work you do matches your values, you will feel greater satisfaction.

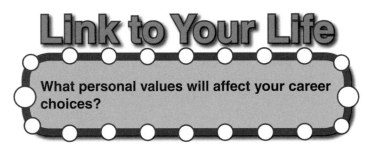

What personal values will affect your career choices?

Goals

Goals are what you want to accomplish in life. They are related to values. Many of the goals you make are based on your values.

Your career choice should help you reach important life goals. That is why it is important to first identify what you really want to do in life. Then you can evaluate a career choice to see if it will help you attain those goals.

What are your work-related goals?

Interests

You will likely enjoy work that you find interesting, 19-4. Therefore, identifying your interests can help you choose a career area. **Interests** are the subjects, activities, or events that a person enjoys. Do you have a favorite class or subject? What hobbies or activities do you enjoy? How do you like to spend your free time? Your answers can help you identify the areas in which your interests lie and the skills you enjoy using most.

In all occupations, a worker is involved to some degree with people, ideas (data and information), and objects. For instance, a homebuilder uses a blueprint that provides information about how the house will be built. The builder also works with people in getting all the materials and constructing the house. Then the builder works with materials and tools to carry out the plan. Making sure the customer is satisfied also requires communicating with people.

Although many jobs involve all three areas, they usually focus on just one. To find an enjoyable career, you will need to know which area interests you most. It is also helpful to know which area you like least.

Interests are learned. They also change as you mature. You really do not know if you have an interest in something unless you are exposed to it. That is why it is helpful to meet new people and try new activities to see what your interests really are. Try talking to people about why they chose their careers or what they like about their work.

Another way to explore your interests is to take an **activities preference inventory**. A preference inventory is designed to help you learn whether your interests are centered on people, ideas, or objects. Your high school guidance department will likely have such a test available.

Investigate Further

What are some jobs in your community that deal mainly with people? with ideas? with objects?

19-4 When work relates to your interests, you enjoy it more. If you work with children, it is very important that you have an interest in their well-being.

Aptitudes

Another factor affecting career choice is your aptitudes. **Aptitudes** are your natural talents. You learn certain skills quickly and easily because you have an aptitude for them, 19-5. In other areas, it may be more difficult for you to learn.

Aptitudes make a difference in what a person is able to learn quickly and easily. Consider your aptitudes when looking at careers. Your guidance counselor can help you measure your aptitudes so you can recognize which careers could be a good match.

Link to Your Life

What are some skills that you are able to learn quickly and easily? What are some skills that are more difficult for you to learn?

Abilities

The final personal factor affecting career choice is abilities. Your **abilities** are skills that you learn and develop. Everyone has certain abilities as a result of training and practice.

19-5 A person with an aptitude for learning computer languages may pursue a career as a computer programmer.

Different jobs require different sets of skills. **Transferable skills** are basic job skills that can be applied in various work situations. Thinking, communicating, problem solving, working well with people, and leading are some examples. The more transferable skills you have, the greater are the number of work opportunities that will be open to you.

Use What You Learn

To identify your abilities, list some of your greatest accomplishments. Then think about what skills you used to achieve those accomplishments. Are any of your skills transferable?

Learning About Careers

Identifying your personality strengths, values, goals, interests, aptitudes, and abilities are important steps in career planning. They reveal your strengths so you can determine the type of work that would best match them. The next step in planning a career is to gather information about careers and occupations. When investigating different career choices, the following factors should be considered:

- job responsibilities
- personality traits needed
- places where employment can be obtained
- skills, training, and education required
- employment outlook
- earnings potential
- working conditions
- potential for advancement

Evaluating each of these factors can help you choose a career that will match your personality and skills and provide opportunities for growth.

Researching Careers

Using the career clusters can help you learn about different careers. **Career clusters** are 16 broad groupings of occupational and career specialties, 19-6. Each cluster includes several career directions, called *career pathways*. All the career choices within a pathway require a set of common knowledge and skills. The career clusters are important because they link school-based learning to career success.

Your school counselor can assist you in identifying the courses you should take to prepare for a career in a certain pathway. Counselors can also provide data on job descriptions, education and training requirements, and average salaries.

Using the Internet is another way to learn about careers. Career information guides published by the government are available online as well as at many locations, including libraries and government offices. Some examples include the following:

- The *Occupational Information Network* (O*NET) serves as the United States' primary source of occupational information. Using the O*NET Web site, http://online.onetcenter.org, you can look for an occupation that matches your skills. You can also search by career clusters, by high growth industries, and by descriptors such as tools and technology.

- The *Occupational Outlook Handbook* (www.bls.gov/oco) describes various occupations, including the education and training needed. It also lists potential pay scales, working conditions, and future prospects for jobs.

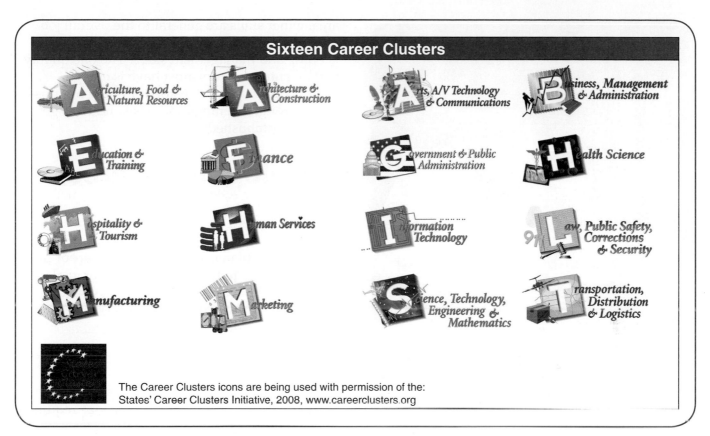

Sixteen Career Clusters

Agriculture, Food & Natural Resources

Architecture & Construction

Arts, A/V Technology & Communications

Business, Management & Administration

Education & Training

Finance

Government & Public Administration

Health Science

Hospitality & Tourism

Human Services

Information Technology

Law, Public Safety, Corrections & Security

Manufacturing

Marketing

Science, Technology, Engineering & Mathematics

Transportation, Distribution & Logistics

The Career Clusters icons are being used with permission of the: States' Career Clusters Initiative, 2008, www.careerclusters.org

19-6 All occupations in the U.S. workforce are addressed within these 16 career clusters.

- CareerOneStop (www.careeronestop.org) is sponsored by the U.S. Department of Labor. It features information on job trends, employment outlook, salary ranges, and education and training requirements.

The *U.S. Department of Labor, Employment and Training Administration*, (www.doleta.gov) also provides career resources and links to related Web sites for skills assessments and career exploration.

Investigate Further

What careers match your values, goals, interests, aptitudes, and abilities?

Factors Affecting Job Outlook

Job outlook is an important factor in choosing a career. You may not be able to find a job if you plan a career in a field with few jobs and many workers.

The *Occupational Outlook Handbook*, O*NET, and CareerOneStop provide information about industries that are growing. You can also learn what skills and knowledge are required for these jobs.

High growth industries are those expected to provide many new jobs. Most of these incorporate new technologies and innovative ideas. As a technology spreads to various industries, new jobs are continually created. That usually means jobs using the old technology disappear.

Career opportunities are also affected by changes in society and the world. For instance, as the older population increases, more social and health services are needed, 19-7. Choosing a career in an expanding field will increase the likelihood of finding a job when you have finished your training.

Link to Your Life

What high growth industries interest you?

19-7 An aging population increases the demand for workers in the health care field.

Considering Entrepreneurship

Have you ever thought of owning your own business? Perhaps you like the idea of being your own boss and setting your own hours. The harder you work, the more you might earn. The opportunity to make all the decisions, make a long-term investment, and reap high rewards is available to entrepreneurs. **Entrepreneurs** are people who are self-employed and earn incomes through their own businesses.

Entrepreneurship involves starting and running your own business. To succeed, a wide range of skills is needed to make the business a success. Some skills are specific to the subject area. Other skills are general to the overall job of operating a business, such as good record keeping and management skills. The one quality that all entrepreneurs must have is energy. Entrepreneurs work nonstop for many months—often through evenings and weekends—to get a business established.

Developing a Career Plan

After deciding what type of work suits you, developing a plan is the next step. A **career plan** is a list of steps to take to reach a career goal. It includes short-term and long-term goals for extracurricular activities, work experience, and education and training, 19-8.

Education and Training

While in high school, you gain some training and skills for work. However, most jobs require further education or more specialized training after high school. There are several options for getting the training and education you will need, depending on the career you choose.

- *An apprenticeship program.* In an **apprenticeship**, the worker learns skills and gains experience while under the supervision of an experienced worker. Some classroom learning may also be required.

- *The military.* The military provides training that can be used in both military and civilian careers. However, the student must stay in the military for the number of years required by the terms of his or her contract.

- *A technical college.* One or two years at a technical college can provide the training needed for many jobs.

- *A four-year degree program.* To be a professional in many occupational fields, a degree from a college or university is needed.

The amount of training and education needed can influence your choice of careers. Your career plan can help you estimate how much time, money, and effort it will take to pursue a certain career.

Career Plan for a Psychologist	
Short-Term Goals	
Education and training	• Take courses in science, math, English, and psychology.
Extracurricular activities	• Participate in math and science competitions. • Participate in student organizations that conduct research-based activities.
Work and volunteer experiences	• Job shadow with a psychologist. • Observe a psychologist administering a standardized achievement test. • Volunteer as a tutor for special education students. • Volunteer or work at a day care center, hospital, mental health clinic, or shelter.
Long-Term Goals	
Education and training	• Earn a bachelor's degree in psychology. • Earn a master's degree. • Earn a doctorate degree. • Complete state certification or licensing requirements.
Extracurricular activities	• Join a psychology student association. • Obtain student membership in a professional association for psychologists.
Work and volunteer experiences	• Become a volunteer research assistant in the psychology department. • Obtain an internship in the psychology field. • Volunteer or work at a hospital, mental health clinic, community center, or shelter.

19-8 A career plan can help you stay focused on the steps toward your career goals.

Student and Professional Organizations

Student and professional organizations offer the opportunity to develop skills while learning about future careers. Participation in such organizations builds transferable skills, including leadership, communication, and problemsolving. Student organizations usually focus on a certain career area, such as business, marketing, health, or trade occupations.

Family, Career, and Community Leaders of America, Inc. (FCCLA) is a student organization that prepares students to be leaders in their families, careers, and communities. Through involvement in FCCLA, you can learn about careers in family and consumer sciences.

Some professional organizations offer memberships at the student level. Being active in a professional organization can help you stay informed about job trends and advancements in your career field. In addition, you will be able to meet professionals in your field who can offer guidance about your career plan.

Portfolios

As you put your career plan into action, it is important to keep a record of your activities, education, and training. A **portfolio** is a collection of materials that document your achievements over time. When preparing a portfolio, include items that demonstrate your academic and career skills, 19-9.

Items to Include in a Portfolio

- Career summary and goals
- Copy of résumé
- List of references
- Letters of recommendation that document career-related skills
- Certificates of completion
- Work samples that show mastery of certain skills
- Writing samples that demonstrate communication skills
- List of awards and special honors
- Descriptions of volunteer work
- List of memberships in student organizations and related activities
- Transcripts, licenses, and certifications

19-9 Your portfolio should demonstrate your career skills to potential employers.

Link to Your Life

What education and training opportunities are you willing to explore as you prepare for a career?

Review Section 19:2

1. List four personal factors that could influence your career choice.
2. Explain the difference between a career cluster and a career pathway.
3. Identify two sources of job outlook information.
4. What do entrepreneurs need in order to establish a business?
5. What are the goals that should be included in a career plan?
6. Explain how a need for training and education could influence your career choice.

section 19:3

The World of Work

Sharpen Your Reading

For each heading in this section, summarize the key points you could share with a friend who is trying to find a job or succeed at a new job.

Boost Your Vocabulary

Make a list of three people you could use as references. Include contact information for each person.

Know Key Terms

networking
résumé
cover letter
interview
references
teamwork
business etiquette
business ethics
sexual harassment
equal opportunity

Right now you spend little or no time in the workplace. During your adult life, most of your time will be spent in the workplace. That is why taking the time now to prepare for a satisfying career choice is so important.

The Job Search

With the right preparation, you can find and secure the job that is best for you. The following steps will help you begin:

- *Gather the information you need to know about yourself.* See 19-10.
- *Find out what jobs are available.* Check newspapers, online job listings, and company and government Web sites.
- *Network with family, friends, and people in your career field.* **Networking** is talking to family members, friends, and other people you know about possible job openings. They may hear about job openings or know someone who works for a company that interests you. Membership in a professional organization can also provide networking opportunities.
- *Identify employers who offer the job you want.* You may locate this information through a library, the Internet, or even the Yellow Pages.
- *Research the requirements needed for each position you consider.* The key requirements are usually listed in each job posting. If no opening is posted, try to identify some of the organization's needs through Internet or library research.

Factors to Know About Yourself
• Personal needs and values
• Commitments
• Life and career goals
• Interests
• Aptitudes and skills
• Noteworthy achievements
• Strengths and limitations
• Memorable experiences
• Personal energy level
• Preferred lifestyle

19-10 **Knowing these factors can help you decide what type of job is best for you.**

Think More About It
What do you think would be the best source of information about job openings in which you might be interested?

Preparing Your Résumé

When you want to apply for a job, you will send a résumé. A **résumé** is a summary of your skills, training, education, and past work experiences. A résumé allows an employer to quickly evaluate an applicant's qualifications, 19-11. Most résumés include the following parts:

- *Worker identification*—your name, address, telephone number, and e-mail address.
- *Work objective*—a statement about the position you seek.
- *Education*—the high school(s) attended and the certificates or diplomas received or in progress. (College graduates need not list their high school.)
- *Experience*—a job history, listing the years worked, title of your jobs, and duties performed.
- *Activities and organizations*—the groups' names and your involvement, achievements, and leadership roles.
- *Special skills*—a list of your special skills relating to the job you seek.

Denon P. Capikrolanka
199 Eighth Avenue
Menomonie, WI 54751
715-555-0123
denonpc@email.com

Employment Objective	Full-time summer employment as an inventory clerk.
Work Experience	**Inventory Clerk** *June–August, 20XX* Menomonie Groceries, Menomonie, WI Received inventory, entered inventory data on computer, stocked shelves, trained new employees. **Stock Clerk** *June–August, 20XX* Menomonie Groceries, Menomonie, WI Stocked shelves with groceries.
Education	Menomonie High School, Menomie, WI, Junior, 20XX
Honors and Activities	Honor roll student President, Computer Club, 20XX Member, Computer Club, 20XX–20XX
Special Skills	Computer programming, database maintenance, graphic design.

19-11 All résumés follow a basic format to allow employers to quickly judge a job candidate's abilities.

Applying for a Job

When you find an interesting job, you will want to apply for it. Usually this requires writing a **cover letter** and sending it with your résumé to the contact person listed in the job posting.

Your cover letter should clearly state the position you seek in about three paragraphs. Indicate how you learned about the position. Then state the foremost reasons why you qualify for the job. Mention the qualities or experiences that are most likely to attract the employer's interest. Do not describe them in the same way the résumé does.

End your letter with a request for an interview, and thank the employer for considering you for the position. Send your résumé with the letter.

Filling Out Application Forms

At some point before or during the interview session, you will be asked to fill out an application form. Completing this form neatly and accurately is important. This form is a test itself. It represents you to the employer and demonstrates how well you follow written directions.

When filling out the form, do not skip any questions. If a question does not relate to you, write "does not apply." Be sure to answer all other questions accurately.

You may be asked for specific names, dates, and addresses—details beyond the facts on your résumé. Create a list of facts about your education, work experience, and outside activities. This list is often called a *personal fact sheet*. Keep this fact sheet with you and refer to it when extra details are needed, such as when filling out application forms. By keeping a list of detailed facts, you will be able to answer any question that arises.

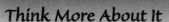

Think More About It
What might an employer think if you do not bring a pen to complete an application form?

Interviewing for a Job

An **interview** gives the employer an opportunity to talk with job applicants. Before an interview, do some homework about the position you are seeking, 19-12. Be able to explain why you want to work for that organization. Be prepared to tell the interviewer what you will be able to do for him or her. If you know what skills and qualities the employer wants, you can stress your strengths in these areas. Also, prepare some questions that show genuine interest.

Be ready to provide a list of references if the interviewer requests it. **References** are people who have direct knowledge of you and your past work record. For references, you should choose at least three people who could give you a good recommendation. (Do not include relatives.) Before you list people as references, be sure to ask for their permission. List your references on a separate sheet of paper, including their names, titles, office addresses, phone numbers and e-mail addresses.

Your appearance at the interview can make a difference in whether you get the job. Cleanliness, neatness, and appropriate apparel are important in any interview. As a rule, observe what the employees of that company wear to work and dress slightly better for your interview.

Send a short thank you note to the interviewer immediately after the interview. You can express appreciation for the interviewer's time and thank him or her for considering you. Your thank you note may be the final step that gets you the job. It shows that you know how to treat people with kindness and respect.

Link to Your Life

What information would you like to know about a company before working there?

Job Success

Most people want to succeed in their work. Learning all the responsibilities of a new job takes time, so do not be too critical of yourself at first.

Interview Tips
Prepare for the interview
• Learn all you can about the employer.
• Prepare some questions to ask about the job.
• Take materials needed for the interview in a folder: pen, résumé, list of references, personal fact sheet to fill out application form, and a notepad with your list of questions.
• Prepare to answer questions the interviewer might ask, such as these:
• Can you start by telling me about yourself?
• Why do you want this job?
• What are your strengths and weaknesses?
• Are you willing to work evenings and weekends?
• What are your future plans?
• Practice your answers to these questions before the interview.
Make a positive impression.
• Wear neat, clean clothes that help you look your best.
• Comb and neatly style your hair.
• Shave or trim a beard.
• Wear makeup sparingly.
• Be sure hands and fingernails are clean.
• Brush your teeth and be sure your breath is fresh.
Be on time for the interview.
• Know the exact time and place of the interview.
• Allow extra travel time to arrive a few minutes early.

19-12 Being prepared, well-groomed, and on time will help you interview successfully.

It may take several weeks to adjust to a new job. The key is to stick to it and work hard at learning your duties.

Of course, your job will likely have some tasks that seem petty and small. Most jobs do. After a period of time, you will be able to see your accomplishments and evaluate your progress, 19-13.

Performance Ratings

Feelings of job success will be influenced by the performance ratings you receive from your supervisor. Most employees are evaluated formally (in writing) once or twice a year. They are rated on how well they do their job and work cooperatively with others. A rating scale of excellent, good, fair, or poor for each area is commonly used.

Besides doing your job well, your conduct on the job is important, too. Being dependable, loyal, getting along with coworkers and supervisors, and following company rules—all merit a high rating.

Succeeding as a Team Member

Learning teamwork is very important. **Teamwork** means everyone does their part to help the group succeed. It requires that members work cooperatively, sharing information and

Keys to Job Success
• Perform your responsibilities with competence.
• Be open to learn from criticism.
• Follow directions.
• Be cooperative with supervisors and coworkers.
• Be courteous; show concern for others.
• Be dependable; avoid unnecessary absenteeism.
• Keep a neat, clean appearance.
• Look for opportunities to advance in your career.

19-13 Positive personality traits can be your key to job success.

keeping each other informed, 19-14. Team members must give constructive input and accept recommendations from each other. When group decisions must be made, the welfare of the whole company must be the first consideration.

Link to Your Life

What activities are you involved in that build teamwork skills?

Business Etiquette

Being mannerly on the job is expected of all employees. Showing respect, being polite, and taking time to listen and communicate clearly is considered appropriate **business etiquette**. Using business etiquette will help you become successful.

One aspect of business etiquette that you will probably use often is introducing people to others properly. Always use the name first of the person to whom you should show the most respect. It may be the company president, a well-respected customer, your supervisor, or an older coworker. For example, you would say, "Mr. Carmichael, I would like to introduce to you my friend, Melissa Bach. She is a reporter with our daily newspaper.

19-14 Working in groups in class can help you develop teamwork skills that help you succeed on a job.

Melissa, this is Mr. Carmichael, the owner of our company." By making proper introductions, you show your ability to treat people respectfully.

Business Ethics

Good character traits are highly valued by employers. When these traits influence business activities, a company and its employees are said to have high standards of **business ethics**. Honesty and integrity are apparent when you do what you say you will. Your teammates and supervisor know that you stand by your words. You do not lie to customers, clients, or coworkers. You do not steal company property such as office supplies. You do not steal time from the company by leaving early or taking extra long breaks.

Employee conduct that reflects high moral principles is important to employers. Companies expect employees to treat everyone in the workplace with respect. They especially ask all employees to avoid behavior that may be viewed as **sexual harassment**. This is unwelcome or unwanted advances, requests for favors, or other verbal or physical conduct of a sexual nature. All forms of sexual harassment are illegal and should be reported to the proper authority within the company. The company handbook given to new employees usually lists the proper procedures for reporting sexual harassment. It also summarizes a company's rules and policies.

Fairness and a sense of justice are important in job decisions that impact others. Employees have a better attitude toward work if they feel they are treated fairly. This is the basis of equal opportunity, which is required by law. **Equal opportunity** forbids the discrimination of workers based on race, color, sex, national origin, age, or disability. Opportunities in the workplace should be open to all qualified individuals. Salaries should be equal for those who perform similar jobs. Companies that focus on workers' abilities report greater loyalty and productivity from their employees.

Think More About It
How can you demonstrate high standards of business ethics?

Terminating Employment

Hard work on the job pays off. It will help you succeed on the job and also help you get a good recommendation when it is time to leave. That is your main goal as you prepare to take another job, moving up the career ladder. You want a good recommendation from your employer to add to your file.

Giving Notice

A two-week notice of termination from employment is accepted as a standard of courtesy in most jobs. Some jobs require more than that. For instance, a teacher is required to sign a contract or an intent to return early in the year. In most cases, employers like to have enough time to fill your position with your replacement by the time you leave, 19-15.

Asking for a Reference

Once you have given written notice of your intent to leave your job, plan to continue working throughout that remaining period. It may be tempting to come in late or skip work when you know the end is near, but your reputation as a dependable worker is at stake. Keep a positive attitude and continue to put forth full effort at your job. Your boss will appreciate it, and your recommendation will show it. Be sure to ask your boss for a written recommendation or reference before you leave so you can add it to your work file.

19-15 Doing your best, even on your last day of work, will persuade your boss to highly recommend you to future employers.

Review Section 19:3

1. List three sources of job leads.
2. What are the parts of a basic résumé?
3. Briefly explain what to write in a cover letter.
4. Describe how to prepare for an interview.
5. List four behaviors that will help you succeed on the job.

Think It Through

Krista's Career Choice

Krista hurried down to the high school guidance office. She had an appointment with a career specialist from the U.S. Army who was visiting the school. She was anxious to discuss careers in her area of interest.

Krista had always been interested in what she called "crawly critters." As a child, she loved to catch caterpillars and put them in a jar. She would watch them eat up the leaves in the jar and eventually spin a cocoon. Her terrarium was home for salamanders, frogs, and toads—whenever she could catch them. She was always careful to treat them gently, for she had great respect for all living things.

Her biology class had really confirmed her interest in living creatures. She did well in that class, finding it easy to memorize all the many details that were required. She had also learned some techniques for studying and classifying her collection of flying insects.

Her biology teacher had asked her to serve as a guide for elementary school field trips in the environmental park. She enjoyed sharing her interest in living things with the children. She would guide the children through the park, pointing out the different species of insects and animals. Then she always ended the tour with a display of her bug collections.

Questions to Guide Your Thinking

1. From this description, what can you tell about Krista's personality? Include her patterns for responding to the environment intellectually, socially, emotionally, and physically.

2. What aptitudes and skills can you identify for Krista?

3. Identify as many career opportunities as you can that would match Krista's interests, personality, aptitudes, and skills. How many of these could she pursue in the U.S. Army?

4. Choose one career that you think Krista would like the most. Describe what work she would do. Explain the training or education she would need. Identify five different potential employers (agencies, companies, or institutions) who employ persons in that occupation.

Chapter Summary

People work for different reasons, such as obtaining income or personal satisfaction. Work can present opportunities for growth. It can bring recognition and increased feelings of worth. The work that you do in your future occupation can help you meet these goals if it is interesting, worthwhile, and a good match with your personality, aptitudes, and abilities.

The career clusters are helpful in identifying broad areas of interest and outlining the knowledge and skills you will need. Career information can be found on the Internet and through your school counseling office. When researching careers, job outlook and entrepreneurship opportunities should be considered. Developing a career plan will help you put your research into action and achieve your career goals.

Being successful in the workplace requires knowing how to find and apply for a job and successfully interview for it. Once a job is obtained, doing the best work possible will help you keep it and advance within your field.

Assess...

Your Knowledge

1. What are the reasons why people work?

2. What factors should a person consider when choosing a career?

Your Understanding

3. How can career choices affect the ability to reach life goals?

4. How can the career clusters help you choose a career?

Your Skills

5. Analyze your personal characteristics—personality, values, goals, interests, preferences for people, ideas, or objects, aptitudes, and abilities—and identify one or more careers that match your strengths.

6. Develop a career plan for a career in a high-growth industry.

7. Complete a personal résumé.

Think Critically

8. Identify four goals that a young adult in your community may have for his or her career. List four possible obstacles to reaching these goals. Then determine four resources that could help the individual reach his or her goals. Present your information in a table. *Choice:* Present your information in a visual drawing or a song.

9. *Writing.* Assess your own personality traits, values, goals, interests, aptitudes, and abilities, and match them to at least three different jobs. Identify the career clusters that relate to the jobs that interest you. In a paper, explain how the characteristics of each job seem ideal for you.

10. Analyze three career areas related to working with individuals and families and identify personality (or temperament) traits that would benefit workers in these careers. *Group option:* Work in a small group and present a skit that demonstrates how certain personality traits would be useful when working with individuals and families.

11. *Financial literacy.* Analyze your lifestyle expectations. Identify a house you would like to own, a car you would like to drive, vacations you would like to take, the number of children you would like to raise, and other aspects of your desired lifestyle. Estimate the average salary needed today to live that lifestyle, and identify five careers that provide it. Write a paper relating your lifestyle expectations to the job you plan to have.

Connect with Your Community

12. Visit a guidance counselor at your school to learn the procedures that can be used to help students identify areas of work that match individual interests, personality, and aptitudes. Identify three postsecondary institutions that provide training in a career area that interests you. *Choice:* Develop a career plan using the information provided by your guidance counselor.

13. **Writing.** Obtain a list of jobs that are open in your community. Choose one job that looks interesting to you. Write a letter of application to that employer, but do not mail it. Instead, submit the letter and a copy of your résumé to your teacher.

14. **Social studies.** Interview a worker from one of the following areas that interests you: a person who works mostly with people, ideas, or objects. Summarize your interview in a report and describe the work performed by the person. Then explain which of the reasons for working are met in the person's work. *Group option:* Work with a partner to complete this activity.

15. **Social studies.** Identify a person in your community who works in a career that interests you. Contact the person and request permission for a day of job-shadowing him or her at work. (If permission is granted, have your school office arrange the job-shadowing experience.) Afterward, write a report describing the various tasks you observed the person doing. Include in your report a description of the specific personality characteristics that help this person succeed on the job. *Choice:* Document your job shadowing experience by taking pictures with a digital camera. Take photos that show the work environment and various job tasks. Create an electronic presentation about the experience and present it to the class.

Use Technology

16. **Writing.** On the Internet, locate a career assessment survey. Take the survey to identify careers that match your interests, abilities, and personality. Print out a copy of the results of the survey. Reflect on the results of the survey in a paragraph, summarizing which of your personal strengths matches one of the careers. *Choice:* Take several different surveys and create a chart that compares the results of each.

17. Assess your interests, aptitudes, and abilities. Gather information related to past and current work and volunteer experiences. Write a résumé emphasizing your skills, personal qualities, courses taken, and experiences that would attract an employer's attention. Using a computer, create and print a final copy of your résumé. *Choice:* Prepare an electronic résumé that could be e-mailed to prospective employers. Use the Internet to find guidelines to follow when creating an electronic résumé.

18. **Research.** Using the Internet, research a career cluster that interests you. Identify five possible occupations within the field, and describe the type of work done in each. List the aptitudes, abilities, and training or education required for each occupation. Also, identify the personality traits needed in each occupation. Present the information in a chart in a table format.

19. **Financial literacy, social studies.** Use the Internet to explore potential jobs throughout the United States and other parts of the world. Select five occupations available in different countries. For each occupation, compare salary ranges in the U.S. to that offered in at least four other countries. Prepare a chart illustrating the comparisons. *Group option:* Work in a small group and have each person work on a different country.

Chapter 20

Balancing Family and Work

Section 20:**1**
Work Patterns

Section 20:**2**
Managing Multiple Roles

Key Questions

Questions to answer as you study this chapter:

- **How can a person balance family and work goals?**

- **How can a person find quality child care?**

Chapter Objectives

After studying this chapter, you will be able to

- **describe** various work patterns for men and women.

- **identify** factors that may affect a family's choice of work patterns.

- **explain** how families can manage multiple roles.

- **describe** various substitute child care arrangements.

- **evaluate** child care services for age appropriate child care.

Life Sketch

When her mother graduated from college, Rita was very proud. The whole family attended the graduation ceremony. Her mother looked so happy as she marched down the aisle in her cap and gown! The job she got as a result of her degree meant more money for the family to spend. They were able to take a family vacation. With their mother working, Rita and her brother Jon both had extra chores to do to help the family. Each night they traded meal, cleanup, and laundry tasks. However, Rita didn't mind because the benefits of her mother's job made up for any extra work.

Lollie lived next door. She did not feel so positive about her mother's job. In fact, she resented it. She hated to come home after school to an empty house. She was alone until her dad arrived at 6 p.m. She was supposed to do homework and housework until then, but she felt too lonely to do anything. Instead, she sat and watched TV to make the time pass quickly. Lollie felt like her parents were always working. She wished her parents could spend more time with her.

Getting Started

Decisions about balancing family and work have different effects on children as well as adults. In Rita's family, both parents working outside the home had a positive effect on the whole family. In Lollie's case, the same circumstances had a negative effect.

Why the difference? Every child is unique and may respond differently to the same situation. Also, parents are unique, too. They have their own personalities, so their responses to the pressures of work and family differ. Families have different resources and skills for managing them. All these factors need to be considered when families make decisions about work patterns.

section 20:1

Work Patterns

Sharpen Your Reading

As you read this section, identify an example of someone you know who fits each work pattern. After reading, share your examples with a partner.

Boost Your Vocabulary

Contact the human resources department of a company and interview them about family-friendly options for their employees. Ask questions using the key terms in this section.

Know Key Terms

flexible scheduling
job sharing
maternity leave
paternity leave
childrearing leave

Families have many factors to consider when making work pattern choices. These include your family goals and values and your expectations for work. The birth of children, employer policies that benefit the work of the family, the roles that family members take, and the earning potential of each family member also affect choices related to work patterns.

Work Patterns for Men

Most men follow *conventional work patterns.* They start working full-time after completing their education. Whether married or single, many work until retirement age or longer. Their work history may be broken by periods of unemployment or changes in jobs. However, they are expected to return to the job market as soon as possible. In general, men are expected to be wage earners so long as they are productive and healthy.

In recent years, some men have chosen an *unconventional work pattern.* In this pattern, the roles for men and women are reversed. The wives are committed to building careers, while husbands spend their time caring for the family, 20-1. However, this work pattern is less common than other types.

20-1 When husbands choose an unconventional work pattern, they are the primary caregivers for the family.

Work Patterns for Women

While men generally follow a consistent work pattern throughout life, the same is not true for women. Depending on their circumstances, most women follow one of three work patterns.

Conventional

When women first started working outside the home, few chose this option as a permanent work pattern. This pattern is similar to the conventional work pattern most men follow. Today, however, increasing numbers of women are choosing to work from the time they finish their education until retirement.

Career to Family-Focused

Some women start work when they leave school and work until they marry or have children. Then they quit their jobs and become full-time homemakers. Women who choose this work pattern tend to be very involved in the work of the family and raising children. They are often involved in their children's education and volunteer work in the community.

Although being a full-time homemaker is considered a work pattern, a homemaker is not classified in government statistics as a working person. The reason is work benefiting the family does not earn an income. This does not mean a homemaker's work has no value. Instead, the opposite is true. Work within and for the family includes such tasks as housekeeping, laundry service, food service, child care, and preschool teaching. These and other homemaker tasks command a wage when the work is done in the workplace for others.

Interrupted Work

An interrupted work pattern is quite common for women. They devote full-time attention to their careers after leaving school, then to their families when children arrive, 20-2. At a later time, they resume their careers. The length of time they stay out of the work field varies. Some may take a maternity leave and then return to work. The length of a maternity leave may be six

20-2 An interrupted work pattern is more common for women than men.

weeks to three months or even longer, depending on the employer. Others may wait until their children are older before they resume their careers.

Think More About It

What impact would it have on our society if work within and for the family earned wages?

Dual-Career Family Work Patterns

Both spouses pursuing careers is called a *dual-career family*. Both work outside the home to earn income. Their jobs place demands on their time, energy, skills, and other resources. In addition, they are responsible for the work of the family. When dual-career families include children, child care must be found while the parents are at work. The home still needs to be managed and household tasks must be done. For these families, balancing family needs and work demands is very challenging.

Choosing a Work Pattern

One work pattern may interest you more than another. One may match your expectations for the roles you will take in the future. Once you marry, however, choices about work patterns become influenced by your partner's desires as well. Couples need to share their thoughts and feelings about work patterns before they consider marriage. During the engagement period, values and goals for work should be discussed. A couple should also discuss their views about work and child care issues as well as their expectations for work.

When children are older, they should also be included in work pattern decisions since they are affected by the choices made. Children may be required to do extra household chores or care for siblings. Positive attitudes are fostered when children are involved in the decision making. It helps when each person can see how the decision will benefit the whole family.

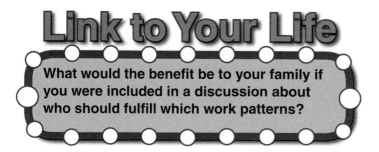

What would the benefit be to your family if you were included in a discussion about who should fulfill which work patterns?

Goals and Values

Choices about family work patterns are influenced by what the family members value highly and want to achieve. Most families want to meet their basic needs for food, clothing, shelter, health care, and transportation. Just meeting basic needs often requires both parents

to earn incomes. Single-parent families often have incomes too low to support their families.

Some people value their work highly and regard it as important to their lives. They like the opportunities for growth, creativity, or self-expression their work provides. Social stimulation or the mental challenge is important. They enjoy opportunities to benefit others through their work. Others place a very high value on being a full-time parent, and make work choices that help them do that.

The Birth of Children

The birth of children significantly affects a family's work patterns. Some families choose to have one parent consistently care for the young children. Other families adjust their work schedules so parents can take turns being home with the children.

The availability of good child care may also affect a family's choice of work patterns. If a family cannot find satisfactory child care during the hours it is needed, the demands of family and work are difficult to balance. Sometimes a parent will choose to provide child care for his or her own children as well as others. In this way, families care for their children while earning extra income.

Employer Policies

Employer policies have a direct effect on a family's choice of work patterns. Most policies set fairly rigid schedules—generally eight-hour workdays, five days a week. Workers must work at the time and place specified by the employer. With rigid work schedules, a worker may need to request special leave to take care of some family responsibilities, such as doctor or dentist appointments. Company policies that allow personal leave without penalizing the employee's work record are helpful to the family.

Some companies offer **flexible scheduling**, which allows workers to choose the hours they work, within reason. For example, employees must be at their work sites during core periods, such as 10 a.m. to noon, Monday through Thursday. Then they do the rest of their work at whatever hours suit them. Such flexibility can help families adjust their schedules so one parent is always home with the children.

Job sharing is another alternative to a rigid 40-hour work week. With this work arrangement, a full-time job is split between two people. This makes more part-time work available to those who want it. Job sharing offers the benefits of working, but allows more time for parenting and household tasks.

Some employers even make child care services available to employees through work-sponsored child care centers, 20-3. They may also have special arrangements when children of employees are ill. These services are extremely helpful because many child care centers do not allow sick children to attend.

Opportunities that permit parents to be away from work while involved in full-time parenting for a specified period have certain titles. **Maternity leave** is when a mother is away from her job to give birth and recover from it. **Paternity leave** is the period when a father is away from his job immediately following the birth of his child. A **childrearing leave** is a longer period of time that a parent may be absent from work to provide full-time care for a young child. Company policies that support employee efforts to care for their families help workers meet both family and work demands.

Think More About It
Which family-friendly work policies do you think are most essential for an employer to have?

20-3 Child care made available by an employer can help workers meet their family and work responsibilities.

The Family and Medical Leave Act

The Family and Medical Leave Act helps parents balance work and family responsibilities. It applies to employers with 50 or more workers, so not all employees are covered. This law allows workers to take up to 12 weeks off without pay during any 12 months for the following reasons:

- having and caring for a baby
- adopting a child or adding a foster child to the family
- caring for a sick child, spouse, or parent
- being unable to work because of serious illness

Roles of Family Members

The roles that spouses take can affect their choices about work patterns. One spouse may be the main wage earner; the other may work part time and carry most of the roles that go with the work of the family—cleaning, making meals, shopping, and doing laundry.

Some families expect the husband and wife to have equal roles as wage earners. Their incomes are considered to be equally important to the family. Other roles of homemaking and providing child care are also shared equally.

Earning Potential

In many families, the potential income of each spouse is a major factor in choices about work. For instance, when a family earns two incomes, they have a higher amount of taxable income. Therefore, they are taxed at a higher rate. Paying more income tax reduces some of the take-home portion of the second income. The cost of child care also reduces the amount of money a second worker actually adds to the family income.

Sometimes families decide that the amount of money left over after taxes and extra expenses is not enough. The family may not benefit from trying to balance the extra demands on time and energy when both spouses work. For other families, the extra income is needed for family expenses, even if the income is small.

Review Section 20:1

1. Briefly describe three different work patterns for women.
2. Explain the term *dual-career family*.
3. List five factors that may affect a family's choice of work patterns.
4. For what four reasons may a person take a work leave under the Family and Medical Leave Act?

section 20:2

Managing Multiple Roles

Sharpen Your Reading

Use a graphic organizer to identify key points and supporting ideas that would help a person identify quality child care for their family.

Boost Your Vocabulary

Interview a child care provider who fits one of the categories listed under key terms. Write a summary of the characteristics of the care offered in that setting. Share your summary with a partner or the whole class.

Know Key Terms

nanny
family child care
group child care
cooperative child care
employer-sponsored child care
latchkey children

Think of the different resources needed to fulfill the role of being a family member. Healthy families are made of members who show love, affection, and appreciation for each other. They spend time together as companions. They are committed to each other, offering support and encouragement. They use good communication skills to express thoughts, share feelings, listen, and solve problems. They work together to build strong family relationships. The goal of healthy family living requires many personal resources from each family member.

Work also places a demand on these resources. Work requires time and effort from your physical, mental, social, and emotional resources. These resources, however, are limited.

> **Think More About It**
> What demands could be placed on a family because of their child's involvement in school activities? in a part time job? in extracurricular events?

Identifying Resources

Managing multiple roles requires planning. People need to plan the use of their resources in order to carry out the responsibilities of their various roles. First, family members need to identify all the resources they have to help them meet their needs. That includes resources inside the family, such as the time, energy, and skills of each member. Resources outside the family may also be needed. Substitute child care, housekeeping services, or laundry services may be necessary to handle the jobs that family members cannot do. Second, families must manage their resources to meet the needs of all family members. That requires flexibility in roles, sensitivity to each other, and cooperation.

Outside resources and management skills become very important as a single parent tries to balance family and work. Good child care at a low cost is a necessity, but it is not always available. Assistance from family and friends can help the single parent manage the home. Within the family, older children are often required to carry a major part of the responsibility for housekeeping tasks and child care.

> **Think More About It**
> What could families do if they always found themselves too short on resources to meet the demands and needs of their family?

Substitute Child Care

The decision to go to work when children are young is often hard for parents. They recognize the importance of a main caregiver in the young child's life and want to fulfill this role. Sometimes one parent will choose to postpone their career plans until the child is older. Some adjust their schedules so that one parent provides care while the other is working. Some are able to take the child to work with them. For many families, though, such options will not work. Instead, they must rely on resources outside the immediate family to meet child care needs.

Finding a quality caregiver who is able to stimulate their child's growth and development is important to parents. Quality caregivers can provide nurturing and stimulation while parents are working. Parents also need to give the child love, affection, and guidance. They need to take time to talk with their child, do activities together, and be a role model. When parents and caregivers work together to provide the best care possible, a child's growth and development usually benefits.

In each community, a variety of child care arrangements may be available. These might include care in the child's home or the home of a caregiver. Child care can also be provided in group settings such as child care centers. Whatever arrangements are considered, the family must carefully decide what is best for their child.

Child Care in the Child's Home

Sometimes child care is provided in the child's own home, often by a grandparent or other relative, 20-4. Usually relatives will have a personal interest in, love for, and attachment to the child. Their previous contact with the child can reduce feelings of insecurity, especially for infants and toddlers. Relatives often have similar childrearing viewpoints as the parents. For these reasons, relatives or close friends are often relied upon to provide child care for infants and toddlers. For older children, parents may consider group care.

Sometimes families are able to obtain the service of a **nanny**. A nanny is a person who comes into the child's home to provide child

20-4 Leaving a child with a close family member can help reduce everyone's anxiety over the separation.

care. A live-in nanny would actually stay at the child's home. This child care service has many benefits for parents who work long hours, travel away from home, or work irregular schedules. The nanny can provide consistent care and often becomes attached to the whole family. However, the cost of hiring a nanny is often too high for most families.

Weigh the Facts

What could be the advantages and the disadvantages of having child care in the child's home?

Family Child Care

Sometimes child care is offered in the caregiver's own home. This is called **family child care**. Children have the benefit of a homelike setting, yet have opportunities to play with other children. The group of children should be small. Children from the same family can be together, even though they are different ages. Family child care may offer flexible hours, which is an advantage to parents who work irregular hours.

Most states have regulations for family child care. Licensing agencies check the number of children permitted, safety, nutrition, and activities. Parents should question whether a family child care program is registered or licensed. They should also inquire about the nutritional program, scheduled activities, and liability insurance in case of an accident. References from other parents who use or have used the service should also be checked before enrolling a child.

Use What You Learn

What could parents do to learn about the quality of care in a family child care if they are new to the community?

Child Care Centers

Care for a fairly large number of children is provided in **group child care** centers. Children have the benefit of interacting with others the same age. Usually child care centers offer educational programs with activities for children in each age group. The facilities and equipment are designed for children. Such centers are usually open during daytime hours. Centers provided by an employer are more likely to have care hours that match various work hours.

Child care centers are licensed by state agencies. They must meet minimum standards for space, nutrition programs, activity programs, group size, and staff. Special facilities must be available for infant and toddler programs. Certain regulations apply to public programs funded by government agencies as well as to private programs.

Cooperative child care centers are organized, managed, and funded by the parents who use a center. Usually the center has a board of parents who handle administrative tasks. Teachers and caregivers are hired to work at the center. Sometimes parents donate services to keep the costs down. Profits from the service are channeled back into the center.

Some child care programs are funded by businesses for their employees who have children. These programs are called **employer-sponsored child care**. Often the child care facility is in or near the work site, so workers can spend breaks and lunch hours with their children, 20-5. This child care service is usually lower in cost since the employer sponsors the program as an employee benefit.

Think More About It

Why might involvement in a cooperative child care center be difficult for most working parents?

Choosing Substitute Child Care

All children need consistent and loving care, both at home and away from home. Parents need to help children make the transition between the two as smoothly as possible. The goal for families and caregivers is to help the child continue to grow and develop in both environments. Choices about child care need to be based on the following:

- needs of the child
- demands of the parents' work schedules
- services available
- family budget

The best way to evaluate a child care program is to visit the home or center. Observe the staff and the children. Evaluate the space and the equipment. Ask for a description of the program and the type of activities offered. The center should provide a warm, nurturing, child-centered environment.

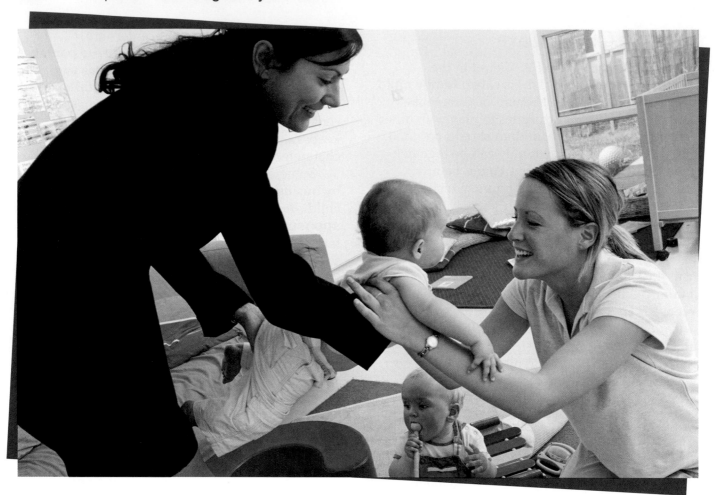

20-5 Parents can easily pick up and drop off their children if an employer-sponsored child care facility is located in the work site.

Specific needs for child care will depend on a child's age and developmental stage. Young infants, toddlers, preschool children, and elementary children need child care with unique qualities. The needs of the young infant and toddler are the most difficult to meet in child care arrangements.

Substitute Care for Infants

Infants need to develop feelings of trust and security in their environment away from home. Adjustment to a caregiver could first be made in the infant's home with a parent present. If that is not possible, the parent should spend time with the infant in the new environment. New sights, sounds, and smells should be added slowly to the infant's environment with the parent present.

Caregivers must enjoy holding, cuddling, and talking to the infant while they provide care. They need to be relaxed and able to spend

time nurturing as well as caring for the infant's physical needs. Parents often choose an extended family member to care for their infant. If none is available, a neighbor, friend, or nanny may be chosen to provide substitute care for the infant.

Use What You Learn

What actions can parents take to help infants develop a strong attachment for their caregiver?

Meeting Toddlers' Child Care Needs

Toddlers also need a secure, intimate environment. Consistent care from one main caregiver is important at this age. Parents can help their toddler adjust to a new caregiver by spending time with the child in the care setting. Taking along a small personal item that belongs to the parent can also increase the toddler's feelings of security. The item is a visual reminder that the parents will return.

In addition to needs for security, a toddler needs to explore the environment and move about. The needs of toddlers can make child care challenging. Caregivers must understand the toddler's need for nurturing one minute and exploring the next. This takes both patience and flexibility on the part of the caregiver.

Substitute Care for Preschoolers

Preschool children between three and five years of age need a greater variety of experiences with both people and objects. They need more opportunities to explore their environment. They need larger spaces to exercise their large muscles. Opportunities to play with other children are important. They enjoy play companions and develop close friendships at this age, 20-6. They are able to feel more secure away from their parents. This opens up more opportunities for child care arrangements.

Child Care for the Elementary Years

Once children start school, parents are responsible for fewer hours of the child's day. However, they still are responsible. How children spend their time after school usually requires a parent's careful attention.

Sometimes children participate in school-sponsored activities directly after the school day. If not, they need someone to whom they are accountable after school. Some families arrange for their child to go to the home of a neighbor, grandparent, or family friend. Others make arrangements for a neighbor or grandparent to check on the child shortly after the child gets home. This may be done with a telephone call or visit.

Latchkey children is a term that refers to children who regularly go home after school to empty homes without adult supervision. They are often alone until a parent returns from work.

Loneliness and boredom are common problems for the child who is home alone. Worry and fear that the parents will not come home on time is another. The way the child spends this time of day should be planned ahead. Parents and child can discuss activities and develop a plan for checking progress. Whatever the activities planned—homework, special hobbies, or household tasks—a method of checking the child's progress should be developed. This helps the child to be accountable for time, and it helps parents set guidelines for the child's activities.

If children go to a child care center or family child care after school, parents should inquire about the activities offered. Elementary-age children need activities appropriate for their age. Some public schools are addressing the problem of latchkey children by offering supervised activities in a relaxed atmosphere in an after-school program.

20-6 Preschool children enjoy opportunities to play with their peers in a child care setting.

the demand is too great, family members must make choices. Sometimes, activities will need to be limited to those most preferred.

Think More About It
How do families get into the position of having too many activities to attend?

Meeting the Needs of Parents

Finding substitute child care that meets both the child's and parents' needs can be a challenge, 20-7. Several factors such as cost, available hours, location, and the quality of the caregivers must be considered. Finding a caregiver who provides quality care at a cost the parents can afford is probably the greatest need of working parents.

Managing Household Tasks

An organized home does not happen automatically. It requires everyone working to the degree that each is capable. The keys to managing household roles are flexibility and cooperation. Family members need to be flexible, because needs and resources change, sometimes daily. They also need to cooperate and work together to determine what tasks to address and how to accomplish them.

Problems develop when one person—often the mother—tries to handle too many tasks. Then, all tasks probably do not get done and she becomes exhausted trying. This often is the dilemma faced by the heads of single-parent families. They do not have other adults with whom to share work and family demands. Task overload can be avoided by developing a family schedule, prioritizing tasks, and following a home management plan.

Develop a Family Schedule

In a weekly family meeting, members can work together to develop a family schedule. Each person in the family can put on the calendar all the extra activities that he or she plans. Then the family can evaluate the calendar to see if any one person's plans are taking too many resources. If

Child Care Service
Parent's Needs
• The service is available when needed.
• The service is easy to reach from home or work.
• The service is within the parent's budget.
• The caregiver has a similar childrearing philosophy as the parent.
• The caregiver is competent.
• The caregiver is willing to talk about the child's progress regularly.
• The caregiver shows love and affection for the child.
• The caregiver appears relaxed and free of anxiety.
Child's Needs
• The child is happy and comfortable with the caregiver.
• The child feels loved by the caregiver.
• The child is developing self-care skills.
• The child is learning about himself or herself, other people, and the environment.
• The child can play alone and with others, too.
• The child has positive attitudes.
• The child knows the limits for behavior.
• The child has a variety of activities to keep busy.

20-7 Child care services should meet both parents' and children's needs.

Prioritize Tasks

Another home management technique is to separate the important tasks that must be done from those less important. The important daily tasks can be written on a primary list, such as preparing meals, doing dishes, or picking children up from school. Family members can divide these tasks according to their schedules, 20-8. Such a plan helps make sure that necessary work gets done.

A second list can be made for less important tasks. These are tasks that need to be done, but may be less urgent. For instance, doing laundry and vacuuming are tasks that probably can be rescheduled for tomorrow.

Follow a Plan

After tasks are listed, the family should establish a plan for completing them. Each family member may be assigned certain tasks. Another idea is to set a certain time aside for everyone to work together until all tasks are completed, such as 9:00 to 11:00 on Saturday mornings. A ten-minute period may be set aside each evening to pick up personal items before going to bed. Such techniques help to put a plan into practice and keep the responsibilities for housework shared among all family members.

20-8 Work responsibilities for the family should be shared by all capable members.

Link to Your Life

What plan does your family have to make sure the work of the family is distributed evenly to all family members?

Using Technology to Manage the Home

There are many electronic devices, appliances, and gadgets that help make the work of the family easier. Technology such as cell phones has improved the ability for families to communicate, no matter what their schedule or where they are. Technology will continue to change. Some new products will help families reach their goals. Some will add challenges for families to manage. All new products come with a price. Family meetings can provide a good time for members to weigh the costs and the benefits of new products to assure balance between the family's needs and resources.

Investigate Further

What new technologies make the work of the family easier? Which ones add responsibilities for the family to manage?

Review Section 20:2

1. Explain why family and work roles need to be managed.

2. List the types of substitute child care available and describe the characteristics of each.

3. List the characteristics of preschoolers that make finding substitute child care easier at this age.

4. Name three resources that working parents may use to care for elementary children after school.

5. List three common responses of latchkey children who are home alone after school.

6. What are two keys to managing household tasks successfully in a changing family?

7. What are three activities that families can use to help manage household tasks?

Think It Through

Balancing Family and Work

Linda and Abby sat at the table, talking with their younger sister, Wendy. They were all excited that the due date for Wendy's baby was near. "What have you decided to do about work?" asked Linda.

Before Wendy answered, Abby chimed in. "It's a hard decision to make. You can be sure of that. I really liked my job at the airport, and we needed the income, too. That's why I transferred to the night shift, so Ed and I could take turns caring for the baby. That way we were both able to keep our jobs."

Linda smiled. "That's a hard schedule to keep! I don't think I could do it. I really enjoyed staying home with Kim the first three months. Then Scott took a three-month leave from his job. After that, our childrearing leave was all used up. We were lucky to get Grace as a babysitter. She comes to our home to take care of Kim. That really works great since we both are gone quite a bit. I have tried to cut down on the time that I have to travel, though. I don't like to be away from the baby so much. I wish Scott could cut back on his schedule, too."

Wendy thought about her sisters. They were raising their families differently from the way they had been raised. She really looked forward to staying home and being a full-time mother. Her job in sales would not allow her enough time at home to raise a family, so she decided to quit. Her husband Bill supported her decision and felt they could manage without her income. They wanted at least one of them to be home with the children. Bill's job was also very demanding, and he would not have much time to help her with the housework. It was a tough decision, but she was sure they had made the right one for them.

Questions to Guide Your Thinking

1. Identify the work patterns of the three sisters: Linda, Abby, and Wendy. What are their husbands' work patterns?

2. In each situation, what factors influenced their choice of work pattern?

3. For each situation, how was the choice of child care arrangements related to the child's needs? Would it be likely that the child's needs were or were not met?

4. How was each choice about child care affected by the demands of the parent's work?

5. How did the work patterns affect the roles taken by the spouses?

Chapter Summary

Work patterns for both men and women have more variations today than in past generations. Several factors enter the picture as choices about work patterns are made in families. Managing multiple roles becomes a greater challenge when both parents hold jobs. Resources such as time and energy become limited. Outside resources such as substitute child care may be required. Families need to consider the needs of each child, the services available, their costs, and the parents' schedules when seeking substitute child care.

In the home, family members must be flexible. They need to share roles and work together to carry out the household tasks.

Assess...

Your Knowledge

1. What factors could affect a couple's work patterns when they are expecting their first child?

2. What should a parent look for when searching for quality child care for the following:

   a. an infant?

   b. a toddler?

   c. a preschooler?

   d. an elementary aged child?

Your Understanding

3. How do personal values and goals affect work patterns when a couple have small children?

4. How can employer policies influence parents' choice of work patterns?

Your Skills

5. Evaluate the following substitute child care program. Explain why this program would or would not meet the needs of both an infant and a toddler. The center is a group child care facility for children of all ages. The space for infants is separated from the other children. When children are able to walk, they are moved to a toddler area. There is a crib for each infant, and the ratio of child care providers to infants is one

to four. The sleep and play areas are in adjoining rooms, with a glass window between the two areas. The center appears clean, and the staff is friendly.

6. Develop a family schedule for one week for the following situation. Both parents work 8 hours a day and commute ½ hour each way to work. The children in the family are ages four, seven, and 12. The youngest child goes to a group child care center. The older children take the bus to school and go to an after-school program. Include the following items in the schedule: shop for groceries, prepare meals, keep up with household chores, drop off and pick up children, help children with homework, do family leisure activities.

Think Critically

7. *Social studies.* Survey three families with different work patterns. Inquire about their reasons for choosing their specific work patterns. Include a question for each of the five factors affecting work patterns. Summarize the results in a table. *Group option:* Work in small groups and combine your individual survey results. Evaluate your data to see if families with the same work patterns have similar reasons for their choices.

8. Imagine your future career and identify your desired work pattern. Explain why you would choose this work pattern. Identify the particular challenges that this work pattern presents to families and explain how you plan to meet those challenges. *Choice:* Present your information in a chart, diagram, poem, or video.

9. *Writing.* Interview your parents and discuss their work pattern decisions. Write a paper discussing their considerations and reasons for their choices. Summarize by expressing your opinion about how well their choices meet the needs of your family.

10. Create a list of indoor and outdoor household tasks. Identify who is likely to carry out each task in a dual-career family with children: mother, father, or one of the children. Then evaluate your list. Would all members in that family experience a balance between family and work demands? Write a paragraph describing

the division of work in the family and suggest ways to create a better balance between family and work demands. **Choice:** Create your list; then exchange lists with a partner for the evaluation and writing portion of the activity.

Connect with Your Community

11. **Social studies.** Prepare a list of questions to ask a panel of working mothers and fathers. Ask questions about how they balance family needs and work demands. **Group option:** Prepare your questions with a small group.

12. **Research.** Research three different child care services in your community. Describe the important characteristics of each, including the caregivers and the environment. Identify the ages of children served, the programs offered, food service provided, and the type of license held or required.

13. **Research.** Choose a company in your community and research their policies related to families (such as sick leave, maternity or paternity leave, childrearing leave, or employer-sponsored day care). Prepare a one-page report describing these policies. **Choice:** Present your information in an electronic presentation.

Use Technology

14. **Research.** Using the Internet, obtain a copy of the regulations for child care services in your state for the following: family child care services; group child care centers; cooperative child care centers; and other types of licensed child care, if any. Prepare a brief written report.

15. Using a desktop publishing program, prepare a flyer to advertise a new child care service, either real or imaginary. Highlight the special features of the service and the age group(s) of the children served. Add pictures and graphics to your flyer.

16. **Research.** Identify a large company that interests you as a possible future employer. Using the Internet, research the company's family-related policies. Use a computer to compile your research into a chart titled "Family-Related Employer Policies." List the name of the employer across the top of the chart and the various policy items down the left side. (Items may include sick leave, maternity or paternity leave, employer-sponsored day care, among other categories.) **Group option:** Work with two other classmates and compile the results of your research in one table. Present your results to the class.

17. Choose one of the following stages of child development: infant, toddler, early childhood, or elementary years. On the computer, prepare a checklist to use when evaluating a child care service for that age group. Visit a center and evaluate it using your checklist. **Group option:** Work in a small group, with each member focusing on one stage of development. Combine the results of your evaluations in a spreadsheet.

Chapter 21

Becoming a Leader in Your Community

Section 21:**1**
Effective Leadership

Section 21:**2**
Effective Groups

Section 21:**3**
Your Role as a Citizen

Key Questions

Questions to answer as you study this chapter:

- **What traits and skills do effective leaders demonstrate?**

- **What does it take for a group to be successful?**

- **How are the rights and responsibilities of citizenship interrelated?**

Chapter Objectives

After studying this chapter, you will be able to

- **identify** the roles and responsibilities of group leaders.

- **distinguish** between various leadership styles.

- **describe** the characteristics of a successful group.

- **plan**, **organize**, and **evaluate** a group meeting.

- **identify** the rights and the responsibilities of a citizen.

- **explain** the need for taxes at various levels.

- **relate** ecologically safe practices and volunteering to citizenship.

Life Sketch

"Why don't you join FCCLA this year?" Amy asked.

"What does that stand for?" responded Julia.

"Family, Career and Community Leaders of America," Amy replied. "It's a great club! We have a lot of fun. We learn about different careers, take field trips, do community projects, and take part in state competitions. You can meet so many people who share the same interests as you."

"I have thought about it, but I'm not sure I have time," Julia said.

"Why don't you come with me to the meeting after school today? We're looking for new members," Amy said.

Julia nodded. Amy's enthusiasm had sparked her interest. "I guess that's the best way for me to decide. I'll call home to let them know I'm staying after school."

"Great!" Amy said. "I'll introduce you to some of the other members at lunch today."

Getting Started

Participating in student organizations will help you develop leadership skills and group interaction skills. These skills can help you at work, at home, and in your community—anywhere you work together with other people. In this chapter, you will learn how group members and group leaders can make a difference in the success of a group.

You will also learn how you can be a leader in your community in your role as a citizen. Learning about the rights and responsibilities of citizenship, exercising your voting rights, and understanding taxes will help you more fully assume this role. In addition, you can make a positive contribution to your community by caring for the environment and volunteering.

section 21:1

Effective Leadership

Sharpen Your Reading

Create a graphic organizer to diagram the qualities of a good leader.

Boost Your Vocabulary

For each style of leadership, identify a person you know who uses that style and summarize how they provide leadership to their group.

Know Key Terms

leader
group
task-oriented leader
authoritarian
democratic
relationship-oriented leader

A **leader** is the person who takes charge in a group. A **group** consists of two or more people interacting in a way that has an effect on each other. The leader of a group strongly influences the thoughts and behavior of the other members. He or she is responsible for helping the group succeed.

Responsibilities of Group Leaders

Effective leaders possess the traits and skills described in 21-1. The first step in developing effective leadership skills is understanding and fulfilling your responsibilities. Effective leaders have four main responsibilities. Their confidence and commitment in meeting these responsibilities can motivate the group to succeed.

- *Identify the group's goals.* Why is the group together? What does the group expect to accomplish? What are the needs of the members?

- *Develop a plan that will help the group reach its goals.* What resources are available? What talents and skills can group members contribute? How can all these resources be managed so the group reaches its goal?

- *Carry out the plan.* Who is going to do what task?

Leadership Traits and Skills

- Has positive self-esteem.

- Shows enthusiasm.

- Sets a good example for others.

- Shows empathy. Listens to group members and recognizes their needs and opinions.

- Motivates the group to work toward a goal.

- Makes decisions and stands behind them.

- Handles problems diplomatically.

- Takes a stand on issues.

- Manages group resources by delegating responsibilities.

- Does a fair share of work; carries out duties.

- Gives credit where due to group members. Praises them for their efforts.

21-1 These skills and traits are needed for a person to assume a leadership role. Which of these do you possess?

- *Evaluate the group's accomplishments.* Did they reach their goal? How could the group work together more effectively?

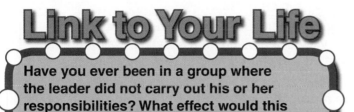

Have you ever been in a group where the leader did not carry out his or her responsibilities? What effect would this have on the way a group functions?

Leadership Roles

As a group leader, you will have several different roles to fulfill. Since your main responsibility is leading the group to reach its goals, you will need to be a good communicator. You will need to direct discussions to find out what your group members are thinking. You will also need to be a motivator to get people enthused and involved. Finally, you will need to be a problem solver. Often problems will come up as you try to meet group goals.

The Leader as a Communicator

All leaders need to practice good communication skills. Skills for sending, receiving, and interpreting messages are necessary so everyone in the group shares the same meaning. Nonverbal messages need to support what is said.

A leader can help others express their ideas by using active listening skills. You can show interest in what each team member has to say. Your comments can encourage people to participate. Reflecting or checking out can be used to help clarify what a person has said. In this way, leaders can make sure the meaning is clear.

Use What You Learn

What are some examples of comments a leader could say that would encourage people to keep talking and share their ideas?

Directing a Discussion

A leader can help team members contribute to the group through discussion. This method can be used to identify a problem or gather information. Discussion can also be used to make group decisions. A good leader tries to encourage everyone's participation. Different techniques can be used to inspire members to share ideas, 21-2.

Effective discussion is directed toward a goal identified by the leader. Others may want to add their ideas, expanding on the nature of the goal. At times, the leader may need to redirect the group to keep it on track.

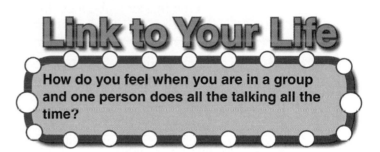

How do you feel when you are in a group and one person does all the talking all the time?

The Leader as a Motivator

One of the main roles of the leader is to get all members of a group involved. When group members are involved, they will have better attitudes toward the group. Also, they will be more supportive in carrying out group activities. The following techniques can help motivate a group.

- *Be persuasive.* People prefer being asked to help instead of being told what to do.
- *Show recognition.* As a leader, you can listen to group members' ideas and include them in setting goals and developing a plan. Also, you can recognize in a special way what group members do for the group.
- *Look successful.* People like to succeed. If group members believe they are part of a successful group, their enthusiasm will increase. In addition, others will want to join.
- *Include friendly competition in group activities.* Competition can encourage members to work together to reach goals.
- *Maintain a democratic environment.* Group members are likely to have a better attitude when their opinions and feelings are

Small-Group Discussion Techniques	
Brainstorming	Members contribute whatever ideas come to mind. All ideas are accepted. No comments are made while discussion is in progress.
Buzz session	Large group is divided into small groups of four to ten people. Each, led by a chairperson, briefly discusses one view of a problem or a situation. Following the discussion, the chairpersons report each group's opinion to the entire group.
Role-playing	Individuals are given fictional, real-life situations to act out in short drama. After the role-play, the group discusses the main objective.
Large-Group Discussion Techniques	
Roundtable	Members sit in a circle or around a table to discuss a topic. A chairperson opens the discussion and summarizes throughout.
Panel	Four to six people form a panel to discuss various aspects of a chosen topic. A moderator introduces the topic and panel members and draws them into conversation. The panel discusses the topic back and forth for the audience's benefit. The audience participates during or after the discussion.
Colloquium	One or more resource people respond to questions from an interviewer and from the audience.
Symposium	Several speakers give a presentation. Each presents information on a different aspect of a topic.
Forum	Speakers present their opinions or point of view on a topic or issue. The audience may ask questions after all speakers have finished their presentation.
Debate	Two speakers or teams present two opposing sides of a controversial issue. After the speakers present their views, the opposing speaker may offer a rebuttal. That speaker tries to point out flaws in the other person's argument. A moderator helps maintain control.

21-2 An effective leader uses these discussion techniques to encourage group participation.

considered. People like to be asked for their opinions, even if another form of action is taken.

The Leader as a Problem Solver

A fourth role of a group leader is seeing that problems get solved. In any group project, unplanned situations will arise. Someone gets sick and cannot complete a task. One part of the project does not come together as quickly as planned. Group members may disagree on how to carry out part of the plan.

Begin by identifying the problem. Encourage group members to discuss their concerns. Listen to and observe the verbal and nonverbal messages that are sent. Use active listening to interpret a clear meaning. Then determine

ownership of the problem. Finally, use the steps of the decision-making process to work out a solution.

Use What You Learn

How could a leader's communication skills either help solve a problem or make the problem worse?

Leadership Styles

All leaders will need to carry out the above responsibilities and roles to some extent. However, the style of leadership that is used can vary with the situation and the structure of the group. Different groups require different kinds of leadership.

Task-Oriented Leadership

One style of leadership focuses on the job that needs to be done. A **task-oriented leader** uses this style when a specific task needs to be accomplished. The leader may break down the task or take suggestions from the group on how to divide it. However, the leader's emphasis is not on how each person feels or thinks about the task. The emphasis is on the job that needs to be completed.

A task-oriented leader is likely to appoint certain people to carry out the plan. Such a leader identifies the skills and abilities of each team member ahead of time. Then the leader makes sure that each part of the job is completed. After the task is done, the leader evaluates the progress of the group. This style of leadership is important when groups are trying to meet certain standards.

Task-oriented leaders may use an **authoritarian** approach to leadership. A leader who uses this approach likes to be in control of the situation and makes most of the decisions.

Sometimes the authoritarian approach to completing a task is most effective. A group of firefighters would not sit down and discuss how to put out the fire. Instead, each person would follow the leader's instructions to complete the task.

Investigate Further

What groups or organizations are mostly task-oriented?

Relationship-Oriented Leadership

Some groups need a more **democratic** style of leadership. In other words, group members need to be involved in making decisions. A **relationship-oriented leader** recognizes this need. This style of leadership places greater emphasis on the feelings, thoughts, and needs of each group member, 21-3.

How would you use this style of leadership if you were the leader of a group planning a class party? Your role would be to guide the group and to get everyone involved in the planning.

Your first step as a leader is to get the group members to help identify the group's goal. A group discussion will help you do this. When the group understands what they are trying to achieve, they are more likely to work together.

During the discussion, you need to listen as members share their ideas. Everyone's opinion is important. Once you understand how each group member feels, you can ask for suggestions on setting a work schedule. Then you can ask for volunteers to carry out specific tasks. Using this positive approach gets everyone involved and motivates the group to reach its goal.

After the class party, evaluate your group's success. Ask the group members to share what worked and what did not work. As a group, decide what could be done better next time.

 How is a task-oriented leadership style different from a relationship-oriented leadership style? In what ways are they similar?

Developing Your Leadership Style

Most people are more comfortable with one leadership style or the other. Many strong leaders use both, depending on the needs of the situation. Developing leadership skills takes time and practice. Your effectiveness in a leadership role will depend on the situation, your personality, and the other group members.

Examine the Situation

What type of situation needs leadership? If you are a task-oriented leader, is it a structured situation? Can the different parts of the task be identified? Will there be specific guidelines to follow? Will you be able to exercise the kind of control you desire?

If you are a relationship-oriented leader, will the situation be challenging? Will you be able to use your creativity as well as the group members'? Are you willing to lead the group in forming its goals?

21-3 A relationship-oriented leader is willing to consider each group member's ideas.

Most situations require a flexible leader. To be flexible, you may need to use parts of each leadership style. Part of the time you may need to focus on group relationships. You may need to encourage group members to add their opinions and ideas. You may need to help the group relax and work as a unit. Then, as the ideas are put together, you may need to become more task-oriented. You may then exercise more control to get the job completed. In these situations, you use skills for both styles of leadership.

Examine Your Personality

Considering your personality traits is an important part of determining your leadership style. If you need to get things done or see a job carried out, you are a task-oriented leader. If you are a person who can guide people to work together, you have a relationship-oriented style. You are able to lead a group to come up with their own ideas and solutions.

How much control do you need? If you are task-oriented, you may want to supervise each phase of a project. On the other hand, you may want others to be responsible for various parts of the project.

How adaptable are you to different situations? Can you use more than one leadership style to lead a group to reach its goal? Greater flexibility can help you succeed in many situations.

Link to Your Life

Analyze your own personality, personal preferences, and leadership skills to identify whether you would prefer to lead with a task-oriented or relationship-oriented style of leadership.

Examine the Group Members

Before you agree to lead a group, it is helpful to evaluate the situation, 21-4. Examine the task to be completed and the relationship that exists between the leader and group members. If you feel that you could fit that role, you may be the one to lead the group to reach its goals.

Guidelines for Evaluating a Leadership Situation
1. Know your leadership style.
Task-oriented:
• Focus on getting a job done.
• Emphasize parts of the task.
• Identify the expected outcome.
• Set specific guidelines.
• Exercise control over group.
Relationship-oriented:
• Focus on feelings and needs.
• Emphasize people.
• Leave some goals open to discussion.
• Allow for creativity.
• Encourage members to share responsibilities.
2. Evaluate the leadership style needed for the situation.
3. Compare your personal preferences with the requirements of the situation.
4. Evaluate whether the group members will support you.

21-4 Deciding whether to take a leadership position with a group requires careful thought.

Consider whether you will be able to get the group members to work together. If they elect you, you probably will have their support. If you are appointed for a position, you may need to determine the group's expectations. Whatever the case, you need the confidence and support of the group members to succeed.

Developing skills for both styles of leadership is helpful for all leaders. The key is to be flexible and use the style that is needed for the situation. Whatever the situation, all leaders need to practice their skills as they work to fulfill their leadership roles.

Review Section 21:1

1. List the four main responsibilities of a group leader.

2. Explain why effective leaders need good communication skills.

3. Describe two small group discussion techniques and two large group discussion techniques.

4. Give one example of a situation in which you would use (A) a task-oriented and (B) a relationship-oriented leadership style.

5. Which style of leadership would you prefer to work under? Describe the characteristics of that style of leadership.

section 21:2

Effective Groups

Sharpen Your Reading

As you read, write a list of the qualities of an effective group member. Underline the qualities that you already demonstrate and circle the qualities that you need to develop.

Boost Your Vocabulary

Find an example of a constitution for a group. Look at the constitution and identify the people required to make this group function.

Know Key Terms

chairperson
secretary
minutes
parliamentary procedure
Robert's Rules of Order
constitution
bylaws
agenda

Some people join a group to make friends. They want to meet new people who share similar interests, 21-5. Learning a new skill motivates others to join a group. A skilled or experienced person may share his or her expertise with other group members. Taking part in a worthwhile project is another reason some join a group. The project may be related to a cause they value or it may meet their needs.

21-5 A shared interest in basketball motivated this group to get together.

You will most likely belong to several groups over the course of your life. As your needs change, the groups to which you belong change. This process continues throughout your life.

Link to Your Life

What are some examples of groups you were in as a child? in the teen years? In what groups do your parents or other family members take part? How do these groups meet different needs?

Qualities of Successful Groups

Successful groups demonstrate teamwork, which means everyone does their part to help the group accomplish goals. For teamwork to take place, all members of a group must be recognized as important. They contribute equally to the group's common goals.

Group Goals

Goals give a group a sense of purpose and direction. Group members know what they are expected to accomplish as a team. Groups are important because they can accomplish what no single member can do in the same amount of time.

An effective group will have clearly defined goals to which group members can relate. Members can see that their personal goals will be met through the group goals. As the team members work together to fulfill group goals, their personal needs are met as well. If a group has no purpose or direction, others might not join.

Leaders guide the group to reach its goals. At the same time, leaders listen to and include the ideas of the team. Active team members participate in reaching goals by attending meetings, working on committees, and supporting group activities.

What are some goals that you could accomplish by joining a group?

Cohesiveness

Active groups are cohesive. They stick together because group members feel they belong to the group. They feel their input is important. They can express their ideas and opinions. They accept each member's contribution. They take part in setting goals and making plans to meet those goals. The group as a whole cooperates and takes responsibility in carrying out tasks. Support within the group brings feelings of satisfaction and keeps the group intact. It also attracts new members into the group.

Setting

Groups are more productive when the setting for the group's activities matches its plans and goals, 21-6. If the group is large, breaking into small teams can promote a good exchange of ideas. Small teams work best at round tables. Then they can look directly at each other as they talk.

Group Structure

Every group needs some type of structure. Group members need to know what is expected of them so they can work to reach goals. Leaders

21-6 This casual setting is effective for informal discussion, but could slow serious decision making.

guide and motivate the group. Group members support their leaders to help make the group successful. This structure helps the group effectively meet its goals.

Roles and Responsibilities of Group Members

Group members are just as important as group leaders. Group members make it possible to complete tasks and reach goals. You can be an effective group member by fulfilling the following roles and responsibilities.

- *Be a clear communicator.* Clear and simple statements can help others in the group understand your comments. Use active listening to make sure you understand what others share. Group members can show respect for each other by commenting only on ideas, not on the person who gave them.

Use What You Learn

How could active listening help you be an effective group member?

- *Be cooperative.* You may need to give up your personal desires in order to reach a group goal. When all members cooperate, they will be more willing to work together for the benefit of the whole group.
- *Be willing to participate.* You need to be willing to express your ideas, even if your suggestions are not carried through in the plan of action. Most group plans have several steps to carry out. As a team member, you need to be willing to help carry out the plan.
- *Control your participation.* Communication in a group first involves paying attention to others. Listen carefully so that you understand the purpose and goal of the discussion. Next, determine what is needed in the discussion and decide whether you have something to contribute, 21-7.

21-7 Knowing when to speak and when to keep quiet can help members contribute to the effectiveness of the whole group.

Think More About It
If one or two group members talk all the time, what effect will it have on the group's success?

- *Be an informed participant.* Knowing what issues will be discussed, what information is needed, and what can be expected will help you contribute to the group.
- *Control your emotions.* Intense emotions lower the chance of sending clear and accurate messages. If, as a group member, you feel your emotions are getting stronger, you may want to be quiet until you feel calm again.
- *Be empathetic to others' emotions.* If another group member becomes upset or angry, suggest that the group take a break. Then the person can go for a walk, get some exercise, and collect his or her thoughts. Try to be respectful of group members and their feelings.
- *Support the group.* Team leaders need the support of the team. Let your leaders know they are doing a good job. They appreciate constructive input that team members have to offer.

Developing the skills of an effective team member is an important task for all workers. You will need these skills on the job. They are an important part of the professional etiquette that will help you succeed in the world of work.

How to Plan, Organize, and Evaluate a Group

Groups provide opportunities for people to learn together. Some experiences build leadership skills. Others provide opportunities for group interaction. Still other experiences are related to the specific goals of the group.

Student organizations provide many opportunities to meet all these needs. Family, Career and Community Leaders of America, Inc. (FCCLA), for instance, is open to students in family and consumer sciences classes.

The group's purpose is to prepare students to be leaders in their families, careers, and communities. This is accomplished through educational experiences in such areas as financial management, career planning, balancing family and careers, leadership development, and community service.

> ## Use What You Learn
> Describe a need that a group could possibly solve if they worked together, and explain how their combined efforts could make a difference.

Planning a Group

Have you ever thought about organizing a club or group? Perhaps you share a common interest with others. You may have identified a personal need you feel could be met in a group. In either case, you and another interested person can easily start a group. Together you can plan the purpose of the group and write down what you want to accomplish. Contact others who might be interested in joining. Use e-mails, newspaper articles, or announcements to let other people know that you want to start the group.

Organizing the Group

If the group will be a local chapter in a national organization, contact the headquarters for information. They will help you get started with step-by-step procedures to follow. If you are organizing a local group, you need to appoint someone to lead the organizational meeting. You can also ask someone to keep a record of the meeting until a secretary is elected.

Elect Officers

Most clubs or groups have at least a president or **chairperson** who leads the other members. Also, most groups have a **secretary**, who records the minutes of each meeting. The **minutes** usually include a description of what happens at the group meetings. There may be other offices that you feel will be needed as well. There may be a vice president who leads the meeting when the president is absent, a treasurer, or various committee members. Officers are usually nominated and elected once a year.

Identify Rules and Procedures

Many organizations follow **parliamentary procedure**. This is an orderly way of conducting a meeting and discussing business. The procedure is detailed in the book **Robert's Rules of Order**.

Following a set procedure helps a meeting progress smoothly. The leader has a format to follow so that items of business are brought up, discussed, and decided. Discussions are orderly. Group members know when they can speak and when to complete business. Voting procedures give members input in making group decisions.

A new group will need to develop a constitution and bylaws. A **constitution** is a formal written statement that governs how the group functions. The constitution usually includes the purpose of the group and the broad goals of the group. It also outlines specific benefits that members will gain from being in the group.

Bylaws state when meetings are held, how often, when elections are held, and what procedures are used. Any other information related to the group's organization can be included in the bylaws.

> ## Think More About It
> What might be some problems that could develop if a group does not follow rules or procedures?

Prepare for Meetings

Successful groups have an agenda for every meeting. An **agenda** is a list of what the group will be doing and discussing at the meeting, 21-8. The group leader should prepare the agenda and distribute it to the group members before the meeting. The leader's copy may be more detailed with specific ideas or questions to guide the members' participation.

The leader or officers can also plan the amount of time needed to complete the agenda. By keeping the agenda concise, most items can be completed during the meeting. No more than one item should be left unfinished. Group members will feel discouraged if they see that too much is left undone.

Group Meeting Agenda

1. Call to order
2. Reading and approval of minutes
3. Officers' reports
4. Committee reports
5. Unfinished business
6. New business
7. Program
8. Announcements
9. Adjournment

21-8 Most meetings follow this order of business, which is based on parliamentary procedure.

Physical arrangements for the meeting should be planned in advance. Tables can be arranged in the most effective way for the work that needs to be done. Any needed supplies should be gathered before the meeting. Breaks should be planned at a logical stopping point in the agenda.

The leader also needs to consider what type of leadership will be most successful. In some parts of the meeting, a relationship style may be required. The group members may need to express personal opinions and feelings related to the plan. At other points in the agenda, the leader may need to be more task oriented to get the job done.

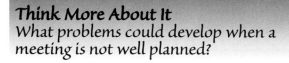

Think More About It
What problems could develop when a meeting is not well planned?

Evaluating the Group

After each meeting, the leader and other officers can evaluate the meeting. A short checklist of evaluation questions works well: What techniques were successful? What areas did not seem to go well? Were there any problems that surfaced in the meeting? If so, how can these be handled in future meetings? How can the group members be encouraged to participate?

An occasional evaluation by the entire group can be valuable. This can be a guided discussion in which all group members answer evaluation questions. Small-group discussion techniques can be used to bring out these opinions. At these evaluation meetings, the purpose and goals of the group should be stated. This reminder can help the members evaluate the various meetings and activities to see if they are truly meeting their goals.

Review Section 21:2

1. List two characteristics of a successful group.
2. Explain how group goals can help a group stay together.
3. List six responsibilities of a group member.
4. Why should a group have clearly defined rules and procedures?
5. Explain the purposes of a group's constitution and bylaws.
6. Suppose you are interested in forming a new group. In your own words, briefly describe how you would plan and organize a group meeting.

section 21:3

Your Role as a Citizen

Sharpen Your Reading

Create two columns with the headings *Citizen Rights* and *Citizen Responsibilities*. As you read, summarize key ideas under the appropriate heading.

Boost Your Vocabulary

Identify where you would vote in your community and find out what you would need to do to register to vote.

Know Key Terms

citizen
register
legislatures
ordinances
felony
misdemeanor
violation
contract
tort
volunteers
mentor

As a citizen, you are a member of an important group—the community in which you live. A **citizen** is a person who formally owes allegiance to a government. Leadership skills and group interaction skills will help you be an active citizen in your community.

Citizens have both rights and responsibilities. The laws of the government protect your rights. You are also responsible to obey these laws. Citizens have the right to be informed about laws that are being considered. They have the right to provide input into decisions made by local, state, and federal government. This input is usually through voting. Writing letters to officials in charge can be another effective way to influence government decisions.

Citizens also have the responsibility to pay taxes. Tax money is used by the local, state, and federal governments to provide a variety of public services. Some examples include fire and police protection, education, and highway maintenance. As a citizen, you also have the responsibility to stay involved in your community and help improve your community by volunteering and caring for the environment.

Think More About It
What could happen to a country if its citizens did not become involved in elections?

Your Voting Rights

The right to vote is one of the most important rights of a U.S. citizen. Voting allows you to express your opinions on public issues. Often this is done by voting for a person who has views similar to yours. When you vote for someone, you are saying, "I choose this person to represent me in government."

Voting enables you to elect leaders at all three levels of government—local, state, and national. The power of your vote makes it important to be informed about candidates running for any government office. Compare their views with your own and then make an informed decision about who can represent you, 21-9.

Registering to Vote

At age 18, you are eligible to register to vote. When you **register**, you are placing your name on the list of citizens who can vote in elections. To register, you must be a citizen of the United States. You must also meet a residency

21-9 Researching candidates is an important step in making an informed voting decision.

requirement. This means you must have lived for at least 30 days in the state and county where you register.

Just before a major election, registration booths are often set up in high-traffic areas to encourage voter registration. At other times, you can register to vote at the government office of the county commissioner, municipal clerk, or election supervisor. Some states also register voters at driver's license facilities. Voter registration forms are available on most state Web sites.

At election time, election officials will check if you have registered. If your name is on the list of registered voters, you will be allowed to vote.

Think More About It
Why is it important to become involved in voting?

Levels of Government and Their Laws

As a citizen, your rights are protected by the laws of the land. You are also required to obey these laws. Laws are written and enforced so that people in the country can live in harmony. Laws are designed to protect the rights and safety of individuals as well as benefit society as a whole. Therefore, laws are passed at the local, state, and national levels.

Lawmaking bodies are called **legislatures** at the federal and state levels. Your input into these laws comes through voting in state and national elections.

Federal Laws

At the federal level, the U.S. Congress is a legislature that makes federal laws. Federal laws apply to the whole country. For instance, there are federal laws against spying, airplane hijacking, mail fraud, and other crimes affecting more than one state. Federal laws also apply to military service, protecting the civil rights of U.S. citizens, and spending federal dollars.

State Laws

At the state level, the state legislature makes laws that apply to that state and its residents. Some examples include laws against robbery, drunken driving, murder, and shoplifting. Other areas include laws about the use of state funds, state highways, motor vehicle registration, and traffic, 21-10. Laws relating to marriage and divorce are also made at the state level.

Local Laws

Local laws are usually called regulations or **ordinances**. These are made by local legislatures such as city, town, or county councils or boards. Zoning regulations, building codes, and curfews for minors are a few examples.

Think More About It
What would it be like if there were no state and federal laws, and all laws were made at the local level?

21-10 Speed limits are an example of a state law.

Types of Laws

The types of laws that federal and state legislatures most often make fall into two main areas: public law and civil law.

Public Law

The laws that govern a person's rights relative to the government are called *public law*.

Constitutional laws refer to the basic laws of the nation. They are based on the U.S. Constitution and the constitutions of the 50 states. They establish freedoms for all citizens. Any new laws cannot go against these basic constitutional laws. If they do, they can be challenged in court and cannot be enforced if found unconstitutional.

Investigate Further

How does having constitutional law benefit individuals at the local level?

Criminal laws refer to punishments for those who break the law. Some laws cover more serious offenses than others, but all are designed to protect society.

A **felony** crime is considered most serious. It is a crime that can result in a sentence of more than a year in prison or even death. Some examples include murder, rape, kidnapping, armed robbery, arson, and sales of illegal drugs.

A **misdemeanor** is considered less serious, such as speeding or disorderly conduct. Such crimes may be punished by a fine or short prison term of less than a year.

A **violation** (sometimes called a *petty offense*) is an act that violates or breaks a local ordinance. For instance, failing to clear the snow off the sidewalk or littering may be violations in some towns. A violation may result in a fine or even a short jail term.

Use What You Learn

In what ways do public laws benefit citizens?

Civil Law

Civil laws govern your rights in relation to other people. Issues such as divorce, child custody, inheritances, and personal injuries are all covered by civil law.

Most civil laws fall into two groups: contract law and torts. Contract laws cover agreements that people make with each other. Torts refer to wrongdoings against another person.

Contracts

There are many situations in life in which you may need to sign a contract. A **contract** is a mutual agreement between two consenting people. For instance, you usually have to sign a service contract when you purchase a cellular phone. A bank will require that you sign a contract to take out a loan to buy a car. Understanding your rights and responsibilities according to the terms of a contract is important.

There are conditions that need to be met in order for a contract to be legal. Both parties must sign the contract agreement willingly. That is, one party cannot force the other party to sign the contract. Also, both parties must be *competent*. This means both parties must be able to understand the terms of the contract and the consequences of accepting those terms, 21-11. State laws define who is considered legally competent.

In most states, you must be at least 18 years of age to be legally bound by a written contract. To make a contract valid, a minor (person under age 18) may have a parent or another adult cosign the contract. Then the adult would be held responsible for the terms of the contract. Minors who lie about their age and sign a contract are legally bound to the contract.

Both parties must give consideration in order for a contract to be valid. *Consideration* means giving up something to obtain something else. For instance, as a renter you would give money to obtain a place to live. A valid contract must relate to a legal activity. For instance, a contract between two parties asking one party to commit a theft or a murder is not valid.

Once you sign a contract, you are legally responsible to abide by it, even if you did not read it or understand it, 21-12. Before you sign your name, carefully read all parts of the contract. Be sure you understand all the terms. Ask for explanations of anything that seems unclear. Keep a copy of the signed contract for your own records.

Link to Your Life

What are some common contracts that you may sign in your lifetime?

Torts

A wrongful act committed against another person is called a **tort**. Some examples include injuries to another person's body, emotional well-being, reputation, property, or business. Another wrongdoing that is considered a tort is *fraud*. Fraud is intentional trickery, lies, or misrepresentation to make a person give up a right or something of value.

Paying Taxes

As a citizen you enjoy many of the services paid for, in part, by local, state, or federal government funds. The money to pay for them is obtained through government taxes. Government funds are used to help pay for the following programs and services:

- public schools, community colleges, state universities, and other educational programs
- social services and welfare programs
- healthcare facilities and services
- police and fire protection and paramedic services
- unemployment and job services

Cellular Service Agreement

Customer Information

Name   Regynald Hall

Address   456 Chayes Court, Unit 210

City, State, Zip   Chicago, IL 60645

Service Information

Mobile #   (321) 456-7891

Plan   Individual Nationwide   Minutes Included   600

Term   24 months

Monthly Fee $59.99

Customer Acceptance

By signing this service agreement, I acknowledge and agree that:

- I am of legal age (at least 18 years old).
- I have read and understand the terms and conditions.
- I give permission to obtain information about my credit history.

Signature   *Regynald Hall*   Date   04/05/20XX

Terms and Conditions

1. Your service begins when you accept by signing this agreement. There is a $40 activation fee for each mobile phone.

2. If you terminate your service before the end of your term, you will be charged an early termination fee of $150.

3. If you cancel your service within 10 days of signing a service agreement, you will not be charged an early termination fee. You will be responsible for paying for all charges, fees, and taxes incurred through the date of cancellation.

4. We can change the terms of this agreement at any time. If we make any changes, we will provide you with 30 days notice. You may terminate service without paying an early termination fee, provided you notify us within 30 days of receiving the notice. By failing to terminate within 30 days, you accept the changes.

5. You will receive a bill summarizing your charges each month. If we do not receive payment in full by the due date, you will be charged a late fee of $6 a month. If we need to use a collection agency to collect payment, you agree to pay any collection agency fees incurred.

21-11 Be sure you understand all of the terms and conditions before signing a contract.

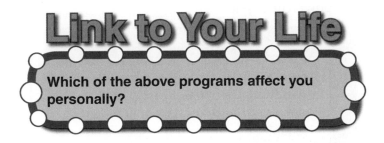

Link to Your Life

Which of the above programs affect you personally?

Government funds provide many other types of programs and services as well. Four different types of taxes help the government raise funds. These include income-based, employer-paid, sales, and property taxes.

Income-based taxes are taken out of your paycheck. Income taxes are used to pay for many state and federal programs and services.

Contract Tips

Before you sign a contract:

- Be sure you understand all the terms of the contract. If you need help, ask for a copy of the contract and take it to a lawyer or consumer-help agency. Have them explain the terms of the contract in language you understand.

- Never sign a contract that has blank spaces in it. Either have the blanks filled in or cross them out.

- Be sure all verbal promises are included in writing on the contract.

- If any changes are made to the written contract, make sure that both you and the other person write your initials next to the change.

- Be sure the total amount of money you have to pay and the amount of monthly payments are clearly stated.

After you sign a contract:

- Always get a copy of the contract after it is signed by both parties. Keep it with your other important records.

21-12 A contract is a legally binding document. Protect yourself by following these tips.

The funds are also used for Social Security and Medicare, which provide income and medical benefits to older retired citizens.

Employer-paid taxes are paid by employers on the employees' behalf. Employer-paid taxes are used for unemployment benefits, as well as Social Security and Medicare.

Sales taxes are used by all levels of government to raise money to pay for the services they provide. The rate of sales tax will vary from one state to another. The rate may also vary within a state as some counties add a county tax. What items are taxable may also vary from state to state.

Property taxes provide funds for education and other services. If you own real estate, a tax assessor will appraise its value for the purpose of taxation. The amount of property tax you must

pay is determined by two factors: the taxation rate in your area and the assessed value of your property.

Paying taxes is one way to be a responsible citizen. It enables you to support programs that benefit you, others in the community, and the country as a whole.

Investigate Further

What items are taxed a sales tax in your county?

Citizen Involvement

Sometimes you may feel that your tax dollars are not being spent wisely. Staying involved in local, state, and federal government issues can help you let others know what you think and feel. You can take a number of steps to be an involved citizen.

- *Check your local newspaper to see when community meetings are scheduled.* These may be school board, county board, or city council meetings. Try to attend as many as you can.

- *Attend area forums held by state representatives.* These are often advertised through mail fliers or the local newspaper. You can become informed about issues being considered at the state level.

- *Write letters stating your opinions.* Locally, write "letters to the editor" for publication in the local newspaper. Contact members of your local government on local issues. Let school board members know your views on school issues. Send letters or e-mails to your representative at the state legislature and to your representatives in the Senate and House of Congress. You may be only one voice, but as one with many others, you can have a powerful impact.

Use What You Learn

What issues in your community are important to you? How could you let others know how you feel about these issues?

Volunteering in Your Community

Volunteers are people who donate their time, talents, and energy to serve others. By volunteering, you can improve your community while making new friends and developing new skills. Choosing a volunteer opportunity that matches your interests is a good way to decide where to devote your efforts. The following examples are just a few ways that you could give back to your community.

- Participate in an outdoor cleanup event at a park or forest preserve, 21-13.
- Distribute food at a food pantry or serve a meal at a soup kitchen.
- Organize a blanket or clothing drive for a shelter.

21-13 Volunteering for a clean-up event at a local park is one way to stay involved in your community.

- Be a mentor for a younger person. A **mentor** is an adviser, teacher, or coach. Programs such as Big Brothers Big Sisters and the Boys and Girls Club exist in some communities and connect younger children with suitable mentors.

You can find out about volunteer opportunities in your community by searching the Internet for local branches of national charities. Joining a service-oriented club at your school is another way to give back to your community. In addition, the community section of your local newspaper may have listings of volunteer opportunities.

Link to Your Life

What skills do you have that you could share with others by volunteering?

Protecting the Environment

Another way to improve your community is to take action to protect the environment. Protecting the environment means keeping water and air clean and preserving a healthy food supply, to name just a few areas. They are important for everyone's health and well-being—now and in the future. As an individual citizen, your actions have a worldwide impact on the environment. Through personal support, by wise purchasing decisions, and through recycling actions, everyone can make a difference.

- *Contact your representatives* in all levels of government and let them know that you support the need to protect the environment.
- *Contact companies* who may have an impact on your local environment to see what they are doing to control pollution.
- *Make wise purchasing decisions.* Choose items that have recyclable packaging like glass, paper, aluminum, and cardboard. Check plastic containers for the recycling symbol. Plastics with a recycling classification of 1 or 2 are easiest to recycle.
- *Choose reusable items* rather than disposable products.

- *Buy only what you will use*, especially items such as cleaning agents, solvents, and paints.

- *Sort recyclable items.* Having items clean and ready for recycling can assist a community recycling program.

- *Follow local regulations* in disposing of nonrecyclable items.

Some communities have a hazardous waste collection drive. They set up collection sites for wastes such as empty paint cans, old cleaning agents, or similar products. The disposal of such items needs to be controlled to protect the environment.

Use What You Learn

What steps can you take to help people in your community be more conscious of protecting the environment?

Review Section 21:3

1. Name three requirements that citizens must meet to vote.

2. What does a citizen accomplish by voting?

3. Describe the difference between a felony and a misdemeanor.

4. List four conditions of a legal contract.

5. List four types of taxes that are collected by local, state, or federal governments. Then give an example of services that are provided through each tax.

6. Describe three steps a person can take to protect the environment.

Think It Through

Using Leadership Skills

A committee of five has been given the task of finding a band for a community festival. Kayla has been appointed the chairperson of the committee.

Kayla's first step was to call each of her committee members. She asked what time would be convenient for them to meet. She also asked if they had any specific concerns about the meeting. Then she asked each committee member to think about some possibilities for a band.

When the committee had the first meeting, Kayla stated its goal: finding a band. Then she asked the group to brainstorm the qualities the band should have. The next step was to think of bands in the area that fit these qualities. This helped them determine the suitable choices available.

Then, Kayla guided the group in evaluating the alternatives. They identified both positive and negative factors for each band. At that point, the committee members felt they needed more information to make a decision. They needed to know which bands were available that night, what kind of music each could play, and what they charged. The committee members agreed to research one band each. Kayla assigned one band to each person. They agreed on the next meeting date.

At the next meeting, each person presented the information they had gathered related to the bands. The group discussed each alternative. Kayla could tell that two committee members favored one band and two favored another. She wondered if she should call for a vote. She did not want to have the committee divided. Instead, she suggested the committee present a report to the large group. As chairperson, Kayla drew up the report for the group, presenting all the factors the committee had identified. Then the large group voted for the band they wanted.

After the large group voted, Kayla implemented a plan. She asked the committee member who supported that particular band to make the contact and confirm the date. Arrangements were made and the band came for the community festival.

After the event was over, the committee met again to evaluate its choice. They discussed the qualities of the band. They shared comments from others about how the band was received. They also discussed whether this band would be a good choice for another event. This evaluation was put into a report and presented to the entire group for future reference.

Questions to Guide Your Thinking

1. In leading the group through the decision-making process, when did Kayla use a relationship-style of leadership?

2. Why do you think she used a relationship-style of leadership in this situation?

3. When did Kayla use a task-oriented style of leadership?

4. Why do you think she used the task-oriented approach?

5. Do you think one style would be more effective than the other? Explain your reasoning.

6. What technique did Kayla use to develop rapport in her group?

7. What technique did she use to get the group members involved?

8. How did she encourage unity and avoid division in her small group?

9. Explain why you think Kayla was or was not an effective group leader.

Chapter Summary

Effective leadership is needed in a successful group. A leader is responsible for seeing that goals are identified and met. Leaders may use a task-oriented style or a relationship-oriented style to meet their responsibilities. The role of leader also requires skills for communicating, directing discussions, motivating members, and problem solving.

Groups are important because they can accomplish what no single person can do in the same amount of time. Many opportunities exist in which people become involved in a group, either as leaders or group members. Active groups depend on good leadership and good membership to be successful.

As a citizen, you are a member of an important group—the community in which you live. Through the right to vote, citizens can provide input into decisions made at local, state, and federal levels of government. Citizens have a responsibility to obey the laws of the land and pay taxes. It is important that individuals be involved in their community by volunteering and caring for the environment. The input of one person, multiplied by many, can have a far-reaching and powerful impact.

Assess...

Your Knowledge

1. What techniques can leaders use to motivate a group?

2. What strategies can help a group be effective?

3. What are the rights and responsibilities of citizenship?

Your Understanding

4. What personality traits are attributed to each leadership style?

5. Give an example of how a civil law could protect a citizen's rights.

6. How can you stay involved as a citizen?

Your Skills

7. Explain what style of leadership you would use to lead a group to clean up a local park. Explain why you would use that style in this situation.

8. What steps would you take to plan and organize a chapter of a national career and technical student organization at your school?

9. Write a legal contract between you and a friend in which you agree to lend him $300 and he agrees to pay you back in one month. If you are under 18, identify what additional steps you would need to take to make this legal.

Think Critically

10. Choose one of the following topics and identify which large group discussion technique you would use to promote that topic. Explain your choice.
    - changing the legal drinking age
    - choosing a career in family and consumer sciences
    - developing effective parenting skills

11. *Research, writing.* Research and write a report on an area of public service that is paid for by tax dollars. Include the following in your report:
    - name of the service
    - specific services provided
    - any fees that must be paid
    - eligibility requirements for the service

12. Identify a need in your school that could be addressed through a classroom club. Form the club. Develop a constitution with a written statement of purpose, goals, and methods of reaching those goals. Specify what officers will be included. Suggest five possible bylaws for the club. *Choice:* Research a current club and report on each of the items above.

13. *Writing.* Think about three different group situations in which you have been involved. Analyze the style of leadership that was used in each group. In a one-page paper, describe each situation and the leadership style used. Then make a judgment regarding the effectiveness of the match between the situation and the style. Make suggestions for improvement. *Group option:* Work with a partner who has been in similar group situations.

Connect with Your Community

14. *Social studies.* Attend a school board meeting and observe the group in action. Describe the members' involvement, the group's setting, the styles of leadership used, and techniques of control that you observed.

15. *Research.* Choose a club that interests you in your community and research the club's background. In a one-page report, identify the purpose of the club, the organizational structure, and the basic points in the constitution and bylaws. Summarize the activities of the group, and identify the needs it meets in group members' lives. Explain the leadership style used by the group leader.

16. Interview a locally elected official, asking him or her to discuss the following topics:
    - the procedure for registering to vote
    - the local government's structure and operating procedure
    - how to become actively involved in local government

    Summarize the results of the interview in writing. Discuss why you think more people do not become actively involved in local government.

17. *Research, writing.* Identify an issue in your community related to protecting the environment. Research various sides of the issue. Then write a letter to the editor of your local newspaper, expressing your position on the issue. Be sure to present information to support your position.

Use Technology

18. *Writing.* Search the Internet to locate current issues addressed by your state government. Choose one issue that particularly interests you. Contact your state representatives via e-mail or a written letter to express your opinions.

19. Use a word-processing program to develop a leader's manual that will help you in future leadership situations. Include one or two pages for each section below. Be creative as you develop each section. Include diagrams, guidelines, lists, pictures, posters, and sample displays. *Group option:* In groups of four, complete the manual and prepare your finished product for posting on a Web site.
    - Section 1. Communication Tips for Leaders
    - Section 2. Guiding Group Discussions
    - Section 3. Techniques for Motivating Teams
    - Section 4. Solving Problems As a Group

20. *Research.* Using a computer, prepare a table listing the services provided by government agencies down the side. Across the top put local, state, and federal levels of government. Complete the table by researching which level of government contributes money to each service. Print out the table and provide a written summary of your opinions on how the three levels of government spend tax dollars.

Connecting with Career Clusters

Business, Management & Administration

Pathways

- General Management
- Business Information Management
- Human Resources Management
- Operations Management
- Administrative Support

Human Resources Manager

Human resources managers and specialists handle the routine tasks of interviewing, hiring, and explaining company benefits and policies to employees. These specialists also provide training opportunities to personnel and help firms make the best use of their employees' skills. Many also write employee newsletters and develop programs to boost employee morale.

A big part of this career is staying informed of laws and guidelines pertaining to equal employment, affirmative action, health insurance, pension planning, and other workplace programs. Human resources managers also negotiate labor issues between workers and managers and resolve employee conflicts.

People in this career work normal office hours, except when labor contracts are being prepared. Most work in an office setting, but may travel extensively to discuss labor contracts or recruit new employees. Human resources positions are found in every industry, with about 13 percent of workers in state, federal, and local government.

A bachelor's degree is needed for entry-level jobs, but specialized and top positions require an advanced degree. Courses in business, psychology, management, labor law, and employee training and development are important.

Career Outlook

A career in human resources requires good communication, persuasion, presentation, and computer skills; a talent for functioning well under pressure, coping with opposing viewpoints, and resolving conflict; an ability to work with people from various backgrounds; and integrity and fair-mindedness.

The overall growth of new jobs through 2016 is expected to be faster than average. Salaries for human resources managers ranged from $51,800 to $145,600 in 2006, with a median salary of $88,510. Salary varies according to the type of employer, level of experience, and area of specialty.

Explore

Internet Research
Find a company that interests you on the Internet and search for information about working in its human resources department. What career information does the site provide? Write a letter (as though you were applying for a job) indicating how you, as a potential human resources specialist, could benefit the business.

Job Shadowing
Spend some time with an employee who handles human resource tasks for a local business, organization, or school. Summarize your impressions of the job in a one-page paper. Report the person's title, and identify 10 qualities the person possesses.

Community Service/Volunteer
Volunteer to referee children's games for a summer camp, youth-group outing, or recreation department program. Afterward, report the type of training you received before starting the assignment and the lessons you learned from the experience.

Project
Identify a problem in your school involving two or more people that needs to be resolved. Then, take on the role of a human resources manager and determine the steps to take to solve the problem. Write a report describing what you would do in each step and how much time the project would take.

Interview
Ask a human resources manager for a 15-minute telephone interview about his or her job. Find out the main responsibilities of the job and the skills required to accomplish them. Also, learn what the job requires in terms of education, training, and experience. Prepare a report summarizing your information.

Part-Time Job
Prepare a training manual that could be used to train a person who does your job. Include techniques that would help the new worker become efficient and productive. Identify training workshops held in the area that could be beneficial to you and similar jobholders.

Unit 6
Managing Your World

Chapter 22

Managing Your Time

Section 22:1
Why Manage Time?

Section 22:2
How to Manage Your Time

Key Questions

Questions to answer as you study this chapter:

- How can time management help a person achieve goals?

- What tools can help with time management?

Chapter Objectives

After studying this chapter, you will be able to

- **identify** the benefits of managing time.

- **relate** the use of time to values and goals.

- **develop** a weekly and daily plan for managing time.

- **analyze** time management tools for their effectiveness in helping you manage time.

Life Sketch

Lea flopped across her bed, exhausted. The after-school basketball game had run overtime. Then she and Terry had stopped to eat after the game. It was eight o'clock already, and she still had a lot to do. She really needed to study for tomorrow's science test. Then she had some math homework. That wouldn't take too long, but the history report was due tomorrow, too!

"Why didn't I start sooner?" she moaned to herself. She thought of the assignment that Mr. Havaro had given two weeks ago. "I always seem to leave these things to the last minute. I just wish I had more time!"

Getting Started

Lea's wish for more time is common to many. Why is time such a valuable resource? Why does it make a difference how a person uses time? Here are two important reasons why time management is important:

- **Time is a limited resource.** The amount of time that each person has is limited. Every person has 24 hours each day. Whatever you do in life, you have to complete it within the time you have.

- **Time is a scarce resource.** Often, there seems to be too little time to do what you want to do. The fact is, not enough time exists to do everything.

Learning to manage your time wisely is a useful skill. Time management can help you do everything you need and want to do. It is a skill you can use throughout your life.

section 22:1

Why Manage Time?

Sharpen Your Reading

As you read, list reasons why you should manage your time and then create a diagram or picture that illustrates each reason.

Boost Your Vocabulary

Before you read, list all the words that come to mind when you think about time management. After reading, create another list of terms that you relate with time management.

Know Key Terms

time management

Because time is limited and the possible uses of time are many, time needs to be managed. **Time management** means controlling the use of time. This includes planning how you will use your time and then carrying out your plan. Learning to use this skill can help you in many ways, 22-1.

The Benefits of Time Management

Managing your time can help you do the following:

- *Accomplish important activities.* Managing your time can help you make choices so you complete important activities first.

- *Balance your activities.* A balance of activities is important for overall good health and development. Time management can help you recognize your priorities and spend time on the important areas of your life.

- *Reach your goals.* Managing your time can help you choose activities that move you down a path toward reaching your goals.

- *Avoid wasting time.* By planning and controlling the use of your time, you can avoid time wasters. Managing your time can help you find more of it to spend in meaningful activities.

Link to Your Life

Who do you know tries to do too many activities? Do you sometimes find it hard to say no when someone asks you to do one more thing?

Time Management and Values

When planning your time, look at the overall picture of your life path and ask these questions: What in your life is important to you? In what activities do you want to spend your time? Your answers will help identify your values.

22-1 This society highly values time. Everyone is expected to put time to good use.

The next question to answer is "How do you really spend your time?" Think of all the activities you do in a day. Ask yourself this question. "Am I really spending time on things that are important to me?" Managing your time can help you make this happen.

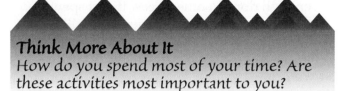

Think More About It
How do you spend most of your time? Are these activities most important to you?

Identifying Your Values

After examining all the activities you do in life, determine which you cannot eliminate or would not want to live without. These activities are ones you value highly. You can identify your values more easily by grouping them under the following categories.

- *Personal activities.* These include eating, sleeping, bathing, and dressing. Time spent for personal growth, such as reading or learning a new skill, is also included in this group.
- *Relationship activities.* All your relationships with parents, siblings, peers, and others are in this group.
- *Work activities.* These include time spent doing productive work. Being a good student by participating in classes and studying is work. You may also perform work at a job or by doing assigned tasks at home.
- *Leisure activities.* These activities involve enjoyment and relaxation. Examples include playing a sport, reading, or doing anything that interests you.
- *Support activities.* These include activities that help and benefit others, such as helping your siblings learn to read or volunteering in your community.

Link to Your Life

How might your values and your use of time change as you grow and mature?

When you plan the use of your time, include activities that are important to you in each of the areas you value. Such planning will help you balance your time across all areas important to your life.

Sometimes you will need to say no to activities that are worthwhile, but not very important to you. This is necessary when trying to manage time according to priorities. By spending time in important activities, you will be happier with what you do. Also, you will avoid wasting time on unimportant activities.

Time Management and Goals

Your plans for the future are usually based on goals formed by your values. When daily activities move you closer to accomplishing goals, you will feel better about yourself, 22-2. You will feel successful and capable, and your self-esteem will increase.

Identifying Your Goals

Much of your time may be spent doing activities that you must do. You may not feel that you are getting close to reaching your goals. Looking at the big picture with your long-term goals can be helpful. Then break those long-term goals into short-term weekly and daily goals. This can help you manage your time on a weekly and daily basis. It can also help you see how daily activities contribute toward your goals.

- *Personal goals.* What goals do you have for yourself? A good appearance? Good health? By identifying these goals—and recognizing the progress you continue to make—you will feel successful.
- *Relationship goals.* What goals do you have for your relationships? Do you spend time with family members and friends to strengthen those relationships? Activities that help relationships grow need to be included in a time management plan.
- *Work goals.* What goals do you have for the work you do? Right now you may feel that getting through school is a big enough goal. How you spend your time now will

22-2 Feelings of satisfaction and success can result when you manage your time to reach your goals.

likely affect your future choices about work. Spending time studying for good grades and taking certain courses will help prepare you for advanced education or training.

- *Leisure goals.* A balance of leisure and other activities is needed. If you spend too much time in fun activities, you will not get enough done in other areas. If you spend too little time in leisure activities, you will feel stressed. Time to relax and enjoy yourself is important for handling the effects of stress in your life.

- *Support goals.* Many worthwhile activities exist in which you could benefit others as well as yourself. Opportunities in your school, community, house of worship, or other areas of service are available. These build valuable teamwork skills that are important to mention in your resume. They also help you keep your life balanced.

Review Section 22:1

1. Explain what is meant by "time is a limited resource."
2. List two benefits of managing time.
3. List five categories of values that determine how people use time.

section 22:2

How to Manage Your Time

Sharpen Your Reading

Preview this section and list the three main strategies for managing time.

Boost Your Vocabulary

Create a list of your upcoming projects or tasks. For each item on your list, identify specific ways to prevent yourself from procrastinating.

Know Key Terms

deadline
procrastinate

Time is used minute by minute. Planning for every minute of every day is difficult, if not impossible! However, planning the use of your time on a weekly and daily basis is much more manageable. It is one way to make the most of your time.

Your Time Management Plan

A time management plan will help you use time wisely and work toward important goals. Your activities will be more meaningful and will help you experience success in your life. The following steps can help you organize a time management plan:

- *Identify your values.* Decide what is really important in each area of your life.
- *Identify your goals for each major value.* Choose two or three major goals to pursue at one time. As you start making progress toward reaching these, other goals can be added.
- *Set a deadline to meet each goal.* A **deadline** is the time at which a task needs to be completed. Record the deadlines on a calendar, showing weekly, monthly, and yearly goals.
- *Break down each major goal into smaller subgoals.* What are the steps that will lead you to reaching each long-term goal? A deadline for each step can help you progress toward your goals as you follow your management plan.

Thinking about the obstacles that might keep you from reaching your goals is also helpful. As you plan your activities, you can take steps to handle or avoid possible obstacles.

Use What You Learn

Why are deadlines important to consider when creating a time management plan?

Your Weekly Plan

Your weekly plan should include a list of activities you want or need to do that week, 22-3. It should also include a deadline for the completion of those activities.

List the activities in order of importance. Activities that must be done this week become top priority. Those that should be done but are not as pressing become medium priority. Those that you want to get done eventually become low priority.

| Weekly Time Management Plan ||
Things To Do	Deadline
Science; read pages 50-62	Sunday
Social studies report	Monday
Clean room	Tuesday
Study for math test	Tuesday night
Buy pizza and chips	Friday night
Call friends for Friday night	Thursday night
Help Dad mow lawn	Saturday afternoon
Go bowling	Saturday night

22-3 A weekly plan should include the activities you want to get done and a deadline for each.

Your Daily Plan

To create a daily plan, divide your weekly goals into smaller steps that can be accomplished each day, 22-4. Number and list these items, putting the most important first. For each day, write down one or two goals that you would like to reach.

Large projects might take several days of work before they are completed. Set aside some time in a daily plan to work on part of a big project. Schedule enough time to work on an activity to make sure it is completed by the deadline.

As you make your daily plan, block out periods of time that are the same every day. These include grooming, eating, and sleeping periods. Then add your top-priority items first and medium-priority items next. If any time is left, add your low-priority items.

Use What You Learn

How could a weekly plan help a person use time wisely on a day-to-day basis?

Avoiding Time Wasters

A well-organized plan is beneficial only when you are able to carry it out. That means avoiding obstacles that prevent you from following your schedule. Some of the major obstacles are time wasters, such as procrastination, interruptions, disorganization, and lack of preparation.

Avoid Procrastinating

Some people waste time because they **procrastinate**. They put off doing a project. Instead of working on the project, they do less-important activities. Then, at the last minute, they hurry to get the project done. Procrastination can lead to mistakes, incomplete projects, and poor-quality work. It also causes stress and anxiety. Avoid procrastinating by dividing bigger projects into smaller tasks to complete each day.

Avoid Interruptions

When you plan work time, plan to carry it out in a quiet place away from interruptions. If you have voice mail on your phone, let your friends leave messages and return the calls after you finish studying. If you are working on the computer, close your e-mail and sign out of instant messaging services and social networking sites.

Link to Your Life

What are some interruptions that you experience when you are trying to work? How could you reduce those interruptions?

Stay Organized

Storing items in a specific place and returning them after each use is a good way to stay organized. If you are organized, you will spend less time searching for items and will have more time to work on reaching your goals.

Be Prepared for Unplanned Events

Unplanned events often become time wasters. An accident may keep you sitting in traffic an extra hour. You may have to wait in the doctor's office while an emergency patient is treated. You can make use of these unexpected periods by always carrying some type of activity with you.

Daily Time Management Plan	
Monday, February 8	
Daily Goals: Read one resource for social studies project.	
Time Schedule	**Things to Do Today:**

Time Schedule		Things to Do Today:
6:15	Shower and dress	5 Call Kallie about Friday party
7:15	Breakfast	3 Practice for band
7:30	Leave for school	1 Regular homework
8:00	School	2 Review for math test
	↓	4 Start on social studies report
3:30	Track practice	6 Pick up clutter in my room
4:30	↓	
5:00	Get home Help prepare dinner	
5:30	Eat dinner	
6:00	Help clean up kitchen	
6:30	Relax Watch TV	
7:00	Do regular homework	
7:30	Review math	
8.00	Read one resource for social studies	
8:30	Practice trumpet	
9:00	Call Kallie Relax and get ready for bed	

22-4 A few minutes spent planning a day can help you reach your daily goals.

It may be a book you want to read or a craft or hobby you like to do. Even if you forget one of these projects, you could use your spare time to think about your overall management plan. What progress have you made toward your goals? What improvements would you like to make? Whether you think through or actually carry out an activity, time is used beneficially, not wasted.

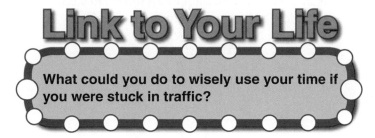

Link to Your Life

What could you do to wisely use your time if you were stuck in traffic?

Time Management Tools

Time management tools can help you organize and save time. They let you get more done with the time you have. You will be able to reach more of your goals as well as carry out tasks that are important to you. This can help you feel successful and enjoy what you do each day.

Personal Calendar

A personal calendar can help you meet deadlines on time. It can also help you remember your appointments and commitments. With a personal calendar, you can plan your priority activities so you progress toward your goals.

Your calendar can be paper or digital, 22-5. It should include yearly, monthly, weekly, and daily goals. It should also include appointments and deadlines.

Using Technology

As technology advances, more and more tools are available to help you save time. Personal computers are often used for time management. A computer can help you save time on many tasks, including the following:

- *Information gathering.* Using the Internet, you can instantly access information about any topic.
- *Financial management.* Many people use a computer to track their personal finances, balance their checkbook, and pay bills. Some financial management programs can be used to create budgets, track spending, and prepare reports for filing income taxes.

22-5 Personal calendars, either paper or digital, can help you keep track of important appointments, activities, and tasks.

- *Filing and recordkeeping.* What types of lists and files do you need to keep? Addresses and phone numbers? Medical costs? Data can be easily entered and sorted using spreadsheets and databases.
- *Automating household tasks.* Some computer programs are designed to store recipes and menus and generate shopping lists.
- *Learning new skills.* Online classes or distance learning courses eliminate travel time to a classroom and provide the opportunity to expand your knowledge and skills.

Personal digital assistants (*PDAs*) offer many of the same capabilities as computers in a portable, handheld format. Using a PDA, you can keep track of your appointments and activities electronically. Some PDAs are also cellular phones and may have wireless Internet access.

The tools you use to manage your time can be as simple as paper and pencil or as advanced as a PDA. Select the tools that are readily available to you and will help you manage your time best. As new technologies are developed, consider implementing new tools to manage your time.

Link to Your Life

What technology tools do you or your friends use? In what ways do they help you save time?

Review Section 22:2

1. List four steps to follow in organizing a time management plan.
2. List the information that should be included in a weekly time management plan.
3. Name four ways to avoid time wasters.
4. Name two time management tools. How can each tool help a person manage time?

Think It Through

Managing Time

Chor felt overwhelmed as she stared at the tall stack of textbooks on her desk. She brought home every book from school for the weekend. She wondered how she was going to get all her work done! She had 28 problems to do for math which were due Monday. She had to read chapter three in science by Tuesday and turn in a chapter outline by Wednesday. She had to give an oral report to her health class on Friday, which had to include library research.

Then she had her piano lesson scheduled on Monday at 4 p.m. She had to practice one-half hour daily for that. Her family expected her to help with household tasks for one-half hour each day as well.

Her friends invited her to go bowling Saturday afternoon and to a movie afterward. On Sunday her family spent several hours at their house of worship. In the afternoon, they planned to visit her cousin and her new baby, who everyone was anxious to see for the first time.

Chor decided she had to get organized. She had to have a plan. How else could she manage to get all those things done on time?

Questions to Guide Your Thinking

1. Identify Chor's weekly goals. Put them in a list and number them in order of importance. What must be done first?

2. Help Chor plan the use of her time in the next seven days (Saturday to Friday) by developing a weekly time schedule.

   - Identify at least one daily goal for each day.

   - Set aside time for studying and music practice on a regular basis.

   - Include specific times for each major project.

   - Include time for the following activities: building relationships, developing hobbies, and helping others.

3. How could use of a computer save time for Chor in the next week?

Chapter Summary

Everyone has the same number of hours in a day, yet most people wish they had more. Since time is limited, managing it is important. Time management means controlling the use of time by making a plan and following it.

Two key aspects of planning are values and goals. A person's values include views about work, leisure, and helping others. When people do what is important to them, their values are influencing their actions and helping them reach their goals. Also, they are more satisfied with life and feel that time has been well spent.

Planning use of time needs to be done weekly and daily. A weekly plan should include all the tasks that a person wants to get done and a deadline for each. A daily plan should include one or two small goals that lead toward reaching a long-term goal.

By avoiding time wasters, individuals can save time and turn it to good use. Time management tools, such as calendars and personal computers, can help people plan and organize their time.

Assess...

Your Knowledge

1. What are the benefits of managing time?

2. What are the steps in developing a time management plan?

Your Understanding

3. How does a person's use of time reflect his or her values?

4. How could a person's use of time impact the ability to reach goals?

Your Skills

5. Develop a time management plan for yourself. Include weekly and daily goals, appointments and activities, and deadlines for projects and assignments.

6. What could be the advantages and disadvantages of using a personal digital assistant (PDA) as a time management tool?

Think Critically

7. *Social studies.* Create a chart or table listing the five categories of values. For each category, list some goals that are common to teens and young adults. Explain how time management could help achieve each goal. *Choice:* Draw pictures that represent each category.

8. *Research, writing.* Research a career of your choice. Write a paper on the importance of time management for success in that career.

9. *Research.* Analyze two time management tools for their value in helping you manage your time. Gather information on their cost, their ease of use, and features that could help manage time. Weigh these features and make a judgment about whether they would be good tools for your personal time management needs. Write a paragraph summarizing your findings. *Choice:* Present your information to the class in an oral presentation.

10. *Math, writing.* Conduct a survey to determine your classmates' use of time. Calculate the average number of hours spent on personal, relationship, work, leisure, and support activities. Then in a one-page paper, compare your use of time with the class averages. Discuss how your use of time helps (or does not help) you reach your life goals.

Connect with Your Community

11. Visit a store in your community where computers are sold. Inquire about software that is available and find out what the software is designed to do. Prepare a list of software that you would recommend for assisting with time management in the home. *Group option:* Work with two or three other students and visit several stores.

12. *Social studies.* Interview a young adult who works full-time. Ask questions related to the use of time in various areas. In a paragraph, compare the working person's use of time to a student's use of time.

13. Take a field trip to a department store or an office supply store. Identify as many time management tools as you can. Prepare a list of these tools along with a description of how they could help you use your time more wisely. *Choice:* Instead of taking a field trip, use the Internet to visit office supply store Web sites.

Use Technology

14. Using the computer, design a one-page weekly time management calendar. Include slots for high-priority items, medium-priority items, low-priority items, daily goals, daily lists, and an hourly schedule. Create your own time management plan for one week using your calendar. *Group option:* Exchange calendars with a partner. Complete your plan on your partner's calendar. Then provide feedback to your partner regarding the effectiveness of the plan.

15. *Speech.* Research a computer program that could be used for home management. Prepare a report for the class and a demonstration of how that program works.

16. *Math.* Keep a daily diary for a week. Record everything you do and how much time you spend at it. At the end of the week, analyze your use of time. Record the number of hours you spent in personal, relationship, work, leisure, and support activities. Show your use of time in a pie chart or a bar graph. *Group option:* Work with a partner and compare your results. Calculate the average amount of combined time you spent in each activity area. Create a pie chart or bar graph that shows your averages.

Chapter 23

Managing Your Money

Section 23:**1**
Your Income

Section 23:**2**
Using a Budget

Section 23:**3**
Banking Services

Section 23:**4**
Using Credit Wisely

Key Questions

Questions to answer as you study this chapter:

- How can a person balance income and expenses?

- What banking services can help with money management?

- How can credit be used wisely?

Chapter Objectives

After studying this chapter, you will be able to
- **describe** sources of income.
- **plan** a budget to help you manage your money wisely.
- **describe** how to use a checking account.
- **relate** interest and liquidity to savings accounts.
- **recognize** guidelines for using credit wisely.

Life Sketch

Sharon and Milo planned to go shopping after work, and their list of needs was long. They had recently rented a larger apartment and needed new furniture. Both had good jobs, so the move to the larger apartment seemed like a good idea. However, it was farther to work for both of them. Since driving each other to work was out of the way, they also felt they needed another car.

During her lunch hour, Sharon bought two lamps on sale and looked at a couch and two chairs. Sharon wanted Milo to see the furniture before she used their credit card to make such a costly purchase.

Sharon wondered how much they would need for a down payment on a car. The dealer said they could buy a new car and finance it through the manufacturer. She knew they would save considerable time if they had their own cars.

Getting Started

Sharon and Milo's needs are common to many young adults. These needs often come all at once—when people first live on their own, are newly married, or start a new job. Meeting all these needs at once may seem important, but spending without a plan can result in financial disaster.

Learning to manage your money will enable you to live within your means and reach your goals. It involves creating a budget, planning the use of your income, and controlling your spending. Understanding and using various banking services can also help you manage your money. In addition, using credit wisely can help you reach your financial goals.

section 23:1

Your Income

Sharpen Your Reading

Create a two-column chart. As you read, list the various ways of earning income in the left column. Write a description of each in the right column.

Boost Your Vocabulary

Compare the interest earned on an investment that is compounded monthly for twelve months to the same investment compounded quarterly for one year. Identify the investment that would earn more interest.

Know Key Terms

gross income
net income
interest
compounding

Income is necessary to be independent and get the goods and services needed to live on your own. Income can come from several sources. You can work for an employer and earn a wage. You can work for yourself in your own business and earn a profit. Income can also come from savings and investments.

Think More About It
What would be the benefits of having income from more than one source?

Income from Work

Most people earn income by working and are paid wages. Wages include payments—in the form of an hourly wage, a salary, or a commission—and any benefits received from an employer. Vacation pay, bonuses, and tips are also considered part of a person's wages.

- *Hourly Wage.* Some workers are paid by the hour. Many beginning workers receive a minimum wage. *Minimum wage*, which is set by the federal government, is the lowest amount per hour that most workers must receive. You can learn what the minimum wage is by contacting a Job Service office or the U.S. Department of Labor.

- *Salary.* A salary is a set amount of money that is paid for all the work that goes with a job description.

- *Commission.* Some wages are paid when a job is done or a service is provided. In sales jobs, commission is often a certain percentage of each sale made by a worker.

- *Profit.* Some people are self-employed and earn an income through their own business. As entrepreneurs, they sell goods or services for money. Profit is the amount of money earned from sales, minus expenses.

Weigh the Facts What might be the advantages and disadvantages of earning each type of income?

At a job, the wage or salary you make is called your **gross income**. However, the amount of money you actually receive is less than your stated income, 23-1. From your gross income, certain paycheck deductions are subtracted. Some of these deductions are required by law, such as federal and state income taxes and Social Security tax, listed as *FICA*. (This stands for the *Federal Insurance Contributions Act*, a part of which goes toward a Medicare tax.) Your take-home pay is your net income. **Net income** is the amount of money left after subtracting the deductions from your gross income.

CIRCOLINI, SAL K.			Social Security No. 131 02 1111
			Check No. 04244

CIRCOLINI, SAL K.
Period Ending   5/12/XX
Hours   20
Rate $10.50

Gross Pay   = $210.00
FICA:
  Social Security   =   13.02
  Medicare   =   3.05
Federal Tax   =   21.00
State Tax   =   6.30
Total Deductions   =   43.37

Net Pay   = $166.63

- -

Coastal Cannery   04244
West Coast Road   May 14, 20XX
West Coast, WA 01234

Pay To The
Order Of   **SAL K. CIRCOLINI** $ 166.63

ONE HUNDRED SIXTY-SIX AND 63/100   Dollars

1st Bank of West Coast
West Coast, WA 01234   *PJ Canner*

23-1 Your paycheck, like Sal's, should reflect deductions for income taxes. Sal keeps the top half as a record of income received and deductions made. The check at the bottom she cashes at the bank.

What are some advantages and disadvantages of being a business owner rather than an hourly worker?

Income from Savings and Investments

Income can also be obtained by placing money in various savings and investment plans. The money earned may be subject to income taxes.

Savings

Money placed in a savings account earns interest. **Interest** is a charge for the use of money, usually expressed as a percentage. Income earned on a savings account is called *interest income*. For instance, if you had $10,000 in a savings account with an annual interest rate of 4%, you would earn $400 in one year. This $400 is interest income. Interest income on a savings account is based on the following four factors:

- total savings
- length of savings period
- interest rate
- type of compounding used

Compounding is when the interest previously earned is added to the total before new interest earnings are figured, 23-2. Therefore, interest is paid on your original deposit plus the amount already earned. Interest may be compounded *annually* (once a year), *semi-annually* (twice a year), *quarterly* (four times a year), or monthly.

Use What You Learn

What is the benefit of having your money earn interest over a long period of time?

How Interest Income Grows								
	Principal		**Interest Rate**		**Time**			**Interest Earned**
	100.00	X	2½%	X	6 months		=	$1.25
1. Increase in principal	200.00	X	2½%	X	6 months		=	$2.50
2. Rate increase	200.00	X	3%	X	6 months		=	$3.00
3. Time increase	200.00	X	3%	X	1 year		=	$6.00
4. Compounded quarterly	200.00	X	3%	X	1 year		=	$6.07

23-2 This chart shows how interest income grows as the following factors are increased: (1) principal, (2) interest rate, (3) length of the savings period, and (4) frequency of compounding.

Investments

Investments include stocks, bonds, mutual funds, retirement accounts, and real estate. Money put into these investments is usually kept there for several years, sometimes until retirement age. Depending on market conditions, some investments can increase dramatically if held for several decades. However, some investments can lose value.

Another way to make money with investments is through buying and selling them, which is called *trading*. The key to successful trading is buying an investment at a low price and selling it at a higher price. While the financial rewards can be high, so are the risks. Consequently, trading is recommended only for experts.

Income During Emergencies

Sometimes people lose their source of income. They may lose their job or become ill or injured. Families may be able to get help from local social service or human service agencies. Some families purchase insurance to provide income during emergencies, such as short-term or long-term disability insurance. Social Security insurance provides income for workers who are disabled, as well as their spouses and children.

Financial experts recommend having enough savings set aside to cover living expenses for three to six months in the event of an emergency. Establishing such an account and contributing to it regularly can help you avoid financial problems.

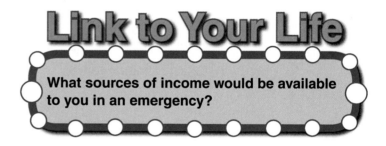

Link to Your Life

What sources of income would be available to you in an emergency?

Review Section 23:**1**

1. Name and describe four ways to earn income from work.
2. Explain the difference between gross and net income.
3. Identify the most common paycheck deductions.
4. List the four factors that affect the amount of interest income earned.
5. What are some income sources that could help families through an emergency?

section 23:2

Using a Budget

Sharpen Your Reading

As you read, create a list of the different pieces of information you would need to develop a family budget.

Boost Your Vocabulary

Interview a parent and ask which items in their family budget are fixed expenses and which items are variable expenses.

Know Key Terms

budget
fixed expenses
variable expenses

A **budget** is a plan for the use of your income. Whether your income is small or large, a budget is a tool that can help you in the following ways:

- control spending so you live within your income
- guide decision making about purchases
- set aside money for special purchases, future plans, and emergencies
- reach financial goals

Your budget will be different from another person's plan for spending, 23-3. That is because a budget is based on personal income, expenses, and plans for savings. Your income may be identical to another person's, but your expenses

will differ because of your needs, values, and goals. These factors will also influence how much you save and how you use your savings.

A family budget will likely include more expenses than an individual budget. Usually, the expenses of all family members must be met with one or two incomes. Involving the whole family in the planning process can lead to greater success in developing a budget.

Think More About It
How might a budget help guide your decisions about making purchases?

Establishing Goals for Your Income

Deciding what you need and want is the first step in planning a budget. Your needs and wants will determine your short- and long-term financial goals.

Most people expect their income to provide for their needs. They need to have food, shelter, and clothing—goals that must be taken care of immediately. However, expecting the best food, clothing, and living conditions are not needs, but wants.

Most people do not have enough money to do everything they need and want at once. By building a savings, they set aside money for the following:

- short-term goals, such as buying a car or taking a vacation
- long-term goals, such as a college education or retirement

Planning and controlling the use of your income by following a budget can help you meet your needs as well as short- and long-term financial goals.

Link to Your Life

What are some of your goals that are needs? What are some of your goals that are wants?

Planning a Budget	
Gross monthly income from paychecks	$3,200.00
Deductions:	
Federal tax	316.20
State tax	175.00
Social Security and Medicare	244.80
Net income	**$2,464.00**
Monthly Expenses	**Amount**
Housing	
Rent (includes water)	$700
Rental insurance	23 ($276/yr.)
Utilities	
Gas	$45*
Electric	67*
Cable	40
Internet access	25
Cellular phone	65
Food	$333*
Personal	
Health insurance	$95
Other medical expenses	25*
Clothing	98*
Recreation and entertainment	125*
Miscellaneous	70*
Transportation	
Car payment	$226
Car insurance	102 ($1,224/yr.)
Gas, oil, tolls	146*
Other	
Student loan payment	$150
Savings	100
Total monthly expenses (*flexible expenses)	$2,435
Balance (income minus expenses)	$29

23-3 This budget might be typical for a young person beginning a career.

Estimating Income

A budget is usually planned by the month. To begin planning, you must first estimate your income. How much money did you make last month? That total should be a guide to how much you will make this month if you expect to do the same amount of work.

Base the estimate on your net income. Also include all other sources of income. These might include bonuses, tips, allowances, gifts, or interest earnings.

Planning Expenses

Your budget should include the categories on which you spend money. Keep a record of your expenditures for a few weeks if you are not sure how you spend it. Receipts can also help you estimate your expenses.

Most people have both fixed and variable expenses. **Fixed expenses** are expenses that are constant each month. Fixed expenses include rent, a car payment, and insurance payments. A weekly lunch ticket or bus ticket is also a fixed expense.

Variable expenses are expenses that change or vary from month to month. A telephone bill may change depending on how many calls a person makes. Clothing costs, food, and other expenses may depend on personal needs and desires, 23-4. You cannot estimate your variable expenses exactly, but the estimate should be as close as possible.

Use What You Learn

How would you include the expense of a yearly insurance payment in your monthly budget?

Planning for Savings

An important area to include in a budget is savings. Financial experts recommend treating savings as a fixed expense. When you get your paycheck, put a certain amount into savings immediately. This helps you control spending, save for future goals, and develop a habit of saving.

23-4 A family's food budget depends on their personal preferences, the cost of groceries, and how often they eat at restaurants.

Making a Budget Work for You

In a well-planned budget, the amounts reserved for spending and saving should equal income. They should never surpass your income.

After preparing your budget, use it for a trial period. Keep track of your income and expenses and compare them with your budget's estimates. If necessary, revise your budget to keep your spending and income in line. If you spend more than you make, some decisions will be needed. How can you cut your spending? Can income be increased?

Making Buying Decisions

A well-planned budget can help you make good buying decisions. For instance, suppose the personal media player you want is on sale. Take a look at your variable expenses. Have you budgeted any amount for this type of expense? Have you set aside enough money in savings for this purchase? If your budget cannot handle the expense, do not make the purchase. Consider setting aside a small amount of money each month until you have enough to purchase the personal media player.

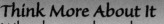

Think More About It
Why do people make purchases on impulse?
Why is it difficult for some people to follow a
budget?

Being Realistic and Flexible

When you plan a budget, you need to be realistic. You need to use figures that truly reflect your income, spending needs, and ability to save. You need to include items that are important to you. A budget is not much help if it looks great on paper but does not match your situation.

Be flexible in your planning. When expenses or income change, you need to adjust your budget to reflect those changes. If income goes up, you will be able to increase your savings, your spending, or both. You may add a fixed expense. If income goes down, you need to adjust expenses and savings to reflect that change. As your financial picture changes, so should your budget.

Using a Computer for Budgeting

Some people prefer to use a computer to track spending habits, 23-5. Spreadsheets can be used to calculate expenses and prepare a budget. Personal finance software is also a helpful budgeting tool. These programs can be linked to

23-5 A computer can help you organize financial data and quickly calculate expenses.

your bank account to automatically download and categorize expenses. If your financial situation changes, your budget is automatically adjusted. The programs also allow you to view reports of spending habits and track progress toward savings goals.

Review Section 23:2

1. List four benefits of planning a budget.
2. Explain the difference between fixed and variable expenses in a budget. Give two examples of each.
3. What is the recommended way to include savings in a budget?

section
23:3

Banking Services

Sharpen Your Reading

Preview this section and list the banking services discussed. As you read about each service, write questions that you could ask at a local bank to evaluate the services provided.

Boost Your Vocabulary

Visit a financial institution's Web site and compare the liquidity of various savings accounts.

Know Key Terms

debit card
overdraft
electronic funds transfer (EFT)
liquidity

Understanding and using banking services can help you manage your money and reach your financial goals. The first step in using banking services is choosing a financial institution that meets your needs. Compare the types of accounts offered at several institutions, as well as the interest rates charged on loans and paid on savings accounts. Also, consider the location of each facility and the business hours.

You should always choose a financial institution that is insured. The Federal Deposit Insurance Corporation (FDIC) insures most banks. The National Credit Union Administration (NCUA) insures most credit unions.

A sign stating "Insured by FDIC" or "Insured by NCUA" should appear by the front window or each teller station, 23-6. This means that each depositor's account is insured for a certain amount, as designated by the FDIC. As a result, the money you deposit up to the insured amount remains safe. You will not lose your money in case the bank is robbed or goes bankrupt.

Checking Accounts

A personal checking account is a safe place to keep your money. It also offers a convenient way to pay bills and make purchases.

Before opening a checking account, investigate the types available and the requirements for each. Opening a checking account usually requires a minimum deposit. Some financial institutions charge a monthly service fee. Others require you to keep a certain amount of money in your account at all times. If your balance falls below the required amount, you will be charged a fee. Free checking accounts may be offered if you also open a savings account.

Use What You Learn

Which factor(s) would be most important to you when choosing a checking account?

23-6 If a financial institution does not state that it is FDIC-insured, your money will not be protected against losses.

Using Checks

Usually, you will have to pay a fee to order checks for your account. When writing checks, avoid errors and chances of fraud by using a pen to properly fill out all the required areas, 23-7. When a check is made out to you, you need to *endorse* it before you can cash or deposit it. This means you sign your name on the back of the check at the top left end. Never endorse a check before cashing or depositing it, and never sign a blank check.

Using Debit Cards and ATMs

A **debit card** is used to immediately withdraw funds from your checking account to pay bills and make purchases—without writing a check. Usually, you will need to enter a security code called a *PIN (personal identification number)* when using a debit card. You can also use a debit card at an *automated teller machine (ATM)* to withdraw cash from your checking account.

Careful use of a debit card can protect against fraud. Keep your card in a safe place. Memorize your PIN and keep it secret. Be sure to report a lost or stolen card to your financial institution immediately.

Managing Your Account

You should always keep accurate records of when you write checks, use a debit card, or withdraw cash from an ATM. Subtract the amounts from your account balance. When you make a deposit, record the amount and add it to your balance. By following these steps, you will always know how much money is in your checking account.

Each month the financial institution will send you a statement showing the transactions that took place in your account. (Some send bimonthly or quarterly statements.) Always compare your records with the statement to be sure your balance is accurate.

Keeping accurate records can prevent you from overdrawing your account. An **overdraft** occurs when you write a check, use your debit card, or withdraw cash from an ATM for more money than you have in your account. If you overdraw, your financial institution will charge overdraft fees. Some financial institutions offer *overdraft protection*, which acts as an instant loan to cover overdrafts to a certain limit. Overdraft protection usually involves additional fees.

Think More About It
Why do you think using a debit card might increase your chances of having an overdraft?

Online Banking

Online banking allows you to monitor your account activity 24 hours a day. You can access your statement, check your account balance,

---

Sal K. Circolini		428
Box 111 West Coast Road		
West Coast, WA 01234		_October 1_ 20 _XX_
Pay To The Order Of _Tilly's Shoes_		$ _49.21—_
Forty-nine and _²¹/₁₀₀_		DOLLARS
1ST BANK OF WEST COAST		
WEST COAST, WA 01234		
MEMO _shoes_	_Sal K. Circolini_	
01010101010 1010 1110001234 0428		

23-7 To prevent fraud, it is important to fill out a check properly.

review deposits and withdrawals, and transfer funds. **Electronic funds transfer (EFT)** allows you to use a computer to move money between accounts. Funds can be transferred between your checking account and other accounts you may have at the financial institution. You can also set up automatic payments for most bills and loans.

Make sure your computer has a secure connection before accessing financial information on the Internet. A *firewall* is a security feature that protects a computer from unauthorized access. Maintaining a firewall and installing antivirus software can help keep your connection secure. Memorize your account passwords and keep them private. In addition, when you are finished with an online banking session, be sure to properly log out from the Web site.

Investigate Further

What types of security precautions has the financial industry taken to ensure the security of online banking?

Savings Accounts

The primary purpose of a savings account is to earn interest on your money. The savings accounts offered by each financial institution may vary. Some institutions have several types. Your choice of a savings account can depend on the following factors, 23-8.

- *Convenience*—Some savings accounts allow you to withdraw money when you want. Others limit the number of withdrawals you can make in a month. Some institutions allow you to transfer money from your savings account to your checking account. Such convenience may influence you to open a savings account at the same place you have a checking account.

- *Interest rate*—The higher the interest rate, the more interest income you will earn. The more often interest is compounded, the more you will earn.

- *Liquidity*—The ability to take out your money on short notice is **liquidity**. Some savings accounts allow you to withdraw money whenever you want and even write checks on the account. These accounts have high liquidity. They usually pay the lowest rate of interest. Other savings plans require that you leave your money in the account for a period of time, but usually pay a higher interest. However, if you need your money before the time is up, a penalty is charged.

Types of Savings Plans

Most financial institutions offer a variety of savings plans. Four common types are discussed here.

- *Regular savings account*—This is the simplest savings account because money can be added or withdrawn at any time. Usually there is a low or no minimum balance and the rate of interest is low.

- *Club account*—This account acts as a budgeting device, requiring a predetermined deposit at specific times, such as saving $10 a week. A club account is planned for a special purpose, such as saving money for a vacation, 23-9.

Comparing Savings Plans		
Types	**Liquidity**	**Interest Rates**
Regular Account	Can withdraw on notice.	Pays lowest interest rates.
Club Account	Can withdraw on club due date.	Interest rates fairly low.
Certificate of Deposit (CD)	Withdrawal depends on terms of CD.	Higher rates for longer terms.
Money Market Account	Less liquid—requires minimum balance.	Rates vary with market rates.

23-8 Savings plans vary in liquidity, and rate of interest. Look for the plan that best suits your needs.

23-9 Club accounts can help families save a set amount each month for a future vacation.

• *Certificate of deposit (CD)*—This is a type of savings certificate that is issued in exchange for a specified minimum deposit. This savings plan requires you to leave your money in the account for a certain period of time. The time can vary from 31 days to several years. This allows you to earn a specific rate of interest, usually more for longer periods. If you withdraw your money before the term ends, a penalty is usually charged.

• *Money market deposit account*—This is a savings plan in which the interest rate may vary monthly. This account often requires a minimum balance. Usually, a limited number of checks may be written on the account each month.

Choosing an appropriate savings plan and saving money every month can help you use banking services to reach your short- and long-term financial goals.

Review Section 23:3

1. List three factors to consider when choosing a financial institution.
2. Explain why you should choose a FDIC or NCUA insured financial institution.
3. Describe the actions a person can take to avoid overdrafts.
4. List three factors to consider when choosing a savings account.
5. Name the type of savings account in which the interest rate may vary from month to month.

section 23:4

Using Credit Wisely

Sharpen Your Reading

Create a graphic organizer by writing the word *credit* in the center of a blank sheet of paper. Draw branches coming out from the center and write a main heading on each branch. As you read, write key ideas under the appropriate branch.

Boost Your Vocabulary

Create a chart with three columns. Write the terms in the first column and the text definitions in the second column. In the third column, write how each term relates to using credit wisely.

Know Key Terms

credit limit
collateral
annual percentage rate (APR)
credit rating

Credit enables people to purchase goods or services and pay for them in the future. Before using credit, you need to weigh its advantages and disadvantages. By doing so, you may find it advantageous for some situations, but not others. These are the main benefits.

- *You can enjoy goods and services before paying for them.* For instance, most people would not be able to purchase a home or even a car if they had to pay cash.

- *In emergencies, credit lets people purchase needed goods or services.* You may have an emergency car repair, for example, but not enough money saved to pay it. Credit can make it possible to get the repair done.

- *Credit is convenient.* Credit cards allow you to charge the purchase of many goods and services, 23-10.

- *Using credit can be safer than carrying large amounts of cash.* For instance, a family may use a credit card on a vacation rather than carry cash. Also, the family will have a record of how much was spent, where, and when.

There are also some potential disadvantages to consider before using credit. If credit is taken for granted, it could lead to financial problems. The disadvantages of using credit include the following:

- *Using credit can encourage overspending.* Credit is convenient—sometimes too convenient. Unplanned spending can easily occur if a person buys on impulse.

23-10 Credit cards offer the convenience of being able to purchase goods and services from the comfort of your own home.

- *Using credit costs money.* Lenders charge people for the privilege of buying now and paying later. Also, the more time people take to repay credit, the more they will pay in interest.

- *Credit reduces future income.* Buying on credit is a promise to pay in the future. However, people sometimes become unemployed or face emergency expenses. They may realize too late that their financial commitments exceed what they are able to pay back.

- *Misusing credit can cause serious financial problems.* Sometimes when payments are missed, the lender may *repossess*, or take back, a purchase. You would lose the money you had already paid for the item. Bankruptcy and a bad credit rating are other financial risks.

How many of these issues do you think people consider before using credit?

Credit Cards

Credit cards are one of the most common ways that people use credit. Many financial institutions, companies, and stores offer credit cards. A credit card has a **credit limit**, or a maximum amount of money that you can borrow. A minimum payment is due each month (usually 2%–4% of the balance). If the balance is not paid off in full, interest will be added. Credit cards are considered *revolving credit*, which means you can continuously borrow and repay money, as long as you stay under the credit limit.

When you have a credit card, you will receive a monthly billing statement. If you find an error, notify the creditor in writing within 60 days of the billing date. Be sure to write to the correct address for billing inquiries. Also include your name, account number, and explanation of the error. You do not need to pay the amount in question until it is settled. However, you are responsible for paying the rest of your bill on time.

If your credit card is stolen or lost, report it at once to the creditor. In such cases, the law limits your responsibility for purchases made

without your permission to $50. Once you have notified the creditor of the loss, you cannot be held responsible for any charges thereafter. Using credit cards wisely can help you avoid financial problems, 23-11.

Loans

Loans are a type of credit often used to finance cars, homes, education, or a new business. When you take out a loan, you borrow a set amount of money and agree to pay it back over time, plus interest. Loans are considered *installment credit*, which means the loan is paid

---

Tips for Using Credit Cards Wisely

- Shop around for a low annual percentage rate and low or no user fees. Fees for credit card services vary from one institution to another.

- Look for an institution that does not charge interest from the time of purchase to the first billing.

- Pay your bill in full each month and avoid interest charges.

- Be aware of institutions that do not charge a yearly user fee, but instead charge each time the card is used.

- Budget your credit spending carefully.

- Pay your bills on time to build your credit rating.

- Keep your receipts and compare them with your monthly statement.

- Notify the institution in writing if any incorrect charges are on your statement.

- Keep a list of your credit card numbers and the issuers' phone numbers in your file, where you can find them easily.

- Report loss or theft of a credit card at once. Call by telephone; then follow up with a letter.

23-11 Following these tips can make credit work for you.

back in equal installments, usually as monthly payments. Knowing the exact terms of the loan before signing any credit agreement is important.

Loans often require collateral. **Collateral** is a form of security on a loan. When you take out a car loan, the car serves as collateral. If a person stops making loan payments, the lender can repossess the collateral.

Investigate Further

What other types of items do lenders accept as collateral?

The Cost of Credit

When you take out a loan or use a credit card, it usually costs more than if you paid cash at the time of purchase, 23-12. That is because lenders charge interest on the amount you owe. The cost of using credit can vary from one lender to another. The *Truth in Lending Act* requires lenders to disclose the exact cost of using credit, including interest and other charges, such as annual fees. Also, lenders are required to disclose the **annual percentage rate (APR)**, which is the annual cost of credit.

Experts recommend keeping credit expenses under 20% of net income. A lower amount is certainly safer. To figure how much credit you can afford, you need to look at your budget. Buying on credit adds another fixed expense. If you do not have enough money to cover a credit payment and other expenses, you cannot afford to buy on credit.

Investigate Further

How do credit card companies fulfill the Truth in Lending Act through billing statements?

Applying for Credit

Credit is offered to people who have a good record of paying their bills on time. They have a regular income and are able to show that future income will likely continue. When you apply for credit, the lender will ask for information about your job, length of employment, and your income. The lender will also check your credit rating.

Credit Rating

Your **credit rating** is a record of how well you paid your bills in the past. To establish a credit rating, you need to apply for credit and use it on a purchase that you could buy with cash. If you are considered a good credit risk, many retail stores will issue a first credit card quite easily. A person can make small purchases and pay the bill each month. This helps build a good credit rating.

The Cost of Credit		
Item purchased	**Time to pay off**	**Real cost of item (approximate)**
$100 boots	11 months	$107
$300 game system	38 months (about 3 years)	$371
$1,500 computer	124 months (about 10 years)	$2,334
$3,000 vacation	162 months (13½ years)	$4,788

23-12 This chart shows the cost of purchasing items using a credit card with an APR of 14% and making the minimum payment every month (3% of the balance).

To keep a good credit rating, you need to pay bills on time. If you make late payments, fail to pay, or have items repossessed, you will have a poor credit score which results in a poor credit rating. Negative information about your credit history cannot be erased from your file. A poor credit rating can result in being turned down for any type of credit.

The *Fair Credit Reporting Act* gives you the right to receive one free credit report annually to verify the information in your report. You have the right to ask the credit bureau to investigate any information that is not correct or complete. The bureau must then correct its records. If you apply for credit and are turned down, you have the right to know the specific reasons why.

The *Equal Credit Opportunity Act* states that certain factors cannot be used against you in determining whether you are granted credit.

These include race, color, sex, age, and marital status. However, you must be old enough (age 18 or 21) to sign a binding contract in your state.

Review Section 23:4

1. Describe two advantages and two disadvantages of using credit.
2. Explain the difference between installment and revolving credit.
3. Explain how the Truth in Lending Act helps the consumer.
4. Explain how a person can build and keep a good credit rating.

Think It Through

Hans and Britta's Budget

Hans and Britta both work and attend college classes part-time. They have tried to keep their spending as low as possible in order to finish school. After graduation, they look forward to finding better paying jobs and higher incomes.

Hans and Britta have a joint gross income of $2,550 per month. Their monthly paycheck deductions equal $222 for Social Security and Medicare taxes, $160 for state income taxes, and $244 for federal income taxes. They also have taken out $5,000 in student loans to help with tuition and living expenses.

Housing in a college town is not cheap, but they found a small apartment for $690 per month. Their electricity and telephone bills average about $150 per month. Heat and water are included in their rent payment. Their food bill is about $400 per month. They pay $110 per month for student health insurance. They drive an old used car that took about $340 worth of repairs last year. They try to put aside money each month in an emergency fund to cover such expenses. They hope the car will keep going until they graduate. Gas and oil expenses add up to about $135 each month. Their car insurance is $900 annually. Britta pays $90 a month to use the local bus system to get to her job.

They spend about $50 each month for entertainment, $125 for textbooks, and as little as possible on clothing or extra household items. To pay tuition costs, they must set aside $400 each month. They hope they can save this money during their last semester to pay for new clothes for job hunting and moving expenses.

Hans and Britta's budget is somewhat different from that of their friends, who also have an income of about $30,000 per year. A financial adviser suggested their friends should plan an average budget, based on the following figures:

Expenses as Percent of Net Income

Rent	28%
Utilities	9%
Food	18%
Transportation and auto insurance	15%
Entertainment	5%
Clothing	4%
Gifts	3%
Household items	5%
Education/reading	2%
Health care and miscellaneous	5%
Savings	6%

Questions to Guide Your Thinking

1. How much net income do Hans and Britta have to budget?

2. How much should they put in savings each month to cover car repairs if expenses will be the same as last year?

3. Prepare a budget for Hans and Britta using the amounts they have set aside for fixed and variable expenses and savings.

4. Compare their budget to the average budget the adviser prepared for their friends. In which areas do Hans and Britta spend more than average? In which areas do they spend less than average?

5. Do you think Hans and Britta could continue with their budget long-term? In which areas are expenses likely to increase over a period of time?

6. If they continue to take out the same amount in student loans for 3 more years, how much will they be in debt when they finish school?

7. How will their student loans affect their financial planning for future goals?

Chapter Summary

Earning and using money are two important life skills. Money needs to be managed so that you are able to live within your means. Money management also helps you reach the goals you have set for yourself.

Using a budget can help individuals and families plan and control spending, make buying decisions, and save money. A well-planned budget can work for you if you follow it. You also need to evaluate it often to make sure it is working. Being realistic and flexible in your planning will enable you to reach your financial goals.

Financial institutions offer a variety of financial services, including checking and savings accounts. Knowing how to choose and use such services is important. It can help you use your income to reach your goals.

Credit allows you to buy now and pay later. Before using any type of credit, you need to consider the pros and cons of credit use. Always know the total cost of using credit and the amount of credit you can afford. Paying bills on time helps you establish credit and keep a good credit rating.

Assess...

Your Knowledge

1. What are the main sources of income?

2. What information is needed to create a budget?

3. What services can be accessed through a financial institution?

Your Understanding

4. Explain why a high interest rate is a benefit when saving money, but hurts you financially when borrowing money.

5. How could a budget help a person make buying decisions?

6. How can credit decisions affect your financial future?

Your Skills

7. If a person earns $10 per hour and works 40 hours a week, what is the gross monthly income? If FICA deductions are 7.65% of gross income and tax deductions are 15% of gross income, what would the person's net income be?

8. Create a budget for yourself if you earned $290 net income every two weeks at a part-time job. Include your current expenses (assuming you don't pay for housing because you live with your family). Determine if you could afford to buy a car with a monthly loan payment of $185.

9. Calculate the amount due on a credit card with a $557 balance and a minimum payment requirement of 3%. If the minimum amount was paid this month, and the card charges a monthly interest rate of 1.5%, what would the balance be next month? How much interest was charged?

Think Critically

10. Completely fill out a credit application form using your current status, age, income, and collateral. *Choice:* In a paragraph, describe why you think a lender would or would not grant you credit. Explain at least three reasons to support your choice.

11. **Research.** Choose two financial institutions in your community and compare the services offered. Judge which bank you would recommend, and in a brief written report, give reasons for your opinion. Include a report with the following information for each institution:

    - list of services

    - description of the most popular checking account, including all fees involved and the interest rate paid

    - interest rate paid on regular savings accounts

    Choice: Present the information in a chart.

12. **Financial literacy, math.** Plan a budget using an income figure close to the amount you expect to make at the beginning of your working career. Use realistic figures for the cost of food and housing in your area. Budget for the following: emergency expenses, one short-term goal, and the long-term goal of buying a home. Figure

what percent of your income you planned for each budget expense. Compare your budget to the case study in "Think It Through" or to Figure 23-3. In what ways is your budget different from the examples?

Connect with Your Community

13. **Social studies.** Interview a self-employed worker. Ask questions about how income and deductions are figured. Prepare a short report summarizing the information.

14. **Research.** Interview a small business owner regarding the financial management of his or her business. How does managing money as an individual differ from managing it for a business? How is a business' credit rating determined? Present your findings in a one-page report. *Choice:* Give an oral presentation to the class and share the results of your interview.

15. Prepare questions to ask a bank representative who has been invited to speak to your class. Think about questions related to online banking, including its benefits and potential security concerns. Summarize what you learn in a paragraph.

16. **Research, writing.** Interview a financial advisor in your community to identify recommendations for amounts to budget for various living expenses. Compare the advice with the recommendations in your textbook. In what categories do they differ, and how might the unique characteristics of your community contribute to the differences? *Group option:* Identify a small group to work with, having each person interview a different adult for the above topic. Combine your information and identify recommended budget amounts in your community.

Use Technology

17. **Research, writing.** Using the Internet, research and prepare a report describing one of the acts of federal legislation designed to protect consumers' credit rights. *Choice:* Use presentation software to compile your research. Give a presentation for the class.

18. **Financial literacy, research.** Search the Internet for credit card offers from three different credit card companies. Create a chart on the computer comparing each card's annual fee, APR, and the penalties or extra charges for late payments. Report your findings to the class.

19. **Financial literacy.** Using computer software for creating budgets, plan a budget for the income you expect to make when you finish your formal education. (Use the earnings estimate found in the Occupational Outlook Handbook.) Print out your budget. Use the Internet to find an apartment in your price range. Print the apartment listing and attach it to your budget. Group option: Work with a partner and search for an apartment that you could afford if you were roommates.

20. **Financial literacy.** Search the Internet for a Web site that figures how expensive a house you can afford on a starting income in the career of your choice. Assume that you will obtain a 30-year mortgage and make the minimum down payment to obtain it. Then, determine how much you would want to spend on monthly payments for 30 years. After the house's price is figured, locate a house in that price range in your area by searching the local newspaper or a realtor's page on the Internet. In a paragraph, describe the house that you believe you could afford.

Chapter 24

Protecting Your Resources

Section 24:1
Consumer Protection

Section 24:2
Protecting the Family Through Insurance

Section 24:3
Protecting the Family Through Savings and Investments

Key Questions

Questions to answer as you study this chapter:

- How can people become informed consumers and protect themselves against fraud?

- What assets should be protected with insurance?

- How can savings and investments help protect a person's future?

Chapter Objectives

After studying this chapter, you will be able to
- **evaluate** sources of consumer information.
- **identify** records that are important for consumer protection.
- **recognize** signs of consumer fraud.
- **describe** various types of insurance.
- **explain** the purpose of an emergency savings fund.
- **relate** savings, investments, and estate planning to family security.

Life Sketch

As Kenneth glanced through the pile of mail on the kitchen table, a colorful envelope caught his eye. "Four compact discs free," it read. All he had to do was join a music club. "That's my kind of deal!" Kenneth thought to himself. He was anxious to join and get the great bargain.

"Did you read the fine print?" his mother asked. "What commitment are you making when you join the club?"

"I don't know," Kenneth replied. He looked closer at the paragraph of fine print on the bottom. As he read it, he realized there was an obligation involved. By signing the offer, he was agreeing to buy at least one new CD each month for the next year.

"One each month!" he exclaimed. "Each costs $16.99 and postage is extra." He quickly calculated the cost just for CDs at $203.88 and decided not to join after all.

Getting Started

You will make decisions about products and services on a daily basis. Some decisions will leave you feeling satisfied and happy with the choice you made. Other times you may wonder why you did not ask more questions before you made your choice.

Families can avoid the loss of some resources by protecting themselves as consumers. They can make informed consumer decisions and know the steps to take when products or services are not satisfactory. They can buy insurance to protect against large financial losses. Managing their money with savings and investments can also increase the family's financial security.

section 24:1

Consumer Protection

Sharpen Your Reading

As you read, outline the key strategies that can help you be an informed consumer and avoid consumer fraud.

Boost Your Vocabulary

Locate and read a warranty. Identify what the warranty agrees to provide the consumer.

Know Key Terms

testimonial
warranty
fraud
Better Business Bureau (BBB)

The main goal for selling goods and services is to make money. Companies may use a free offer to introduce their products to you. However, they make money by getting you to buy their goods and services. Understanding how to protect yourself as a consumer is important. A *consumer* is a person who uses goods and services.

In most cases, you will pay a fee for those goods and services. For instance, when you buy a hamburger at a fast-food restaurant, you are paying for both the hamburger (the goods) and for someone to cook and serve it to you (a service). In one small product, you are buying both goods and services.

To protect yourself against consumer losses, you need knowledge about consumer products, services, and advertising. You need to keep family records to protect your rights under consumer laws. You need to recognize practices that may be deceptive. Also, you need to know how to handle your complaints about a product or service.

Use What You Learn

What are some examples of goods that you consume? What services do you consume?

Be an Informed Consumer

To make wise buying choices, you need knowledge about the product or service you want to buy. With that information, you can choose the product or service that best meets your needs. That knowledge can come from advertising, labels, warranty statements, independent testing results, friends, and government agencies.

Recognize Advertising Techniques

The information from an advertisement may or may not help you make an informed decision, 24-1. When advertising presents information about the quality, price, or availability of a product, it can be quite helpful. Companies use advertising to get their products noticed through the following techniques:

- providing factual information
- making a product comparison
- using an endorsement
- showing an attention-getter
- associating the product or service with a common setting
- using an emotional appeal

Some ads appeal to social and emotional desires rather than provide facts about the product. They appeal to a person's desire to

Advertising Methods	
Factual information	Describe scientific facts about a product; emphasize brand, price, quality, or features
Product comparisons	Compare a product with a competitor's brand
Endorsement (testimonial)	Have a well-known person promote the product
Attention-getters	Use comedy, cartoons, or a catchy song to get your attention
Association	Present a product in a common setting—such as at work, in the home, at a party, or after a game—to associate the product with your environment
Emotional appeal	Appeal to desires for love, popularity, wealth, power, or security

24-1 Advertising uses different methods to achieve the goal of persuading consumers to buy products.

be attractive, popular, secure, wealthy, sexy, or powerful. Others may appeal to a person's desire to identify with a well-known individual. These ads use a **testimonial**, which is an endorsement of the product by a famous person.

If an advertising appeal truly provides information that helps you find a good value, it is worth considering. However, if an appeal simply catches your interest but provides no information, recognize that you need to get facts from elsewhere. Only then can you make a logical decision.

a written statement from the manufacturer about the conditions under which an item will be repaired or replaced free of charge. A *full warranty* covers all parts and labor for a specified period of time. A *limited warranty* provides less protection for the buyer. It may cover only the cost of parts or just the labor to repair the item. Some companies require that you pay the cost of returning the item to the service center. Read warranties carefully so you know exactly how much protection is included with each purchase.

Use What You Learn

What products can you identify that are promoted by a testimonial from a famous person?

Read Labels for Information

Labels can be a good source of information about a product. They can provide information about quality, expected performance, size, and price. Many labels also provide information about the selection, safety, and use of the product. Labels can be a tool for comparing one product with another, 24-2.

Compare Warranty Coverage

Different companies provide different warranties on their products. A **warranty** is

24-2 Comparing quality, features, price, and warranty can help a consumer make a wise buying decision.

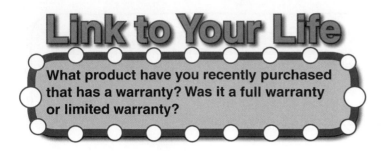

Check the Results of Independent Testing Organizations

Information about products and services can be found in reports by independent testing organizations. *Consumer Reports* is a magazine that presents the results of tests and evaluations by Consumers Union (CU). CU checks products and services from the consumer's point of view. Its magazine is a leading source of comparative buying information for consumers.

Some organizations test appliances, tools, and building materials according to national and international safety and performance standards. The best-known organizations are Underwriters Laboratories (UL) and CSA International, the two largest testing organizations in the world. Products that meet current safety and performance standards display a UL or CSA symbol in the instruction guide and other product materials. Both organizations test products that operate on gas or electricity.

Consult Friends and Government Agencies

Friends can provide information about past experiences with products and services. Sometimes their evaluation is correct. At other times, their evaluation of an experience may be more emotional than logical. Either way, each person has the potential to influence up to 200 other consumers with such information. The reputation of a business or company is important.

Booklets with information about many consumer purchases are available through local, state, and federal government agencies. The Cooperative Extension Service, a division of the U.S. Department of Agriculture, provides helpful information on various topics. You may also be able to access consumer buying tips through your local consumer protection offices.

Think More About It
What is the benefit of talking with an older person about a purchase you plan to make?

Keep Family Records

"Where is the sales receipt for my MP3 player?" Colleen asked her mother. "It doesn't work anymore, and I need to return it. I bought it only two months ago!"

Colleen's question is important if she wants to get her recent purchase replaced or repaired for free. Most likely, it is still covered by the manufacturer's warranty. For instance, it may cover parts and labor to repair any defect within 90 days of the date of purchase. Without the sales receipt, Colleen will not be able to prove when the purchase was made.

There are several more reasons to keep family records organized. Some records are needed for planning a budget and filing required tax returns. Others prove personal identity, marital status, or work records. Yet others prove ownership of important possessions, accounts, or policies.

Organizing Records

An organized home filing system can help a person find important information when it is needed, 24-3. It may consist of a simple box with folders or envelopes, a cabinet with drawers, or a purchased filing cabinet. Whatever system is used, family records should be kept up-to-date and organized according to a simple filing scheme so documents can be found quickly.

A *safe-deposit* box is a storage area in a vault at a financial institution. It should be used for important records and valuables. Such records include contracts, insurance policies, stock certificates, property deeds, and a copy of a will.

Using a safe-deposit box protects your valuables from loss due to fire or theft in your home. A fee is charged for use of a safe-deposit box. You gain access to the box with a key given to you by the financial institution, which keeps a duplicate.

Records to Keep in a Home File	
Personal	• Information such as names, birth dates, and place of birth of family members • Social security numbers of family members • Documents such as birth certificates, marriage certificate, social security cards
Employment	• Contracts and other work records • Records of employee benefits, pension funds, social security deposits, and paycheck withholding taxes
Financial Planning	• Records of income, expenses (filed by the month or by each category in the budget), and savings
Taxes	• All records of income, including interest income • Receipts for deductible expenses (keep for 3 years) • Receipts for property taxes, interest paid on a home mortgage, gifts to charity, medical bills, and business-related expenses • Canceled checks, which serve as proof of payment
Banking	• Records of banking services • Documents such as canceled checks, bank statements, deposit slips, savings certificates, and reports of interest income • Copies of loan agreements • Record of loan payments
Credit	• Copy of credit agreements • List of credit card numbers • Records of purchases and payments
Family Security	• Health, life, disability, home, and auto insurance policies • Records of payments on these policies • A copy of a will (the original is usually filed with a lawyer)
Consumer Purchases	• Warranties and original dated sales receipts • Serial number and model number of large purchases • Booklets with service information

24-3 A well-organized home file gives you easy access to important consumer information.

Think More About It
What is the benefit of having an organized home file?

Avoiding Consumer Fraud

A **fraud** is intentional trickery, lies, or misrepresentation to make a person give up a right or something of value. A fraudulent salesperson often seems kind, polite, friendly, knowledgeable, and sincere. The deal sounds so convincing, and the prices seem so cheap. The person seems honest and may even make you feel guilty for not taking advantage of such an offer. Once the money is paid and the person leaves, however, you are left with something less than promised and your money is gone.

Older adults are often a target for fraudulent practices. They may live alone and delight in having someone stop and talk to them. They may feel obligated to buy because the person was so nice. They may not take the time to check out the person's credentials. Potential cases of fraud can be avoided by following good consumer buying guidelines, 24-4.

The Federal Trade Commission and Better Business Bureaus provide valuable information about scams in progress and ways to recognize them. They also help consumers know what to do if they become victims of fraud.

Avoiding Identity Theft

It is easy for someone to steal from you if they have your personal information. Criminals with access to your social security number, credit card numbers, bank account numbers, and PINs can commit *identity theft*. They can use this information to make purchases or open accounts in your name. Do not use this information online unless you are on a secure line. At ATMs, make sure that people standing nearby cannot see the numbers you enter.

If someone e-mails you asking for such confidential information, do not reply to them. This is known as *phishing*. Do not click on any hyperlinks provided; delete the message. Avoid opening e-mails from people you do not recognize. If someone calls you and asks for such information (even if they sound sincere and legitimate), hang up. Only give out confidential information to people *you* have contacted and that you know have a legitimate need for such information. Shred any documents or receipts you do not need that show your name, address, or credit card information.

Handling Consumer Complaints

If you are not satisfied with a purchase or service, there are several steps you can take.

Tips for Consumer Buying

- Do not buy on impulse. You may end up buying an item you really do not need or want.

- Beware of deals or claims that make too many promises. If it sounds too good to be true, it probably is.

- Buy only from dealers with a good reputation.

- Get a written warranty that states under what conditions the product can be returned, replaced, or repaired.

- Do not sign contracts or agreements you do not understand.

- Beware of the line "Many of your neighbors have bought this product." Some salespeople will flip through a chart listing neighbors' names and an amount they have purchased or invested. If the sale is legitimate, you will have time to check out these claims with your neighbors.

- Beware if you have been "specially chosen" for a good deal. That is a line to catch your interest.

- Do not put any money down to hold your special selection or deal. Too often, people never see that money again.

- Report all incidents of fraud. A report to the Better Business Bureau (BBB), Consumer Protection Agency, or District Attorney may help you get your money back. It will help others who will take the time to check for a salesperson's past reputation.

24-4 Avoid consumer fraud by practicing good consumer buying habits.

1. Return to the place of purchase. Take the product with you, if you can. Also take your sales receipt proving when you bought it and how much you paid.

2. Contact the company's main office in writing and explain your complaint. E-mailing is acceptable, but write the e-mail using a formal language and style. See 24-5.

3. Seek help from a consumer agency like your local Better Business Bureau. **Better Business Bureaus (BBBs)** are nonprofit organizations sponsored by private businesses. They attempt to help consumers resolve their complaints with local merchants.

Being an informed consumer can help you make wise buying choices when you are in the marketplace. It can help you avoid potential cases of fraud. When you do have problems with products or services, you will be able to protect yourself from financial loss.

Review Section 24:1

1. Describe five techniques advertisers use to influence people to buy a product.

2. List four sources where consumers can obtain information about a product or service. Rate the sources according to their likelihood of offering reliable, factual information.

3. Explain the difference between a full and limited warranty.

4. Explain why it is important to keep the original dated sales receipt of an item under warranty.

5. List five examples of items and information that should be kept in your home file.

6. What three steps could you take to handle a consumer complaint?

7. How does the Better Business Bureau help consumers in a community?

Complaint Letter Format

Your address
Your city, state, zip code
Today's date

Company contact (person's name and job title)
Company name
Street address
City, state zip code

Dear Mr., Mrs., or Ms. (person's name):

I purchased (name of product with model number and serial number) on (date of purchase). I made the purchase at (name and address of store).

I have been dissatisfied with the product because (state the problem). I would appreciate your (state what action you would like them to take). I have enclosed copies (do not send originals) of my receipt, warranty, canceled check, and model and serial numbers (use those that apply).

I am looking forward to hearing from you soon to get this matter resolved. I will wait four weeks before seeking assistance from a third party. You can contact me at the above address or at the following phone numbers (home and work numbers and times when you can be reached).

Sincerely,

(your signature)
Your name

24-5 Many businesses will gladly refund a customer's money if the person is dissatisfied with a product or service.

section 24:2

Protecting the Family Through Insurance

Sharpen Your Reading

As you read, develop a checklist for each type of insurance. Include key points you should know or questions you should ask before agreeing to buy that type of policy.

Boost Your Vocabulary

Create a chart with four columns. Put each key term in the first column. In the second column, write the text definition for each term. In the third column, give an example of that term. Then Interview the person in your family who handles insurance. Ask them what they know about each term. In the fourth column, write information you learn from your interview about that term.

Know Key Terms

insurance
premium
policy
liability
financial responsibility law
medical payments coverage

bodily injury liability
uninsured motorists protection
property damage liability
collision insurance
comprehensive physical damage
deductible
no-fault insurance
face value
guaranteed replacement value
basic medical insurance
major medical insurance
group health insurance
term insurance
whole life insurance
modified whole life insurance
universal life insurance

When Lola came home from school Thursday afternoon, she had no idea how her life was about to change. Her dad had been in a car accident on the way home from work. He was pronounced dead on arrival at the hospital. Suddenly, their family had become a single-parent family. Their lives were torn by the tragic event.

Such events do happen. They may be due to perils (dangers) such as an accident, storm, violence, or illness. There is always a chance that such an event could affect you or your family, resulting in a loss.

Buying Insurance

Insurance is a form of protection against financial loss. This protection is purchased from an insurance company. The company charges a fee called a **premium** to assume a financial loss that is described in the policy. The **policy** is a contract between the insurance company and you as a *policyholder*.

A basic policy will describe the exact risks against which you are being insured and the dollar amount of your protection. If you want more coverage for other risks or perils, you may be able to add extra insurance. This extra protection is added to the policy as a *policy rider*. Knowing what coverage a basic policy provides and the risks included by any riders is important, 24-6.

When people buy insurance, they are putting their money together into a pool. When one policyholder gets sick or has an accident, money

24-6 Most families purchase several types of insurance to protect them against the risk of loss of their costly purchases, such as a home and vehicle.

is taken from the pool to cover the expenses. The goal is to have enough money in the pool to cover the needs of the members. If many people have high expenses at the same time, the pool runs dry. When the pool gets low, insurance rates increase.

Financial Loss Risks

Risk of financial loss comes from several sources. There is the risk of damage to personal property such as a car or home. Protection against such losses can be purchased with car and home insurance. There is the risk that you may lose your health or life. Protection against the financial burdens that result from such losses is purchased through health, disability, and life insurance.

Investigate Further

How much money would your family need to live for one month without any income? What insurance do they have that would provide this money?

Liability Risks

You may also have liability risks. **Liability** is the legal responsibility for another person's financial costs due to a loss or injury. You can become legally responsible if the loss or injury results from your neglect. For instance, if the work you do for a business could result in a loss to someone, you would need to carry liability insurance. This coverage would protect you against the liability risk. You are responsible if the loss is caused by your property (such as your car or your dog). A loss caused by a person for whom you are responsible, such as your child, is also your responsibility. Protection against these liability risks is purchased with your property insurance.

Link to Your Life

What are some actions that could cause loss to another person's property? Do you have liability insurance for any of those actions?

Insuring Your Car

All states have a **financial responsibility law**. Such laws require drivers to prove that they are able to pay for the cost of any damages or injuries that might be caused in an auto accident. Most people could not cover large costs out of their own funds. Instead they carry auto insurance.

Auto insurance provides protection against the risks of bodily injuries and property damage. As a driver, you have the risk of hurting yourself and others. You risk being hurt by someone else. You also risk damaging someone else's property, damaging your own property, or having your property damaged by someone or something else. These risks can all be covered in an automobile insurance plan.

Use What You Learn

What are some examples of injuries or damages that occur as a result of automobile accidents?

Bodily Injury Risks

Your risks for bodily injuries can be protected under three different sections in your insurance policy. These three sections include medical payments coverage, bodily injury liability, and uninsured motorists protection.

Medical payments coverage pays for the medical expenses resulting from injuries to you and others in your car should an accident occur. It also covers you if injured as a passenger or pedestrian. The coverage pays no matter who is at fault.

Bodily injury liability protects against major financial losses resulting from an accident for which you are responsible, 24-7. The insurance pays medical costs, legal expenses, lost wages, or compensation for suffering. The total of these losses can be hundreds of thousands of dollars. Protection against such loss is very important.

Bodily injury liability coverage is usually stated on a policy as part of three numbers, such as 50/100/25 or 100/300/100. The first

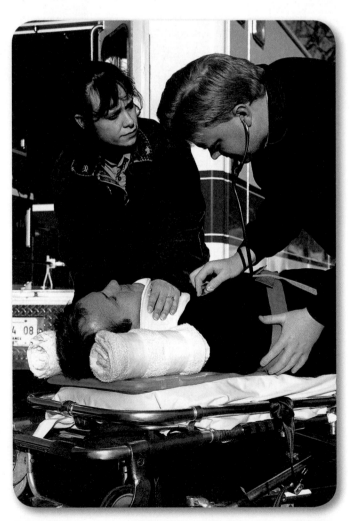

24-7 The person at fault in an accident is responsible for the costs of injuries to others.

two numbers of the liability coverage are for bodily injury liability. The third number is for property damage liability. The first number is the maximum amount (in thousands of dollars) that the insurance company will pay for one person in an accident. The second number is the maximum amount that will be paid for all people injured in an accident. Many companies recommend 100/300 coverage to protect against costly accidents.

24-8 Collision insurance covers damage to the insured's vehicle.

Investigate Further

How much protection for bodily injury liability do you think a person needs?

Uninsured motorists protection covers bodily injuries to you and your family caused by someone else. It does not cover property damage. If someone driving without car insurance injures you or a family member, the medical costs are covered. This insurance also protects you if the driver carries insufficient insurance to cover the cost of your injuries.

Property Damage Risks

Your car and the items in it are possible property damage risks. The same is true for any items your car may hit, such as someone else's car or property. Your car may also be damaged by hail, wind, a storm, a falling tree, or other perils. These risks are covered by property damage insurance.

Property damage liability is protection to cover losses to someone else's property caused by you and your vehicle. The amount of your coverage is stated as the third number of the liability limits. The policy of 50/100/25 covers damage to someone else's property for $25,000.

Collision insurance covers the cost of damage to your car when it is involved in an accident, 24-8. The amount of coverage depends on the vehicle and its worth. The most you can collect is the retail value of your car at the time of the accident. What if someone else is at fault for the accident? Your insurance company will try to collect the repair costs from that person's insurance company.

Comprehensive physical damage covers the risk of damage to your car by perils other than collision. For instance, the damage caused by a fallen tree is covered under comprehensive damage. Damage from perils such as fire, theft, glass breakage, falling objects, vandalism, wind, hail, or animals are usually included.

Think More About It
Why do you think the liability part of an auto insurance plan is the most costly part of insurance?

Costs of Automobile Insurance

The cost of your car insurance will depend on several factors. The amount of liability coverage you carry will be a major factor. Other factors that will affect how much you pay include the following:

- type of car owned
- your home address
- your driver classification

How Much Liability?

The more protection you buy, the higher the premiums will be. Less coverage would equal lower insurance premiums. The insurance company is charging you for the amount of risk they are taking.

The legal limits for liability vary from state to state and are lower than adequate for most situations. Legal advisers recommend 100/300 for bodily injury liability while 25/50 is legal in most states. Also, property damage liability of $50,000 or $100,000 is recommended rather than the $5,000 or $10,000 that is legal in most states.

Link to Your Life

What would happen if you did not carry enough liability insurance to cover the cost of an accident? Who would be responsible to pay the damages?

How Much Is the Deductible?

In insurance policies, a **deductible** is an amount that the insured person (you) has to pay before the insurance company pays any money. For instance, suppose an accident resulted in $1,500 in damages to your car. If you had a $250 deductible, you would be responsible to pay the first $250. The insurance company would pay the remaining expense of $1,250. If you carry a high deductible, it will lower the cost of your collision and comprehensive insurance.

Investigate Further

How might a person decide how high a deductible to carry?

What Is the Retail Value of Your Car?

Coverage for collision and comprehensive damage depends on the value of your car. The year, make, and model determine the value. The amount the company will pay for damages will not be greater than the retail value of your car at the time of the accident. Do not insure your car for more than it is worth. If your car has little retail value, you may decide not to carry collision or comprehensive insurance and save the expense. Insurance is costly for sports cars, luxury cars, and other cars that are stolen frequently. Insurance companies charge for the risk they will be taking.

Where Do You Live?

The risk of loss from accidents or theft varies from one location to another. Insurance companies keep charts that show the risk of loss in your area. Your insurance premium will be higher if you live in areas of high risk. The risk is greater, for instance, in large cities than in small cities. It is greater in a city than in a rural area.

What Is Your Driver Classification?

Insurance companies will compare you with other drivers to determine how risky it will be to insure you. The classification you are given will depend on your age, sex, marital status, driving record, and driving habits.

Young unmarried males tend to have more accidents, 24-9. As a result, if you are a young unmarried male, you will be classified in a group that pays higher premiums. What if you had a number of accidents or received tickets for traffic violations in the past three years? That poor driving record would put you in a classification with those who pay higher premiums.

24-9 A young unmarried male is a high insurance risk and will pay higher premiums for car insurance.

Your risk of having an accident increases the more often you drive. That risk will be reflected in your insurance premium. For instance, if you drive to work or school every day, your premium will be higher than if you just drive your car for pleasure.

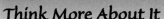

Think More About It
How might your driver classification affect how much deductible you decide to carry?

Reducing Car Insurance Costs

The expenses of auto repairs and high liability settlements have caused auto insurance rates to increase rapidly. To help keep costs down, drive carefully within the law and keep your driving record clean. Good grades can also make a difference with insurers.

If your family has more than one car insured with a company, you may be able to get a discount. Some companies offer discounts for completing a driver education course, not smoking, and driving fewer miles than the average. Choosing a higher deductible on your policy will also lower your premium.

Comparing one insurance company with another can help you find the best rate. However, remember the importance of having good coverage. Giving up important coverage to save a few dollars on the premium may cost you more later.

No-Fault Insurance

Some states have **no-fault insurance** plans. These are an attempt to keep the costs of auto insurance down. No-fault insurance mainly applies to a person's liability for bodily injury to others. It eliminates the legal process of proving who is at fault in an accident. The actual costs of medical expenses, lost wages, and related expenses are covered by each person's own insurance.

Think More About It
How could a person prepare before an accident occurs to cover the cost of a high deductible?

Insuring Your Home

To protect against financial loss due to damage to a home and its contents, families purchase homeowner's insurance. Two basic types of coverage are provided: property protection and liability protection.

Basic property protection coverage insures you against certain dangers. These include fire or lightning, windstorms or hail, explosions, riots, aircraft, vehicles, smoke, vandalism, and theft. It covers the damage or loss of your home and your personal property (such as home furnishings and clothing). A *loss-of-use protection* may be included. This means the family's living expenses will be paid while the family's own home is being repaired or rebuilt.

Most policies also include liability protection in case someone is hurt on or by your property. If you or your property accidentally damages someone else's property, it provides this coverage as well.

Knowing exactly what your insurance company will pay in case of a loss is important. Some policies provide *replacement cost*. This means they will replace what was damaged up to the face value of the policy. The **face value** of your policy is the largest amount the company will pay for a loss. Other policies insure for the actual cash value of the property at the time of the loss.

For instance, you may carry insurance on your entertainment system for a loss due to theft or fire for up to $600. Nine months later, your entertainment system is stolen. The present cash value of your entertainment system may be $500, even though a new one costs $600. The insurance company will pay only $500 (present cash value) unless your policy states that replacement value is covered. Then it will pay the $600. If replacement cost is now $700, the company will only pay $600 because that is the face value of your policy.

Some policies offer **guaranteed replacement value**. Then the company replaces the item even if the cost of the new item is higher than the face value of the policy. With guaranteed replacement value, the insurance company will pay the $700 for your entertainment system if that is the cost of a new one.

Do you think the coverage provided by a policy with guaranteed replacement value would be worth the additional cost in insurance?

Renter's Insurance

Even if you do not own a home, you still face the risk of loss by renting an apartment or house. Renters should carry insurance to cover loss of personal belongings and property that they have inside the home. Liability protection should also be considered since there is a risk that guests may be harmed by your property. If someone slipped in your shower or was bitten by your dog, any financial liability you might incur would be covered.

How Much Property Insurance?

An insurance plan should cover the risks that could produce serious financial hardship. How do people protect against large property losses and yet keep the cost of their insurance down? Some choose a policy with a deductible. When a loss occurs, the person has to pay an amount equal to the deductible before the insurance pays any of the loss. A deductible results in lower insurance premiums. The higher the deductible amount, the lower the premiums are.

A home should be insured for enough money to cover the cost of rebuilding it, 24-10. The value of the land and the cost of the foundation do not need to be included. Most companies will not consider a home fully insured unless it is covered for at least 80 percent of its replacement costs. If the owner is insured for less, the company will not pay the full amount, even if the claim is a

small one. For instance, a homeowner insures a $200,000 home for $150,000. Then the owner has a $10,000 loss. The company will only pay 75 percent of the claim.

The amount of insurance and the types of insurance that a person carries should relate to that person's needs. Property risk will depend on what the person owns and what losses can be afforded. If there is a debt on the property, the loaning agency will require property insurance.

Filing an Insurance Claim

When you have a loss, filing a claim properly is important. This requires some prior record keeping on your part. With the proper papers in hand, file an insurance claim by following the appropriate steps. See 24-11.

Insuring Your Health

Without good health, working at a job, caring for a family, or even caring for yourself is difficult. Making daily living choices that contribute to good health is the best method of protecting your health. However, at some time in your life you likely will need to obtain health care, which can be very costly. For this reason, you need to be covered by some form of health plan.

Health Insurance

Insurance companies offer two types of health coverage: basic medical and major medical. **Basic medical insurance** covers the cost of hospital expenses such as room, board, and nursing services. It also pays for services such as X-rays, medications, and lab tests. It may also pay some of the costs of the doctor's services.

Major medical insurance protects the family against large losses due to a major illness or serious injury. A major medical policy usually starts paying when the basic medical insurance stops. In some cases, the major medical policy may start paying after a deductible has been met. For instance, a person may have to pay the first $250 of a medical bill. Then the major medical policy may pay a percentage of the medical costs up to a certain amount. Beyond that, the insurance company pays the entire bill up to the limit of the policy.

24-10 The cost of rebuilding a home can be estimated by measuring the square footage of usable floor space. Multiply this number by current square-foot construction costs for new homes in the area.

Group Health Insurance

Group health insurance policies are available through employers, unions, and professional associations. These group policies provide more coverage at a lower cost than individual policies. Employers may pay all or part of the insurance costs. Although groups can provide health insurance for members in different ways, many choose HMOs or PPOs.

- *Health Maintenance Organizations (HMOs)* differ from traditional health insurance companies. Rather than pay medical bills, this organization of medical personnel and facilities provides health care services to its members. If you belong to an HMO, you or your employer pays a monthly amount to the organization. Then when you need health care, you go to a doctor associated with the HMO. Depending on your plan, there usually are additional charges for services, called *co-payments*.

- *Preferred Provider Organizations (PPOs)* offer another option for health care. A PPO is an organization of doctors and/or hospitals. They contract with the insurance company or employer to provide health care services to group members for certain fees. If patients choose to go elsewhere for health care, they pay higher fees.

Managed care describes methods insurance companies use to lower medical expenses. One technique they use is to set a "customary and reasonable charge" for medical procedures. If your doctor charges more than the insurance company allows, you must pay the difference.

Before choosing an HMO or a PPO, be sure to check what services are provided, where they are offered, and how much they will cover.

Filing an Insurance Claim

- Keep an up-to-date file of your insurance policies. Be sure family members know where the files are.

- Keep receipts from purchases to prove the value of your property. Also keep an inventory of all personal property.

- Contact police as soon as you have property loss. Be sure to obtain a copy of the written police report describing your loss.

- Write down the names, addresses, and telephone numbers of people involved in an auto accident. Include witnesses as well. Get the license plate number(s) from the other car(s) and get the driver's license number(s).

- Contact your insurance agent as soon as possible.

- In the event of property loss or damage, locate original receipts to determine original costs. Obtain estimates to repair the property or get estimates of the value of the property. Share your information with your agent at the insurance company.

24-11 To file an insurance claim for a property loss, follow these steps.

What provisions are made for emergency health care if you are not able to reach your preferred provider or assigned doctor? Compare the costs and services with other health care providers and insurance companies. Then choose the plan that will work best for you.

Think More About It
In what ways do you think HMO and PPO programs benefit a medical organization?

Controlling Health Insurance Costs

Health insurance has become a large expense for many families. There are several things you can do to control your health care costs.

Take steps to keep healthy. Health insurance costs increase the more people use health care. Preventive care can help you avoid many major health problems. Some insurance policies include wellness checks.

You can save on health insurance by carrying a policy with a higher deductible. Your monthly premiums will be lower. However, you will need to budget some money to cover your deductible should you become ill.

You might consider opening a *health savings account (HSA)*. An HSA allows you to save money for health care expenses without paying taxes on that income. People who carry an HSA often carry higher deductibles and thereby have lower premiums. The money they save on premiums is put into the HSA.

Investigate Further

How could having regular checkups by a doctor save you money over time?

Disability Insurance

Disability insurance protects against loss of income if a person becomes disabled, 24-12. Some policies cover disability due to accident; some include disability due to illness. The amount of income the policy pays will vary, some paying 70 to 90 percent of a person's regular income. The waiting period before benefits begin will also vary. Check the details of a disability policy to know what protection you have.

Insuring Your Life

Life insurance protects against the loss of income due to death. Its main purpose is to provide income for family members (spouse, children, elderly parents) who depend on the wage earner's income.

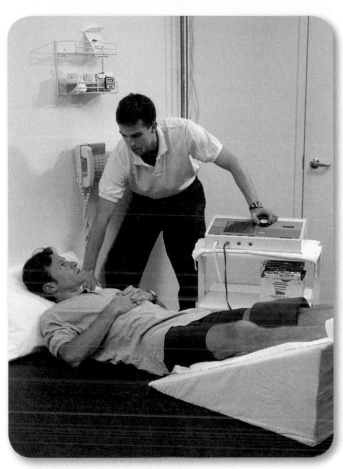

24-12 Loss of income due to an accident or illness can mean financial disaster if a wage earner has no disability insurance.

There are two main types of life insurance: term and cash value. Policies may have many different names, but they all represent variations or combinations of these two.

Term Insurance

A **term insurance** policy insures your life for a set number of years. The term may be one, five, ten, or more years; then it expires. Term insurance gives you the most protection for the least amount of money. Premiums are lower during the early years and higher as you grow older.

A term policy is taken out for a certain *face amount* indicating the amount of insurance purchased. At death, the policy pays a death benefit to a *beneficiary*, who is the person named in the policy to receive the money. In a term policy, the death benefit is equal to the face amount of the policy. For instance, if you buy

a $100,000 term insurance policy at age 25, the death benefit to your beneficiary is $100,000 if you should die.

Some companies may require that employees have a physical before renewing the policy each new term. If the employee's health is poor, the company may not renew the policy. A *guaranteed renewable term policy* is a variation that may interest some people. With this policy, the employee would not have to meet the company's medical standards after each term.

Think More About It
Why might term insurance be a good choice of family protection for a young couple with preschool children?

Cash Value Insurance

Cash value insurance provides coverage for a death benefit just as term insurance does. It also acts as a type of savings plan and has a cash value. The cash value of the policy is the amount you would receive if you should drop or surrender the policy. In the early years, the cash value grows slowly. The longer you hold the policy, the more the cash value will increase. However, the death benefit remains the same, even if the cash value increases.

The cash value can be used in several ways:

- You could take out a loan from the insurance company based on the cash value of your policy.

- You also could turn in (surrender) your policy and the company would pay you the cash value.

- If you wanted to stop paying premiums, you could buy a certain amount of protection for a certain number of years (paid-up insurance).

- The cash value could also be put into an *annuity*, which provides you a guaranteed income for life.

Whole life insurance is the best known form of cash value insurance. In a straight whole life policy, the premium stays the same as long as you carry the policy. The cost of the protection is spread evenly over the years of the policy. This occurs even though the risk of death is less during the younger years.

Modified whole life insurance policies have premiums that are lower during the early years. For instance, a Modified 3 policy means that after three years the premium will go up.

Understanding the difference between cash value insurance and term insurance will help you choose the plan that is best for you, 24-13. Cash value insurance is a type of forced savings plan, but the interest rate paid is usually quite low. The difference in premium costs between term and cash value insurance could produce a higher return in a savings or investment plan. To get the most protection for the money, consider term insurance.

Link to Your Life

What would be the benefit of purchasing a whole life insurance policy when you are young and keeping it your entire life?

Combination Plans

Many insurance companies have developed plans combining term and cash value policies to appeal to consumers wanting higher interest rates. The most common type of plan is **universal life insurance**, which combines both term and cash value policies. If you bought a universal life policy, you would pay a set premium each month. Part of the premium goes toward the death benefit protection (term part of insurance). The company also deducts an amount for administrative costs. The remaining amount earns a variable rate of interest. This adds up to form the cash value part of the policy.

When considering a universal life policy, be sure to ask what rate is charged for the death benefit. A regular term policy usually offers the same amount of protection for a lower premium.

Also ask what the administrative costs are. Most companies charge a one-time fee for setting up the policy. They may charge a percentage of all premium payments to pay for company expenses. Also, they may charge a fee for withdrawing funds from your cash value. All these costs reduce the amount that actually earns interest.

	Term Insurance	Cash Value Insurance
Advantages	Has lower premiums in the early years	Has constant premiums over the years
	Provides more coverage with fewer dollars	Cannot be canceled because of age
		Builds a cash value
	Can be flexible by being converted to cash value insurance	Has increases in value that are tax free
		Is a type of forced savings
Disadvantages	After a certain age, policy cannot be renewed	Early premiums are higher even though risk of death is low
	Premiums increase when a person reaches an older age bracket	A person may not carry enough protection because costs are higher
	No buildup of cash value	Higher interest rates may be available in other investments
		Comparing rates of return is difficult because of administrative costs

24-13 Comparing life insurance can help you determine which policy best suits your needs.

Comparing the interest earned on a universal life policy is difficult if you do not know how much the administrative costs will be. Some companies advertise high rates of return. However, the return is paid only on part of the money you have paid in. (Remember, part of your money is deducted for company expenses.) Your rate of return may be less than what you could receive by putting the same amount into an investment plan.

How Much Life Insurance Is Needed?

What is the extent of the family's financial loss with the death of a wage earner? This question must be answered in order to determine how much life insurance coverage a family needs. The death benefit can provide funds for funeral and burial expenses. It can provide funds for family living expenses during the years that children are growing up. Such funds can also provide income for the surviving parent after the children are grown.

The size of the death benefit should relate to the policyholder's responsibilities in these areas. In a family with children at home, higher amounts of life insurance are needed on a wage earner. When there are few or no dependents, less life insurance is needed.

If a family has a good savings and investment plan, it probably needs less return from life insurance. That is because these funds can be used to provide income for the family.

Review Section 24:2

1. Explain how auto insurance and homeowner's insurance can protect the family.
2. Describe the steps you should take if you had a laptop stolen from your home or apartment.
3. Identify the purpose of a major medical policy. Explain how it differs from an HMO.
4. Explain why term insurance is the best buy for a young family with a limited income.
5. Explain how a universal life policy differs from a straight cash value policy.

section 24:3

Protecting the Family Through Savings and Investments

Sharpen Your Reading

Identify key points about each type of investment. Then summarize how each protects the family.

Boost Your Vocabulary

Create a chart with the terms *bonds*, *stocks*, *mutual funds*, and *real estate* in the first column. In the second column, write the text definition of each term. Search online or in a newspaper and identify some examples of each term. Write the examples in the third column. In the fourth column, rate each example that you identified as a high-risk or low-risk investment.

Know Key Terms

bonds
stocks
mutual funds
estate
trust

Savings and investments can increase a family's financial security. Some funds can be set aside in a liquid account for emergency needs. These funds provide security against a short-term loss of income or fairly small but unexpected bills.

Money for long-term savings can be invested. Investment plans have the potential of earning more income. Long-term plans tend to earn a higher rate of interest. Some are designed to provide income at a later date, such as after retirement. Savings and investment plans are an important part of protecting the family and increasing financial security.

An Emergency Savings Fund

An emergency fund equal to at least three months income can help families handle unexpected bills and emergencies. Such a fund also helps wage earners get through periods of no income because of illness or loss of a job. For instance, payments on a loan, rent, or insurance still need to be made. Food, heat, electricity, gas, and other items still need to be purchased. An emergency fund can help individuals get through such common events.

For most people, building such an emergency fund takes time. A certain sum must be set aside each month until the fund is established. Other goals may have to be delayed for a while. Money for an emergency savings fund should be put into a liquid account—one from which it can be withdrawn whenever needed. Check around and get the most interest income for the liquid account you choose.

Think More About It
Why might people fail to develop an emergency fund?

Benefits of an Emergency Fund

Being prepared for an emergency provides a sense of security and lessens anxiety. Unexpected costs will not destroy all the progress a person has made saving for other goals. An emergency fund will make it easier to stick to a budget. Also, it protects families against financial disaster.

Investments

Some people receive a lump sum of money at once to invest, such as an income tax return. For most, though, putting aside enough money to begin an investment account usually takes time and regular saving. Also, it takes time to research investments to find those that match the investor's goals. For these reasons, many people never even begin an investment account. Consequently, they miss out on reaching their long-term financial goals.

When choosing an investment plan, you need to know what you want the investment plan to do for you. Also, there is usually some measure of risk involved, and you must decide how much you can tolerate. Often the payoff is greater for a riskier investment than a safe one. If a risky investment succeeds, you could make a great deal of money, but if it fails, you could lose it all.

You also need to examine your financial situation. Do you have enough money, a three-month reserve, in an emergency fund? An investment fund cannot serve as an emergency fund since investments are not liquid. This means you will probably have to wait a while to get your money out of an investment plan.

Bonds, stocks, mutual funds, and real estate are four common types of investments, 24-14. Learning a few basic facts about each may help you reach your future financial goals.

Investigate Further

How do investments help build a family's financial security?

Bonds

Sometimes corporations or governments need to borrow money. To do this, they may sell bonds. A **bond** is a written pledge to pay back the money plus interest in a certain period of time. At that time, the bond *matures*.

Three types of bonds are available to investors. The federal government sells *U.S. Government bonds* to provide money for its activities and finance the national debt. Local governments sell bonds to finance community projects, such as a library, school, or bridge. These are called *municipal bonds*. Corporations issue *corporate bonds* to help finance their business activities.

The U.S. government issues several types of bonds. Some are for long periods of time, such as 15 to 20 years. Some are issued for large amounts of money. A common bond in which most workers are able to invest is the *U.S. savings bond*, considered a secure investment. When you buy a U.S. savings bond, you are lending your money to the U.S. government. The U.S. Treasury Department issues these bonds through various financial institutions. The government pays back your money plus interest when the bond matures.

The rate of interest earned on bonds can vary, but a minimum rate is guaranteed. If you redeem or cash in your bond before maturity, you earn a lower interest rate. The interest earned on government bonds is exempt from state and local income taxes. Also, you do not have to pay federal income tax on that interest income until you redeem the bond.

When buying any type of bond, investigate who is issuing the bond. You will want to find out whether the bond will be a safe investment. Will the company or government agency be able to pay back the bond? Will they be able to pay the interest?

You can check the risk of the investment through a rating agency. Bonds are rated according to the risk involved with the investment. The soundest investments with the least risk receive a triple A (AAA) rating. As the risk increases, the bond rating goes down to a B or C. The riskiest bonds are rated CCC.

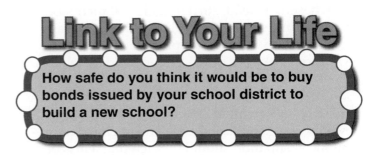

How safe do you think it would be to buy bonds issued by your school district to build a new school?

Types of Investments	
Bonds	• Involve lending your money to a government agency or business for a period of time
	• Provide interest on your money when the bond matures
	• Are as safe as the financial condition of the agency or business
Stocks	• Involve buying into a company and becoming part owner
	• Earn dividends on the company's profits
	• Must be sold to end the investment
	• May earn a profit or take a loss upon sale
Mutual Funds	• Involve a pool of money from several people, which is put into a variety of investments
	• Entail different requirements for withdrawing money or selling it
	• Are as safe as the investments made
Real Estate	• Involves property such as a home, land, or rental unit
	• Usually increases in value over time
	• Must be sold to "liquidate" the investment and get your money back
	• Involves maintenance costs and property taxes which must be handled by the investor

24-14 Learning a few basic facts about investing may help you reach your financial goals faster.

Stocks

A **stock** is a share in the ownership of a company. When people buy stock in a company, they become *stockholders*. All stockholders are part-owners, and they share in the success of the company. However, if a business fails, stockholders may lose their investment.

Stockholders are paid *dividends* from the earnings of the company after all other obligations are met. If the company is profitable, the stockholder can earn a profit from his or her investment. If the company has a bad year, no dividends may be paid.

A company is not required to pay back the money a stockholder pays when the stock is purchased. Instead, stockholders sell their stocks to other investors. If the value of the stock has gone up, they can make a profit. Sometimes the value of stock goes down. If stockholders sell their stock at such a time, they can take a large loss.

People should not invest money in stocks unless they can afford to take the risk that goes with such a purchase, 24-15. That means their financial situation should be such that a loss of funds would not cause them financial disaster.

Investigate Further

How would you decide if you had enough money to invest some in stocks?

Mutual Funds

A **mutual fund** is a group of many investments purchased by a company representing many investors. Each person may invest only a small amount of money. Altogether, the sum can be large. The mutual fund is used to buy a variety of stocks, bonds, CDs, and other securities. Shareholders in a mutual fund receive earnings (or losses), usually on a quarterly basis.

One benefit of a mutual fund is that the money is invested into a variety of investments. In that way, a loss in one investment can be balanced by profits in another. When selecting a mutual fund, matching your investment goals with an appropriate fund is important. Also evaluate the management and past performance of any fund you might consider.

24-15 Stocks can be very profitable, but only to those who truly understand the risk involved and can afford to take it.

A *money market fund* is a type of mutual fund that invests in short-term high-yield securities. (It is different from a money market deposit account that is offered and insured through a bank.) Money market funds often pay higher interest rates than regular savings accounts. However, they are not insured. That means there is more risk. Therefore, it is important to know where the funds will be invested. When money market funds are invested in government securities or reputable companies, the risk is not high.

You can buy shares in such funds through various financial institutions. They provide various methods for making withdrawals or selling shares. These options should be investigated before you deposit money in the fund.

If you only had a small amount of money to invest, would you choose a mutual fund or a bond?

Real Estate

Do you view home ownership as an investment? Some may not see it as such, but it is. Real estate in the form of a home, land, or rental property can be a good and safe investment. However, as with any investment, some risk is involved.

Most real estate increases in value over time. The value of a home tends to keep up with *inflation* (an increase in the general level of prices). Thus, the selling price of a home can yield a profit over the purchase price. Also, property taxes and interest on a home mortgage can be deducted from income taxes. In these ways, homeownership can both make money and save money for the investor, 24-16.

Some risk is involved with a real estate investment, however. Sometimes real estate does not increase in value. Instead it may *depreciate*, or lose value. This may occur even when the property is well maintained. Generally, the local economy is the biggest factor in determining property values.

24-16 A home often is the biggest investment most people make.

When choosing housing, checking the value of other property in the area is important. Consider the location. Is it near schools, shopping centers, or community recreation areas? Check the zoning laws for the area to determine whether future changes could affect the property value. For many, a well-chosen piece of property will be the best investment they make.

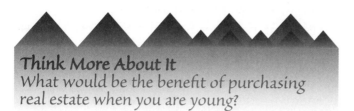

Think More About It
What would be the benefit of purchasing real estate when you are young?

Retirement Funds

Many people put money into investment funds to provide an income when they retire. Such a plan is usually offered through a company pension plan. Other people may set up an *individual retirement account (IRA)*. The cash value of a whole life insurance policy can also provide retirement funds at age 65. Such retirement plans help increase financial security for older people.

The payout options for retirement plans vary. At a specified age, usually 65, a person may withdraw the money from a retirement fund as a lump sum. Another option is to receive the retirement savings in installments as a monthly check. Often reduced retirement payouts are available to those who retire early.

Purchasing an annuity is another payout option for a retirement plan. An *annuity* is a type of investment that provides guaranteed income for life. An annuity may be purchased with a single payment, as some workers may do at retirement. It can also be purchased with regular payments over several years. Some annuities stop providing a payout when the retired person dies. Other annuities continue payments to a spouse or dependent until the amount in the annuity is gone.

Financial Planners

A financial or investment planner can help you make wise investment choices. When choosing a financial planner, select a person who has been trained in securities, insurance,

taxes, real estate, and estate planning. A financial planner should have the proper credentials, such as *Certified Financial Planner (CFP)* or *Chartered Financial Consultant (ChFC)*. This person should also have a good reputation with local bankers, accountants, and lawyers.

Avoiding Investment Fraud

Investment scams always claim to help you get rich quickly, but take your money and do just the opposite. You need to cautiously invest by dealing only with reputable companies and individuals.

No one is immune to being a target of an investment scam. Young couples know they need to start investing when they are young to provide financial security for their family. Middle-aged families feel the need to increase their funds for a child's college education or their retirement. Older adults often have some money to invest, but they realize that costly medical bills could occur quickly. Anyone can become a target for those who promise fast or high returns. Following some fundamentals of investing can help people avoid investment fraud.

- *Good investing takes time and knowledge.* An investor should take the time to learn about a possible investment. If they cannot afford the risk, they should find a safer investment.
- *Check the company's reputation.* Consult with other financial institutions. Check with your local Better Business Bureau. Inquire at your state or local consumer protection office.
- *Do not pay out any money until you have completed your investigation and made a final decision.* Do not give money to a salesperson to hold your option to buy. You may never see that money again, 24-17.
- *Watch out for claims that sound too good to be true.* High profit almost always involves high risk. If an investment salesperson promises low risk and high profit, do not invest.
- *Do not buy when pressured to make an immediate decision.* Good investments reap profits over a period of time. They are not going to disappear overnight.

24-17 Cash transactions are especially risky because they leave no paper trail. When making an investment, use a check so you will have a record of the purchase with the cancelled check.

- *When investing in real estate, do not buy without checking out the property.* Be sure you know what you are buying, where it is located, and any repairs it may need. Check for the value of other property in the area and the taxes.

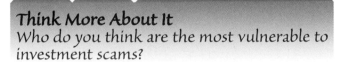

Think More About It
Who do you think are the most vulnerable to investment scams?

Wills and Estate Planning

Most people spend a lifetime working to build financial security. What happens to their assets (money and property) upon their death? Developing plans during their lifetime assures that assets will be distributed to their beneficiaries as they wish. Known as *estate planning*, this process requires an understanding of wills, trusts, and estate taxes.

Wills

Every adult should have a will. A *will* is a legal document stating a person's wishes for distributing all money and personal property after death. The people who receive the money or property are called *beneficiaries*. Without a will, a person's property is distributed by the state according to the state's laws of descent. These laws will vary from one state to another. A legal will is the only way to be sure that the estate is handled as the person wishes.

A will may be handwritten or formal. A handwritten will is dated and signed by the person in his or her own handwriting. A formal will prepared by a lawyer is preferred because a lawyer knows all the legal aspects involved.

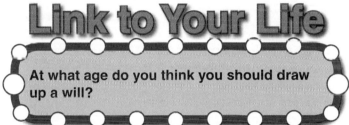

At what age do you think you should draw up a will?

Estate Planning

Your **estate** is the sum of all your personal property, including savings, investments, and insurance benefits. At this time of your life, your estate may be very small. However, during retirement your estate may be very large, especially if you have been involved in estate planning.

Estate planning is the process of building financial security for you and your beneficiaries over your lifetime. Most people use savings, investments, and insurance to build their estate, 24-18. Estate planning also includes an orderly transfer of your assets to your beneficiaries upon your death. This is done through legal documents such as wills or trusts.

A **trust** permits the transfer of property or income from you to a second group (trustee) for the benefit of your beneficiaries. The trustee

24-18 Estate planning can help you build a comfortable life. It also assures that your assets will be divided according to your wishes in the case of death.

manages the assets of the trust on behalf of the beneficiaries.

Trusts are created for different reasons. They may be used when the beneficiaries are too young to manage the property or income. Some people set up a trust when their estate is large. Others do so to set guidelines for future management of their estate. Consulting a lawyer is the best way to determine whether a trust could be helpful in managing your estate.

A Letter of Last Instruction

An important final item in estate planning is a *letter of last instruction*. This serves as a guide for family members so they know what plans have been made and where important papers are kept. It should include the location of the will, the safe-deposit box, and its key. A list of bank account numbers, insurance policies, investments, and trusts is important as well. A list of homeowner records, loans to be paid, debts to be collected, and desired funeral arrangements can also be included. Such information is helpful for family members as the estate plan is carried out.

Review Section 24:3

1. Name three benefits of building an emergency savings fund.
2. Name and briefly describe the four common types of investments.
3. Explain how an annuity can provide security for a retired person.
4. Name one reason why a will is an important part of family protection.
5. List the three most common types of personal property that are part of an estate.

Think It Through

Consumer Beware!

When Lars answered the door, a middle-aged gentleman introduced himself. He was from the Midtown Roofing Company, whose main office was in the next town, 20 miles away. They were canvassing older homes in the area, he told Lars, and they could offer him a good bargain. That was because they would be reroofing several homes in Lars' neighborhood. The salesperson showed him a stack of bids for homes in the area. Lars recognized several names.

He thought maybe he should take advantage of the opportunity. The salesman described the qualities of the shingles they would be using. The product sounded good. The company offered a lifetime guarantee. Lars agreed to the offer, signed the contract, and paid $1,000 down for the work that would be done.

A month later, Lars tried to contact the main office. He had not heard anything from the company. However, the phone number had been disconnected. Lars became concerned. He contacted the Office of Consumer Protection in his area and explained his situation. The agency agreed to check into the company.

When the agency contacted Lars, they did not have good news. The company was no longer in business. The owner had left the area and could not be located. They were sorry for the loss, and explained that some of Lars' neighbors had also lost several thousand dollars.

Questions to Guide Your Thinking

1. What steps should Lars have taken before considering the salesman's offer?

2. When the salesman asked for a down payment to hold the offer, how could Lars have protected himself?

3. What warning signs of potential fraud did Lars fail to recognize?

4. What questions should Lars have asked about a "lifetime" guarantee?

5. What other steps could Lars take to try and get his money back?

Chapter Summary

The risk of financial loss has led to increased interest in protecting the family. Sizable losses can be prevented when consumers keep adequate records to prove what they have done (made payments and purchased certain items). Some losses can be avoided by requiring that companies guarantee a certain quality in their products. If quality or performance is missing, complaining and requesting compensation can help the consumer avoid loss.

Families can protect themselves against financial loss by purchasing insurance. It may be purchased to protect against loss due to some property risks, personal risks, or liability risks. A family's need for such protection will depend on what risks they can afford to absorb.

Savings and investments can increase family security. Short-term savings can supply the money needed for unexpected bills, or a short-term loss of income. Long-term savings and investments can earn a higher rate of return for the family. However, money in such accounts cannot usually be accessed immediately in an emergency. Investments can be a source of income for the future such as during retirement.

Insurance, savings, and investments can help a person build an estate. A well-planned estate can provide for family security even after a person's death.

Assess...

Your Knowledge

1. What are three ways people can protect themselves against consumer fraud?

2. What are the types of insurance that most families need?

3. What are the two main types of risks protected by car insurance?

4. List four common types of investments.

Your Understanding

5. How can a person become an informed consumer?

6. Why does a person need to carry insurance even if he or she does not own very much?

7. Explain how a person's age could impact their cost of car insurance and their cost of life insurance.

8. Why would a person choose a life insurance policy that also served as a savings plan?

9. How could savings and investments help a person reach life goals?

Your Skills

10. Carry out a personal-risk assessment for yourself. Identify your needs for protection in all areas (property, liability, health, life); analyze your current sources of protection (insurance, savings); and summarize the overall state of your financial security.

11. Assume your renter's policy has a face value of $50,000, a deductible of $500, and a premium of $125 per year. How much would the insurance policy pay out if lightning struck the apartment and destroyed your $1,000 laptop computer?

12. Analyze two different investments and rate them for their effectiveness in protecting a family's financial future. Compare the interest they can earn and the safety of the investment.

Think Critically

13. **Research.** Acquire information on life insurance policies from two different insurance companies. Make a chart comparing the features of both companies' policies. Summarize their similarities and differences in a written report and make a recommendation for the policy you would choose. *Choice:* Present your information in a chart, visual representation, or flyer.

14. **Speech.** Write a sample letter of complaint for a consumer product or service. Then present your concern to the class. Explain your complaint and exactly what action you are asking the company to take. *Group option:* Lead the class in a discussion about what action they think the company will take.

15. **Reading.** Read a magazine or newspaper article on a consumer topic. Write a summary of the article, citing the author's title or position, and turn it in with a copy of the article. Critique the article for the following: opinions versus

facts, soundness of information supporting the author's main points, soundness of assumptions made, and final judgment or decision.

16. *Writing.* Evaluate five advertisements for the type of techniques/methods used to promote the product or service. Locate at least three different types of techniques. Clip or describe each advertisement and attach a summary of the technique(s) used. *Choice:* Evaluate each ad's effectiveness (or lack of it) in accomplishing the following: helping you become an informed consumer; encouraging you to try the product or service. *Group option:* Complete the activity with a partner.

Connect with Your Community

17. *Financial literacy.* Invite a financial planner to your class as a guest speaker. Ask the planner to discuss insurance needs for families at different stages in the life cycle. After the presentation, summarize these insurance needs in a one-page report.

18. *Research.* Research the sale of bonds in your community or state. What bonds are being sold? Into what will the money be invested? What interest rate is being paid? Prepare a report for your class summarizing your findings. *Choice:* Present your information in a chart or diagram.

19. *Financial literacy, math.* Compare the value of homes today to the value of the same homes five years ago. Gather information for several neighborhoods or communities in your area. (Real estate offices can be a good source of such information.) Describe how the values of homes have changed. *Group option:* Complete the activity with a partner or small group.

20. Contact your local Better Business Bureau or office of consumer protection to learn about the leading fraudulent practices or consumer concerns in your area. Make a brief oral report to the class.

Use Technology

21. *Social studies.* Using stock market reports on the Internet, identify five stocks that rose in value in the last year. Also identify five stocks that lost value in the last year.

22. *Research.* Using the Internet, locate an article that discusses a fraudulent telemarketing practice that is currently taking place. In a paragraph, summarize the article and identify steps to take to avoid being a target of this fraudulent practice.

23. *Financial literacy.* Using a computer program, prepare a table listing various brands of a product you plan to buy. Compare at least three brands. Acquire information about the product from the Internet as well as from labels, friends, and independent testing agency reports. Across the top of the table, list various qualities of the product, such as price, warranty coverage, and the company's policy on customer satisfaction. Summarize your report by judging which brand you feel is the best buy, giving data to support your choice.

24. *Social studies.* Design an advertisement for a product of your choice using a computer program. Include three types of appeals in your advertisement.

Meeting Your Nutritional Needs

Key Questions

Questions to answer as you study this chapter:

- **What foods should people eat to stay healthy?**

- **How can people use MyPyramid to develop personal eating plans?**

- **How can people make good choices in the grocery store?**

- **How can people handle food safely?**

Chapter Objectives

After studying this chapter, you will be able to

- **identify** the nutrients needed by the body and the importance of each.

- **plan** nutritious meals using the MyPyramid food guidance system.

- **select** menu items that are part of a healthful eating plan.

- **interpret** and use food label information as a buying guide.

- **explain** principles for selecting, storing, and preparing foods in each food group.

Life Sketch

"All you can eat for $8.99," flashed the sign over the door of the restaurant.

"Sounds good to me," Joseph called out. "Let's stop here and eat. I can really get my money's worth."

Cindy sighed. "Eat again?" she thought to herself. They'd had pizza before the game. Now a buffet!

Ramon replied, "It's a great place to eat! They have a huge salad bar and fresh rolls. And the shrimp is the greatest! And it's all you can eat!"

Cindy laughed as Joseph pulled into the restaurant. "I guess I'll have the salad bar. They'll go broke if everyone eats like you do!"

Getting Started

People eat for several different reasons. Socially, you might get together with friends and family and eat to celebrate special events. Emotionally, some foods make you feel good or special. You enjoy eating them. Culturally, you may like recipes that have been passed down for generations in your family. You may prefer foods that are traditional in your cultural background. Physically, the food you eat makes a difference in your health and well-being.

Your body needs certain amounts of foods daily. Eating without regard to your body's needs can affect your health, energy, looks, and performance. Not getting enough nutrients hinders the body's growth and prevents it from fighting disease. Eating too much food often results in problems with weight control. Knowing what your body needs and how to choose, store, and prepare food to meet those needs is important.

section 25:1

Your Nutritional Needs

Sharpen Your Reading

As you read, develop a chart with four columns. In the first column, identify the nutrient and its text definition. In the second column, identify sources of each nutrient. In the third column, list why your body needs that nutrient. In the fourth column, identify signs of too much or too little of that nutrient in your diet.

Boost Your Vocabulary

Locate several labels of foods that are sources of different nutrients. Group the labels by the amount of key nutrients they provide.

Know Key Terms

nutrients	enzymes
carbohydrates	antibodies
glucose	minerals
cholesterol	vitamins
saturated fats	water-soluble vitamins
unsaturated fats	fat-soluble vitamins
trans fatty acids	calories
complete protein	nutrient dense
incomplete protein	

Food is a source of nutrients for the body. **Nutrients** are chemical substances the body needs to carry out its various functions. Nutrients provide energy, regulate body functions, and promote growth and development. Since no one food contains all the nutrients needed by the body, a variety of foods must be eaten every day. This will help you get all the nutrients you need.

At least 40 different nutrients have been identified. These can be grouped into six major categories: carbohydrates, fats, protein, vitamins, minerals, and water. A basic understanding of these nutrients will help you make healthful food choices.

Carbohydrates

Carbohydrates are nutrients that provide the body with a major source of energy, 25-1. Carbohydrates include sugars, starches, and fiber—all foods of plant origin. If you eat more carbohydrates than you burn, your body will convert them and store them as fat.

Sugars

Sugar is used by the body as a quick source of energy. Food sources such as ripe fruits and vegetables and honey contain sugar. Sugar is also a common ingredient in candy and frostings. Food labels sometimes list terms such as *glucose*, *fructose*, *lactose*, *maltose*, and *sucrose*. These are all types of sugars.

Starches

Starches are more complex than sugars. They take longer for your body to use as an energy source. They are found in fruits, vegetables, breads, cereals, pasta, dry beans, and nuts.

Fiber

Dietary fiber does not supply your body with energy, but it does aid in digestion. Fiber is found in cellulose as well as pectins and gums.

Cellulose is the fibrous material found in plants. Cellulosic fibers are important to the body—not for nutrients, but for the way they aid digestion. These fibers swell up in the intestine and provide bulk so the intestines function well. Such fibers are found in whole grains and cereals, fruits, and vegetables.

25-1 Whole-grain breads and cereals are valuable sources of carbohydrates, also providing fiber, vitamins, and minerals.

Pectins and *gums* are dietary fibers that are water soluble. They chemically act in a way that results in the liver removing cholesterol from the bloodstream. This is helpful for a healthy heart and circulation system. Apples, citrus fruits, and some vegetables are common sources of pectin. Oatmeal, dried peas, and beans are sources of gums.

Investigate Further

Why is eating oatmeal advertised as a way to lower blood cholesterol?

How does your body use carbohydrates? The body converts carbohydrates into **glucose**, the substance called *blood sugar*. Glucose is then

burned for energy. The glucose in sugar moves quickly into the bloodstream. Starches are a better source of energy because the glucose is released into the bloodstream more slowly. Then the body has a source of energy for a longer period of time.

Fats

Fats are also a source of energy to the body, 25-2. Energy is provided when fats are broken down into fatty acids and burned along with glucose. Fats also have other roles. They help maintain healthy skin and cell membranes. Some fats are needed for brain development. Fats carry certain vitamins throughout your system. They also form a layer of protection for internal organs and act as insulation for the body.

Several fatty acids are essential to your body. However, your body can make all but two: *linoleic acid* and *linolenic acid*. These can be found in sources such as corn oil, soy oil, and cottonseed oil. A lack of fats in the diet could slow growth and result in unhealthy skin. Too much fat in the diet results in weight gain and possibly heart disease.

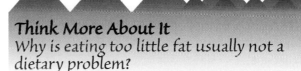

Think More About It
Why is eating too little fat usually not a dietary problem?

25-2 Fats are found in many foods, such as butter, salad dressings, nuts, and fatty meat.

Cholesterol

Cholesterol is a fat that helps the liver make bile, vitamin D, and sex hormones. The liver makes about one to two grams of its own cholesterol each day. Cholesterol is also found in foods of animal origin, such as organ meats and dairy products. Cholesterol is important to the body. However, too much cholesterol in the bloodstream can clog arteries and increase the risk of heart disease.

Types of Fatty Acids

There are two types of fatty acids: saturated and unsaturated. **Saturated fats** are the fatty acids present in meats and dairy products. They are usually solid at room temperature. Saturated fats are also found in coconut oil and palm oil. Saturated fats in the diet increase the level of cholesterol in the bloodstream. They therefore increase the risk of heart disease.

Unsaturated fats are fatty acids found in vegetable oils such as corn, soybean, canola, and olive oil. They are also found in fish oils. These are liquid at room temperature.

When vegetable oils are processed into solid fats such as margarines and shortening, their chemical structure is altered. This process, *hydrogenation*, creates **trans fatty acids**, or trans fats. These fatty acids also increase the risk of heart disease.

Investigate Further

How can foods advertised as containing no cholesterol still increase the risk of heart disease?

Proteins

Proteins are made of building blocks called *amino acids*. At least 20 amino acids have been identified. The body can produce 11 amino acids, which are called *nonessential*. However, nine must come from the proteins in food and are therefore called *essential amino acids*.

A **complete protein** contains all of the essential amino acids the human body needs.

Meat, poultry, fish, eggs, milk, and other dairy products are complete proteins.

Plant proteins lack one or more essential amino acids. These are called **incomplete proteins** and are found in dry beans, dry peas, nuts, and seeds. However, certain plant proteins can be paired to contribute all the amino acids of a complete protein, 25-3.

The body uses amino acids in various combinations to make more than 50,000 different proteins. Body proteins are present in every cell. They are needed to build and repair cells and to make the DNA that carries genetic information. **Enzymes** are proteins used to direct chemical reactions in the body. **Antibodies** are proteins that fight off disease. Proteins also carry nutrients in the blood and maintain the balance of fluids in the body.

The body can use protein to provide energy. This happens if the body is short on glucose. It will burn protein and even break down muscle and other tissue to provide fuel for energy.

Use What You Learn

Why is protein so important in a breakfast meal or morning snack?

Complementary Protein Combinations		
Kidney beans	and	Rice
Lentils	and	Pasta
Chickpeas	and	Brown rice
Peanut butter	and	Whole-grain bread
Tahini or hummus	and	Whole-wheat pita bread
Legume soup (lentils, split peas, white beans, red beans, garbanzo beans)	and	Whole-grain bread

25-3 Protein combinations such as those shown above can provide all the essential amino acids needed for a balanced diet.

Minerals

Minerals are inorganic elements found in the earth's crust. They are also found in our bodies in small amounts. The body needs minerals to make strong bones and teeth. Minerals are needed to balance the amount of fluid in the body and transmit nerve impulses. Together with enzymes, minerals are involved in most of the body's major functions. Therefore, getting all the essential minerals in adequate amounts is necessary.

A deficiency of an essential mineral will affect the body in some way. It may be in growth, deterioration of bones or teeth, weakness, loss of appetite, or poor health in other areas.

All minerals are *toxic* (harmful) at high levels. A diet that includes a variety of foods is not likely to provide a toxic level of a mineral. However, taking large doses of minerals as a supplement could be dangerous. For healthy bodies that need the normal quantities of minerals, a variety of foods is the best source.

Calcium

One disease related to a lack of calcium in the diet is osteoporosis. *Osteoporosis* means *porous bones*. Bones deteriorate and become porous if the body does not get the needed amount of calcium daily. Eating foods rich in calcium, such as milk, milk products, and fruit juices with added calcium, can help prevent osteoporosis. Physical activity is also beneficial.

Iron

The body uses iron to build new red blood cells, help burn fuel for energy, and carry oxygen in the blood. A deficiency of iron results in loss of energy, weakness, and fatigue, a condition called *anemia*.

During a teen's years of rapid growth, the need for iron increases. For women, the need will remain high through most of life due to the loss of blood during menstruation. On a regular basis, women need to replace twice as much iron as men. During pregnancy, a woman's need for iron increases three to four times.

Many foods are excellent sources of iron. Iron is found in liver and other meats; shellfish; dark green, leafy vegetables; cooked dry beans; and whole-grain or enriched breads and cereals.

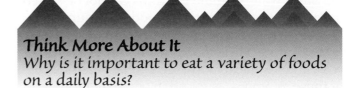

Think More About It
Why is it important to eat a variety of foods on a daily basis?

Vitamins

Vitamins are organic compounds that are essential to health, 25-4. They are required in tiny amounts, but without them deficiency diseases result. Vitamins are involved in regulating the action that takes place in cells. They directly affect growth, reproduction, digestion, and good health. Vitamins are either water-soluble or fat-soluble.

Water-Soluble Vitamins

Vitamins that cannot be stored in the body—B-complex and C vitamins—are called **water-soluble vitamins**. The B and C vitamins are found in watery parts of food, and work in water-filled parts of cells.

Water-soluble vitamins are easily destroyed during food preparation by excess heat. Some are destroyed by light. Often they are thrown away, as when the water used to cook vegetables is drained off. Proper storage and food preparation are necessary to preserve water-soluble vitamins.

25-4 A good source of vitamin C, such as citrus fruits or juices, should be included in your daily diet.

Since water-soluble vitamins cannot be stored in the body, you need to eat foods that supply these vitamins every day. Excess amounts of water-soluble vitamins leave your body along with body wastes. However, excess quantities of these vitamins, as found in some dietary supplements, may be harmful. The body may not be able to process super high doses effectively.

Use What You Learn

What would be the benefit of eating raw fruits and vegetables instead of those that have been cooked?

B-Complex Vitamins

The *B-complex vitamins* are a group of related vitamins that have slightly different functions. Some key B vitamins are thiamin, riboflavin, niacin, and folate. In general, they help the body use energy foods and other nutrients. They contribute to healthy nerves, appetite, digestion, and red blood cells. Good sources of B vitamins include whole-grain breads, cereals, meats, and fish.

Vitamin C

Vitamin C helps the body fight infection and heal wounds. It also works with calcium to create and maintain healthy bones and teeth. Vitamin C also helps in blood formation and strengthening blood vessel walls. Citrus fruits such as oranges, grapefruit, and lemons are excellent sources of vitamin C. Other fruits and dark green vegetables such as broccoli are good sources of vitamin C.

Fat-Soluble Vitamins

The **fat-soluble vitamins**, which include vitamins A, D, E, and K, can be stored in the body. They are found in a variety of foods such as liver, fish, dairy products, and oils. Dark green and yellow vegetables are good sources of vitamins A and K.

Each of these vitamins serves an important function. *Vitamin A* promotes healthy growth and is especially important for the development of healthy bones, teeth, skin, and hair, 25-5.

Vitamin D is known as the sunshine vitamin. The body can make vitamin D when the skin is

25-5 Vegetables such as broccoli and carrots are good sources of Vitamin A.

exposed to sunlight. Vitamin D is also important for strong bones and teeth.

Vitamin E is found mostly in fats and oils. It is also found in leafy green vegetables and whole-grain cereals. This vitamin protects cell membranes and aids in the use of energy foods. *Vitamin K* is important in helping blood to clot properly.

Fat-soluble vitamins are not dissolved or destroyed in the cooking process. They travel through the body in fats and are stored in the body's fatty tissue. Consequently, the body has access to these vitamins over a period of time. However, taking large doses of these vitamins can be harmful. Toxic levels can build up in the body.

Link to Your Life

Which vitamins do you probably get sufficiently from foods you eat? Which vitamins might be lacking in your diet? Why do you think this is the case?

Water

Water is also considered a nutrient as it serves several important functions in the body. Water, which makes up over one-half of normal body weight, is a vital part of many body fluids. It forms part of the blood and helps carry nutrients to the cells. It helps carry away waste products. Water also helps regulate body temperature through perspiration.

Your body uses large quantities of water every day. Water is lost through perspiration and the elimination of wastes. Overall, two to three quarts of water are lost each day.

Lack of water can have a negative effect on your body's performance. If your intake of water is too low, you may begin to feel tired, hot, and achy. You may feel bored and find it hard to concentrate.

Lack of water also can have a negative effect on your health. You can survive without food for days, even weeks, but you can only survive a few days without water. Ten percent water loss can result in kidney failure. Twenty percent water loss results in death.

You replace water in your body by eating food and drinking fluids. At least eight glasses of water or other beverages, such as juice and milk, are recommended daily. Foods also add water to the diet. Some foods have higher water content than others. These include soups, watermelon, and oranges. Beverages high in caffeine cause the kidneys to expel more water than is normal.

Use What You Learn

What is the benefit of keeping a water bottle with you in class?

Calories

Calories measure the amount of potential energy in food. The body is able to obtain energy from carbohydrates, fats, and protein. One gram of fat yields nine calories of energy. One gram of either carbohydrate or protein yields four calories. Carbohydrates and fats provide most of the energy the body needs. Protein provides the remainder.

When choosing energy foods, you should try to get at least 55 percent of your calories from carbohydrates. No more than 30 percent of your calories should be met through fats. By limiting your intake of fats, you can eat more

carbohydrate and protein foods for the same number of calories. You can also decrease your risk for health problems related to excess fat in the diet.

Foods that are **nutrient dense** provide a good supply of nutrients in proportion to calories. For instance, grilled chicken, a baked potato, green peas, and a whole wheat roll would make a nutrient-dense meal. Foods that are high in calories and low in nutrients provide *empty calories*. Foods that are deep fried, greasy, sticky, or sweet may be energy rich, but provide few other nutrients. If you eat more calories than your body uses each day and do not stay active, you may gain weight. If those calories are gained from empty-calorie food, you still could be lacking important nutrients in your diet.

Link to Your Life

Which of your favorite foods are mostly empty calories?

You can see why a variety of foods is needed to obtain all the nutrients the body needs. (See the chart in 25-6 to review the functions and sources of essential nutrients.) Your body needs these nutrients in a balanced amount. Nutrients work together to carry out their functions. If one is missing, another may not be able to do its work. Too much of one nutrient may hinder the work of another. Some even are toxic when taken in very large doses. Therefore, choosing a balanced diet with a variety of foods to meet your nutrient needs is important.

Review Section 25:1

1. List the six essential nutrients and explain one important function of each.

2. Identify the main reason for eating a variety of foods.

3. What is the difference between a nutrient-dense food and a food with empty calories?

Key Nutrients		
Nutrient	**Function**	**Sources**
Carbohydrates	Supply energy Provide bulk in the form of cellulose (needed for digestion) Help the body digest fats efficiently Spare proteins so they can be used for growth and regulation	Sugar: Honey, jam, jelly, sugar, molasses Fiber: Fresh fruits and vegetables, whole-grain cereals and breads Starch: Breads, cereals, corn, peas, beans, potatoes, macaroni products
Fats	Supply energy (most concentrated energy in food) Carry fat-soluble vitamins Insulate the body from shock and temperature changes Protect vital organs Add flavor and satisfying quality to foods Serve as a source of essential fatty acids	Butter, margarine, cream, cheese, marbling in meat, nuts, whole milk, olives, chocolate, egg yolks, bacon, salad oils, dressings
Proteins	Build and repair tissues Help make antibodies, enzymes, neurotransmitters, hormones, and some vitamins Regulate fluid balance in the cells and other body processes Supply energy, when needed	High-quality proteins: meat, poultry, fish, eggs, milk, other dairy products Low-quality proteins: cereals, grains, peanuts, peanut butter, lentils and legumes
Vitamins • Vitamin A	Helps keep skin clear and smooth and mucous membranes healthy Helps prevent night blindness Promotes growth	Liver, egg yolk, dark green and yellow fruits and vegetables, butter, whole and fortified milk, fortified margarine, Cheddar-type cheese
• Vitamin D	Helps build strong bones and teeth in children Helps maintain bones in adults	Fortified milk, butter, and margarine; fish liver oils; liver; sardines; tuna; egg yolk; the sun
• Vitamin E	Acts as an antioxidant that protects membranes of cells exposed to high concentrations of oxygen	Liver and other organ meats, eggs, leafy green vegetables, whole-grain cereals, salad oils, shortenings, other fats and oils
• Vitamin K	Helps blood clot	Organ meats, leafy green vegetables, cauliflower, other vegetables, egg yolks

(Continued)

25-6 Knowing the functions of various nutrients and their food sources can help you balance your daily food needs.

Key Nutrients		
Nutrient	**Function**	**Sources**
• Vitamin C	Promotes healthy gums and tissues Helps wounds heal and broken bones mend Helps body fight infection Helps make cementing materials that hold body cells together	Citrus fruits, strawberries, cantaloupe, broccoli, green peppers, raw cabbage, tomatoes, green leafy vegetables, potatoes and sweet potatoes cooked in the skin
• Thiamin	Helps promote normal appetite and digestion Forms parts of the coenzymes needed for the breakdown of carbohydrates Helps keep nervous system healthy and prevent irritability Helps body release energy from food	Pork, other meats, poultry, fish, eggs, enriched or whole-grain breads and cereals, dried beans
• Riboflavin	Helps cells use oxygen Helps keep skin, tongue, and lips normal Helps prevent scaly, greasy areas around the mouth and nose Forms part of the coenzymes needed for the breakdown of carbohydrates	Milk, all kinds of cheese, ice cream, liver, other meats, fish, poultry, eggs, dark green leafy vegetables
• Niacin	Helps keep nervous system healthy Helps keep skin, mouth, tongue, and digestive tract healthy Helps cells use other nutrients Forms part of two coenzymes involved in complex chemical reactions in the body	Meat, fish, poultry, enriched or whole-grain breads and cereals, peanuts, peanut butter, dried beans and peas
• Vitamin B-6	Helps nervous tissue function normally Plays a role in the breakdown of proteins, fats, and carbohydrates Plays a role in the reaction in which tryptophan is converted to niacin Plays a role in the regeneration of red blood cells	Liver, muscle meats, vegetables, whole-grain cereals
• Folate	Synthesizes DNA Guards against giving birth to babies who suffer brain or spinal cord injuries	Dark green leafy vegetables, liver, legumes, oranges, cantaloupe, broccoli, most enriched breads and grain products fortified with folic acid
• Vitamin B-12	Protects against pernicious anemia Plays a role in the normal functioning of cells	Eggs, fish, liver and other meats, milk, cheese

(Continued)

25-6 Continued.

Key Nutrients		
Nutrient	**Function**	**Sources**
Minerals • Calcium	Helps build bones and teeth Helps blood clot Helps muscles and nerves work Helps regulate the use of other minerals in the body	Milk, cheese, other dairy products, leafy green vegetables, canned fish eaten with the bones
• Phosphorus	Helps build strong bones and teeth Helps regulate many internal bodily activities	Protein and calcium food sources
• Iodine	Promotes normal functioning of the thyroid gland	Saltwater fish, shellfish, iodized table salt
• Iron	Combines with protein to make hemoglobin Helps cells use oxygen	Liver, lean meats, egg yolk, dried beans and peas, leafy green vegetables, dried fruits, enriched and whole-grain breads and cereals
Water	Aids in proper digestion Plays a role in cell growth and maintenance Plays a role in all chemical reactions in the body Lubricates the joints and body cells Helps regulate body temperature	Liquids such as water, milk, clear soups, coffee, tea, fruit juices, other beverages Most foods, especially fruits and vegetables

25-6 Continued.

section 25:2

Planning What You Eat

Sharpen Your Reading

Draw a graphic organizer that looks like the MyPyramid triangle. As you read, identify good sources and recommended daily amounts for a person your age and size for each food group.

Boost Your Vocabulary

Go to the MyPyramid Web site at **www.mypyramid.gov**. Enter your age, gender, and activity level to learn how much food you need daily from each food group. Also enter your height and weight for more accurate information.

Know Key Terms

MyPyramid

How much of each nutrient do you need to maintain a healthy body? This question is important because you have different needs at different stages of the life cycle. Your needs also vary depending on your sex, body size, and lifestyle.

MyPyramid

MyPyramid is a tool developed by the U.S. Department of Agriculture to help people make more healthful food and physical activity choices.

This plan sorts foods of similar nutritive values into groups. Eating the suggested amounts of foods from each group daily will provide you with the nutrients you need. See 25-7.

Note how the foods that should make up the largest part of your diet form the largest parts of MyPyramid. MyPyramid includes the following groups:

- grains
- vegetables
- fruits
- milk
- meat and beans

Nutrient-rich foods are found in each of these five food groups. By choosing carefully from each group, you can avoid consuming too many calories, too much fat, or added sugars. By eating the recommended amounts from each group, you can meet your nutrient needs.

Link to Your Life

Do you eat foods from all five of these food groups daily?

Grains

The *grains group* includes bagels, English muffins, biscuits, pancakes, noodles, macaroni, rice, cereals, tortillas, and other grain products. These foods are low-fat sources of complex carbohydrates. Whole grains provide B vitamins and fiber as well. Many products in the grains group are fortified or enriched with B vitamins and iron.

Vegetables

The *vegetable group* includes all forms of vegetables—fresh, canned, frozen, dried, and juices. Vegetables provide an important source of vitamins, minerals, and dietary fiber. Some vegetables also supply starch for energy. Foods in this group include broccoli, spinach, carrots, squash, corn, and cabbage.

25-7 MyPyramid illustrates how the different food groups work together to form a balanced diet.

Fruits

Like the vegetable group, the *fruit group* is a high-fiber, low-fat source of vitamins and minerals. All forms of fruit and fruit juices are part of this group. Grapes, bananas, apples, peaches, citrus fruits, melons, and berries are all found in the fruit group. At least one serving of fruit per day should be high in vitamin C.

Milk

The *milk group* includes foods that are good sources of calcium, riboflavin, protein, and many other nutrients. During the teen years when growth is rapid, three cups of milk are needed daily. Other dairy products can be substituted for milk to meet a person's calcium needs.

Meat and Beans

The *meat and beans group* is a major source of protein, iron, and B vitamins. Beef, pork, lamb, chicken, turkey, and tuna are part of this group. Meat alternates, which include dried beans, peas, and lentils; peanuts; and eggs, are also part of this group.

Fats, Oils, and Sweets

Some of the foods you probably like to eat are not included in these five groups. Butter, gravies, salad dressing, and mayonnaise are considered *oils*. These foods are included in MyPyramid with recommendations to use them sparingly. They do not represent a food group. Fats, oils, and sweets add flavor and variety to meals. However, eating too many of these high-calorie foods may result in weight gain.

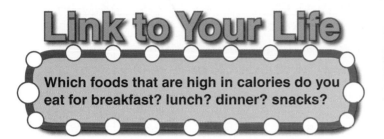

You need to choose a variety of foods each day. No single food group provides all the nutrients your body needs. Think of the different groups in MyPyramid as members of a team. Each team member is needed to carry out a specific role. Without each member's contributions, the team cannot win. The body needs nutrients from a variety of foods in order to carry out its functions. A "winning" body means good health, energy, and the abilities to grow new cells and fight off disease.

Recommended Amounts

How do you know how much you need from each group daily? That depends on your age, sex, height, weight, and activity level. These factors influence your specific nutrient and calorie needs. By going to the MyPyramid Web site (www.mypyramid.gov) and entering your age, gender, height, weight, and activity level, you can learn how much food you need daily from each food group. The chart in 25-8 gives eight calorie levels and the amounts from each food group appropriate for each level. Try to eat at least the minimum amount recommended for each food group to get essential nutrients.

Select carefully from each food group to get maximum nutrition. For instance, choose lean meats and low-fat dairy products. Rather than juices, opt for whole or cut-up fruits since they provide fiber. Keep a supply of fresh and frozen vegetables on hand. Limit processed vegetables and those with added sauces and seasonings. Look for whole-grain breads and cereals, which

are also high in fiber. Limit the amounts of fats, oils, and sweets you add to your foods. Following these tips will help you get the nutrients you need for a healthy body.

Planning Meals

What is your daily eating pattern? Some people eat three meals a day. Others eat one meal and several snacks. Some eat off and on all day. Whatever your eating pattern, choosing foods that will meet your nutrient needs is important. Knowing what, when, and how much you eat can help you plan.

Eating Patterns

If you eat three meals a day, you can plan your meals using basic meal patterns. For breakfast, you may eat a bowl of cereal, a slice of toast with peanut butter, orange juice, and a glass of milk. Lunch could include a chicken sandwich, carrot sticks, an apple, and a glass of milk. Dinner could be spaghetti with tomato sauce, meatballs, green salad, Italian bread, and a glass of milk. A serving of fruit for dessert or a snack will complete the recommended number of servings for teens. If you are active and need more servings, the number of servings of pasta, bread, cereal, vegetables, and fruit can be increased.

Instead of three meals daily, some individuals eat smaller snacks several times a day. This eating pattern is called *grazing*. It is important that the foods you choose are high in nutrients rather than just calories. For example, you might start the day with orange juice. The following are good grazing foods: muffins, bagels, toast, chicken fingers, carrot sticks, crackers and cheese, cold meat sandwiches, salads, vegetables and dip, and three or four fruits throughout the day. It is possible to meet the daily requirements if you plan your eating to include servings from the MyPyramid. Whether meals or snacks, everything you eat needs to be included in your food plan.

Recommended Daily Intakes

Food Group	1,800	2,000	2,200	2,400	2,600	2,800	3,000	3,200
Fruits	1.5 cups	2 cups	2 cups	2 cups	2 cups	2.5 cups	2.5 cups	2.5 cups
Vegetables	2.5 cups	2.5 cups	3 cups	3 cups	3.5 cups	3.5 cups	4 cups	4 cups
Grains*	6 oz-eq	6 oz-eq	7 oz-eq	8 oz-eq	9 oz-eq	10 oz-eq	10 oz-eq	10 oz-eq
Meat and beans*	5 oz-eq	5.5 oz-eq	6 oz-eq	6.5 oz-eq	6.5 oz-eq	7 oz-eq	7 oz-eq	7 oz-eq
Milk	3 cups	3 cups	3 cups	3 cups	3 cups	3 cups	3 cups	3 cups
Oils	5 tsp	6 tsp	6 tsp	7 tsp	8 tsp	8 tsp	10 tsp	10 tsp

*Servings in these groups are ounce-equivalents (oz-eq). The chart below shows what counts as an ounce-equivalent.

What Is a Portion?

Grains Group

Count as one ounce-equivalent:
- 1 slice of whole-wheat bread
- 1 cup of ready-to-eat cereal
- 5-7 small crackers
- ½ cup of cooked pasta or rice

Milk Group

Count as one cup portion:
- 1 cup fat-free or low-fat milk or yogurt
- 1½ ounces natural cheese
- 2 ounces processed (American) cheese
- 2 cups cottage cheese

Vegetables Group

Count as one cup portion:
- 1 cup broccoli, raw or cooked
- 1 large tomato
- 1 medium baked potato
- 2 cups romaine lettuce

Meat and Beans Group

Count as one ounce-equivalent:
- 1 ounce cooked lean meat, poultry, or fish
- 1 egg
- ½ ounce of nuts
- 1 tablespoon peanut butter
- ¼ cup dried beans or peas

Fruits Group

Count as one cup portion:
- 1 cup canned fruit or fruit juice
- 1 small apple or medium banana
- ½ cup dried apricots
- ¼ of a medium cantaloupe

25-8 Choosing the recommended amounts for your calorie level from each food group can help you eat a balanced diet.

Use What You Learn

What steps can people take to plan nutritious meals without spending a lot of time?

Eating Out

Today, the lifestyle of many people includes eating meals away from home. More women are working outside the home and have less time to prepare meals. Family members live active lives and keep individual schedules. Eating out has become a common event.

Fast-Food Restaurants

Many Americans enjoy the convenience of eating at fast-food restaurants. These restaurants often feature fast service, low prices, and a limited menu. However, many of the foods served are high in saturated fats, calories, and sodium. Too much of these foods are not healthy for any food plan.

Your knowledge of good nutrition can help you make wiser choices from fast-food menus. For instance, a grilled chicken sandwich on a whole-wheat bun provides a serving of meat and two servings of bread. (It is also lower in calories and fat than a cheeseburger.) A tossed lettuce salad with fresh vegetables provides a serving from the vegetable group. It is also a no-fat, high-fiber choice. Low-fat milk or low-fat shakes (if made with dairy products), instead of soft drinks, can also contribute nutrients to your meal.

Knowing that customers are becoming more health conscious, many fast-food restaurants now offer salad choices or a salad bar. Again, watch the extras you tend to put on these foods: mayonnaise, salad dressing, and dips.

The key to meeting your nutrient needs when eating out is to choose healthful foods from each food group, 25-9. Remember, only you can control what you order off the menu. These tips may be helpful in making these choices:

- Avoid eating too many fried foods, such as French fries, onion rings, or doughnuts. Look for lower-fat options, such as grilled or baked items.

- Sweet or very rich foods provide mostly calories and few nutrients. They should be avoided or eaten in small amounts. Try a bagel or English muffin instead of a sweet roll. Substitute frozen yogurt for ice cream.

- Take advantage of salads and side dishes made of fruits and vegetables. If you choose a high-fat dressing or sauce, ask for it served on the side. Add only enough to flavor the food, not smother it.

25-9 Develop good nutrition habits when eating out. Choose a variety of foods from the menu in moderate amounts, and avoid too much fat or salt.

 What choices might be healthful alternatives to your fast-food favorites?

Meals eaten away from home can account for most of a person's daily food consumption. To get all the nutrients needed to stay healthy, try to balance your fast-food choices with other selections during the day. By selecting carefully from a menu, you can make healthful eating a lifetime habit.

Dining Etiquette

Whether you are eating alone or with others, practice the rules of dining etiquette. This way you will not embarrass yourself with bad table manners when it is important to make a good impression. Knowing proper table etiquette can help you remain at ease while on dates and at work-related functions.

Using good table manners is a way of being considerate of others. If you use proper etiquette every day, it will become a habit. Practice good etiquette by following the basic guidelines in 25-10.

Review Section 25:2

1. List the five food groups in MyPyramid and identify the major nutrients each provides.

2. Identify a one-day eating plan for a person whose calorie intake is 2,200 calories. List specific amounts of each food.

3. Describe how snacks or meals eaten at a fast-food restaurant can be included in an eating plan.

Good Table Etiquette
• After sitting, place the napkin in your lap.
• Wait for the host to begin eating.
• Use eating utensils in the order they are placed on the table starting from the outer edge.
• Keep your elbows off the table while eating.
• Eat slowly and quietly, keeping your mouth closed while chewing your food.
• Do not talk or drink with your mouth full.
• Place your knife or fork on your plate after use, not on the table.
• Never use your own silverware to take food from the serving dish.
• Do not reach across the table or in front of another diner. Ask to have the food passed to you.
• Hold water glasses near the base.
• Try to eat a small portion of each food served. If you cannot, leave it.
• Do not place any food, such as rolls or bread, on the table. Place them on the bread or dinner plate.
• When finished eating, place your knife across the plate rim and the fork parallel to it.
• At the end of the meal, place your napkin to the left of the plate.

25-10 By knowing good table etiquette, you avoid the awkwardness of not knowing how to behave in a social meal setting.

section 25:3

Shopping for Food

Sharpen Your Reading

As you read each topic, summarize how the information can help you make good choices when shopping for food.

Boost Your Vocabulary

Visit a grocery store and compare the costs of two similar products, using the unit price. Compare a national brand, a house brand, and a generic brand.

Know Key Terms

Daily Values
house brand
unit price

"Remember, you'll be cooking tomorrow," Dan's mother reminded him. "Check to see that we have everything you need."

Before You Shop

Dan knew he had to get organized before he went shopping. He decided to plan the menu first, check for supplies, and then make a shopping list.

Plan Your Menus

Dan planned a simple menu: spaghetti, meatballs, salad, and Italian bread. "That shouldn't be too hard," he thought. He included foods from the meat, bread, and vegetable groups. He also would serve low-fat milk to drink.

Check Your Supplies

The next step was to check the supplies he needed. He decided to make a list. Dan was surprised to see how long his list became. He needed several ingredients for the meatballs. The supplies of milk, eggs, margarine, and spaghetti were low. Besides, his mother had also given him a list of items she needed.

Make a List

Prepare a shopping list before shopping, just as Dan did. It saves you money and time. You stick to your food budget, buy only what you need, and avoid making extra trips for forgotten items. Listing the items in the same order as they are arranged in the store is helpful, too. That way you can proceed through the store quickly, 25-11.

Another helpful tip is to check your local newspaper before you shop. Newspaper ads can help you identify items that are on sale or in season. These are good items to include in your meals. They can help you keep food costs down.

25-11 Making a list can help you get your shopping done quickly without forgetting any items.

Use What You Learn

How do you think a list could help you and your family when shopping for food?

Food Labels

One of the keys to informed shopping is reading food labels. Several items are required on food labels to help inform the consumer about what is being eaten.

Government regulations require the following on all food labels:

- common name of the product
- form of the product, such as whole, shredded, or cubed
- net contents or net weight, including the liquid in which food is packed
- name and address of the manufacturer, distributor, or packer
- list of ingredients in descending order by weight
- nutrition label

Link to Your Life

How could this information help you make an informed choice when shopping for food?

Nutrition Labels

Nutrition information is required on the labels of all packaged foods. All nutrition labels follow a required format, 25-12. Look on the label for the heading *Nutrition Facts*. You should find the following information under *Nutrition Facts*:

- serving size, stated in both household and metric measures
- the number of servings found in the food product container
- nutrition information for one serving of a product
- total calories per serving, followed by the number of calories from fat

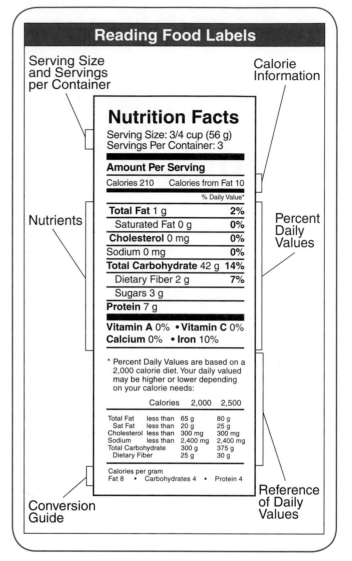

25-12 Food labels provide a variety of information that helps consumers make informed choices.

In addition, certain nutrients must appear on the nutrition label: total fat, saturated fat, cholesterol, sodium, total carbohydrate, dietary fiber, sugars, protein, vitamin A, vitamin C, calcium, and iron. Food manufacturers may also choose to list additional nutrients if they follow required guidelines. The label must include the metric weight of each listed nutrient in a serving of food stated in either grams (g) or milligrams (mg). Amounts are also expressed as a percent Daily Value.

Think More About It
Why do you think the government is so strict about having the above information on food labels?

Daily Values

Daily Values are reference numbers used to help consumers see how food products fit into the day's nutrient needs. Your Daily Values are based on the number of calories you need each day. The percent Daily Values on food labels are based on a 2,000-calorie diet. If you need more than 2,000 calories per day, your Daily Values will be higher. Therefore, a serving of a food product will provide less of your Daily Values than the percent shown on the label. On the other hand, you may need less than 2,000 calories per day. In this case, food products will provide a larger percent of your Daily Values than shown on labels.

Look at the percent Daily Values of the foods you eat throughout the day. This will help you determine whether you are meeting your daily nutrient needs. The percent Daily Value can also be used to compare the nutritional content of various foods.

Near the bottom of a nutrition label, a reference of Daily Values is given for two calorie levels: 2,000 and 2,500. This shows the maximum amount of fat, saturated fat, cholesterol, and sodium recommended. It also shows the minimum number of grams of total carbohydrate and dietary fiber needed for a healthful diet.

At the bottom of the label, an optional conversion guide may appear. It states the number of calories provided by a gram of fat, carbohydrate, and protein. The numbers make it possible to figure how many calories in a food come from these components.

Use What You Learn
How do you think consumers could use the percent Daily Values on food labels?

Product Dating

Product dating helps you select foods that are fresh, wholesome, and top quality. Two types of dating are important to know. A *sell by* date shows how long the manufacturer recommends grocers keep the product on the shelf. A *use by* date is the last date manufacturers recommend consumers use the product for peak quality. However, foods stored properly should still be wholesome and safe to eat for a period after the dates expire.

Link to Your Life
How would you use product dating to help you decide whether to use a product?

Managing Your Food Costs

Food costs take a significant portion of the family income—as much as 25 percent. Spending less on food, then, can help you reach other family goals.

Using sale items and advertised specials in your food plan can help you get the food you need at lower prices, 25-13. Buying foods in season and preserving them by canning or freezing can also add savings to your food budget over the year. Sometimes manufacturers' coupons can be used to reduce the price you pay for an item.

You can also make selections that help you save money. For instance, a can of whole tomatoes costs more than chopped or stewed tomatoes. If the form makes no difference in your recipe or meal plan, choose the cheaper one. Fresh, in-season foods generally cost less than processed foods. You will save money by buying foods that you prepare versus purchasing foods that are ready to eat.

25-13 Planning meals around sale items is a good way to manage food costs.

Convenience Foods

When time is short and your schedule is busy, you may prefer some convenience foods. These are products that are partially prepared and require minimal preparation. Although you save time by using them, you generally pay more for the added convenience. It is usually cheaper, though, to use convenience foods than to eat out at a restaurant.

Food Brands

Products carry one of the following name brands: national, local (or house), or generic. Generally, national name brand products have the highest prices. This is because manufacturers spend more money on packaging and advertising. National advertising promotes the product, but it also increases the cost of the product.

House or local brands are generally less expensive to buy. A **house brand** is a product offered by a particular store. The store may belong to a chain of stores. Local brands may be cheaper due to less distribution costs.

Generic brands cost less than national or house brands. One reason for the savings is that items are packaged in plain containers. They display only the required labeling. Nutritionally, they are the same as other brand name items. However, they may be lower in quality. For instance, food items may be in pieces rather than whole, or uneven in sizes and shapes. Also, flavor and appearance can vary considerably from one container to the next, or one season to another.

Use What You Learn

What are some house brands available in your local grocery store?

Unit Pricing

How can you compare the cost of one product with another, or one brand with another? Some stores make it easier for you by using unit pricing. A product's **unit price** is the cost per unit, weight, or measure. This price is often stated on a shelf label next to the product, 25-14.

With unit pricing, you can compare the cost of foods quickly and easily. You can determine if the larger size of a product is cheaper per ounce than the smaller size. You can compare if a house brand is a better buy than a sale-priced national brand. If your store does not offer unit pricing, you can figure out this information yourself. Divide the cost of the product by the net weight stated on the package. The result will be the cost per unit. Be sure to compare equal units. For instance, compare the cost per ounce of one product with the cost per ounce of another.

Many of your choices will be guided by cost and influenced by personal preference. Making informed choices can help you buy foods that contribute to a nutritious eating plan.

25-14 Which product is the best buy? By comparing the unit prices on these products, you can see one is more economical than the other.

Use What You Learn

Figure the unit price (price per pound) on hamburger that costs $9.00 for a three-pound package.

Review Section 25:3

1. Name three steps to follow before going shopping for food.
2. What nutrients are required to be listed on a nutrition label?
3. Explain the two types of dates on products that are important to know.
4. List four ways people can manage their food costs.

section 25:4

Handling Food

Handling food involves storing, preparing, cooking, and serving food. Skills for preparing, cooking, and serving food can help you make interesting and appealing meals. More importantly, food should be handled in a way that keeps it safe for human consumption. Only then can food contribute to your health and well-being.

Sanitation

Whenever handling food, a clean environment is essential. **Sanitation** refers to practices that prevent bacteria from multiplying and causing illness.

Good sanitation begins with good personal hygiene and kitchen cleanliness.

- *Wash your hands for 20 seconds.* Use warm soapy water to wash before and after handling food or food utensils.

- *Keep the work area clean.* Wash counters before and after you prepare food on them. Wipe off eating areas before and after you eat.

- *Keep raw, cooked, and ready-to-eat foods separate.* This guideline applies during food shopping, preparation, or storage. It is especially important when handling raw meat, poultry, fish, shellfish, or eggs. Cooking kills bacteria, but some may remain on a cutting board, utensil, or platter. Do not allow the drippings from these raw foods to touch other foods.

- *Keep foods at safe temperatures.* Bacteria grow most rapidly at room temperatures, 25-15. That is why hot foods should be served hot, and cold foods served cold. Thaw meats in the refrigerator to prevent the growth of bacteria. Store leftovers in the refrigerator as soon as you finish eating. Dairy products such as cream pies and custards must also be kept chilled until eaten.

Think More About It
In what settings is it most difficult to keep hot foods hot and cold foods cold?

Foodborne Illness

A **foodborne illness** results from eating food that has not been handled correctly. Vomiting, diarrhea, and stomach cramps are the most common symptoms of foodborne illness. The degree of severity varies from person to person. Foodborne illness can last for a few hours or a few days. Some cases can develop complications, linger for months, and possibly cause death. Thousands of cases of foodborne illness go unreported because they are mistaken for flu. All who handle food—growers, truckers, processors, sellers, and preparers—have an obligation to keep food safe.

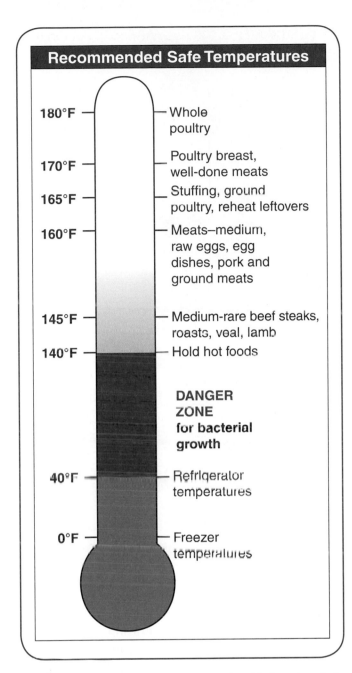

Recommended Safe Temperatures

180°F — Whole poultry

170°F — Poultry breast, well-done meats

165°F — Stuffing, ground poultry, reheat leftovers

160°F — Meats—medium, raw eggs, egg dishes, pork and ground meats

145°F — Medium-rare beef steaks, roasts, veal, lamb

140°F — Hold hot foods

DANGER ZONE for bacterial growth

40°F — Refrigerator temperatures

0°F — Freezer temperatures

25-15 Food safety is dependent on food being stored at and cooked to proper temperatures.

Food Storage

Food should always be stored properly in the refrigerator, freezer, and kitchen cabinets. Proper storage will help prevent foodborne illness.

Refrigerating Food

Perishable foods are foods that spoil easily and must be kept at refrigerator temperatures. These foods include meats, eggs, dairy products,

any leftovers, and some fruits and vegetables. Refrigerator temperatures should be set at 35°F to 40°F. To package foods properly, use tightly covered containers, food storage bags, plastic wrap, or foil.

Freezing Food

Freezer temperature should be set at 0°F or slightly lower. A freezer can be used to store foods for longer periods. Foods should be wrapped in moisture- and vapor-proof wrap, put in freezer bags, or sealed in airtight containers. Label and date the packages so you know the contents and date of freezing.

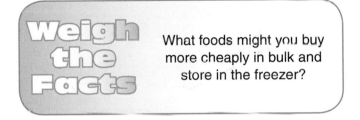

Weigh the Facts

What foods might you buy more cheaply in bulk and store in the freezer?

Storing Food at Room Temperature

Food that does not require refrigeration can be stored on the shelf. A cool dry place is recommended for shelf storage. However, once cans and jars have been opened, the food should be stored in the refrigerator. Packages or boxes of dried food products such as pasta should be resealed or transferred to sealed containers. Of course, kitchen shelves and cabinets should be free of insects and rodents.

Food Preparation

Becoming a good cook takes practice and good recipes. Following some general principles for handling food can help you serve meals that are tasty, nutritious, and appealing.

A good cookbook can give you step-by-step directions for preparing and cooking a large variety of foods. Generally it is important to follow the directions exactly. Once you try a recipe, you may want to make slight variations next time. For instance, you might add spices or herbs that your family prefers, 25-16.

25-16 Encouraging family members to help with food preparation assures meals that everyone will enjoy.

Understanding principles of food cookery can help you be a successful cook. Common problems in food cookery can be identified with specific food groups. Being aware of these potential problems and knowing how to avoid them can help you prepare successful products. Also, nutrient loss is a problem when foods are cooked. Knowing how to preserve nutrients when cooking can help you serve nutritious meals. Following are a few basic guidelines for preparing various foods.

Dairy Products

Since dairy products are protein foods, they should be cooked at low temperatures. The proteins in milk are affected by heat. When milk gets too hot, it can scorch and burn easily. It will also curdle if the cooking temperature is too high or if ingredients high in acids, enzymes, or salts are added. (Acids are found in foods such as tomatoes, lemons, and oranges.) Prevent scorching and curdling by using low heat. Heating milk in the top of a double boiler is helpful. Thickening milk before adding acids also prevents curdling.

When cooking with cheese, avoid overcooking. This makes the cheese tough and rubbery. Cut cheese into small pieces so it will melt faster; then add it near the end of cooking. Sprinkle cheese on a casserole after the casserole is baked. Then return it to the oven for a few minutes to melt the cheese. A medium to medium-high power setting is used to melt cheese in the microwave. Higher settings can cause it to become tough and rubbery.

What are some of your favorite foods that include milk or cheese as ingredients?

Eggs

Eggs are the source of a protein that cooks more quickly than other protein foods. Moderate temperatures are recommended. Accurate cooking times are also important. Overcooking will cause eggs to become tough and rubbery. Poaching, scrambling, and frying are just a few of the common methods of preparing eggs.

Use What You Learn

At what temperature should your favorite egg dish be prepared?

Meats

The cooking method used to cook meats depends on the cut of meat. Some meat cuts are more tender than others. These cuts can be cooked with higher temperatures for a short period of time using *dry-heat cooking methods*. These include roasting, baking, grilling, or broiling.

Moist-heat cooking methods work well with less-tender cuts of meat. A less-tender cut has more connective tissue that makes it tough. Connective tissue needs to be softened by cooking slowly with moisture over low heat. Marinating or cooking meat in an acid, such as tomato or lemon juice or vinegar, will tenderize connective tissue. A powdered meat tenderizer sprinkled over the meat before cooking also breaks down connective tissue. Pounding meat with a meat mallet is another way to tenderize tougher cuts.

Choosing the cooking method that is appropriate for the cut of meat is essential. The right method helps bring out the most flavor and tenderness in meat.

Weigh the Facts If you want to grill a cheaper steak that is a little tough, what could you do to make it more tender?

Fruits and Vegetables

Fruits and vegetables are high sources of vitamins and minerals if properly prepared, 25-17. The following are some tips for preparing fruits and vegetables and preserving their nutrients:

- Serve fruits and vegetables raw when you can. Cooking destroys some nutrients, particularly vitamin C.
- Leave the skins on fruits and vegetables.

Tips for Handling Fruits and Vegetables

- Buy fresh, crisp produce.
- Serve raw if possible.
- Leave peelings on when you can.
- Do not soak in water before cooking or serving.
- Cook with a small amount of water.
- Do not rinse after cooking.
- Use cooking water in soups and sauces when you can.

25-17 Following these tips for handling and cooking can reduce loss of essential vitamins and minerals.

- If you need to peel or cut fruits and vegetables, do so just before serving. Foods prepared in advance and exposed to air or soaked in water will lose nutrients.

- Cook with a small amount of water. Use the cooking water in sauces, soups, and gravies to prevent nutrient loss. If you cook fruits, serve the liquid with the fruit as a juice.

- Fat-soluble vitamins (A, D, E, and K) will not dissolve in water, nor are they destroyed by heat.

Investigate Further

What foods that contain high amounts of vitamin C are not usually cooked?

Rice and Pasta

Rice and pasta products come with cooking directions on the box or container. Rice is cooked in a tightly covered container. As it cooks, it absorbs the water and swells. Do not rinse rice after it is cooked or water-soluble vitamins will be rinsed off and lost.

Pasta is cooked uncovered. A cover will cause the pasta to boil over. Be sure to use a large amount of water for cooking pasta or it will become sticky. You can tell if pasta is done by cutting it with a fork or tasting it. It should be tender but still firm. If you cook pasta too long, it will become limp and sticky, lose its shape, and lose nutrients. Avoid rinsing pasta after it is cooked or more nutrients will be lost.

Review Section 25:4

1. Name two proper sanitation practices to follow when handling food.

2. Explain why it is important to put leftovers in the refrigerator right after a meal.

3. Explain how the effect of heat on protein influences cooking temperatures for dairy foods and eggs.

4. Compare dry-heat cooking methods with moist heat cooking methods for meats.

5. Which vitamins are not destroyed by cooking?

Think It Through

Making Daily Food Choices

April stood and looked at the menu. She and her friends had stopped to eat at the local fast-food restaurant before they went to the game. "What should I have?" she wondered. She heard Tom order six cheeseburgers, three large orders of fries, and an extra-large soft drink.

"Wow, he must be hungry!" she thought. She looked back at the menu. "Hamburgers, fish, chicken, salads, shakes, yogurt—they really have a variety."

April thought back over the day. What had she eaten so far? She'd had cereal and milk for breakfast; a hamburger, fries, apple, and milk for lunch at school; and a cola and a bag of chips after school. What did she still need in her daily food plan?

Questions to Guide Your Thinking

1. How many servings of each food group has April eaten so far in her day? (Assume she ate one serving of each food she consumed.)

2. How many more servings of each food group does she need to meet her daily food plan?

3. What foods from the fast-food menu would you suggest she order?

4. How do these foods fit into her food plan for the day?

5. With this meal, will April's food plan for the day be complete?

6. What would you suggest she have for an after-game snack?

Chapter Summary

Your body needs a variety of nutrients in balanced amounts in order to carry out its functions and prevent illness and disease. A simple plan for healthy eating is to include a variety of foods from each of the food groups. Choose the number of servings to match your daily needs. All you eat should be a part of this plan, whether you eat at home, eat at fast-food restaurants, or snack. Choosing foods low in calories and high in nutrients can help you avoid empty calories.

One of the benefits of eating at home is that you can control your diet. You can plan meals and prepare foods in ways that allow you to get needed nutrients and avoid excess calories. Food labels and open dating on products can help you determine nutritious and wholesome choices in the supermarket. Skills for preparing foods can enable you to serve meals that are nutritious, appealing, and enjoyable to eat.

Assess...

Your Knowledge

1. What are the six main nutrients? Describe what each does for the body.

2. List two good sources of each of the six main nutrients.

Your Understanding

3. How can food labels help a consumer make good choices while shopping?

4. How should food be handled and stored to help avoid foodborne illness?

5. How does the cooking temperature affect dairy, egg, and meat products?

Your Skills

6. Develop a personal eating plan for one week using the MyPyramid tool to identify your personal needs.

7. Analyze your peers' table manners in your school cafeteria and make recommendations for improvements based on good table etiquette.

8. Use unit pricing to determine which of the following is the better buy:

   A. Six 8-ounce cans of tomato sauce for $2.40 or three 16-ounce cans for $2.25.

   B. One 64-ounce bag of grated cheese for $12.00 or an 8-ounce bag of cheese for $2.00.

Think Critically

9. **Writing.** Write a paragraph describing your present eating habits. Explain why they are or are *not* adequate to meet your daily needs for nutrients. If *not* adequate, include changes you could make to improve your nutrient intake.

10. **Science.** Using the five food groups from MyPyramid, plan a menu for one day. List the foods you would eat and how much you need of each food to meet your daily nutrient needs. Include meals and snacks.

11. **Science.** Develop a three-day menu that a family could use for a healthful eating plan. *Choice:* Develop a menu for a family with young children.

12. **Math.** Analyze the nutrition label from a food product. Copy the list of nutrients given on the label. Write the percent Daily Value given for each nutrient. Use the following chart to compute the percent of your Daily Values provided by a serving of the food product. *Group option:* Compile the data gathered by four students, tabulate the data in a chart, and make a judgment about which product is most nutritious.

Population Groups	Daily Calorie Needs	Multiply Percent Daily Values on Food Labels by
Active women	2,200	1.1
Active men	2,800	1.4

Connect with Your Community

13. **Research, social studies.** Evaluate several menu items offered at a local fast-food restaurant. List nutrients provided and the number of calories per serving. *Group option:* Compare your findings with a partner who evaluated a different restaurant. Draw some conclusions about nutrients and calories in the menu items at the two restaurants.

14. **Research.** Visit a supermarket. Identify and record the advertising and promotion techniques used to spark sales of various products. Create a table or chart to illustrate your results. *Choice:* Write a summary about which techniques are used most often to promote food products in this supermarket. *Group option:* Compare information from three different stores and identify differences in strategies used to promote products.

15. **Math, research.** Visit two different grocery stores. Compare the costs of three different forms of a food (fresh, canned, partly processed, and ready-to-eat). Draw some conclusions about your comparisons. *Choice:* Compare the unit cost of three brands of a particular food item. Note any differences in added ingredients. Also note any differences in brands available in the two stores. *Group option:* Compare your findings with those of a classmate. Does your partner have similar conclusions?

16. **Research, social studies.** Interview an extension agent from your county's Cooperative Extension Service office. Ask questions about the leading eating-related problems in the county. Ask about resources your community has for helping families meet their daily food needs. Prepare a report presenting your information. *Choice:* Present your information to the class as a poster, flyer, or slide presentation.

Use Technology

17. **Writing.** Using the Internet, locate an article related to a current issue dealing with food safety and handling. Print out a copy of the article and summarize it in your own words.

18. Log on to the MyPyramid Web site at **www.MyPyramid.gov**. Click on the subject *MyPyramid Plan*. Enter your age, gender, and physical activity to generate your personal pyramid plan. Print the PDF version and summarize the following in a paragraph: your recommended daily amounts for the five food groups, oils, discretionary calories totals, and physical activity.

19. **Writing.** Search the Internet for information on a current nutritional issue such as cholesterol, dietary fiber, or dietary supplements. Identify various points of view on the issue. Analyze the data supporting each point of view and summarize your information in a report.

20. **Science, math.** Using a recipe analysis program, choose a recipe, develop a shopping list, and identify the nutrients one serving of the food will provide. In a written paragraph, identify the main ingredients in the recipe and the related food preparation principles. *Choice:* Prepare the food dish.

Chapter 26

Maintaining Your Health and Well-Being

Section 26:1
Today's Health Problems

Section 26:2
Maintaining a Healthful Weight

Section 26:3
Physical Activity and Health

Section 26:4
The Use and Abuse of Harmful Substances

Key Questions

Questions to answer as you study this chapter:

- What do people need to do in order to stay healthy?

- How can a person maintain a healthful weight?

- How can decisions about tobacco, alcohol, and other drugs affect a person's health and well-being?

Chapter Objectives

After studying this chapter, you will be able to

- **relate** lifestyle choices to common health problems.

- **differentiate** between healthful and harmful eating habits.

- **describe** the factors influencing ideal weight.

- **compare** weight control to food intake and physical activity.

- **identify** the effects of dieting, physical activity, tobacco, drugs, and alcohol on health.

Life Sketch

Pepe and Alayna, both in their teens, are interested in sports. Pepe is anxious to build stronger muscles so he can win the wrestling meet. He also wants to keep his weight down so he can compete in a lower weight class.

Alayna is concerned about becoming fatigued in her long-distance race next week. She is also concerned about her appearance. She has become very slim with all her running, but she dares not eat more in case she might gain weight.

Ramona and Phil work all day. Ramona works in an office. The work is intense and stressful. At the end of the day, she usually has a headache. She knows she needs exercise, but she is exhausted by the time she gets home.

Phil's doctor tells him he needs to lose weight. He is thirty pounds over the ideal weight for his height and body size. Phil's risk for heart disease is high. Both his blood cholesterol level and his blood pressure are high.

Jeanette is retired from her job. She lives alone. She takes a one-hour walk each day as part of a plan to help control her diabetes. Her friend, Delores, walks with her. Delores has heart problems and needs the physical activity to strengthen her heart.

Getting Started

You may know people who have similar problems. Today, such health concerns are common in this society. Finding out the facts when looking for answers to health problems is important. There are no quick-fix techniques, diets, or cure-alls—even though many products may be sold as such. Research has shown that lifelong eating and physical activity patterns dramatically affect a person's quality and length of life. Heredity also plays a part. Choosing healthful eating habits, getting needed physical activity, and avoiding harmful substances can help you develop and maintain good health.

section 26:1

Today's Health Problems

Sharpen Your Reading

Create a chart with three columns. As you read, identify a current health problem in the first column. In the second column, list the major causes of each. In the third column, write some strategies you can use to prevent this health problem.

Boost Your Vocabulary

Search online for a list of known carcinogens. Add this list to your chart for causes of cancer.

Know Key Terms

arteriosclerosis
hypertension
cancer
carcinogens

In recent years, Americans have taken greater interest in developing healthful lifestyles. For many, the results of this trend are good news. The life expectancy of children born today has increased. Of concern, however, is the increase in number of deaths due to liver diseases like cirrhosis. This disease is often associated with the consumption of alcohol. It is one of the leading causes of death for 25- to 44-year-olds.

For older adults, heart disease and cancer are still major killers. These diseases impact all ages. Obesity, a major nutritional disorder in this country, increases a person's risk for other diseases. This chapter takes a closer look at some of these leading health risks.

Heart Disease

Heart disease hinders the heart's ability to function. The risk of heart disease increases with high levels of blood cholesterol, high blood pressure, obesity, and cigarette smoking. Two common causes of heart disease are arteriosclerosis and hypertension.

Arteriosclerosis

A major cause of heart disease is the hardening of arteries. The major type of hardening of the arteries is known as **arteriosclerosis**. Fatty deposits called *plaque* form on the inner walls of the arteries. This cuts off the flow of blood to the heart and can result in a heart attack. A heart attack occurs when a coronary artery becomes completely blocked. Plaque forms when diets are high in fat and cholesterol. Eating foods low in fat and cholesterol can help reduce the risk of heart disease.

Think More About It
What are some examples of foods a person should avoid if he or she is at risk for heart disease?

Hypertension

High blood pressure, or **hypertension**, also raises the risk of heart attack, 26-1. This occurs when blood pressure stays above the normal range. It causes the heart to work harder as it moves the blood through the circulatory system. High blood pressure increases the risk of stroke. A stroke occurs when the pressure on the small vessels in the brain causes them to break. As a result, the blood supply to the brain is cut off and nerve cells cannot function.

26-1 Blood pressure can be measured by a trained health professional or at home using a digital monitor.

Hypertension can be treated in different ways. Reducing excess weight, limiting sodium (salt) in the diet, and taking drugs that lower blood pressure are three methods commonly used.

Investigate Further

How could regular physical activity help prevent high blood pressure?

Cancer

Cancer is a disease in which there is abnormal uncontrolled cell growth. This growth of cancer cells destroys healthy tissue. Many

factors, including health and diet, contribute to a person's risk of cancer. There are about 100 kinds of cancer. The areas of the body most affected are skin, breast, lungs, digestive organs, and colon.

Causes

Uncontrolled cell growth seems to result from a change in a cell's DNA. Radiation can change DNA. That is why ultraviolet rays in sunlight can cause skin cancer. Chemicals can change DNA, too. Such chemicals, called **carcinogens**, are found in soot, asbestos, tobacco, some drugs, and other substances. Diet plays a significant role in the development of some types of cancer as well.

Link to Your Life

With what types of cancer are you most familiar? Do these seem to be common in your family or community?

Body Defenses

The human body has several natural defenses against carcinogens. Liver enzymes are able to inactivate some toxic substances. Some foods such as cabbage, broccoli, and cauliflower contain certain chemicals that stimulate the liver to produce these enzymes. In addition, the body uses *antioxidants*, such as vitamins A, C, and E, to prevent substances called *free radicals* from harming body tissue. The body also protects itself from harmful substances by eliminating wastes. *Insoluble fibers* (the bulk in vegetables and bran) help the large intestine remove these substances more quickly from the body.

Sometimes these body defenses are not effective, and a cancerous growth forms. Cancer can develop slowly and be undetected for years. Watching for early warning signs of cancer is important for early treatment, 26-2.

Use What You Learn

What are some examples of foods that are high in antioxidants?

Early Warning Signs of Cancer
• A sore that does not heal
• Unusual bleeding
• A lump in the breast or other areas
• Bowel and bladder changes that persist
• A cough that persists
• Difficulty in swallowing
• Changes in a wart or mole

26-2 If you notice any of these danger signals, see your doctor.

Preventing Diet-Related Health Problems

Heart disease and cancer sometimes are related to what people eat. The most common nutritional disorder in the United States is *obesity*. Obese people are overweight to the point that their health is at risk.

The *Dietary Guidelines for Americans*

In response to the nation's many diet-related health problems, the government issued the *Dietary Guidelines for Americans*. The U.S. Departments of Agriculture and Health and Human Services jointly developed them. The *Guidelines* should be followed by everyone age two and older. The *Guidelines* encourage people to develop and maintain healthful life habits through nine main topics, each with Key Recommendations, 26-3.

Adequate nutrients within calories needs. Many people consume more calories than they need. Unfortunately, these are often empty calories—they come from foods that are low in nutrients. Instead, choose foods that are high in nutrients but lower in calories. Using MyPyramid as a guide can help you choose nutrient-dense foods.

Weight management. To manage weight, balance the calories you eat with the calories you use in physical activity. For people who are already at a healthy weight, the goal is to

maintain that weight. People who are overweight or obese should focus first on not gaining more weight, then on losing weight. Even a small weight loss begins to lower health risks.

Physical activity. Physical activity is an important part of becoming physically fit and maintaining good health. Physical activity will be discussed in detail in Section 26:3, *Physical Activity and Health.*

Food groups to encourage. This guideline stresses the need for fiber and other nutrients found in vegetables, fruits, and whole grains. The health benefits include lower risk of chronic disease. Milk and milk products are also emphasized to help maintain healthy bones.

Fats. Although fats are an important nutrient, too much fat can contribute to health problems. You need the benefits of fat—such as fat-soluble vitamins and essential fatty acids—but without consuming excess calories. Therefore, fat intake should account for 20 to 35 percent of the calories you eat. Only 10 percent of calories should come from saturated fats. Also limit your intake of trans fats and cholesterol.

Carbohydrates. Carbohydrates should come primarily from fresh fruits and vegetables, whole grains, and legumes. Limit your intake of foods high in sugars and sweeteners. These often contribute empty calories to your diet.

Sodium and potassium. Too much salt increases blood pressure and contributes to health problems such as heart disease and stroke. Sodium occurs naturally in many foods, so use salt sparingly when cooking. Check nutrition labels when buying packaged and canned convenience foods, which are often high in sodium. In addition, eating potassium-rich fruits and vegetables can help reduce the effects of salt on blood pressure.

Alcoholic beverages. Alcohol contributes to many health problems, including liver disease and high blood pressure. Alcoholic drinks contribute calories, but few nutrients. Alcohol consumption is also a factor in many accidents.

Food safety. As you read in Chapter 25, handling food safely is important to prevent foodborne illness. Wash hands carefully when preparing or serving food, and wash all work surfaces with hot soapy water. Keep foods separated to prevent cross-contamination. Cook food to proper temperatures. Chill perishable foods as quickly as possible.

Dietary Guidelines for Americans
Adequate Nutrients With Calorie Needs
• Consume a variety of nutrient-dense foods and beverages within and among the basic food groups. Choose foods that limit the intake of saturated and trans fats, cholesterol, added sugars, salt, and alcohol.
• Meet recommended intakes within energy needs by adopting a balanced eating pattern, such as MyPyramid.
Weight Management
• To maintain body weight in a healthy range, balance calories from foods and beverages with calories expended.
• To prevent gradual weight gain over time, make small decreases in food and beverage calories and increase physical activity.
Physical Activity
• Engage in regular physical activity and reduce sedentary activities to promote health, psychological well-being, and a healthy body weight.
• Achieve physical fitness by including cardiovascular conditioning, stretching exercises for flexibility, and resistance exercises or calisthenics for muscle strength and endurance.
Food Groups to Encourage
• Consume a sufficient amount of fruits and vegetables while staying within energy needs. Two cups of fruit and 2½ cups of vegetables per day are recommended for a reference 2,000-calorie intake, with higher or lower amounts depending on the calorie level.
• Choose a variety of fruits and vegetables each day. In particular, select from all five vegetable subgroups (dark green, orange, legumes, starchy vegetables, and other vegetables) several times a week.
• Consume 3 or more ounce-equivalents of whole-grain products per day, with the rest of the recommended grains coming from enriched or whole-grain products. In general, at least half the grains should come from whole grains.
• Consume 3 cups per day of fat-free or low-fat milk or equivalent milk products.
Fats
• Consume less than 10 percent of calories from saturated fatty acids and less than 300 mg/day of cholesterol. Keep trans fatty acid consumption as low as possible.
• Keep total fat intake between 20 to 35 percent of calories, with most fats coming from sources of polyunsaturated and monounsaturated fatty acids, such as fish, nuts, and vegetable oils.
• When selecting and preparing meat, poultry, dry beans, and milk or milk products, make choices that are lean, low-fat, or fat-free.
• Limit intake of fats and oils high in saturated and/or trans fatty acids, and choose products low in such fats and oils.

(Continued)

26-3 Following the Key Recommendations of the *Dietary Guidelines for Americans* can help you and your family achieve good health.

Dietary Guidelines for Americans

Carbohydrates

- Choose fiber-rich fruits, vegetables, and whole grains often.
- Choose and prepare foods and beverages with little added sugars or caloric sweeteners.
- Reduce the incidence of dental caries by practicing good oral hygiene and consuming sugar- and starch-containing foods and beverages less frequently.

Sodium and Potassium

- Consume less than 2,300 mg (approximately 1 teaspoon of salt) of sodium per day.
- Choose and prepare foods with little salt. At the same time, consume potassium-rich foods, such as fruits and vegetables.

Alcoholic Beverages

- Alcoholic beverages should not be consumed by some individuals, including those who cannot restrict their alcohol intake, women of childbearing age who may become pregnant, pregnant and lactating women, children and adolescents, individuals taking medications that can interact with alcohol, and those with specific medical conditions.
- Alcoholic beverages should be avoided by individuals engaging in activities that require attention, skill, or coordination, such as driving or operating machinery.

Food Safety

To avoid microbial foodborne illness:

- Clean hands, food-contact surfaces, and fruits and vegetables. Meat and poultry should not be washed or rinsed.
- Separate raw, cooked, and ready-to-eat foods while shopping, preparing, or storing foods.
- Cook foods to a safe temperature to kill microorganisms.
- Chill (refrigerate) perishable food promptly and defrost foods properly.
- Avoid raw (unpasteurized) milk or any products made from unpasteurized milk, raw or partially cooked eggs or foods containing raw eggs, raw or uncooked meat and poultry, unpasteurized juices, and raw sprouts.

26-3 Continued.

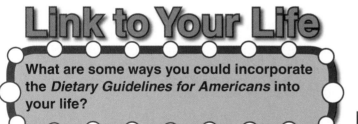

What are some ways you could incorporate the *Dietary Guidelines for Americans* into your life?

You will notice that the *Guidelines* reflect many of the nutrition and food safety principles discussed in Chapter 25, "Meeting Your Nutritional Needs." For example, when you follow the weight management and physical activity recommendations, you take steps to maintain a healthful weight. By following the *Guidelines*, you will build healthful eating habits and enjoy good health. You will also reduce your chances of getting certain types of cancer, diabetes, stroke, and osteoporosis—the leading causes of death and disability among Americans.

Review Section 26:1

1. List three common health problems and describe how the risk of each can be related to a person's lifestyle.

2. Summarize each of the nine sections of the *Dietary Guidelines for Americans*. Explain why each guideline is important for good health.

section 26:2

Maintaining a Healthful Weight

Sharpen Your Reading

Outline the steps for maintaining a healthful weight.

Boost Your Vocabulary

Create a chart with each key term in the left column. In the second column, write the text definition for each term. In the third column, explain how that term is related to a person's ideal weight.

Know Key Terms

ectomorphs
endomorphs
mesomorphs
basal metabolic rate (BMR)
steroids
anorexia nervosa
bulimia nervosa

Young people are usually very concerned about their appearance. Concerns about how much they weigh occupy their thoughts. Many teens see themselves as being overweight, while others wish to gain weight.

Maintaining a proper weight is a challenge for many people. What is your healthful weight range? Who decides what is ideal? Americans spend much of their time, energy, and money trying to change their body weight. As a result, weight control has become big business.

Determining Your Ideal Weight

Your ideal weight is no specific number. Instead, it is a weight range within which your health is not affected one way or the other. Extremes either above or below that range could be harmful to your body.

Your ideal weight depends on many factors, including your age and bone structure. It can also depend on your genes, which determine the number of fat cells you have at birth. Genes also affect the way you tend to store most of your fat.

Body Frames

The size of your body frame is determined by your bone structure. People who have small bones and a slender, angular build are classified as **ectomorphs**, 26-4. Of course, their ideal weight will be less than a person with larger bones. **Endomorphs** are people with a large frame. They usually have a more rounded shape. **Mesomorphs** are between the two with a medium-sized bone structure.

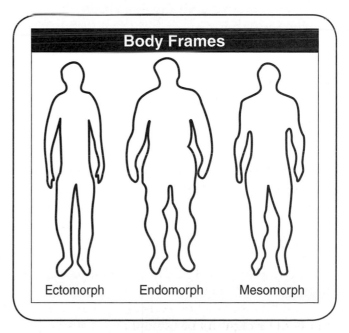

Body Frames

Ectomorph Endomorph Mesomorph

26-4 People who are the same height but have different body builds will have different ideal weights.

Link to Your Life

How would you expect your bone structure to affect your ideal weight?

Visual Tests

The easiest way to tell if you are overweight or underweight is to just look at yourself in the mirror. Rolls of fat or bulges are signs of being overweight. Some flabbiness may be due to poor muscle tone, which could be corrected with physical activity. If your hipbones and ribs protrude, you may be underweight.

Another way to determine if your weight is right is by using the *pinch test*. This test measures the amount of fat stored under your skin. Do the test by gently pinching the skin at the back of your upper arm or at your waistline. The fold should measure about ½ inch if your weight is normal. If the fold measures more than this amount, you may be overweight.

Think More About It
Why might the mirror test or pinch test result in a person drawing inaccurate conclusions about his or her ideal weight?

Body Mass Index Charts

There are no charts showing ideal weights for teens since teen bodies are still growing. Teens grow and mature at different rates, so weight charts are developed for adult bodies, which have finished growing. These charts show the appropriate weights for people of different heights. A term for the relationship of weight to height is *body mass index (BMI)*. See the chart in 26-5 for adult BMIs in the *Healthy Weight* range.

Investigate Further

Find the healthy weight range for adults who are your height.

In the BMI index, there are two ranges beyond the *Healthy Weight* range: *Overweight* and *Obesity*. *Overweight* refers to people who are up to 10 percent over their desirable weight range. *Obesity* is defined as being at least 20 percent above ideal weight. *Underweight* people weigh 10 percent less than their ideal weight. Of all the types of weight problems, obesity has the most serious health risks. The heart and lungs have to work harder in an obese body. The muscles and bones are under extra strain. The extra fat hinders the body from cooling itself, and the body perspires more easily. Obese people may tire easily and find exercise difficult. They also have a higher risk of heart diseases, high blood pressure, cancer, and diabetes.

Being underweight can have health risks, too. Feeling tired, becoming ill frequently, and lacking strength may result.

To determine your body's ideal weight, find out what weight is realistic for your body. Setting realistic goals for your weight can help you avoid health risks from too much or too little weight.

Think More About It
What are some reasons people may think they weigh too much, even if they are within their healthy weight range?

How Your Body Uses Calories

Knowing how your body uses calories can help you maintain a healthful weight. Calories measure the amount of potential energy in food. Energy can be obtained from carbohydrates, fats, and proteins. The body uses energy to maintain normal life processes, which include basal metabolism and muscular activity.

Basal Metabolism

Your body needs energy to carry out its basic life functions. For instance, your heart beats, you breathe, and your blood continues circulating. Your **basal metabolic rate (BMR)** is the rate at which your body burns calories for these *basal*, or basic, functions. This rate is measured when the body is at rest.

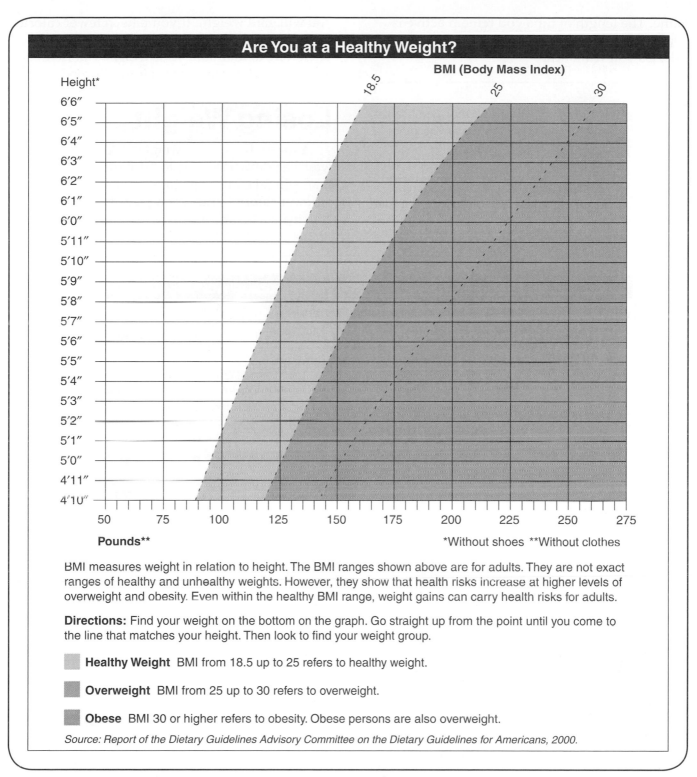

Are You at a Healthy Weight?

BMI (Body Mass Index)

Height*

*Without shoes **Without clothes

Pounds**

BMI measures weight in relation to height. The BMI ranges shown above are for adults. They are not exact ranges of healthy and unhealthy weights. However, they show that health risks increase at higher levels of overweight and obesity. Even within the healthy BMI range, weight gains can carry health risks for adults.

Directions: Find your weight on the bottom on the graph. Go straight up from the point until you come to the line that matches your height. Then look to find your weight group.

Healthy Weight BMI from 18.5 up to 25 refers to healthy weight.

Overweight BMI from 25 up to 30 refers to overweight.

Obese BMI 30 or higher refers to obesity. Obese persons are also overweight.

Source: Report of the Dietary Guidelines Advisory Committee on the Dietary Guidelines for Americans, 2000.

26-5 The body mass index illustrates how additional pounds can become an unhealthy weight, no matter what height a person is.

Muscular Activity

When you awake, body activity increases. The need for energy also increases. Some activities use more calories than others, 26-6. For instance, you will burn more calories walking to school than sitting and riding to school on a bus. The more intensely you take part in an activity, the more calories you burn. Shooting baskets, for example, uses fewer calories than playing a basketball game. The length of time you remain active is a factor, too. The longer you exercise, the more calories you will burn.

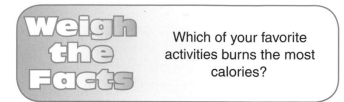

Which of your favorite activities burns the most calories?

When you take in more calories than you use, your body stores excess calories as fat. As a result,

you will gain weight. If you take in fewer calories than your body uses, you will lose weight. Therefore, to maintain your weight, calorie intake must equal the number of calories burned, 26-7.

Losing Weight

Your body can lose weight in more than one way. The desired way is to burn more calories than you take in so fat stores are used. Taking in fewer calories and getting regular physical activity is a healthful way to do this.

Average Calories Burned per Minute in Activity					
Activity	**Average Calories Burned**		**Activity**	**Average Calories Burned**	
Sitting	1		Roller skating	7	
Standing	2		Canoeing (4 mph)	7	
Walking (2 mph)	3		Dancing	7	
Cycling (5 mph)	3		Tennis (singles)	8	
Golfing	4		Walking (5 mph)	8	
Vacuuming	5		Cycling (11 mph)	8	
Pushing light mower	5		Water skiing	8	
Walking (3 mph)	5		Splitting wood	8	
Bowling	5		Snow shoveling	8	
Cycling (6 mph)	5		Jogging (5 mph)	9	
Badminton (doubles)	5		Touch football	9	
Swimming	5		Handball	9	
Badminton (singles)	6		Basketball	10	
Volleyball	6		Ice hockey	10	
Tennis (doubles)	6		Squash	10	
Aerobic dancing	6		Cross-country skiing (5 mph)	10	
Raking leaves or hoeing	6		Running (5 mph)	10	
			Cycling (13 mph)	10	

26-6 The intensity of an activity determines how many calories are used per minute.

Daily Calorie Needs for Teens				
	Age Groups	**Height (feet, inches)**	**Weight (pounds)**	**Daily Calories Needed***
Males	11 to 14	5'2"	99	2,500
	15 to 18	5'9"	145	3,000
	19 to 24	6'0"	160	2,900
Females	11 to 14	5'2"	101	2,200
	15 to 18	5'4"	120	2,200
	19 to 24	5'5"	128	2,200
*Based on light to moderate activity				

26-7 In this chart, teens' daily calorie needs are based on age, height, weight, and activity level. These allowances are necessary for maintaining health and well-being.

Successful Weight Control

The best and safest way to lose weight is by eating less while being more active. About 3,500 calories must be burned to lose one pound of fat. Therefore, a goal of losing one pound a week without increasing activity would require eating 500 fewer calories per day. However, by increasing activity, the goal can be accomplished with a less severe calorie reduction. For instance, by burning an extra 200 calories through exercise, only 300 calories per day need to be cut from the diet to accomplish the goal.

Here are some easy guidelines to help you cut calories in your diet, yet maintain healthful eating habits.

- *Avoid high-fat foods.* Watch out for greasy or fried foods, thick milk shakes, and creamy sauces and gravies. Remember, fat provides nine calories per gram—more than twice the calories of one gram of carbohydrates.
- *Eat complex carbohydrates.* These include whole-grain breads and cereals, vegetables, and fruits. Complex carbohydrates help you get the nutrients you need without excess calories. They also provide fiber, which eliminates the feeling of hunger by providing a sense of fullness.
- *Eat more low-calorie foods.* Look for foods that are crisp and crunchy (raw vegetables and fruits). Low-fat or fat-free milk, seasoned broths, lean meats, and unsweetened juices are other choices.
- *Eat a wide variety of foods from all five food groups.* This will help you get the nutrients your body requires.
- *Watch portion size.* The average sandwich with two slices of bread contains two servings from the grains group, not one. The abundance of food in the United States tends to make people unaware of serving size. This unawareness is a common cause of eating too much and taking in too many calories.

Cutting Calories and Your Basal Metabolic Rate

When you begin to cut back on calories, your body will automatically lower its BMR to protect itself. "Famine coming!" That is the signal fewer calories mean to your body. It wants to keep its fat stores, which makes weight loss harder. This is where physical activity comes into the picture. Physical activity offers many weight-loss benefits. It burns calories, strengthens muscles, and increases your BMR for up to 12 hours.

If you lose weight slowly, you will be more apt to keep it off. A pound a week is a good goal. To lose that pound, you would need to burn 3,500 calories more per week than you took in. If weight is lost too rapidly, you are likely losing water and muscle.

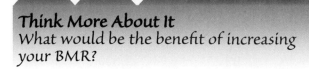

Think More About It
What would be the benefit of increasing your BMR?

Fad Diets

Many dieters look for quick fix ways to solve their weight problems. *Fad diets*, which are diets popular for a short time, often promise quick, effortless weight loss. Promises of a slim body persuade people to spend their money for diet products and programs, books, and weight-reducing gadgets. Many such diets are more harmful than helpful. They may result in a breakdown of muscle and other tissue, produce toxic side effects, and even result in death.

Extremely low-calorie diets can be risky, especially for growing teens. They can deprive you of important nutrients. Some fad diets emphasize one food or food group and eliminate the others. Liquid formula diets are sometimes recommended in place of meals. Fasting, which is going without food for days, is the most dangerous of all.

Use What You Learn
What are some popular fad diets?

Here is an example of how a fad low-carbohydrate diet can affect your health. Carbohydrates are often blamed for weight gain, but they are the major source of glucose for the body. Your body needs glucose to fuel your brain and central nervous system. If you do not take in any carbohydrates, at first your body will use glucose stored in your liver, but that will go quite fast. Then the body uses protein to produce glucose for a short period of time. This process results in toxic levels of poisonous ammonia in the blood. If protein is missing in the diet, the body will break down muscle (including heart muscle) and other protein tissues.

After two or three days without carbohydrates, the body will produce ketones from its fat supplies. Ketones are toxic. Too many ketones produce *ketosis*, a condition that can result in a coma or even death.

The body needs a balance of nutrients in order to carry out its functions, 26-8. Fad diets always upset that balance one way or another.

Investigate Further

How might fasting have similar effects on the body to that of the fad low-carbohydrate diet?

Diet Aids

Many diet aids—pills, capsules, or patches—are ineffective and unsafe. Some aids promise to "burn" or "flush" fat from the system. Some pills may help suppress appetite but have harmful side effects. For instance, amphetamines are addictive and can affect the heart and nervous system. Research has shown that people may lose some weight with the aid of diet pills, but the loss

26-8 Eating a variety of foods will help you get the balance of nutrients your body needs.

is temporary. As soon as they quit using the pills, they quickly regain the lost weight. Other diet aids similar to amphetamines are sold over the counter. A range of side effects from these aids has been identified, including anxiety, dizziness, and increased blood pressure.

Most people will struggle with losing weight at some time in their lives. Weight loss is a hard task—it requires self-control to reduce calories and increase exercise. However, the benefits of both looking and feeling better help motivate people to maintain their ideal weight.

Gaining Weight

Fewer people seek to gain weight than lose weight. People are considered *underweight* if they are more than 10 percent under their ideal weight. They appear thin. Hipbones will likely protrude, and bones in the rib cage are obvious. Underweight is often from eating too little food.

During times of rapid growth, a teen may appear underweight if more calories are used than taken in. The appetite usually increases at times of rapid growth, and the body returns to an ideal weight shortly thereafter.

Using and Abusing Steroids

Many teen boys have a natural desire to grow faster and be bigger, 26-9. Some want to gain weight to improve their appearance or enhance their athletic performance. Those who look for quick ways to achieve such results may be tempted to use and abuse steroids. **Steroids** are a synthetic version of testosterone, a male hormone. They are normally prescribed by doctors to patients for treating cancers and other conditions. The illegal use of steroids is a growing problem among teens, especially athletes.

Steroids are illegally obtained and used by athletes to build muscle and body strength. Teens who compete in athletics may be tempted to use steroids. They do help muscles grow bigger and

26-9 Weight training is a healthful way for teens to build muscle and strength.

stronger. However, using any type of steroids in athletic competition is illegal.

Teens who illegally use steroids today rarely realize their negative long-term effects. In men, they cause premature balding, the growth of breasts, and decreased size of sexual organs. Females take on male characteristics. Steroids can cause facial hair to grow, breasts to shrink, the voice to become husky, and menstruation to stop. For young people, using steroids can stunt normal bone growth. Steroids cause a person to be more aggressive. Long-term abuse of steroids can result in liver disorders, heart problems, strokes, and possibly cancer.

Think More About It
What are the pressures that might influence a young person to try steroids?

Eating Disorders

Sometimes people need to gain weight but suffer from eating disorders. People with these disorders can actually die of starvation if help is not obtained in time.

Eating disorders have both physical and psychological causes. To correct these disorders, both causes must be addressed. Nutritional needs (physical) must be met, and the attitudes that led to the disorder (psychological) must be changed. The two most common eating disorders are anorexia nervosa and bulimia nervosa.

Anorexia Nervosa

Anorexia nervosa is self-starvation often caused by an irrational fear of being overweight. This eating disorder is common to females between adolescence and young adulthood. It affects one in every 200 American teenage girls.

Anorexia nervosa results from a fear of being overweight and also an inaccurate evaluation of present body weight. Even though they are very thin, people with anorexia nervosa see themselves as fat. They refrain from eating and may even dislike food. This results in dramatic weight loss and *amenorrhea* (menstruation stops).

Bulimia Nervosa

Bulimia nervosa is also an eating disorder that involves a concern about weight and a fear of not being able to control eating. It is characterized by sessions of binge eating, when large amounts of food are consumed uncontrollably. The food binge is kept secret by the bulimic eating alone. Then purging takes place by vomiting, use of laxatives, diuretics, and fasting.

People with bulimia nervosa may be depressed, knowing the behavior is not normal. The first outward signs of the behavior may be extreme fluctuations in weight. Continued purging results in harmful physical effects. These may include an inflamed esophagus, dental problems (from the stomach acids), urinary infections, colon damage, heart problems, and kidney failure. Tendencies toward bulimia are more common than anorexia. Both boys and girls have reported habits of binge eating and purging.

Think More About It
What societal pressures may result in anorexia nervosa or bulimia nervosa?

Treatments

People with anorexia nervosa and bulimia nervosa need help to change these eating disorders. If evidence of such eating patterns appears, a family doctor should be consulted, 26-10. Medical help must be obtained, at least at first, to treat the malnutrition. Since both eating disorders are psychological in nature, counseling is usually needed to change behavior patterns.

Signs of Eating Disorders

- Extreme weight gains and losses
- Frequent changes in weight
- Hiding food
- Eating alone
- Skipping meals
- Frequent nausea, bloating, or constipation
- Fear of gaining weight
- Menstruation stops
- Browning of teeth due to loss of dental enamel
- Puffiness in face

26-10 Eating patterns of teens may vary from day to day. However, a combination of several of these signs could indicate an eating disorder.

Review Section 26:2

1. Identify the factors that could make a difference in determining your ideal weight.
2. Describe the biological process in which the body gains and loses weight.
3. Explain how your body would respond biologically to a famine.
4. Describe the role of physical activity in weight control.
5. Name three harmful effects of following a fad diet or using diet aids.
6. Describe two common eating disorders.

section 26:3

Physical Activity and Health

Sharpen Your Reading

Summarize the benefits of physical activity.

Boost Your Vocabulary

List some examples of each type of exercise.

Know Key Terms

aerobic exercise
anaerobic exercise

You may be one of many teens who are neither overweight nor underweight. Athletes work out to perform better in sports, but you may not be that interested in being an athlete. Why should physical activity be important to you? What does physical activity include?

Physical Activity

When you hear the words *physical activity*, what comes to your mind? You may picture organized exercise programs. You may think of joining a gym, playing on a sports team, or planning structured workouts. However, the most recent government guidelines focus on expanding this mindset.

Physical activity is any bodily movement that burns calories. Therefore, you actually get physical activity through many of your daily actions as well as exercise programs, 26-11. These actions include housecleaning, gardening, walking, and climbing stairs.

In the past, many everyday chores involved physical labor. Unfortunately, today's technology and modern conveniences seem to encourage inactivity. Household appliances make doing chores almost effortless. Cars are used most often for transportation. Hobbies such as playing video games and surfing the Internet may require sitting for long periods. At malls and offices, taking elevators or escalators is quicker than using stairs. For all these tasks, only a minimal amount of physical activity is necessary.

26-11 Taking stairs whenever possible is one way to add physical activity to your lifestyle.

Adding Physical Activity to Your Day

MyPyramid and the *Dietary Guidelines for Americans* emphasize the need for daily physical activity. (In the MyPyramid symbol, the figure walking up the stairs represents physical activity.) Both sources recommend that teens accumulate 60 minutes of moderate physical activity most days of the week, preferably daily. A moderate physical activity is any that requires about as much energy as walking two miles in 30 minutes. Note that the 60 minutes of activity can be *accumulated.* This means you do not have to do an hour of physical activity at one time to benefit from it. Any physical activity done throughout the day counts toward your 60-minute goal. However, each segment of activity should be at least 10 minutes long.

Adults need to accumulate at least 30 minutes of physical activity most days to help reduce the risk of disease. To lose weight or maintain a loss, adults should accumulate at least 60 minutes of activity daily.

If reaching this goal every day seems difficult, try making small changes in your lifestyle to add more physical activity. For instance, walk to a bus stop that is farther from your house. Take your dog for walks. Use stairs instead of elevators. Instead of driving, walk, skate, or cycle to places when possible. When you must travel by car, park farther from your destination and walk the distance.

Working Out

In addition to regular physical activity, many people enjoy taking part in organized exercise routines or sports teams. You may prefer to work out alone, exercise with others, or use equipment. Your favorite sport may be tennis, basketball, swimming, or soccer. You may enjoy a yoga or dance class. No matter what your preferences are, choose activities you like to help make physical activity an enjoyable lifetime habit.

Aerobic Activities

Aerobic exercise is an activity done at a moderate pace for fairly long periods using the large muscles. *Aerobic* means *with oxygen.* The term refers to activities that keep pace with the supply of oxygen your lungs can deliver. Aerobic exercises make you breathe faster and deeper, taking in more oxygen. Examples include brisk walking, running, rope jumping, swimming, and bicycling. As you practice these exercises, you develop *cardiorespiratory fitness*—strong lungs, heart, and blood vessels. Aerobic exercise is most effective when the activity is sustained for at least 20 minutes each time. Strenuous aerobic exercise is good for strengthening heart muscles, improving respiration (breathing), and controlling weight, 26-12.

Link to Your Life

What activities do you enjoy that are types of aerobic exercise?

Anaerobic Activities

Anaerobic exercise uses muscles to produce a sudden burst of power. Examples include doing push-ups, hitting a tennis ball, or lifting weights. The all-out muscle exertion lasts for about 90 seconds, leaving muscles very tired. This form of exercise develops muscle strength and endurance as well as lean muscle tissue. A routine in which you exercise various muscles will help you build power and speed. Strengthening your muscles also puts more pressure on bones and causes them to strengthen, too.

Some exercises enable you to move your muscles and joints to their fullest extent. This makes movements such as bending, twisting, and stretching easier and more graceful. Warm-up exercises before a strenuous workout fulfill this goal. Stretching exercises improve flexibility. Staying strong and flexible helps older persons reduce their risk of falling and breaking bones. Lifting small weights is one way to include strength building in your routine.

Getting Started

Many health clubs and community park districts provide pools, sports, and exercise classes. Weight machines provide opportunities to build various muscles and bones. Machines such as stationary bicycles provide aerobic exercise. The social aspects of meeting with others to exercise can help some stick to an exercise program.

26-12 Aerobic exercise improves muscle tone and increases muscle mass, thereby strengthening the heart.

The importance of exercise to a more healthful lifestyle has led some families to include such machines in their homes. The convenience helps them make exercise a regular part of their daily routine.

However, remember that it is even more important to adopt an active lifestyle and keep active. Taking part in active leisure activities or developing active family hobbies can help families keep physically fit throughout life.

The Benefits of Physical Activity

Physical activity can help you feel better—more alert and energetic. That may surprise you, since physical effort takes energy. When your body is active, you increase your intake of oxygen. More oxygen reaches the brain, and you feel more alert. You can relieve both physical and psychological stress through physical activity. That is why being active is a good idea, even if you are tired or depressed.

Think More About It
Why might people need physical activity the most when they feel the least like doing it?

In addition to the health benefits, physical activity can help you become more agile, improve your body image, and benefit your appearance. Being active can help build your self-confidence.

Physical activity helps your body function more efficiently, 26-13. This will help it do a better

26-13 When you develop an active lifestyle, you are contributing to an overall healthful plan for living.

job of protecting you from illness and disease. Activity strengthens muscles, including the heart muscle. It lowers pulse rate and blood pressure and reduces the risk of heart disease. Physical activity also helps prevent osteoporosis. The body will not build stronger bones if it does not need to. Activity places demands on the bones, and the body will respond by increasing bone density. Physical activity also helps joints remain flexible as you grow older. Greater health benefits can be obtained through more vigorous, sustained activity.

Review Section 26:3

1. Explain the difference between anaerobic and aerobic exercise.
2. List seven ways that physical activity can benefit health.

section 26:4

The Use and Abuse of Harmful Substances

Sharpen Your Reading

Create two columns in your notes. List the various harmful substances in the left column. As you read, identify the health effects of using these harmful substances in the second column.

Boost Your Vocabulary

Choose one of the key terms. Write a paragraph describing what it would be like to live with a person who had problems related to that term.

Know Key Terms

emphysema
depressant
alcoholic
drug
addiction
withdrawal

Most of this chapter has focused on developing positive health habits—eating right, controlling your weight, and exercising regularly. However, some other habits are *not* positive and pose a significant risk to health. These include the use and abuse of harmful substances such as tobacco, alcohol, and other drugs. These substances affect the body physically. They also affect a person emotionally, mentally, and socially. Using harmful substances affects your entire person. Even so, people who use such substances may pressure you to do so as well. They may encourage you to fit in with a group, escape your problems, or celebrate special occasions.

Your decisions about using such substances need to be informed decisions based on facts. Personal opinions, gut-level feelings, or a friend's opinions are not enough. Your decisions about tobacco, alcohol, and other drugs can affect you for the rest of your life.

The Effects of Tobacco on Health

Smoking is a major health problem in the United States. Over 400,000 Americans die prematurely each year from the effects of smoking cigarettes. Smoking contributes to lung cancer, coronary heart disease, chronic bronchitis, and emphysema. It is easy to see how smoking could affect your health when you look at what it will do to your body, 26-14.

Smoking Cigarettes

When you inhale on a cigarette, the hot tip of the cigarette reaches about 1,800°F. At that temperature, several chemical reactions take place, releasing about 4,000 different chemicals. The most damaging of these chemicals include the following:

- *Nicotine* is the addictive drug in the smoke. It constricts the blood vessels, putting stress on the heart.
- *Tar* is a brown sticky mass formed from the weight of all the chemicals as they cool in the lungs. Some chemicals in tar are known to cause cancer. Also, the lung tries to rid itself of the tar and actually destroys itself.
- *Carbon monoxide* in smoke combines with the hemoglobin molecule in the blood much faster and easier than oxygen does. That means the blood carries less oxygen, which

may cause a person to feel light-headed, tired, or short of breath. Carbon monoxide stays in the blood up to six hours after the person stops smoking.

- *Hydrogen cyanide* is only one of the poisonous gases in cigarette smoke. It paralyzes and kills the part of the lung's lining that sweeps away the mucous. A buildup of mucous results, causing a persistent hacking cough.

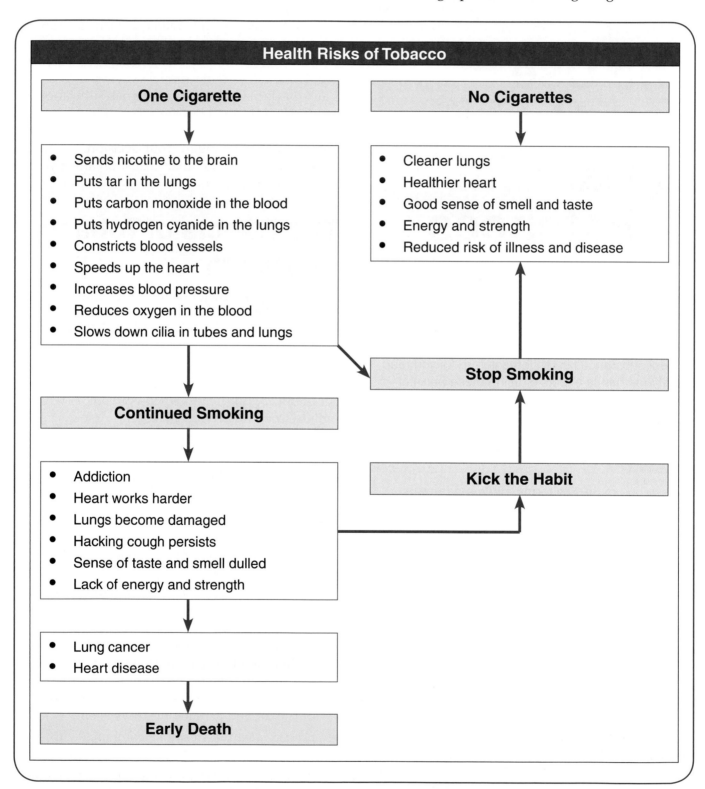

Health Risks of Tobacco

One Cigarette

- Sends nicotine to the brain
- Puts tar in the lungs
- Puts carbon monoxide in the blood
- Puts hydrogen cyanide in the lungs
- Constricts blood vessels
- Speeds up the heart
- Increases blood pressure
- Reduces oxygen in the blood
- Slows down cilia in tubes and lungs

Continued Smoking

- Addiction
- Heart works harder
- Lungs become damaged
- Hacking cough persists
- Sense of taste and smell dulled
- Lack of energy and strength

- Lung cancer
- Heart disease

Early Death

No Cigarettes

- Cleaner lungs
- Healthier heart
- Good sense of smell and taste
- Energy and strength
- Reduced risk of illness and disease

Stop Smoking

Kick the Habit

26-14 A decision not to use tobacco can lead to better health and reduced risk of disease.

The effects of smoking build up over time, resulting in chronic health problems and even death. **Emphysema** is a progressive disease in which the walls of the lungs are destroyed. A person with emphysema finds it increasingly harder to breathe. Lung cancer involves an uncontrolled growth of abnormal cells. Smoking also contributes to coronary heart disease as it constricts the flow of blood through the blood vessels.

These diseases cannot be cured, and may lead to early death. However, if a person stops smoking before these diseases develop, many of the harmful conditions in the lung improve.

Use What You Learn

Why do you think people use tobacco when it contains so many harmful chemicals?

Secondhand Smoke

Secondhand smoke is produced by a smoker but inhaled by someone else. It consists of smoke from a burning cigarette as well as the smoke exhaled by the smoker.

Secondhand smoke gives nonsmokers the same chemicals that smokers inhale, 26-15. It causes a faster heartbeat, higher blood pressure, and increased levels of carbon monoxide in the blood. It can also have toxic effects on the lungs, resulting in breathing problems and lung diseases.

Investigate Further

Why are incidences of asthma higher in children whose parents smoke?

Smokeless Tobacco

Snuff and chewing tobacco increase the risk of cancers of the mouth. Whether it is dipped (put between cheek and gum) or chewed and spit, the cancer-causing chemicals affect the tissue. There is no such thing as harmless tobacco.

26-15 Smoking is banned in many facilities because of the problems to others posed by secondhand smoke.

Choosing Not to Use Tobacco

The facts about smoking led the U.S. surgeon general to require tobacco products be labeled with health warnings. To protect those who want to breathe clean air, many laws prohibit smoking in public areas. Young people under the age of 18 cannot purchase cigarettes. This is a federal law.

If you have chosen not to smoke, stick to your decision. You have the right to healthy lungs and clean air. You will not run out of breath as fast as a person who smokes. Your clothes will not smell, and your teeth will not yellow. Think of the money you will save. A person who smokes a pack of cigarettes in a day spends about $1,500 a year on cigarettes. A heavy smoker may spend twice or even three times that much. The benefits of not smoking go beyond reducing the risk of ill health.

Benefits of Quitting

A major problem for those who want to quit smoking is their addiction to nicotine. However, more than 33 million people in the U.S. have overcome their addiction and quit smoking. Within 12 hours after the last cigarette, the body begins to heal itself. Levels of carbon monoxide and nicotine go down. Heart and lungs begin to repair the damage caused by the smoke. Within a few days, a renewed sense of smell and taste returns. In time, the smoker's hacking cough will disappear. Feelings of energy and strength return. Breathing is easier. Quitting has helped many people reduce their risk of death from smoke-related illnesses.

Think More About It
What factor do you think can have the greatest impact on encouraging people to quit smoking?

The Effects of Alcohol on Health

If you consume alcohol in any form, it will affect you. Alcohol will enter your bloodstream rapidly. It does not require digestion. Within a few minutes, it will reach all parts of your body. If your stomach is empty, alcohol will be absorbed even faster than if you have food in your stomach.

How Alcohol Affects the Body

The main effect of alcohol will be on your brain and spinal cord. Alcohol is a powerful depressant drug. A **depressant** will slow the activity of your brain by knocking out control centers. Your reflexes will be slower. The coordination of different parts of your body will be hindered. Your interpretation of messages will not be accurate. Judgment will be poorer. You may make choices and respond in ways you normally would not, 26-16.

Even one drink can bring about these chemical effects, but you may not notice them. In fact, your brain may interpret the results as improved ability. You may be more daring and more confident to take chances that could hurt

you and others. Continued drinking will increase the chemical effects, causing obvious physical and mental impairment.

Investigate Further

Which centers in the brain are affected by alcohol? How does this keep a person from having good judgment and making good decisions?

The body breaks down alcohol in the liver at the rate of about one-half ounce per hour. That is about the amount of alcohol in one drink. There is no way to speed up the liver to burn alcohol faster. Drinking coffee, exercising, and eating do not help. The brain's functions will only return with time, after the liver breaks down and burns the alcohol in the bloodstream.

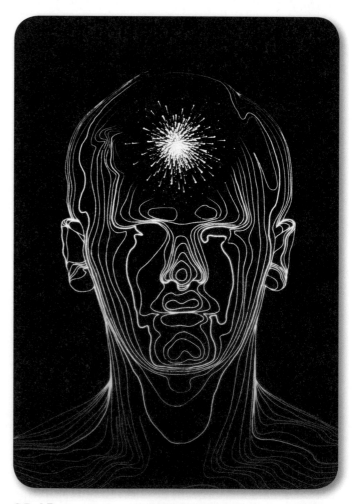

26-16 By affecting the brain's control centers, alcohol dulls a person's senses and ability to think.

Alcohol-related accidents are the number one killer of teens. Alcohol is responsible for nearly half of all traffic deaths, nearly half of all fatal falls, and more than half of all homicides.

How Alcohol Affects Relationships

Your use of alcohol will affect your social and emotional responses. Brain cells control these responses. Brain cells dulled by alcohol result in fewer inhibitions. You may feel happy and relaxed, but also more jealous, quickly angered, and aggressive. Your actions may hurt relationships, bring you embarrassment, and even result in arrest.

Your desires to reach your goals may be dulled by alcohol. That may lead to skipping school or ignoring homework. Your overall social and emotional growth will be stifled if you use alcohol to escape your problems rather than solve them. You may also become dependent on alcohol.

Use What You Learn

How does the use of alcohol affect a person's ability to control his or her emotional responses with logical thinking?

Alcoholism

As with any drug, using alcohol can become addictive. An **alcoholic** becomes addicted to alcohol and cannot control his or her use of it. About one out of every 10 drinkers is at risk of becoming an alcoholic. Personality changes make living with an alcoholic difficult.

Alcoholism strikes men and women of any age, social group, and community. People become alcoholics by experimenting with alcohol, then using it more often. Eventually they come to depend on alcohol as a crutch. As they become more and more dependent, alcohol takes control of their lives. They cannot get along without it.

Throughout history, people have used alcoholic beverages with meals, at social gatherings, and for celebrations. The danger in drinking alcohol for any occasion or purpose is that people fail to recognize it as a harmful drug. They fail to identify how easily it is abused.

Even though it is against the law, teens may begin to use alcohol at such social gatherings or celebrations. They may also continue its use and become dependent on it.

Think More About It

How can the use of alcohol in society result in alcohol abuse?

Using alcohol never solves problems. It often makes them worse. Alcohol slows the natural inhibitions that help you say no to other drugs. Drugs and alcohol increase the effects of each other. Combined, they are extremely dangerous, sometimes ending in death. Alcohol may also hinder your ability to say no to sexual pressures in a relationship. The use of alcohol can even hinder your ability to say no to more alcohol. Alcoholism may result.

About one in five teenagers have experienced problems as a result of drinking. Some of the consequences of alcohol use are listed in 26-17. It is never too late to decide not to drink any more alcohol.

Consequences of Alcohol Use
Alcohol can
- impair thinking and reasoning
- affect coordination
- be addicting
- stifle emotional growth
- hurt relationships
- cause embarrassment
- harm reputation
- produce hangovers
- cause absenteeism from school and work
- result in arrest
- cause health problems, including birth defects, cancer, brain damage, mental disorders, loss of sexual function, liver damage, and death

26-17 Before taking an alcoholic drink, consider the consequences. Drinking alcohol can cause many types of physical and mental health problems.

Some of the reasons young people give for saying no to alcohol are shown in 26-18. Do not let others pressure you into drinking. Realize you are a unique and special person who does not need alcohol to be somebody. Believe in your ability to handle your problems. Become involved in activities. Talk about the pressures to drink with family members and friends who can encourage you to stick to your decision.

The Effects of Drugs on Health

"Just once won't hurt." You may have heard that line from someone trying to convince you to experiment with a drug. Do not believe it. People have died from that first experiment with drugs.

A **drug** is any substance that chemically changes structures or functions in a living organism. Misusing and abusing drugs has become a crisis in the United States. The instant effects it produces on the body's mental and physical state encourages some people to experiment. For teens, their reasons for using drugs are much like the reasons given for alcohol abuse. It is a way to "tune out" problems and "tune in" feelings of excitement.

Teens do face many stressors in the growing years. Pressures to succeed, look great, and be accepted are common. Drugs, however, do not

---

Reasons for Saying No to Alcohol

- I don't run from my problems; I solve them.
- I have confidence in my abilities.
- I like to be in control of my body.
- I don't need alcohol to have fun.
- I value my health and my life.
- I like to drive.
- I want to avoid the consequences of saying yes.

26-18 These responses may help you say no the next time someone offers you alcohol.

---

solve problems; they only add to them. Thinking through the consequences of drug misuse and abuse is important to avoid making decisions that could harm your body.

Drug Use, Misuse, and Abuse

If you look in your medicine cabinet at home, you may find a variety of drugs. *Over-the-counter drugs* are those you can buy without a doctor's prescription. *Prescription drugs* are those prescribed by a medical doctor and purchased at a pharmacy. Such drugs can be used to cure or control a medical problem. They are used to improve physical or mental health.

Some people use drugs incorrectly. They may take a sleeping pill intended "for occasional use only" every night. Later they wonder why they cannot get to sleep without the drug. They may take a laxative in order to maintain their weight when eating high-calorie foods. Drugs with beneficial uses that are used incorrectly are *misused*.

When drugs are used in ways for which they were not intended, they are *abused*. For instance, if a person uses a cold medicine to get to sleep, that drug is being abused. If a person uses a tranquilizer to avoid facing up to problems, it is drug abuse. The drug is being used for a purpose other than its intended use.

Using drugs can lead to physical dependence on them. This is called **addiction**. The body physically has a need for the drug. If this need is not met, the body goes through **withdrawal**. Discomfort, nausea, pain, and convulsions may accompany the withdrawal, even resulting in death.

Some drugs create a *psychological dependence*. The person desires the feelings that the drug gives and relies on the drug to feel good. In addition to physical and psychological dependence, the drug abuser builds a tolerance to many drugs. Higher doses are needed to get the same effects. The abuser becomes more dependent, and the need for drugs becomes greater. Common names, street names, and specific effects of these drugs are listed in the chart in 26-19.

Commonly Abused Drugs			
Type of Drug	**Common Name**	**Street Name**	**Effects**
Hallucinogens	Marijuana	Pot, tea, grass	Psychedelic drugs, affecting the mind: cause changes in perception and consciousness; reduce coordination and reflexes; impair judgment; distort time and distance; may cause hallucinations—seeing things that are not there
	LSD	Acid, cubes	
	Mescaline	Peyote, cactus	
	Dimethyltrytamine	DMT	
	Psilocybin	Mushrooms	
	Hashish	Hash	
Stimulants	Cocaine	Snow, coke, flake, crack	Stimulate or speed up the central nervous system; deplete chemicals between nerve cells; result in the body not able to send a signal on its own; severe depression and nervous exhaustion result; can cause seizures and heart attacks, deteriorate the lungs, impair and kill liver cells
	Amphetamines	Pep pills, bennies, uppers	
	Methamphetamine	crystal meth, ice, glass	
Depressants	Barbiturates	Downers, yellow jackets, red devils, phennies, barbs	Relax the central nervous system; cause slow responses, slurred speech, confusion, and staggering; easily overdosed; can result in death
	Tranquilizers		
	PCP (phencyclidine)	Angel dust	
Narcotics	Heroin	Horse, H, junk, smack, dope	Depress the central nervous system; cause drowsiness, slurred speech, impaired coordination, constricted pupils, constipation, and slow reflexes
	Codeine	Schoolboy	
	Morphine	Morphine, hocus	
	Methadone	Dollies, doll	
Designer Drugs	MDMA	Ecstasy	Chemically made to avoid present definitions of drugs that are illegal; destroy neurons in the brain; can result in stiffness, impaired speech, rigidity, tremors, paralysis, and death
	MDA, MDE	Essence	
	Fentanyl	China White	
	Rohypnol	Roofies	
	GHB	Goop	
	Meperidine	Synthetic heroin	
	Demerol		
	TP, MPPP		

26-19 This chart details the most commonly abused drugs.

Investigate Further

What are some drugs that are commonly used for medicinal purposes in the home? Could any of these be abused?

Types of Abused Drugs

Drugs that are often abused include hallucinogens, stimulants, depressants, narcotics, and designer drugs. *Hallucinogens* are psychedelic drugs that affect the mind, causing a person to see objects that are not there. *Stimulants* speed up the central nervous system. *Depressants* relax and *narcotics* depress the central nervous system. They both cause slowed or impaired responses. *Designer drugs* are chemically made to avoid the present definitions of drugs that are illegal. However, they are very dangerous and can destroy brain cells.

Use What You Learn

Why do you think some teens are drawn into experimenting with drugs?

Choosing Not to Abuse Drugs

There will be times when you feel down, lonely, perhaps unaccepted. There will also be times when pressures to succeed are great. Someone may suggest a quick cure—a way out of your problems. Will you be able to say no?

Consider the consequences of using drugs. Drugs are not a method of solving problems. Instead, they lead to more problems such as impaired judgment, destroyed brain cells, and lapses in memory. Reflexes get slower. Major organs are destroyed, and the result is early death. Problems are solved by seeking solutions and taking action. High self-esteem, personal standards, and values can help you make healthful choices for living. Strong skills for making decisions and reaching your goals will assist you as well.

Review Section 26:**4**

1. Explain how the four most harmful ingredients in cigarette smoke affect the body.
2. What is secondhand smoke? Whom does it affect?
3. Give four ways that alcohol affects relationships.
4. Explain the difference between drug misuse and drug abuse.

Think It Through

Making Weight

Rod's face was pale and haggard as he peered into the school cafeteria. The smell was almost more than he could bear. "Two more days to make weight!" he thought. "Then I can eat again."

Rod was trying to reach the lower weight class for the upcoming wrestling match. Although he was thinner than average for his body size, he was trying to lose four more pounds this week. He was allowed to drink water, but food was off-limits. Once a day, he drank a liquid supplement that was supplied by his wrestling coach. After wrestling practice, he would sit in a steam room to sweat off more weight. The big match was only two days away, but Rod was feeling weak and sick. He wondered how well he would really do, even if he made the lower weight class.

Questions to Guide Your Thinking

1. Describe the methods Rod is using to try to lose weight.

2. What are the immediate biological effects on the body of these weight-loss methods?

3. How might his attempt to reach a lower weight class affect his overall goal of excelling in athletic performance?

4. What suggestions can you make that would increase Rod's chance of success in winning the wrestling match?

5. For Rod, what might be the long-term effects of repeated crash dieting?

Chapter Summary

The goal of maintaining family health and well-being is important. Following certain guidelines can reduce the risk of major killers such as heart disease and cancer. These include having healthful eating habits, maintaining ideal weight, and getting adequate physical activity. Another important guideline is avoiding toxic substances.

Eating disorders such as anorexia nervosa and bulimia nervosa prevent people from getting the nutrients they need. Being overweight also increases health risks. The health risks of obesity are lessened by reducing weight to a healthier level through physical activity and changes in eating patterns.

Substances such as tobacco, alcohol, and other drugs harm the body physically, emotionally, and socially. Many people, including teens, struggle with the consequences of using them. The stress of daily living, feelings of loneliness, and a desire to be accepted may influence some to escape problems through drugs. High self-esteem, strong values and standards, and personal goals can help people make wise choices for healthful living.

Assess...

Your Knowledge

1. List three early warning signs of cancer.

2. What are the nine main topics of the *Dietary Guidelines for Americans*?

3. Why is a person more apt to keep weight off if he or she loses it slowly?

4. How does alcohol affect the body?

Your Understanding

5. How do the *Dietary Guidelines for Americans* help people maintain their health and well-being?

6. How does physical activity contribute to health and well-being?

7. How can the use of alcohol negatively affect interpersonal relationships?

Your Skills

8. Manuel decides to take up playing tennis. He plays three days a week for 60 minutes each day. If Manuel keeps his other activities the same and does not increase his food intake, how long will it take him to lose five pounds?

9. Comisha's favorite meal is a cheeseburger with fries, regular soda, and a chocolate shake. If Comisha eats foods as these on a regular basis, what effect could her diet have on her health?

Think Critically

10. Clip several newspaper articles or magazine articles about one of the health issues discussed in this chapter. Prepare a collage with these articles and write a summary of the concerns related to this health issue in your community. *Choice:* Present your information to the class in an oral report.

11. *Writing.* Write a paragraph in which you identify your ideal weight range and explain why that range is your match.

12. *Science, math.* Prepare a weight-loss plan, listing the food you eat and describing physical activities that could help you lose weight. Identify how much weight you should be able to lose per week on this plan. *Group option:* Work with a partner to develop the plan and prepare a flyer to promote the plan to the class.

13. *Writing.* Search the Internet for three weight-loss plans. Write a summary of each plan. Then evaluate the plans for nutritional adequacy. Create a table using the plan names as top headings and the criteria used to evaluate them as side headings. Summarize how well each plan follows the Dietary Guidelines for Americans. *Group option:* Work in teams of three with each person evaluating one plan. Share your evaluations with one another. Then complete your table and analyses as a team.

Connect with Your Community

14. **Speech.** Interview a fitness instructor on how to start a personal exercise program. Prepare a report to present to the class.

15. **Research.** Survey the various fitness programs in your community. Identify the types of equipment they offer, other services they provide, cost of service, and other information you can identify about each program. **Choice:** Prepare a table for the various fitness programs in your community and their services.

16. **Science.** Search the Internet for information on one form of substance abuse and prepare a report on the harmful effects of that drug. Identify any community resources available to help a person overcome the problems related to the use of that drug. **Choice:** Present your information in a flyer, an electronic presentation, a poster, or an oral report.

17. **Writing.** Interview a counselor or law enforcement officer on drug and alcohol abuse in your community. Write a summary of concerns about these issues in your school and your community. Make recommendations for ways to prevent problems related to drug or alcohol use in your community. **Group option:** Prepare and record a public service announcement.

Use Technology

18. **Speech.** Search the Internet for consumer alerts related to diet issues. Share a summary of the consumer alert with the class.

19. **Research.** Search the Internet to locate information on a known carcinogen. Research and prepare a report, describing what it is, where it is found, and how it affects the body. **Choice:** Present your information in a poster, electronic presentation, or flyer.

20. **Writing.** Search the Internet for recipes that appeal to you and meet the recommendations of the Dietary Guidelines for Americans. Create a one-week menu using these recipes. **Group option:** Work with other members of your class and compile a recipe book with your recipes and menu plans.

21. **Math.** Record your food intake for three days and determine the average number of calories you consumed per day. Use a dietary analysis program to identify the number of calories that came from simple carbohydrates, complex carbohydrates, protein, and fat. Compare your food intake to the Dietary Guidelines for Americans and recommend more healthful choices you could have made. **Group option:** Work with a partner to analyze your diets and identify common concerns in your dietary habits.

Chapter 27

Managing Your Wardrobe

Section 27:1
Choosing Clothing

Section 27:2
Caring for Clothing

Life Sketch

"I love these jeans!" Cory exclaimed. "They're really in style! All the kids are wearing them."

Cory's mother looked closely at the jeans. They certainly didn't look special to her—rather worn, faded, low hung, almost like something she might have worn in the '80s. She shook her head, trying not to show her amusement.

Key Questions

Questions to answer as you study this chapter

- How can a person choose clothing to meet personal needs?

- How can a person care for clothing?

Getting Started

Most young people want to dress "in style." They want to wear clothes similar to those their peers wear. Some of those clothes, such as Cory's jeans, may be short-lived fads. Other clothing, such as a dress shirt with a button-down collar, can be in style for many years.

Clothing choices need to be based on more than just "what's in." You will likely be more satisfied with your clothes if they suit you and your lifestyle. Simple care requirements can also add to your personal satisfaction with your clothing choices.

Chapter Objectives

After studying this chapter, you will be able to

- **explain** the difference between styles, fads, and fashions.

- **relate** the elements of design—line, texture, and color—to clothing selection.

- **identify** criteria for planning a wardrobe.

- **interpret** information on clothing labels.

- **describe** procedures for caring for clothes.

section 27:1

Choosing Clothing

Sharpen Your Reading

Create a graphic organizer with the words *choosing clothing* in the center. From the center, draw a line for each topic in this section and identify key points to remember when choosing clothing.

Boost Your Vocabulary

Create a chart with four columns, and put each of the terms in the left column. Then look in your closet for examples of each term. In the second column, write the example from your own clothing. In the third column, write any additional information you learn about that term.

Know Key Terms

style
high fashion
fad
wardrobe
accessories
basic garments
extenders
label
fiber
hangtags

Your clothing choices will be influenced by those around you. However, your personal needs should guide you when you make choices about which clothes to buy. Your clothes should enhance your natural coloring and flatter your body lines. They should coordinate with other items in your wardrobe, and match your lifestyle and your budget. Skills for choosing clothing are lifetime skills, ones you will use over and over throughout your life.

Styles, Fashions, and Fads

The term **style** refers to a particular design, shape, or type of apparel. Style is determined by the features that create the apparel's appearance. For instance, classic styles are those that remain popular for many years. A double-breasted jacket, dress shirt, and turtleneck sweater are examples of classic styles. The overall lines stay much the same from one year to the next.

Variations in a style are often based on high fashion designs. **High fashion** refers to original clothing designs made by well-known designers in New York, Paris, and other major fashion centers. These designer originals are very expensive. The cost of high fashion designs is beyond the budget of most consumers.

Each season, clothing manufacturers adapt the high fashion ideas to design less expensive clothing. The lines, textures, and colors are similar to those used in the high fashions. The clothes you buy are an interpretation of the latest fashion or style.

Trendy clothing that is very popular for only a short time is called a **fad**. Fads tend to be exaggerations of fashion designs. The lines of a style are carried to an extreme. Color combinations may be bold and contrasting. Fads catch the interest of buyers who desire something different or want to make a statement. When young teens want to identify with a group, fads are often used to make that statement.

Think More About It
Why do people pay extra money to have clothes with a designer label? In which category do most of the clothes worn by your peers fall?

How Clothing Speaks

The clothing a person wears sends a variety of nonverbal messages to others, 27-1. What does your clothing say about you? You can use clothes to tell others about yourself or show your uniqueness. If you want to be like your friends and peers, you may choose clothing styles similar to what they wear.

Home sewing can allow you to express your creativity and design unique clothing. Taking sewing lessons and choosing simple, stylish patterns can help you learn to create basic garments. You can select the colors, styles, and fabrics that suit you.

Clothing reflects your personality and self-concept. The way you dress affects the first impression others form of you. An attractive appearance is important in making a positive first impression. Clothing can also reflect how you feel about yourself. Knowing that you look good can help you feel at ease. It can give others an impression of your confidence and authority. It can make you stand out from others. If you choose, your clothes can help you blend into a group.

27-1 Teens like to express themselves through the clothes they wear.

Link to Your Life

What first impression do you want your clothes to give to others?

A garment's line, texture, and color—the basic elements of clothing design—also communicate a message. Clothes that look good on you use line, texture, and color to enhance your best features. Choosing items that complement each other is also important. Clothes that will be worn together should have appealing colors plus similar lines and textures.

Line

In clothing design, line gives direction. The most important line to consider is your silhouette (the outline of your body). By knowing this, you can use clothing design lines to show your best points. You can even give the illusion of having a different body shape than you really have.

The lines in clothing may be either structural or decorative. The silhouette plus the seam lines within the garment are *structural lines*. Other lines, added through colors, prints, or ornaments, are *decorative lines*. Lines lead the eye to a point of emphasis. Vertical lines make a person appear taller and thinner. Horizontal lines make a person look shorter and wider. A curved line can give a soft and graceful effect.

Use What You Learn

How do thin vertical stripes in a garment affect the way a person looks?

Texture

Texture refers to the way fabrics look and feel on the surface. Just as with design lines, the types of textures you choose can help you emphasize your good points.

Fabric textures range from bulky to smooth, shiny to dull, or stiff to soft. Some have a fuzzy, nubby, looped, or raised texture. These textures add bulk, making the body appear larger. Smooth, soft fabrics appear less bulky. Such fabrics hang or drape to form slenderizing curves. Shiny textures add weight or size because the surfaces reflect light, 27-2. Dull surfaces absorb light, so they do not draw attention. Some fabrics are flat on the surface and may be dense, firm, and even stiff. Smooth crisp fabrics can be used to achieve crisp, straight lines in clothes. They can give an impression of formality and control. Clothing with smooth textures conveys comfort, openness, or relaxation.

Use What You Learn

What textures would you choose if you wanted to look smaller in size?

27-2 Clothes with shiny textures reflect light, while clothes with smooth textures and vertical lines absorb light and create a slenderizing effect.

Color

Each person has a range of colors that are most attractive for him or her. The colors that are included in your range will depend on your skin tone, eye color, and hair color. Colors that enhance your natural coloring are most flattering. They help you to appear lively and attractive. Colors that do not have the same base as your natural coloring will draw color from your face, making you look pale.

Clothing colors send psychological messages. The warm colors of red, orange, and yellow give a feeling of excitement and cheerfulness. The bold or intense use of these colors draws attention to the body. Warm, bright colors appear to advance, making the body seem larger.

The cool colors are green, blue, and violet. They give a quiet, restful feeling. Cool colors appear to recede, or move into the background, making a person seem smaller. Dark or dull colors also make a person seem smaller. Because they absorb light, they convey a feeling of warmth. Dark colors, such as black, navy, or dark brown, can give a message of authority and confidence.

White and light colors reflect light. This makes objects look larger. Lighter colors also give a feeling of coolness, so they are often worn in warm climates.

Think More About It
What are your favorite colors to wear and how might they affect your interactions with others?

Wardrobe Planning

Wardrobe planning can help you choose clothing that looks good on you, fits right, and matches other clothing in your closet. It involves taking a look at what you already have in your wardrobe. Your **wardrobe** includes all the clothes you have to wear, including accessories. **Accessories** are the items you wear with your clothes, such as shoes, handbags, belts, scarves, and neckties. Once you know what you have, you can decide what additions to make. A plan for buying what you need can help you put the total picture together. Then you, too, can look well coordinated, no matter what you choose to wear.

Wardrobe planning can save you time. When you get dressed, the items in your wardrobe will go together. Whatever you choose to wear will look good on you. You will save time when you shop, too. You will know what items you need and the characteristics of each item.

Wardrobe planning can save you money, even though you may spend more for each item you buy. That is because you will not have a closet full of clothes you do not wear. Many people waste money on purchases that they wear once or twice. They may not even wear them at all because the clothes do not look right, fit right, or match anything else. A few well-chosen items can give you an attractive, flattering wardrobe.

27-3 Taking an inventory of all the items in your closet is the first step in wardrobe planning.

Link to Your Life

What clothes do you have in your closet that you never wear? Were they planned purchases?

Looking at What You Have

Start your wardrobe plan by taking a wardrobe inventory, 27-3. This is a detailed list of everything you already have, including all garments and accessories. The next step is to sort everything in your wardrobe into three groups:

- items worn often
- items worn occasionally
- items not worn in the past year

Look at the clothes you often wear. These items probably fit well, match your coloring and body structure, and suit your lifestyle. Take note of these favorite items. You will want to look for similar styles, textures, and colors in future purchases as well.

Next, take a look at the clothes you wear only once in a while. Is there a reason that you do not wear them more? Is the fit not right, or is it the color? Is the style wrong for you? Does it not match your other clothing? Try to determine if you could make some changes in those clothes so you would wear them more often.

Finally, look at the items you have not worn in the last year. Clothing in this group is taking up space in your closet, but not meeting your needs. Some specialty items, such as a formal dress or suit, you may want to keep. However, in most cases, you should get rid of clothes you do not wear.

This wardrobe evaluation should leave you with a list of clothes you like and can wear. The next step in wardrobe planning is to decide what you need to do to meet your clothing needs.

Use What You Learn

What clothes do you have that fit into each of the wardrobe groups?

Meeting Your Clothing Needs

Every time you shop, you likely see many items you want. However, there is a difference between what you need and what you want. Items you cannot get along without are needs. Wants are the extra items you would like to have, but do not really need. The items you need most go at the top of your priority list for clothing purchases.

The next step in developing a wardrobe plan is to list all your activities since your clothing needs depend on them. Next to each activity, identify what garments you have for that activity. Some items are **basic garments**. These are the garments worn most often. Basic garments should be classic styles and neutral colors that will have a long-lasting fashion life. They should also be top-quality items so they last.

Next to your list of basic garments, list the less expensive items you use to expand your wardrobe. These are called **extenders** and are often purchased in brighter, bolder colors. You will get the most wear out of your clothes if you have extenders that you can mix and match.

The next list in your wardrobe plan is for accessories. Include all the accessories you use in each activity. With a well-planned color scheme, you will need only a few accessories to complete your outfits.

The final step in your wardrobe plan is to plan future purchases. Add to your plan a list of items you need or want to buy. Make the list complete even though you know you cannot buy them right away. This way, you can identify items that will go together to give you a complete wardrobe. Then prioritize your list. Decide which item you need to buy first. Then number the remaining items from most to least important.

By following these suggestions, you will have a wardrobe plan similar to the chart in 27-4. It will guide your future clothing purchases.

Investigate Further

Do your basic garments meet the standards for having a long-lasting life?

My Wardrobe Plan					
My Activities	**Basic Garments**	**Extenders**	**Accessories**	**Item I Need to Buy**	**Priority Number**
School	1 pair dress jeans 1 pair black pants 1 denim skirt 2 sweaters 2 cotton shirts	1 pair dress jeans	Long necklace Athletic shoes Black shoes (casual)	1 pair jeans 1 pair gray pants	2 4
Work Part-time at Hardee's	1 pair gray pants	2 striped shirts 2 knit shirts 1 polka dot top	Black shoes	1 pair of gray pants (same as above)	4
Sports	1 sweat suit 1 swimming suit	2 t-shirts	Athletic shoes	1 pair shorts	3
Church and Special Events	1 dress 1 black skirt 1 black jacket 2 sweaters (same as above)	1 white blouse 1 striped shirt (same as above)	Black shoes (dress) Silver necklace	1 gray skirt 1 red plaid skirt	6 5
Outdoor Clothing	1 lightweight jacket		Wool scarf Wool gloves	1 winter coat	1

27-4 A wardrobe plan can help you evaluate your clothing needs. Use it to determine what you need and which items should be purchased first.

Buying Clothing

Wise use of your resources—money, time, and personal skills—can help you stretch your clothing dollar. If you have your own income, you can set aside some money each month for clothing purchases. You may have to save a while to make major purchases. When money is set aside, you can take advantage of good buys that suddenly become available.

Developing a plan for buying clothes can help you make better wardrobe choices. The quality of each item you purchase is an important factor to consider. If an item looks good on you and fits well, you will wear it many times.

Your Shopping Plan

Some people spend much of their shopping time checking to see what is on sale. Store managers count on those people buying items because "they are a good deal." However, clothing purchases are good deals for you only if they achieve the following:

- fit into your wardrobe plan
- meet your fabric care requirements
- are constructed well enough to last through wear and laundering

When planning to shop, start with your clothing needs list. Make a note of the color needed and the amount you can afford to spend on each item. Think about where you want to shop for the items on your list. Plan to purchase basic items first. Then if time and your budget permit, you can purchase extenders and accessories. Try not to shop at the last minute for a needed item. Otherwise you may opt for a quick purchase rather than make a careful selection.

The Right Fit

Getting the correct fit is important for a garment to look and feel right for you. A well-fitting garment should have some ease to allow for movement. Depending on the activity for which the garment will be worn, some items will need more ease than others. A shirt or blouse should have ample room across the chest, shoulders, and back. You should be able to raise your arm and bring it across your chest without it

pulling across the back. Be sure that buttons close without gaping. You should be able to lift your arms over your head without the shirt pulling out of your waistband. Pants should not wrinkle or crease at the front crotch. The seat area should fit smoothly, without bagging.

Think More About It
Why is it important to try on clothes before buying them?

Clothing Labels and Hangtags

A clothing **label** is permanently attached to the inside of a garment. Some garments today are tagless, meaning they do not have a sewn-in label. If you do not see a clothing label sewn into the garment, look for the same information to be stamped somewhere on the garment.

By law, certain information is required on the garment:

- *Fiber content*—A **fiber** is a long, thin strand that makes up the content of a fabric. Fabrics are made of natural fibers, manufactured fibers, or a combination. The percentage of each fiber in a garment must be listed on the label, 27-5.

- *The country of origin*—The country where the garment was assembled.

- *Care instructions*—Proper care methods must be clear, complete, and readable for the normal life of the garment.

Investigate Further

Why do you think the government requires all labels to display the same information on clothing sold in the United States?

The larger tags attached to clothing, which are not required by law, are **hangtags**. Much of their information is promotional, to help sell the product. Companies may add trademark names, brand names, size information, or information about the fabric construction and special finishes.

Characteristics of Natural and Manufactured Fibers				
Natural Fibers				
	Fiber Name and Source	**Good Characteristics**	**Poor Characteristics**	**Care**
Protein Fibers	Silk (cocoon of silkworm)	Luxurious Strong Drapable, soft Absorbent Resists wrinkles	Damaged by perspiration, deodorants, perfumes, hairspray, bleach Weak when wet May water spot	Dry cleaning is safest Some fabrics may be hand washed; however, color loss can occur Do not rub surface as damage to fibers can occur Iron wrong side, moderate temperature
	Wool (sheep)	Does not build up static Strong, durable Resists wrinkles Absorbent Resistant to fading and perspiration Warm	Absorbs odors Not moth resistant Not washable unless treated Weaker when wet	Usually dry-cleaned May be machine washed if treated Use cold water, gentle cycle
Cellulosic Fibers	Cotton (cotton plant)	Strong, durable Comfortable Absorbent Does not build up static	Does not spring back into shape Wrinkles easily without special finish Shrinks unless treated or preshrunk	Machine washable if colorfast May shrink if washed or dried at high temperatures Usually ironed at high temperatures
	Linen (flax plant)	Cool, comfortable Absorbent Natural luster Strong, durable	Wrinkles easily Shows wear in areas of abrasion Shrinks unless treated or preshrunk	May be machine washed and dried Check manufacturer's instructions due to shrinkage variations Can be dry-cleaned Iron at high temperature
	Ramie (plant similar to flax)	Dyes well Absorbent High luster Stronger and stiffer than linen Cool, comfortable	Shrinks Wrinkles easily	Check manufacturer's instructions due to shrinkage variations

(Continued)

27-5 Silk, wool, cotton, linen, and ramie are the natural fibers most often used in clothes. Manufactured fibers were created to duplicate and improve the characteristics of natural fibers.

Characteristics of Natural and Manufactured Fibers				
Manufactured Fibers				
	Generic Name	**Good Characteristics**	**Poor Characteristics**	**Care**
Cellulosic Fibers	Acetate	Excellent drapability Luxurious feel and appearance	Poor resistance to abrasion Wrinkles easily	Dry-clean for best results Can machine wash but wrinkles are difficult to remove Iron at low temperature
	Rayon	Cool, comfortable Highly absorbent Good sheen Soft drapability Dyes well Versatile	Lacks strength May stretch or shrink Heat sensitive Poor resistance to soil and abrasion Wrinkles unless treated	Retains appearance best if dry-cleaned Iron at low temperature
Synthetic Fibers	Acrylic	Soft, warm, woollike Lightweight Resists wrinkles Quick drying Retains shape	Surface tends to pill Builds up static electricity Does not absorb moisture	Machine washable and dryable Use fabric softener to reduce static
	Nylon	Exceptionally strong Abrasion resistant Crease resistant Soft, lustrous Retains commercially heat-set pleats Resists stretching and shrinking Accepts dyes well	Builds up static electricity Heat sensitive Does not absorb moisture May pill White fabric may gray or yellow	Machine washable Use fabric softener to reduce static Iron at low temperature
	Polyester	Durable Resists wrinkling Versatile Retains commercially heat-set pleats Resists stretching, abrasion, shrinking	Builds up static electricity Does not absorb moisture Absorbs oils and grease readily May pill	Usually machine washable Use fabric softener to reduce static Remove oily stains immediately with solvent or detergent solution
	Spandex	Elastic Strong Lightweight Soft Resists abrasion	Heat sensitive Chlorine bleach will cause loss of strength and yellowing	Hand or machine wash and dry Do not use chlorine bleach Iron at low temperatures

27-5 Continued.

Judging Quality

A garment that is well made will last longer and give you better wear than a poorly constructed one. Well-made garments may cost more, but this is not always the case. Even expensive garments can be poorly made. Judge each garment carefully. Poorly made garments will show wear more quickly. They will end up with ripped seams, lost buttons, or broken zippers—all of which take time and money to repair.

Buy the best quality you can afford. Rather than considering the actual price, determine the cost per wearing. You can figure this by dividing the original cost by the number of times you will probably wear the item. If it is well made, the item will have a longer life. If it has flattering lines, textures, and colors, you will enjoy wearing it often. The following details are signs of good quality clothing.

- *Seams.* Look for smooth, flat, pucker-free seams. Where threads have pulled tight and created puckers, they will likely break and create holes in your seams.

- *Hems.* The hem edge and stitches should not show on the right side of the garment unless they are decorative. In addition, the edge of the hem should be finished to prevent raveling.

- *Fasteners.* Buttons should be spaced evenly along the opening of a garment and securely attached. Zippers should stay closed even when the garment is stretched.

Use What You Learn

Why is it important to inspect a garment carefully before you make a purchase?

Clothing the Family

The clothing budget must include the needs of all family members. Developing a wardrobe plan for each member with a list of clothes to purchase is helpful. Prioritize the lists, putting each person's most important needs

first. All family members want clothing that is comfortable, attractive, and suitable for their various activities. However, clothing needs of family members change throughout the life cycle.

Infants need comfortable, practical, and safe clothes. Comfort is part of helping them feel secure. Selecting fabrics that are washable, easy-care, and durable is also important.

Safety is another important factor when choosing infant clothing. Avoid buttons or trims that could be pulled off and swallowed by the infant. All infant sleepwear must meet federal government standards for flame-resistance.

Young children need clothing that provides comfort as well as freedom of movement. Extra room is needed in armholes, pant legs, crotch, and seat. Loose-fitting, one-piece styles are good choices as they allow room for growth.

Children are very active, and their clothing will receive much wear. Clothes need to be made of durable, sturdy fabrics. They will need to be laundered often. Soil and stain-resistant finishes are best.

Comfortable, easy-care clothing that meets individual needs can help older adults and people with disabilities maintain their independence. Health problems or illness can lead to difficulty in getting dressed. Clothes that are easy to manage, with large openings and front closures can help. Fasteners should be easy to open and close. Lightweight, warm fabrics work well for people with circulation problems. Selecting appropriate clothing can help people care for themselves as much as possible, and build feelings of esteem and worth.

Review Section 27:**1**

1. Explain how high fashions and fads are related to current style trends.

2. What is the most important line to consider when choosing clothing?

3. Briefly explain the differences between basic garments, extenders, and accessories.

4. List the information that should be on your shopping list when you shop for clothing.

5. Name the information required by law on clothing labels.

section 27:2

Caring for Clothing

Sharpen Your Reading

As you read, create a checklist of strategies for keeping clothes looking their best.

Boost Your Vocabulary

Create a chart of laundry aids. Visit a store where laundry aids are sold and read the labels on different types of products. From the labels, list the uses for each product.

Know Key Terms

soap
detergent
bleach

When you get home late, where do your clothes go—on the floor or in a pile on a chair? Do they lie there all night in a wrinkled heap? If so, they will need to be laundered, ironed, or dry-cleaned before you can wear them again.

When you leave your clothes in a heap, the threads become bent in many directions, resulting in wrinkles. If you hang up your clothes, the lengthwise threads will hang in straight lines. This decreases wrinkles. Giving your clothes a vigorous shake before you hang them up also straightens those threads. It will decrease wrinkles, shake off loose dust and dirt, and move air into the creases and folds.

Caring for your clothes properly will help you protect your investment. Proper care can save you time and money because you cut down on the number of washings or dry cleanings needed. Overall, your clothing will last longer because a high number of washings or cleanings can shorten a garment's life.

Think More About It
What are some reasons why people may not take the time to hang up their clothes?

Washing Clothes

Clothes are easier to clean if you wash them when lightly soiled instead of heavily soiled. When soil gets in and around fibers, it can weaken them. Check the care label on a garment to see if any special washing or drying procedures are required, 27-6. Then use the following steps to launder your clothes. Proper care procedures can extend the life of your garments, keeping their original size, shape, color, and overall appearance.

Sorting Clothes

Separating clothes by color, fabric, and the amount of soil is an important step. The following tips will help you prepare clothes for washing:

- *Wash whites alone.* Synthetic whites pick up color from other clothes and become gray or yellowish.
- *Wash dark or bright-colored clothes alone.* They might fade or bleed onto other items.
- *Separate clothes by fabric type and garment construction.* Delicate items need a gentle wash cycle, while sturdy clothes need stronger washing action.
- *Separate clothes that easily shed lint from those that easily pick it up.* For example, towels and fleece bathrobes shed lint, while dark colors, synthetics, corduroy, and suede finishes quickly pick it up.
- *Separate lightly soiled clothes from those heavily soiled.* If washed together, the soil from heavily soiled clothes may be deposited

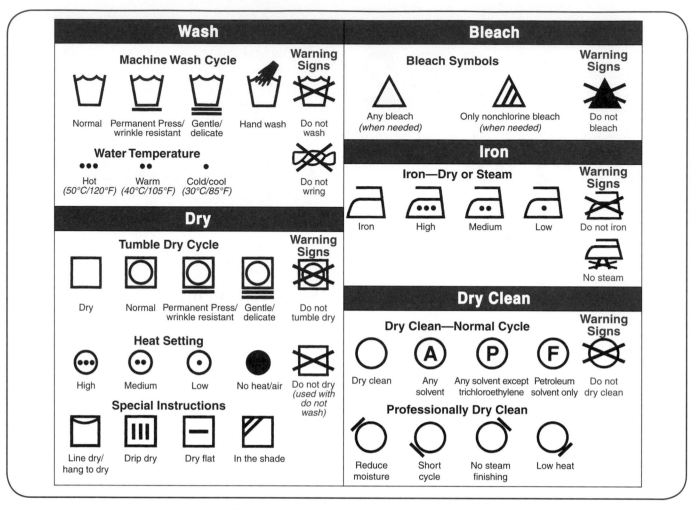

27-6 Understanding the symbols on clothing labels can help you know how to care for your garments.

on the lightly soiled clothes. Do not wash polyester or nylon fabrics with oily or greasy items. These synthetics have a tendency to attract oil and look spotty.

- *Sort clothes by the temperature of the wash water needed.* Hot water can be used for white and colorfast fabrics and heavily soiled loads. Although hot water may cause colors to fade, it removes soil best. Cold water should be used for dark colors that bleed. It can also be used for lightly soiled loads and delicate items. Warm water provides good cleaning for most wash loads, especially for synthetic fibers and permanent press finishes.

Use What You Learn

What would be the benefit of doing laundry with other family members?

Removing Stains

Spots on clothing need to be removed as quickly as possible. Once set, they may never come off, 27-7. The first step is to remove any residue. You may be able to blot, towel, sponge, or scrape off the residue.

Liquid detergent and water will remove water-based stains. Prewash soil removers may be effective on washable synthetics that tend to hold oily stains. Test your stain removal method on a hidden area of the garment first. Also, never iron over a stain or expose it to heat. The heat could permanently set the stain.

Selecting Laundry Products

A variety of laundry products are available to help care for clothes. Choose only the products you need. Choose products that are compatible with your clothes and the hardness of your water.

27-7 Immediately rinsing clothes in warm water can prevent water-based paint stains. Once the paint dries, it cannot be removed.

Prewash sprays or sticks are available for removing stains prior to washing. In fabrics made of synthetic fibers, such as polyester or nylon, oily stains can be hard to remove. A prewash product can be effective on these stains as well as on fabrics with a permanent-press finish.

Soaps

A **soap** is a cleansing agent made from natural products. Mild soaps may be recommended for washing silk and wool or fabrics with antistatic finishes. Some bar soaps work well for removing certain types of stains prior to washing. Soaps do not work well in hard water. They react with the minerals in hard water to form cloudy white solids. Soaps are biodegradable, which means they break down naturally when disposed. They do not harm the environment.

Detergents

Detergents generally clean better than soaps. They are made with *surfactants*, chemicals that allow water to penetrate soiled fabrics more easily. Detergents loosen and remove soil from clothes with the washer's agitation. Detergents also dissolve and suspend the removed soil in the water.

Enzymes are proteins that speed up chemical reactions. They are used in laundry products to help break down certain soils and stains. Enzymes are found in some detergents and presoak products.

Bleach

Bleach is a chemical mixture used to whiten and brighten clothes and remove stains. There are two types of bleaches: chlorine and nonchlorine. They do not remove soil, but oxidize it, making soil invisible. Bleaches also break down oils.

Chlorine bleach is the most widely used and least expensive bleach. It whitens clothes and fades the color of most fabrics. It can also be used to disinfect and deodorize clothes. Do not use chlorine bleach on silk, wool, mohair, or spandex. Chlorine bleach reacts with the fibers and destroys them. The bleach can destroy flame-retardant finishes, reduce the effectiveness of permanent-press finishes, and cause white polyester to yellow. If chlorine bleach is used too often, it will weaken the fibers and shorten the life of a garment. Used correctly, it can be a useful laundry aid. Enzymes are inactivated by chlorine bleach, so be careful not to use them together in a wash load.

Nonchlorine bleach releases oxygen in the water to give a gentle bleaching action. Sometimes it is called an oxygen bleach or all-fabric bleach. This type is considered to be safe for all fabrics. If used properly, it is safe for most colors as well. Although considered less effective than chlorine bleaches, it does contain builders to increase the cleaning power of detergent.

Care labels on clothing may state "No bleach" or "No chlorine bleach." Be sure to follow the label guidelines when using bleach. Clothing that has been bleached must be rinsed thoroughly to get the bleach out and stop the oxidizing action.

Use What You Learn

In what situations would you consider using bleach in your laundry?

Fabric Softeners

Fabric softeners were first used to prevent clothes from becoming stiff and scratchy when dried. In addition to softening fabrics, they reduce static electricity, which is common in synthetic fibers, 27-8. Different fabric softeners are available for use in the wash cycle, the rinse cycle, or the dryer. Liquid softeners used in the rinse cycle transfer the most softener to fabrics. Softeners used in the dryer come in the form of sheets that tumble with the clothes. They act on the outer surface of the fabric. They are also effective in reducing static.

Drying Clothes

Clothes may be machine dried or hung to dry. With either method, shake items as you remove them from the washer. This helps straighten the fibers, loosen wrinkles, and speed the drying process.

When placing items in the dryer, do not overload. This will cause wrinkling. Be careful not to overdry your clothes in a dryer. The natural fibers need to retain some moisture. If too dry, garments wrinkle and synthetic fibers build up static. To avoid wrinkles from setting, hang garments as soon as you take them from the dryer, especially synthetics.

27-8 Fabric softeners reduce static electricity in addition to softening clothes.

Review Section 27:2

1. What techniques can help remove wrinkles from clothes after you wear them?
2. Explain why clothes should be separated by color, amount of soil, and fiber content before laundering.
3. What can you do to prevent stains from setting on your clothes?
4. Which type of bleach is safe for all fabrics?

Think It Through

Clothing for a Job Interview

Sandy and Joel both planned to apply for a job at a local restaurant after school. At lunch Terry remarked, "Are you two going to your interviews looking like that?"

Sandy and Joel looked at each other. "What do you mean, Terry?" Sandy asked. "Don't we look okay?"

"Well, the restaurant is such a formal place," commented Terry, "I thought you would really dress up to go to a place like that."

Sandy looked at her sweatshirt and jeans. They were clean, but she knew what Terry meant. She looked at Joel in his T-shirt and cut-off jeans.

"Maybe it would be best to hurry home after school and change first," she said to Joel.

Questions to Guide Your Thinking

1. What messages would Sandy and Joel's clothes give to an interviewer?

2. Why would Terry's opinion of the restaurant make a difference in what Sandy and Joel would wear to an interview there?

3. What would you suggest that Sandy and Joel wear to the interview?

4. What type of clothing would you suggest they wear to interviews for the following jobs?

   A. child care worker

   B. retail salesperson

   C. office worker

5. What impact do you think clothing choices could have in the workplace?

Chapter Summary

Most young people and adults want to appear up-to-date in their clothing choices. Even though style preferences may change from one year to the next, basic garments with classic lines will serve a person for many years.

Planning a wardrobe requires taking a clothing inventory and developing a plan for new purchases. Choosing clothing with lines, colors, and textures that suit you can help you develop an interesting and flattering wardrobe. Items in your wardrobe will more likely mix and match with harmony. Well-fit and well-made garments may cost more. However, they will last longer and need fewer repairs. You will wear them more, getting your money's worth out of your investment.

When buying clothes for other family members, consider their special needs. When shopping, look at clothing labels and hangtags. They can be a key to understanding a garment's wear and care. Follow correct laundering procedures to maintain the life of your garments.

Assess...

Your Knowledge

1. Describe how the lines, textures, and colors of clothing can make a difference in the way a person looks.

2. What are the signs of good-quality clothing?

3. What techniques lengthen a garment's life?

Your Understanding

4. In what ways does clothing send messages to others?

5. How can a wardrobe plan help a person make wise shopping decisions?

6. How could the information found on a garment label help you decide whether to purchase it or not?

Your Skills

7. Analyze your personal characteristics and identify clothing lines, colors, and textures that will help you look your best.

8. A label lists the fiber content of a shirt to be 100% polyester, and the recommended care on the label is "dry clean." What questions would you ask yourself before you spent money to have it dry cleaned?

9. Analyze your personal habits for caring for your clothes. List the habits that help you make your clothes look their best. Then identify which habits you need to change to make your wardrobe look better and last longer.

Think Critically

10. Using magazines, newspapers, or old catalogs, find pictures of clothing that illustrate line, color, and texture. Create a poster using these pictures. Under each picture write how the line, color, or texture might affect other's impressions of a person wearing the garment.

11. Complete a self-analysis and describe the lines, textures, patterns, prints, and colors most attractive for you. Put together a poster illustrating these elements that would enhance your wardrobe. *Choice:* Write a summary of the elements of clothing design that most suit you.

12. *Science.* Find samples of clothing made from 3 different fibers. Identify the fiber and summarize the qualities of that fiber. Then describe how those qualities match (or do not match) your expectations for how each garment should wear.

13. *Science.* Take a large fabric or old piece of clothing that you can use for a staining experiment. Stain various sections with grease, ketchup, grape juice, grass stain, chocolate, iodine, and other substances that cause cleaning problems. Subject a portion of each stain to a different laundry aid and document its effectiveness. Prepare a chart of the various stains and laundry aids you used, rating their stain-removal ability as effective, somewhat effective, or ineffective. *Group option:* Complete this project with a partner.

Connect with Your Community

14. *Writing.* Interview a person you know who has special clothing needs. Write a report describing those needs and explain how the person meets them. *Choice:* Share the results of your interview with the class in an oral presentation.

15. Visit a department or grocery store that carries laundry aids. Prepare a chart of all the laundry aids you can find, identifying the purpose or recommended uses of each.

16. Prepare a shopping list of two to four major items from your clothing needs list. Include characteristics you want in each item (color, texture, fabric construction, structural or decorative details, durability, comfort, and care requirements). Visit at least two stores in your community and make specific requests to see items meeting those characteristics. Summarize your experience in a paragraph, describing how easy it was to find what you wanted. Also describe the salesperson's knowledge of the characteristics you examined.

17. *Research.* Visit a clothing store and analyze five clothing labels on similar garments (for example, five dresses or five sweaters). List the information provided by each. Describe how you would expect the garment to perform. From the label, identify how you would care for the garment. Summarize by writing a paragraph on the current design trends displayed by the garments, the common fibers used, and the laundry methods most often recommended. *Group option:* Work with a group of classmates to gather the information from ten garments. Then compile your data in a table and present your findings to the class.

Use Technology

18. Use a computer program that allows you to use a digital photo to view various styles and colors on your body. Identify styles and colors that are most attractive for you. Present your information in a poster or a paragraph.

19. Search the Internet for a Web site specializing in color analysis. Identify clothing colors that are most attractive for a person with your hair, eye, and skin coloring. Prepare a color chart with the colors that enhance your personal coloring. *Choice:* Create a collage of photos from clothing magazines that shows the colors that would work for you.

20. *Writing.* Visit a Web site selling clothing online. Write a paragraph describing the clothing selection available, information on garment care, the ease of ordering, and the company's return policy. *Choice:* Create an electronic presentation for consumers that explains important tips to remember when shopping for clothing online.

21. Using a computer spreadsheet, develop a wardrobe inventory. List your clothing items down the left side. Then make three columns titled *Worn Often*, *Worn Occasionally*, and *Rarely Worn*. Check the appropriate column that describes each item. Turn in your inventory with a plan to complete your wardrobe and a description of your future purchases.

Chapter 28

Managing Your Housing

Section 28:**1**
Locating Housing

Section 28:**2**
Maintaining Your Living Space

Key Questions

Questions to answer as you study this chapter:

- How can a person locate and obtain affordable housing?

- What needs to be done to maintain a living space?

Chapter Objectives

After studying this chapter, you will be able to

- **describe** how housing meets people's needs.

- **identify** different types of housing.

- **compare** methods of obtaining housing.

- **identify** guidelines for choosing furniture and appliances.

- **determine** ways to maintain a safe and healthy living environment.

Life Sketch

The work was hard, but Rosa and Don didn't seem to mind. They were making his parents' basement into an apartment. It was going to be Don and Rosa's first home!

Don's parents bought the materials. Don and Rosa did most of the work. Simple partitions divided the space. They painted the walls, made curtains, and put throw rugs on the floor. Used furniture was a bargain at local garage sales.

Although their new home was not a fancy and expensive place, they were pleased. The rent was low. They had been able to organize and furnish the space to meet their needs. Their furniture seemed sturdy enough to last a while. They would both be finished at the technical college in a year. Maybe then they could afford to look for a bigger place and better furnishings.

Getting Started

Don and Rosa's need for inexpensive housing is common to many newlyweds. They still had to finish their education. Their income was low. They did not have any money saved to buy a home or expensive furnishings. Their choices of housing were limited. However, their new home would satisfy their lifestyle and needs.

Housing is more than a place to live. It includes the building itself plus all that is in and near it. The furnishings, neighborhood, and community are all part of it. Housing creates a total environment that affects every aspect of people's lives.

As a family's needs change throughout the life cycle, their housing choices often change as well. Married couples, like Don and Rosa, often start out with affordable housing. Couples with children often need to look for more spacious housing located near playgrounds and schools. After the children have grown and moved away from home, the family's needs change again. In the retirement years, families often choose smaller, less expensive housing.

Within your home, developing skills for maintaining a living space can help you meet your needs efficiently. Understanding guidelines for selecting household items can help you choose high-quality, energy-efficient products that are accessible to all family members. Knowing how to clean and maintain your home can help you make your home a comfortable, enjoyable, and efficient place to live and work.

section 28:1

Locating Housing

Sharpen Your Reading

Review the headings for this section and use them to develop an outline. Under each heading, list key ideas related to locating and obtaining housing.

Boost Your Vocabulary

Obtain two samples of leases from different apartments and compare them for different requirements.

Know Key Terms

lease
security deposit
down payment
mortgage

You most likely will move several times during your life. That means you are likely to make several housing choices. Your choices will be affected by factors including your lifestyle, taste, and income. Your housing needs and the types of housing available will also influence your choices.

Functions of Housing

Housing serves an important function by helping you fill your needs and express your values. Most people expect their housing to meet their personal physical, emotional, and social needs as well as family needs.

Meeting Physical Needs

The physical needs that are met by housing include shelter, protection, and safety. People want housing to provide shelter from the outside climate and protection from weather extremes. They expect to feel safe and secure from potential dangers, both outside and inside the home. People also use housing to meet their personal needs for eating and sleeping.

Link to Your Life

How does your current housing situation meet your physical needs?

Satisfying Emotional Needs

Sometimes you may want to be alone, away from the pressures of school, work, or other people. Housing can provide that personal and private space. Your personal space is the space within your home that you call your own. An individual bedroom, personal chair, or corner desk may provide this comfort and privacy, 28-1.

Another emotional need all people share is the need for self-expression, which housing can help to satisfy. By designing and decorating a personal space, you create an area that reflects your personality.

Meeting Social Needs

Housing provides spaces for meeting social needs that involve interaction with others. Such gathering places include the kitchen, dining room, or family room. These spaces promote social activities such as talking, playing games, eating, and entertaining guests.

Indoor and outdoor living spaces can be arranged for enjoying recreational activities. Indoor spaces can promote reading, listening to music, or playing games. Outdoor spaces such as a yard or play area accommodate active sports and games.

28-1 Housing satisfies emotional needs by providing a private space for personal activities such as studying, reading, or working on hobbies.

Types of Housing

Many different types of housing are available. The type you choose will depend on what is available in your price range that best meets your personal needs. The two main types of housing available are single-family dwellings and multifamily dwellings. Both groups offer numerous styles at a wide range of prices to meet a variety of needs.

Single-Family Dwellings

A *single-family dwelling* is a structure that houses one family. *Freestanding houses* are the most common type of single-family home. This type of home is not connected to another unit. Most families prefer a freestanding home because of the freedom and privacy it provides.

On the other hand, this type of house requires more exterior care. Lawns, shrubs, sidewalks, and driveways all increase the amount of time needed to care for the home.

Attached houses are single-family homes that share at least one wall with the adjacent dwelling. Examples include town houses and duplexes.

Town houses are built in rows or clusters, with several units joined together. Most town homes have their own entrance and yard area. Duplexes are two single-family houses attached

together. This type of housing is usually less expensive than a single-family home because less land and building materials are used.

Investigate Further

What type of single-family housing is available in your neighborhood?

Multifamily Homes

Structures that house more than one family are considered *multifamily dwellings*. Each family lives in a separate unit within the building. Apartments and condominiums are common examples of housing in this group. In areas around the country where space is limited, this is an efficient and necessary form of housing.

An *apartment* building is the most common type of multifamily dwelling. Each apartment unit is rented. The condition and cost of apartments can vary greatly. Features often vary, too. Some may come fully furnished or have laundry and extra storage facilities. Recreational facilities such as tennis courts and swimming pools may be available.

In a *condominium*, each unit is purchased as though it were a separate home. All owners belong to the condominium association. Common areas such as hallways, parking areas, and recreational facilities are shared. Maintenance on these common areas as well as insurance on the building is provided by the condominium association, 28-2. Condominium owners usually pay a monthly fee to cover maintenance costs.

All multifamily dwellings usually have some restrictions. Noise restrictions, for instance, are designed to protect everyone's rights for privacy and quiet. Although these restrictions may limit individual freedom, they protect the rights of everyone in the building.

 **Weigh the Facts** In your community, how do the costs of living in a rental apartment compare to the costs of living in a condominium? Are both types of housing available?

28-2 Buying a condominium enables a person to invest in real estate, yet avoid the tasks of maintaining the yard and building.

The Cost of Housing

You need to know what type of housing you can afford before you start looking. Should you rent or buy a home? Your decision will be affected by the following factors:

- annual income
- lifestyle
- family size
- family members' ages
- housing availability in the area
- housing preferences
- job mobility (how often you change jobs)

The cost of housing includes many expenses. First, there is the cost of monthly payments for rent or to repay money borrowed to buy a house. Utilities, taxes, insurance, furnishings, and repairs must also be considered. Utility charges include electricity, natural gas, water, sewer, telephone, and garbage disposal services. Cable and Internet services could also be included. These costs vary depending on usage. Basically, the more services you use, the higher your housing costs will be.

Sometimes people cannot afford the type of housing they really want. As a result, they may need to take another look at their needs and priorities. They may need to compromise and choose another alternative. Cost is often the biggest factor in determining which housing

choices a family can consider. Therefore, obtaining affordable housing that meets a family's needs and expectations requires careful thought and planning.

Think More About It
Why might the monthly cost of living in a single family home be higher than the cost of living in a rented apartment?

Renting a Place to Live

Single people, young married couples, and retired people often choose to rent a unit in a multifamily dwelling. People who move frequently for work may also choose to rent.

Reasons for Renting

One reason for renting is cost. The monthly cost of renting is usually more affordable than owning a home. Monthly rent payments may include some utilities. Renters do not need a large sum of money for a down payment. They also do not have property taxes to pay or the cost of maintaining the building. Most apartments provide major appliances and some are furnished. This saves the renter the cost of major purchases.

Convenience is also a common reason for renting. Renters do not have to worry about doing repairs. If the roof leaks, it is the landlord's responsibility to fix it promptly. They do not have to take care of a lawn or clear sidewalks. Also, renters have more freedom when they need to move. Once they give the landlord notice of their leaving, according to the terms of their contract, they can leave anytime thereafter.

Another reason for renting is location. Rental units can be found in urban, suburban, and rural areas. They may be close to work, school, family, friends, cultural facilities or child care facilities, 28-3.

Investigate Further

Are there any rental units in your community that are close to your school and appealing to families? What is the cost for these types of rental units?

28-3 Close access to a child care facility may influence a housing decision for young parents.

Finding an Apartment to Rent

The Internet and local newspapers are good places to look for apartment listings. You can also talk to friends, relatives, and coworkers. Let them know you are looking for a place to rent. Larger cities or suburbs often publish apartment guides. These guides describe locations, features, and sometimes rental costs of larger complexes.

When you find an apartment you like, check the overall condition of the facility inside and outside. Take a tape measure along and measure the room sizes. Make sure it has the space you need. Check the door widths. That is important if you already have furniture to move in. Flush the toilet. Turn hot and cold water faucets on and off. Note any drips or leaks. Open and close windows to make sure they operate smoothly. Check the general upkeep of the building. Are the hallways clean and well lighted? Are the grounds kept neat and clean?

If you are interested in the apartment and some things need repair, write them down. Arrange to have the landlord make the repairs before you sign a lease.

Think More About It

Why is it important to thoroughly check out an apartment before you sign a lease?

The Lease

A **lease** is an agreement between the renter and the landlord. It is a legal contract that states all the terms and conditions of the agreement, 28-4. A renter is also called a *tenant*. A tenant has the following rights:

- use the rental unit in agreement with the landlord's rules
- occupy the rental unit without unjust interference from the landlord
- know the name and address of the landlord or legal agent representing the landlord
- live in a property that meets building codes and is kept in reasonably good repair
- be informed of unhealthy or unsafe conditions
- receive prompt return of any security deposit

Landlord practices are regulated by state law. In general, a landlord has the following rights:

- determine the amount of rent
- set rules and regulations for the tenant
- collect payment for damages to property
- refuse to rent to tenants with pets
- inspect the premises, but only at reasonable times and after advance notice is given to the tenant

Use What You Learn

Why would it be important to review a lease carefully before signing it?

The Security Deposit

When tenants sign a lease, most landlords require payment for the first month of rent plus a security deposit. A **security deposit** is a sum of money equal to one or two month's rent. The security deposit insures the landlord against the risk of loss due to unpaid rent or damages to the building. If renters break their lease, they usually lose their deposit. If there is no damage to the apartment when the renter moves out, the deposit is returned. Minor wear and tear on the apartment is not considered damage.

WB-20 APARTMENT LEASE
Approved by Wisconsin Real Estate Examining Board

Nelco Forms
P.O. Box 10208
Green Bay, WI 54307-0208

APARTMENT LEASE

	1	This lease of the apartment identified below is entered into by and between the Landlord and Tenant (referred to
	2	in the singular whether one or more) on the following terms and conditions:
PARTIES	3	Tenant: *Raoul Doe* Landlord: *Sawdusky Realty*
		Ilse Doe
		Agent for maintenance, management:
		name *Mike Manning*
		address *1210 Fixit St.*
		Anytown, USA
		Agent for collection of rents:
APARTMENT ADDRESS	10	Building address: name *Lisa Brown*
		street *1000 Collect St.* address *1000 Collect St.*
		Anytown, USA
		city, village/town *Anytown,*
		Agent for service of process:
		name *Myra Lee*
		county *Anycounty* State *St* address *508 Process St.*
		Anytown USA.
TERM	24	Apartment number: *208*
	25	Lease term: *8/1/xx to 8/1/xx* ~~Month to Month~~ (strike if not applicable)
	26	First day of lease term: *8/1/xx* Last day of lease term: *8/1/xx One Year Later*
RENTALS	27	Apartment: $ *950.00* per *MO.* Other: *Garage Sp.* $ *30* per *MO*
	28	Payable at *Apt. 101, 1000 Collect St.* on or
	29	before the *First* day of each *Month* during the
	30	term of this lease.
UTILITIES	31	Utility charges, other than telephone, are included in the rent, except: *Heat And*
	32	*Electricty*
	33	which Tenant
	34	shall pay promptly when due. If charges not included in the rent are not separately metered, they shall be allo-
	35	cated on the basis of: *Separate meters are installed*
	36	
SPECIAL CONDITIONS	37	Special conditions: *No Pets*
	38	
	39	
	40	
RENEWAL OF LEASE TERM	41	(Strike clause 1 or 2; if neither is stricken clause 2 controls.)
	42	1. This lease shall be automatically renewed, without notice from either party, on identical terms for a like suc-
	43	cessive lease term unless either party shall, at least 45 days before the expiration of the lease, notify the other
	44	in writing of the termination of the lease. However, Landlord must, at least 15 days but not more than 30 days
	45	prior to the time specified for giving the notice as herein set forth notify Tenant in writing of the above
	46	provision for automatic renewal or extension.
	47	~~2. This lease shall be automatically renewed, without notice from either party, on identical terms, except that it~~
	48	~~shall be a month-to-month tenancy.~~
ASSIGNMENT SUBLETTING	49	Tenant shall not assign this lease nor sublet the premises or any part thereof without the prior written consent of
	50	Landlord. If Landlord permits an assignment or a sublease, such permission shall in no way relieve Tenant of
	51	Tenant's liability under this lease.
SECURITY DEPOSIT	52	Upon execution of this lease Tenant paid a security deposit in the amount of $ *950.00* to be held by
	53	*Sawdusky Realty*
	54	If the person holding the security deposit is a licensed real estate broker, acting as agent, it shall be held in the
	55	broker's trust account. The deposit, less any amounts withheld, will be returned in person or mailed to Tenant's last
	56	known address within 21 days after Tenant vacates the premises. If any portion of the deposit is withheld, Landlord
	57	will provide an accompanying itemized statement specifically describing any damages and accounting for any amount
	58	withheld. Failure to return the deposit or provide a written accounting within 21 days will result in the waiver of
	59	any claim against the deposit. The reasonable cost of repairing any damages caused by Tenant, normal wear and
	60	tear excepted, will be deducted from the security deposit. Tenant has 7 days after the beginning of the lease term to
	61	notify Landlord in writing of damages or defects in the premises; no deduction from Tenant's security deposit
	62	shall be made for any damages or defects of which notification is given. Landlord will give Tenant a written
	63	description of any physical damages charged to the previous tenant's security deposit as soon as such description is
	64	available. (If none, so specify_____.) (Strike paragraph if no security deposit is paid.)
VACATION OF PREMISES	65	Tenant agrees to vacate the premises at the end of the lease term or the extended lease term, and promptly deliver
	66	the keys to Landlord.
LANDLORD'S RIGHT TO ENTER	67	Landlord may enter the premises at reasonable times and with 12 hours advance notice, with or without Tenant's
	68	permission to inspect the premises, make repairs, show the premises to prospective tenants or purchasers, or to com-
	69	ply with any applicable law or regulation. Landlord may enter with less than 12 hours advance notice upon specific
	70	consent of Tenant. No advance notice is required for entry in a health or safety emergency or where entry is neces-
	71	sary to preserve and protect the premises from damage in Tenant's absence.
ABANDONMENT BY TENANT	72	If Tenant shall abandon the premises before the expiration of the lease term, Landlord shall make reasonable efforts
	73	to re-lease premises and shall apply any rent received, less costs of re-leasing, to the rent due or to become due on this
	74	lease, and Tenant shall remain liable for any deficiency. If Tenant is absent from the premises for three successive
	75	weeks without notifying Landlord in writing of such absence, Landlord, at Landlord's sole option, may deem the
	76	premises abandoned.
DISPOSAL OF TENANT'S PROPERTY	77	If Tenant shall leave any property on the premises after vacation or abandonment of the premises, Tenant shall be
	78	deemed to have abandoned the property, and Landlord shall have the right to dispose of the property as provided
	79	by law.
TENANT OBLIGATIONS	80	During the lease term, as a condition to Tenant's continuing right to use and occupy the premises, Tenant agrees
	81	and promises:
USE	82	1. To use the premises for residential purposes only by Tenant and Tenant's immediate family.
	83	2. Not to make or permit use of the premises for any unlawful purpose or any purpose that will injure the reputa-
	84	tion of the premises or the building of which they are a part.
	85	3. Not to use or keep in or about the premises anything which would adversely affect coverage of the premises or
	86	the building of which they are a part under a standard fire and extended insurance policy.
	87	4. Not to make excessive noise or engage in activities which unduly disturb neighbors or other tenants in the build-
	88	ing which the premises are located.
PETS	89	5. Not to keep in or about the premises any pet unless specifically authorized as a special condition in this lease.
GOVT. REG.	90	6. To obey all lawful orders, rules and regulations of all governmental authorities.
MAINTENANCE IMPROVEMENTS	91	7. To keep the premises in clean and tenantable condition and in as good repair as at the beginning of the lease
	92	term, normal wear and tear excepted.
	93	8. If obligated to pay for heat for the premises, to maintain a reasonable amount of heat in cold weather to prevent
	94	damage to the premises, and if damage results from Tenant's failure to maintain a reasonable amount of heat
	95	Tenant shall be liable for this damage.

WB20   NTF 0074

28-4 In rental situations, both the landlord and the renter have rights. These are generally stated in a written lease.

You can protect your security deposit by taking a few precautions before you move into the apartment. List any damaged or very worn items. List needed repairs. Describe the cleanliness of the unit. Have the landlord sign and date this memo. Give a copy of the memo to the landlord, but keep the original. When you move, repair any damages you have caused. Clean the unit and show your list to the landlord. This should help you get your full security deposit returned.

Breaking a Lease

A lease obligates the renter to pay the rent until the term expires. If you move early, you still have to pay the rent unless the landlord finds another tenant. If you need to break a lease, check with your landlord to find out exactly what is required. Some require 60 to 90 days notice to find someone else to rent the unit. You may be able to sublet the unit to someone else if the landlord approves your choice of tenant.

Good communication between renter and landlord can help keep the experience a positive one for all. Sometimes even if you try to work things out with your landlord, problems result. When things go wrong, it is best to get legal advice or consult your local housing board.

Use What You Learn

Before you sign a lease, why is it important to make sure you can afford your choice of housing?

Home Ownership

Many people want to own their own homes. Ownership offers many advantages, including financial benefits. On the other hand, some financial disadvantages also exist.

Advantages of Home Ownership

Home ownership provides an emotional sense of security and freedom, 28-5. Homeowners do not have to be accountable to a landlord for what they do in the home. They can paint, remodel, or have pets. These freedoms are usually limited in a rental situation.

28-5 A desire for privacy motivates many families to own their own home.

Home ownership is an investment in real estate. If the value of real estate goes up, your investment will be worth more. Before buying real estate, evaluate the community and the neighborhood to make sure that home values are not declining. Check to see what the community has to offer. Work opportunities, schools, medical facilities, churches, and recreational facilities are some factors to consider. These can help real estate maintain or increase in value.

Home ownership has several financial benefits. The interest you pay on a home loan can be deducted on your federal income taxes. You may also be able to take deductions for the property taxes you pay. Such deductions could decrease the amount of income taxes you owe.

Think More About It
What would be the advantage of living in the same home for many years?

Disadvantages of Home Ownership

The initial cost of buying a home can be high. A portion of the purchase price of the home is needed for a **down payment**. This must be paid at the time the house is purchased. The rest of the money is borrowed from a lending institution and becomes the mortgage. A **mortgage** is a contract between a borrower and a lender. The home is listed as *collateral*, which is a form of security for the loan. Most lending institutions charge a fee for the mortgage.

Other expenses include closing costs and insurance. *Closing costs* are the purchasing and financing costs paid at the time the mortgage is loaned. The family must come up with the money to pay these costs when they buy the house.

Once the home is purchased, there is the commitment to pay monthly mortgage payments and property taxes. Failure to make mortgage payments on time can result in the loss of the home and the investment. Homeowners must also pay for upkeep and repairs on the home. In order to maintain the value of the home, the owner must keep the home in good condition.

It takes time to sell a home when the owner wants to move, 28-6. A buyer must be found. Certain legal and financial matters must be settled. Real estate agents handle these aspects of selling a home, usually for a percentage of the selling price of the home.

Financing a Home

Few people have enough money to purchase a home with cash. For most families, it takes several years of saving just to get enough money for a down payment. Home buyers generally turn to a lending institution to finance the purchase of a home.

When choosing a lender for your home mortgage, check out all the policies and procedures that could affect you, even if your circumstances should change. Check out the interest rates and the amount needed for a down payment. Ask whether there are any penalties for paying off the mortgage early. Also, ask about their policies if you make a late payment or miss a payment.

Small differences in lenders can make a large difference on the total amount you pay for your home. Even a ¼ percent difference in the interest rate can significantly affect the total interest paid over the years.

Investigate Further

What are the current interest rates for mortgages in your area?

Insuring Your Home and Belongings

Whether you own or rent your housing, insurance can protect you against the risk of financial loss. Renters and homeowners risk the loss of their possessions to hazards such as fire, theft, and vandalism. For such risks, they need property protection.

Homeowners and renters are also responsible for any injury to others or to others' property caused by their own property or possessions. For more information on homeowners insurance and renter's insurance, see Chapter 24, "Protecting Your Resources."

Review Section 28:1

1. Explain how housing needs may change over the family life cycle.
2. Give examples of how housing can meet physical, emotional, and social needs.
3. Explain the difference between a single-family dwelling and a multifamily dwelling.
4. Explain the differences between an apartment and a condominium.
5. Give one reason why people choose to rent a home.
6. Give three examples of a landlord's rights and also a tenant's rights as stated in a written lease.
7. List one advantage and one disadvantage of home ownership.

28-6 It often takes a great deal of time to sell your own home.

section 28:2

Maintaining Your Living Space

Sharpen Your Reading

As you read this section, create a list of home maintenance tips that you could apply in your current living situation. Summarize how each tip would improve your living space.

Boost Your Vocabulary

Find pictures of furnishings and appliances that demonstrate universal design.

Know Key Terms

universal design

Often young families struggle with the costs of furnishing and maintaining a home. Making choices with quality, accessibility, energy efficiency, and costs in mind will help you meet your housing budget. Keeping your living space clean and orderly can help you meet the needs of the family for a safe living environment.

Furnishing Your Home

Remember, your home is a reflection of you. The furnishings and appliances you select should reflect your personality, values, and lifestyle.

Your decision-making skills will help you decide which choices best meet your needs.

Develop a Buying Plan

Furnishings and appliances can be expensive items. A plan for acquiring them can help you avoid costly purchases that you regret. Think of all the items that are put away in an attic or sold at a garage sale. Most likely, these rarely used items were unplanned purchases.

Before you buy, develop a plan, 28-7. List the items you want, and consider the cost and the quality of each. High-quality items will last longer than those of lower quality. They will also be more expensive. Consider how much money you can spend now and how much should be put aside for later purchases. Think about recycling possibilities if you choose an inexpensive item now, but plan to replace it later. For instance, outdoor furniture could be used indoors until you can afford to buy a better quality. When you are ready to replace it, you then have what you need to furnish your patio or deck.

Guidelines for Choosing Furniture

A piece of furniture may be beautiful, functional, and inexpensive. However, if it is the wrong size or style, it will not be a wise purchase. These factors and others should be considered before purchasing furnishings.

28-7 Comparison shopping on the Internet can help you estimate how much furnishings will cost.

- *Function.* Some items serve only one function, while others can serve several. If you purchase furniture with flexible functions, you will need to make fewer purchases. This is helpful if your finances are very limited or space is small.

- *Space considerations.* How much space do you have? Remember to leave space for traffic patterns through a room. People should have a clear path to pass from one room to another.

- *Comfort.* Personal comfort is important in choosing items such as a bed mattress, chair, or sofa. Try out the furniture to make sure it matches your needs.

- *Portability.* Furniture should be easy to move for cleaning and rearranging. It is also important for families who move often. Lightweight furniture that stacks makes packing, shipping, and resettling easier.

- *Quality of construction.* Check pieces of furniture carefully before you buy. Overall, quality furniture should have sturdy construction to give lasting service.

- *Care requirements.* Choose furniture that matches your lifestyle, including the time and money your family has available for care.

Selecting Appliances

Several appliances are indispensable for helping with household tasks. A range, refrigerator, freezer, dishwasher, washer, and dryer are considered major appliances because they are large and expensive. Portable appliances, which can easily be moved from place to place, are also helpful. These include microwave ovens, toasters, and electric mixers.

Once you know which appliance you need, careful planning can help you choose from among the many models available.

- *Features and costs.* These are key factors to consider. What features best suit your needs and budget? Consider the cost of the appliance in relation to the features it offers.

- *Size.* Consider the size of the appliance and the space you have available. What hookups will the appliance need?

- *Energy usage.* The cost of an appliance only begins with its purchase price. Your monthly utility bills will reflect the appliance's energy use. Energy-saving appliances often cost more, but save money in the long run by using less energy. Look for the yellow EnergyGuide label displayed on major appliances to compare operating costs, 28-8. By comparing models of similar size and performance, you can see which cost less to operate.

- *Warranty coverage.* Check the warranty coverage provided. If you narrow down your appliance choices to two models with similar features and prices, the one with the better warranty coverage is often the better buy.

Planning for Universal Design

Considering universal design when planning your living space will make your home more comfortable for yourself and others. **Universal design** is the concept of creating products and living spaces that are easy for everyone to use. People of all ages and abilities benefit from universal design.

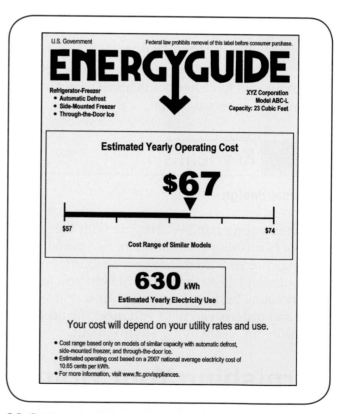

28-8 When buying a major appliance, check the Energy-Guide label to determine the estimated yearly cost of using the appliance.

Some elements of universal design are structural, such as wide doorways and entrances without steps. However, you can incorporate nonstructural elements by selecting items for your home with the following features:

- appliances with front-mounted controls
- side-by-side or freezer-under style refrigerators with pull-out drawers
- front-loading washers and dryers, 28-9
- microwave ovens with high-contrast displays and minimal programming requirements
- cabinets with pull-out shelves
- touch lamps that operate without switches
- handheld shower heads
- chairs with raised seats

Universal design accommodates the needs of all family members throughout the life cycle as well as people with disabilities. Keeping this concept in mind when furnishing your home will increase the comfort and accessibility of your living space both now and in the future.

Conserving Energy in the Home

Energy conservation begins at home. Rising energy costs and limited energy resources are two reasons to practice conservation. Using energy-saving appliances, proper insulation, and recycling are just a few steps you can take to help protect the environment and save money, too.

Use Energy Wisely

Heating and cooling appliances use the most energy in the home. Heat is used for activities such as cooking, heating water, drying clothes, and heating homes in the winter. Cooling is accomplished by refrigerators, freezers, and air conditioners. When you buy energy-saving models of these appliances, you can make the biggest dent in your current and future utility bills.

When using appliances, operate them efficiently to conserve energy. For example, bake several items instead of just one—perhaps a main dish and a couple side dishes. Run the dishwasher when it is fully loaded.

28-9 Raised, front-loading washers and dryers are easy for family members of all abilities to operate.

Also, know what you are looking for before opening the refrigerator and freezer doors. Trying to decide what to eat with doors wide open empties the cold air and forces a refrigerator to work harder.

Use Proper Insulation

Well-insulated housing will cost less to heat or cool. Good insulation acts like a thermal blanket to keep the house warm in winter and cool in summer. Walls, floors, ceilings, doors, and windows should be properly insulated. These measures help maintain year-round comfort. If you are renting, talk with your landlord about possible ways to conserve energy with more insulation, or caulking around doors and windows. Heavy insulated fabrics for curtains can also help conserve energy loss through windows.

Recycle Waste

Garbage pickup is another household cost that can be reduced by using recyclable materials as much as possible. Recyclable items include paper, glass, aluminum, steel, cardboard, and some plastics. Check plastic containers for the recycling symbol.

Your efforts to control the amount and type of waste you create will help in several ways. By controlling waste, you help reduce the excessive volume currently going into landfills, 28-10. You encourage manufacturers to package more products in recyclable containers, thus conserving raw materials. Also, by emphasizing recycling, fewer raw materials are used. This helps preserve more for future generations.

28-10 Recycling at home helps reduce the amount of waste sent to landfills.

Cleaning Your Living Space

How often should you clean? That depends on the use of the space. Some tasks need to be done daily. Clutter should be picked up every day to avoid accumulation. Identify areas where clutter tends to pile up and plan a way to organize the space.

Dishes should be washed daily so they do not attract bugs and insects or become sources of bacteria that could make family members sick. Tasks such as scrubbing toilets, cleaning sinks, and washing floors—should be done often enough to remove the germs that accumulate from daily use.

A cleaning schedule can help you keep your home healthful and safe. First, identify the tasks that need to be done and determine how often they should be completed. Then set aside time each day to complete the tasks. Involving all family members can help accomplish cleaning tasks without taking too much of one person's time.

Review Section 28:2

1. Identify four guidelines used for choosing furniture.
2. Give examples of three ways to incorporate universal design when furnishing a home.
3. Describe two ways to practice energy conservation at home.
4. What is the first step in developing a cleaning plan?

Think It Through

Buying a House

Michael and Opel live in a small one-bedroom apartment, but hope to buy a house soon. They both earn good salaries and have managed to save $10,500 in the last three years. Their baby is due in two months so they will need more space for their soon-to-change lifestyle. Opel plans to take three months off from work when the baby arrives.

Michael and Opel found a three-bedroom house in a quiet neighborhood for $250,000. A playground and a school were nearby. Their commute to work would be short. They thought the house would meet their needs for several years.

Michael and Opel know they must decide whether to continue renting. However, they both wonder if this is really the right time to buy a house.

Questions to Guide Your Thinking

1. What types of housing alternatives can you identify that would meet Michael and Opel's present needs?

2. Michael and Opel must consider the alternatives of renting an apartment or buying a house. Using the decision-making steps from Chapter 4, list the pros and cons they must consider for renting and for buying.

3. Choose one alternative and explain why you would recommend it as a decision for Michael and Opel.

Chapter Summary

Housing serves several functions for people. Your expectations for housing may vary depending on your needs, interests, personal taste, and lifestyle. The types and costs of available housing will also influence your choice. The decision to buy or rent is affected by many factors and should be considered carefully.

Several factors should be considered when you buy furnishings and appliances. Using the decision-making steps can help you make choices that meet your needs and tastes. Planning for universal design will make your home comfortable and accessible for everyone.

Conserving energy at home can help you lower costs and protects the environment. In addition, having a plan for keeping your home clean and orderly can contribute to overall satisfaction with your housing.

Assess...

Your Knowledge

1. List and explain three reasons for choosing to rent a living space.

2. What are the advantages and disadvantages of owning your living space?

3. What monthly and yearly expenses need to be included in the costs of housing?

Your Understanding

4. Explain how two different types of housing could meet the needs of a young family with children.

5. In what ways might the housing needs of a young married couple be similar to the housing needs of a retired couple?

6. How does a lease protect both the landlord and the tenant?

Your Skills

7. Make a recommendation for a type of housing that could meet the specific needs of a young single person starting a career. Explain how your choice could meet those needs.

8. Develop a plan for keeping your current living environment clean and orderly. Include daily, weekly, and monthly tasks.

Think Critically

9. *Research.* Compare a homeowner's and a renter's insurance policy. Write a report describing the similarities and differences.

10. *Writing.* Write one paragraph listing your personal expectations for housing. Then describe the housing features you would choose to meet each expectation. Find two listings for housing that would meet those needs and explain how each would do so. *Choice:* Compare your current housing situation to your personal expectations. Explain what you would like to change to better meet your needs.

11. *Financial literacy, math.* Research the various costs of housing-related expenses, such as a monthly cable bill, a monthly telephone bill, costs of garbage disposal in your community, cost per kilowatt for electric service, an average monthly heating or cooling bill for an apartment, estimated cost of insurance for a rental unit, and an average monthly rental payment. Add up these payments and then identify how much monthly take-home income you would need if your housing costs equaled 37% of your income.

12. *Writing.* Use the Internet to locate sample lease agreements. Analyze two different leases, and identify their similarities and their differences. In a paragraph, explain which lease you would prefer to have as a tenant.

Connect With Your Community

13. Visit a furniture store in your community. Choose one item and evaluate it for its function(s), space needed, comfort, portability, quality of construction, and care requirements. Summarize your evaluation in a paragraph.

14. **Research.** Research current waste disposal requirements in your city or state. Prepare a poster providing information about your local waste requirements, plus promoting additional steps families could take to reduce the amount of waste they produce. *Choice:* Present your information in a brochure or a community service announcement.

15. **Financial literacy.** Locate two listings for local rental units. Contact the landlords and gather information about the following: length of lease, restrictions, services provided, extra facilities offered, security, and monthly rent payment. In a short summary, explain which rental unit you recommend as the best choice for a single person on a limited income, giving reasons to support your choice.

16. **Research.** Interview a waste management expert from your city or county board to discuss waste disposal problems in your area. Prepare a report in which you explain all sides of the waste disposal issues facing your community, and make recommendations that community members could follow to address the issues. *Group option:* Work in a small group, with each member of the group researching a different aspect of the local waste disposal problems. Present your information to the class in an electronic presentation.

Use Technology

17. **Research.** Use the Internet to research the principles of universal design. Create a brochure for consumers that explains how to incorporate these principles when furnishing a home. *Choice:* Create an electronic presentation instead of a brochure.

18. **Financial literacy.** Using the Internet, locate real estate agencies in your area. Identify houses for sale that would be affordable for someone in your income bracket when you begin your career. Figure how much money is needed for a minimum down payment on a 30-year mortgage and the resulting monthly payments. Also find out the first year's real estate tax bill.

19. **Research.** Locate a Web site for two major appliance companies. Compare the features, warranties, cost, energy usage, universal design features, and services available for a major appliance from each company. Write a brief report about which appliance you would choose and why. *Choice:* Summarize the appliance comparison information in a chart or table.

20. **Financial literacy.** On the Internet, locate a site that will compare for you various loans, interest rates, and mortgage payments for the amount of money you would need to purchase a home. Create a chart listing the loans you researched, interest rates, amount of mortgage payments, and length of loan. Print out a quote for buying the house, including the total cost of finance charges over the life of the loan. *Group option:* Work with a partner as you research various loans. Then have each member print out a quote and finance charges for a different house.

Chapter 29

Managing Your Transportation

Section 29:**1**
Modes of Transportation

Section 29:**2**
Buying and Owning a Car

Key Questions

Questions to answer as you study this chapter:

- What forms of transportation are available?
- What should a person know before buying a car?
- What are the costs of car ownership?

Chapter Objectives

After studying this chapter, you will be able to

- **analyze** different modes of transportation.
- **relate** personal lifestyle to transportation choices.
- **develop** a checklist of factors to consider when purchasing a car.
- **identify** the basics of maintaining a car.

Life Sketch

Lou walked to school every day. Usually she didn't mind, but today was cold and rainy. She envied those who rode in a warm, comfortable car.

"Even a ride in one of those old rusty cars wouldn't be bad on a day like today," she thought. She wondered if she would ever be able to afford her own car.

"A shiny red sports car would be nice. Everyone would be jealous." Then she thought about how much fun it would be to give her friends a ride.

Getting Started

Lou's dreams of owning her own car are not unusual, yet a car is only one mode of transportation. People can travel from one place to another in several ways. They make choices about transportation because of their own needs and wants, and the options they have available. Transportation choices are influenced by each person's lifestyle.

A car is a major financial purchase and, therefore, should be an informed purchase. There are many factors to consider when choosing, financing, and maintaining a car. If you become a car owner, it will be your responsibility to make good decisions in each of these areas.

section 29:1

Modes of Transportation

Sharpen Your Reading

Draw a graphic organizer with each mode of transportation being one segment of the graphic. As you read, add the benefits and disadvantages of each mode.

Boost Your Vocabulary

Search the Internet for various options in the moped category. Identify pros and cons for each option.

Know Key Terms

mopeds
car pool

Within one day, you may use several forms of transportation. You may walk to the bus stop and ride the bus to and from school. After school, you may ride your bike to a friend's house. Later, you may ride in a car to your soccer match. Each form of transportation has certain advantages and disadvantages.

Walking

Walking is one way to get from one location to another. It is not costly, and it is good exercise, 29-1. It may not always be comfortable, especially in weather extremes. If the distance you need to travel is far, walking can be too slow. Walking

29-1 Walking is one form of transportation that contributes to a healthful lifestyle.

after dark or near risky areas may be unsafe. While walking is an option at some times, it is not at other times.

Biking

Biking is a fairly low-cost form of transportation. You can purchase a well-made bike for a relatively low price. Biking is good exercise, is faster than walking, and does not pollute the air. A bike does not take much parking space.

Link to Your Life

What might be some disadvantages of biking as a mode of transportation where you live?

Mopeds and Motorcycles

Mopeds and motorcycles are other transportation options. They vary in size and potential speed. A license is required to drive them on the road. Since they are motorized vehicles, insurance is also needed.

Mopeds are motorized bikes that are small, lightweight, and easy to handle. Motorcycles are usually bigger and faster than mopeds. Mopeds and motorcycles are cheaper to run than cars. Safety is a major concern since they offer no protection to the rider in an accident. Some states require the use of helmets on riders and passengers to help protect against head injuries.

Investigate Further

What are some advantages and disadvantages of using mopeds and motorcycles as modes of transportation?

Public Transportation

Buses, trains, and subways are common forms of public transportation systems. They can transport many people in a fast and efficient manner, which helps keep the cost per person low. Traffic and parking problems are decreased. They spare the community of air pollution by creating less than would develop if everybody drove their own vehicles.

Public transportation is not always convenient or available, however. Trains and buses run on set schedules so if you miss one, you must wait for the next. Sometimes there is "standing room only" when you travel, or a long walking distance to pickup or drop-off points. Such inconveniences prompt people to get their own cars.

Think More About It
What would be the long-term impact if safe, reliable public transportation was not available in a large city?

Cars

Owning a car may be a priority goal for you. It increases a person's freedom to come and go as desired. A car gives people the pride of ownership. It can be a status symbol and can even communicate a part of your identity, 29-2. Besides cars, there are many other styles including vans, sports utility vehicles, and trucks.

Cars are expensive to own and operate. In addition to the purchase price of the car, there are sales taxes, title and registration fees, and insurance costs. In addition, there are routine expenses such as gas, oil, and possibly parking fees. Eventually car owners have repair costs to pay.

Some people cut the costs of using their car by participating in a car pool. In a **car pool**, several people who work at the same location and live near each other take turns driving to work.

Even though the costs are high, many families own one or more cars. For some, a car is needed to do their job. Most depend on their vehicles to get them to and from work. For many, the convenience of going where and when they want is a major factor for car ownership.

29-2 Cars often become symbols of status and independence for the driver.

Decisions About Transportation

Getting back and forth to school, work, home, shopping, and other activities is a routine part of life. However, without reliable transportation, getting around is difficult and sometimes impossible. When deciding your own transportation, consider the following guidelines:

- *Identify your needs.* Where do you need to go? How far is it from where you live? Ideal transportation for one person may not work very well for another.

- *Determine your options.* What choices are available to you? Evaluate each option to see how well it could meet your needs.

- *Look at costs.* The cost of each option may affect whether it is an alternative for you. Consider the costs of daily, weekly, and monthly use of different forms of transportation.

- *Consider personal desires.* Do you prefer to walk, bike, or use public transportation? Do you want to own a car, or would you rather not have the expenses and responsibilities of car ownership?

- *Consider other factors.* How does each option rate for comfort, convenience, and safety? Does public transportation run near your home? How often would weather be a problem if you rode a bicycle, moped, or motorcycle? Is traffic heavy during the times you travel? Is there a place to park a car if you drive?

Your needs, wants, and available options will affect your transportation choices. For instance, you may need a car and prefer a sports model. However, if you do not have the money to buy a sports car, it will not be one of your transportation choices.

Review Section 29:**1**

1. List four different modes of transportation and their advantages and disadvantages.

2. Name five factors that could affect a person's choice of mode of transportation.

section 29:2

Buying and Owning a Car

Most people will purchase a car some time in their life. You may purchase your first car with the help of a family member or friend. Being informed about buying a car can help you make a choice that will meet your needs and match your desires.

Cars vary in performance, comfort, appearance, and price. A car's condition, warranty offered, and repair costs can also vary from one model to another.

Buying a Car

Cars can be found for sale in your local paper, in local dealerships, on the Internet from dealerships, and online from individual owners.

When buying a car, know something about its features and how they compare to those of other models. Understand how a car's value is figured in order to buy the car at the lowest possible price. The costs of financing, insuring, and maintaining the car need to be considered. Taking a look at how Tami and her father bought her first car will help you see the many decisions involved. She began by comparing features, car ratings, prices, and warranties.

Features

Tami and her father started their car search by looking at some local dealerships. They looked at new and used cars. Some were full-sized; others were compact or midsize. Tami and her father listened to salespeople talk about makes, models, engines, gas mileage, alternative fuels, electric cars, transmissions, and warranties. Tami wondered how she could ever make a choice.

Tami's father, however, was not in a hurry. "Let's take time to look around," he said. "Let's see what's available and at what cost. We want to make the best choice we can for you."

Tami discovered that cars have many different features. Her problem was to decide which features were important to her. What size did she want? The subcompact and compact models were small, but then she really did not need much room. Their estimated miles per gallon (MPG) of gasoline were high. A high MPG meant the car would use less gas, and she knew that would help her keep her operating costs lower. However, her father was concerned about her safety in case of an accident. The midsize cars were larger and still got fairly high gas mileage. The standard-sized models were even larger. Although safety was less of a concern in a standard size, Tami noticed that their MPG ratings were much lower. She felt that a midsize car would be right for her.

Tami learned that cars come with *standard features* that are included in the basic price of the car. For other features, called *options*, she would pay extra, 29-3. Manually adjusted seats are a standard feature. Power-adjusted seats are an option that increases the price of the car. Tami noticed that extra features could add several hundred dollars to the price of a car.

Performance Features	
Engine size	
❏ 4 cylinder	
❏ 6 cylinder	
❏ 8 cylinder	
Transmission	
❏ Automatic	
❏ Manual (4-speed, 5-speed)	
❏ Four-wheel drive	
❏ All-wheel drive	
Fuel Types	
❏ Gas	
❏ Diesel	
❏ Electric	
❏ Hybrids	
Power steering	
Electric steering	
Power brakes	
Anti-lock brakes, traction control	
Comfort, Safety, and Convenience Options	
Keyless entry	MP3 compatibility
Keyless ignition	Power door locks
Cruise control	Power seats
Alarm system	Heated seats
Satellite navigation system	Rear window defroster
Air conditioning	Interval wipers
Dual temperature controls	Tinted glass
	Side air bags
AM/FM stereo, CD player	Hands-free wireless phone system
Satellite radio	
Appearance Options	
Alloy wheels	
Special trim	
Leather upholstery	

29-3 Some car features are offered as standard equipment. Others are offered as optional equipment, which increases the basic price of the car.

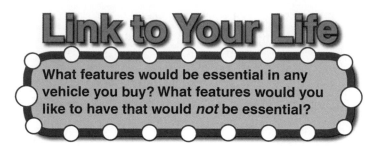

Link to Your Life

What features would be essential in any vehicle you buy? What features would you like to have that would *not* be essential?

Ratings

As part of gathering information, Tami and her father went online to www.consumerreports.org. They looked up recent test reports on cars by Consumers Union, an independent consumer testing agency. It inspects, drives, and crash-tests popular car models to rate each vehicle. These ratings are combined with readers' experiences with the cars. The results can be found online and in *Consumer Reports* magazine. Guides for evaluating both new and used cars can also be found in the reference section of the public library.

The Price of a Car

Tami was learning about cars, especially about the variation in prices. New cars had a **sticker price**, which was found on the sticker on the window. The sticker price included the basic price of the car, costs of transportation and shipping, and costs of extra options on the car.

Used cars sold by dealers also displayed a window sticker with information about the car. In addition, the used car sticker provided a **disclosure statement**. It contained a list of general items and safety equipment that had been inspected for defects.

Tami and her father found several used cars that were in their price range. Three of them interested Tami. Their next step was to check the *NADA Official Used Car Guide*, often called the "Blue Book." Tami and her father checked the Web site www.nada.com to check the retail value of the three cars. The *Guide* is also published monthly by the National Automobile Dealers Association (NADA). Copies can usually be found in school or public libraries. Newer cars *depreciate* (go down in value) each month, so be sure to check a current issue of the NADA guide.

Lending institutions and dealers use the monthly publication to help them figure the value of a used car or truck. The *NADA Guide* lists trade-in, retail, and loan values for most makes and models eight years old or newer. The *trade-in* value is wholesale price. That is the price a dealer should give you if you trade in a used car on a newer model. The *retail value* is the worth of a car in average condition. The *loan value* is the amount that a lending institution will loan to a person to buy that car.

Think More About It
What could be the advantage of looking for cars on the Internet?

The *NADA Guide* also states amounts that should be added to or subtracted from the value of the car. Additions are made when a car has extra features or low miles. A mileage chart states how much should be added to that car's value. High mileage, on the other hand, lowers the car's value. If the car needs repairs, the cost of those repairs is also subtracted from the stated values. Tami and her father wrote down the information for the cars that interested them. They included the trade-in, retail, and loan values for each car on their list.

Warranties

Tami's father was also concerned about future repairs on the auto. He knew that Tami would not have much money to save for repairs after paying her monthly car payment, gas, and oil. New cars had *full warranties* from the manufacturer that provided free labor and parts for a certain number of miles or period of time. Some required that the repairs be made by the factory-authorized dealership that sold the car. Some became invalid if the owner failed to perform the specific maintenance requirements listed by the manufacturer. Tami compared the warranties because they varied with each manufacturer. Some were much better than others.

Some used car dealerships offered warranties as well. Most were *limited warranties*, which cover only specific items for a limited period of time, often 30 days.

Others sold the car "as is." That means no warranty was offered. Even so, an *implied warranty* was still in effect. All states have laws stating that

any item sold for a special purpose must fulfill that purpose. That means if a car is sold to run as a car, then it must do so for a reasonable period of time. Just how much an implied warranty would cover would be determined in court. When a car is sold "as is," a thorough inspection by a qualified mechanic is important for the buyer's protection.

Some dealerships, both new-car and used-car, offer service contracts. For a set fee, they provide a warranty that covers the services stated in the contract.

Investigate Further

What items do you think would be most important to have covered in a warranty when you buy a car?

The Condition of the Car

Two of the cars Tami liked were priced close to the *NADA Official Used Car Guide* price. One was several hundred dollars higher. Even so, they decided to check the condition of all three cars. Perhaps the one was priced higher for a good reason.

They checked the condition of each car's exterior and interior. They checked under the hood, and took them for a test drive, 29-4. Tami liked the highest priced car the best. It was clean, had been newly painted, and handled well on the road.

Tami's father asked for permission to take the car and have another mechanic check it over. Even though he had to pay for the inspection, he knew that it was important to have another opinion. Tami's dad also knew they could purchase a vehicle history report through the NADA Web site.

He called the credit union where he had taken out loans in the past. He gave the loan officer the year, make, model, and mileage of the car. He asked how much they would loan on that car.

Think More About It
Why might a person want to talk to the previous owner of a used car?

Tips for Evaluating a Used Car	
Outside	**Inside**
• Check for major dents or signs of accidents.	• Look for wear on pedals and steering column.
• Inspect trunk and spare tire.	• Check for operation of dash lights and accessories.
• Check tire tread wear.	
• Observe smoothness of springs and shocks.	• Check instrument panel for operation of gauges.
• Check operation of doors and windows.	
• Look for leaking fluids under vehicle.	• Start engine and check power accessories such as radio, wipers, and heater.
Engine	**Road Test**
• Check for leakage of radiator fluids and overheating.	• Let vehicle warm up.
	• Test-drive on familiar road.
• Check oil level and signs of leaks.	• Check brakes at different speeds.
• Check radiator cap; look for cracks and repairs on radiator.	• Listen for smoothness of acceleration and transmission.
• Check for oil in coolant.	
• Check battery and cables.	
• Expect a smooth, clean start.	

29-4 When buying a used car, you may be able to judge its condition by checking these areas.

Comparing the Price

Tami and her father were ready to make an offer on the car. The *NADA Official Used Car Guide* retail value of the car was $4,550, yet the sticker price was $4,750. The car seemed to have been well cared for by the previous owner. The seats did not show much wear, the tires were in good condition, and it seemed to run smoothly. They felt the car was in their price range.

The credit union agreed to loan $3,325 on the car. Tami had saved $1,000, and her father offered to help her with $1,000. The title fee, loan filing fee, registration fee (license plates included), and sales tax on $4,700 equaled $329 (these vary by state and locale). See an example in 29-5. Tami's insurance payment was $300. Tami and her father agreed that $4,700 was the amount she could pay for the car, 29-6.

Tami's dad asked the salesperson why the car was listed above the average retail value of $4,550. The salesperson responded by showing them the maintenance records of the previous

owner. It did appear that the car had been well maintained. Tami's dad then offered $4,700 as the highest Tami could pay for the car. The salesperson accepted the offer and the sale was finalized.

Financing a Car

The cost of Tami's car was more than the price they offered the dealer. The sales tax and other fees had to be paid at the time of purchase. Tami also had to buy insurance for the car. When Tami and her father figured how much they could pay for the car, they had to allow for these additional costs.

Sources of Financing

Tami and her father considered their options for obtaining a car loan. Banks and credit unions are common sources of financing auto loans. Some car loans are available through dealerships.

Tax Statement	1. Full purchase price	4700.00
	2. Less trade-in allowance	——
	3. Amount subject to tax (line 1 minus line 2)	4700.00
Dealer's Statement	4. Tax Due (5% of line 3)	235.00
	5. County Sales Tax if applicable (0.5% of line 3)	23.50
Fee Computation	6. Municipal or County Vehicle Registration Fee (Wheel Tax) if applicable	——
	7. Title Fee ($21.50), (replacement = $30.00)	21.50
	8. Loan filing fee ($4)	4.00
Certification	9. Registration fee	45.00
	10. Intrastate	——
	11. Counter service fee	——
	TOTAL DUE	**$5,029.00**

29-5 There are several extra costs when purchasing a car. These costs will vary from one area to another.

1. Tami determined how much she had available to spend and additional expenses:

Sources of Money		Expenses	
Credit Union	$3,325.00	Title fees	$ 21.50
Savings	1,000.00	Loan filing fee	4.00
Father	1,000.00	Registration	45.00
		Sales tax	258.50
		Insurance	300.00
Total Money Available	$5,325.00	Total Expenses	$ 629.00

2. Then she subtracted the expenses from the total money available:

	Total money available:	$ 5,325.00
	Total costs of other expenses	− 629.00

3. Total amount available to purchase the car: $4,696.00

29-6 Before you make an offer on a car, determine the total amount of money you have available for the purchase. Subtract the amount you will need for sales tax, title, registration fees, and an insurance payment. (Note: Fees vary from state to state.)

Terms of the Loan

It is important to know the terms of a loan before you make a decision to buy. This information can help you know the dollar amount you can pay for a car.

What is the annual interest rate for the loan? What down payment is required? How much will the monthly payment be? Can the loan be paid off early without a penalty? What happens if you default and cannot make a payment? This information can help you figure out the total cost of buying the car.

Tami borrowed the money from the credit union, but her father had to cosign the note. That way, she had the chance to build her credit rating. In addition, the credit union had the security of her father's credit rating to back the loan.

The amount Tami will pay for the car over the term of the loan increases the total cost of her car. Over the three year loan, she will pay $731.27 in interest and $3,325 in principal. The other terms of her loan were clearly stated on the loan agreement as follows:

- annual percentage rate (13.4%)
- total finance charge ($731.27)
- amount she borrowed ($3,325)
- total amount she will have paid at the end of three years ($4,056.27)
- amount due per month ($112.67) to repay the loan

How important is it to save money ahead of time before you need to buy a car?

Leasing a Car

At some time in your life, you may consider leasing a car. **Leasing** is a method of automobile financing in which you make a monthly payment for the use of a vehicle. The lease usually covers a short period of time, such as two or three years. A lease is usually obtained on a new car with little or no down payment. The monthly costs are less than the payments on a loan for a new car.

The disadvantage of leasing a car is that when the lease is up, you do not own the vehicle. The leasing company takes the car back. They will also charge you additional amounts if the car decreased in value more than expected. For instance, if you put a high number of miles on the car, you will be charged an additional fee.

People may choose to lease a vehicle for several reasons. They may feel it is important to have a new vehicle every two or three years with no major repair risks. They may wish to pay no down payment and have lower monthly payments. However, for the long term, they may pay more money for transportation. They will never reach the point of having paid off their car and therefore having no monthly payments.

Whether you are considering buying or leasing a car, make sure to gather as much information as possible. Identify your needs, determine your options, look at costs, and consider your personal desires.

Maintaining Your Car

Repair costs for vehicles can be major expenses, especially if the car is not cared for regularly. Even new cars require routine maintenance to keep major repair costs down. A schedule for such maintenance is included in the manual that comes with the car.

Routine Maintenance Costs

You should budget money for regular car maintenance. Such care can prolong the life of your car and save you headaches over the years.

Learn to check the fluid levels in your car on a regular basis, 29-7. Use your car owner's manual to find out how and when to do these checks. Check the level of motor oil in the engine and antifreeze in the overflow tank attached to the radiator. If you have an automatic transmission, be sure to check the automatic transmission fluid. Be aware of liquid spots on the floor or ground where you park your car. They can be signs of leaking oil, antifreeze, transmission fluid, or brake fluid. Recognizing these problems early before major damage can save you money.

Check the owner's manual for recommended times for routine maintenance. If you need to obtain a manual, most owner's manuals can

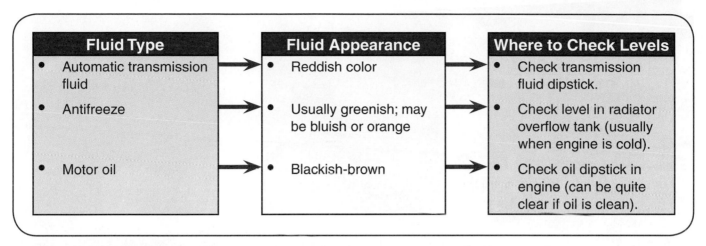

Fluid Type	Fluid Appearance	Where to Check Levels
• Automatic transmission fluid	• Reddish color	• Check transmission fluid dipstick.
• Antifreeze	• Usually greenish; may be bluish or orange	• Check level in radiator overflow tank (usually when engine is cold).
• Motor oil	• Blackish-brown	• Check oil dipstick in engine (can be quite clear if oil is clean).

29-7 Know the types of fluids used in your car and check their levels regularly. Driving with low levels can cause major damage.

be downloaded or purchased online from the manufacturer's Web sites.

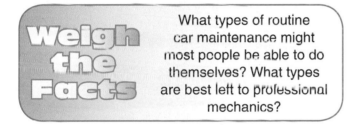

What types of routine car maintenance might most people be able to do themselves? What types are best left to professional mechanics?

Major Maintenance Costs

Some of the larger expenses of car ownership include tires, batteries, brakes, exhaust pipes, and mufflers. If you drive a used car, you might want to set aside money in a car repair fund for these expenses.

New tires can give you many miles of safe driving. Tires that show wear should be checked often. Side-to-side bars will be visible when a tire is worn to $\frac{1}{16}$ of an inch of tread. Tires should be replaced if they are worn down to these bars.

Under normal conditions, batteries on a new car will last approximately four years. You may choose to buy a warranted battery. If it fails before the warranty runs out, the cost of the new battery is usually prorated.

Brake linings and pads may last up to 40,000 or more miles. Checking brakes is part of a regular maintenance schedule. The sound of

scraping metal is a sign that your brakes need repair. Exhaust pipes and mufflers also wear out, especially in areas where roads are salted in the winter. These are also checked on a regular maintenance schedule.

Car maintenance and repairs can be a major budget item. Therefore, you will want to choose a reliable service and repair shop. The mechanic or a service writer in larger shops will write up a service contract. When you sign the service contract, you are agreeing to have the specified work done at the quoted price. Be sure to leave a phone number where you can be reached in case the repair shop needs to contact you.

Review Section 29:2

1. Make a list of various features a person could find in a car.

2. Name two reliable sources of consumer information that can be valuable to a car buyer. What type of information does each provide?

3. Briefly describe the information provided on the window sticker of a new car.

4. What information is found on a used car disclosure statement?

5. List the various costs of owning a car.

Keeping up regular maintenance on your car can help keep the costs of major repairs down.

Think It Through

Buying a Used Car

Vernon was anxious to buy his own car once he started his new job. "It would be so convenient," he thought, "rather than always asking for a ride." His parents agreed they would feel better if Vernon had a reliable car, so they offered to help him with a down payment.

Vernon shopped around for a used car and found a Chevrolet Cavalier that fit his needs. The asking price was $5,495. The car features included automatic transmission and air conditioning. Optional features included cruise control, power door locks, power windows, and a power sunroof. Vernon went to the library and used a consumer used car guide to figure the car's value.

Questions to Guide Your Thinking

Vernon used a chart from a used car guide, similar to the one below. With the information, he was able to figure the loan value and retail value of the Cavalier. Use the example below to answer the questions:

1. What is the average retail price of this car with its optional features, assuming it is in good clean condition?

2. Why is it important for a seller to verify the odometer reading on a used car? If this car had over 150,000 miles on it (considered high for its age), how should Vernon adjust his offer?

3. If a lending institution was willing to loan $500 less than trade-in value for this car, how much could Vernon borrow for this car? Remember to add options to obtain final trade-in value.

4. How much would Vernon need to borrow from his parents for the down payment if he had saved $500?

5. What questions could Vernon ask the seller about the previous owner?

200X Chevrolet Cavalier–L4–AT– PS–AC–FWD*	Clean Trade-In	Clean Retail
Base Price	$3,475	$4,825
Optional Features:		
Add aluminum/alloy wheels	+75	+100
Add cruise control	+50	+75
Add power door locks	+50	+75
Add power sunroof	+275	+325
Add power windows	+50	+75
Deduct manual transmission	−325	−325
	$	$

*Key to Abbreviations: 200X–year manufactured; L4–four cylinder engine; AT–automatic transmission; PS–power sunroof; AC–air conditioning; FWD–front wheel drive.

Chapter Summary

For most people, transportation is an important part of maintaining their lifestyle. Their choices of transportation may vary depending on needs, desires, and the options available. Walking and biking may be chosen for short distances and good exercise. Public transportation may be chosen for an efficient and fairly low-cost way to move in heavily populated areas. Many choose to own and operate their own cars to transport themselves when and where they want.

Purchasing a car can be a major decision. Comparing features, prices, and warranties is important in choosing a car that will best meet your needs. Checking the condition of a used car is important. This can protect you from purchasing a car that needs many repairs.

The purchase price of the car is only the beginning of car-related expenses. Routine and major maintenance costs are normal for all vehicles, both new and used. Making informed purchases and budgeting for such expenses can help a person manage these car-related costs.

Assess...

Your Knowledge

1. List two modes of transportation (other than a car) and the advantages and disadvantages of each.

2. What are five factors that a person should consider when buying a car?

3. List three resources a person should check before buying a used car.

Your Understanding

4. How can information in the *NADA Official Used Car Guide* help a person make a decision when buying a car?

5. How could information from a consumer testing organization like Consumers Union help a person make a good choice when buying a car?

6. How can people estimate the cost of car ownership when planning their budget?

Your Skills

7. Raoul is graduating from high school and going to a college 50 miles from his parents' home. He will be living in a dorm on campus. Analyze what type of transportation Raoul will need after graduation. Identify other information you would need in order to make a decision.

8. Evaluate a car of your choosing. Use the Internet or library resources to identify pros and cons of this particular choice.

Think Critically

9. *Writing.* Write a paragraph describing a ride in a subway, school bus, or other public transportation system. *Choice:* Explain why you would or would not choose that form of transportation if you had another option.

10. *Research, writing.* Search the Internet and library for resources that promote biking as a form of transportation. Write a paragraph persuading a friend to choose bike riding more often as a mode of transportation. *Choice:* Present your information in a persuasive poster or flyer.

11. *Financial literacy.* Assume that you want to buy a car. Develop a plan with the various steps to follow in making your decision, obtaining financing, and purchasing the car. Include a checklist of features and options important to you. Calculate the monthly cost of owning this car.

12. *Financial literacy.* Using your expected starting income for when you complete your education, figure how much per month you could afford to spend on a car payment. Then, using that sum, figure how much you could afford to spend on a vehicle. Identify three vehicles that are in that price range.

Connect with Your Community

13. *Research.* Interview a mechanic to identify the steps the mechanic takes to evaluate the condition and value of a car. Summarize your findings in a report.

14. Interview a mechanic, service writer, or service manager of a dealership about what steps a person should take to maintain a car. Present your information in a poster that can be hung in your classroom. *Group option:* Invite a mechanic, service writer, or service manager to class as a guest speaker. Prepare questions to ask the speaker about maintaining a car. As a group, summarize the speaker's recommendations in a poster format.

15. *Financial literacy.* Interview an insurance salesperson in your community to identify how your particular choice of a car could impact the cost of insuring that car. *Choice:* Create a chart comparing different makes, models, and years of vehicles for the same type of coverage.

16. *Research.* Visit two or more dealers in your area and obtain copies of warranties they provide for used cars and new cars. Compare the parts and services covered by each. Present your findings in a report. *Group option:* Work with a partner to gather the information and prepare the report.

Use Technology

17. *Writing.* Use the Internet to locate a Web site offering used cars for sale. Write a paragraph describing the information provided on the site and any concerns or issues that you can identify related to buying a vehicle online.

18. *Research.* Search the Internet for a major automobile manufacturer. Look over the various vehicles they offer, their options, and the services they provide. Identify a vehicle that you would like to buy and write a description of it, noting the options you would add and the car's total cost. *Choice:* Compare this information with the cost of purchasing the same car at a local car dealer.

19. *Math, financial literacy.* Locate a Web site related to financing a used car. Enter the cost of the car you identified and print out various payment plans based on four-year and five-year loans. Compare the total cost of purchase at various interest rates, including a low-interest rate loan from the manufacturer and a loan from your local bank. *Choice:* Compare the difference in total costs between a new car (with a lower rate of interest) and one that is five years old (lower cost but higher rate of interest).

20. *Math, research.* Search the Internet for leasing information on your dream car and compare the costs of leasing this car to purchasing it. *Choice:* Show your comparison in a spreadsheet, calculating columns to indicate the total costs of each choice at the end of 3 years and then again at the end of 6 years.

Connecting with Career Clusters

$inance

Pathways

- Securities & Investments
- Business Finance
- Accounting
- Insurance
- Banking Services

Personal Financial Advisor

Personal financial advisors help individuals and families assess their financial needs and identify available options for meeting them. The financial advisor's job includes gathering financial information, analyzing it, and making recommendations that address each client's unique goals. Saving for a major expense, such as a house, a child's college education, or retirement, are topics commonly covered.

Financial advising requires a complete analysis of a consumer's financial status and a discussion of short- and long-term plans. The advisor can identify problem areas and recommend alternatives. The advisor also examines the short- and long-term tax consequences of various courses of action.

Personal financial planners may work for a financial institution, insurance company, or investment firm. Many are self-employed, teaching evening and weekend classes in money management to bring in new clients.

A college education is recommended, with coursework in finance, business, accounting, statistics, and economics. Advisors may also obtain a Certified Financial Planner credential. Advisors who sell insurance, real estate, or other financial or legal services will need to satisfy the requirements of whatever licenses are required.

Career Outlook

Mathematical, computer, analytical, problem-solving, and communication skills are necessary. The personal financial advisor also needs to be self-confident, detail-oriented, mature, and able to work independently; as well as familiar with the economy, tax laws, and money markets.

Much faster than average employment growth is expected. An aging population requiring investment and retirement advice is a key reason for the growth. The median income of financial advisors in 2006 was $66,120. Differences in commissions, bonuses, and hourly rates affect earnings, which can range from $32,300 to $145,600.

Explore

Internet Research

Research the steps involved in obtaining a Certified Financial Planner credential. Visit the Certified Financial Planner Board of Standards, Inc. Web site for information. Develop a career plan for a person pursuing credentialing as a Certified Financial Planner.

Job Shadowing

Spend time with a banker, insurance agent, real estate agent, or financial planner. Write a report on the methods he or she uses to help customers and clients stay calm when discussing money matters.

Community Service/Volunteer

Volunteer to present a seminar on using credit wisely to an audience of students your age, such as your class or a local youth club. Seek advice from a personal financial advisor or your family and consumer sciences teacher.

Project

Research a famous person who became wealthy and analyze his or her financial habits. Describe the person's accomplishments in life and attitude toward money.

Interview

Choose three people of different generations and interview them about the methods they use to save money. Also, ask if they use a financial planner. Write a report comparing the money-saving methods used and their varying degrees of success.

Part-Time Job

Obtain a job working as a bank teller. Keep a journal identifying various aspects of money management that you experience on the job.

Glossary

A

abilities. Skills that a person learns and develops as a result of training and practice. (19:2)

abstinence. Not having sexual relations. (7:2)

accessories. Items worn with clothing, such as shoes, handbags, belts, scarves, and neckties. (27:1)

accommodation. When a spouse agrees to accept and live with his or her partner's differences. (9:1)

acquaintances. People who are known, but are not close friends. (6:1)

acquired immune deficiency syndrome (AIDS). A disease caused by a virus that attacks the cells that normally help the body fight off infection and other diseases. (7:2)

active interaction. Physical and verbal exchanges between two people. (9:2)

active listening. Giving the message sender some type of feedback. (5:1)

activities preference inventory. A test designed to help people learn whether their interests are centered on people, ideas, or objects. (19:2)

addiction. Physical dependence of the body on a drug. (26:4)

adult day care. A program that transports older adults from their homes to centers that provide daytime group activities. (18:3)

aerobic exercise. An activity done at a moderate pace for fairly long periods using the large muscles and that keeps pace with the supply of oxygen delivered by the lungs. (26:3)

agencies on aging. Organizations that help plan, fund, and coordinate senior citizen services. (18:3)

agency adoption. Adoptions handled through public or private adoption agencies. (10:3)

agenda. A list prepared by a group leader that outlines what the group will be doing and discussing at the meeting. (21:2)

aggressive. A type of behavior that includes yelling, name-calling, criticizing, pushing, shoving, and possible violence. (6:1)

alcoholic. A person who is addicted to alcohol and cannot control its use. (26:4)

alienated. Feeling alone, without hope, or cut off from others who care. (16:1)

alimony. A financial settlement paid to a spouse. (17:2)

alternative. A possible choice to consider when making a decision. (4:2)

amniocentesis. A test in which a sample of amniotic fluid is removed from a woman's uterus to examine the cells cast off by the fetus for birth defects. (11:2)

amniotic fluid. The fluid inside the amniotic sac that enables the fetus to move easily, serves as a cushion and thermostat, and aids in delivery. (11:1)

amniotic sac. A membrane that surrounds and protects the fetus until birth. (11:1)

anaerobic exercise. An activity that uses muscles to produce a sudden burst of power. (26:3)

anemia. A condition of weakness and fatigue caused by an iron-deficient diet. (10:1)

annual percentage rate. The annual cost of using credit. (23:4)

anorexia nervosa. An eating disorder that involves self-starvation often caused by an irrational fear of being overweight. (26:2)

antibodies. Proteins that fight off disease. (25:1)

anxiety. The uneasy feeling people experience when they believe something terrible will happen. (3:2)

Apgar scale. Tests used to measure the overall physical condition of a newborn. (11:4)

apprenticeship. A position in which the worker learns skills and gains experience while under the supervision of an experienced worker. (19:2)

aptitudes. A person's natural talents. (19:2)

arteriosclerosis. Hardening of the arteries caused by fatty deposits called *plaque* forming on the inner walls of the arteries. (26:1)

artificial insemination. A medical procedure in a syringe is used to deposit sperm directly into the uterus to cause pregnancy. (10:3)

assault. A threat to cause physical harm to a person. (15:3)

assertive. When a person uses I-statements, direct eye contact, and genuine expressions and gestures to let other people know what he or she thinks or intends to do. (6:1)

associative play. Type of play in which two or more children play at one activity that is not organized. (13:3)

attitude. Learned behaviors that people develop as they interact with their environment. (3:1)

authoritarian. An approach to leadership that puts the leader in control of making group decisions. (21:1)

autonomy. The newborn's realization that he or she has control over his or her own body and is a separate person. (12:3)

B

Babinski reflex. The newborn's instinct to extend the toes when the soles of the feet are stroked. (12:3)

barrier to divorce. Fears or pressures that keep a couple from moving ahead with a divorce. (17:1)

basal metabolic rate (BMR). The rate at which the body burns calories to carry out basic bodily functions. (26:2)

basic garments. Clothes that are worn most often. (27:1)

basic medical insurance. Insurance that covers the cost of hospital expenses such as room, board, and nursing services. (24:2)

battery. The use of force resulting in physical contact with a person that the individual did not permit. (15:3)

Better Business Bureau (BBB). A nonprofit organization sponsored by private businesses that attempts to help consumers resolve their complaints with local merchants. (24:1)

birth defect. A condition that exists from birth and limits the ability of a person's body or mind. (11:2)

blaming. A pattern of communication in which people accuse others for everything that goes wrong as a way of preserving their own self-esteem. (5:2)

bleach. Chemical mixture used to whiten and brighten clothes and remove stains. (27:2)

bodily injury liability. Type of insurance that protects against major financial losses resulting from an accident for which the policyholder was responsible. (24:2)

body language. The expression of thoughts, feelings, and emotions through body movements, such as facial expressions, gestures, and body motions. (5:1)

bond. A written pledge to pay back money borrowed plus interest in a certain period of time. (24:3)

bonding. The close feelings of attachment between a newborn and his or her parents. (11:4)

brainstem. Part of the brain that controls life functions such as the beating of the heart and breathing. (2:1)

breech birth. Birth in which the baby is positioned buttocks first for birth. (11:3)

budget. A plan for the use of income. (23:2)

bulimia nervosa. An eating disorder that is characterized by sessions of uncontrolled eating followed by vomiting. (26:2)

bullying. Using aggressive behavior to intentionally harm another person. (6:1)

business ethics. A guiding set of moral values that influence high standards in business activities. (19:3)

business etiquette. Showing respect for others, being courteous, and taking time to listen and communicate clearly. (19:3)

bylaws. Additional guidelines for group activities that state when meetings are held, how often, when elections are held, what procedures are used, and any other information related to the group's organization. (21:2)

calories. A measure of the amount of potential energy in food. (25:1)

cancer. A disease in which abnormally uncontrolled cell growth destroys healthy tissue. (26:1)

car pool. An arrangement in which several people who work at the same location and live near each other take turns driving to work. (29:1)

carbohydrates. Nutrients that provide the body with a major source of energy. (25:1)

carcinogens. Chemicals that can change a cell's DNA and cause cancer. (26:1)

career. Refers to the work done over several years while a person holds different jobs within a particular career field. (19:1)

career clusters. Sixteen broad groupings of occupational and career specialties. (19:2)

career ladder. A series of jobs in which each builds on the experiences of the previous step. (19:1)

career plan. A list of steps to take to reach a career goal. (19:2)

carrier. A person who has a recessive gene for a certain disease and can pass the disease on to his or her children, but who does not have the disease. (1:2)

cerebellum. Part of the brain that controls automatic movements. (2:1)

ceremonial wedding. When friends and family witness the couple's vows taken before a religious official. (8:3)

certified nurse-midwife (CNM). A registered nurse who is trained to provide health care for normal pregnancies and births. (11:2)

cervix. The opening to the uterus. (11:1)

cesarean delivery. A surgical method of delivering a baby through an incision in the mother's abdomen. (11:3)

chairperson. A group leader who may also be called a president. (21:2)

character. Guidelines developed as part of the socialization process that serve as a person's personal judge for every situation that he or she faces. (2:1)

checking out. When questions are used to clarify a message. (5:1)

child abuse. Any physical or mental threat or injury to a child under the age of 18. (15:3)

childrearing leave. A period of time that a parent may be absent from work to provide full-time care for a young child. (20:1)

child support. Payments that a noncustodial parent is legally required to pay toward the expense of raising children under 18. (17:2)

chlamydia. A sexually transmitted infection that can damage a woman's reproductive organs; one of the most common bacterial STIs in this country. (7:2)

cholesterol. A fat that helps the liver make bile, vitamin D, and sex hormones, but can clog arteries and increase the risk of heart disease when there is too much. (25:1)

chromosomes. Rod-shaped particles that carry heredity information from each biological parent to the child. (1:2)

chronic illness. A medical problem that cannot be cured. (16:3)

citizen. A person who formally owes allegiance to a government. In return, he or she gains rights and responsibilities that are protected by the laws of the government. (21:3)

civil ceremony. When family members and a few friends witness a couple's wedding vows taken before a judicial officer. (8:3)

closed adoption. Type of adoption in which the child does not know the identity of the birthparents and an adoption agency makes the decisions. (10:3)

collateral. A form of security on a loan in which the lender can repossess goods if a person fails to make payments. (23:4)

collision insurance. Insurance that covers the cost of damage to the policyholder's car if it is involved in an accident. (24:2)

communication. An exchange of information between two or more people involving the sending and receiving of messages through spoken or written words, facial expressions, or gestures. (5:1)

community-based day care. A program of activities for older people who are still somewhat independent. (18:3)

compensation. A technique in which a person focuses on a strength to make up for a weakness in another area. (3:1)

complementary qualities. Differences between people that attract one person to another and benefit the relationship. (8:2)

complementary role. Each person in a relationship takes on a role that supplies what the other person lacks. (8:3)

complete protein. Contains all the essential amino acids the human body needs to take in via food. (25:1)

compounding. When interest previously earned is added to the total before new interest earnings are figured. (23:1)

comprehensive physical damage. A type of insurance that covers the risk of damage to the policyholder's car by perils other than collision. (24:2)

compromise. A give-and-take method of resolving differences where both people give in a little to reach a solution that is satisfactory to both. (5:3)

conception. The moment of becoming pregnant when one sperm and one egg unite. (11:1)

concession. When one spouse gives in to the other rather than working to reach a joint agreement. (9:1)

conflict. When two people disagree on an issue. (5:3)

conflict resolution. A communication skill that encourages a better understanding of the other person's point of view, helping to resolve conflicts in a positive way. (5:3)

consequence. The end result of a choice. (4:2)

constitution. A formal written statement that explains a group's purpose and goals and governs its functions. (21:2)

contagious disease. Disease that is easily spread from one person to another. (13:4)

continuum. A way of representing the parts of a whole across a lengthy time period, such as a marriage relationship from beginning to end. (9:1)

contract. A mutual agreement between two consenting people. (21:3)

conversion. Transferring an emotion into a physical symptom. (3:1)

cooperative child care. Centers that are organized, managed, and funded by the parents who use them to care for their children. (20:2)

cooperative play. Type of play in which children work together to reach common goals. (13:3)

coping behavior. Planned behavior that helps the family adjust as quickly as possible to changes that have taken place. (16:3)

cortex. Part of the brain that controls thinking, decision making, and judgment. (2:1)

cover letter. A letter sent with a résumé to express interest in a job. (19:3)

credit limit. The maximum amount of money a person can borrow on a credit card. (23:4)

credit rating. A record of whether or not a person has paid his or her bills on time. (23:4)

crises. Experiences or events that cause people to make major changes in their lives. (16:1)

crises events. Major changes in a person's life that require major changes in behavior. (3:2)

crisis-care centers. Safe shelters for abused children. (15:3)

cultural heritage. Learned behavior that is passed from generation to generation. (1:3)

cultural identity. The way a person sees himself or herself as a member of a specific cultural group. (14:2)

custody. The rights and responsibilities of providing for the children's care until the children reach age 18. (17:2)

cyberbullying. Using technology, such as the Internet or cell phones, to send hurtful or threatening messages to another person. (6:1)

Daily Values. Reference numbers used to help consumers see how food products fit into the day's nutrient needs based on the number of calories needed each day. (25:3)

date rape. Sexual intercourse with a dating partner against one person's will. (7:2)

deadline. The time at which a task must be completed. (22:2)

debit card. A card used to immediately withdraw funds from a checking account without writing a check. (23:3)

decision-making process. A step-by-step method to guide thinking when a planned decision is needed. (4:2)

deductible. Payment of a predetermined amount by the policyholder before the insurance company pays any of the loss. (24:2)

defense mechanisms. Methods people unconsciously use to deal with life situations; may hide or balance people's feelings and actions. (3:1)

democratic. A style of leadership in which group members are involved in making decisions; when each member's feelings, thoughts, and needs are considered. (21:1)

democratic decision making. Process in which group members take part in the selection of one choice and help carry out the plan of action. (15:3)

dendrites. Fingerlike extensions of neurons through which information is sent to the nerve cells. (1:2)

depressant. A label given to drugs that slow the activity of the brain by knocking out control centers. (26:4)

depression. An overwhelming attitude of sadness, discouragement, and hopelessness that can cause difficulty in making decisions and in trying to lead a normal life. (3.2)

detergent. Cleaning agent made from chemicals that generally cleans better than soaps. (27:2)

developmental task. A skill that society expects of individuals at various stages of life. (1:1)

direct attack. A method used to face a problem, recognize it, and try to solve it. (3:1)

disability. An impairment that interferes with certain mental or physical abilities. (16:3)

disclosure statement. A document that provides important information a buyer needs to know in order to make an informed purchase decision. (29:2)

displacement. Taking out feelings on someone or something else rather than face the real problem. (3:1)

distracting. A pattern of communication in which people ignore unpleasant situations and put them aside as not really being important. (5:2)

diversity. The unique qualities of people from different cultural backgrounds; another term for multiculturalism. (6:3)

down payment. A portion of the purchase price of a home that must be paid at the time of the purchase. (28:1)

drug. Any substance that chemically changes structures or functions in living organisms. (26:4)

dual-career family. Type of family in which both husband and wife pursue careers outside the home while maintaining their family roles. (14:3)

E

ectomorphs. People who have small bones and a slender, angular build. (26:2)

elder abuse. Intentionally or knowingly causing an elder person to suffer physical harm or injury, unreasonable confinement, sexual abuse, or a lack of services or medical treatment to maintain health. (18:3)

electronic funds transfer (EFT). A system that allows a person to use a computer to move money between accounts. (23:3)

embryo. The first two months of the development of the zygote. (11:1)

emotional abuse. Actions by a parent or caregiver that interfere with a child's development and damages self-esteem. (15:3)

emotional development. A developmental process that refers to the ability to experience, express, and control emotions. (2:1)

emotional divorce. Withdrawing from the relationship to fulfill emotional needs outside the marriage. (17:2)

empathy. When a person puts himself or herself in another person's shoes to imagine what that person is feeling or thinking. (6:1)

emphysema. A progressive disease in which the walls of the lungs are destroyed, making breathing difficult. (26:4)

employer-sponsored child care. Care offered for children of employees that is funded by the employer. (20:2)

endometriosis. A disease in which uterine tissue grows outside the uterus, often resulting in pain and infertility. (10:3)

endomorphs. People with large frames and rounded shapes. (26:2)

engagement. The final stage in the dating process leading to marriage. (8:3)

entrepreneurs. People who are self-employed and earn incomes through their own businesses. (19:2)

environment. A person's surroundings and everything in them, including human and nonhuman factors. (1:3)

enzymes. Proteins used to direct chemical reactions in the body, including digestion. (25:1)

equal opportunity. A requirement in the workplace to treat all people fairly regardless of race, color, sex, national origin, age, or disability. (19:3)

estate. The sum of all a person's personal property, including savings, investments, and insurance benefits. (24:3)

ethics. Moral principles or standards a person uses to judge what is right or wrong. (2:1)

extended family. Several generations of one family living together in one home. (14:3)

extenders. Less expensive items used to expand a wardrobe. (27:1)

external stress. Stress caused by factors outside the family. (16:2)

extrovert. A person who is very outgoing and confident and enjoys being with people. (2:2)

F

face value. The largest amount an insurance company will pay for a loss, as determined by the type of policy purchased. (24:2)

fad. Trendy clothing that is very popular for only a short time. (27:1)

family. Two or more people living in the same household that are related by blood, marriage, or adoption. (14:1)

family child care. Child care that is provided in the caregiver's own home. (20:2)

family life cycle. Stages in the life of a family that extend from marriage to the death of a spouse. (15:2)

family routines. Small events that are repeated on a regular basis in the family. (15:3)

family system. The interactions of all family members with one another and the effects of these interactions. (15:1)

family traditions. Established patterns of behavior or customs handed down through generations. (15:3)

family tree. A list of several generations of blood relatives. It is often used to trace hereditary factors and traits from one generation to another. (1:2)

fantasy. Defense mechanism in which people use their imaginary thoughts as an escape to fill their personal needs. (3:1)

fat-soluble vitamins. Vitamins A, D, E, and K, which can be stored in the body. (25:1)

felony. A serious crime that can result in a sentence of more than a year in prison or even death. (21:3)

fetal alcohol syndrome (FAS). A pattern of physical and mental birth defects in children born of alcoholic mothers. (11:2)

fetus. The name for a growing baby during the last seven months of pregnancy. (11:1)

financial responsibility law. Law that requires drivers to prove their ability to pay for the cost of any damages or injuries that might be caused in an auto accident. (24:2)

fixed expenses. Expenses that are the same each month. (23:2)

flexibility. The quality of being willing to change and negotiate differences. (8:1)

flexible scheduling. An employee benefit that allows workers the ability to choose their work hours, within reason. (20:1)

fontanels. Six soft spots on the head of a newborn where the skull bones have not yet fused together after allowing the head to flex while traveling through the birth canal. (12:3)

foodborne illness. Illness caused from eating food that has not been handled correctly. (25:4)

foster care. Temporary care for children under 18 years of age. (15:3)

fraud. Intentional trickery, lies, or misrepresentation to make a person give up a right or something of value. (24:1)

gene. The basic unit of heredity that determines human characteristics or traits. (1:1)

genetics. The scientific study of heredity. (1:2)

genital herpes. An incurable and widespread STI caused by a virus that produces painful sores or blisters. (7:2)

genital warts. Small bumps or clusters of bumps in the genital area caused by a virus. (7:2)

germs. Disease-causing organisms. (13:4)

glucose. The substance called *blood sugar* that the body makes from carbohydrates and uses for energy. (25:1)

goal. Something a person wants to have or achieve at a certain point. (4:1)

gonorrhea. A sexually transmitted infection caused by bacteria that can produce damage to the male and female organs resulting in sterility. (7:2)

grasping reflex. The newborn's instinct to tighten his or her wrist as a response to stimuli. (12:3)

gross income. A person's total wage or salary before any deductions are made. (23:1)

group. Two or more people who interact and have an effect on each other. (21:1)

group child care. Care provided for a number of children, usually of the same age, in a child care center. (20:2)

group dating. Several boys and girls spend time together, developing friendships with others in the group. (7:1)

group health insurance. Insurance policies available through employers, unions, and professional associations that provide more medical coverage at a lower cost than individual policies. (24:2)

group homes. Places available for children or teens who live in abusive families. Counselors provide care and counseling to cope with problems stemming from abuse. (15:3)

group values. The ideals and beliefs that are important to a specific group of people within a culture. (4:1)

guaranteed replacement value. The assurance that an insurance company will replace an item even if the cost of the new item is higher than the face value of the policy. (24:2)

guidance. All that parents do and say as they influence their children's behavior in a positive way and lead them into maturity. (13:2)

hangtags. Information attached to a garment that is used to help sell or promote a product and must be removed before wearing. (27:1)

hepatitis B. A sexually transmitted infection caused by a virus that attacks the liver; can also be transmitted by exposure to infected blood. (7:2)

heredity. The sum of the qualities that are passed to a person from his or her ancestors. (1:2)

high fashion. Original clothing designs made by well-known designers in New York, Paris, and other major fashion centers. (27:1)

home health care. Assistance given to elderly or ill people with personal and housekeeping chores from nursing aides and assistants.

home study. Process in which an agency or a social worker conducts an evaluation of a couple's home to determine its suitability for a child. (10:3)

homogamy. A principle suggesting that people who have many similarities, or much in common, are more likely to have a satisfying marriage. (8:2)

hospice care. Physical, emotional, and spiritual care designed for a dying person. (18:3)

hostility. When a couple continually argues or quarrels without settling conflicts or agreeing on solutions. (9:1)

house brand. A product offered by a particular store. (25:3)

human immunodeficiency virus (HIV). The AIDS-causing virus, which attacks cells that normally help a person fight off infection and disease. (7:2)

human papilloma virus (HPV). A sexually transmitted infection that infects the skin and mucous membranes and can cause genital warts or cancer. (7:2)

human resource. A personal quality and characteristic that comes from within a person; also a person who provides support in some way. (4:1)

hypertension. High blood pressure, which can raise the risk of heart attack. (26:1)

I

idealization. Valuing someone or something far more than its true worth. (3:1)

immunizations. Injections or drops given to a person to prevent a specific disease. (13:4)

impotency. The inability to have sexual relations. (17:2)

in vitro fertilization (IVF). A procedure that involves removing an egg from the mother's ovary, fertilizing it with the father's sperm, and implanting it in the mother's uterus. (10:3)

incomplete protein. Plant proteins that lack one or more essential amino acids. (25:1)

independent adoption. Adoptions arranged privately, usually through a physician or lawyer. (10:3)

independent living. An option for teens whose parents agree to give up legal control; only for mature, emotionally stable teens who can provide for themselves financially. (15:3)

individual education plan (IEP). A special plan set up by parents and school staff members for the education of a child with special needs. (13:4)

infatuation. A strong feeling of attraction that tends to be self-centered or one-sided. (7:2)

infertility. A couple's inability to conceive a child after trying for a year or more, or a woman's inability to carry a child to full term. (10:3)

insurance. A form of protection against financial loss. (24:2)

intellectual development. A development process that refers to the growth of the brain and the use of mental skills. (2:1)

intelligence. A person's capacity for mental activity. (1:2)

interest. A charge for the use of money, usually expressed as a percentage. (23:1)

interests. The subjects, activities, or events that a person enjoys. (19:2)

internal stress. Stress that comes from inside the family. (16:2)

international adoption. Type of adoption in which a family adopts a child from another country. (10:3)

interpersonal adjustments. When couples learn to adjust to each other's differences. (9:2)

interview. A meeting in which an employer talks with a job applicant. (19:3)

introvert. A person who is shy, withdrawn, and anxious about meeting new people. (2:2)

I-statements. Expressing thoughts, feelings, and ideas from a personal point of view. (5:1)

J

job. A position in which a person works to earn an income. (19:1)

job sharing. A full-time job split between two people. (20:1)

joint custody. Arrangement in which both parents in a divorce share the rights and responsibilities of legal custody of their children. (17:2)

L

label. A tag permanently attached to the inside of the garment that states the fiber content and care instructions. (27:1)

labor. The contractions of the uterus during the birth process. (11:4)

lactation. The production of milk in the breasts. (11:3)

Lamaze method. A birthing technique in which the mother is taught to focus on breathing techniques to relax her muscles. (11:3)

latchkey children. Children who regularly go home after school to an empty house or apartment. (20:2)

leader. The person who takes charge in a group and is responsible for helping the group succeed. (21:1)

lease. A legal contract between the renter and the landlord that states the terms and conditions of the agreement. (28:1)

Leboyer method. A birthing technique that focuses on making the baby's transition into the outside world more gradual by providing a comforting environment similar to the internal environment. (11:3)

legal divorce. The ending of a marriage through the legal process. (17:2)

legal separation. A legal agreement for a couple to live apart, divide their property, and provide for their children. (17:2)

legislatures. Law-making governmental bodies. (21:3)

liability. The legal responsibility for another person's financial costs due to a loss or injury. (24:2)

life span. A person's path from birth until death. (1:1)

lifestyle. The way a person chooses to live. (19:1)

limbic system. Four main structures in the brain that control emotions and hormone production; eating, drinking, and sleeping; and long-term memory storage. (2:1)

liquidity. The ability to withdraw money from an account on short notice. (23:3)

long-term goal. Something a person wants to have or achieve in the distant future. (4:1)

M

major medical insurance. Insurance that protects the family against large losses due to a major illness or serious injury. (24:2)

marital adjustment. The process couples use to modify their relationship as needed throughout their married life. (9:1)

marital roles. Responsibilities a person may be expected to fulfill after marriage, such as spouse, friend, wage earner, cook, caregiver, or housekeeper. (9:2)

marriage counseling. Meeting with a professional to try to improve a couple's relationship. (9:3)

marriage enrichment programs. Programs sponsored by community service agencies or religious or educational groups to help couples strengthen their marriages. (9:3)

material abuse. The misuse of an elder person's property or financial resources. (18:3)

maternity leave. A period of time in which an expectant mother leaves her job to give birth and care for the newborn. (20:1)

maturation. The emergence of physical characteristics through the growth process. (12:1)

mature love. A long-lasting, caring, and giving type of love. (7:2)

media. Sources of information and entertainment that include television, radio, movies, videos, newspapers, magazines, and the Internet. (1:3)

medical payments coverage. A type of insurance that pays the medical expenses resulting from a car accident. (24:2)

Medicare. A federal program that helps older people in paying their medical bills. (18:2)

mentor. A person to look to for guidance and encouragement. (21:3)

mesomorphs. People with medium-sized bone structures. (26:2)

middlescence. The years between the ages of 40 and 65. (18:1)

midlife crisis. An event caused by trouble adjusting to the changes that occur during the middle years of life. (18:1)

milestones. Major accomplishments within each area of development. (12:2)

minerals. Inorganic elements found in the earth's crust and which the body needs to make strong bones and teeth. (25:1)

minutes. A written description of what took place at a meeting. (21:2)

misdemeanor. A less serious crime that may be punished by a fine or short prison term of less than a year. (21:3)

modeling. Acting in a way that sets a good example for children to follow. (13:2)

modified whole life insurance. A form of cash value insurance in which the premiums are lower during the early years. (24:2)

mopeds. Motorized bikes that are small, lightweight, and easy to handle. (29:1)

mortgage. A contract between a borrower and a lender to finance the purchase of a house. (28:1)

motor development. The physical movements that a child makes as development proceeds. (12:2)

multiculturalism. A society with people of different cultural backgrounds. (6:3)

mutual funds. A group of many investments purchased by a company representing many investors. (24:3)

MyPyramid. A tool developed by the USDA to help people make more healthful food and physical activity choices. (25:2)

N

nanny. A person who comes into the child's home to provide care. (20:2)

natural consequences. The normal result of an action. (13:2)

neglect. Failure to give a child proper shelter, clothing, food, medical care, supervision, love, and affection. (15:3)

negotiation. A communication process in which people alternate between sending and receiving messages for the purpose of reaching a mutually agreeable solution. (5:3)

net income. The amount of money left after subtracting deductions from gross income. (23:1)

networking. Talking to family members, friends, or acquaintances about possible job openings. (19:3)

neurons. Nerve cells in the brain. (1:2)

neurotransmitters. Chemicals in the synapses that allow messages to be carried from one neuron to another. (1:2)

no-fault divorce. A legal term for a divorce in which neither spouse is blamed for the divorce. (17:2)

no-fault insurance. Insurance that eliminates the legal process of proving who is at fault in an auto accident. The actual costs of medical expenses, lost wages, and related expenses are covered by each person's own insurance. (24:2)

nonhuman resource. An item available to help a person reach a goal, such as money, a car, tools, time, or information. (4:1)

nonverbal communication. A way of sending and receiving messages without using words, such as through body movements, facial expressions, and eye contact. (5:1)

normative stressors. Everyday events that cause stress. (3:2)

nuclear family. Traditional family structure that includes a married couple and their children. (14:3)

nurturing environment. Environment in which children feel secure, protected, satisfied, and loved. (13:1)

nutrient dense. Providing a good supply of nutrients in proportion to calories. (25:1)

nutrients. Chemical substances the body needs to provide energy, regulate body functions, and promote growth and development. (25:1)

O

obesity. Condition in which a person is at least 20 percent above ideal body weight and has excess body fat. (12:1)

obstacle. Something that stands in the way of achieving a goal. (4:1)

obstetrician-gynecologist. A specialist who provides medical and surgical care to women. The obstetrician provides mainly pregnancy care. (11:2)

occupation. Type of work. (19:1)

onlooker play. Type of play in which toddlers watch other children play but will not join in. (13:3)

open adoption. Type of adoption in which birthparents may select and meet the adoptive parents and the adopted child will have information about his or her birthparents. (10:3)

ordinances. Local laws or regulations. (21:3)

overdraft. When more money is withdrawn than is available in an account. (23:3)

ovulation. The process in which the ovaries release a mature egg. (10:3)

pair adjustment. When a couple adjusts their individual lifestyles to have a satisfying life together. (9:2)

pair dating. When two people spend time as a couple building their friendship. (7:1)

parallel play. Type of play in which children play side-by-side without interacting with each other. (13:3)

parenting. Using skills to care for and raise a child to adulthood. (10:1)

parliamentary procedure. An orderly way of conducting a meeting and discussing business. (21:2)

passive. Going along with whatever is said or done in a group. (6:1)

passive interaction. When a person is involved only as an observer or listener. (9:2)

passive listening. Hearing words without listening for meanings. (5:1)

paternity leave. A period of time that a new father is absent from his job immediately following the birth of his child. (20:1)

pediatrician. A medical doctor who specializes in the care of children. (13:4)

peers. Other people in a person's age group. (1:3)

pensions. Funds paid by employers to former employees who contributed to a special retirement fund while they were employed. (18:2)

perishable foods. Foods that spoil easily and must be kept at refrigerator temperatures. (25:4)

personal boundaries. Limits for behavior that a person will accept in a relationship. (7:1)

personality. The sum of all inherited and learned behavioral traits that combine to make a person unique. (2:2)

petitioner. The person who files for divorce. (17:2)

physical abuse. The intentional hurting of a person's body, causing physical injury. (15:3)

physical development. A developmental process that refers to the body's physical growth, which affects height, weight, and internal body systems. (2:1)

pileup effect. Stress that builds up and ends in a crisis. (16:1)

placating. A pattern of communication in which people say or do things just to please others or keep them from getting upset. (5:2)

placenta. Organ in which the pregnant woman's blood vessels meet with the baby's capillaries to allow the transfer of oxygen and nutrients to the fetus and the removal of waste products from the fetus. (11:1)

planned decision. A decision that requires more time and energy to make the best choice. (4:1)

policy. A contract between the insurance company and the policyholder. (24:2)

portfolio. A collection of materials that document achievements over time. (19:2)

preeclampsia. A condition during pregnancy that includes swelling and high blood pressure; also called *toxemia* or *pregnancy-induced hypertension (PIH)*. (10:1)

premium. A fee charged by an insurance company to assume a financial loss that is described in the policy. (24:2)

problem ownership. Identifying the person who is most bothered and affected by a problem. (5:3)

procrastinate. Putting off doing a project until the last minute. (22:2)

project. To plan or estimate ideas for the future. (4:1)

projection. Placing the blame for failures on others. (3:1)

property damage liability. Protection to cover losses to someone else's property caused by the policyholder and his or her vehicle. (24:2)

puberty. An adolescent growth spurt that occurs at the time when reproductive organs mature. This sexual maturity takes place when certain hormones are released in the body. (2:1)

Punnett square. A scientific method used to determine what possible gene pairs may result from combining two genes. (1:2)

quarantine. Confinement to the home or away from other people until the contagious stage of a disease is past. (13:4)

R

rape. Forced sexual intercourse. (7:2)

rapport. A balanced, harmonious atmosphere between two people. (6:1)

rate of development. The speed at which that child proceeds through a developmental pattern. (12:1)

rationalization. Explaining weaknesses or failures by giving socially acceptable excuses. (3:1)

receiver. Hears and interprets the message during communication. (5:1)

redirecting. Focusing a child's interest from one activity to a more acceptable one. (13:2)

references. People who have direct knowledge of a person and his or her past work record. (19:3)

reflecting. Repeating in your own words what you think was said. (5:1)

register. When a citizen shows documents to prove that he or she has the right to vote in elections and fills out the required forms. (21:3)

regression. Returning to childish or immature behavior when difficulties or frustrations occur. (3:1)

reinforcement. Praising a child who does well in order to encourage continued behavior. (13:2)

relationship-oriented leader. A leader who places emphasis on the feelings, thoughts, and needs of each group member (21:1)

resiliency. The body's ability to adjust to setbacks and make changes to survive and reach maximum growth and development. (1:3)

resource. Anything available to help carry out decisions and reach goals. (4:1)

respondent. The spouse against whom a divorce is filed. (17:2)

responsible parenting. Making choices that will help a child develop fully in all areas of life. (10:2)

résumé. A summary of a person's skills, training, education, and past work experiences. (19:3)

retirement. The ending of paid employment. (18:2)

Robert's Rules of Order. A book that details the process of parliamentary procedure. (21:2)

role. A way of acting to fulfill certain responsibilities in life, most often taught by the family. (2:1)

role overload. Having too many roles and responsibilities to carry them out well. (17:3)

role sharing. A way of handling responsibilities by partners working together to carry out a task. (8:3)

romantic love. The exhilarating feeling that can spark a relationship to then grow into mature love. (7:2)

rooting reflex. Survival instinct of a newborn to suck when hungry. (12:3)

routine decision. Decisions made every day without much thought. (4:1)

S

sandwich approach. When a criticism is expressed between two positive statements. (9:2)

sanitation. Cleanliness and hygiene practices that prevent bacteria from multiplying and causing illness. (25:4)

saturated fats. The fatty acids present in meats and dairy products that are usually solid at room temperature. (25:1)

scapegoating. Blaming someone else for a problem instead of taking ownership. (15:3)

secretary. A person who records the minutes of each group meeting. (21:2)

security deposit. A sum of money equal to one or two month's rent that a renter pays before moving in and is returned upon moving out, provided there is no damage. (28:1)

self-concept. The mental picture people have of themselves; their opinions about or views of themselves. (2:2)

self-esteem. The way a person feels about his or her self-concept; a feeling of high or low value and importance, depending on one's self-concept. (2:2)

self-identity. A sense of individuality. (1:1)

self-perpetuating cycle. The process of attitudes producing actions that may cause those same attitudes to increase. (3:1)

self-talk. Brief comments a person makes in his or her mind that can be either negative or positive. (3:1)

sender. Transmits or sends the message during communication. (5:1)

separation anxiety. Infants' fear of being any distance from parents, or the fear that parents who leave will not return. (12:3)

sex roles. A culture's definition of how males and females should behave. (3:2)

sex stereotypes. Widely held beliefs about the characteristics shared by all members of one sex. (3:2)

sexual abuse. Any sexual contact or interaction by an adult with a child or teenager; can be physical or nonphysical. (15:3)

sexual harassment. Any unwelcome or unwanted advances, requests for favors, or other verbal or physical conduct of a sexual nature. (19:3)

sexually transmitted infections (STIs). Infections that are passed from one person to another through sexual contact. (7:2)

Shaken Baby Syndrome. A form of physical abuse in which brain damage is caused by a fast and forceful shaking of an infant. (15:3)

shelters. Short-term places of safety that provide an escape from a family crisis. (15:3)

short-term goal. Something a person wants to have or achieve in a relatively short amount of time, such as a day or week. (4:1)

sibling. A brother or sister. (1:3)

significant adults. Nonparental adults who play some important part in a person's life. (6:3)

single living. A lifestyle in which a person lives alone. (14:4)

single-parent family. Family structure that includes one parent and one or more children. (14:3)

soap. A cleansing agent made from natural products. (27:2)

social development. A developmental process that refers to the way people relate to others around them. (2:1)

social security. A federal program run by the Social Security Administration that is designed to give retired or disabled people some source of income. (18:2)

socialization. The process through which children learn behavior that is acceptable in their society, including the beliefs and standards of that society. (2:1)

solitary play. Type of play in which babies tend to play alone and ignore other children playing nearby. (13:3)

split custody. An arrangement in which children are divided between the divorced parents. (17:2)

standards. A measurement of progress toward meeting goals or determining whether a goal has been reached. (4:1)

startle reflex. Newborns' instinct to throw out their arms, draw back their heads, and stretch out their legs when surprised. (12:3)

states of the newborn. Patterns in which newborns respond to the environment. (12:3)

steady dating. A commitment to date only one person. (7:1)

stepfamily. Family structure that consists of a husband and wife, one or both of whom have been married before, and any children from previous marriages. (14:3)

stepparent. The new spouse of a parent with children from a previous marriage. (17:3)

stereotype. An oversimplified opinion or prejudiced attitude. (3:2)

steroids. A synthetic version of the male hormone testosterone. (26:2)

sticker price. The basic price of a car, including the costs of transportation and shipping and the costs of extra options on the car. (29:2)

stocks. A share in the ownership of a company. (24:3)

stranger anxiety. An infant's reaction of crying in fear when an unfamiliar person is near. (12:3)

stress. The body's response to the events of a person's life that cause physical, mental, and emotional tensions. (3:2)

stressors. Life events that cause the body to react. (16:1)

style. Refers to a particular design, shape, or type of apparel. (27:1)

subgoal. A step that brings a person closer to achieving a long-term goal. (4:1)

substance abuse. Drug or alcohol abuse.

substitute family. Non-relatives who encourage or help a person in a way that family members would if they were present. (9:3)

sudden infant death syndrome (SIDS). The unexplained death of a healthy baby that stops breathing and dies in its sleep. (11:3)

Supplemental Security Income (SSI). A federal program that provides extra income for people who are age 65 or older, blind, or disabled. (18:2)

support network. Relatives who help each other with child care, parenting, and daily problems. (6:2)

surrogate mother. A woman hired by a couple to carry the couple's child to birth. (10:3)

swimming reflex. The newborn's instinct to make swimming movements in water. (12:3)

symbols. Thought-picture of objects. (12:2)

synapse. Space between the dendrites of two neurons. (1:2)

syphilis. A sexually transmitted infection caused by bacteria that produce a sore called a chancre. (7:2)

task-oriented leader. A style of leadership that focuses on specific tasks needing to be accomplished. (21:1)

teamwork. Work done by several members doing their parts to help the group succeed. (19:3)

technology. The practical application of knowledge; the process of using knowledge to solve problems. (1:3)

temperament. Consistent, predictable behavior based on inborn patterns of response. (2:2)

term insurance. A policy that insures a policyholder's life for a set number of years, but builds no cash value. (24:2)

testimonial. An ad in which a product is endorsed by a famous person. (24:1)

time management. Controlling the use of time. (22:1)

time-out. A form of guidance in which a child spends time alone to think quietly about his or her behavior. (13:2)

tort. A wrongful act committed against another person. (21:3)

traits. Inherited characteristics. (1:2)

trans fatty acids. Fatty acids whose chemical structures are altered when vegetable oils are processed into solid fats such as margarines and shortening. (25:1)

transferable skills. Basic skills that can be applied from one work situation to another. (19:2)

trust. A legal document that permits the transfer of property or income from the investor to a second group (trustee) for the investor's beneficiaries. (24:3)

ultrasound. A technology that uses sound waves bouncing off the fetus to produce an image of the fetus inside the womb. (11:2)

umbilical cord. A shaft of blood vessels that carries oxygen, nutrients, and antibodies to the growing fetus while eliminating waste products. (11:1)

unconditional love. The ability to love another under any circumstance, such as the love of a parent for a child. (10:2)

uninsured motorists protection. Insurance that covers bodily injuries to the policyholder and family members if an accident is caused by someone who has no insurance. (24:2)

unit price. The cost of a product per unit, weight, or measure. (25:3)

universal design. The concept of creating products and living spaces that are easy for everyone to use. (28:2)

universal life insurance. A policy that combines both term and cash value life insurance. (24:2)

unsaturated fats. Fatty acids found in vegetable oils such as corn, soybean, canola, and olive oil, that are liquid at room temperature. (25:1)

values. All the ideals and beliefs that a person considers important and that influence his or her decisions and actions. (4:1)

variable expenses. Expenses that change or vary from month to month. (23:2)

verbal communication. The use of words as in speaking and writing to send and receive messages. (5:1)

violation. An act that violates or breaks a local ordinance and can result in a fine or short jail term. (21:3)

violence. Any physical act intended to harm another person. (15:3)

visitation rights. Arrangements for the noncustodial parent in a divorce settlement to visit the children. (17:2)

vitamins. Organic compounds that are essential to health. (25:1)

volunteers. People who donate their time, talents, and energy to serve others. (21:3)

vows. Statements that specifically express a couple's commitment to each other. (8:3)

wardrobe. All the clothes a person has, including accessories. (27:1)

warranty. A written statement from the manufacturer about the conditions under which an item will be repaired or replaced free of charge. (24:1)

water-soluble vitamins. Vitamins that cannot be stored in the body. (25:1)

whole life insurance. A form of cash value insurance in which the premium stays the same during the life of the policy. (24:2)

withdrawal. Discomfort, nausea, pain, and convulsions that occur when a person stops using an addictive drug. (26:4)

work. Any activity that results in a useful product or service; accomplishing a goal. (19:1)

zygote. The cell that is formed when a sperm and egg unite. (11:1)

Index